THE LAST KING OF POLAND

by the same author

CHOPIN, A BIOGRAPHY
PADEREWSKI
THE POLISH WAY

THE
LAST KING
OF
POLAND

Adam Zamoyski

JONATHAN CAPE
LONDON

First published 1992
© Adam Zamoyski 1992
Jonathan Cape, 20 Vauxhall Bridge Road, London SW1V 2SA

Adam Zamoyski has asserted his right
under the Copyright, Designs and Patents Act, 1988
to be identified as the author of this work

A CIP catalogue record for this book
is available from the British Library

ISBN 0-224-03548-7

Typeset by Computape (Pickering) Ltd, Pickering, North Yorkshire
Printed in Great Britain by
Butler and Tanner Ltd, Frome, Somerset

Contents

Contents

Maps

Family Trees

vi

Preface

*A*lthough an enormous amount has been written about various aspects of his reign, there is no satisfactory comprehensive biography of Stanisław Augustus in any language. This is not surprising. The subject is so immense that it would require two fat volumes to begin to do it justice. My overriding feeling in writing this book has been one of frustration at not being able to dwell at requisite length on the many threads that make up this exceptional story. Much more needs to be written about Stanisław's political activities, about his influence on the hundreds of people with whom he worked and corresponded, about Polish politics, about the diplomatic kaleidoscope that swallowed up the Polish Commonwealth, about the relationship between the political awakenings in Poland, America and France, about the connections between the arts, sciences and thought that produced the cataclysms at the end of the century, and about the economic factors that underlay all of these. More work needs to be done in the archives and libraries of Poland, Russia, Germany and Austria before the real causes and effects of those events, and Stanisław's part in them, can be properly assessed. I can but hope that this book might be a step in that direction.

I have based my work principally on Polish and Russian archival sources, though for the latter I relied heavily on the remarkable 146 volumes of the *Sbornik Imperatorskovo Russkovo Istoricheskovo Obschestva*, as considerations of time and expense prevented me from delving into archives in Russia.

Preface

Dates are given in new style throughout, for simplicity's sake. I do not give the nobiliary titles borne by some Polish families, as these were rarely used at the time, and can only confuse the foreign reader as to the relative standing of families. Polish names appear in their original form, and I use the spelling of *Seym* current at the time in preference to the modern *Sejm*. Stanisław himself is called Stanisław August in Polish, Stanislas-Auguste in French, and usually Stanislas Augustus in English. Since he was actually Stanisław II, to which he added 'Augustus' in an allusion to his immediate predecessors and to the Roman emperor Augustus, I have decided to refer to him as Stanisław Augustus.

I owe a debt of gratitude to the librarians and staff of the Archiwum Główne Akt Dawnych and the Biblioteka Narodowa in Warsaw, the Biblioteka Czartoryskich in Kraków, the Bibliothèque Polonaise in Paris, and the Polish Library and Polish Research Centre in London. I am grateful to Prince Philippe Poniatowski for permission to view the Poniatowski papers at the Archives Nationales in Paris. I am also grateful to Miss Joanna Wódke and Mr Jerzy Gutkowski of the Royal Castle in Warsaw for their assistance with obtaining the pictorial material. I should like to thank Mr Trevor Allen for the hard work he put into drawing the maps.

I am deeply indebted to Dr Andrzej Ciechanowiecki, Professor Andrzej Rottermund, and particularly Professor Andrzej Zahorski and Professor Isabel de Madariaga, for reading and commenting on my manuscript. I should also like to thank Shervie Price and Roger Hudson for their editorial help.

Adam Zamoyski
June, 1992

1

Bedchambers and Cabinets

On the night of 28 December 1755 Stanisław Poniatowski, the twenty-three-year-old secretary to the English ambassador in St Petersburg, set off on a clandestine escapade that was to alter the course of history.

He left his lodgings secretly, climbed into a sleigh with Lev Alexandrovich Naryshkin, and drove towards the Winter Palace. The sleigh stopped a little way from the palace, and Poniatowski followed his companion on foot through the snow to a side entrance. They passed a sentry, climbed the servants' staircase, and went into the private apartments of the Grand Duchess Catherine Alekseyevna. Naryshkin, who bore the rank, appropriately it seems, of Gentleman of the Bedchamber to the grand duchess, showed him in and then vanished. Poniatowski was nervous at meeting her alone for the first time. He was also terrified. He had heard stories of savage punishments meted out to those who had incurred imperial displeasure, and visions of Siberian mines haunted him.

In the bedroom he found a young woman of twenty-five, dressed in a simple white satin gown trimmed with lace and pink ribbons. 'She had reached that moment when beauty is at its height in any woman to whom it has been granted. With black hair, she had a complexion of radiant whiteness and a high colour; she had large, prominent and very expressive blue eyes; long black eyelashes, a Greek nose, a mouth that seemed to beg for a kiss, perfect hands and arms, a slender figure, tall rather than small, a vivacious yet deeply noble deportment, a pleasant voice and a laugh that was as gay as her humour,' he wrote. 'Such was the mistress who became the arbiter of my destiny.'[1]

That night they became lovers. Seven years later, she became Empress of all the Russias, and two years after that she used her influence and her troops to place Stanisław Poniatowski on the throne of Poland. 'These two philosophical beings seem made to be united,' wrote Voltaire, dreaming of a match that would give birth to a great northern utopia.[2] Yet the story that began in love and mutual esteem ended forty years later in misunderstanding and recrimination. Catherine humiliated Stanisław, carved up his kingdom, and erased the name of Poland from the map of Europe.

This did not come about as a result of some lovers' tiff. It stemmed from a collision of reasons of state, from the conflict of some of the strongest personalities ever to sit on European thrones, and from the political upheavals that shook the Continent in the second half of the century and culminated in the French Revolution. Poniatowski's reign was to see not only the demise of Poland, but the transformation of the whole of Central Europe and the rise of a system of power-relations that governed political life for the next two centuries.

The eighteenth century was punctuated with wars – the Northern War, the Wars of the Spanish Succession, of the Polish Succession, of the Austrian Succession, the Seven Years' War, the Turkish Wars – each involving the whole of Europe. These wars were the levers of diplomacy, and their objectives and prizes were negotiable. So were alliances. Prussia's favourite tactic under Frederick the Great was to goad an ally into starting a war, and then change horses and collect a prize from the injured side for having come to its rescue. France had two distinct diplomatic networks pursuing sometimes diametrically opposed aims. Which course was ultimately embraced depended on the whim of a monarch and his advisers, and sometimes on little more than the temper of a royal mistress.

Sheaves of alternative projects cluttered the shelves of every chancellery. Dubious justifications for claiming some province could be run up at short notice and brandished at opposing diplomats like newly dealt cards. The diplomats were often not natives of the country they represented but Baltic barons or Italian marquesses who treated their assignments in terms of professional pride rather than patriotism. They skirmished daily at balls, banquets and at tables of ombre or piquet.

They played a convoluted game, making use of spies, courtesans, venal postmasters, servants and tradesmen in order to obtain intelligence, purloin letters or plant disinformation in the enemy camp. They worked in a curious interplay of dishonesty and probity, and while bribes were often given and taken quite openly, everything had to be done with the requisite decorum. Correct form, titles and above all precedence had to be scrupulously observed.

Two states stand out as consistently successful players of this game, a reflection of their well-defined aims and strong motivations. Russia absorbed decaying states on her periphery through a combination of military saturation and able diplomacy, driven by the demands of a state structure that seemed to subordinate even her rulers. Prussia, which began the century as a mere electorate, managed to treble in size and turn herself into a powerful kingdom, by thrifty management, crafty diplomacy and military success, all of which were tightly harnessed to the fulfilment of a family's dynastic dream.

Between these two expanding states lay the Polish Commonwealth, comprising the Kingdom of Poland, the Grand Duchy of Lithuania, Royal Prussia and the vassal Duchy of Kurland. It was the largest state in Europe after Russia, but it was also the most passive. It had fallen into sharp decline, and after the death of King Jan III Sobieski in 1696 became a diplomatic and military playground for other states. They decided who would sit on its throne. The Poles' chosen rulers, the Bourbon Prince de Conti, and later Stanisław I Leszczyński, were seen off by foreign troops, and from 1697 to 1763 the throne was occupied by Augustus the Strong and then his son Augustus III, both Electors of Saxony of the Wettin dynasty. They reigned in Poland by the grace of Russia. By the Treaty of Warsaw (1717) Russia turned Poland into a demilitarised zone with a skeletal army of 18,000 men, and guaranteed to defend her territorial integrity. Theoretically an independent country, Poland had become in effect little more than a protectorate. Her king could go to war as Elector of Saxony, but the Polish Commonwealth remained neutral.

This state of affairs was the product of a curious evolution. In the sixteenth century the Kingdom of Poland and the Grand Duchy of Lithuania had turned themselves into a republic or commonwealth, in which the entire nobility, the *szlachta*, represented the source of power. The monarchy was retained by making the throne elective and absorb-

3

1 The Polish Commonwealth in 1764

ing the king into the constitutional structure. But the process was interrupted by a series of wars in the seventeenth century and subsequently distorted. Poland and Lithuania were ruled as one but retained their separate ministries, treasuries and armies. The centrifugal tendencies implicit in this encouraged regionalism and weakened the very notion of the state. The essence of all political activity became the struggle *inter majestatem ac libertatem*, as the szlachta obsessively defended their rights against imputed encroachments by the Crown. The szlachta's right to protest against royal absolutism was perverted into the *liberum veto*, which permitted a single deputy to bring the whole parliamentary process to a standstill. The right of a province to confederate against central dictates became a licence to start civil war. None of the state's institutions was strong enough to guarantee continuity or public order: even the judiciary was democratically elected.

The political structure of the Polish Commonwealth was like a house that had been gutted by fire before it was completed. A fatal combination of economic, intellectual and moral decline within Polish society

4

vitiated all attempts at repairing it, and the situation was institutional-
ised by the two neighbouring states, for whom a sick and powerless
Poland was convenient. With a population of 10 million, invaluable
mineral resources, agricultural capacity that could feed half the Continent and enough forest products to build and equip all the navies of
Europe, Poland was too rich a prize to be allowed to fall into any single
pair of hands, and potentially too powerful to be allowed to revive.

Happily for Russia and Prussia, the Poles showed few signs of
wishing to alter this state of affairs. To outsiders, they seemed determined to remain in the Middle Ages. In England and the Netherlands,
the transition from medieval attitudes to modernity was accomplished
through the Reformation. France underwent a philosophical reformation in the eighteenth century which achieved the same result. Other
Catholic states, such as Spain and Portugal, did not break the mould
until the nineteenth. In Poland, the Reformation had created a profoundly secular culture, but this process had been reversed before it had
time to set, with the result that the two traditions co-existed. Polish
social and political life therefore consisted of a conflict between lay,
modern and national perceptions, and religious, archaic, hierarchical
ones.

At the root of this political culture lay a strong democratic instinct
inimical to central authority and a conviction that all government was
tyranny. The szlachta, which made up some 10 per cent of the population, was a caste rather than a class, and it included paupers as well as
fabulously wealthy magnates. But it clung tenaciously to a theoretical
equality, which endured only in its personal liberties and its political
rights. Rich and poor alike kept a jealous watch for any threat to these.
The Russian protectorate was convenient because it precluded the
development of central government in Warsaw, which meant no state
interference with the liberty of the individual and minimal taxation.
Poland's state revenue was one-seventy-fifth that of France, and the
entire budget was smaller than England's revenue from stamp-paper.[3]
Parish-pump wisdom held that since Poland threatened nobody,
nobody would bother to threaten her back, while the mutual jealousy
of her neighbours would prevent any one of them conquering her. The
foreign armies which regularly passed through the country caused little
disruption, and were a source of profit.

Polish grain, cattle, horses and cloth were indispensable to her warring neighbours and commanded high prices. Every year a multitude of boats laden with grain or timber was floated down small rivers to the Bug and the Vistula and thence to Gdańsk, to the Warta and thence to Stettin, or the Dvina to Riga for shipment. In winter over 500 corn-laden sledges would arrive at Königsberg every day. Herds of horses and cattle were driven across the country, to Silesia or Brandenburg. The easy profits obscured the fact that Polish agriculture was hopelessly backward. Only half of the land was cultivated, and its productivity, acre for acre, was one-sixth that of English farmland.[4] Land values in some parts of the country went up tenfold in the second half of the century. Poland's terms of trade – the real value of the commercial results of production – improved steadily as new methods of production made foreign manufactured goods cheaper in relation to foodstuffs and raw materials. It is estimated that between 1600 and 1750 the terms of trade of the magnates went up threefold, those of the landowning szlachta twofold, and those of the peasants were reduced by three-quarters.[5] The peasants were not, in theory, serfs that could be bought and sold. But, whether they were landowning or labour-renting they floundered in chronic poverty, and the rights that distinguished their condition from serfdom became academic.

In the 1750s Frederick the Great of Prussia began to take forage, horses and even recruits without paying for them, or, worse, paying for them in debased currency. He hit on the idea in 1753, and began to flood Poland with coinage whose silver content was up to 70 per cent lower than face value. Before everyone learnt to recognise the bad coins, an estimated 200 million złoty (twenty-five times the annual budget) had been siphoned out of the country in silver alone.[6] This impoverished the country, and the resulting shortage of reliable currency impeded economic recovery.

The cities, which had flourished during the Renaissance, were devastated by the wars of the seventeenth century and their potential for recovery was undermined by unfavourable legislation and lack of political representation. The szlachta had encouraged the large Jewish community to set up a virtual monopoly on internal trade, which inhibited the development of a native merchant class. The landed szlachta saw no reason to spend money in Poland, since foreign goods were cheaper. This had a suffocating effect on the development of industry. Only in western Poland and the city of Gdańsk was there an entrepreneurial class indulging in industry to any significant extent: the largest industrial complex in the country belonged to the bishopric of Kraków, the richest in Europe after Strasburg and Toledo. Magnates set up factories on their estates, but this was in order to force the local peasants to spend their money in the company store, and had the effect of cutting these areas off from the national market. The magnates were also, in effect, the only banks in Poland, since only they had capital to lend, and only they, with their well-fortified palaces and private armies, provided a secure deposit. As a result, lesser szlachta would lodge their savings with them, at a rate of interest.

What had evolved was a grotesque form of baronial feudalism based on capital. And the political implications of this were magnified because there was no state structure in Poland. In most countries, penniless noblemen took service with the state, either in the army or the administration. In Poland the only alternatives were to enter the Church or to take service with a magnate. Thus it was the magnate who saved the poor nobleman from the ignominy of having to turn to trade and lose his standing, and he who gained military and political power in the process.

Having curbed the power of the Crown and reduced the parliament, the *Seym*, to a talking-shop, these oligarchs ran the day-to-day business of the country as they liked. It was they, and not the king, who decided who would get the lucrative starosties (Crown lands granted for life to the deserving on condition they paid a quarter of the revenues to the Treasury). They arrogated the best to themselves and awarded others to their followers. The magnates also exercised a monopoly over the higher offices of state. These all provided opportunities for graft, and those of Treasurer and *Hetman* (commander-in-chief) for embezzlement as well, but their principal attraction was the prestige they carried. The same went for the titles of count or prince picked up at foreign courts, which were not legally valid in Poland. Aped by the lesser szlachta, who vied for purely honorific and obsolete titles, such as Ensign of Mazovia or Cup-bearer of Sandomierz, these magnates lived out their own dynastic aspirations in a kaleidoscope of baroque splendour.

There was a score of them who were richer than any other private individual in Europe, and they knew no law but their own. They passed their time in increasingly lavish and eccentric amusements in order to escape the boredom that was the concomitant of their lack of education. A Sułkowski, bored by the colourlessness of game-birds in Poland, imported parakeets by the shipload from Africa for his shoots. A Radziwiłł divided his private army of 6,000 in two, put one of his courtiers in charge of half of it, and then made war on him. 'Nowhere is there a more magnificent nobility, and nowhere such bad citizens,' commented Bernardin de Saint-Pierre.[7]

Others saw it differently. 'The manner in which the Polish magnates lived, their power, the consideration which they enjoyed, all this struck me and convinced me that there was no condition to be envied more than that of a grandee of Poland,' wrote Alexander Vorontsov, future chancellor of Russia, who spent several months in Warsaw in 1758.[8] Foreign governments pensioned the magnates in an effort to control the internal affairs of the country, but their money had little effect, as the magnates acted according to their own reasons of state. They milked Versailles and St Petersburg, and did exactly as they pleased. Poland, in the words of one English traveller, had fallen 'into a state of almost total aristocracy'.[9]

'This republic had considerable standing and weight in Europe at the time,' opined Vorontsov. 'Although its condition did not permit it to play an active role in foreign affairs, I do not see that such a role is essential to the happiness of a nation.'[10] There was certainly something to be said for the absence of state interference, and an English diplomat coming from Prussia 'found the air of a Republic refreshing' by contrast.[11] But any such advantages were the result of indolence rather than idealism, underpinned by a stagnant educational system. The sons of magnates for the most part eschewed school altogether, and were taught the rudiments of a life of unruly drunkenness by local clerics or foreign charlatans. Apart from colourful family mythologies, the only part of their education that was strictly applied was the inculcation of all the forms and ceremonies of post-Tridentine Catholicism.

Polish society flattered itself that it was ardently attached to the Faith of Rome, and this was certainly reflected in the amount of time and effort spent in elaborate religious ritual, which flourished in pilgrimages and processions, and in the erection of magnificent shrines and churches at every turn. But religious orthodoxy co-existed with laxity of morals, and a strong mystical tradition with the most cynical observance. Morals were rigid in the recesses of the countryside and loose in Warsaw, where divorce was rife, and where, in the words of the visiting English diplomat Wraxall, 'Women of the first distinction derive more pride and respect from the rank or qualities of their lovers, than from those of their husbands.'[12]

Warsaw received enthusiastic praise from all travellers, who found it cosmopolitan, refined and joyful. But the rest of the country presented a depressing aspect, with appalling roads and filthy inns, villages of crumbling wooden hovels and sleepy decrepit towns. The manor-houses of the szlachta were little better. They were typified, in the words of a French traveller, by 'a great number of servants and horses, and almost no furniture; an oriental luxury and none of the amenities of life'.[13] The magnates inhabited magnificent palaces stuffed with French furniture and fine pictures, but these were imported baubles bearing little relation to the landscape in which they nestled, and often even less to the cultural level of their owners. These, for the most part, clung to a set of values and a cultural identity defined as 'Sarmatism'. This was based on an erroneous historical thesis that the szlachta were not Slavs at all, but the descendants of a noble warrior race, the Sarmatians, who had allegedly conquered Poland in the Dark Ages. This theory, which underlined the szlachta's racial superiority over every other class and accommodated the taste for things oriental that had swept Poland in the previous century (giving rise to, among other things, their distinct-ive dress), produced a mongrel growth of a culture that sanctioned extravagant behaviour and a xenophobic conviction that Polish was best.

Such attitudes did not go entirely unchallenged. A tenuous move-ment for national regeneration manifested itself in the 1720s and 1730s through a number of books and pamphlets advocating reform and exhorting society to save the country before it was too late. Their tenor was hardly revolutionary. They referred to the past, suggesting measures intended to revive, or at most develop the constitution, which, like all existing systems, was believed to be nearly perfect. Foreign models could not be invoked: all the other major states of Europe were monarchies, and therefore 'tyrannical' in the eyes of the szlachta. Thus all reform programmes steered an uneasy course between the Scylla of despotism and the Charybdis of anarchy.

The disciples of reform realised that the key was education. This was monopolised by the Jesuits and assorted clerical scholastics, who kept the country's four universities, ten academies and ninety-odd colleges wedded to the philosophical outlook of the counter-Reformation. In this they were ably supported by the mendicant orders, who went about the country preaching bigotry. A few magnates attempted to give their offspring a modern education, and a small academy at the enlightened court of the exiled Stanisław I Leszczyński at Lunéville in Lorraine offered free education for the sons of those who believed in such things.

Yet it was from the ranks of the Church that the reformers sprang. Stanisław Konarski, a Piarist priest (the *Fratres Scholarum Piarum*, founded by Joseph of Calasanza, known variously as *i Scolopi, Piarons* and Piarists) who had travelled widely and absorbed Locke's *Thoughts Concerning Education*, returned to Poland in the 1730s bent on changing the system. He met a kindred soul in Andrzej Załuski, Bishop of Kraków, who had amassed a vast library and attempted, and failed, to reform the Jagiellon University in Kraków. Together with the bishop's brother, Józef, himself Bishop of Kiev and also founder of a great library, they began publishing – first the laws and constitutions, which people knew only by rumour, then the classics of political literature, which explained how they should work, and then Polish literature from the past, which helped reveal the true meaning of words. In 1747 the Załuski brothers endowed their pooled library and gave it to the nation.

In 1740 Konarski opened a new school, the *Collegium Nobilium*, which removed the sons of magnates from the corrupting influence of their homes and gave them a modern education. He then reformed the twenty-eight colleges run by the Piarists in Poland. The language of instruction was changed from Latin to Polish; modern languages, political studies and cartesian philosophy replaced theology and rhetoric, and debates and dramatics were also included. Panicked by the competition, the Jesuits followed suit, introducing modern subjects into their sixty-six existing colleges and founding their own versions of the *Collegium Nobilium* in Warsaw, Wilno, Lwów, Lublin and Ostróg.

Following on the heels of education, the movement for reform and regeneration gathered in strength in the 1750s, and came to fruition with the election of Stanisław Poniatowski to the throne in the following decade.

It came too late. The Polish Commonwealth had fallen so far behind her neighbours that only a miracle could have saved her. It would have needed to be a double miracle, restoring power and wealth to the state at home, and ensuring the benevolence of her neighbours. The second of these was the least probable. A pasquinade that appeared in the London press in 1763, just as the peace conference at the conclusion of the Seven Years' War was to convene, admirably catches the policies and possibilities of the European powers:

Hôtels pour les Ministres des Cours Étrangères:

De l'Empereur; À la Bonne Volonté, rue de l'Impuissance.
De Russie; Au Chimère, rue des Caprices.
De France; Au Coq Déplumé, rue du Canada.
D'Autriche; À La Mauvaise Alliance, rue des Caprices.
D'Angleterre; À la Fortune, Place des Victoires, rue des Subsides.
De Pologne; Au Sacrifice d'Abraham, rue des Innocents, près la Place des Dévots.
De Prusse; Aux Quatre Vents, rue des Renards, près la Place des Guinées.
De Suède; Au Passage des Courtisans, rue des Visionnaires.
Des Princes de l'Empire; Au Roitelet, près de l'Hôpital des Incurables, rue des Charlatans.
De Württemberg; Au Don Quichotte, rue des Fantômes, près la Montagne en Couche.
D'Hollande; À la Baleine, sur le Marché aux Fromages, près du Grand Observatoire.[14]

European diplomacy was devoid of any sense of collective responsibility, and those powers with no direct interest in Poland left her to the tender mercies of her neighbours. Russian reason of state could not countenance a strong Poland, while Prussia was almost pathologically afraid of a Polish resurgence. Poland was acceptable to both only if she remained impotent. Ultimately, it was the political and cultural renewal taking place in Poland that condemned the country to annihilation at their hands.

The annihilation of Poland in 1795 brought Russia into the very centre of Europe and established her as the greatest continental power for a century. The territories she acquired from Poland between 1772 and 1795 had a population of nearly 40 million by 1914, forming one-third of the population of European Russia. Prussia also gained manpower. More important, she acquired prosperous territories and linked up her own provinces, which gave her a power-base from which to pursue her nineteenth-century apotheosis. The demise of Poland therefore stands in very close connection to the unification of Germany and the outbreak of the two world wars in the twentieth century. While Austria gained relatively little from the partitions of Poland, her share in the loot placed her in an ambivalent role.

The dismemberment of Poland, coinciding as it did with the French Revolution, gave the three powers a common interest in the suppression of liberalism and socio-economic evolution, which in turn arrested economic growth. It was this that created the division between Eastern and Western Europe, and even if the watchtowers have been dismantled, this does not affect the deep social and economic differences which create that division.

2

Stars and Signs

*T*he man who would reign over the demise of Poland was not elected in Catherine's bed. The path that led him to the steps of the throne was not direct, yet every curve and obstacle along it brought him nearer the throne in a way that could easily justify his own belief in predestination. It started with his birth, on 17 January 1732 in a country house at Wołczyn. Although it stood in a formal garden intersected by a canal with a fountain representing Neptune and his suite, surrounded by a park in which roamed fallow deer – an ensemble that reminded one contemporary faintly of Versailles – the house itself was an unpretentious wooden structure. The child's father was a fifty-six-year-old general of mediocre lineage, but his mother was of the blood of kings. It was as though Providence, that concept which was to hold the future king in thrall throughout his life, had taken a hand in the event, reproducing a parentage with curiously Christ-like connotations.

Stanisław was fascinated by these, and equally by the constellation of the heavens at his nativity, which was meticulously recorded. He was born in Capricorn, in a year when Saturn was in the ascendant. This god, together with his attributes – such as the black horse and the yew tree – would recur throughout his life and feature prominently in his artistic arrangements. Saturn is the sign of the return of the golden age, and astrologers deduced from the stars that the child would have a great future, strewn with obstacles over which he would triumph.[1]

A skein of legends was woven around Stanisław's origins. There was a story that a passing Italian doctor from Messina called Antonio Fornica had looked at the baby and prophesied that one day he would be king. Similar prophecies were attributed to a Swedish cabalist and an ancient rabbi. It was said that his father was the bastard son of a Lithuanian magnate of the Sapieha family and a local peasant girl, or even a poor Jewish girl. Some Poniatowskis later retaliated by forging a genealogy which used the bull in their coat-of-arms as a link with the Italian noble house of Torelli, which also sported a bull in its arms as well as its name. The Torellis were then tenuously traced back to a warring duke of Saxony in the ninth century.[2]

The reality was more prosaic. General Stanisław Poniatowski came from a family of minor szlachta, the Ciołeks, who settled on the estate of Poniatowa near Lublin in the fifteenth century. They sold Poniatowa in 1620, and moved south to the Rzeszów region. Franciszek Poniatowski, the general's father, managed not only his own estates but also those of the magnate Hieronim Lubomirski. He acquired more property in the region of Kraków, held local honorific posts, and served in the army when the need arose (he was wounded at the relief of Vienna from the Turks under King Jan III in 1683). He had four children. The two younger ones were, in traditional fashion, destined for the Church, while the elder two, Józef and Stanisław, were educated in Kraków, and then, in 1690, aged fifteen and thirteen respectively, sent off to Vienna under the care of a cleric.[3]

From Vienna, where they spent a couple of years learning German, they were supposed to travel on with their tutor, but they turned out to have minds of their own. The Emperor was massing an army for war with the Turks, and the two young men enlisted as volunteers. Stanisław distinguished himself at the battle of Temesvar, and was promoted to command a company in the regiment of Michał Sapieha, a Lithuanian magnate serving under Prince Eugene of Savoy. When the war ended with the treaty of Karlowitz in 1699, Poniatowski returned to Poland with Sapieha, who took him under his wing. Sapieha arranged a marriage for him with a supposedly wealthy widow, but this turned out to be a financial disappointment, and the couple soon separated.

The Sapieha clan were making one of their perennial bids for political control of Lithuania, which was vigorously resisted by the Radziwiłł family. Matters came to a head in November 1700, when the 3,000-strong army of the Sapiehas faced their rivals in pitched battle at Olkieniki. They were routed, and they began to cast about for allies. They did not have to look far. Charles XII, the eighteen-year-old king of Sweden, had been challenged by a formidable alliance of Peter I Tsar of Muscovy, the king of Denmark, and Augustus II Elector of Saxony and king of Poland. He defeated the Danes and then Tsar Peter, at the battle of Narva in Livonia. In the winter of 1701 the Sapiehas despatched Poniatowski to Charles XII's camp with a plea for help. The following year Charles invaded Lithuania and took the Sapiehas under his protection. Their rivals appealed to Peter, who also obliged by invading. A civil war ensued, as Peter and Charles moved their quarrel into Poland. Charles forced Peter's ally Augustus II to abdicate the Polish throne, and arranged the election of the Polish magnate Stanisław Leszczyński as King Stanisław I.

Charles XII had quickly spotted Poniatowski's qualities, and took him into his own service, making use of him as both soldier and diplomat. In 1709 Poniatowski accompanied Charles on his invasion of the Ukraine and took part in the fateful battle of Poltava, in which the Swedes were routed. Charles was badly wounded and in imminent peril of being taken prisoner. Poniatowski rallied a handful of troops, placed the king on a stretcher slung between two horses, and fought his way out of the trap. By the time they were free of the Russian pursuit, they had only twenty men left, and Poniatowski had no less than seventeen cuts and bullet-holes in his tunic. They were now in the wilds of the Ukraine, with no food and no allies. Poniatowski managed to persuade some Cossacks to join them, and led the whole group to the safety of Turkish territory beyond the Dniester. He himself went on to Istanbul and persuaded the Porte to make war on Russia.

The army the Turks sent turned out to be unwilling to fight, principally because Peter had managed to bribe its commander, the Grand Vizir. Back to Istanbul went Poniatowski, to conspire – with ministers, women, harem doctors, and anyone else who might have any influence – to get the commander dismissed. His efforts were crowned with success, and a new Vizir was appointed. The Turkish army advanced and Poniatowski could see victory within reach, but then the new Vizir decided to negotiate with the Russians. Undeterred, Poniatowski tried, and nearly succeeded, in raising a mutiny against the Vizir and taking command himself.

The Turks made peace with Russia in 1711. This opened the door for Russia to extend her hegemony over Poland. A weakened Augustus recovered the Polish throne, King Stanisław I went into exile, and Charles returned to Sweden. Poniatowski continued to serve him in various capacities. He saved his life in battle a second time at Rügen in 1715, and was eventually given the post of governor of Charles' province of Zweibrücken in Germany in 1718. Charles' death shortly afterwards left Poniatowski without a job. His reputation was such that he was approached on behalf of George I of England and by the Regent of France, but he decided to return to Poland. He made his peace with Augustus II, and was immediately put to work by his new master on various diplomatic missions. It was in the course of one of these, in Brunswick in 1720, that he met Michał Czartoryski. This meeting decided his future.

The Czartoryskis were descended from the Grand Dukes of Lithuania, one of whom ascended the Polish throne in 1386 and founded the Jagiellon dynasty. But their branch of the family had dwindled to financial and political insignificance over the centuries, and had only just begun to recover its position. A rich marriage in 1693 had put Kazimierz Czartoryski back on the political map, and his children began to annexe extensive territories on it. There were five of them. One became a bishop, one an abbess, and the three others, Michał, August and Konstancja, were to forge Poland's political destinies. On 14 September 1720, only a few months after meeting Michał Czartoryski, Stanisław Poniatowski married his sister Konstancja. The young Czartoryskis were just starting out on their political career, and in the person of Poniatowski they welcomed a skilful and experienced ally. They nurtured ambitious plans for the reform of the Polish Commonwealth, but their first priority was to manœuvre themselves into a position of strength.

In 1721 Poniatowski became commander of Augustus's court troops, and it was the wish of the king that he should in time become the Grand Hetman of the Crown. But when the king attempted to give him this post in 1728, the Potocki family, who felt it to be their preserve, made so much trouble in the Seym that he had to leave the post vacant. Poniatowski was made Crown Regimentary instead, effectively commander-in-chief of the Polish army. Three years later, in 1731, he was given a seat in the Senate, as Palatine of Mazovia. The Czartoryski brothers had also attained positions of power, and acquired a following of friends and clients, the beginnings of a political party. Since it was led jointly by the two brothers and their brother-in-law, it was known as the Czartoryski Family, or simply as the *Familia*. By 1733 the Familia felt strong enough to press for Poniatowski's appointment as hetman once more, as well as for a number of constitutional reforms. They were working closely with the king, who was eager to reassert his independence from Russia. But Augustus II died unexpectedly shortly after the Seym opened.

Russia, Prussia and Austria favoured the election of his son Augustus to succeed him, but the Familia had other plans. Initially they considered trying to get August Czartoryski elected, but when the ex-king Stanisław Leszczyński announced his candidature, they threw their support behind him. His cause was espoused by France, whose king Louis XV was married to his daughter, and was backed up by France's allies Sweden and Turkey. In Poland itself the support of the Potocki faction was purchased at the price of Poniatowski's agreeing to let them have the hetman's baton.

Leszczyński was duly elected King Stanisław I of Poland, and Voltaire composed an ode of joy. But within days Russian troops were on the march. On 5 October 1733 less than 1,000 szlachta were assembled outside Warsaw under Russian guard and forced to elect Augustus. Once again, there were two kings in Poland, one supported by Russian troops, the other by detachments of szlachta dispersed all over the country. King Stanisław and his supporters fell back on Gdańsk to await the arrival of a French fleet. Although she had declared war over the Polish succession, France was more interested in wrenching provinces from Austria than helping Stanisław, and no fleet appeared in the Gdańsk roads. He eventually fled the encircled city in disguise, and made his way to France. Ironically, he was given one of the provinces France gained from Austria, the duchy of Lorraine and Bar, in which to reign as titular king.

The Familia were left in Gdańsk to make their peace with King Augustus III, which would not be easy. Poniatowski had been in worse straits. He quickly worked out how to gain the support of Russia, whose influence was paramount in Poland. The Tsarina Anna had promised to make her favourite, Ernest Bühren (Biron), Duke of

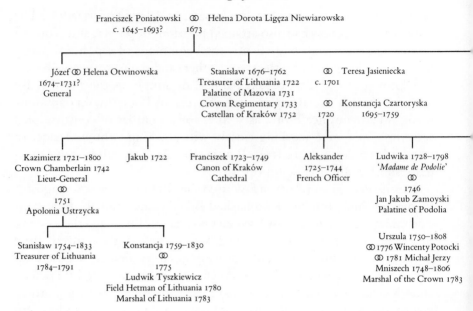

Franciszek Poniatowski ⚭ Helena Dorota Ligęza Niewiarowska
c. 1645–1693? 1673

Józef ⚭ Helena Otwinowska
1674–1731?
General

Stanisław 1676–1762 ⚭ Teresa Jasieniecka
Treasurer of Lithuania 1722 c. 1701
Palatine of Mazovia 1731
Crown Regimentary 1733 ⚭ Konstancja Czartoryska
Castellan of Kraków 1752 1720 1695–1759

Kazimierz 1721–1800
Crown Chamberlain 1742
Lieut-General
⚭
1751
Apolonia Ustrzycka

Jakub 1722

Franciszek 1723–1749
Canon of Kraków
Cathedral

Aleksander
1725–1744
French Officer

Ludwika 1728–1798
'Madame de Podolie'
⚭
1746
Jan Jakub Zamoyski
Palatine of Podolia

Stanisław 1754–1833
Treasurer of Lithuania
1784–1791

Konstancja 1759–1830
⚭
1775
Ludwik Tyszkiewicz
Field Hetman of Lithuania 1780
Marshal of Lithuania 1783

Urszula 1750–1808
⚭ 1776 Wincenty Potocki
⚭ 1781 Michał Jerzy
Mniszech 1748–1806
Marshal of the Crown 1783

1   The Poniatowskis

Kurland. This was technically a Polish fief, and the appointment needed the assent of the Polish Seym. Poniatowski wrote to Anna offering to obtain this for her. By September 1734, he was receiving cordial letters from her, and by December she was writing to Augustus insisting that he treat Poniatowski and his family with due respect. At the same time, Poniatowski approached Augustus, explaining that only the Familia could bring the remainder of Leszczyński's supporters round to his cause.

Augustus could hardly ignore the benefits of such an arrangement. He was a profoundly indolent man who avoided all serious pursuits and handed over the business of governing Saxony to a former lackey, Count Heinrich Brühl. The only question he ever asked his minister, very frequently, was: 'Brühl, have I enough money?' to which the answer was always: '*Oui, Sire!*'[4] By one disreputable means or another, the minister kept up the flow of cash, and that was all that mattered. Anyone who promised to make life easy for Augustus in Poland could expect a sympathetic hearing, and by the early 1740s Poniatowski had manœuvred the Familia back into favour. In 1752 he was made

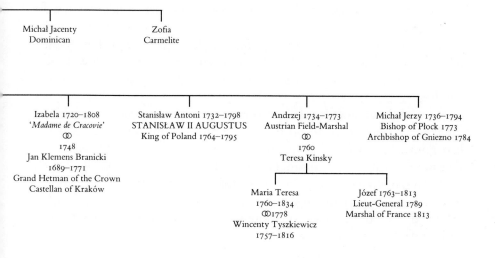

Michał Jacenty	Zofia
Dominican	Carmelite

Izabela 1720–1808
'Madame de Cracovie'
⚭
1748
Jan Klemens Branicki
1689–1771
Grand Hetman of the Crown
Castellan of Kraków

Stanisław Antoni 1732–1798
STANISŁAW II AUGUSTUS
King of Poland 1764–1795

Andrzej 1734–1773
Austrian Field-Marshal
⚭
1760
Teresa Kinsky

Michał Jerzy 1736–1794
Bishop of Płock 1773
Archbishop of Gniezno 1784

Maria Teresa
1760–1834
⚭1778
Wincenty Tyszkiewicz
1757–1816

Józef 1763–1813
Lieut-General 1789
Marshal of France 1813

Castellan of Kraków, the highest temporal post in the Senate, an honour that set the seal on his career.

Poniatowski's was a remarkable life by any standards. 'He was a man of extraordinary merit,' wrote Voltaire, 'a man who at every turn in his life and in every dangerous situation, where others can show at the very most only valour, always moved quickly, and well, and with success.'[5] The words Voltaire chose are very telling. Poniatowski was perceived as an ideal modern man by people of the Enlightenment, because his highest attributes were not old-fashioned virtues, but intelligence and successful decision-making. He was a pragmatist who gauged his aims by the bounds of the possible, not a quixotic champion of lost causes. Fundamentally irreligious, he was guided by a rationalist view of what was good, and showed energy and conviction in its pursuit. He was the perfect *honnête homme*. He was trusted by the kings he served, and he kept the respect of the exiled Stanisław Leszczyński after he had taken service with Augustus. Personal gain was not as important to Poniatowski as to most of his contemporaries, and he did not take the opportunity to amass great wealth.

He fitted the ideal of the *honnête homme* too in that he was a model husband and father. His marriage to Konstancja Czartoryska may have been a great social and political coup, but it was also a love-match, and the two remained a tender and loving couple to the end of their lives. Such marriages were unusual in the eighteenth century, and so was the care and attention given by the parents to the upbringing of their eight children.

None of them quite lived up to their father. But they all inherited his intelligence, they were all brought up with the same set of ethics that had guided him through life, and they were all expected to fend for themselves. The two daughters were brought up to make brilliant marriages. Two of the sons were destined for the priesthood. The other four were to be prepared for careers in public life, a preparation which involved a modern education, some foreign travel, military service, and political work at home.

The eldest child, Kazimierz, was perhaps the most gifted and most closely resembled his father, but lacked his moral qualities. The second, Franciszek, was well-launched on a career in the church by the time he died, aged only twenty-six. The third, Aleksander, was the father's favourite, and showed promise as a soldier. 'If God preserves him, he will one day be a great general,' the proud father wrote to Konstancja from Paris in 1741.[6] But he was killed in battle at Ypres three years later, aged nineteen. Then came the two daughters, Ludwika and Izabela. The sixth child, born in 1732, was Stanisław, and he was followed by Andrzej, who became a soldier, and Michał, the youngest, who was to become Primate of Poland.

Although their father ultimately attained the highest offices, his future was anything but certain when the children were growing up. They were therefore not brought up comfortably on some country estate to slip easily into a world which belonged to them by rights. Their education was disrupted in 1733, when the eldest was twelve and Stanisław only a year old, as the Familia found themselves engaged in the civil war over the Polish succession. And most of the next decade saw the family living out of the way in Gdańsk, while Poniatowski gradually mended his bridges. In 1734, the baby Stanisław was actually kidnapped by Józef Potocki, who was incensed that Poniatowski had abandoned Leszczyński's cause so quickly. But in the following year, the child was returned to Gdańsk and the tender care of his mother.

Konstancja was a deeply religious woman. She was referred to by some as 'the hail-cloud' on account of the severity of her looks, but she was a kind and loving mother, and positively doted on her favourite, Stanisław.[7] She exercised a strong influence over the education of all her children, but when his turn came, hers became the dominant one, since the father was often away from home. She reacted strongly against the accepted manner of educating young noblemen, which consisted in letting them run wild until their teens, and then giving them a smattering of surface accomplishments. In some cases, even these were dispensed with. Karol Radziwiłł, a contemporary of Stanisław's and the head of one of the most powerful families in Lithuania, was kept away from books, but not from the bottle, with the result that he was an alcoholic by the age of twelve. He was taught to read as an afterthought during his teens, by the curious method of metal letters hung up in a tree as targets for pistol-practice.

Konstancja's determination to give her children a thorough education took her to the opposite extreme. Stanisław's education began very early, and it was entrusted to eminent scholars, such as the Gdańsk historian Gotfryd Lengnich. As Stanisław later explained, 'She applied herself above all to give my soul a temper of austerity and to elevate it, which, as she intended, raised me above the normal behaviour of children, but which also gave rise to several of my defects; I began to think of myself as being superior to my fellows, because I was not prone to the usual faults of children, and because I knew many things which they had never been taught. I became a little person who seemed very arrogant.'[8]

He was a delicate, even sickly, child, and this encouraged her to keep him away from what she believed to be at best a waste of time, and at worst a corrupting influence – other children's company. She taught him to think, to treat life as a challenge, both moral and rational, and to despise ignorance and stupidity. Since the latter were the norm among his contemporaries, this set him apart. 'As a result of always seeking only perfect companions', he later observed, 'I ended by speaking with no one.'[9]

In 1739 the family moved from Gdańsk to Warsaw, where they occupied a spacious mansion Poniatowski had built on Krakowskie

Przedmieście, the city's principal artery. They lived a comfortable but quiet life, spending the holidays on the modest estate of Malczyce in Podolia (Poniatowski had sold Wołczyn to August Czartoryski in 1744). The seven-year-old Stanisław now abandoned the Polish costume and donned French dress to face the world and go to school. His education was entrusted to the Theatine Fathers. Theirs was an unusually liberal programme, heavily marked by the ideas of the Enlightenment. It was, in the 1740s, the only Catholic establishment in Poland to use Polish as the language of instruction, and the only one which taught modern philosophy. Along with the traditional subjects, and a range of scientific ones, Stanisław learnt French, in which he quickly became fluent, German, Italian, and English.

He was exposed to some singular influences during these first years in Warsaw. The Principal of the Theatine priests, Father Antonio Portaluppi, was irreligious and had a reputation for depravity. According to one contemporary, he lived in 'a beautifully arranged apartment closed to the profane, but well known to all the Italian ballerinas and singers of the Warsaw stage'.[10] Additional education was provided by individuals such as the Abbé Allaire, a freethinking Frenchman in the service of Poniatowski, who was later to be tutor to the regicide Duc d'Orléans, *Philippe-Égalité*. Count Hermann Keyserling, the Russian ambassador in Warsaw and a friend of Stanisław's father, contributed lessons in logic and mathematics. Later, the boy was taught military studies by Colonel Thoux de Salverte, an active Rosicrucian and one of the founders of Freemasonry in Poland. These people were all either Deists, freethinkers, or devotees of the secular ideals of the Enlightenment, and their influence was in apparent contradiction to Konstancja's principles. But, for all her piety, she was far from orthodox in her beliefs. Her confessor, Father Śliwiński, who was also Stanisław's spiritual instructor, was a quietist, even a Jansenist at heart, believing in predestination.

The child's mind was soon overloaded, not only with information, but with the philosophical and theological concepts fashionable at the time. He had a breakdown at the age of twelve as a result of trying to resolve questions of predestination and free will. He soon recovered, but this joyless education left enduring marks. 'I was, you might say, never allowed the time to be a child: it is as if one took the month of April out of the year,' he later wrote.[11] The whole tenor of his education suggested the futility of combating fate, stressed the virtue of resignation, and undoubtedly helped to develop the passive streak which friends often noted in Stanisław. The heavy dose of philosophical fatalism drummed into him at such an early age imbued him with a lasting melancholy and a sense of the pointlessness of human life.

By the middle of his teens, he was, by his own confession, overeducated, excessively submissive to his parents, in awe of their qualities, and incapable of taking an interest in anything that was not intellectually worthy. He was more at ease in the company of older people and women than that of his peers. He lacked gaiety and often seemed preoccupied or even depressed. This was compounded by the fact that he was small, stocky and clumsy.

When he was sixteen his father decided it was time to make a man of him. To the old general, a military campaign was 'worth all the academies on earth', and the two older boys had already been subjected to the experience. In 1748 a Russian army was marching across Poland to take part in the War of the Austrian Succession, and Poniatowski arranged for Stanisław to go with it.

But just as he was about to set off, news came of the signature of the preliminaries of peace at Aix-la-Chapelle. Stanisław was disappointed. 'Any man called to lead a nation and who has not known war is like a man to whom nature has refused one of the five senses,' he later commented.[12] Since the preparations had been made, it was decided he would go anyway. Even if he could not take part in a campaign, he could at least see assembled armies and meet a few of Europe's great generals. Foreign travel was always instructive, and it was felt that as well as being worthy of curiosity, the United Provinces of the Netherlands, as a republic, held particular relevance for Poles. He set off in the spring of 1748, accompanied by an old German soldier who had ended up as a factotum for the Poniatowskis. The parents probably had the example of their eldest son in mind – Kazimierz had been sent off over eight years before to campaign under the Maréchal de Saxe, and while he had distinguished himself in battle, he had also turned into something of a profligate – and they made Stanisław solemnly swear that he would not gamble, drink wine or marry.

Thus armed against the perils of the outside world, Stanisław left home. He travelled through Prague, Bayreuth, Frankfurt and down the Rhine to Cologne. On 10 June he reached Aix-la-Chapelle, where he met some of the statesmen assembled for the peace congress, most notably Count Wenzel Kaunitz, the Imperial minister. Thence he went to Maastricht, to see Marshal Löwendahl's army, and on to Brussels, to meet the Maréchal de Saxe, who received him with much honour, in recognition of his father and his brother Kazimierz. Stanisław toured camps, battlegrounds and sites of sieges in the Low Countries and Flanders; everywhere he was cordially greeted by commanders who had served with or against his father in one or other of the wars of the last thirty years.

From the military point of view it was a waste of time. The armies he saw, mostly French, were enjoying the leisure of peacetime, and the officers were engaged in amateur theatricals rather than exercises. Löwendahl took him rabbit-shooting and invited him to come to Paris. But there were other things to catch his attention. He visited shipyards, factories, banks and botanical gardens, taking in all the usual 'curiosities' on the way, and if most of the things he saw made only a superficial impression, the progress and prosperity in evidence all around him set him thinking about the backwardness of Poland.[13] And while exploring the Dutch cities he discovered the pleasures of art. 'I would get entirely carried away while looking at a Rubens or a Van Dyck,' he wrote.[14] In Brussels he bought a little painting, and felt he had acquired something priceless. The picture was probably Pompeo Batoni's repentant Magdalen, which later hung above his bed, and it awakened in him the joy of collecting that was to develop into a passion.[15]

With his return to Poland in October 1748, the sixteen-year-old Stanisław began his political apprenticeship. The Familia were strong in the Seym and in favour at court, and they attempted to implement a programme of reforms which had been set out by Stanisław's father in 1744 in a pamphlet entitled *Letter from a Country Gentleman*. It proposed an increase in the army, to be paid for by a reorganisation of the fiscal system, and measures lifting some of the social and economic restraints on city-dwellers with a view to encouraging trade and industry. On the constitutional side, the programme included limiting the power of the liberum veto, the introduction of salaries for deputies to the Seym, and the reform of the judiciary. On the face of it, there should have been no problem, since Poniatowski's pamphlet was answered by another, written by a member of the rival faction, Antoni

Potocki's *Appeal to Men of Every Condition*, which voiced similar thoughts.

Matters were not that simple however. The Potocki and Radziwiłł families were suspicious of the Familia's real intentions, while the neighbouring powers were wary of any Polish proposals. 'It is in my interest that matters should remain in a state of some confusion in Poland, and that no Seym should maintain itself,' Frederick of Prussia wrote to his agent in Warsaw.[16] As a result, the Seym was broken up by a veto before the reforms could be proposed.

The Familia's response was to consolidate their position further, and try again. Michał Czartoryski was now Vice-Chancellor of Lithuania, where he had a great following, his brother August was Palatine of Ruthenia, his other brother Teodor was Bishop of Poznań, Poniatowski was Palatine of Mazovia, while their Flemming, Massalski, Ogiński, Mostowski and other allies were entrenched in various key posts. Almost as important as offices were the starosties which gave them and their supporters financial bases. Between them, the members of the Familia were in possession of an impressive number of these, and, being in favour at court, could procure others for supporters or would-be supporters. Another avenue of political manœuvre was the dynastic marriage. Stanisław's sister Ludwika had recently been wedded to Jan Zamoyski, Palatine of Podolia, and in November 1748, on his return from the Netherlands, Stanisław attended the marriage of his other sister, the eighteen-year-old Izabela, to Jan Klemens Branicki, the sixty-year-old Palatine of Kraków and Field Hetman of the Crown. The wedding was held jointly with that of Michał Czartoryski's daughter Aleksandra to Michał Sapieha, Palatine of Podlasie. But even this impressive array of power and influence, behind which was ranged a strong parliamentary party, was powerless against a solitary veto, and the Familia's programme was blocked once again in the Seym.

Stanisław was politically apprenticed to his uncle Michał Czartoryski, who initiated him into the business of keeping clients and allies in line, and gaining appointments or favours for those who could be of use to the cause. Morale was low in the wake of the recent failure, and Stanisław's first direct political experience was unedifying. In October 1749 he was sent down to Piotrków for the elections to the post of Marshal of the Supreme Tribunal of the Crown, and was a

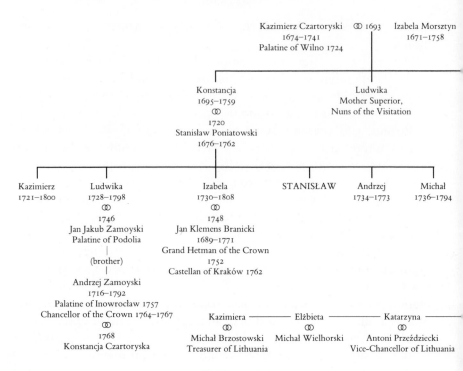

Kazimierz Czartoryski ⚭ 1693   Izabela Morsztyn
1674–1741   1671–1758
Palatine of Wilno 1724

Konstancja   Ludwika
1695–1759   Mother Superior,
⚭   Nuns of the Visitation
1720
Stanisław Poniatowski
1676–1762

Kazimierz   Ludwika   Izabela   STANISŁAW   Andrzej   Michał
1721–1800   1728–1798   1730–1808   1734–1773   1736–1794
           ⚭   ⚭
          1746   1748
     Jan Jakub Zamoyski   Jan Klemens Branicki
     Palatine of Podolia   1689–1771
          | Grand Hetman of the Crown
      (brother)   1752
          | Castellan of Kraków 1762
    Andrzej Zamoyski
      1716–1792
  Palatine of Inowrocław 1757
Chancellor of the Crown 1764–1767   Kazimiera ——— Elżbieta ——— Katarzyna ——
         ⚭   ⚭   ⚭   ⚭
      1768   Michał Brzostowski   Michał Wielhorski   Antoni Przeździecki
  Konstancja Czartoryska   Treasurer of Lithuania   Vice-Chancellor of Lithuania

2   The Familia

witness to the events which marked the nadir of Polish political life. The Familia sent prodigious numbers of supporters, while the Potocki faction bolstered their ranks with a few regiments of private troops. This nearly led to a pitched battle in the church where the electoral meeting was held. Kazimierz Poniatowski, who was leading the Familia faction, saved the situation through courage and tact, but the constitution of a Supreme Tribunal was prevented for the first time in the country's history. Stanisław did not know whether to be more amazed at the travesty of politics he had seen or at the indifference with which the outcome was accepted. In the following year, he was elected to the Seym, but this was promptly dissolved by a veto from one of the Potocki faction.

Stanisław was depressed by the futility of this activity, and he was not enjoying life in Warsaw. He found working with his uncle Michał demanding as well as dull. The austere Poniatowski house

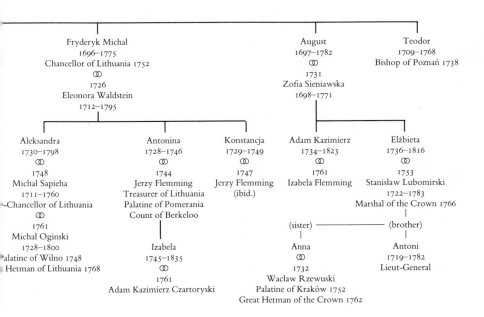

Fryderyk Michał 1696–1775 Chancellor of Lithuania 1752 ∞ 1726 Eleonora Waldstein 1712–1795			August 1697–1782 ∞ 1731 Zofia Sieniawska 1698–1771	Teodor 1709–1768 Bishop of Poznań 1738

Aleksandra
1730–1798
∞
1748
Michał Sapieha
1711–1760
-Chancellor of Lithuania
∞
1761
Michał Oginski
1728–1800
alatine of Wilno 1748
Hetman of Lithuania 1768

Antonina
1728–1746
∞
1744
Jerzy Flemming
Treasurer of Lithuania
Palatine of Pomerania
Count of Berkeloo

Izabela
1745–1835
∞
1761
Adam Kazimierz Czartoryski

Konstancja
1729–1749
∞
1747
Jerzy Flemming
(ibid.)

Adam Kazimierz
1734–1823
∞
1761
Izabela Flemming

(sister) ——————— (brother)

Anna
∞
1732
Wacław Rzewuski
Palatine of Kraków 1752
Great Hetman of the Crown 1762

Elżbieta
1736–1816
∞
1753
Stanisław Lubomirski
1722–1783
Marshal of the Crown 1766

Antoni
1719–1782
Lieut-General

hold offered little to stimulate a young man in the eighteenth year of his life, and he seems to have had no close relationship with any of his siblings apart from Kazimierz, who doted on him. But Kazimierz was eleven years his senior and much taken up with political activities of one sort or another. He held the influential rank of Crown Chamberlain, in 1744 he was made a knight of the Order of the White Eagle, and he had his eye firmly focused on the hetmanate as the ultimate goal of his career. He was the leading skirmisher of the Familia in the Seym and one of its best negotiators out of it. Handsome, extrovert, active and temperamental, he was hardly the ideal companion for the farouche adolescent.

Stanisław was finding it difficult to make friends, being 'of a disposition that easily adopts a decisive tone', in Kazimierz's words. 'Do not expose yourself to a discussion with him, yet do not indulge him too much,' Kazimierz advised his sister Ludwika Zamoyska when their brother went to stay with her. 'When he has hurt someone by his criticism or his misplaced wit, you will be able, if you show much kindness and friendship, to make him see the harm he can do himself, and that he daily does himself; and I assure you that if you accompany your gentle admonitions with professions of the interest you take in everything that regards him, he will take it all in very good heart, and will even be grateful to you for it,' he went on. 'I have often found this to be so when I have had occasion to speak my mind to him . . . as for me, I have high hopes for him, and I love him very dearly.'[17]

Stanisław was showing all the signs of adolescent alienation. Things were not made any easier by the fact that he was also in poor health, perhaps as a result of depression. In 1749 he fell ill. The family grew alarmed. Count Keyserling, the Russian ambassador and family friend, suggested that he be sent to consult a Doctor Lieberkühn in Berlin, for whom he professed great veneration. So in the early months of 1750, Stanisław set off for the Prussian capital. He spent a couple of months there. The cure did indeed do him good. What did him much more good was the influence of someone he met there, someone who would be probably the greatest single influence in his life.

3

A Second Father

Stanisław's impressions of Berlin were far from favourable. He had two interviews with Frederick the Great, who had 'the embarrassed air of a man who feels he should always speak more brilliantly than others and fears he might not succeed; he had an anxious look, haggard eyes, a nervous countenance, dirty clothes – in all not a very noble figure'.[1] While he admired the architecture of Sans-Souci, Stanisław deplored the scruffiness and the meanness he saw in the royal apartments. He found Berlin society depressing. Most of the menfolk seemed to be perpetually absent on active service, while the ladies suffered from a 'voltairomania' which rendered them vulgar rather than entertaining in his eyes. The only person he did like was the English ambassador, whom he met on 9 July 1750 at a dinner given by Count Bülow, the Saxon minister in Berlin.

Sir Charles Hanbury Williams was an intriguing figure. A wealthy Monmouthshire gentleman, he had married well, represented his county in Parliament, and in 1744 became a Knight of the Bath. He wrote poetry and was prized as a conversationalist. A school friend of Henry Fielding, he numbered among his close friends people such as Sir Hans Sloane, Horace Walpole, Henry Fox, the first Lord Holland, and his brother Stephen, later Lord Ilchester. His notorious affairs with actresses, his outrageous behaviour, and his caustic wit made him a prominent member of the gilded set (which included his cousin George Selwyn, Sir Francis Dashwood and John Lord Hervey) that founded the Society of Dilettanti and the Hell-Fire Club. His enemies imputed secret vices to him, and priggish nineteenth-century historians depicted him as the epitome of the corruption and perversion they saw as the essence of the eighteenth century. But his friends revered him, and Walpole considered him 'a bright genius, dangerously great'.[2] He certainly had a dangerous capacity for offending people, and his vicious poetic squibs eventually made it politic for him to find an honourable escape from London. The result was that in 1747, at the age of thirty-nine, he was posted ambassador to the Court of Saxony at Dresden, and in 1750 to that of Berlin, which he hated. He thought Frederick II 'the compleatest Tyrant that God ever sent for a scourge to an offending people', and found Berlin society very dull.[3]

The reticent Stanisław was struck by the cultivated and witty Welshman. Williams had already met Kazimierz Poniatowski, to whom he took a great liking, and he was intrigued by his little brother. Among the many contradictory traits of his complex character was a pronounced avuncular streak, and this immediately focused on the awkward youth, of whom he saw much over the next three weeks.[4] His inclination was undoubtedly backed up by professional consider-ations. Stanisław's family were the foremost party in Poland, and Williams' mission was to further a Russo-Austro-Saxon rapproche-ment based on a stabilisation in Poland. Stanisław was therefore a useful contact, and when the young man left Berlin Williams proposed that they should keep up a correspondence on matters of mutual interest, and gave him a set of cyphers for the purpose.

As soon as England had begun to take an interest in the affairs of the region, the Familia sought to engage her on their side. Stanisław was therefore encouraged to cultivate Williams. When, a few months later, Williams arrived in Warsaw for the Seym, the Czartoryskis hardly let him out of their sight. Stanisław would call on him in the mornings to take him to lunch with August Czartoryski at Wilanów or dinner at the Branicki Palace. Williams was enchanted. 'Of all the countries I was ever in, I think I like the manner of living here the most,' he wrote to Henry Fox in London. 'You meet with numbers of sensible people with whom one converses agreeably, and numbers of noble houses always open to one. I could name five or six, where they all live better and more at their ease than in any parts of Europe I have seen . . . I could stay here with pleasure for some months. The ladies are hand-some and polite to a degree, and, tho' educated at home in the forests of

Lithuania, have all the noblest carriage and are as accomplished persons as I ever met with.'[5] He was impressed by the Familia, particularly August Czartoryski, 'a man of good sense and clear judgment, of great resolution and courage', as he reported to his superiors. He was more cautious about Michał, but liked Jerzy Flemming, and particularly old Poniatowski, 'a great friend of mine, & tho' near fourscore as active as he was at eighteen'.[6]

In 1751 Williams was back in Dresden, and it was partly on that account that it was decided Stanisław should go there. He was overjoyed at the opportunity to escape from the drudgery of party politics at home and to see the renowned Saxon court. In the autumn he set off for Leipzig, where he found Augustus, his queen Maria-Josepha, who was, in Williams' characteristically succinct phrase, 'ugly beyond painting and malicious beyond expression', and Count Brühl, who remained unmistakably parvenu in his frills and diamonds.[7] Always in high spirits, Brühl was a cool, implacable schemer, and operated through a web of cronies and spies, playing people off against each other and keeping his royal master isolated from anyone who might expose his titanic embezzlements. Happily for Stanisław, Countess Brühl took a liking to him. The king conferred the title of gentleman of the bedchamber on him, and invited him to accompany the court to Hubertusburg for the hunting season. This was the happiest part of the year for Augustus. It was also the occasion for an idyllic holiday for his court, for, as Stanisław put it, 'the life one led at Hubertusburg could honestly be described as delicious'.[8]

The term 'hunting' is perhaps misleading. The obese Augustus did not tear about the countryside in pursuit of the nimble stag. After Mass at eight o'clock he drove to an ample breakfast in the forest. Those who could do so then mounted up and moved off with the hounds, followed at a leisurely pace by the king and queen in their carriages. 'The blue, yellow and silver uniform of the court, the fine horses, the carriages filled with the ladies of the Queen's suite, and above all the extreme beauty of that forest of three leagues in diameter, criss-crossed by twenty-four rides straight as a die, gave this diversion the appearance of a party,' Stanisław explains.[9]

After the hunt, everyone went back to change and rest before the exertions of the evening, which included music and banquets. Before retiring for the night Stanisław would spend an hour or two in conversation with Williams. One only has to read Williams' letters to appreciate the appeal such causeries must have held for the nineteen-year-old Stanisław. Williams combined the frivolity which his parents denied with the intelligence that most of his Polish acquaint-ances lacked. A cultivated man with a generous, secular outlook, he felt an almost missionary urge to help gifted young people expand their horizons. He had an enormous influence over young men such as his diplomatic secretary, Harry Digby, later Earl Digby, and Lord Essex, who was to marry Williams' daughter. Stanisław presented a chal-lenge he could hardly fail to take up.

Stanisław craved the avuncular influence, which compensated for certain shortcomings in the young man's relationship with his father. Indeed, Williams would later call him his 'adopted son', and was as proud as a father of the rapid progress he made. He began filling in the gaps in his education, and, in Stanisław's own words, 'helped a great deal to give me in the *grand monde* a consideration and an aura of maturity that my age still denied me'.[10] Stanisław was an ideal pupil, voraciously storing every morsel of knowledge in his capacious memory – he remembered everything about people he met, and could quote Shakespeare and Milton at the drop of a hat. 'You will be surprised to see a person of nineteen years of age so formed and so knowing as this young gentleman,' Williams wrote to Robert Keith, his colleague in Vienna, at the end of November 1751.[11]

Williams deplored the streak of melancholy in Stanisław's char-acter, and the tendency towards resignation implanted by his upbring-ing. He challenged his fatalism and urged him to assert himself. Stanisław's outlook was transformed by the friendship, and for the first time in his life he began to enjoy himself actively. 'I was in good health, I had little money, but enough for my needs, I had no worries, I was living in a very beautiful place, in a beautiful season, in very fine company,' he recorded. 'I have never in my life been as happy as I was during those six weeks.'[12]

Vienna, where Stanisław went next, seemed remarkably dull in comparison. The court was austere and formal, deeply marked by the stiff Spanish etiquette inherited of old. Maria Theresa's piety cast a gloom over everything, and the only amusement permitted was card-games, which Stanisław detested. Fortunately, he had the companion-ship of Harry Digby, with whom he had travelled from Saxony, and soon fell into an adolescent romance with Angelika Kotulinsky, a lady-in-waiting to Princess Victoria of Savoy, with whom he exchanged solemn vows. His parents heard about it before he had even left Vienna, and on his return to Warsaw at the end of 1751, they knocked out of his head all thoughts of pursuing an engagement to a young lady who, well-born though she was, represented nothing either financially or politically.

The round of political activities Stanisław was obliged to resume back in Poland seemed more sterile than ever. But his morale was sustained by a regular flow of letters from Williams and Digby. They addressed him as 'Mon cher Palatinello' (when his father was promoted from Palatine of Mazovia to Castellan of Kraków, he became their 'cher Castellanino'), and regaled him with advice, gossip and, during the Dresden carnival in February 1752, a certain amount of smut.[13] 'The young Poniatowskis have a hereditary right to surmount all difficulties,' wrote Digby with bravado in response to a fit of despondency.[14]

In the spring of 1752, Stanisław was elected to the Treasury Commission for Mazovia, which spent its time in drinking and idleness rather than auditing accounts. In the summer he stood for election to the Seym which was to meet at Grodno that autumn. This was an exercise in futility, since it was known that Augustus hated having to go to Lithuania, and would find somebody to sabotage the proceedings so that he could return home as quickly as possible.

Although elections to the Seym were no model of democracy, there were no rotten boroughs in the English sense. 'For several days before the seymik [the regional electoral assembly], one had to reason from morning till night with the rabble, admire their chatter, appear to be enchanted by their dismal wit, and on top of that continually embrace their dirty and lousy persons,' Stanisław recalled. 'In lieu of relief, one had, ten or twelve times a day, to go and *confer* with the grandees of the county, that is to say to listen, in an atmosphere of the greatest secrecy, to the details of their little domestic quarrels, humour their mutual jealousies, embrace the cause of their promotion to the dignities of the district, concert with them how much and to which of the most noble electors one had to give ready money, and breakfast, dine, tea and sup with them, at tables which were as badly cleaned as they were poorly served . . .'[15]

This was not the worst. After eight days of canvassing he and his victorious colleague, Antoni Glinka, had to celebrate their election at the nearby home of the Starosta of Maków.

The old Starosta, gout-ridden and incapable of movement, had no further aim to his existence beyond drink; his wife was the object of the most tender desire of the lord Glinka, who, a widower himself, could hardly wait for her to become one; in the interim, he had entrusted her with his daughter from an earlier marriage, aged eighteen, plump, white, a real Cunégonde . . . Glinka proposed a ball to these two ladies, who with him and myself made up a lone foursome, while the old husband represented the assembly. The place for the dance was a sort of wooden portico on half-rotten boards some twelve feet square, supported on four posts, where the family would come to take the air at the door of the house. The Starosta installed himself in a corner; a single tuneless fiddler occupied the other, and Glinka and myself held the floor with the two ladies from six o'clock in the evening till six o'clock in the morning. At the end of each dance Glinka raised a toast, bowing to the old Starosta, who joined him faithfully, draining his glass to the last drop, each one to my health, and since I did not drink, I would bow deeply each time. No, if I had not seen it with my own eyes, I would never have believed it possible. The hands moved right around the clock, and Glinka did not stop dancing and drinking; he only, on three occasions, made reductions to his attire, each time very humbly begging my pardon; he first removed his belt, then his coat, then his *żupan*, or vest; in the end he was only in his shirt, and to go with his voluminous Polish breeches and his shaven head, he donned the dressing-gown of the lady of the house, who delighted in all these charming gentilities. At six o'clock in the morning I begged for mercy; with great difficulty I obtained permission to retire to a separate room, where I had only just had time to change my shirt, when the lady of the house, along with my guide and his daughter, made a new irruption into it; I almost went down on my knees to obtain that I should be allowed to rest.[16]

To cap it all, his carriage broke an axle and one of a fine team of horses recently given by his father died on the way back to Warsaw.

Stanisław was greeted with a thundering admonition from his father, who 'forgot for a quarter of an hour that I was now invested with the sacred dignity of a parliamentary deputy, and predicted that I would never make a decent gentleman, because I did not know how to value what I was given, and above all because I did not know how to look after horses, whose merit, nobility and all other qualities I was duly reminded of.'[17]

Stanisław stood in awe of his father. Relations with his mother remained very close, and he wrote to her regularly whenever he was away from home, laying bare all his thoughts and feelings. Both were excessively strict with Stanisław, alarmed as they were at the way Kazimierz was developing. His talents and abilities were undeniable, but his cynicism, his violent temperament, and his profligacy worried them. He had also, in the previous year, married against their wishes. Neither the seventy-six-year-old patriarch nor the doting mother could be expected to understand the feelings and desires of the twenty-year-old Stanisław, and this made Williams' friendship all the more welcome. Williams had become a fast friend of the whole family. He gave Kazimierz two English horses, and his father a couple of Irish wolfhounds. Konstancja was sent gifts of English beer, and she reciprocated with Polish sable caps for Harry Digby.

Beneath the pleasantries lay a solid political motive. England wanted to take Saxony out of France's orbit and tie it in with Russia. The best way of doing this, and at the same time of preventing France and Prussia from muddying the waters during the interregnum after the eventual death of Augustus III, was to arrange for the election of his son Frederick Christian to the Polish throne during the father's lifetime. The Familia were prepared to help if they could obtain reforms and a dominant position for themselves out of it. There was no constitutional precedent for such a move, so the Familia, Williams and the Russian ambassador Keyserling began to consider achieving their ends through a confederation backed by Russian arms and English money.[18]

The first step was to capture all vacant offices for supporters of the Familia at the forthcoming Seym. Williams arrived in Warsaw in August, and at the beginning of September he set off for Grodno in the wake of the king. The royal party stopped at Białystok, the residence of Jan Klemens Branicki, Stanisław's brother-in-law. 'It is a good house, much like Ditchley (Ld Litchfield's) only bigger & the wings much larger,' wrote Williams to his brother. 'There is a large village close by it which is all made up of little tenements pretty well furnished for the reception of strangers, and when I was there it was brim full, for we were not so few as 800 persons lodged and fed by the Master of the house. As Great General [hetman], he has his Guards like a King. I was lodged in one of the wings & before my window there was drawn up every morning a company of Janissaries exactly dressed like those of the Sultan, & at 5 of the clock I was usually awaked by Turkish musick which is very bad.'[19]

The marriage which the Familia had so carefully arranged had proved disappointing. The hetman neglected his wife Izabela, who consoled herself in the arms of his right-hand man, Andrzej Mokronowski. Branicki was a worthy and by no means unintelligent man, but he had little education, and he resented being steered by the cultivated Czartoryski brothers. He was drifting away from them and pursuing his own policy. He spared no effort in his desire to gain the favour of Augustus, and he knew what kind of sport the king liked. The day's shooting he arranged at Horoszcz was entirely to the king's taste, as Stanisław explains:

Wild animals, brought in cages and released in the groves of this charming place, were forced to climb along wooden ramps with tall sides to the tops of the trees which line the canal. There they found a pivoting trap which, by projecting them over the water at a height of thirty yards, gave the king the opportunity of shooting wolves, boars and bears in full flight. Hounds waited at the bottom of the trees, to chase them, across water or land, until such time as the king thought it proper to kill them. One of the bears, encountering a boat, climbed up onto its prow in order to escape the hounds; young Rzewuski, brother of the Marshal, and Saul, first secretary at the Saxon Ministry of Foreign Affairs, withdrew quickly to the back of the boat, and along with the boatman who steered it they made it lean backwards so far that it capsized on its end. The bear flew through the air for a second time and fell into the water beside these gentlemen, who had quite a fright, and whose adventure delighted the king to an extraordinary extent.[20]

Another day's sport was organised in the forest of Białowieża. More than 3,000 beaters drove a herd of bison and an assortment of other game into an enclosure in the middle of which stood a raised stand from which the king, the queen, and their sons the princes Xavier and Charles disposed of forty-two bison and twenty-five elks, according to Williams' calculations. The court dutifully applauded the royal prowess. But the greatest applause went elsewhere, as Stanisław records: 'A stag had the honours of the day. He entered the enclosure with his female and proceeded to marry her in the presence of the king and the queen, who averted her eyes, and returned safe and sound into the depths of the forest through the throng of a thousand spectators.'[21]

A few days later the whole party moved on towards its destination. Grodno, the second city of Lithuania, was a decrepit dump. 'Usk is a Paris in comparison,' Williams wrote to his brother in Wales.[22] There was a peeling castle, two brick palaces, seventeen monasteries and churches, a sea of Jewish hovels, and a collection of wooden houses, most of them mere shells which came to life as they were filled with fine furniture and hangings for the duration. With its unpaved streets and rudimentary buildings, the little town was like the encampment of some sybaritic army. 'Tho the town is no bigger than Usk nobody makes a visit but in a coach and six,' wrote Williams. 'The Palatines come hither travelling like the ancient patriarchs, with their families, their household, their furniture, their dependants, their servants, their herds and their flocks. Their beds and their kitchen utensils come with them. In short everything that is absolutely necessary. I have lived here a month without being able at any price to purchase a chamber pot.'[23] Williams, who had never known anything of Poland but the sophisticated luxury of Warsaw, was appalled by the 'barbarous country' he found it to be.

Stanisław and his English friends lodged with Jerzy Flemming, Treasurer of Lithuania, but spent most of their time at the various assemblies hosted by Michał Radziwiłł, Hetman of Lithuania and Palatine of Wilno, who owned one of the two brick palaces. The mixture of squalor and refined luxury in this abode gave it the air of 'a poorhouse in triumph', and the dim-witted though affable host was cut out to fit. 'He would have been happy to have the whole Commonwealth to dinner and supper every day, as long as people appeared to respect him,' Stanisław noted.[24]

The Seym did not last long. The only thing the magnates were interested in was a number of new appointments that had to be made. Who they went to would be decided by horse-trading between themselves and Brühl. While this went on, the deputies in the Seym were allowed to 'harangue each other pointlessly, with no purpose and no aim, playing to the gallery and killing time', in Stanisław's words. A deputy from Kiev made a particularly stupid peroration, and Stanisław made his maiden speech in response. 'I seemed to be in the right, and in favour with the assembly; this yielded no effective results, but it helped to give me confidence and to get me noticed.' A stop was called to this the moment the appointments had been agreed. A deputy was given a present by Augustus and told to veto the Seym. The Marshal made a fine speech expressing surprise and sadness, Stanisław and a number of deputies signed a statement of protest, and the king set off for Dresden, delighted at having had to spend no more than two weeks in Grodno.[25]

The Seym had been a defeat for the Familia, who failed to obtain any important offices. Goaded on by the new French ambassador, the Comte de Broglie, by Franciszek Bieliński, most of the Potocki clan and his own son-in-law Jerzy Mniszech, Brühl had managed to turn his royal master against the Czartoryskis and their friends, and their influence at court came to an abrupt end. This suited Williams as little as it suited the Familia. Throughout the winter and spring he conferred and plotted with Keyserling, and in July 1753 they presented to their courts a legally watertight plan for a confederation to force the election of Frederick Christian and put the Familia back in the saddle.[26] Williams wrote to Lord Newcastle and obtained for them a formal profession of the English court's friendship and protection.[27] But while this afforded them some measure of security, the Familia were powerless.

The setback at Grodno brought out a number of tensions. The relationship between Michał, August and Stanisław Poniatowski had worked on the basis of a sound division of roles. Michał was the policy-maker, August lent wisdom and money to the enterprise, and Poniatowski was the executive. With time, Michał took less notice of the ageing Poniatowski. By 1752, when Poniatowski was made Castellan of Kraków, he was less active and, after the Grodno débâcle, retired altogether. Relations were soured by the fact that years before, when Poniatowski had been Crown Regimentary, he had ceded the colonelcy of the Royal Footguards to August, on the condition that August would cede it to Poniatowski's son Kazimierz when the latter came of age. When the time came, however, August avoided honouring the agreement. As the power of the Czatoryskis grew, so did their conception of their own grandeur. The Poniatowskis were treated more and more as poor cousins.

The young Poniatowskis felt this keenly, and resented their uncles for it. Stanisław did not like Michał Czartoryski. He was a hard-working, strong-willed man, good at party-political work, very popular on account of his sociability and his kindness. In Lithuania, his power-base, he stood out from the brutish and venal Radziwiłłs as a model of classical probity and wisdom. But he could be caustic at times, and he was a hard taskmaster. He was also vain. August was a much more likeable person, with 'a sort of magic in his demeanour', as Stanisław put it. 'Nobody has more than he the gift of flattering the pride, of enslaving the heart and the minds of trusting characters.'[28] As a young man, he had seen service on the galleys of the Order of Malta, and subsequently fought under Prince Eugene of Savoy. He had made the single greatest contribution to the Familia's fortunes by marrying, after three years' bitter rivalry with a number of other suitors, Zofia Sieniawska, who was the heiress to two vast fortunes, her father's and her late husband's. Although lazy and comfort-loving, August was a brilliant administrator and adroit in political affairs. But Stanisław disliked and mistrusted him. The feeling was mutual. It was based on very personal factors, and their first major clash inflicted a humiliation on Stanisław that he would never forget.

Stanisław's upbringing had deprived him of easy contact with people, particularly those of his own age. One significant exception was his cousin, August Czartoryski's youngest daughter, Elżbieta. They saw much of each other in their teens, and a natural sympathy soon turned into 'a close and very tender friendship'. Elżbieta was serious-minded and sensitive, and gradually the two drifted into an intimacy which Stanisław described as 'the sweetest pleasure of my heart'.[29] His papers dating from this period are littered with fumbling amorous verse, fragments of love-letters and tender scribbles that testify to stirrings of an extraordinarily sentimental and melodramatic cast.[30]

Elżbieta's father frowned on the friendship. With the usual dynastic

considerations in mind, he arranged her marriage to Stanisław Lubomirski, the scion of the senior branch of one of the richest and
potentially most influential families in the land, a valuable ally for the
Familia. Although Lubomirski was an intelligent and personable man
in his early thirties, Elżbieta disliked the idea of marrying him. Her
father assumed that it was on account of her feelings for Stanisław.
Stanisław claimed that August was in love with his daughter and
resented him out of jealousy. Certainly, for August there could have
been no question of wasting such an asset as Elżbieta on someone as
insignificant as Stanisław. It hardly needs to be added that the social
difference, which had played no part in 1721, when the Czartoryskis
were poor, loomed large now that they had established their position.
Elżbieta duly married Lubomirski in June 1753, and Stanisław was
sent abroad on a long tour for good measure.

4

Paris and London

S tanisław was not sent on a Grand Tour in the English manner. The very fact that his goals were Paris and London rather than Naples and Rome makes it clear that it was not ruins and paintings he was after, but political education. He had been brought up in a milieu which talked continually of reform, and the desire to revive the Commonwealth was the principal purpose of all those he worked with. And while the Poles would never be persuaded to embrace any foreign model outright, a knowledge of them was deemed essential. All the regimes of Europe at the time could be roughly reduced to two types, the absolutist monarchy, and the parliamentary state. The theoretical source as well as the best example of the first was France, and of the second England.

He set off in March 1753, travelling by way of Vienna, where he stopped for a couple of months. He met Williams and Keyserling, who were there on diplomatic business, and in their company he took a more favourable view of the place. From Vienna he proceeded to Dresden with Williams. One evening, at the opera, Stanisław was rudely shoved aside by a young man who wanted a better view. He demanded an apology, which the other, a haughty young prince of the house of Liechtenstein, would not tender. Stanisław had no option but to challenge him to a duel. Williams was impressed by Stanisław's conduct. 'He will never seek a quarrel, he will never avoid an encounter, and he will always defend his honour,' he noted.[1] But the Maréchal de Saxe, who had seen the affront, made Liechtenstein apologise.

Stanisław continued on his journey, travelling to Hanover with Williams, who was on his way back to England for the elections, and then on his own to The Hague. There he made the acquaintance of the British minister, Colonel Joseph Yorke, and the Dutch statesman Count Bentinck, with whom he struck up an immediate rapport. Bentinck was very taken by Stanisław's accomplishments, and predicted 'an extraordinary destiny' for him.[2] He introduced him to many people in Holland, including merchants and bankers, the first such contacts the young man had ever had. Stanisław revisited various parts of the country, taking a more informed interest this time, concentrating on factories and shipyards, and taking copious notes on commercial matters. At length he made for Paris, where he arrived at the end of August.

'My debut in France has been more successful than I had expected,' Stanisław wrote to a friend in Poland in November.[3] There was no reason why it should not have been so. 'Nature has not done as much for him (I speak of his person) as the care which has been given to his education,' Williams opined in a pen-portrait composed a couple of years later. He considered that while 'the head is fine', his face was a little too pale, that 'his hips are too wide and his leg not well turned'. But he pointed out that Stanisław was extremely clean, dressed well, and looked like a lord. 'He has contrived to improve on all the good things that Nature has given him and to correct or hide all that was not to his advantage, and as a result can pass for a handsome man,' Williams affirmed. 'He is not built to dance well, yet he dances well.'[4] 'One cannot speak too highly of him,' the Duchesse de Brancas wrote to Countess Brühl. 'His conversation is agreeable, and far above that of most of our Frenchmen . . . There is nothing that does not interest him and of which he does not speak well, without ostentation, with modesty.'[5] Williams also noted that Stanisław was 'capable of learning everything and of understanding everything'.[6] He had certainly understood some basic truths about the Parisians:

In a place like Paris, where so many people are occupied throughout their lives with mere nothings, they attach a great value to the knowledge of a thousand little things, new expressions, anecdotes, and various skills in the daily commerce of life, which distinguish them from the profane foreigners and elevate the elegance of France

42

above all; one must respect these mysteries. One must deserve to be initiated to them by degrees: it is very useful to know them so as not to commit any gaucherie, but just as necessary to appear not to know them, so as to have the merit of humility before those to whom one expresses the wish to learn them, by treating them as masters. A foreigner starting out in Paris would be well advised, more than in any other capital, to pretend to regard himself as a being inferior to the sublime minds inhabiting it, because they like to condescend.[7]

Stanisław had letters of introduction to people in the highest places and, as everywhere, his father's renown opened doors. It was with an old friend of his father's that he stayed while he was in Paris. Though she was hardly an exalted personage, she was famous throughout Europe and something of a curiosity. Marie-Thérèse Rodet was the daughter of a footman, and had been married at fourteen to the forty-nine-year-old manufacturer François Geoffrin, who died in 1749 leaving her comfortably off. She was completely uneducated and rarely opened a book, but, as Marmontel wrote, 'the knowledge of life was her supreme science', and she built a remarkable reputation on it.[8] Having nothing else to do, she began to frequent Madame de Tencin's famous salon. She understood little of what the great figures who met there were talking about, but she listened quietly and soon acquired the knack of dealing with intellectuals. When Madame de Tencin died, she inherited her salon. The likes of Marmontel, Helvétius, Fontenelle, Voltaire, Montesquieu, Diderot, D'Alembert, Julie de Lespinasse, the Abbé Raynal and Grimm, gathered at Madame Geoffrin's house on the rue Saint Honoré on a Wednesday afternoon, with occasional foreign visitors, such as Horace Walpole and David Hume. On Mondays, she held a similar salon for artists, frequented by Boucher, Van Loo, Vien, Vernet, Quentin de La Tour and Chardin. She was an energetic woman in her mid-fifties, soberly dressed, and she seems to have provided the perfect maternal foil for the swollen egos that visited her, sometimes teasing or even bullying them, but never venturing into their discussions. People sometimes mocked her lack of learning, but an invitation to her salon was considered an intellectual accolade. Hume said it was a pleasure to be scolded by her.[9]

Madame Geoffrin smothered Stanisław in affection, perhaps in memory of her own son, who had died aged ten, and he was quite happy to call her '*maman*' as she demanded. Her knowledge of life and intuitive wisdom must have been most welcome to the young man venturing into the strange world of the French metropolis, while her salon provided him with an easy introduction to the luminaries he craved to meet. He always attended her literary Wednesdays, but for some reason she did not let him in on the artistic Mondays. He nevertheless absorbed a great deal of French artistic culture, as the future was to show.

Stanisław also had another 'home' in Paris. This was the house of Madame de Besenval, née Bielińska, a first cousin of his mother. The late Baron de Besenval had been France's ambassador at the side of Charles XII of Sweden and subsequently Stanisław I of Poland. His son Pierre, ten years Stanisław's senior, had acquired some repute as a soldier, but his later career did not vindicate this, and he has gone down in history as the commander of the Swiss Guards who failed to succour the Bastille on 14 July 1789. His only other claim to fame are his erotic *Contes* published posthumously. He was a witty fashionable young man, and a delightful companion for Stanisław, who also appears to have had a romantic entanglement with Besenval's sister, the widowed Marquise de Broglie. Their friend Count Friesen, a nephew of the Maréchal de Saxe, was another regular companion of Stanisław's in Paris.

It was Besenval who introduced him to the Duc de Richelieu, and it was Richelieu who presented him to Louis XV. The king, as was his wont, was anything but effusive, but the queen, Marie Leszczyńska, received Stanisław cordially. Although she hardly knew Poland, she affected great homesickness, and insisted on speaking Polish throughout their lengthy interview. She was not the only member of the royal family with Polish connections. Stanisław had to pay his respects to the Dauphine, a daughter of Augustus III, and to the Prince de Conti, whose grandfather had been elected king of Poland but prevented from ascending the throne by the armed intervention of Augustus II. For over a century the Conti line of the house of Bourbon had been destined by French diplomacy for the Polish crown, and it was said of the current prince that he would still be dreaming about it three days after the end of the world.

The member of the royal family who appealed most to Stanisław was the libertine Duc d'Orléans. He also enjoyed the company of

Mademoiselle de Charolais, the daughter of the Duc de Bourbon, who had taken it upon herself to debauch Louis XV, personally selecting most of his mistresses – with the notable exception of Madame de Pompadour, whom Stanisław saw 'in the full flower of her beauty'.

Stanisław explored Versailles in the king's absence with a couple of Englishmen of his own age who were just completing their Grand Tour, William Legge, the second Earl of Dartmouth, and Frederick North, Earl of Guilford, the future Prime Minister better known as Lord North. He then followed the king to Fontainebleau. Stanisław was fascinated by the workings of the French Court, a bewildering power-structure of unparalleled splendour in which the king presided over a curious mixture of bedroom intrigue and government. He found an authoritative source of information on the subject in the Duchesse de Brancas, first lady of the Dauphine. She was a Versailles veteran who still remembered Louis XIV and had known Madame de Maintenon. Stanisław loved listening to her stories and explanations of court ritual. It was people such as her, the Duchesse de Luxembourg, the Maréchal de Noailles and the ninety-seven-year-old Fontenelle among the literary, who made up for some of the other disappointments of Paris. 'They say it takes two years to acquaint oneself with Paris,' he wrote to a friend in Poland. 'But I believe that one can know the French quite passably after four months here; they copy each other so closely that there are very few different moulds amongst them.'[10]

Something he found tedious in Paris, as he had in Vienna, was the preponderance of card-playing in society. There was a rumour, repeated by several more or less contemporary diarists, that he lost so heavily at cards that he could not pay and was locked up in the Petit Châtelet prison until Madame Geoffrin came to bail him out. It seems unlikely that such a rumour could have persisted without any foundation, but given Stanisław's dislike of card-games and his natural profligacy, it seems more likely that, as some sources state, he simply ran out of money and was threatened with prison by one of his creditors.[11]

Stanisław was disappointed with the lack of gravitas he found in French society. Like many liberal-minded people in Europe, he had been horrified by the dissolution, in January of that year, of the *Parlement* of Paris and the exile of its members, and he expected to find *bien-pensant* Parisians in uproar, yet the matter was hardly mentioned.

Court circles seemed interested only in what went on in their rarefied world, and the intellectuals did not seem to care much for politics either. When Stanisław met Montesquieu at Madame Geoffrin's, he waited in awe to hear words of wisdom, but found only triviality. The author of *de l'Ésprit des Lois* chose to entertain the company by singing a ditty about Madame de la Vallière.

After six months in Paris, he was looking forward to moving on. 'I have an idea that is perhaps false,' he wrote to his friend, 'that there are in most Englishmen enough good and bad things to make up three Frenchmen, and that in consequence, one needs three times as much time to get to know the English as the French.'[12] He had liked much about Paris, but his feelings were ambivalent. In the event, they were to be completely overshadowed by his experiences in England.

He left in the last days of February 1754. The first thing he noticed on arriving at Dover after a nine-hour crossing during which he was copiously sick, was the quality of the drinking-water. For someone who hardly touched wine, six months of the notoriously bad and scarce water in Paris had been something of a torture. By the time he reached London, other impressions were crowding his mind.

He rented rooms in Suffolk Street off the Haymarket, and promptly called on Sir Luke Schaub, a Swiss native of Basel who had become a naturalised Briton and represented his adopted country as ambassador in Paris and later Vienna, and was a long-standing friend of Stanisław's father. At his house in Bond Street, where he had a fine collection of pictures, Schaub introduced him to Lord Chesterfield. Stanisław thought him a little dotty, but Chesterfield was impressed by the Pole. 'You do not travel like most young people', he commended him, and later invited him to return to England.[13]

Williams was in Wales canvassing and did not appear in London until May. He entrusted his 'adopted son' to his wife. She was born Lady Frances Coningsby, and had married Sir Charles in 1732, but ten years later, after producing a son and a daughter, they had parted, never to see each other again, although they remained on excellent epistolary terms. Stanisław quickly became her 'violent favourite', as she wrote to her husband, 'for he has none of the English brutality about him', and she and her daughter Charlotte provided him with all the feminine attentions he could have wished for.[14] But they were not alone in this, as Horace Walpole explained in a letter to a friend:

T'other night, a description was given me of the most extraordinary declaration of love that was ever made. Have you seen young Poniatowski? He is very handsome. You *have* seen the figure of the Duchess of Gordon, who looks like a raw-boned Scotch metaphysician that has got a red face by drinking water. One day at the Drawing-room, having never spoken to him, she sent one of the foreign ministers to invite Poniatowski to dinner with her for the next day. He bowed and went. The moment the door opened, her two little sons, attired like Cupids, with bows and arrows, shot at him; and one of them literally hit his hair, and was very near putting his eye out, and hindering his casting it to the couch

   Where she, another sea-born Venus, lay.

The only company besides this Highland goddess were two Scotchmen who could not speak a word of any language but their own Erse; and, to complete his astonishment at this allegorical entertainment, with the dessert there entered a little horse, and galloped round the table; a hieroglyphic I cannot solve. Poniatowski accounts for this profusion of kindness by his great-grandmother being a Gordon; but I believe it is to be accounted for by . . . [15]

Stanisław's principal interest in London was political, as his letters home reveal. He watched the parliamentary election in the Westminster constituency, in the course of which he was embraced by an old hag selling oysters, which must have reminded him of his own electioneering in Poland, and was alarmed by the mob that gathered on these occasions. He was presented to King George, who had heard of him through Williams and received him graciously. He went to the Houses of Parliament, where he could observe at his ease the workings of a system which interested him vitally. 'I was not a little surprised to find this chamber, of which I had formed such an august impression,' he wrote of the House of Lords, 'so inferior in material terms, to both the size and the beauty of our Polish Senate Chamber,' but he was impressed by the level of debate.[16] As he sat in the gallery, he was recognised by the Lord Chancellor, Lord Hardwicke, the father of Colonel Yorke, Minister at The Hague, and formally greeted on behalf of the whole assembly.

Stanisław became particularly friendly with Lord Hardwicke's second son, Charles Yorke, who was to follow in his father's footsteps and become Lord Chancellor himself, and who had just entered Parliament in 1754. He was a brilliant young man ten years Stanisław's senior, and a willing guide. He took him along when he went to Bath to see William Pitt, who made a strong impression on Stanisław. Another who interested Stanisław from the political point of view was Lord Lyttelton, whom he met through his Paris acquaintance Lord Dartmouth. The amiable, literary and slightly absent-minded Lyttelton had just joined the Duke of Newcastle's ministry. They spent many evenings talking of different political systems, and Stanisław expounded with ardour his desires and plans for reforming his own country. Lyttelton sketched out 'an imaginary republic' for Poland, with Stanisław at its head, and later congratulated himself on having predicted the future.[17]

Stanisław did all the things tourists did. He went to Westminster Abbey several times, where he copied out some of the inscriptions on the graves, and also to the golden gallery at the top of St Paul's, where he scratched his name.[18] He called on the notorious Miss Chudleigh, the bigamous Duchess of Kingston, famous for her appearance at a ball wearing only a transparent shift. He went, with Jacob Sievers, a young secretary at the Russian embassy whom he had befriended, to the debtors' prison to visit the deposed self-proclaimed king of Corsica, Theodore I.[19] One of Stanisław's new acquaintances, Lord Strange, son of the Earl of Derby, a very rich but exceedingly scruffy young man who was very active in Parliament, took him to a cock-fight, as well as to a Shakespeare tragedy. The cock-fight made Stanisław think of a witches' sabbath, but the play had a profound effect on him. He had read plays by Shakespeare, and even translated part of *Julius Caesar* as a school exercise, but he had never seen one performed. 'I took to this spectacle the memory of all the fine rules of the three unities, the observance of which gives the French dramatic poets reason to think themselves superior to the English,' he wrote, 'but I confess that the more of Shakespeare's plays I saw, the more I felt a heretic on this point.'[20] The only area in which he remained insensitive was music, for which he had no ear, and he refused an invitation to go with young Charlotte Hanbury Williams to hear Handel's *Messiah* at the Foundling Hospital. He visited Bath with Charles Yorke, stopped at Wilton, went to see Stonehenge, spent a day in Oxford, and admired the gardens of Stowe, where he stayed with Lord Temple, Lord Lyttelton's father-in-law. The gardens strongly influenced those he later laid out in Poland, but he could not muster the dogmatic passion with which the English embraced the cause of the natural landscape. When he ventured a regret for the odd straight line, canal or fountain, he found himself almost forfeiting the goodwill of his host.

Stanisław admitted to being disposed 'to admire and like the English and almost all their tastes and their manner of being', but he did have reservations.[21] Apart from the cock-pit, he was horrified by the education system. He noted that the only incentive to learning was the cane, and that no manners or principles of civility were instilled in young men. But he was enchanted by English society, which was not as split, as it was in France, between the court, the city and the literary. His own position in Polish society made him warm to a family like the Yorkes, who seemed to embody all that was best in the concept of *noblesse de robe*. He was strongly attracted to them both individually and as a family, and spent much time at their house, whose atmosphere reminded him of his own home. Their self-esteem was based on achievement and work, and each one of them was a useful member of society, unlike most of the people he knew in Poland or those he had met in Paris. France had undoubtedly had a profound effect on him, stimulating his aesthetic sense and developing his taste. But England exerted a far greater influence on the development of his thought, and lent him a new self-assurance. On the Continent, it was his birth and connections that placed him, while in England he felt he was respected for what he was and the promise he showed – indeed, more than one person in England prophesied a great future for him.[22]

He was all the more vexed when, in June 1754, he received a letter from his father telling him to return home at once. Reluctantly, he obeyed, and after only four months in England, he sailed from Harwich for The Hague. There he ran out of money, and had to wait until his parents sent him enough for his journey, through Hanover and Dresden, back to Warsaw. His mother was overjoyed to see him back, but his father began to heap reproaches on him. He had displayed a complete inability to husband his resources, and had spent too much money. Just before leaving he had taken possession of the substantial Starosty of Przemyśl, which his father had purchased for him, and this should have provided for his needs. But whenever he had money he threw it around liberally, and his parents had had to bail him out several times in the course of the year. Stanisław was annoyed when he discovered that this had been the only reason for his recall from England. He had assumed that his presence was required by the Familia for the Seym of that autumn. In fact, his father would not let him stand for election, since his Czartoryski uncles were preparing to do battle against his brother-in-law Jan Branicki, now Grand Hetman of the Crown, and Stanisław Poniatowski did not want him to get involved.

The Familia had been caught out in an intrigue over the disputed entail of Ostróg. This had been created in 1609 out of the vast lands of Prince Janusz Ostrogski, who left detailed instructions as to who should inherit if his own family were to die out. If all the branches he specified were to become extinct, as indeed happened, the entail was to go to a senior Polish Knight of Malta, who was to use its resources in the defence of Poland against the Infidel Tatars and Turks. In the event, the entail had been appropriated by a distant relative belonging to the Sanguszko family, and the matter festered, surfacing at every Seym. Apart from various Poles, interested parties included the Order of Malta, the Papacy, Spain and France. In the 1720s, August Czartoryski, himself a Knight of Malta, had tried to gain possession.

In 1753, while Stanisław was in Paris, the Czartoryskis had constructed an elaborate deal whereby the debt-ridden Janusz Sanguszko ceded the entail to them in return for their taking over his debts. This aroused widespread outrage, since the entail was viewed as being public business, and the feelings were ably exploited by the Familia's enemies. They managed to get Hetman Branicki on their side, since there was a military aspect to the matter, and he occupied the estate with Crown troops. The matter came up in the Seym, and the judgment went against the Czartoryskis.

The affair underlined that the Familia were not as free from venality as they liked to pretend. At the same time, they found themselves in a political wilderness, out of favour at court and powerless to affect policy. Williams, who had followed Augustus to Warsaw for the Seym, found them 'in as low a condition as possible'.[23] He had taken trouble to convince his government that they were worth backing, and while there had been some resistance in London to getting involved in Polish affairs, the Familia was accepted as the English faction in Poland. Their being out of favour reflected badly on England, as did the fact that Brühl was showering favours on the French ambassador, and that Branicki was showing off a snuff-box sent him by Louis XV. The English Secretary of State asked the Russian Court to exert its influence on their behalf. This Russia duly did, hinting to Brühl that she would be prepared to support the Familia with arms if necessary. The Familia wanted Williams to be sent to St Petersburg, in which post, they reckoned, he would be ideally placed to support them, and Stanisław wrote to all his English friends recommending the idea.[24]

'Upon my return to Poland, I was obliged to revise all the ideas and the hopes that I gave voice to in England,' he wrote to Charles Yorke.[25] He was depressed because, instead of implementing sensible policies and reforms, all the Familia could do was fight for its own survival. Over the previous two years people had repeatedly encouraged his ambitions by predicting a bright future for him, and only recently Williams had written assuring him that he would become 'a great figure', but at the moment he seemed to be getting nowhere. Williams warned him to 'correct those few strokes of what the French call *Humeur* that you still have about you', but Stanisław found himself sinking back into ill-tempered gloom.[26]

He had by now made a few friends in Polish society, including August Sułkowski, the eldest of four sons of a former favourite of Augustus III. Sułkowski was a baffling character, both venal and principled, with 'the face of an ape' and unbridled ambition, but he was highly cultivated, which is probably why Stanisław befriended him. The same was true of the brothers Fryderyk and August Moszyński, natural grandsons of Augustus II. Another new friend was Franciszek Rzewuski, an amusing dilettante who became a lifelong and faithful friend. They did their best to raise Stanisław's spirits and to encourage him to taste the pleasures of Warsaw, but he was in no mood for it. 'First of all, my severe upbringing had kept me away from all sordid commerce,' he recalled. 'Then the ambition to get ahead and to maintain myself in what one calls (in Paris) good company, had preserved me during my travels.'[27] As a result he was utterly inexperienced in the arts of gallantry, and was astonished when Franciszek Rzewuski announced that a greatly sought-after Warsaw beauty had set her heart on him, making him guess who it might be. 'I named every lady in Warsaw before the one who, by her extreme gaiety, her youth and her fashion, seemed to me to have the least in common with a man as melancholy and as morose as I was with everyone then, and who had never spoken a word to her.' The lady in question was Joanna Sapieha. He was flattered by her interest, and while he was not attracted to her, he felt obliged to go through the motions required by gallantry. 'I was very new, and I took everything literally . . . she found it very amusing to unfreeze a sort of twenty–two–year–old misanthrope.'[28] She teased him mercilessly for a couple of months, and then left Warsaw to join her husband in the country for the winter, leaving him in a state of confusion.

He was also seeing his cousin Elżbieta Lubomirska daily, and their feelings for each other flourished under the umbrella of intellectual affinity. 'She always seemed to agree with me on every matter. We had the same way of seeing things; whether they were people, events, books, the arts, or amusements. We would discuss everything together, and we always met in our tastes and our judgments . . . [she] had my heart, my esteem and my confidence. I found more sense and feeling in her than I have in any other woman; she seemed then to be above all the weaknesses of her sex, so much so that she seemed to belong to a superior order of being, who made my happiness just by deigning to speak to me.'[29]

At the beginning of 1755 Stanisław went to Wilno for the elections to the Supreme Tribunal of Lithuania, to witness another parody of political life. Michał Radziwiłł, Palatine of Wilno, was determined to push his son Karol, aged eighteen and barely literate, into the post of Marshal of the Tribunal. The city was patrolled by armed gangs and Radziwiłł household troops, and those who were not of the Radziwiłł camp were prevented from casting their vote. Radziwiłł was duly elected. Shortly after, Stanisław went to Fraustadt on the Polish border nearest Saxony. Augustus III was constitutionally obliged to hold a Senate Council, which had to sit on Polish territory, but as he disliked leaving Dresden for long, he held it just inside Poland. Stanisław was there to be invested with the titular honour of Steward (*Stolnik*) of Lithuania, which his brother Kazimierz had obtained for him. Although the Familia were out of favour at court, Kazimierz was in a strong position. Brühl knew of the disagreements with his uncles, and wanted to detach him from the party, a situation Kazimierz knew how to exploit.

Joanna Sapieha had also come to Fraustadt with her husband and she again enticed Stanisław into paying court to her. She arranged a tryst one night when the affair was to be consummated, but at the critical moment her husband turned up. Stanisław dived behind a screen in her bedroom, where he had to spend the rest of the night, and returned to Warsaw feeling foolish.

In the middle of April, Stanisław received a letter from Williams informing him that he had just been named ambassador to St Petersburg. He had rented a mansion on the Nevsky Prospekt, opposite the Winter Palace. 'I am endeavouring to make it very comfortable, for there is not much society here, and one is obliged to live very much at home,' he wrote to friends in England. Lord Chesterfield sent him a goldfish for company.[30] But Williams craved company of another sort, and he invited Stanisław to join him in the capacity of secretary. Stanisław was overjoyed at the idea, which promised a long stay with his mentor and an opportunity to see the Russian Court. He had no difficulty in obtaining his parents' approval, and arrived in St Petersburg at the end of June 1755. 'The time of my first sojourn in Russia, in the house of the Chevalier Williams,' he later wrote, 'was for me an education of an entirely new kind.'[31]

5

Catherine

*P*rovidence could hardly have chosen a more interesting moment to turn Stanisław's steps towards St Petersburg. The young man stumbled on to a stage that was being set for a drama that would decide the future of Russia. The country was ruled by the Empress Elizabeth, the younger daughter of Peter the Great. She was a huge woman, with an appetite for carnality, and a concurrent streak of religious devotionalism in which only she failed to see the inconsistency. She was imperious, suspicious and capricious, though not as cruel as her predecessor Anna. She was then under the influence of her favourite, Ivan Ivanovich Shuvalov, known in English diplomatic correspondence as 'Monsieur Pompadour', but she governed through her chancellor, Aleksey Petrovich Bestuzhev Ryumin, a wily old fox who was already thinking of ways of securing his future after her death. The succession was often a matter for speculation in Russia, and in this case with good reason.

Elizabeth had obtained the throne by a palace coup that toppled her baby great-nephew, Ivan VI, who still mouldered in a dungeon. Although Elizabeth herself had no direct heir, she had her nephew, the Duke of Holstein, brought over and installed as the prospective Tsar, under the name of the Grand Duke Peter Fyodorovich. 'He was not stupid, but mad, and as he liked to drink, he upset thereby the little brain he had,' according to Stanisław. 'A great smoker of tobacco, endowed with a puny lanky figure, dressed usually in a Holstein uniform, but sometimes in town clothes, always of such ridiculous style and poor taste, that he looked either like a soldier of fortune, or a dandy in an Italian comedy.'[1] He was besotted by Frederick the Great, and spent a great deal of time drilling his unfortunate guards or playing with tin soldiers.

He had been given a wife in the person of Princess Sophia of Anhalt-Zerbst, renamed the Grand Duchess Catherine Alekseyevna, whom he generally ignored, with an occasional lapse into active malice. She was an intelligent and sensitive young woman trapped in a danger-ous alien environment, and she was humiliated daily by her boorish husband. She had been seduced by one of his gentlemen in waiting, Sergey Vasilyevich Saltykov, and briefly found solace in what she believed to be his love. But he soon tired of her and seized on the opportunity of a mission abroad to drop her. She was left lovelorn, humiliated and pregnant. The child was born in September 1754, and christened Paul.

Stanisław was presented to the Empress Elizabeth on 23 June 1755, and delivered the greetings of the Familia, expressing their hope that she would continue to support them in Poland. On 29 June, the grand duke's nameday, he and Williams went to his country residence at Oranienbaum to pay their respects. He was impressed by 'the astonishing prodigality of this court', and wrote home effusively about 'the good reception' he was meeting with in every quarter.[2]

As Williams had complete confidence in his 'political son', Stanisław was shown all secret documents and used to encode des-patches to London. St Petersburg was a diplomatic cauldron in which the representatives of several nations fished for choice morsels as a new European crisis loomed, and from his position Stanisław was able to learn much about the workings of diplomacy. Chancellor Bestuzhev, a terrifying figure 'with a mouth which opened to reveal only four stumps of teeth, and a pair of small flashing eyes', seemed well-disposed to Stanisław.[3] The vice-chancellor, Mikhail Larionovich Voront-sov, was pro-French in his sympathies, and on his guard against the Familia's agent in the suite of the ambassador of France's traditional enemy.

Stanisław was befriended by Lev Alexandrovich Naryshkin, gentleman of the bedchamber to the Grand Duchess Catherine, and the soul of a young clique at court. Naryshkin soon began dropping hints to the effect that the grand duchess liked the look of him. Stanisław's own impression was that she was very 'Prussian', and more interested in politics than men, but Williams knew otherwise. On the very first meeting at Oranienbaum on 29 June, he had sat next to Catherine at dinner. She had noticed Stanisław dancing, and had asked about him in a manner that was not lost on the experienced Welshman. Stanisław was reluctant to believe any of it, but when Catherine herself said a few gracious words to him at a court function, his interest, and possibly his emotions, were aroused. But he was afraid of venturing after them. At one ball, a general standing beside him remarked, looking at the dancing Catherine, 'a fellow would happily suffer a few lashes of the knout for a woman like that'.[4] Stanisław was not so sure.

Williams was keen to win the sympathies of the young court to the English interest, and he struck up a friendship with Catherine. He quickly discovered that she was short of cash for her personal expenses, and his superiors supplied him with the necessary funds, which he channelled into her pocket.[5] In her attraction for Stanisław he must have seen a perfect avenue through which to further this influence. But Stanisław still hesitated, for another reason. 'By a remarkable peculiarity, I had to offer, although I was aged twenty-two, that which no other person had had,' he wrote. Whether this means that he had never made love to a woman at all, or whether it is a pious untruth based on his never having consummated a love worthy of the name, he was certainly gravely lacking in amorous experience.[6]

With the onset of winter, the grand-ducal pair moved from Oranienbaum back to St Petersburg. Peter was spending most of his time with his mistress, Elizabeth Vorontsov, and Catherine was left very much to her own devices. The Winter Palace was conveniently close to the Naryshkin residence. On the dull winter nights, Naryshkin would bring Catherine, disguised as a man, to his sister Anna's apartment, where they would amuse themselves in a small group of friends. On the night of 17 December she found Stanisław among them. 'The evening passed in the wildest manner imaginable,' she recorded, and they decided to spend the following evening in Catherine's private rooms, which they sneaked into by the back stairs.[7] Observed in the free and easy atmosphere of this group of friends, Catherine appeared a good deal less 'Prussian', and Stanisław's fears melted before his growing attraction. 'Soon I hazarded a note, to which Naryshkin brought me a reply on the morrow,' writes Stanisław. 'At

1 Stanisław's parents, Stanisław and Konstancja, portrayed here by
Bacciarelli as the ideal of parenthood

2　Stanisław at the age of fourteen, by Niederman

3　The Krakowskie Przedmieście in Warsaw, with the Poniatowski town house on the right, from a painting by Bellotto

4　The house at Malczyce, where the family spent their holidays

5 August Czartoryski, by an unknown artist

6 Franciszek Salezy Potocki, one of the great opponents of the Familia, pictured here in all the Sarmatian splendour of his assumed importance

7 A seymik taking place in a church, from a sepia drawing by Jean Pierre Norblin de la Gourdaine

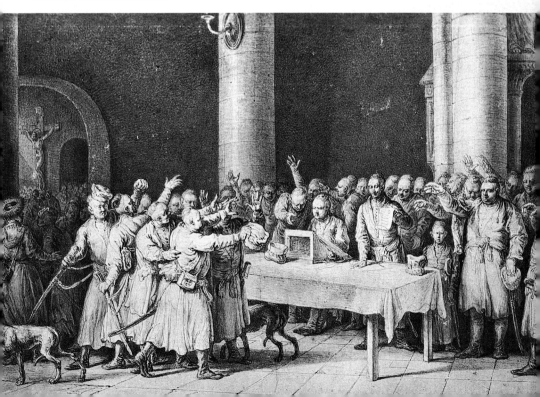

8 Janissary of a Polish
magnate's bodyguard, by J. B.
Le Prince

9 Augustus III in Polish dress,
wearing the Order of the White
Eagle, by Louis de Silvestre

10 The *cour d'honneur* at
Białystok

11 Catherine the Great, from a medal struck in 1765

12 Elżbieta Lubomirska, from a pastel by an unidentified artist

13 Stanisław in the late 1750s, from a damaged pastel by an unidentified artist

14 Stanisław's brother Kazimierz Poniatowski, by Bacciarelli

15 Sir Charles Hanbury Williams, by an unidentified artist

16 *Opposite page* A preparatory oil sketch for the coronation portrait, by Bacciarelli

17 Miniature depicting probably Kazimierz Poniatowski in the new uniform of the Royal Horseguards designed by Stanisław

18 Fireworks celebrating Stanisław's name-day on 8 May 1766

19 Glorification of Stanisław as patron of the arts and sciences, an unfinished ink wash and tempera drawing by Franciszek Smuglewicz, *c.* 1766

that moment I forgot there was a Siberia.'[8] On 28 December he went to her apartment, conducted by Naryshkin, and they became lovers.

If the original attraction had been based on Catherine's need and Stanisław's ambition, the affair quickly blossomed into something entirely different, and they were both a little surprised at the intensity of feeling they evoked in each other. In the terrifying jungle of the Russian court, Catherine had known only fear, suspicion and betrayal, and it was a novel experience to be loved for herself, by a man as tender, honest and sensitive as Stanisław. He had experienced only the emotional confusion inherent in the unavowed and distorted relationship with Elżbieta Lubomirska, the fumbling infatuation with Angelika Kotulinsky, the largely epistolary badinage with the Marquise de Broglie, and the futile coquettry of Joanna Sapieha. He now found himself in love with an equally sensitive yet forthright woman who gave her affection freely and lavishly, expecting only his in return. There can be no doubt that there was a pronounced physical element in the affair. Catherine was strong and energetic, and loved violent exercise, while Stanisław was full of pent-up frustrations which found release in her arms. But the most important element was a marked affinity they discovered in their natures and their thoughts.

Stanisław found in her a temperament 'which allowed her to move with ease from the most madcap, the most childish games, to arithmetical tables, undaunted by the hard work or the texts themselves'.[9] This meant that he could communicate with her at his own rather serious level and discuss the things that interested him. Books had provided a constant refuge during her worst moments in Russia, and while Stanisław introduced her to a number of works by Voltaire and others, she was already well-read in contemporary literature. To young people like them, the Enlightenment was like a new religion. It uplifted and bound them together in an intellectual and sensory exclusivity. At the same time, Catherine's zest for life and her ability to accommodate frivolity with gravity helped the hitherto excessively serious Stanisław to attain a more satisfactory psychological balance. At her request, he sketched out a self-portrait which is worth quoting in full:

I would be happier with my figure if I were an inch taller, had a better made leg, a less aquiline nose, a slighter mouth, better eyesight, and if my teeth showed better. It is not that I would consider myself very handsome if this were the case, but I would not wish to be more so; for I believe that I have a noble and very expressive physiognomy, and an air of quality and distinction in my movements and bearing that can make me noticed anywhere. My shortsightedness often gives me an embarrassed and gloomy air, but this does not last, and then my countenance has the defect of appearing too proud. The excellent education I received helped me to palliate the defects of my figure and my mind, and to profit from both over and above their real value. I have enough wit never to be behind in any conversation, but not enough to lead one very often or for very long, unless my feelings are engaged, or the taste that nature has given me for everything that touches on the arts. I am quick to perceive the ridiculous and the false in all their guises, to spot people's tricks, and I have often been too quick to make them feel it. I hate bad company by inclination. A strong vein of laziness has prevented me from developing my talents and my knowledge as far as I might have. When I work, it is under inspiration. I either do a great deal all at once, or nothing at all; I do not commit myself easily, and that makes me appear more able than I am. As for what is normally called the conduct of business, I usually show too much candour and eagerness, and as a result I often commit blunders. I can judge an affair, I can find the fault in a project or in him who carries it out, but I need a word of advice or a brake to prevent me from committing the same fault myself. I am extremely sensitive, more so to sadness than to joy; and melancholy would certainly take a hold on me if I did not carry in the depths of my heart the presentiment of a great future happiness. Born with a vast and ardent ambition, ideas of reform, of glory and of being useful to my country have become as it were the canvas on which I apply all my affairs and my whole life. I did not think that I was made to love women. I attributed the first attempts I made in that direction to particular circumstance, but then, at last, I found tenderness, and I love with such passion that I feel that were my love to suffer any reverse I should become the most miserable man on earth, and would give way to total discouragement. The duties of friendship are sacred to me, and I take them very far; if a friend of mine does me wrong, there is nothing on earth I will not do to stop myself from breaking with him, and for a long time after he has offended me, I remind myself that I have obligations towards him. I believe myself to be a very good friend, yet it is true that I am only intimate with very few people, although I am always infinitely grateful for any kindness. Although I am very prompt to discern the defects of my fellows, I am strongly inclined to excuse them with a reflection that I have often made. This is that whatever view one takes of oneself, if one examines oneself with great impartiality, one can find within oneself some very humiliating affinities with the greatest crimes, which perhaps only need a very strong temptation to make them flourish if one does not guard them very severely. I like to give, and I hate restraint, and as a result I am not very apt at looking after what I have. I do not keep my own secrets as well as those of others, on the subject of which I am extremely scrupulous. I am very compassionate. I am so eager to be loved and to meet with approval, that my vanity would be excessive were it not that the fear of ridicule and the ways of the world had taught me to control myself on that score. I do not lie, through principle as much as through a natural aversion to falsehood. I am not what you might call pious, far from it, but I can honestly say that I love God and often address myself to Him, and I have this pleasing idea that He likes to do good things for us when we ask it of Him. I have the good fortune to love my father and my mother by inclination as much as from duty. Whatever idea of revenge that might spring up in the heat of the moment I should be unable to carry out; pity would triumph, I think. One often forgives out of a sort of weakness as much as any loftiness, and I am afraid that this will one day lead me to fail in the execution of many of my projects. I like reflection, and I have enough imagination to amuse myself on my own, without a book, particularly since I have been in love . . . [10]

Although they saw a great deal of each other and danced together at court balls, the affair remained a closely guarded secret, known only to Williams and a few of Catherine's intimates. The lovers corresponded through Naryshkin and Williams, and notes were sometimes carried by trusted tradesmen, such as the Venetian jeweller Bernardi, whose comings and goings aroused no suspicion.

This arrangement could not last indefinitely. One day in the summer of 1756, Stanisław went to Oranienbaum in the company of Count Horn, a young Swede. The grand duke had gone off to get drunk at a gamekeeper's wedding, leaving Catherine and Naryshkin to entertain the two guests. When they walked into her private quarters, a little dog rushed out of the bedroom, made a great show of defiant barking at Horn, and then started leaping up at Stanisław, licking his hands affectionately. 'My friend, there is nothing so treacherous as a little dog,' said Horn to Stanisław, taking him aside. 'The first thing I always do with women I love is to give them one, and it is always through the dog that I discover if there is another more favoured than me. The rule is strong and certain. You saw yourself how that dog wanted to eat me, me whom he did not know, while he could not contain his joy at seeing you again; for it is very clear that this is not the first time you have been in that room.'[11] The probability was that sooner or later the empress would come to hear of the affair, and then anything might happen. As a private individual, Stanisław was vulnerable to drastic punishment, or at best summary expulsion.

His position in the English embassy offered no diplomatic protection, and indeed only complicated matters. There were strains developing between the ambassador and his young friend. Towards the end of April 1756, Williams suddenly lost his temper over nothing and told Stanisław to get out of his house. Stanisław left the room, and stood on the terrace wondering in despair what to do next. Williams eventually followed him out and a tearful reconciliation took place. It has been suggested that Williams and Stanisław might at some stage have been lovers. This is unlikely, and to jump to conclusions over the closeness of their relationship is to misunderstand completely the sensibilities of the age. The relationship was indeed one of close intimacy and emotional intensity, and it must have been difficult for the lonely, nearly fifty-year-old Williams to watch his protégé in the paroxysms of satisfied love. Williams may also have been suffering from the first symptoms of the mental derangement that was to lead to his death only three years later.

More important was the changing political situation. Williams' principal task had been to conclude an Anglo-Russian treaty, and while he had achieved this in September 1755 with Bestuzhev's help, the signature in January 1756 of the Convention of Westminster between England and Prussia upset everything. The Seven Years' War had just broken out, and England was bound by alliance to two of the principal opponents: Russia and Prussia. Bestuzhev and Williams now found themselves trying to accommodate the contradictions. As both Williams' secretary and as the Familia's unofficial representative, Stanisław was caught on the horns of the same dilemma. To make things worse, France, which had no diplomatic relations with Russia, had sent a secret agent by the name of the Chevalier Douglas to St Petersburg. Among other things, he was spying on Williams and Stanisław with a view to exposing them as working against Russian interests.

One solution was for Stanisław to return to Poland and then mobilise all his own, Williams' and Catherine's combined influence to persuade Augustus III to nominate him as the envoy of Saxony to the Russian court. This fitted well with his family's desire that he should take part in that year's Seym. Accordingly, Stanisław set off for home after just over a year's stay in St Petersburg. He had an unpleasant moment when a Russian officer caught up with him in Riga. To his relief, the man had been sent post-haste by the empress not to arrest him, but to present him with a gold snuff-box as a mark of her favour. Elizabeth had also written to Augustus III commending Stanisław's conduct.

He stopped at Dyneburg in order to get elected for Livonia to the forthcoming Seym, and reached Warsaw in good spirits, assuming he would soon be back in St Petersburg. But Augustus had things to worry about other than Stanisław's plans, since Saxony had been invaded by Frederick of Prussia. By the autumn of that year Augustus was cut off from Poland, and the Seym could not sit. Stanisław was stranded in Warsaw.

Catherine poured out her despair in daily letters to Williams, begging him to do something. Williams realised that only Bestuzhev could obtain Stanisław's return, by writing to Brühl and asking him to arrange it as a personal favour. He therefore paid the chancellor a visit at the beginning of September and told him about the affair between Stanisław and Catherine. Bestuzhev was aghast, and thought the young Pole 'devilish brave' to carry on such a risky liaison. He welcomed the opportunity to make himself useful to the grand duchess, but he was in two minds about whether he wanted the Pole back in the place. 'He fears Poniatowski and his enterprising genius,' Williams explained to Catherine.[12] But Catherine now decided to have a go at the chancellor herself. On 11 September she wrote to Bestuzhev that she wanted Stanisław back. 'You may be absolutely certain that I shall press to a finish with all the firmness with which nature has endowed me,' she wrote, adding that 'his return, under your special care, is the price which I place on my present friendship and my future protection.'[13]

Bestuzhev had for some time been angling for an English pension, and London had recently authorised Williams to pay out large sums to promote English interests. In Williams' perception, these took second place to the happiness of his young friends. 'One thing I promise you,' he wrote to Catherine. 'The Chancellor will never have a penny of his pension until Poniatowski returns. I shall quarrel with him, I shall make my court quarrel with him. I shall do everything for you and my friend.'[14] In the event, a certain amount of the English subsidy was diverted, at Catherine's request, directly into Stanisław's pocket.

Williams' original interest in Catherine had turned into a paternal concern for her. He gave her practical advice, and encouraged her to think of assuring her own future. By the spring of that year they were reviewing schemes for a coup d'état by which she might take power herself.[15] Although he was doing it for her sake, he linked Stanisław's future with hers. 'I flatter myself that, one day,' he wrote to her in November, 'you will make him King of Poland.'[16] While there had been much talk of a brilliant future, and Williams had commented on Stanisław's 'unbridled ambition', this is the first time the subject had been put in specific terms, and the tone of the letter suggests that the three of them had talked about it.

Williams' health was declining dramatically, and he often suffered from harrowing migraines. He was beginning to feel old and spent, and kept asking to be recalled, but he was determined to help the young lovers. The three of them had grown very close, united by a mixture of feelings that surface in the surviving correspondence. This was a highly dangerous exchange of letters, in which, as well as the cypher, they used a code, with Williams addressing Catherine as '*Monsieur*', referring to Bestuzhev as '*le patron*' and Stanisław as '*le damoiseau*'. Stanisław refers to Catherine as '*Colette*' and in Williams' letters she is 'the Countess of Essex' (his daughter's married name). The lovers refer to him as '*la sagesse*', which matched their feelings for him. 'I love you as my second father,' wrote Stanisław from Warsaw. 'It is a name which I owe you for so many reasons that I shall never change it.'[17]

Stanisław had known him for six years, but Catherine had only a year's acquaintance with him, yet she agreed to follow his counsel blindly in everything – eloquent evidence of Williams' remarkable ascendancy over young people. It also testifies to the strength of her passion for Stanisław, as do the terrifying risks she was taking. For Williams was her only lifeline to Stanisław, and her only hope of getting him back. And she knew Williams would do everything to bring him back, if only for his own sake. 'A friend so close, a confidant so wise and discreet are invaluable,' Williams wrote to her. 'How useful he would be to me at this moment, he who shares all my sorrows and my joys, who loves me disinterestedly, who is attached to me for no reason, and who esteems me simply because he knows me! It is true that I have a father's tenderness for him, he is mine elect, my adopted, and I applaud myself every day as I see that both my own judgment and you approve my choice.'[18]

One obstacle to his return that nobody had foreseen came from Stanisław's own family. 'My mother's love for me makes her ardently desire the same thing that I do; while her religious scruples, which have become very strong, force her to say *"non consentio"*,' Stanisław wrote to Williams on 17 October.[19] Konstancja had learnt of her son's amorous entanglement, and decided that to allow him to return to St Petersburg was to abandon him to a life of debauchery. Her authority over her son was considerable, as was his love and respect for her. 'I have found myself in the most horrible predicament that I have ever had to face in my life,' he wrote to Catherine. 'I dashed my head against the walls, shrieking rather than weeping.'[20] Catherine turned to Williams for counsel. 'His mother loves him,' he explained. 'She is intelligent, but very bigoted. But I have more credit with her than anybody and I shall use all of it on this occasion.'[21] Stanisław confided his troubles in Jerzy Flemming and his uncle August, and they, determined not to let Konstancja's morality get in the way of the Familia's politics, took it upon themselves to break down her objections. She continued to voice her qualms tearfully, but finally allowed him to follow his own instincts.

At the end of October 1756 Stanisław was nominated Envoy Extraordinary to the Court of St Petersburg by Augustus III, and shortly after invested as a knight of the White Eagle. (The story goes that when handing him the insignia, Augustus gave him those specifically meant for the monarch by mistake. Although it is probably inaccurate, it was later discreetly but insistently put about by Stanisław, as one more proof of his predestination.) But there were complications. Although Prussia was at war with France, the diplomats of both countries did share the one aim of crossing Stanisław's plans. The French ambassador in Dresden, the Comte de Broglie, was doing his utmost to prevent Stanisław's posting to Russia. The Prussian resident in Warsaw tried to persuade Augustus and Brühl to rescind the nomination. When he failed in this, he turned to Hetman Branicki, who was by now working for the French interest. They decided to kidnap Stanisław.[22]

On 13 December 1756 Stanisław set out for St Petersburg, taking as his secretary Jacek Ogrodzki, long-standing friend and aide to his father. Along the way he received a warning that a detachment of Branicki's hussars was lying in ambush further up the road. He took another route, and on 4 January Catherine, who had got wind of the plot and was in 'mortal terror' for her lover, rapturously announced his arrival to Williams.

The joy of being reunited with his love was mitigated by the circumstances of Stanisław's new position. His mission was to negotiate Russian military assistance for Augustus against Prussia. His instructions from the Familia were to persuade Elizabeth that the army's march through Poland should be a demonstration of Russian support for them. At his first audience with the empress, on 11 January 1757, Stanisław made a fine speech about the Prussian 'Hydra', which delighted Elizabeth and impressed Catherine. But it did little to allay the suspicions of the permanent Saxon chargé d'affaires, who treated him as an unwelcome supernumerary, or his master Brühl, or the French diplomats who had at last been accredited, all of whom believed Stanisław to be a double agent in the service of the English. With Russia's accession to the Franco-Austro-Saxon alliance against Prussia shortly after Stanisław's return, in January 1757, the French party in St Petersburg felt strong.

The most painful aspect of the situation was that as England was allied to Prussia he could not be seen to have close relations with the English ambassador. Stanisław lived alone, in a house Williams had found for him opposite the Kazan Church, and he could only rarely visit his friend. Williams was confined to his bed for three months that winter, so they could not meet at court. But Williams continued to watch over the lovers. 'Be very circumspect in your interviews with Poniatowski, and above all see him at his own house, or at that of a third person, but *never at your own*,' he admonished Catherine. 'If you go out at night and are recognised, it will only make the world talk and create suspicion. But, if he were caught entering your house, the game is up and his fate is sealed.'[23] At the same time, he took a solicitous interest in their happiness. 'The wish is very near my heart, Monsieur, that your son should have a brother,' he wrote to Catherine on 22 March. 'Dare I ask if there is one on the way?'[24] There was.

Flushed with happiness, Stanisław and Catherine grew careless. He was meeting Williams, in secret, but a little too often, and he actually arranged trysts with Catherine at the apartment of Williams' new secretary, Thomas Wroughton, whom he had befriended. All this was carefully watched and recorded. French diplomacy, in the persons of the Marquis de l'Hôpital in St Petersburg and the Comte de Broglie in Dresden, was determined to remove Stanisław from the scene. L'Hôpital and Vice-Chancellor Vorontsov gathered evidence, with the aim of proving that Williams was using Stanisław to urge the young court to bring Russia into alliance with Prussia. Their suspicions of Williams, whom they referred to as 'the black fox', were not groundless, as he had indeed managed to set up a secret correspondence between the grand duke and Frederick of Prussia.[25] In September, they saw their chance. After his victory at Gross-Jägersdorf on 30 August 1757, Field-Marshal Apraxin failed to pursue his advantage, allowing the Prussians to retreat in good order. Apraxin was a protégé of Bestuzhev and Catherine, and was known to be in correspondence with them. Suspicions of treason were aroused, and the French suggested that out of loyalty to the English, Stanisław had subverted Catherine and Bestuzhev.

Williams' diplomatic position had become untenable. He had been requesting permission to leave for months, and finally obtained it in July 1757. His departure was foiled several times by illness, and he did not get away until October, leaving behind a weeping Catherine and a disconsolate Stanisław. Catherine was now heavily pregnant, so she could be of little help. Bestuzhev was in a shaky position. Stanisław found himself alone in the face of growing hostility. French diplomacy triumphed. Broglie in Dresden persuaded Brühl to recall Stanisław, who received his notification on 9 November.

The French triumph was short-lived. During a court reception on 19 November the empress publicly asked Stanisław why he had been recalled. He replied that his court was acting under pressure from France. Elizabeth declared herself to be quite satisfied with his behaviour, and, turning to Bestuzhev, instructed him to demand a written explanation from the French. Two days later news arrived of the shattering defeat of the French armies by Frederick of Prussia at Rossbach on 5 November. Suddenly, the boot was on the other foot. France's prestige collapsed, and with it the influence of Vorontsov and l'Hôpital. Everyone at court started being friendly to Stanisław, and their treatment of him only became more fawning when Elizabeth suffered a stroke. The prospect of the succession loomed, and all thoughts were on Catherine. Everyone now knew on whom Catherine's thoughts dwelt.

Bestuzhev began to make contingency plans for a coup which would bypass the grand duke and place Catherine on the throne. He resented Stanisław's presence, but Catherine forced him to write to Brühl, expressing his indignation at Stanisław's recall, adding that it was a personal insult to him, Bestuzhev. Brühl could hardly countermand the recall so soon, so he merely instructed Stanisław to delay asking for a farewell audience. Stanisław spent much of the time at home feigning illness, but he continually saw Catherine, who was also homebound on account of her pregnancy. He would spend the evenings in her bedroom, where she had arranged a screen in such a way that whenever anyone appeared she could hide her clandestine guest. On the night of 9 December she gave birth to Stanisław's daughter, who was christened Anna Petrovna. He probably never saw the child, who was held over the font by the empress herself and then whisked away to be looked after by wet-nurses. The grand duke was tremendously pleased, though he had no reason to think the child might be his, and set about holding celebration parades.

When Catherine recovered her health, the lovers began to enjoy themselves once again. Stanisław would leave his sleigh and enter the palace through the back entrance as he had done on his first visit, wearing a wig and a large cape. Usually the sentry let him pass without a word, but if challenged he would say he was one of the grand duke's musicians. Sometimes he would stop his sleigh outside and wait for Catherine, who would come down in man's attire to join him, and they would either go for a drive or return to his apartment.

Danger was never absent. Once, an officer started wandering around his sleigh, asking questions. Stanisław pretended to be a sleepy foreign lackey awaiting his master, praying that Catherine would not appear before the officer went away. He confesses to having been in a sweat despite the arctic frost. On another occasion, they returned to find that her chambermaid had inadvertently locked Catherine's apartments, and they had to creep about the back stairs of the palace looking for someone who could let her in discreetly. The most terrifying moment for Stanisław came one day when they were flying along in the sleigh and one of the runners hit a boulder. Catherine was hurled out into the snow, where she lay motionless. Stanisław was convinced she was dead as he rushed to pick her up. Luckily she was only suffering from mild concussion.

The beginning of the year 1758 was a heady time for Stanisław. He was just approaching his twenty-sixth birthday, he was happily in love, and the prospects beckoning through the haze of possibility before him were stunning. The dream was, however, rudely shattered on the night of 25 February 1758. Stanisław came home from the theatre to find Bernardi, the jeweller who often carried letters between him and Catherine and Bestuzhev, waiting for him. Bernardi informed Stanisław that Bestuzhev had just been arrested, and that the police were searching the jeweller's house at that moment. He begged Stanisław to hide him, but was persuaded that the best course was to go home innocently.

Stanisław immediately sent word to Catherine. 'After reading this note, a succession of thoughts, each more unpleasant than the last, crowded into my mind,' Catherine recorded.[26] That evening they both attended a ball, as though nothing had happened. Catherine went to it with 'a dagger in the heart'. By then she knew that her aide-de-camp Yelagin and her close friend Adadurov had also been arrested, though it was still not clear on what suspicions. She had managed to destroy all papers in her possession that touched on politics or diplomacy on receipt of Stanisław's note, but she had no idea whether anything damning had been discovered among those of Bestuzhev or the others. At the ball, Prince Nikita Trubetskoy, the procurator who was in charge of questioning the chancellor, whispered in her ear that she was in the clear so far. Stanisław managed to approach her for long enough to tell her to meet him at the theatre two days later, so that they could co-ordinate their actions.

It soon became clear that Elizabeth had been alerted to Bestuzhev's machinations. Stanisław realised that if anything incriminating him were discovered, his diplomatic immunity would avail him little. He dashed off a letter to Brühl asking for permission to leave, and in the mean time took to his bed, feigning illness. There followed a terrible two months for Stanisław and Catherine. Bestuzhev was being questioned over and over again, as were Yelagin, Adadurov, Bernardi and Catherine's chambermaid, who knew every detail of her affair with Stanisław. He was determined not to be caught unawares if the interrogations yielded something, and managed to carry on a secret correspondence with the incarcerated Bestuzhev. All those interrogated held up equally well, and since nothing specific was found against anyone, Adadurov and Yelagin were released, and Bestuzhev was stripped of his honours and exiled to his country estate. Bernardi was imprisoned in Kazan and never freed. Stanisław gave the jeweller's wife and children the money to return to Venice, and paid her a pension for the rest of her life.[27]

Stanisław was forced out of his retirement at the end of March, when Friedrich Brühl, the minister's son, arrived in St Petersburg. Stanisław was called upon to escort him. Then, on 10 April, Prince Charles of Saxony, the son of Augustus III, arrived for a three-month visit. He had come to seek Elizabeth's backing for his plan to become Duke of Kurland. This Elizabeth duly agreed to, much to the annoyance of Stanisław and the whole Familia, who had tried to sabotage the visit. Prince Charles was aware that the Familia were ill-disposed towards him, and viewed Stanisław with the utmost suspicion.[28] Shortly after the prince's arrival, Stanisław received the permission he had requested to leave his posting whenever he wished.

He soon regretted having asked for it. On 4 June, Catherine was summoned by Elizabeth, and in the course of what must have been a charged interview between two women of no mean will, she managed to convince the empress of her innocence. The tension melted away, and Stanisław and Catherine could resume their meetings. Stanisław was required to stay with Prince Charles at the summer residence of Peterhof, which was close to Oranienbaum, and to visit the court often in numerous company, where he was less noticeable. The summer season, their recent brush with danger and their feelings all got the better of them. They became less guarded, even reckless.

On 6 July Stanisław set off to see Catherine in a cabriolet with a Russian driver who did not know him, and his own valet on the box behind. It was one of the white nights of the north. At a turning in the road, they met the grand duke with his mistress Elizabeth Vorontsov, the vice-chancellor's niece. The grand duke asked the driver who was in the cabriolet. The valet quickly interjected that it was a tailor, and they were allowed to proceed. But Elizabeth Vorontsov had recognised the 'tailor', and began to taunt the grand duke, who suddenly erupted into a fury.

Stanisław spent a few blissful hours in the arms of Catherine at a bathing pavilion, but as he emerged, he was surrounded by three horsemen with sabres drawn. They dragged him off to an isolated hut by the shore in which the grand duke was waiting. Stanisław thought he was going to die. 'The Grand Duke asked me if I had . . . his wife,' Stanisław wrote. He denied the charge categorically. 'Tell me the truth,' persisted the grand duke, 'for if you are truthful, everything can be arranged; if you deny it, you will have a very unpleasant time.' Stanisław continued to deny any guilt, and the grand duke left him in the hut under the guard of two soldiers. A couple of hours later, Stanisław's heart sank as the door opened to admit Alexander Shuvalov, the grand inquisitor, chief of the Secret Chancery. 'As if to increase the terror which the name of his office inspired alone, nature had endowed him with nervous spasms which horribly disfigured his already hideous face whenever he was concentrating on something,' Stanisław recorded. After a brief interrogation, Shuvalov let him go, and Stanisław went back to Peterhof. Not wishing to draw undue attention to himself by returning at six in the morning, he climbed, by mistake, through the window of a Russian general who was just shaving. Stanisław lay low for a couple of days, wondering what would happen next. Although nobody said a word, he could see by the faces of everyone he met that they knew he was in trouble. Even the Marquis de l'Hôpital reported back to Versailles on the subject.[29] Catherine wrote, saying that she was doing her utmost to calm down her husband. But Peter was volatile, and Stanisław was terrified.

A few days later, during a ball at Peterhof, Stanisław decided to take the bull by the horns. He invited Elizabeth Vorontsov to dance with him. 'It is in your power to make certain persons very happy,' he said to her during the minuet, to which she replied: 'It is almost done.' She told him to go to the pavilion of Mon-Plaisir, where the grand-ducal pair were staying the night, an hour after midnight, and to wait in the garden. When the ball was drawing to a close, Stanisław asked a tough-looking young Pole in Prince Charles's suite to accompany him. He was a minor nobleman by the name of Ksawery Branicki, but no relation to Stanisław's brother-in-law the hetman. 'God knows where our walk will end,' Stanisław warned Branicki, who declared himself ready for anything.

They waited on the terrace while Peter sat drinking and smoking with some friends. Eventually Elizabeth Vorontsov came and told them to follow her in. The grand duke seemed in fine spirits. 'You are mad not to have taken me into your confidence from the beginning,' he said to Stanisław. 'Had you done so, none of this nonsense would have taken place.' Stanisław agreed weakly, and then complimented him on the brilliance of his military strategy in having caught him, which pleased Peter. 'But since we are all now good friends, there is someone missing here,' he exclaimed. He left the room, dragged Catherine from her bed, only allowing her the time to throw a shift over herself, and produced her before Stanisław. 'Well, here she is,' he said, 'I hope that everyone is happy now.'[30]

Stanisław was very happy, although time was slipping by and his departure could not be delayed much longer. His relationship with Catherine had grown so deep that he believed it would endure separation and transcend circumstance. Others believed it would not survive his departure. The French foreign minister Choiseul suggested replacing him with a secretary of the French embassy, to wit the Chevalier d'Éon. (Stanisław, who sometimes fenced with him, had no inkling, any more than did Choiseul, that d'Éon was a woman.) The two lovers had discussed various different plans for the future, but they had settled on nothing, leaving it to circumstance. But Stanisław believed he could easily arrange a new posting to the Russian court soon, and when he left St Petersburg on 14 August 1758 he did not suspect that he would not see Catherine again for thirty years.

6

King-in-Waiting

The period following Stanisław's return to Warsaw in the autumn of 1758 was not a happy one. He felt frustrated, agitated about the future, and quickly sank into a splenetic melancholy. At court he had to endure the ribald jokes and prurient questions of Augustus III, in society the sneers of his political enemies, and at home the silent reproach of his mother. His Russian exploits had made him an object of interest to the ladies of Warsaw, but he ignored them 'with a chivalrous stoicism that could have featured in the finest of novels', as he put it.[1]

The only companion of his woes was Elżbieta Lubomirska. She was now twenty-two years old, and one of the most beautiful women in Warsaw. Blinded by his love for Catherine, Stanisław strayed further into intimacy with her. 'Virtue itself seemed to reassure me, and believing that I was only speaking with an angel, my very own guardian angel, I fell so deeply in love with her, without realising it, that I do not think I have experienced a stronger feeling in my life,' he would write.[2] She was herself far from happy, suffering from 'excessive sensibility' and bouts of nervous depression which affected her health. Stanisław's muddled but violent feelings agitated her, and she was in a state of near-hysteria when she left for Paris with her husband in the summer of 1759. 'This journey that I have desired so much, and which should be distracting me in so many ways, leaves me cold,' she wrote from Kraków, their first stop. 'Tell me what you are doing, what you will be doing, what you do every day, and whom you see.' Two weeks later, from Vienna, she wrote that she was in such a state of nervous depression that she could hardly go out. On 10 July, still from Vienna, she voiced the fear that even if she did get better, she was not frivolous enough to enjoy Paris, and felt that she would only be able to face it if he were at her side. Stanisław advised her against going there at all, suggesting Holland and England instead, but to Paris she eventually went, in October.[3]

With her gone, Stanisław had nobody to turn to for consolation when grief struck again. In late October he set off to see his parents at their estate of Malczyce, but on reaching the little town of Janów two miles away, he found his mother's coffin in the church. She had died two days before, on 27 October 1759. His despair was such that when his father handed him the box in which she had kept all his letters to her, he threw it on the fire, an action he bitterly regretted later. It was a year of loss. In the spring he had heard of the death of his daughter Anna in St Petersburg, and in November of that of Sir Charles, who took his own life in Chelsea on 2 November 1759.

Old Stanisław Poniatowski withdrew further into himself, which did not make him any the more tractable, and only a couple of months later Stanisław had to accompany his brother Andrzej down to Malczyce to lend moral support. Andrzej, who had been fighting with distinction for Austria in the Seven Years' War and had recently been wounded, wished to marry the well-born but impoverished Teresa Kinsky, whom he had met in Vienna. The old man was determined that his son should make a brilliant and financially sound match. It took all Stanisław's arguments, all the pleading of Andrzej, and the personal intervention of the Empress Maria Theresa, who was fond of the girl and later stood godmother to their first child, to break down his opposition. As the couple had little money, Stanisław gave Andrzej all the diamonds he had brought back from St Petersburg.

Kazimierz had also retired to the country. That autumn he had broken with the court party, as a result of a quarrel during a banquet given by Brühl. The minister had arranged a surprise, in the shape of a firework display that issued from the pudding. Unfortunately, the fireworks went wrong and singed Kazimierz's eyebrows. He was seized by a violent rage, and left the table cursing the minister roundly. He buried himself at Malczyce, where only Stanisław visited him.

Stanisław now lived with his Czartoryski uncles in Warsaw, and went with them to their estate at Puławy for the summer and to Wołczyn, where Adam Czartoryski's marriage to Izabela Flemming took place in November 1760. Stanisław had drawn closer to his cousin Adam. They spent dull winter days at Puławy studying Polish history and talking about their plans for the future. There was little else to do. The Familia were becalmed in the political doldrums, and a great question-mark seemed to hang over the country.

The Seven Years' War was into its fifth year. Although Augustus III was one of the principal belligerents, Poland was theoretically neutral, and after Saxony had been overrun by Frederick of Prussia, he took refuge in Warsaw, where he skulked in the Saxony Palace. He was sixty-four years old, and his obesity was not conducive to long life, so the prospect of another election loomed. As a result, Warsaw was becoming a centre of diplomatic attention. Even Spain, which had hitherto seen no need for anything more than a chargé d'affaires, sent an ambassador, Count de Aranda, later famous as Charles III's reforming minister. Maria Theresa transferred Count Mercy d'Argenteau from his embassy in St Petersburg, England was represented by the distinguished diplomat Lord Stormont, and France now sent the Marquis de Paulmy, son of the late French foreign minister d'Argenson. Paulmy, who represented the nation which traditionally took Polish elections most seriously, and who would be dictating policy to both Mercy and Aranda when the time came, had a rather bizarre brief:

France has for many years incurred immense and entirely fruitless expenses, either in order to give Poland kings who would have had a title without any power; or in order to break up parliaments which could not fail to be broken up by themselves, or to pay its partisans who, by their weakness, the opposition of their rivals supported by neighbouring Powers, and by the distance separating them from the Dominions of the King, could not render any significant service to His Majesty, and which, in turn, could not be assisted by the forces of France, in consequence of which all the money which we have spent in Poland has served only one party against another . . . Bearing in mind these considerations, it is evident that France's conduct in Poland has been highly ineffectual in dealing with a polity that can only be considered as an anarchy; but since this anarchy is convenient to the interests of France, her entire policy towards this kingdom

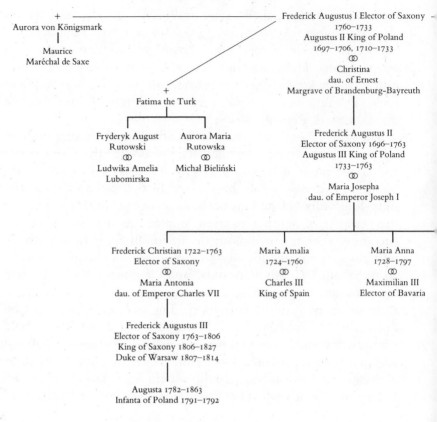

3   The Saxon Kings of Poland

must concentrate now on maintaining it, and on preventing any
Power from increasing its dominions at the expense of those of
Poland.[4]

But while the ambassador of His Most Christian Majesty arrived
with instructions to do nothing, this did not mean that Louis XV was
not interested. France had backed Stanisław Leszczyński against the
Saxon candidates to the Polish throne. When that had failed, she
resigned herself to supporting the Saxons. But Louis XV dreamt of
putting his cousin the Prince de Conti on the Polish throne at the first

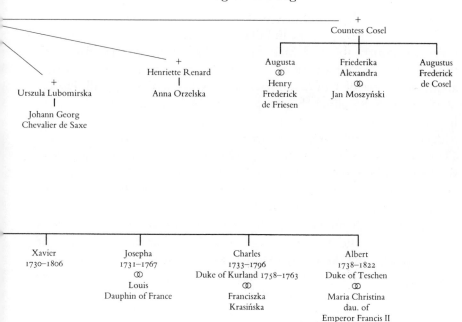

Xavier	Josepha	Charles	Albert
1730–1806	1731–1767	1733–1796	1738–1822
	∞	Duke of Kurland 1758–1763	Duke of Teschen
	Louis	∞	∞
	Dauphin of France	Franciszka	Maria Christina
		Krasińska	dau. of
			Emperor Francis II

opportunity. Since his daughter-in-law, who was Augustus III's daughter, and the Maréchal de Saxe, who was Augustus's natural brother, might object, and since his own wife might demand why, if he was not going to back his Saxon relatives, he did not choose to support her father, the ex-King Stanisław, Louis told no one of his plans. He primed selected diplomats, all of whom were sworn to secrecy, especially in relation to the foreign minister. This conspiracy, known as *Le Secret du Roi*, ramified within the French diplomatic corps throughout the 1740s and 1750s, sowing confusion. One of the most active members of the *Secret*, and a devoted supporter of the Prince de

Conti, was Broglie, posted to Warsaw as French ambassador in 1752. He built up France's prestige in Poland, helped to oust the Familia from favour at court, and had Stanisław recalled from Russia. But with time he changed his opinions and decided that France should forget about the Prince de Conti and back the Saxon dynasty after all. He left Warsaw in 1758, telling the chargé d'affaires Durand to 'try to conciliate in the most adroit manner possible the points on which the secret orders differ from those which come through the normal channel'.[5] Quite how that was to be done he did not explain. Paulmy was not in the *Secret*, although his secretary Pierre Hennin was, and what with his absurd instructions, it is not surprising that he was, in Hennin's words, 'drifting like a ship with no sails'.[6]

This only confirmed the Familia's view that France was unreliable as an ally. They would not easily forget how she had let down the cause of Stanisław Leszczyński and their own. Since Austria followed France's lead, there was little point in seeking her support. They saw Prussia as the greatest danger threatening Poland, since she could have no interest in promoting its regeneration – quite the reverse. This left Russia. Russia was there anyway, with several thousand troops guarding her magazines in Poland, and was enmeshed in Polish affairs by treaty. She was vitally interested in excluding others from Poland, and might be interested in strengthening it. The decisive factor for the Familia was that Russia would feel obliged to intervene in Poland whatever happened, so it would be best to base their policy on hers.

At the same time, if and when Russia did decide to take a hand in Polish affairs, she would have to prepare her ground and neutralise potential rivals. She would not wish to defy Prussia, and the Familia therefore applied themselves to cultivating Frederick's resident in Warsaw, Gedeon Benoit, a Hanoverian of Huguenot origin. An important element in this jigsaw for the Familia, and particularly for Stanisław, was England. They felt that she might act as a moral arbiter over Russia and Prussia if she could be persuaded to act jointly with them. Lord Stormont was less sanguine than his predecessor on the extent of English interest in Poland, but he remained an active supporter and friend of the Familia. It was a disappointment when, in May 1761, he was transferred to Vienna, but they hoped an experienced diplomat would replace him. Adam Czartoryski was sent to England in 1757, and again for several months in 1761, to meet people and make himself known, and was widely received as the future king of Poland.

The Familia worked as a party, and at this stage they were canvassing jointly for the party and its policy. The question of who was to be their candidate for the throne was not openly broached, although it must have been discussed endlessly among individual members. The uncles were grooming Adam for the post. His trips had cultural motives too, no doubt, but their primary aim was to promote him as an eligible figure. In 1759 he had gone to St Petersburg for a prolonged visit, and was addressed by the empress as 'dear cousin', which augured well. The Familia's popularity was growing at home, and many Poles accepted the idea that August Czartoryski or his son Adam might succeed Augustus III.

As Stanisław's chances appeared to fade in Poland, he yearned all the more for St Petersburg. He had been hoping for a new posting there ever since he left, and he remained in close contact with Catherine – the two exchanged more than a hundred letters in 1759 alone, conveyed secretly by Lord Stormont, Mercy, or the Baron de Breteuil, French ambassador in St Petersburg, who was close to Catherine and Stanisław. By the beginning of 1760, things were looking promising. Brühl was not averse to sending Stanisław to Russia, and French diplomacy now decided, for tortuous reasons of its own, to encourage such a posting. But Chancellor Vorontsov made his feelings known to the French foreign ministry, and Brühl was instructed that Poniatowski was not wanted in St Petersburg. Stanisław learnt of this through the French chargé d'affaires Durand in June 1760.[7]

As hopes of seeing Catherine in the immediate future receded, time and reality began to take effect. Stanisław had slipped into what was apparently a purely carnal affair with Sophie Leullier, a French courtesan. He then embarked on a liaison with Jadwiga Ciechanowiecka, a young widow who had caused havoc in Lithuania, where her fatal beauty had started a family feud costing more than a hundred lives over the years. When he left St Petersburg, Catherine had given him 'permission' to have the odd fling, as she realised it would be difficult for him to remain chaste at his age. 'For two and a half years I did not take advantage of it, and I gave repeated assurances to that effect,' Stanisław wrote. 'When, at last, this austere chastity reached its term, I had the quite superfluous sincerity to confess the fact . . . The reply came that, in truth, *this unhappy event had been long expected, but that it would be borne with equanimity.*'[8]

Catherine must have read Stanisław's confession with some relief. In 1760 she had met a dashing young officer, Grigory Grigorievich Orlov, and she was strongly attracted to him. Alone in the welter of palace politics, with the alarming prospect of her husband's accession looming, the need for a tough champion outweighed sentimental considerations. Orlov was not only recklessly brave, he and his brothers were popular officers in the army, and in a crisis the army would be the decisive factor. They became lovers, probably at the beginning of 1761. Catherine had acquired a partner, with whom she fell in love. Stanisław had erred from the path of strict devotion not through love, and it did not alter his feelings for Catherine. He certainly did not alter his perception of the unique affinity of souls that had united them, and that he believed would survive everything. He assumed she saw things the same way.

The one person with whom he could have forgotten Catherine, Elżbieta Lubomirska, had returned from Paris towards the end of 1760 a changed person. 'She, who before her departure had never held an opinion different from mine, not only argued with me often after her return, but did so with ill-humour,' noted Stanisław. 'All her tastes began to change: she who had liked only the English and serious books and occupations, came back much more French, more infatuated with fashion, and more ready to receive, with a sort of gratitude, anyone who flattered her.' She treated him with a coquettry that brought out the real feelings underlying the relationship. 'It was then I knew what jealousy is,' he wrote. 'I caught myself more than once groaning in solitude, almost howling with rage.'[9]

On 5 January 1762 the Empress Elizabeth finally died. The grand duke succeeded her as Peter III, and immediately set about sowing chaos. He reversed Russian foreign policy overnight, abandoning the anti-Prussian coalition, which effectively saved Frederick from humiliating defeat. He issued decrees of astonishing eccentricity, making himself increasingly unpopular, and finally convincing even the sceptical that he was unfit to rule. Catherine feared that sooner or later he would repudiate her if she did not account for him first. Stanisław was anxious. His instinct was to go to St Petersburg to help her. 'I beg you earnestly not to hasten here, as your presence in these circumstances would be perilous for you and very harmful to me,' she wrote on 2 July.[10] She was already engaged on a plan of the utmost danger that materialised a week later, on the night of 9 July, when a coup d'état engineered by the Orlovs placed her on the throne and imprisoned her husband.

Stanisław heard news of the coup at Puławy, whither he had retired to hide his anxiety. He set off for Warsaw at once. As he waited for the ferry over the Vistula, he met his returning messenger, who handed him a letter from Catherine. He broke the seal there and then. It was dated 13 July, and began: 'I am sending Count Keyserling to Poland immediately to make you king after the death of the present one, and in the event that he could not succeed on your behalf, I wish it to be Prince Adam.'[11] He read no further, but immediately raced back to Puławy. There he read the whole letter out to his uncles and his cousin Adam. It was very long, describing in detail the events of the night of 9 July, and telling of her fears and her hopes.

The uncles were delighted. Here at last was a frank and definite assurance of support, and the fact that Adam was mentioned in the same breath as Stanisław seemed to indicate that it was not out of love but out of political conviction that the new empress was supporting them. But Adam was to disappoint his father's ambitions. As they left the room together, he took Stanisław aside and told him he had no wish to be king. He said that he would immediately write to Countess Bruce, Catherine's close friend, with whom he had had an affair during his stay in St Petersburg, telling her to persuade Catherine to erase him from her plans and think only of Stanisław.

Stanisław penned Catherine a long letter, full of enquiries about her plans and advice on how she should proceed. He sent it off through the Austrian ambassador, Mercy, and was soon in receipt of a reply, dated 9 August, in which she stated that she could not correspond freely with him without running great risks. Her position was by no means secure. She was an usurper, and she was technically only a caretaker for her son, the child Paul. A few days after the coup, Peter was killed in mysterious circumstances by his guards, so opponents had no lack of ammunition against Catherine, and she had to keep the loyalty of those who had elevated her. She was being watched, and could not afford to arouse suspicion. Apart from anything else, she was extremely busy. 'To tell you all the internal secrets would be an indiscretion; I cannot

... I shall take heed of all your recommendations,' she answered. 'Write to me as little as you can, or better, not at all, without necessity, above all without hieroglyphs.'[12] Stanisław ignored her fears, and merely sent her a set of cyphers so they could correspond in code. A major misunderstanding had arisen between them. Stanisław underestimated the degree to which she had matured and emancipated herself. He also failed to realise that she now had to fuse her own plans with Russian reasons of state. He kept showering her with advice, presuming on her need for his guidance, and repeating his willingness to come and help her. He also, apparently, fished for some sort of declaration on her feelings for him. She deflected his advice and suggestions, and evaded mention of her sentiments, but he refused to take her hints, and this began to exasperate her:

> You read my letters with little attention. I have told you and repeated that I would be exposed to the most terrible risks from all sides if you set foot in Russia. You say you are in despair; I am surprised at you, for after all every reasonable man must come to terms with circumstances. I cannot and will not explain myself on many things ... All the troubles in the world can still assail me, and your name and your arrival are capable of producing the most disastrous consequences. I have repeated to you, and I say it again; you wish me to flatter your feelings; I cannot do so, and I will not; I need to summon up such firmness a thousand times every day ... Adieu. Be assured that I conserve a special feeling for you and for everything that concerns you, and let me solve my own troubles.[13]

Stanisław was disturbed. Catherine's caution in communicating with him meant that he did not know her exact intentions, and her ambassador's behaviour did not reassure him. It is difficult to know how committed she was, and there is some evidence to suggest that at one stage she shifted her preference to Adam Czartoryski as her candidate for the throne. Yet she repeated her intention of making Stanisław king in letters to his uncles, and one to his father.[14] But old Stanisław Poniatowski never saw this. He had begun failing that summer, and Stanisław and his youngest brother Michał took turns to look after him. He prepared for his death like a general for a battle, installing the coffin-maker in the house so that he could keep an eye on him. He told Kazimierz that two of three prophecies that an old fortune-teller had made had come true, and that the third was all but consummated, but he did not say what it was. He died on 28 August 1762.

His father's death would have done nothing to alleviate Stanisław's mounting insecurity. His repeated suggestions that he might go to St Petersburg in secret, if necessary, irritated Catherine. 'I advise you against secret journeys, as my conduct cannot be secret,' she wrote in November. 'I am half dead with fear on account of the letters you send me.'[15] She had good reason to be afraid. At the beginning of December, Breteuil's messenger was attacked and almost killed on the road to St Petersburg, and the entire diplomatic bag rifled. Luckily for Catherine, Stanisław's letter to her was found lying in the snow unopened. Cypher or no cypher, the correspondence was a source of terrible danger to her. 'Since I have to speak plainly and you have resolved to ignore what I have been telling you for six months, the fact is that if you come here you are likely to get us both massacred,' she wrote.[16]

She wanted him to concentrate his attention on Poland, where there was now plenty to do. Stanisław had taken over from his brother as the parliamentary leader of the Familia, displaying not only great eloquence, but also a sense of timing and tactics. He had taken part in the Seyms of 1760 and 1761, adroitly playing the role of tribune and rabble-rouser at the expense of the court party, and meeting with much popular approval. Later that year, accompanied by Adam Czartoryski, Stanisław Lubomirski and his own youngest brother Michał, he went to Piotrków for the elections to the Tribunal, to push through the marshalcy of the Familia's ally Andrzej Zamoyski. At the Seym of 1762 he again led the attack, by challenging the legality of young Friedrich Brühl's election as deputy for Warsaw. This provoked fury from Brühl's Mniszech and Potocki supporters, and sabres were drawn on both sides of the chamber. There was to be no fighting, however, and the battle continued with words, as Karol Radziwiłł heaped abuse on Stanisław. The Familia then approached Brühl's father and proposed withdrawing their challenge if he gave certain offices to their supporters. Brühl refused, and retaliated by trying to impeach Stanisław on the grounds that he had exceeded his brief while Saxon envoy in St Petersburg. The Seym broke up in uproar after a few days.

A few weeks later, Stanisław went to Wilno with Jerzy Flemming, to lead the Familia's faction at the elections to the Tribunal of Lithuania. Karol Radziwiłł brought 3,000 soldiers as well as large numbers of henchmen who physically prevented opponents from entering the building to cast their votes. Stanisław and Flemming were shot at when one group of Radziwiłł's men stormed the house where they were staying.

All this was grist to the mill of the Familia. For thirty years they had been trying to change things by parliamentary means, showing scrupulous regard for constitutional legality, but it had got them nowhere. The country, which had drifted aimlessly for so long, was likely to fall apart completely if something were not done soon. They were coming to the conclusion that drastic action was necessary. As the king's health deteriorated, his family grew alarmed at their isolation, and began to cast around for allies.

Maria Antonia, the wife of Augustus's son Frederick Christian, approached the Familia through Andrzej Poniatowski in Vienna, offering them any terms they demanded in return for their support. Frederick Christian was prepared to allow the Familia virtually to rule Poland for him as long as he could obtain the throne. But the Familia did not want more of the same, and they had now found in Russia the backing they needed to bring about real change. On 15 February 1763, on the same day that the peace of Hubertusburg brought the Seven Years' War to an end, Catherine put her plans for Poland to her council, and Stanisław's candidature for the Polish throne became Russian policy.

The Familia had decided that there was no point in waiting for Augustus' death, and decided to seize power through a confederation backed by Russian force and English money. With every other power licking its wounds from the recent war, outside intervention seemed unlikely. Catherine instructed Keyserling to back them. He was to let it be known in Poland that if anyone lifted a finger against the Familia, she would not hesitate to 'fill Siberia with my enemies and let loose the Zaporozhian Cossacks'.[17] She immediately ordered a few detachments into Lithuania to cow the Radziwiłłs, but she did not wish to commit large bodies of Russian troops. The confederation was planned for the end of July 1763, and in the spring the Familia started raising troops, a task greatly facilitated by the recent end of the war, which left thousands of redundant soldiers scattered around central Europe. In Lithuania their allies Michał Kazimierz Ogiński and the Massalski brothers did likewise. Stanisław worked on a manifesto and a programme for the confederation. Kazimierz Poniatowski was hauled out of his country retreat and involved in the military preparations. Memoranda on every aspect of the plan were produced for Keyserling and Catherine. She was feeling pleased with herself as she had just succeeded in ousting Charles of Saxony from Kurland, replacing him with the former duke, Ernest Bühren, without any trouble. Foreign affairs seemed to promise her much fun.

But the conduct of foreign policy was the object of a power-struggle between the old ex-Chancellor Bestuzhev and Nikita Panin, a former diplomat who was to become Catherine's foreign minister, and since Poland was Catherine's first major venture abroad, this contest came to a head over how to conduct affairs there. Bestuzhev favoured backing a Saxon candidate for the Polish throne in alliance with Austria. Panin favoured a Pole who would owe everything to Russia, but he recoiled from a confederation to dethrone Augustus. He advised Catherine against getting involved in something that might lead to war, and suggested she prepare her ground diplomatically. England and Prussia both wanted an alliance with Russia. But England was afraid of involvement and wary of the Familia's designs. In the summer of 1762 she had scaled down her representation in Warsaw, replacing Stormont with Thomas Wroughton, with the rank of resident. English diplomats in the area were instructed to 'give the appearance of full harmony' with their Russian colleagues, but not to commit themselves.[18] It was this fence-sitting by the English that forced Catherine to look to Prussia. Frederick was more than happy to get involved, but did not want the Familia to gain power by their own devices, and declined to support their confederation.[19] Catherine got cold feet, and bowed to Panin's advice. On 25 July she wrote to Keyserling telling him to halt all preparations for the confederation and to rein in the Familia, and on 7 August she followed this up with another letter, stating that nothing should be done until Augustus III died.[20]

The news came at the very worst moment for the Familia. Not only did they have to abort the whole meticulously prepared operation, they had to consider the possibility that Catherine had decided to drop them altogether, despite her cordial assurances to the contrary. Stanisław received several letters affirming that she was unchanged in her intention of placing him on the throne, and she sent him money. But he took her hesitation and her caution personally. His heart must have told him that if she cared she would act with greater determination. He was so discouraged that he thought of distracting himself with some foreign travel. He had always wanted to go to Italy and see Switzerland, and to visit Voltaire at Ferney on the way.[21]

The Familia's preparations earlier in the year had not gone unnoticed, and the sudden lull gave the impression that something had gone wrong. In the absence of definite outward signs of Russian commitment, the Radziwiłł and Potocki factions suddenly felt brave, and took every opportunity to bully adherents of the Familia. When the time came for the elections to the Supreme Tribunal, Stanisław, Adam Czartoryski and Stanisław Lubomirski went to Piotrków to face a large and confident Radziwiłł-Potocki faction, emboldened by the presence of thousands of supporters. What promised to be an unpleasant confrontation was averted by the news that Augustus III had died on 5 October. Catherine could now proceed with her plan of arranging the election of Stanisław. But with the throne at last vacant, the whole of Europe became involved to a greater or lesser extent, and she had to tread warily.

Stanisław's principal rival was Frederick Christian of Saxony. As he was married to the Emperor Joseph II's sister, he enjoyed the approval of Austria. One of Frederick Christian's own sisters was married to King Charles III of Spain. He also had the support of Turkey, which feared the possibility of Stanisław ascending the throne and marrying Catherine, thereby creating an alliance that would overwhelm Turkey. Above all, Frederick Christian could count on France, whose Dauphin was married to his sister. His support in Poland itself was patchy. It included the Radziwiłł, Potocki, Mniszech and other families of the court party, but its mainstay, Stanisław's brother-in-law Hetman Branicki, was in two minds as to what he should do. Branicki felt that if Frederick Christian failed and a Pole were to get the crown, that Pole should be himself. At seventy-four he was a little too old for the job, but he was very popular. Nor was he the only Pole with ideas on the subject. One of the Lubomirskis announced that he would stand, but he was generally ignored. And Michał Kazimierz Ogiński, Michał Czartoryski's son-in-law, began to dream of the crown for himself.

Ogiński went to St Petersburg, where he fell in with the Danish Minister Baron von der Osten. Stanisław knew Osten from his own sojourn in the Russian capital, and they had remained on cordial terms. 'His behaviour, his principles and his figure are equally ignoble,' the English ambassador Lord Buckinghamshire warned Stormont. 'Unquiet, intriguing, the most brazen liar there ever was, he is always after something, something bad by preference.'[22] Osten nevertheless enjoyed Catherine's confidence. He was clearly working against Stanisław while showering him with letters pledging his active support.[23] Michał Czartoryski bombarded Ogiński with letters telling him to leave St Petersburg, but Catherine flattered his hopes, and even gave him the Order of St Andrew. She claimed that she was keeping him out of the way in Stanisław's interest, but Stanisław could not be sure.[24] Nor could he be sure that his uncle and cousin had entirely given up their royal ambitions. Adam Czartoryski had recently repeated his assurance that he did not want the crown. But many of the Familia's supporters wanted to see him or his father on the throne, and August had made no renunciation.

Throughout that year, Stanisław had been prey to continuing anxieties. He was cruelly torn between his ambition and his emotional fantasies, and there were moments when he no longer knew what he really wanted. On the one hand, he wanted to be king. It was a prospect that few men's vanity could resist. It was also a means to an end, an end that had fired him from his earliest years – the regeneration of Poland. On the other hand, he wanted Catherine. It was now five years since he had seen her last, and he knew that she had another lover. But he found it emotionally convenient to ignore the implications, and he may have believed, as did Breteuil, one of his main informers on events in St Petersburg, that 'it is impossible to conceive, in view of the rude stupidity of [Orlov], that the taste of this princess for him could possibly go beyond the satisfaction of the senses'.[25] Stanisław himself had just, in the late spring of 1763, embarked on an affair with Elżbieta Szydłowska which was by no means a passing flirtation, yet this had little effect on his deeper feelings, which appear to have become sublimated to an unreal level. What had probably been little more than an idle fantasy entertained by the two lovers as they caressed each other in the back of a sleigh flying through the Russian winterscape – that he would become king of Poland so that they could marry each other – had become a recurring dream in Stanisław's life after their separation. Only through such a solution could he combine the two great desires of his life. 'I loved you with the deepest and the most genuine tenderness which perhaps has ever been, and I loved you solely for yourself,' he wrote to her on 2 November. 'If I desired the throne, it was because I saw you on it.'[26] And as it was being continually pointed out to him that such a union was out of the question, he considered forfeiting the throne for the sake of his love. 'Do not make me king, but bring me back to your side,' he wrote to her, more than once, that winter.[27] He even tried to persuade himself that he could do more good for Poland from a dominant position in St Petersburg than from the throne in Warsaw.

While he struggled to make up his mind between conflicting desires he resented the fact that he had become an object of policy. It was a policy increasingly formulated by Keyserling, the Familia and Panin, rather than, as he would have liked, Catherine and himself. He sent his friend Franciszek Rzewuski to St Petersburg as his own envoy in an attempt to create a direct line of communication, but this did not help. He complained that it was Keyserling and not he who received letters and instructions from Catherine and concerted her policy in Poland. Keyserling treated him merely as the Familia's candidate, to be piloted into the desired position. Aiming to gain support for Stanisław in Poland on the one hand, and to allay Turkish fears on the other, Keyserling suggested that he should marry one of the daughters of Franciszek Potocki, Palatine of Kiev. Stanisław was furious. He expressed 'extreme repugnance' at the idea, and reproached Keyserling bitterly for entertaining it.

Things were to get worse. Keyserling was attached to the Czartoryskis, and Panin feared that he would be too easily manipulated by them. He also resented the fact that Catherine corresponded with Keyserling directly. Since he could not get her to replace him, he suggested that he be given an assistant. The man chosen for the job was Panin's twenty-nine-year-old nephew, Prince Nikolay Vassilievich Repnin. He was sent to Warsaw ostensibly as an assistant to Keyserling, but in effect as a watchdog.

Repnin arrived in Warsaw on 21 December 1763. On the very next day he called on Stanisław, to tell him that he had instructions to work for his election. Yet another link had been introduced into the chain of communication with Catherine, and Stanisław's position grew more impersonal as it became more official. It was through Repnin that Catherine thanked Stanisław for the case of truffles he had sent her for Christmas.[28] Intimate gestures were now out of order, and lovers' dreams had been superseded by international politics.

7

The Election

On 17 December 1763 Stanisław's rival Frederick Christian died unexpectedly. His death threw the Saxon party into disarray. But that would not make the opposition to Stanisław any less determined, and on 23 December 1763 a conference was held in Stanisław's appartments to concert policy. It was attended by Keyserling, Repnin, Stanisław's brothers Kazimierz and Michał, his uncles Michał and August, his cousin Adam, Stanisław Lubomirski and Andrzej Zamoyski. Repnin repeated his instructions to strive for the election of Stanisław, and if for one reason or another this should prove impossible, that of Adam Czartoryski.

The question arose at what stage they should appeal to Catherine for military support. Stanisław declared that he could not accept the presence of Russian troops in Poland, since this would impugn the legality of his election. 'If Russian troops do not come here, you will not be king,' remarked Keyserling, to which Stanisław retorted: 'I would rather not be king, than give grounds for reproach.' Michał Czartoryski and Andrzej Zamoyski told him that it was not a question of his pleasure, and that he was the candidate of a party which had worked for years to place its man on the throne. Stanisław gave way after a few well-chosen words of protest.

His sudden obsession with legality was probably meant for the record, and he later asked some of those who had been present to confirm his unwillingness to countenance Russian intervention.[1] He had never baulked at the idea of Russian support in the past, and had few scruples on the methods to be used to attain his goal. 'As long as the result is good, then I do not think it is worth binding ourselves with supposed rules in such matters, which are by their nature irregular, for such binding can prove harmful, or at least delaying to the business in hand,' he wrote to Ignacy Massalski, Bishop of Wilno, in April.[2] And notwithstanding his professions to Catherine that he would prefer to be at her side rather than mount the Polish throne, he could not quite quench his ambition. In a long memorandum to her composed in December 1763 he pointed out why Ogiński was not a credible candidate for the throne, and reminded her that Adam Czartoryski had declined it for the third time.[3]

Whenever his monarchical ambition did wane, it was strongly bolstered by his brother Kazimierz and a growing number of supporters such as Ksawery Branicki, the daredevil he had met in St Petersburg, Franciszek Rzewuski, August Sułkowski and Ignacy Krasicki, a cultivated young magnate just starting out on a clerical career, all of whom were looking forward to rich pickings under his rule. On 4 January, he laid before Keyserling and Repnin a set of 'conditions' under which he could rule, including an annual subsidy from Russia, the transfer of the four Guard regiments from the hetman's command to the Crown, and a guarantee of the monarch's continued right to make all appointments. He then sent off a formal request for troops to Catherine, technically to be on lease to the Familia.[4] At the same time, he was discussing with the architect Jakub Fontana his plans for rebuilding the Royal Castle.

'In regard to the family of Czartoryski I can positively assure you that there is the utmost union in favour of Poniatowski,' the English resident Thomas Wroughton reported.[5] Nor was there any doubt at this stage about Russia's choice. Panin, whose influence was paramount, had opted for Stanisław, and had informed Russia's allies. Keyserling's attachment to the Czartoryskis made him favour August or his son, but he could not fan any real ambition from their smouldering self-esteem. In the early spring of 1764 he asked Stanisław to consider stepping down in favour of his uncle August, suggesting that perhaps the older man might make a better king. But Stanisław dismissed the idea.

It was not just the glory that lured him on. While an element of vanity cannot be denied, his principal spur had always been the ardent desire to regenerate Poland. And now that this lay within his grasp, he would not be deflected from his purpose. The programme of the Familia was one of reform based on bringing the constitution up to date and ridding it of abuses such as the veto, without altering the fundamental republican nature of the Polish system. If anything, it aimed to diminish the influence of the Crown, by stripping it of the prerogative of nominating ministers and other officials. Stanisław had come to the conclusion that Poland had fallen so far behind not merely because of a few abuses and shortcomings, but because her decentralised republican structure was inappropriate for such a large country. The example of England, where the love of liberty was as keen as in Poland, was ever present in his mind. What Poland needed in his opinion was more than reform – it needed transformation into a state capable of developing economically and defending itself militarily.

In the spring of 1763 he had sketched out his ideas in an essay entitled *Anecdote Historique*, which took the form of an imaginary political testament by King Władysław IV (1632–48). It envisaged an hereditary monarchy, strong cabinet government, a permanently sitting Seym representing more than just the szlachta, and the creation of a salaried administration. The most important element for him was a stronger Crown.[6] The essay's semi-literary form suggests that Stanisław may have intended to publish it, but in the first instance he gave a copy to the Danish diplomat Osten, who happened to be passing through Warsaw on his way to St Petersburg, asking him to give it to Catherine. He wanted to apprise her of his intentions and needed to know her reactions, but it appears that she never saw it.

The first months of 1764 were spent in canvassing. The Archbishop Primate of Poland, who automatically became head of state, interrex, on the death of a king, had called elections for the spring. The seymiks would elect deputies to a Convocation Seym, whose task it was to fix the rules and vet the candidates for the election to the throne. It would then dissolve itself, handing over to an Election Seym, comprising every member of the szlachta who wished to turn up. After the election of the new king, the deputies of the Convocation Seym would re-assemble as the Coronation Seym, and start ruling. Hetman Branicki had called out the Crown troops and taken command of those Saxon units stationed in Poland. In spite of his great age, he marched about the country at their head in a show of force. Others of his faction resorted to open intimidation. Karol Radziwiłł burst into the palace of Bishop Massalski, and threatened to kill him if he did not stop canvassing for the Familia. 'And remember that I have a hundred thousand ducats in reserve with which to go to Rome to ask for absolution,' he added.[7]

The Familia monitored these illegalities, and when they had enough material, they got the Primate, Archbishop Władysław Łubieński, to call on Russia to protect law and order. A couple of thousand Russian troops entered Poland in March, and went about in detachments of about 150 men, showing their presence. The only major confrontation took place at Grudziądz, where General Khomutov was stationed with 2,000 soldiers guarding a Russian magazine left over from the Seven Years' War. Since a pre-election seymik was to be held there on 27 March, he withdrew his men from the city. But then Hetman Branicki turned up with 800 soldiers, and started intimidating the voters. Andrzej Poniatowski, who was organising the Familia campaign there, was attacked, but Khomutov marched back into the city and forced Branicki to withdraw. This and a similar showdown at Bydgoszcz ensured that the Familia achieved an overall majority of forty-five seats in the Convocation Seym. But the very ease with which things were proceeding produced reactions outside the country which were to have heavy consequences.

One was that Frederick of Prussia had begun to get worried. He had been angling for an alliance with Russia since February 1763, and the Russians had been dragging their heels in responding to his proposals. The only immediate benefit of the alliance for them was to guarantee Prussian co-operation over Poland. But Frederick had already made it clear to France and Austria that he supported Catherine, and now it looked as though she was going to get all the benefits of the proposed alliance without having to sign it. By November 1763 he began to wonder whether he had not been duped, and he looked around for ways of forcing Russia's hand.

He did not have to look far. In November 1763 the envoy of the Porte Resmi Ahmad Efendi arrived in Berlin with the aim of obtaining Prussian support against Stanisław's candidature, which Turkey feared. Frederick regarded the arrival of the Turk and his huge retinue as an expensive nuisance, and his first wish had been to get rid of them all as quickly as possible. But by the beginning of December, he was detaining them with lavish feasts and inviting the envoy to come and stay with him at Potsdam, an unusual honour. Foreign diplomats in Berlin, well acquainted with Frederick's avarice, watched in astonishment and reported back to their courts. It was not long before the St Petersburg chancellery was asking itself whether Frederick was not indeed about to sign a treaty with Turkey. It seemed thoroughly unlikely, but it was a terrifying prospect for Russia to be attacked by Turkey and Prussia just when she was engaged in promoting her candidate in Poland in the teeth of French, Austrian and Saxon opposition. Russia had no option but to take Frederick's posturings seriously, and at the end of January generous proposals winged their way from St Petersburg.[8]

Frederick had his alliance, and the hapless Turk was unceremoniously seen off. In fact, Frederick had got more than he had asked for. The treaty signed on 11 April 1764 was ostensibly a defensive-offensive alliance guaranteeing the mutual safety of the two countries. But among its secret clauses was an undertaking to act jointly to prevent any change to the status quo in Poland, and to guarantee the throne to Stanisław. What it meant was that Frederick had become Russia's partner as guarantor of the country's constitution, a role hitherto jealously guarded by Russia. It was a major mistake for Russia, and a catastrophe for Poland. The delighted Frederick despatched Prince Carolath as ambassador extraordinary with the Prussian Order of the Black Eagle for Stanisław. Neither Stanisław nor the Familia suspected this of being an ill omen.

The Convocation Seym opened on 7 May. Warsaw was ringed by Russian troops, estimates of whose numbers vary from 4,000 to 7,000. Another 2,000 troops in the grey and green uniforms of the Czartoryskis took up positions in the capital itself.[9] Andrzej Poniatowski was in command of detachments around the Castle, while Kazimierz supervised the deployment of the rest. There was vociferous indignation from the Hetmans Rzewuski and Branicki, Karol Radziwiłł and Franciszek Potocki, all but 700 of whose soldiers had been denied entry into Warsaw by the surrounding Russians. But when summoned by the Primate to order the Crown troops back to barracks and restore the artillery to the arsenal, the hetmans refused. When, on the following day, Adam Czartoryski was elected marshal of the Seym, noisy protests turned into violent confrontation, and swords were drawn in defiance. But the hetmans' faction were not cut out for heroics. Branicki was too proud to start arguing in the Seym, Radziwiłł was all drunken bluster, and Potocki was 'a brave man when he was strong, but a coward in danger', according to one of his supporters.[10] They and their allies stormed out of the chamber. A number of senators and deputies recorded formal complaints in the Warsaw statute books, and then left Warsaw.

The Seym, which was now under the Familia's control, proceeded to suspend the hetmans from office and vested temporary command of the army in August Czartoryski. Most of the units accepted his command, although a few regiments remained loyal to Branicki. Kazimierz Poniatowski was sent in pursuit. He cornered Branicki's forces near Lublin and, after a short skirmish, arranged a capitulation. Having laid down his arms, Branicki went to Hungary to nurse his spite. Karol Radziwiłł followed him. Kazimierz then followed the retreating Franciszek Potocki into Podolia, where he persuaded him too to disarm. Kazimierz's diplomatic behaviour was censured by August Czartoryski.

It was inspired by Stanisław, who was already thinking of himself as a monarch, and wanted to act like one, rather than like the partisan of a political party. He had gone to great lengths throughout the preceding months to placate Hetman Branicki, approaching him through his sister, who was the hetman's wife, and also through her lover Andrzej Mokronowski, who, as well as being Branicki's right-hand man, was also in the *Secret*. It was partly out of vanity that he wanted to be elected with the greatest possible legitimacy and consensus, but he also realised that the confrontation tactics of the Familia jeopardised chances of gaining a broad base of support for his programme later. That is why he told Kazimierz to treat Branicki, Radziwiłł and Potocki as leniently as possible. It was also why he kept a low profile during the Convocation Seym, in which he sat as deputy for Mazovia, along with Teodor Szydłowski, the father of his current mistress. It was incumbent on him to initiate the legislation recognising the imperial title of the Russian monarchy, which only the Commonwealth and France still ignored, and it was a small gratification for Stanisław to be able to send Catherine news of the recognition of her title. It was with a good deal less pleasure that he pushed through the recognition of Frederick's royal title. Otherwise, he avoided doing

93

anything that might prejudice people against him. Instead he devoted much time to canvassing for his cause and trying to mend bridges, often using the wives in order to bring their husbands round to him. But in the midst of this, one particularly important bridge suddenly collapsed with fracas.

Stanisław believed that in the long term Poland would have to emancipate herself from the influence of Russia and Prussia, and this she could only do with the support of powers such as Austria, France and England. Shortly before the death of Augustus III he had called on the French ambassador's secretary Pierre Hennin, whom he knew to be in the *Secret*. He assured him that although he was Russia's candidate for the throne, he did not intend to be a Russian puppet. He told him of his plan to regenerate Poland economically and politically, and to re-establish her independence, all of which would require the support of France. He asked Hennin to pass this information on to Louis XV, and suggested that it would be helpful if France did not encourage Hetman Branicki. Hennin, an experienced diplomat who knew Poland well, passed the information on to Versailles with his favourable comments.[11] Stanisław called week after week to find out whether a reply had come to his proposals, but none came.

Louis XV could not make up his mind. His foreign minister Choiseul, who was eventually informed by some exasperated member of the *Secret*, was interested, but reacted in a characteristically muddled way. He instructed Paulmy not to offend Stanisław and the Familia, but to carry on ostensibly supporting their rivals.[12] As a result, Paulmy found himself delivering strong statements on behalf of the pro-Saxon magnates, and sending notes to Stanisław assuring him that France would recognise his election.[13] Choiseul also despatched General Monet, who was not in the *Secret*, to promote understanding between the Familia and France. Monet arrived in January 1764, and his presence at the side of the Familia caused consternation among their opponents, who began to heckle and insult Paulmy and Hennin, neither of whom knew what Monet was up to or why. France now had three diplomatic representatives in Poland, two of them with diametrically opposed sets of instructions, and the third, the only intelligent one and the only one who was in the *Secret*, with no instructions at all.[14]

The showdown at the opening of the Convocation Seym demanded a reaction from France, which had to come down in support of one side or the other. But her policy was in such a tangle that Choiseul could think of no better way out than withdrawing his ambassador. On the morning of 7 June, Paulmy called on the Primate, who received him formally in a room crowded with ministers and senators. Paulmy announced his recall, based on the rather curious pretext that the very body of the Commonwealth had been 'torn apart and rendered in-substantial' by the events at the beginning of the Convocation Seym. The Primate, who during an interregnum represented in his person the Crown and Commonwealth of Poland, asked him whether this meant that France no longer recognised the Commonwealth. Paulmy referred to his instructions and affirmed this to be the case. Thereupon the Primate declared that since the ambassador of His Most Christian Majesty did not recognise the Commonwealth, the Commonwealth could not recognise the ambassador, and bade him farewell as a private individual, with a '*Bonjour, Monsieur le Marquis de Paulmy!*'[15]

It was what is known as a diplomatic incident. The honour of the Commonwealth and the majesty of Louis XV had both been insulted. Paulmy left Warsaw at once. Hennin and Monet had to go too. Vienna withdrew Mercy in solidarity, and Spain recalled her chargé d'affaires (Aranda had left a few months before). Their departure virtually cut Poland off from Europe, which alarmed Stanisław, who valued diplomacy and had hoped to make use of it to bolster Poland's position. Now it would depend above all on his relations with Russia. He was again assailed by his old regrets concerning Catherine, and on 27 May he wrote her a letter full of lover's complaints. But this time, other doubts showed through the sorrow:

I beg you, I conjure you, give me an answer, and say something to console me. I need it, and more perhaps than you think. You are making me king, but are you making me happy? You cannot take away from me the memory of the happiness which I once knew, nor the desire to recover it. One does not love twice the way I loved you, and what is left to me? An emptiness, a terrible ennui at the bottom of my heart which nothing can fill. What about ambition, you may say. Oh, I do not know how others are made, but to me ambition seems a very futile thing when it is not supported by serenity and contentment of the heart. And what a throne! What glory! Am I in a position to do the slightest good? Will you allow me to? But what do you care about all that, if you do not love me? You think you are acquitting yourself before those who know the past by giving me a crown. Do you really believe that in the bottom of your heart? If that is so, then your heart resembles mine very little . . . Is it possible that you are really happy with yourself and with your situation? Is it possible that another than me loves you as completely, as truly as I? . . . Ah, Sophie, Sophie, you have made me suffer cruelly.[16]

What transpires from this letter, which may never have been sent, is something he had never touched on before – namely that the withdrawal of her love and her apparent coolness might signify a corresponding withdrawal of her trust in him, and a change of attitude to his plans for Poland once he was king. The question, quite simply, was whether an unloving Catherine would allow him to rule as he wanted. Stanisław had sent his friend Franciszek Rzewuski to St Petersburg to act as a go-between, but he really wanted to meet her himself, believing that an interview would clarify everything. In June 1764 she went to visit Riga, and he wanted to join her there. But Catherine was being closely watched for signs of her marital intentions. Some had thought that she ought to strengthen her position by marrying the great-grandson of Peter the Great's elder brother, Ivan VI, swept from the throne by Elizabeth in 1741 and cast into Schlüsselburg prison, where he still languished. But in July 1764, he was killed during an attempt to liberate him, and this alarmed those, such as the Turks, who feared that she really did intend to marry Stanisław.

The issue came up in Poland too. One of the Convocation Seym's duties was to draw up the *Pacta Conventa*, the set of conditions under which the prospective monarch was to rule. Many of these did not change from one election to the next, but some were specific, and in this case there would have to be one concerning his freedom to marry. In July, Frederick of Prussia wrote to his ambassador in St Petersburg, Count Solms, that the best way of allaying Turkish fears and defusing French threats was by forcing Stanisław to 'marry some Polish woman'.[17] And Keyserling officially told Stanisław that Russian support was conditional on his marrying a Pole. At one stage Panin varied this, and suggested a Russian princess.[18] 'Make my cousin king, and leave me free,' Stanisław wrote to Panin in despair towards the end of August.[19] But Panin had no intention of complying. He had recently been alerted by Repnin that August Czartoryski was scheming to swing matters at the last moment so as to be elected himself, and Panin did not want to see that at all.[20] On 24 August Stanisław received a letter from Rzewuski in St Petersburg stating that Catherine had made it plain that she would never marry him.[21] Stanisław nevertheless resisted all attempts to bully him into other matches, partly because his marriage could be a diplomatic asset in the future.

While he wished to remain absolutely loyal to Catherine personally, he felt no such loyalty towards her country, and his first priority remained the good of Poland. Combining these sentiments was a problem, and it seems to have placed enormous stress on him at this point. One of the reasons he kept coming back to the idea of marrying Catherine was probably that only such a solution could reconcile them. But if he was not to marry her, then he must think not so much of his own position, but of his country's position with reference to other courts. The Familia's view of the situation was more clear-cut. They intended to use Russia's support in order to achieve aims which were to them far more important than any considerations of political or personal loyalty to her ruler. They took a more earthy view of the relationship between Stanisław and Catherine, and a more realistic one of its future. They concentrated on exploiting the existing situation in order to initiate their policies.

The Convocation Seym was due to end on 23 June, having taken the measures necessary for the election. But the Familia wanted to start ruling immediately, while the foreign powers were too busy watching each other to concentrate on what was happening inside the country. The Familia therefore decided to prolong the Seym, through the process of confederating it. A confederation could be proclaimed outside the Seym, as a formal expression of protest at Crown or Seym policy. But when it was proclaimed by a majority within the Seym, it bound that assembly to carry out a certain policy, in the interests of which procedure was simplified and the veto banned. This was easy to justify to Keyserling and Repnin, on the grounds that it kept the whole country under control in the run-up to the election. On the day it was to close, therefore, the Seym declared a general confederation under the marshalcy of August Czartoryski. A number of deputies and senators refused to join the confederation. But this made little difference, and the Seym went on sitting throughout the summer, in the course of which it passed a batch of fundamental reforms.

On 27 August the Election Seym opened. For legality's sake, the confederation was suspended and all Russian troops (there were a total of 14,000 in the country as a whole, and probably no more than about 4,000 around Warsaw) were ordered to move away from the capital and keep out of sight for the duration of the election, which was to take place on 6 and 7 September. The election would not be contested. The Saxon party had collapsed, with most of its leaders in self-imposed exile. Hetman Branicki had made one last attempt to rob Stanisław of the throne, by proposing to Frederick of Prussia that he seize it for his brother Prince Henry. But Frederick was not interested.[22]

Stanisław went about canvassing to the very end, trying to gain the support of magnates who, although not in open opposition, could not bring themselves to take part in the election of an inferior. On 6 September, he drove round the election field to greet the voters. The centre of the field was taken up by an enclosure reserved for the senators, dominated by an empty throne standing on a small dais. The 25,000 szlachta who had turned out to vote surrounded this enclosure, drawn up in military formation under the banner of the palatinate in which they lived.

On the following day they again formed up in the same manner, and then the Primate arrived in an open carriage 'gleaming in every quarter from gold, crimson velvet and braid, drawn by four horses with golden head-dress and coachman and outrider also gleaming with braid'.[23] He drove up to the szlachta of the palatinates of Poznań and Kalisz, and stood up in his carriage. 'Greetings to my worthy lords and brothers on this election field,' he began. 'I ask you what is the will and the assent of the most illustrious palatinates of Wielkopolska in the matter of whom I should nominate as our King and Master?' The Palatine of Kalisz and the Castellan of Poznań (the Palatine of Poznań, Antoni Jabłonowski, had stayed away) replied that they did not wish to have any king other than Stanisław Poniatowski, Steward of Lithuania. The szlachta of the two palatinates shouted: 'Aye! Vivat!' The Primate then drove on to the next palatinates. When he reached the Palatinate of Kiev, he found that Franciszek Potocki, who had come back to take part in the election out of fear of displeasing Russia, could not bring himself to utter the name of Poniatowski, and merely declared that he agreed with the others. When the Primate reached the

Palatinate of Ruthenia, August Czartoryski clearly answered that he wished to have as his king and master Stanisław Poniatowski, but according to one witness 'went very pale in the face' as he did so.[24]

The Primate then drove into the enclosure, and standing on the empty throne in the centre, again asked whether they wanted Poniatowski as their king. He was answered by a roar of assent, so he declared the election accomplished and intoned the *Te Deum* which was taken up by all those present, to the accompaniment of guns thundering out the salute. He then set off for the Poniatowski mansion, followed by the whole assembly.

As he had to stay away from the election field on that day, Stanisław had lunch with Elżbieta Lubomirska. She admitted that she would have liked to see her father or her brother on the throne, but 'Destiny has decided in your favour, and I tell myself that it is for the best, and I desire it to be so from the bottom of my heart, as sincerely and as tenderly as I embrace you.'[25] Scarcely had she said this, when the cannon sounded from the election field. Stanisław hurried back to his own lodgings.

He received the Primate and the Marshal of the Election Seym with a speech in which he likened the act of the election to a christening, which turns the ordinary mortal and sinner into a reborn and innocent instrument of his people and of God. It was a way of saying that he would shed his private interests and antipathies for the good of his people, and he invited them all to treat him henceforth as a generous father, forgetting past antagonisms. In this spirit of reconciliation, he announced that he would reign under the name of Stanisław II Augustus, bringing together the rivalries that had separated the cause of Stanisław Leszczyński and his own from that of the Saxon kings, and taking the opportunity to proclaim the Augustan grandeur that he hoped would attend his reign.[26]

He then mounted a horse – a black horse, alluding to Saturn – and rode forth amid cheering from the populace to the church of St John, where a solemn *Te Deum* was sung. From there he went, on foot, to the Royal Castle, holding his hands out to be kissed by the throng that lined his path. 'It is as though God had given him a special guardian angel for this day,' August Czartoryski said to his daughter, 'for both in his words and in his deeds he has not said or done either more nor less than exactly what was demanded.'[27]

Stanisław kept up this perfect measure, and a few days later, at the solemn swearing of the *Pacta Conventa* in the Church of St John, he made an impromptu speech which ended with a characteristically moving harangue: 'Great God! You who willed me in the post in which I now find myself, You do nothing in vain. You gave me this crown with the ardent desire of restoring the state. Accomplish Your design, let the voice of my prayer reach You. Accomplish, Great God, Your design, and pour into the hearts of the whole nation that love of the public good with which mine overflows!' The congregation burst into tears, and even Franciszek Potocki was blubbering with emotion.[28]

Stanisław had been elected unanimously, and 5,584 voters had endorsed the election. Even those who had viewed the Convocation Seym as irregular had to admit that it was the freest and most legal election since that of Jan III almost a century before. It had been accomplished 'in a spirit of unity, calmness and humility not seen in this kingdom for ages', commented someone not well disposed to Stanisław.[29] There had been no violence, and the only casualty of the whole proceedings was a broken leg from a horse-kick. Many of the magnates who had turned up their noses at him nevertheless seemed prepared to tolerate him, and he believed he could gradually win them over.

On the very evening of the election, Stanisław wrote to Catherine announcing the outcome, and her reply, dated 25 September, was everything he could have wished for. 'I owe you very sincere congratulations on this happy event,' she wrote, 'much less for the acquisition of a throne, than for the open field which is laid before you to do all manner of good according to the extent and the superiority of your talents.'[30]

8

Stanislaus Secundus
Augustus Rex

For his coronation date Stanisław chose 25 November, St Catherine's day. The ceremonies began on the eve, when he processed to the Church of the Holy Cross, attended by a large cavalcade. There he made his confession and heard Mass. Early the following morning, the archbishop of Lwów and the marshal of the court helped to robe him in the semi-religious garb of a white alb and shirt, a cape and sandals. Preceded by senators bearing the crown, orb and sceptre on velvet cushions, and by the standards of Poland and Lithuania held by the two court ensigns, he walked under a canopy carried by four senators along a wooden pavement covered in red cloth to the Church of St John, where the Primate awaited him.

After entering the Church, Stanisław swore to fulfil his duties as king, then prostrated himself on the floor while a litany was recited. When he rose two bishops removed his top garment, and he knelt on a cushion for the anointing. The Primate made the sign of the Cross on his head with holy oil. The bishops lifted the wide sleeves of his shirt for the same to be done to his wrists and elbows, and then unbuttoned the back so the Primate could anoint him between his shoulder-blades. Stanisław was then vested with his coronation robes, the chain of the White Eagle and the royal cape of crimson velvet lined with ermine, and knelt as the Primate started the Mass. Just before the Gospel, the Primate handed him the sword of state, with which Stanisław, turning to the assembly, made the sign of the Cross, then, assisted by two bishops, he placed the crown on the head of the kneeling

Stanisław. The newly anointed and crowned king was handed the orb and sceptre, and conducted to the throne. The Primate called out 'Long live the King!' three times, and Stanisław's friend Ignacy Krasicki, recently named royal chaplain, delivered a sermon. The Mass resumed, while the choir intoned a cantata composed specially for the occasion.[1]

The king returned to the Castle with the crown on his head and the orb and sceptre in his hands. There followed a banquet for all the senators, ministers and Seym deputies. On the following day, Stanisław was led under a canopy carried by city councillors to the Town Hall, to be greeted by delegations from all the cities of the Commonwealth. The president of Warsaw presented him with the keys of the city, and Stanisław knighted six of the councillors and another four from Kraków, before being escorted back to the Castle by the uniformed members of the guilds. That evening the whole city was illuminated with elaborate decorations and triumphal arches. Stanisław mounted a horse and rode round to see the lights before giving a ball for the leading citizens at the Castle. The following night saw more illuminations, as the burghers gave a feast for all comers at the Town Hall. On the fourth day, Stanisław rode in solemn procession to the Church of the Holy Cross for Mass, preceded by the Treasurer of the Crown, who cast handfuls of silver coins into the crowd. With this the ceremonies of the coronation came to an end.

Stanisław was back in the dilapidated and virtually unfurnished Castle, face to face with the realities of his position. He was now King of Poland, Grand Duke of Lithuania, Duke of Ruthenia, Prussia, Mazovia, Samogitia, Kiev, Volhynia, Podolia, Podlachia, Livonia, Smoleńsk, Siewierz, Czernychów, and overlord of Kurland. On 31 December Ernest Bühren, the son of the Duke of Kurland, knelt before him in a formal act of homage amid medieval ritual and pomp. But, unlike so many of his subjects, Stanisław had no court, few servants, and no establishment apart from 1,200 soldiers of the Royal Guard and a pension from Catherine. His income would, when it began to flow, consist partly of revenues from Crown lands and partly of a civil list voted by the Seym. For the first couple of months he had to rely on a caterer to bring in his lunch and dinner. These less than exalted arrangements were symptomatic of his position as a whole.

The nature of the Polish monarchy was an accretion of centuries of precedent rather than planning. There was no well-oiled state machinery in place to receive the incoming elect, as there is in any democracy. A court had taken shape over the centuries, but more than sixty years of Saxon rule had allowed it to wither. The two Augustuses had spent most of their time in Dresden, and they brought their own court with them whenever they visited Poland. Stanisław's first task was therefore to create the structure through which he could function as a monarch. But this apparently straightforward task immediately brought him face to face with a number of wider constitutional issues and political niceties, as well as personal problems.

His position was fraught with ambiguity, complementing the ambiguities inherent in the status of the throne of Poland itself. How far he succeeded in becoming a king was inextricably bound up with how far a king of Poland at this time could be said to be a king. This question was made all the more difficult to answer in view of the changing face of monarchy throughout Europe. In the seventeenth century, the king, whether he was a great man or a mere icon, had been the sole and absolute source of all power, the personal embodiment of the state. This was no longer the case. The Divine element still attached to monarchy but the notion of Divine Right could only be sustained as a pious fiction. The kings of England and Sweden were bound by constitutional systems, and even absolute monarchs had seen their freedom to rule personally eroded. Even that ultimate absolutist Catherine had to tread warily. The exercise of personal power had become a complicated business, and the monarch was becoming more deeply enmeshed in these complications. Nevertheless, he remained the mainspring of government.

In Poland, the government consisted of King, Senate and Seym together. Being one of the three 'estates' of the Seym, the king could not stand aloof, but had to take part in its political work. The ministers, while nominated by the king, were the executive officers of the Seym. And while the king's residence was the seat of government, this was only so by virtue of the fact that the Senate and Seym met there. The Castle was, officially, 'the residence of the King and the Commonwealth'. Thus, even disregarding the elective nature of his office, the position of the king of Poland was unique. He was the chief executive of the system, not the godhead of a system that sprang, so to speak, from his very existence.

Stanisław's travels and diplomatic service had taught him much about how courts worked, how they generated power and upheld the majesty of the monarch through elaborate ritual. Above all, he appreciated that the creation of courtly structures had everywhere played a vital part in the transition from feudal societies to centralised modern states, by turning regional potentates into courtiers, and eventually into servants of the Crown and the state.

In their day-to-day existence, these courts were like extended families, in which large numbers of loosely related people cohabited in a perpetual tussle over favours and precedence. The only thing that prevented matters getting out of hand was the presence on the throne of a father-figure, one who was not so much a demi-god as the symbolic hand and voice of God. The monarch was accepted as the ultimate source of judgment, and when he clapped his hands to call the family to order, they obeyed. His authority derived from his arbitrary power, and from the general consent to invest his person with a god-like role. Fear went hand-in-hand with ritual. And the ritual was very important. The king had to be unapproachable, a being who could not be judged by the same canons as others.

The position of a king of Poland was radically different. He was the anointed of God, but only by virtue of his election. He ruled by the will of the people, not by the grace of God. He could not impose judgment by himself, or punish arbitrarily. He did not even enjoy the universal royal prerogative of the pardon. In spite of this, he could often inspire much of the same worship as did a king of France. This was easier when he came, as did most of Poland's elected rulers, from a reigning house. Preposterous creature that he was, Augustus III benefited from the aura of royalty, and was treated with as much deference as any monarch in Europe. This would not be the case with Stanisław.

He was just a private individual who had suddenly been elevated. Nor was his elevation itself the result of anything that could inspire particular respect; quite the reverse in fact. He was surrounded by a large family, of which he was by no means the senior member, and he could not hope to exercise Divine authority over relatives and friends who knew him intimately. Since the job itself was so subtle and so ill-defined, he could not just mould himself to it. He had to create it himself as he went along. And since he had strong ideas of his own on the subject, the Polish monarchy would be redefined by his reign. He was, in effect, undertaking two tasks, the first to turn himself into a monarch, the second to recreate the Polish monarchy itself in a new form.

Stanisław's vision of the Polish monarchy was conditioned by its ancient traditions, many of which were present in the ritual of the coronation, in which every action alluded to some aspect of the monarch's relationship to God and his fellow-beings. The practice of anointing at the coronation was falling into desuetude in many countries, but in Poland it remained, along with the other ecclesiastical allusions, the central feature of the ceremony. And while Stanisław caused something of a sensation by refusing to wear Polish dress for his coronation, he did not tamper with the archaic prescription of the clerical garb of alb and sandals at the start of the ceremony. This stressed the Polish king's status as a prelate, and his proximity to the Church and to God. His refusal to wear Polish dress was dictated principally by vanity, as it normally demanded closely cropped hair, and he was very proud of his long tresses. In order to scotch grumbling, he had taken the precaution of getting six doctors to sign a document to the effect that a sudden haircut would expose him to illness.[2] But his rejection of the Sarmatian style was also an aesthetic statement and a modern and cosmopolitan gesture. It turned out to be a political mistake. To traditionalists his 'Spanish' costume of white silk and lace was insulting, and it aroused 'laughter and contempt' among the ill-disposed.[3]

Stanisław's vision of his kingship was also influenced by his view of himself as an instrument of Providence. While his brothers tried to enhance their credentials by faking ancient pedigrees, Stanisław only underlined the integrity of his father, and the semi-royal status of his mother. The inference was that, like Christ, he had come into the world through a worthy vessel rather than from a long line of human excellence, and been chosen to rule over his peers by Divine intervention. Since he could point to no fact, other than his election, that might induce people to regard him as in any way different from other mortals, he resorted to symbol and allegory. The trappings and language of legitimacy assumed vital importance for him.

On the more practical side, his style of kingship would be decided largely by his intentions, which were to transform Poland. In 1763, while he waited and dreamed, his near-contemporary, the future Emperor Joseph II, was penning his *Rêveries*. They revealed his aim of centralising the state and creating 'absolute power to be in a position to do all the good which one is prevented from doing by the rules, statutes and oaths'.[4] Stanisław craved the same ends, but such means were out of the question. Not only because an elected monarch, and one who could do nothing without the permission of Russia, would never be able to carry this out, but also because such methods went against the grain of Polish political culture, and he was himself strongly marked by this heritage. In Poland, transformation could only be achieved through consensual processes, and he would in effect have to lead a political movement to carry it through. This he was eminently qualified to do. He had been returned to the Seym six times, sat on various commissions and taken part in every political process over the past fifteen years, so he understood as no other Polish monarch ever had the workings of the system. But this very fact precluded him from creating any kind of royal distance between himself and his subjects. He made himself accessible to all who might help him, and went out of his way to persuade and conciliate those opposed to his aims. Thus in a sense he began his reign as a somewhat paternalistic prime minister, standing above all on his merits and those of his programme rather than on any notion of a divine right to rule.

Stanisław's vision and his intentions were built on a discrepancy and a contradiction. The discrepancy was that while he made himself believe and wanted others to believe that he had been placed on the throne by Divine Providence, he had in effect ascended it through an armed coup. This meant that while he expected his subjects to follow his lead with a degree of filial trust and submission, they would continue to see him as a latent despot. The contradiction was that while he embarked on his reign in much the same spirit as a head of government does after a successful election, he also wanted to elevate himself above politics and to institutionalise the Crown as the embodiment of the state. This confusion undermined his own attempts at defining his position and his image.

Although there was no court in existence, there was a whole series of titles left over from an earlier age, such as Kazimierz's title of Chamberlain and Stanisław's own of Steward. For the most part, these titles were purely honorific. But that of Marshal of the Court, both for

Poland and for Lithuania, carried ministerial rank, and the incumbents had the duty of superintending the royal finances. One of Stanisław's first actions was to get the Seym to release them from this obligation, thereby freeing his private establishment from the political control of the Seym. He then set about creating his royal household, superintended by his own marshal, Kazimierz Karaś. Including the Chamberlain's department, the lackeys, footmen and *frotteurs*, the kitchens, bakery and pantry, the stables and huntsmen, the aides, the medical department, and the fire watch, Stanisław's establishment quickly grew to some 600 people, excluding the Guards.

While this establishment could satisfy the day-to-day requirements of existence, he also needed a body of trustworthy officials who would constitute the power-base on which he could build his political edifice and the machinery through which it could function. For this he intended to draw on people untainted by party affiliations, which meant taking into his service foreigners and Poles belonging to the poorer sections of the szlachta or even the merchant classes, in order to create a sort of service nobility. Independently of this, he aimed to enlist the support of the middle-rank szlachta by favouring them rather than the magnates. He ordered a couple of comfortable travelling-carriages in Paris, intending to visit the provinces and seek out support over the heads of the magnates who hemmed him in at Warsaw.

Before he was actually elected, he set up a private chancellery, the *Gabinet*, under Jacek Ogrodzki, to manage his personal political business. While its essential function was to run his private relations with foreign courts and to act as his private seal for internal business, it became, in effect, the central office of his political party. One of his first actions as king was to set up the *Kamera*, a directorate to administer the Crown lands and his own property. The scope of these bodies was strictly limited by circumstances, but they employed up to fifty people between them, mainly because he wanted to retain and put to work capable young men who might form the nucleus of a future state administration. He also set up a Military Office under General Byszewski to superintend appointments.

He instituted a body of royal pages, drawn from the poorest szlachta, who were given a free education while they attended him at court, and who would, he hoped, grow up as devoted supporters. He also borrowed the foreign habit of nominating honorary gentlemen of the bedchamber. In May 1765 he created the Order of St Stanisław, which greatly increased the range of favours he could grant. The szlachta were generally hostile to such foreign-style distinctions, which undermined their theoretical equality, but vanity triumphed. The red sash of the order would be prized by provincial nobles who could not aspire to the blue sash of the White Eagle.

The most important single institution he brought into being, at the beginning of 1765, was the Cadet Corps. This conformed to a pattern much favoured in Europe at the time, and was specifically designed to provide the state with military and administrative cadres. It took in young men between the ages of eight and twelve, and kept them for seven years, during which time they received a thorough education. Although the Corps was run on military lines and both military study and training formed an essential part of the curriculum, there was also a legal and administrative specialisation. Stanisław intended the Corps to have 200 pupils, but chronic shortage of funds kept the number down to about seventy-five. Adam Czartoryski was named Commander, and he composed a 'catechism' of civic virtue and a pedagogical programme for it. He also, more than once, helped it out financially.

What is apparent in all this is that Stanisław was confusing two aims: the one of creating an independent service nobility devoted to the state and the Crown, and the other of building up a personal political following. This was self-defeating as people came to regard anyone who served the king as a member of 'the court party' or a 'royalist' rather than as a civil servant.

The same ambivalence was present wherever Stanisław attempted to marry discrepant concepts. While trying to build up an aura of royalty, Stanisław sought to project an image of himself as a citizen-king, whose only credentials were his intentions, his intelligence and his ability. He bore this out by his approach to people of lesser condition, particularly professional people and foreigners. Stanisław's sympathy for foreigners is arresting, and touches on something deeper. He was interested in any stranger who turned up in Warsaw, and took a large number into his service. The Gabinet was full of them, for obvious reasons. One of the original members was Karol Boskamp, a Dutchman who had served as Frederick II's agent in Istanbul. In 1765 the Gabinet took in Gaetano Ghigiotti, a former secretary to the Papal

Nuncio. In the same year he was joined by the twenty-three-year-old Swiss Maurice Glayre, who was to become one of Stanisław's most trusted collaborators. Others, such as Stanisław's former teacher Thoux de Salverte and the Welshman Charles Lee, later an American revolutionary general, were employed without official status on various diplomatic missions.

It was not only in the diplomatic sphere that Stanisław employed foreigners. In 1765 he brought over the Swiss Marc Reverdil as reader. His poor English marred Stanisław's enjoyment of *Tristram Shandy*, and he was promoted to librarian instead. Reverdil travelled to Poland in the company of another of Stanisław's foreign acquisitions, Dr Johann Boeckler, who became his personal physician. To command his Guards, Stanisław selected General Friedrich Coccei, a Prussian who had served in the English army. A more significant appointment was that of John Lind, a clergyman's son from Essex and close friend of Jeremy Bentham, to the important post of head of studies at the Cadet Corps.

Stanisław managed to establish relationships of mutual trust and esteem more easily with foreigners than with his own countrymen. He wrote an enormous number of letters, and his best, both in their descriptive quality and in their emotional honesty, are written to correspondents who stood outside Polish life. Writing to them seems to have been a sort of therapy for Stanisław, who bared and weighed his thoughts before them with candour. One reason for his preference for foreigners was undoubtedly that they knew their place and treated him as a monarch, which most of his compatriots found difficult. But there were deeper causes. Stanisław was an educated cosmopolitan gentleman, while most of his peers were arrogant boorish magnates with whom he did not feel at ease. Those whom he did choose as his friends, such as Sułkowski, Rzewuski or Krasicki, were temperamentally brought closer to him by their youth, and in the case of Ksawery Branicki, by the fact that he was no magnate. As they grew up and assumed position and wealth, they mostly drew away from him. Stanisław was not a grandee by nature, and he preferred the company of the *honnête homme* or the *galantuomo*. When Casanova turned up in Warsaw in 1765, he too found ready access and entertained hopes of becoming a permanent secretary to the king.

'The king would dine in his private apartments, admitting people to his table without due consideration of person or rank, so much so that a distinguished deputy, senator or minister might find himself sitting beside a painter, a doctor, or even some adventurer,' Stanisław Lubomirski observed with disapproval.[5] It was true. There were formal court dinners once a week. Every other day Stanisław would let Karaś do the honours at the Marshal's Table, to which various dignitaries were invited, while he himself sat down to what were virtually working lunches in his dressing-room with no more than a dozen select people. He would also permit people to come and talk to him informally in his private rooms while he was being dressed, although he liked to use this time for being read to. Members of his court, deputies to the Seym, men of business, or enterprising visitors had little difficulty in gaining some informal admittance. His uncles and the new Chancellor Andrzej Zamoyski lectured him on the subject and suggested a more reserved and formal style of behaviour, but he ignored them.

In this respect, he saw himself as another Henri IV of France, straightforward, unceremonious, and at home to any good man. He also wanted to project this image abroad, and to gain for himself and his country the approval of the outside world. Frederick of Prussia had courted the *philosophes* for reasons of propaganda. He corresponded with and pensioned a number of famous publicists, in the knowledge that this contact lent him stature, and that their sophistries could be counted on to cover up his sins. Catherine, whose illegal accession to the throne had been poorly received by European opinion, followed suit in an attempt to rehabilitate herself and justify her policies.

Stanisław had prepared his propaganda in advance, and took every opportunity to broadcast throughout Europe the legitimacy of his election. He wrote to his English friends, that they might pass on the message that he was going to turn Poland into a progressive constitutional monarchy, and urged them to come and help him. He invited Voltaire to come to Poland, he sought the friendship of Grimm and Diderot, and he sent detailed material on Poland to the editors of influential periodicals such as the *Gazette de Leyde* and the *Courrier du Bas-Rhin*. He was to be grievously disappointed. Intellectuals are not impressed by righteous weakness.

Stanisław was acutely aware of the weakness of his position. His diplomatic experience, if not his instinct, told him that his future depended on his relations with the outside world. His first preoccupation was to remove from his election the taint of Russian manipulation. Only then could he hope to placate France, reassure Turkey, and establish cordial relations with Austria. And it was only if he established a close relationship or even an alliance with Austria that he could hope for any semblance of independence from Russia. Finally, it was only if he was wholeheartedly recognised by the major powers that he could curb the magnates. He knew only too well from his own experience how every great family having its own foreign policy had rendered the country ungovernable. It was only if no foreign court would speak to them that the Radziwiłłs or the Potockis would resign themselves to his rule. He worked assiduously at establishing agencies abroad, even where formal diplomatic relations were impossible. In Turkey, for instance, he set up a school of oriental languages as a cover for his agent Karol Boskamp. By 1766, he had permanent agents in Prussia, Austria, Rome, England, Holland, France and Turkey, and one official envoy, Jakub Psarski in St Petersburg.

The diplomatic scene at the moment of his accession could hardly have been less favourable to his plans. With the end of the Seven Years' War in 1763 a new pattern of alliances began to emerge. On one side stood the Catholic powers: France, Spain, Austria, and their allies Naples, Saxony and Turkey. On the other was the so-called 'Northern System', consisting of Russia, Prussia and Denmark, with England hovering beside them. Catherine and Panin wanted Poland as a subsidiary ally, neither too weak nor too strong, which could be used against Turkey or Austria if the need arose. In line with this, Repnin had produced a plan in the summer of 1764 for a defensive alliance which would allow the Polish army to be increased to 50,000 men.[6]

Poland did not fit naturally into this Northern System, and while Stanisław was keen to enter into alliance with Russia, in return for which he hoped to gain licence to improve the governance of his kingdom, he also wanted to achieve a degree of independence. But the only Catholic state to recognise his election was the Papacy. The key to breaching this wall of disapproval was Austria. Immediately after his election, Stanisław despatched his brother Andrzej to Vienna with a letter for Maria Theresa and another to be passed on to Louis XV. But while she received him cordially, the Empress could do nothing until Louis XV's ruffled sensibilities were smoothed. Hennin, now residing

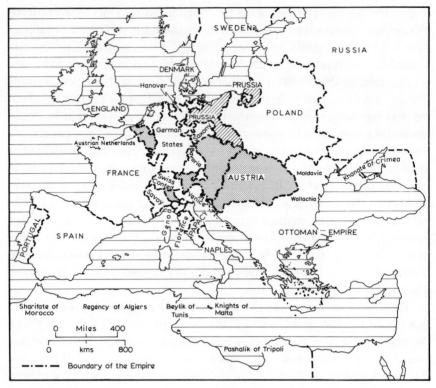

2   Europe at the End of the Seven Years' War

in Vienna, was not authorised to accept the letter for his king. After a
month of fruitless efforts, Andrzej returned to Warsaw. Stanisław had
also decided to despatch a diplomat to Turkey, with English conni-
vance.[7] But Turkey was a traditional ally of France.

The problem of establishing relations with France was one of immense intricacy, in view of the fiasco she had created over the election.
One of the first letters Stanisław wrote after his election was to the
ageing Stanisław Leszczyński, then Duke of Lorraine, asking for his
spiritual blessing, and affirming, when he got it, that: 'Your goodwill,
Sire, is a part of my heritage.'[8] With the titular king of Poland and his
daughter the queen of France on his side, Stanisław could have hoped
for some consideration at Versailles. But the French court, humiliated
by the loss of its colonies in Canada and India in the previous year, was

in a state of dudgeon over its self-inflicted loss of face in the matter of the Polish election. The Prince de Conti was still dreaming of the Polish throne, and the Dauphine was nursing her spite over her brother's failure. Furthermore, France had to show solidarity with her supporters in Poland, such as Branicki and Radziwiłł, who were still smarting from their defeat.

In these circumstances, Madame Geoffrin became an invaluable asset. Two days after his election, Stanisław wrote to his *Chère Maman*, announcing his success and adding that 'One of the things that I desire the most, and certainly more than you can imagine, is the friendship of the King of France.'[9] He artfully slipped in various items of information, such as that he had shown restraint in dealing with Branicki and Radziwiłł, and hoped to conciliate them. 'I have not seen the Empress for six years, and I have very little hope of ever seeing her again,' he wrote beguilingly. 'It is a very painful privation for me, but one on which, as on many other counts, I have to make a quietus.'[10] He knew that his letters would be shown, read out and passed on, and much of the information in them was designed as a set of signals to the French court. He also sent her a copy of his letter to Louis XV which Hennin had refused to accept, so she could let its contents be known at Versailles. Her response revealed all the pride of a mother whose son has landed a good job, so much so that Madame du Deffand began to refer to her as 'the queen mother of Poland'. She eagerly set to work in his cause, and she grew quite cross when she discovered he was also using his other contacts in Paris. One of these was his old colleague, the Baron de Breteuil, who asked Choiseul to send him to Poland. This would have suited Stanisław, since he was also trusted by Catherine. But the French Court could not bring itself to do anything positive. 'With respect,' Stanisław wrote to Madame Geoffrin in March 1765, 'your policy maunders, while mine can only wait.'[11]

Negotiations with Austria continued, through the good offices of Lord Stormont and Count Canal, the ambassador of Sardinia, who were concerned not only with obtaining Austrian recognition of Stanisław's election, but also with trying to engineer a rapprochement between Austria and Russia over Poland in order to counterbalance the Prussian influence there. In October 1765 Andrzej Poniatowski returned to Vienna as the Envoy of the Commonwealth, and met with success. On 1 December 1765 Count

Colloredo arrived in Warsaw to present the Empress' congratulations on Stanisław's accession. There was even talk of a marriage between Stanisław and the Austrian Archduchess Elisabeth.

A bachelor king begs many questions, and in the case of this one, the possible answers were portentous. Stanisław had abandoned any hope of seeing his old dream of a marriage to Catherine come true, although dreams do have a habit of living on in the subconscious for a very long time, and it was to haunt him more than once in later years. Now that he was king, he realised that his marriage was of crucial importance to his own future and that of his country. The *Pacta Conventa* stated that his prospective bride 'ought to be of the Catholic Roman Faith, by birth or vocation, with a preference for the privilege of Polish blood'.[12] His own preference was for a Habsburg archduchess, who would bring the twin benefits of securing the friendship of Austria and making him more respectable at home – kings of Poland had married Habsburgs for centuries. Failing that, he would have liked a Bourbon princess, who would bring much the same benefits with the added bonus of a cultural link with France.

But he felt that in view of the nature of his relationship with Catherine, he had to defer to her. He did not realise to what extent she and her ministers viewed the issue as being their political rather than her personal business. Catherine herself seems to have had no strong feelings on the matter. Panin suggested that Stanisław marry the daughter of the king of Portugal, which would, through Portugal's alliance with England, cement Poland's position within the 'Northern System'.[13] Stanisław was soon in receipt of a likeness of the nineteen-year-old Dona Maria Francisca, with an accompanying note assuring him that 'she is much handsomer than her portrait, which cannot possibly express the delicacy of her complexion'.[14] Another candidate was Princess Christina of Mecklemburg, the elder sister of the queen of England.

What neither Panin nor Catherine was prepared to tolerate was Stanisław's marrying a Habsburg or a Bourbon, which would effectively breach the system. They watched his diplomatic efforts with suspicion, and in 1765 Panin grew alarmed. August Sułkowski, who was to set off for Versailles in order to establish official relations, was halted by order of Russia, and forced to send a letter pleading in-disposition as an excuse. This further annoyed Louis XV, who responded by ordering Vienna and the Porte to have nothing to do with the Poles.

Diplomatic isolation was not easy to break out of without freedom of action, an army and strong finances. But the trappings of monarchy provided an unofficial language through which messages could be communicated and mutual respect established. Saxony had been a political and military disaster for over a century, yet it still figured on the diplomatic map, largely because the court of Dresden was, in the first half of the century, the grandest and most sophisticated in Europe. France continued to look down on Russian victories, and still refused to recognise the Romanovs' imperial title, but the magnificence of St Petersburg was beginning to take effect. Art had become the most tangible expression of a community of civilisation that had replaced the old concept of Christendom, and Stanisław intended to claim a place for Poland in that community, while building up an environment of grandiose proportions in order to give himself the aura of royalty he lacked and to put him on a level to speak to other monarchs. These considerations fed on his vanity and on his aesthetic sense, and he wasted no time.

He summoned the Roman painter Marcello Bacciarelli from Vienna, and made him superintendent of his artistic works. He also recruited the services of the Swedish portraitist Per Krafft, the Swiss Anton Graff, two Frenchmen settled in Warsaw, Jean Pillement and Louis Marteau, the Polish-born miniaturists Vincent de Lesseur and Jozef Kosiński, the young Aleksander Kucharski, and the decorator Jan Bogumił Plersch. In the first instance, he put them to work on dozens of royal portraits, in order to project a public image of himself as king.

Stanisław's paramount need was a new palace. The Castle was an architectural warren spreading from a small medieval core, transformed in the 1600s, and neglected for the best part of a century. Since it was a public building, housing the Seym on the ground floor and the Senate on the first, it had suffered so much wear and tear as to be virtually a shell. The Saxon kings had built the large Saxony Palace for themselves in another part of the city. Stanisław intended to do better. In 1764, within weeks of his election, he bought the derelict castle of Ujazdów just outside Warsaw, which he saw as his future Versailles or Caserta. He planned to rebuild this on a scale that would proclaim the personal grandeur of the monarch as distinct from his position within the constitutional framework. As his intentions were restrained by financial considerations, he began with the more pressing business of refurbishing the Castle, accentuating its function as the seat of government. It was to be no mere restoration, but a total, superb transformation. He had given the matter much thought already, and he knew what he wanted.

In this instance he abandoned his model Henri IV, and, like most eighteenth-century monarchs, took the Sun King, Louis XIV, as his paradigm. At the same time, he was strongly marked by his experiences of the baroque court of Dresden, by the French style, and by his own interest in antiquity – in 1762 he had written to the king of Naples asking for drawings and plans of the excavations at Herculaneum. All these elements are clearly detectable in the way he approached the challenge of the Castle. He put to work two home-grown architects, Jakub Fontana and Efraim Szreger, whom he could supervise and influence, and one French one, the latter an inspired choice that testifies to Stanisław's originality and artistic sense.

While in Paris he had spotted some of the early work of the as yet little-known Victor Louis, who would come into his own twenty years later as the architect of the Palais-Royal and other prime examples of Louis XVI style. Stanisław contacted Louis through the merchant Kazimierz Czempiński immediately after his election, and summoned him to Warsaw. He was delighted with his choice, describing Louis as 'a noble, prolific and wise genius', and explaining to Madame Geoffrin that while 'he has corrected my taste on several subjects, he accepts the ideas of others when one proposes good ones to him'.[15] Louis executed over a hundred drawings in close consultation with Stanisław and, having absorbed the king's taste and intentions, returned to Paris in 1766 to work out the details.

The results of all this planning were seven projects for the rebuilding of the Castle, five by Fontana, one by Szreger and one by Louis. The general tendency of all of them, which reflects Stanisław's specific requirements, was to create a monumental structure, with façades imposing by their regularity, and enhanced by grand forecourts approached by converging avenues. They all required demolition of parts of the old city in order to create the sense of distance that would enhance the symbolic importance of the buildings. They all alluded to Versailles and the Louvre, fusing the baroque with the classical in a statement that was cosmopolitan, modern and strongly monarchical. They also constituted a shattering break with tradition. These projects mirror Stanisław's view of how the Polish monarchy should redefine itself, and they also, in their treatment of the parliamentary parts of the building, reflect his vision of the constitutional aspects of that monarchy.

The same is true of the interiors projected by Louis. He suggested a typical *appartement de parade*, centred on a state bedroom with a raised bed behind a balustrade, designed for the *levée*. The ceiling was to depict Hercules wedding Hebe and being received into Olympus, an allusion to the deification that Stanisław wished to insinuate as coming with the election. The senators' antechamber, which preceded the throne room, was another focus for his special attention. He invented a richly thematic composition centred on a series of paintings which, after much thought, he decided to entrust to Charles André Van Loo and François Boucher. 'I would like, if possible, the spectator to be struck at the first glance by the ideas of justice, emulation, magnanimity and concord which these paintings will bring to mind,' he wrote to Madame Geoffrin, and he insisted that the artists send their sketches for his comments before embarking on the work.[16] They refused to comply, so the paintings were executed by Joseph Vien, Noël Hallé and Jean Louis Lagrenée instead. Perhaps the most interesting of the projects to come from the tandem of Stanisław and Louis was the Senate chamber itself. It was Stanisław's idea to take the Roman Pantheon as a model, and that of Louis to make it oval. The chamber was overlooked by seven statues of Polish kings, whom Stanisław spent a long time selecting. The throne was to be raised and strongly accentuated, with a line from Horace, *Rex eris, si recte facies*, inscribed over it.

None of these projects saw the light of day. Apart from some minor refurbishment, the only room that Stanisław rebuilt in the first two years was his study, which was decorated in chinoiserie by Jean Pillement around six portraits by Per Krafft; of Catherine, Stanisław's sisters, his sister-in-law, and his two cousins Elżbieta Lubomirska and Izabela Czartoryska. But while waiting for the opportunity to start rebuilding, Stanisław went ahead and ordered furnishings, including some torchères from Philippe Caffieri. Louis had suggested a still unknown artist, Jean Louis Prieur, who sent drawings for furniture, as well as bronzes, chandeliers and clocks which delighted

Stanisław by their incorporation of Hellenistic elements into an otherwise monumental Louis XIV style. He promptly ordered a number of Prieur's projects, as well as some tapestries, which arrived in 1766 and 1767.

The amount of time Stanisław devoted to these matters is astonishing in view of the political workload, which he certainly did not neglect. And buildings and furnishings were not the only aspects of the royal environment which absorbed him. While he was prevented by lack of funds from going ahead with the reconstruction of the Castle, he turned his mind to creating a courtly atmosphere amid the ruins and lending lustre to his presence in other ways. He designed sumptuous liveries in the Poniatowski colours of crimson and green for his servants, and glittering uniforms for the Royal Guard. He held parades and military exercises, visited schools, and even attended village weddings. Although he had no ear for music, he appointed Jan Stefani *kapellmeister* and retained an orchestra. He also made much of Domenico Cimarosa during the latter's sojourn in Warsaw in 1765. His developed sense of allegory and his experiences at the courts of Dresden and St Petersburg went hand-in-hand with his love of pleasure, to create elaborate pageantry and courtly amusements that projected an image of himself as the Elect of Providence and of God, the shining hero prince of classical poetic drama. He attached great importance to symbol of every kind, and if he wanted to buy the Duke of Cumberland's famous horse King Herod in 1766, it was for what it could bring him in terms of legitimacy. Similarly, it was not out of mere Anglophilia that he tried to persuade the Duke of York, visiting various German courts in 1765, to come to Warsaw.

It was at home that he faced the greatest difficulties in asserting his royalty. Many traditional republicans who believed in the theory that Poland's safety lay in anarchy took it to its logical conclusion, suggesting that the throne should be abolished altogether, so as to remove the unsettling international crises that attended every election, and because it was felt that all kings by definition seek to extend their powers. Even without such theoretical bases, most of the magnates felt a pronounced reluctance to accept anyone above themselves, and there were no physical arguments that could be used against them. Franciszek Potocki, master of an estate of more than 3 million acres and 130,000 peasants, was, with a court of 400 and an income of 3 million złoty, in a position to live better than the king.[17] So was Karol Radziwiłł, whose income of 5 million złoty was over three times that of the richest English dukes, the Bedfords and the Devonshires. These people were Stanisław's social superiors, and his elevation stuck in their throats. Some, like Karol Radziwiłł, refused to recognise Stanisław as king and went into self-imposed exile. Others, like Hetman Branicki, buried themselves on their estates. The rest were merely disdainful, and they showed this by staying away from court and spreading malicious gossip, referring to the king contemptuously as 'Augustulus', 'His Poniatovian Majesty', or 'King Ciołek'. But even where there was no jealousy, no spite, no feeling of social superiority, many of his subjects felt an entirely understandable personal right to disagree with him and to ignore the fact that he was the anointed of God when they did so. Even people who were not ill-disposed to him found it difficult not to view him as an upstart who had achieved his position through the ignoble channel of Catherine's bed.

There was a trace of jealousy or at least sour grapes within his own family, for there can be no doubt that the Czartoryskis nurtured right up to the very end a vague hope that the crown might fall into their hands. According to Stanisław, August took his son Adam aside at the first royal audience and said: 'Well, you fool! You spurned the crown when it was within your grasp; look how well it suits your cousin – it is too late for you now!'[18] Adam himself showed no signs of envy. 'If great genius, superior qualities, and the finest feelings in a king of Poland were sufficient to ensure the happiness of this nation, then ours would have nothing more to wish for,' he wrote to the English diplomat Robert Murray Keith.[19]

These problems were compounded by Stanisław's character and upbringing. He was neither distant nor imperious, ruthless nor vengeful. He was sensitive and often showed it – by weeping, as all men did in that age of *sensibilité*. He was naïve, almost gullible. He lacked presence, and was acutely conscious of his own weaknesses. Most of his peers had been brought up as little sovereigns within their own circumscribed spheres. He had no experience of managing either a fortune or dependants. He had been brought up to make a career for himself, much as his father had done, and this involved the skills of the courtier – service, flexibility, patience – not those required of a king.

And yet he had set himself the task of reviving a nation, recreating a state, defining a constitution, and, most difficult of all, turning himself into a monarch. 'I know full well what I have to do, but it is a terrible prospect!' he wrote to Madame Geoffrin. 'Patience, circumspection, courage! and again: circumspection! That is my motto.'[20]

20   The Kazimierz Palace, in which the Cadet Corps was housed, from a watercolour by Zygmunt Vogel

21a & b   Medal presented to graduates

22   Stanisław admitting boys to the Cadet Corps, from a painting by Norblin

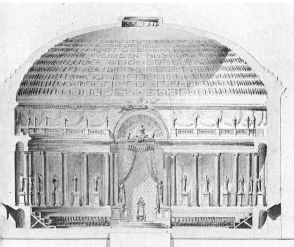

23   Szreger's project for the main façade of the Castle, 1767

24   Louis' project for the Senate Chamber, 1765

25.   The reality; a carriage (centre) is just disappearing down the alleyway leading to the Castle, the only visible part of which is the turreted dome in the top right-hand corner. From a painting by Bellotto.

26   Louis' project for the king's bedroom, 1766, clearly designed for the levée

27   Console, clock and two candlesticks designed by Louis for the royal bedroom

28   Pillement's rococo decoration of the king's study, incorporating portraits of the most important women in his life

29 Michał Czartoryski, from a
print by I. F. Mylius after
Silvestre

30 Stanisław Lubomirski, by
Bacciarelli

31 Andrzej Zamoyski, after
Bacciarelli

32 Stanisław's lifelong friend
Franciszek Rzewuski, from a lost
portrait by Pompeo Batoni

33 Repnin in 1765, from a
miniature by an unidentified
artist

34 Izabela Czartoryska in 1768,
by Per Krafft

35 Figures in the Saxony Gardens, by Bellotto

36 Fête champêtre at Powązki

37 Stanisław in a domino, by J. B. Lampi the elder

38 Primate Podoski receiving a client, or rather his wife, while his mistress looks on, from a pen and wash drawing by Daniel Chodowiecki

39 Medal struck (prematurely) to commemorate the emancipation of the dissenters, 1768

40 Ball in a magnate's Warsaw residence, by Norblin

41 A Cossack after looting a church, watercolour by an unidentified artist

42 The fanatical Dominican Marek Jandołowicz, who helped to turn the Confederation of Bar into a crusade, from a painting, now lost, by an unidentified artist

43 Confederate cavalry skirmishing with Russian grenadiers, a watercolour by Aleksander Orłowski

9

The Constraints of Monarchy

*I*n his memoirs, Stanisław writes that the period between his election and his coronation was the happiest in his life. Congratulations and good wishes flooded in from all quarters. 'I can see Poland rise from the ashes, and I see her resplendent, like a new Jerusalem!' enthused Madame Geoffrin. 'Oh my dear son! My adorable king! Your spirit will now have an open field and boundless means, it will no longer be agitated by unfulfilled passions and continual contradiction.'[1] Joseph Yorke prophesied that Stanisław's reign would be 'blessed by history', and that he would go down as one of the greatest kings.[2] Similar sentiments were echoed at home. 'I am sure that my compatriots will never repent of the choice they have made,' Ignacy Krasicki assured him.[3] A number of people, such as Kajetan Sołtyk, Bishop of Kraków, who had sided with the Saxons and walked out of the Convocation Seym, now accepted his kingship and agreed to work with him. But as soon as the Seym resumed, only a week after the coronation, Stanisław was disabused.

The first days of the Convocation Seym before the election had opened a new era in the political life of the country. The noisy confrontations between the rival factions on 8 May had quickly given way, after the departure of the principal malcontents, to a businesslike atmosphere that affected even the Familia's opponents. As the Seym had confederated, majority voting obtained, which permitted the Familia to direct matters in their own way. As soon as the tumult had died down, Andrzej Zamoyski delivered an epoch-making speech.

Leaning heavily on the ideas of Montesquieu, he pointed out the way to restore the state to health. He then moved on to the spiritual condition of the nation, declaring that 'it is necessary to form the heart, to form the mind', after which he addressed himself to the ailing economy. 'The sale of materials and the purchase of goods impoverishes, the purchase of materials and the sale of goods enriches,' he lectured the astonished deputies. He called for the abolition of the veto, the creation of an executive council made up of senators and deputies, and the introduction of salaries for all deputies and state officials – which would allow the lower ranks of the szlachta to take part. He urged reform of the administration, the fiscal system, the educational system, the laws by which cities were taxed and governed, and suggested various limitations to the servitude of the peasants, and the granting of freedom to those who had done ten years' military service.[4]

After this declaration of intent, the Familia concentrated on pruning measures. These included placing the auditing of the state revenues in the hands of a commission elected by the Seym, and of suspending the right of veto in the matter of the passing of the accounts. When one considers that the treasurers had been the only ones with access to the accounts, which they embezzled extravagantly, and that no audit had been passed by the Seym since 1726, because the treasurer simply got one of his henchmen to use the veto, one can appreciate what a revolutionary measure this was. A similar commission was placed in charge of the army. The Familia's plan was to circumscribe the power of veto by gradually squeezing it out of various administrative areas, on the principle that these areas should be considered as judicial rather than political functions of the Seym, and in the judiciary, the power of veto had never applied.

Other reforms passed by the Convocation Seym included the abolition of the deputy's oath to obey the instructions given by his constituents, the so-called binding mandate, the introduction of closed sessions of the Seym in important matters, of harsher criminal penalties for the szlachta, stronger executive powers for courts of law, the limitation of private armies to 300 men, a curtailment of the legal exemptions enjoyed by szlachta possessions in cities, the standardisation of weights and measures, and, most important, the adoption of a General Tariff. This replaced all duties levied on goods as they passed through cities, over bridges and through provincial customs, with a single tariff, consisting of 2 per cent on Polish produce sold inside the country, 10 per cent on exports, and a sliding scale of 4 per cent to 12 per cent on all imports. Apart from simplifying the system, in the fiscal year of 1765–6 the tariff brought in several times the amount yielded by all those it replaced.[5]

The Seym suspended its sessions for the election and coronation. It reopened on 3 December 1764, and reconfederated. Stanisław wanted to forge ahead with more reforms. 'If he could, he would in the space of a single day reform the whole country, the whole nation,' reported the Papal Nuncio, Eugenio Visconti.[6] This brought him into conflict with his collaborators. The most active were Michał Czartoryski, supported by Stanisław Lubomirski, and Andrzej Zamoyski. All three now took a cautious approach. They argued that the considerable reforms carried out by the Convocation Seym should be allowed to sink in and yield some benefits before the next stage was embarked on. They were wary of ruffling the sensibilities of the szlachta on the one hand, and of arousing the suspicions of the neighbouring states on the other. They were also alarmed at the way Stanisław seemed to spawn new projects every day, many of them poorly thought out.

The Familia saw themselves as a political party which had won an election, and Stanisław not so much as their leader, more as their executive figurehead. Stanisław saw things otherwise, and his programme was significantly different from theirs. This divergence of views was exacerbated by the intrusion of personal factors: a hint of hauteur tinged with jealousy on the part of the Familia, and a touch of arrogant self-assertion on Stanisław's. While he valued his uncles and wished to show them respect, he also wanted to make it clear that he would not be their instrument.

Stanisław's brothers had thrown themselves into his cause with devotion, and this only made matters worse. Kazimierz strongly backed his intention of governing independently, and worked hard at gaining support for him, openly stating that the road to preferment lay through him and the king, rather than through the Familia. They found this galling. They had been obliged to make promises to their supporters in order to get Stanisław elected, and now found themselves having to queue for favours. Kazimierz enjoyed rubbing salt into the wound. At the Coronation Seym he had, on instructions from his constituents, demanded the princely title for the king's brothers and their descendants, and this had been granted, to the thinly masked distaste of the Czartoryskis and Lubomirskis. Stanisław Lubomirski was further mortified when the rich starosty of Spisz, which was to fall to him according to the arrangements made by the Familia, was given instead to Kazimierz.

Matters were made worse by Stanisław's attempts to gain the favour of former opponents. With their long experience of managing a large political clientele, the Familia viewed with dismay the ease with which Stanisław bestowed offices on people in an effort to buy their goodwill. A typical gesture, aimed to placate the Saxon sympathisers, was Stanisław's granting of the Generalcy of the Artillery to Friedrich Brühl. The Familia felt such favours should be withheld until tangible service had been rendered, and that he was unwittingly building up the influence of people who were by no means proven friends. Nor was Stanisław's choice of friends always good. He was right to single out and promote people such as Joachim Chreptowicz, an able and wise man who was to serve him and Poland well for three decades, Antoni Tyzenhauz, a clever and loyal young man who would build up Stanisław's following in Lithuania, Antoni Przeździecki, a Familia supporter known as 'the rhinoceros' on account of his bull neck and huge nose, Fryderyk and August Moszyński, the clever though mercurial illegitimate grandsons of Augustus II, and Jan Borch, Palatine of Livonia. He would get little effective help from Franciszek Rzewuski, a man of many talents but no backbone, or Ignacy Krasicki. For all his genius, the newly created Bishop of Warmia would fail Stanisław politically. Undoubtedly his most misguided preference was for Ksawery Branicki, a man of mean background and few talents, possessed only of the brute charm of the affable, swashbuckling, bibulous blockhead, whose relationship to Stanisław was that of a miscreant if devoted dog.

During the interregnum the Familia had held regular meetings to discuss policy, and when he ascended the throne, Stanisław continued this tradition by instituting daily conferences of a council composed originally of the two chancellors Andrzej Zamoyski and Michał Czartoryski, together with Antoni Przeździecki, Vice-Chancellor of Lithuania, August Czartoryski, Stanisław Lubomirski, and his own secretary Jacek Ogrodzki. He soon brought in his brothers. Kazimierz tended to force issues and drive the king to assert himself. Andrzej, who was now a field-marshal in Austrian service but also commanded the Royal Guards, had a view on everything and gave it, while his wife gossiped and intrigued in the background. Michał, who had moved into the Castle with his brother, brought up the rear. He was a clever man with a caustic wit that made him a number of enemies. The next addition to this cabinet was the new Vice-Chancellor of Poland, Andrzej Młodziejowski, whose allegiance, if that is the right word, meandered between the king and the Russian embassy. According to Stanisław Lubomirski, 'The opinions of these newcomers were not only often in contradiction to those of the original members, causing disputes and delays, but they also gave rise to diffidence between the king and his ministers.'[7] According to Stanisław, the conferences, instead of being a source of good counsel, became sessions during which his uncles told him what to do. The sensible Chancellor Zamoyski, a sort of Polonius to Stanisław's Hamlet, seems to have particularly irritated the young king on occasion. The Familia felt that they had lost control. 'This league of the king's brothers was made up of other creatures, and influenced by women's counsel,' complained Lubomirski.[8]

It was not that some particular mistress held sway. Stanisław remained faithful to the memory of Catherine in that he never gave himself wholeheartedly to another woman. But he adored the company of women and he was by no means abstemious. He did not dismiss mistresses when he embarked on new affairs, and had a remarkable talent for keeping attachments of varying intensity going at the same time. During the first years of his reign he remained deeply involved with Elżbieta Szydłowska and Jadwiga Ciechanowiecka, who bore him a son as late as 1773. He also began an affair with Izabela Czartoryska (her husband, otherwise occupied, used to drop her off at the Castle for him in the evenings), who bore him a daughter in 1768. He kept up his more down-to-earth liaisons, such as that with Sophie Leullier, while his relationship with Elżbieta Lubomirska continued to ebb and flow in intensity. He was a very attractive man and clearly an accomplished lover. He was also a king. As a result, he did not lack feminine attention. At least two more Sapiehas, a Potocka, and the beautiful Anna Lubomirska wended their way through his affections and his bed during these first years of his monarchy, as well as a number of less exalted ladies and passing actresses, some of whom were moved into the Castle, while others were set up in houses near by. These ladies had ready access to the king, as did his sisters and his gossipy sister-in-law, Andrzej's wife, Teresa. Many of them did not like each other. Elżbieta Lubomirska and Izabela Czartoryska were locked in a perpetual feud, which Stanisław was always trying to patch up. Others jockeyed for position among themselves. Some played at politics or lent themselves to the interests of husbands or other lovers. Stanisław could hardly fail to be enmeshed in their affairs and rivalries. From this flowed intrigue, and the fear that what was said in council was not entirely secret.

Stanisław's management of his finances was another source of concern to his uncles. Although the fortunes of magnates such as the Czartoryskis or Lubomirskis were truly fabulous, they were not boundless, and they could not sustain political influence without careful husbanding. Stanisław had not been brought up to manage a fortune and had no natural aptitude for it, being impulsive and generous. He at once began spending on a lavish scale. He was in such a hurry to put in hand projects which had matured in his mind during the long years of forced inactivity, that he initiated as many as he could, without planning for their economic sustenance. He also dispensed largesse to individuals on a vast scale. He supported various worthy causes and people, and only two days after his election was granting bursaries to the painter Kucharski for his studies in Paris and to Anna Rajecka, who was studying under Greuze. But much of his generosity was lavished on less worthy objects. Stanisław was a soft touch, and in his readiness to relieve hardship he could be remarkably undiscriminating. Casanova found no difficulty in getting 200 ducats out of him simply by saying that he was strapped for cash, and another thousand a year later to cover his debts.

But analysis of the king's accounts reveals that it was the court which swallowed up the lion's share. Of the total expenditure of 4,630,940 złoty in 1769, the largest single item was the Royal Guard, which cost 509,000, but the kitchen, pantry, cellar and bakery taken together cost 597,000, while horses and stabling for the court cost 412,000 – beside which the 329,000 that went on rebuilding the Castle and the 454,000 that went towards establishing factories seem remarkably modest.[9] Stanisław Lubomirski, a wealthy man descended from generations of great spenders, was horrified at the lack of method in the king's finances.[10]

Since the Treasury was empty and the country's fiscal services were in chaos when he came to the throne, Stanisław was dependent on the pension granted by Catherine for the first year. But this could not keep pace with his expenditure. He borrowed from Poles, raised loans in Genoa, the Netherlands and England, and attempted to start up a national lottery. He was nevertheless obliged to seek further subsidies from Catherine. Stanisław's uncles and his ministers repeatedly warned him against drawing too heavily on her purse, pointing out that he would be accused of being her 'stipendiary'. Michał Czartoryski and Zamoyski offered to help him organise his finances better, but he saw this as unwarranted interference. 'I do not look into the accounts of others, and nobody should meddle in mine,' he snapped back at them.[11] It was a statement they could not argue with, but they were worried that his profligacy put a powerful and humiliating weapon in the Russian ambassador's hands.

Keyserling had died a few days after the election, and Repnin stepped into his shoes. Stanisław tried to place his relations with Russia on a regular diplomatic footing, but Catherine and Panin found it easier to delegate policy to Repnin than to issue him with specific instructions at every turn, and they politely ignored Stanisław's envoy Franciszek Rzewuski and his successor Jakub Psarski. The ambitious and energetic Repnin preferred this arrangement to that of a mere ambassador passing messages this way and that.

Repnin was a remarkable man. He was only thirty years old. Clever, cultivated and intrepid, he could draw on great reserves of charm, but he was very much the product of the Russian court, and his position of power in Warsaw went to his head. 'Everything favoured him, and universal success contributed to spoil what was at heart an excellent nature,' according to Stanisław.[12] The English diplomat James Harris found him 'a worthy man, very feeling and humane, of great natural parts, and very agreeable'.[13] But he soon grew high-handed and, when crossed, he would flare up into violent rages and trample all forms of civility. He compensated for the blind obedience he owed to his masters in St Petersburg by abusing his power in Warsaw, and revealed, in the French historian Claude Rulhière's felicitous phrase, the nature of 'an insolent slave'.[14] He quickly sized up the king's character and recognised his weaknesses. He found no difficulty in insinuating himself into his confidence. He gauged the strength of the king's feelings for

Catherine, and used his position to play upon them, thereby extending his influence considerably. 'The similarity of their ages, of their tempers and of their love of pleasure drew the king to the ambassador, and their daily contact turned this into a friendship,' Lubomirski noted.[15] Another thing which linked them was their common interest in women. They not only succeeded each other as lovers of the same ladies, but in some cases even seem to have shared them. Taking all these things into account, it is obvious that the king could not begin to stand on his dignity with the ambassador, could not even avoid giving him an audience, since Repnin would just walk into his private rooms. Stanisław's uncles warned him against such familiarity, but there was little he could do to prevent it. He lacked the presence to impose distance, and he could not openly challenge Repnin, who was the ambassador of Poland's only ally.

Repnin missed no opportunity of making trouble between the king and his uncles, which was not difficult, since their views often diverged. Stanisław felt that they did not support him enough, and taxed Michał Czartoryski with disloyalty. 'We do not wish to appear in the public's eyes as creatures of the court, which would do us no honour,' replied Czartoryski.[16] In this attempt to safeguard their reputation, Stanisław saw only spiteful defiance, and he explained it to himself as the fruit of resentment at having failed to secure the throne for themselves. But what really worried them was the dangerous course he was steering with respect to Russia.

Stanisław trusted in Catherine's goodwill, and believed that he could depend on Russia as a partner and ally while pursuing Polish reasons of state. He did not see these as being incompatible with Russian interests, as he did not realise to what extent Panin, and increasingly Catherine herself, had come to consider Poland as little more than a Russian dependency. Nor did he have any inkling of the secret clauses of the Russo-Prussian treaty regarding Poland. That is why he determined to carry on with his programme and push through further curtailments of the veto, against the advice of his uncles.

The matter had to be approached with caution, since the one thing all Poland's neighbours were agreed on was to preserve the consti-tutional status quo. In May 1764 Russia and Prussia had issued their latest joint declaration to that effect. Undeterred by this, Stanisław had in the course of the summer before his election put it to Catherine and Panin that what he wanted was not the abolition of the *liberum veto*, only of the '*liberum rumpo*', that is to say of the constitutionally dubious habit by which a veto cast during a debate automatically annulled the whole session, and prevented even those bills which had been voted unanimously from becoming law. He argued that the change he envisaged would not diminish Russia's ability to obstruct any measure she did not like, but would facilitate the passing of those she did want to see brought in.[17]

Panin liked the idea, and Catherine saw no objection. But because of their alliance with Prussia, they had to inform the Prussian ambassador in St Petersburg, Count Solms. He did not like the sound of it at all. 'This project', he wrote to Frederick on 18 September, 'gives rise to the suspicion that those who propose it may have hidden motives.'[18] His superiors in Berlin, Finckenstein and Hertzberg, agreed. On 6 October Frederick wrote to Solms instructing him to do everything possible to quell the idea.[19] Neither Catherine nor Panin was inclined to have their policy dictated to them. But the Russo-Prussian alliance of 1764 had in effect made Frederick the co-protector of Poland, and on 30 October 1764 he wrote to Catherine, warning her that the proposed reforms might turn Poland into a threat to her neighbours in the future. He reminded her that as guarantor of Poland's political freedom, she had a right, not to say a duty, to intervene.[20] A few weeks later, prompted by the arguments of Frederick and also, apparently, by those of the Orlovs, Catherine changed her mind.[21] There was to be no more constitutional change in Poland.

Frederick would not let matters rest there. In January 1765, he pulled a new trick out of his hat. Through his resident in Warsaw, Benoit, he announced that the General Tariff passed by the Poles was illegal, since all measures relating to customs should, according to the Treaty of Wielawa (1657), be agreed mutually between Poland and Prussia. The Poles replied with documentary refutation of his case, showing that there had been many unilateral changes by both sides since then, and that the treaty had been superseded by others. In March Frederick responded by building a customs-house at Marienwerder, where his territory touched one bank of the Vistula, and exacting by force a duty of 10 per cent from every boat carrying goods down to Gdańsk.

Stanisław turned to Catherine to intervene as Poland's ally. Frederick's action reflected badly on her theoretic hegemony in Poland, and she was irritated by his high-handed manner.[22] She insisted that he dismantle the customs-house forthwith and open negotiations with Poland. This he duly did, and Poland and Prussia each delegated a commission to discuss the issue. Stanisław also tried to involve England, whose mercantile interests were at stake, and he was helped in this by the fact that the already sympathetic English resident Thomas Wroughton's personal effects had been ransacked and taxed on their way to Warsaw, in flagrant disregard of his diplomatic status. In tones of outrage he urged his government to make a stand on the matter, but nothing came of it.[23]

The behaviour of Frederick had forced Stanisław to make early use of the Russian alliance, which placed him further in Catherine's debt. It also threw him into closer contact with her ambassador in Poland. This upset his delicate balancing-act and exacerbated the divergence of views with the Familia. They were growing more and more alarmed at his policy, but he ignored them, feeling that he knew better. He often did, but his impatience and inability to humour his advisers produced unwonted confrontations, at least one of which gave rise to a major disagreement as well as highly unfortunate consequences for the country.

As a result of Frederick's monetary depredations, it had become necessary to revalue the Polish currency and mint enough new coinage to allow trade to revive. The main problem was to fix its gold and silver content so that it could hold its own against other currencies. Stanisław appointed a commission, consisting of the two chancellors, Lubomirski, and several others, under the presidency of Jan Borch, and tenders were invited from contractors. The first to come forward was a Berlin banker named Schweigert. Stanisław liked his scheme and decided to award him the contract giving him an advance before the commission had had time to consider it fully. When they had, they rejected Schweigert's proposal, and opted for another, put forward by an entrepreneur from Saxony. Stanisław stuck to his guns, supported vigorously by his brother Kazimierz and Ksawery Branicki, and ignored the commission's protests.

Schweigert tried to go back on the terms of his contract, which forced Stanisław to abandon his scheme. Although he did not lose face, he sustained a heavy financial loss, as the banker went back to Berlin with the advance in his pocket. Stanisław nevertheless continued to support Schweigert's calculation of the silver value of the

Polish złoty at the rate of 18 to the ducat, and in this he was supported by some members of the commission, notably Aleksander Unruh and Fryderyk Moszyński. But Borch and the rest of the commission wanted to pin its value at the rate of 16.75 to the ducat, which corresponded to the rate current throughout the Empire. Stanisław argued that since most Polish commercial transactions passed through Gdańsk or the Prussian dominions, where the silver content of the equivalent coin was 18 to 1, this would create a state of affairs in which a Prussian merchant could exchange his gold ducat for a greater weight of silver in Poland than anywhere else, which would tempt him to buy up Polish silver coinage. He was proved right by events. The issue was decided against him in 1766, and the result was that over the next twenty years approximately 40 million out of the 43 million silver złoty coins minted were siphoned off abroad, mainly to Prussia, where they were melted down, merely aggravating the chronic currency shortage.[24]

Stanisław had gravely mishandled the matter. An understandable desire to act decisively had led him to upset procedure and undermine the very notion of administrative formality he was trying to encourage. He did not appreciate this, and he would repeat the same mistake in the future more than once. All he could see was that he had been crossed, and wrongly. It added further cause for discontent and recrimination between him and his ministers, but one must be careful not to exaggerate the importance of the tensions, which were an inevitable consequence not only of the relationship between the people involved, but also of the extraordinary tempo at which they worked for the regeneration of the country.

The first year of Stanisław's reign had transformed the country beyond recognition. A proper budget was voted for the first time, and by 1766 it produced a surplus. In 1767 55 per cent of state revenues, a larger amount than ever before, was spent on the army, and the remaining 45 per cent on funding the Cadet Corps, the diplomatic service and other civil institutions. In 1764 the old Krasiński palace was purchased to house government bodies, which hitherto functioned in the back rooms of the private residences of the ministers involved. Renamed the Palace of the Commonwealth, it proclaimed the existence of a state administration which had not existed before. Stanisław wanted to complement this by a revision of the duties and powers of all officials. He attempted to eliminate some of the duplication which resulted from the dualism between Poland and Lithuania, by combining some of the functions, but this aroused regional resentments, so he shelved the proposal. He was planning to revise the constitutional position of Gdańsk in relation to Poland, and drawing up a charter framing the prerogatives of other cities and their inhabitants. At the back of his mind lurked a plan to recodify the laws.

Before the year was out, the Cadet Corps was founded and housed in the old Kazimierz palace, also purchased by the state. The army, which had fallen to a ludicrous 12,000 men, a staggering proportion of them officers, was modernised. As the treaty of 1717, confirmed by the Russo-Prussian agreement of 1764, did not allow him to keep more than 18,000 men under arms, Stanisław decided to treat the army as a specialised cadre which could be expanded quickly in emergency. He cashiered supernumerary officers, restructured the infantry, and increased the ratio of artillery. With his own money, he built a cannon-foundry in Warsaw, which was producing guns, caissons and ammunition by 1767. The Seym voted a project to construct a bridge over the Vistula at Warsaw, and established a company of pontooners to tackle the job. Work began on a wide-ranging programme of improving the main roads all over the country, and the postal service, including staging-posts and inns, was brought up to a standard that surprised travellers by its speed and efficiency.

Stanisław's intention of extending the resources of the Crown, combined with his chronic shortage of funds and his desire to develop the country economically, impelled him to look at every economic possibility. His proposal that Crown rights to search for mineral deposits be extended met with a less than enthusiastic response from the Seym, but he set up a foundry on the Crown estate of Sambor, and in 1768 an ironworks at Ruda on the Brześć estate. He also founded a private cloth-mill on his own land at Zaleszczyki in Podolia. In March 1765 he appointed Antoni Tyzenhauz to the management of the Crown estates in Lithuania, with a brief to develop manufacturing industry there. In 1766 he founded the Wool Manufacturing Company, a joint-stock venture with 120 shares, under the presidency of Andrzej Zamoyski, with the aim of developing this staple industry on a large scale.

Stanisław's mind raced far ahead of what he could achieve immediately, and his papers reveal the extraordinary versatility of his interests. They are full of projects for canals, roads and factories. Countless foreign entrepreneurs and correspondents fed this enthusiasm, and even Casanova contributed a project for a soap factory. Stanisław's mood was contagious. August Sułkowski founded a miniature cadet corps at his estate of Rydzyna and set about introducing manufacturing industry there. Fryderyk Moszyński produced an avalanche of projects, while Bishop Massalski was establishing factories in Lithuania. The country had begun to wake up.

It was an intellectual awakening as much as anything else. Throughout the 1750s Konarski's reforms percolated through the schooling system, so that by the end of the decade a significant proportion of the country's youth was getting a modern education. The decade also saw the publication of historical materials and classics of literature, as well as a number of influential new works, such as a book on Polish usage by the Jesuit Franciszek Bohomolec, and a history of Poland by Gotfryd Lengnich, Stanisław's erstwhile teacher, the first such work to reject myth and legend. In 1758, a periodical entitled *Economic and Scientific novelties, or a magazine of all the sciences necessary to human happiness* had begun to appear, edited by Mitzler de Kolof, an enthusiast of things new and literary. He was emulated by others, and a number of periodicals started up over the next couple of years. By far the most important development, however, was the publication, between 1761 and 1763, of the four volumes of Konarski's *On the manner of effective counsel*, which was at once a textbook of logical thought, a primer of public and political conduct, and a political manifesto suggesting a redrafting of the constitution to accommodate permanent cabinet government. It was accompanied by the publication in Polish of Montesquieu's *Considérations sur les causes de la grandeur des Romains et de leur décadence*, a fitting subject for the Poles to ruminate. These ruminations were further stimulated by Pyrrhis de Varille, tutor to the children of Barbara Sanguszko, whose *Political Compendium*, published in 1762, undermined the accepted view of Poland's past, and demonstrated the relation between the decline of royal power and that of the country.

With Stanisław's accession to the throne, these hesitant movements were invested with official backing. In 1765 Stanisław had a medal struck in honour of Konarski, with the inscription *Sapere Auso*. With the king's support, Mitzler de Kolof set up a Literary Society which began publishing Polish literature. Stanisław was determined to reach a larger number of people, and in the first three months of his reign, he established the first public theatre in Poland. He rented the Saxony opera-chamber, engaged an Italian entrepreneur called Carlo Tomatis, and booked three companies, Italian, French and Polish. The Warsaw public was now exposed to the plays of Goldoni, Corneille, Racine and Voltaire, as well as to the didactic comedies of Franciszek Bohomolec (written originally for performance in Jesuit colleges) the elegant classical tragedies in the French style and comedies in the manner of Molière composed by Hetman Wacław Rzewuski, and the works of other Polish dramatists.

A landmark in Stanisław's campaign to spread light through the nation was the launching of a new periodical, *Monitor*, in 1765. He commissioned Ignacy Krasicki to sketch out publishing policy, and placed the editorship in the hands of Bohomolec. *Monitor*, which appeared twice a week, was modelled on Addison's *Spectator*, and often lifted copy straight from it, but it also printed excerpts from French writings, as well as Polish poetry and essays, including polemical pieces inspired, or even written by, Stanisław himself.

Many of the people Stanisław employed to further his educational plans were Jesuits, and there can be no better example of his pragmatic approach than the relationship he built up with them. 'I use the Jesuits to help me drag the nation out of its barbarism,' he confided in Saint-Saphorin, the Danish minister in Warsaw. 'They have such a vehement desire to be in at court and to dominate there, that there is nothing they will not do to achieve this end, and according to this principle, while they remain Catholic zealots in Rome, they serve me in this country as only Protestants could.'[25] The reference to Protestants was not inapt, for the cause of enlightenment was inextricably locked in combat with religious bigotry, which dictated views on everything from the constitution to natural sciences. Stanisław was fundamentally religious, but both his home upbringing and the influence of Williams had conspired to give him a somewhat Protestant outlook. He was more of a deist than a Catholic, while remaining in many ways strongly attached to the traditions of Rome. He rejected the more superstitious elements of Church teaching, and despised the mendicant orders, which propounded these most actively.

He was fully aware that to open the mind of the Polish nation at this time was to take on the whole established Church. Since there were no intellectual cadres outside its ranks, Stanisław used those men of the cloth whom he could subvert. He encouraged the Jesuit Karol Wyrwicz to start work on a book comparing the political systems of the world which caused a sensation when it was published in 1768, and he encouraged the Piarist Konarski to write a work on comparative religions which ridiculed bigotry and won him the enmity of the Papal Nuncio when it appeared in 1769. In 1764 he appointed the Jesuit Marcin Poczobut to manage the new Observatory at Wilno. He commissioned other members of the Society to start work on a scheme dear to his heart, that of producing an accurate atlas of Poland, and to elaborate plans for an academy of fine arts that he intended to found in Warsaw.

'I am only thirty-three years old,' he wrote to Madame Geoffrin after a year on the throne. 'I can probably count on another thirty years of life; one can do many things in thirty years . . . ' But he was frustrated by limited resources and the lack of understanding and support he found in many quarters. 'There is one thing that I can see coming, against which I try to brace myself, and that is the ill-humour that the continual opposition of people, the circumstances, and my own temperament, compounded by an awful emptiness in the heart, encourage in me more and more,' he wrote to Madame Geoffrin. And he could not stifle a lingering regret at seeing his emotional life subsumed by his public role. 'Oh! Maman, it is sad to feel that one's heart is used up, and that one will never love again with that fullness of feeling, with that intoxication which prevents one from seeing any defect or wrong, either in the idol or in one's worship of her!'[26]

His despair was premature, for while he could not attempt to scale the heights of emotional intensity reached with Catherine in the company of the many women who now engaged his affections – and in some cases probably no more than his lust – his emotional balance was to be upset once more by Elżbieta Lubomirska. Since the surviving correspondence between them consists of undated notes, it is difficult to reconstruct this tempestuous relationship, but, as she assured him in one of these, apparently written soon after his election, 'nobody appreciates you, nobody loves you with greater tenderness, and nobody esteems you as much as I; it is the constant sentiment of my heart'. She admitted to drifting away from him, but, as she put it, 'the returns are always in your favour, and always redouble my tenderness for you'.[27] She was certainly engaged on one of her 'returns' in the middle of 1766, and Stanisław was now resisting his natural impulse to let himself go. 'I must keep a cool head in everything at all times,' he wrote to Madame Geoffrin, explaining that 'my heart would run away only too fast if I let myself go . . . I must not give myself to anything or anyone without reserve.' But this reserve did not come naturally, and it made him suffer.[28]

Stanisław drowned his self-pity in hard work, which explains the remarkable fecundity of his projects and initiatives during these first years. He also assuaged it by playing very hard. The social life of Warsaw was curiously informal in some ways, and the Saxony Gardens were the centre of amusements that were more egalitarian than anywhere in Europe. The king would promenade there without attendants or guards. He would encounter Repnin lying under a tree reading a book, and groups of people from every level in society walking about or sitting on the grass. The gardens were open to anyone, and in the evenings, they were a venue for masked balls organised by the king, by various aristocrats, or by entrepreneurs. In the latter case, admittance was paid for at the gate, in the former, there would be a couple of soldiers to prevent anyone who was too scruffy or too drunk from joining in. 'There could be nothing more enchanting than these balls,' wrote a German visitor. 'Some parts of the Gardens, lit up with coloured lanterns, created a magical contrast with the deep shadows of other areas. Under the great tent people danced the *polonaise*, in others it was the *anglaise* or the *contredanse*. Polite merriment reigned everywhere, and the mask allowed greater freedom, enhancing the pleasure, since it allowed all classes to approach each other for a while.'[29]

These balls were daily events during the carnival, which Casanova, an expert at least in such things, found very much to his taste. 'The Carnival was very brilliant,' he wrote. 'People from every corner of Europe seem to have arranged to meet there.'[30] His memory of it was somewhat marred a couple of weeks later when, after trading insults with Ksawery Branicki over their respective mistresses, Casanova challenged him to a duel, and wounded him in the gut. While Branicki hovered between life and death, a lynch-mob of his supporters scoured

Warsaw for the unfortunate Italian, who had to hide and then flee the city.

Stanisław also enjoyed more exclusive and elaborate courtly amusements which he devised himself. In the summer months, these often consisted of trips down the Vistula, sometimes with a small group of ladies in gondolas, for a picnic at Bielany or Saska Kępa (a pretty Dutch farm laid out by Augustus II), sometimes in magnificent barges bearing not only a sizeable court but also entire orchestras. Then there would be *fêtes champêtres*, amateur theatricals on the river-bank and firework displays.

But while people noted him dancing in his domino until four in the morning, apparently the soul of the party, they often recorded that Stanisław did not seem happy at heart.[31] Often, he would avoid public entertainments and, particularly in winter, spent his days hunting with his uncle August at Wilanów and his evenings quietly supping with one of his less trying mistresses. At other times, he retreated for a few days to the Crown estate of Kozienice, where he would exhaust himself by tracking wild game through the snow all day long. But he never let up on his work, rising early, and using every minute of the day to improve himself and his country.

10

A Matter of Faith

$\mathcal{S}$hortly after signing their treaty of alliance in April 1764, Catherine and Frederick had issued a joint declaration asserting their intention to protect the interests of their respective co-religionists, the Orthodox and the Protestant citizens of Poland. They agreed 'to instruct their ministers residing in Poland to make the appropriate representations and to insinuate in the strongest terms, both to the Commonwealth during the interregnum, and to the new king after his election, that the aforementioned dissenters, both noble and of lesser condition, should be heard and re-established in accordance with the general and fundamental constitutions of the Commonwealth.'[1]

The Polish Commonwealth was the only major state in Europe which had consistently tolerated the free practice of all religions by its citizens. During the Reformation the unhindered spread of every creed and the influx of religious refugees from other lands had produced a situation in the sixteenth century where Catholics were in a minority among Orthodox, Calvinists, Lutherans, Jews, Muslims and a number of minor sects. There was no disability attached to any religion, and every post in the Commonwealth, except that of king, was open to all. In the following century, the Poles drifted back towards Catholicism, guided by the Jesuits. In doing so they were only following a trend manifest throughout Europe. The wisdom of the age was that too much diversity undermined national unity, and in an ethnically mixed country such as Poland, held together by very little in the way of centralised administration, a religion of state was an important cement. Some sects such as the Quakers and the Arians, who had sided with the Protestant Swedes against Poland, were expelled. It became illegal to leave the Catholic faith for another. In 1717 a decree forbade the building of new non-Catholic places of worship, and the rebuilding of those which had been abandoned. In 1733, non-Catholics were banned from the Senate and the Seym, from sitting as judges or holding starosties, but not from military ranks.

The Orthodox and Protestants in Poland were therefore better off than dissenters in most European countries, in many of which they were not allowed to own land or practise their faith at all. The disabilities concerned eligibility for office, and therefore affected only the szlachta, few of whom were dissenters anyway. Most of the Orthodox szlachta had in the previous century converted to Catholicism or joined the Uniate Church – which kept the Eastern rite but acknowledged the Pope. And there were no more than about a thousand Protestant szlachta within the Commonwealth.

Worse than the disabilities was the harassment of dissenters which had begun over the last decades. The Catholic clergy seized on every opportunity to declare an Orthodox Church to be illegal, to accuse an Orthodox priest of some petty crime, to ban a religious procession and to persuade some bigoted country magistrate to save his soul by penalising the dissenters. In the cities, Catholics treated Protestant merchants or artisans as undesirable foreigners and used religion as a pretext in their professional rivalry. In the south-east of the country there was a running battle between the clergy of the Orthodox and Uniate Churches.

The Orthodox Bishop of Mohylów, Jerzy Koniski, had attended Catherine's coronation in 1762 and implored her protection. This made her realise that she had what were in a sense subjects of her own within Poland. If she could introduce them into the political body, then she would have acquired one more lever of influence there, as well as gaining popularity at home. In Russia, she was exerting strong state control over the Church, so it would be useful to her to pose as its defender abroad. Frederick also liked posing as the defender of the oppressed, particularly when this involved having a go at the Catholic Church, which he loathed with all the vehemence of a true *philosophe*. The kings of Denmark and England were invited to join in the

Russo-Prussian declarations on behalf of the Protestants, which they gladly agreed to do.

Declarations were one thing, bringing about a change of attitude in Poland quite another. When, in deference to Catherine's wishes, Stanisław had brought the matter up at the Convocation Seym, there was a predictable howl of pain from the bishops and a xenophobic outburst from the deputies. 'The feeling against the naturalisation of foreigners, the oppressive contempt for the lower orders, and religious intolerance are the three strongest national prejudices I have to fight against,' he complained to Madame Geoffrin, adding that 'one has to proceed with caution'.[2] Everyone seemed to appreciate this. In April 1764, Repnin wrote to Panin that lifting the disabilities of the dissenters 'would appear to be a difficult, and perhaps impossible thing to achieve'.[3] Panin agreed that it was 'unrealistic', and that forcing the issue would only make Russia unpopular.[4]

Catherine took his point, and in October declared that she would be happy if the dissenters remained barred from the principal charges, but would like to see them allowed to stand as deputies to the Seym or as judges. Failing that she could accept the largely symbolic concession that a couple of them could be nominated to the post of local magistrate (*Starosta Grodowy*). But she told Repnin to pursue the matter, explaining that 'my reputation is involved'.[5] This was unfortunate.

The issue was highly inconvenient to Stanisław, as it jeopardised his own political programme. Everything he was doing was revolutionary. He was tampering with time-honoured practices, which caused offence and aroused suspicion in many quarters. If he now embraced this deeply emotive cause on Catherine's behalf, it could only swell the existing resistance and confirm people in their fears that he was an instrument of Russian policy.

At the same time, he perceived that the issue gave him a lever over Catherine. In the autumn of 1764 he explained to her that the enfranchisement could be carried out with greater ease if the veto were abolished, as he was suggesting.[6] But Catherine had just decided, at Frederick's insistence, not to allow this. She nevertheless expected Stanisław to act on the dissenter issue. Stanisław did not appreciate to what extent she felt involved in the matter, and he little realised that she would see it as a litmus-test of his loyalty to her. He stalled her demands with pious utterances and much shrugging of shoulders at popular prejudice.

In July 1765, the Orthodox Bishop Koniski submitted a list of grievances. He named 200 churches and monasteries in Uniate hands which he wanted returned to the jurisdiction of the Orthodox hierarchy. He demanded the restoration of all ancient freedoms and privileges, including the right of Orthodox clergy to be tried exclusively by their own religious courts, the repeal of various taxes, full freedom of religious ceremonies, the right for children of mixed marriages to follow the Orthodox faith, and the opening of all public offices to Orthodox szlachta.[7] He also wanted a seat in the Senate for himself alongside the Catholic bishops. The demands were preposterous, and Catherine had no intention of supporting them. If the Orthodox were made too comfortable in Poland, they would cease to require Russian protection. Worse still, the steady drift of Russian peasants into Poland would turn into a flood.[8] Stanisław pointed out that if Koniski were given a seat in the Senate, the Uniate bishops would have to be admitted as well. Catherine preferred to see neither get a seat.[9] But she did want some abrogation of the dissenters' disabilities.

Stanisław set up a commission to investigate the grievances brought up by Koniski, which gave him several months' respite, but the matter could not be put off indefinitely. It had grown into a stumbling-block in relations between Poland and Russia, and affected the negotiations with Frederick over the General Tariff, which had reached stalemate. While in the previous year Catherine had urged Frederick to yield, in January 1766 Panin made it plain that she would no longer support the Poles, and that they had no option but to abolish the Tariff altogether.[10] Stanisław despatched Rzewuski to St Petersburg once again in an attempt to sort things out with Catherine, but she was not inclined to talk to him.

In April, she sent the senior Russian diplomat Kaspar von Saldern to Warsaw to assess the situation. Repnin's assurances that he had everything under control, the ageing Primate Łubieński's pliability and Stanisław's protestations of loyalty led Saldern astray and convinced him that the disabilities of the dissenters could be lifted without too much trouble. Saldern's real goal was Berlin, where he was to reassure Frederick on the point of Catherine's plans for Poland. She was hoping to strengthen Stanisław's position, increase the Polish army and turn the country into a more useful ally, as she anticipated a war with Turkey. Frederick did not like the sound of this at all. He suggested giving Stanisław more money to play with and leaving Poland in a state of political 'lethargy'.[11] Stanisław sensed Russia's need of him and her disagreement with Prussia. This made him more confident of his position, as did a number of other developments that summer. Saldern's visit was followed and completely overshadowed by another, apparently trivial, that caused a stir throughout Europe.

Madame Geoffrin had wanted to come to Warsaw from the moment of Stanisław's accession, and he encouraged her in the undertaking, knowing the publicity value of such a visit. 'You will find your son very occupied (which is not a bad thing in itself), but almost always unhappily occupied, making plans and drawing up details of projects without ever having the satisfaction of succeeding,' he warned her. 'Always crossed by prejudice or by ill will, both that of my compatriots and of foreigners, whatever good I intend to achieve I am prevented from executing by the lack of power, both as a king limited by a jealous democracy, and as the leader of a defenceless nation.'[12]

She left Paris at the end of May 1766 in the company of Stanisław's envoy to the French court Feliks Łojko. She arrived in Vienna on 7 June and stayed there for a week, entertained by the Chancellor Prince Kaunitz, who knew her of old and also addressed her as *Chère maman.* Maria Theresa received her at Schönbrunn with great honours; the Emperor stopped his carriage and walked over when he saw her in the gardens. Frederick wrote from Berlin asking her to come, while Catherine declared that she would 'cast all the diamonds on earth into the river' if that could bring her to St Petersburg.[13] Madame Geoffrin was met on the borders of Poland by an officer sent by Stanisław with a bevy of servants and cooks, a set of furniture to be installed at every inn at which she stopped, silver plate, fine linen and delicate provisions, 'and generally everything it is possible to imagine to make my journey most comfortable'.[14]

The ludicrous royal progress of this footman's daughter provides a fascinating insight into the bizarre relationship that bound despots and intellectuals, and the fatuous self-importance of the latter. 'Madame Geoffrin's journey to Warsaw has been a subject of interest and conversation everywhere throughout the course of the summer,' noted Grimm in his *Correspondance*, describing it as 'an enterprise of great beauty'.[15] Marmontel and D'Alembert concurred, while Voltaire sententiously decreed that 'your journey will be in France a great moment for all those who believe in thought'.[16] Even Walpole was badgering Madame du Deffand for the latest news of 'la Geoffrinska'.

She reached Warsaw on 22 June, and as her carriage swept into the courtyard of the Castle, Stanisław was at the foot of the stairs to greet her with a warm embrace. He installed her in an apartment furnished like her own in Paris, and attended to her every need. It was a summer of endless festivities. There were operas and plays given by Stanisław, and *fêtes champêtres* hosted by Kazimierz in his newly laid-out gardens at Solec. But Madame Geoffrin was not taken in by Stanisław's show of gaiety. 'It is a terrible condition to be king of Poland,' she wrote to D'Alembert on 23 July. 'I dare not tell him how unhappy he seems to me . . .'[17] She found him overworked and beset by depressing realities. She felt she was there to shed Parisian wisdom and light, and could not resist giving advice which, since she understood nothing about Polish politics, only served to irritate Stanisław. What she had expected to find one can but guess at, but she was deeply disappointed. Stanisław's pragmatic attitude to the dissenter issue must have struck her as indecently un-'philosophical'.

The visit, which lasted until the middle of September, proved a strain for both of them. They even quarrelled on a couple of occasions, notably after August Czartoryski had misreported to her some remark of the king's about her artistic taste. But such clouds were soon dispelled, and they did not occlude the praise she heaped on Stanisław in letters to her friends in Paris. These were, of course, read out in salons and assemblies, and communicated to the 'thinking world'. His public image received a tremendous boost from it. 'You are, Madame, with a king who, alone of all kings, owes his crown to his merit, and your journey does you both honour,' wrote Voltaire from Berlin, adding that if he had been in better health he would gladly have gone with her.[18] Marmontel, writing from Paris, acclaimed Stanisław as 'a great king', D'Alembert expressed his admiration, and Voltaire presented his compliments to 'a king who is truly worthy of being one'.[19] This sort of thing was music to Stanisław's ears.

More important were the diplomatic aspects. Madame Geoffrin's journey drew attention in France to the fact that this enlightened monarch was being studiously ignored by Versailles, and helped to bring about a long-awaited event. That summer, the Marquis de Conflans, French ambassador to Berlin, came to Warsaw to deliver the compliments of Louis XV on Stanisław's election. It was little, and it was late, but it was a start. Conflans stayed only two weeks, and there was no mention of a minister being posted, but an agent of the *Secret* called Gérault settled in Warsaw.

Madame Geoffrin was genuinely fond of her royal 'son', and Stanisław was deeply attached to the old lady. He was sorry to see her go in September. 'I found, when I woke up this morning, my castle and my day empty; I have been left all alone, very alone, silent, my heart gripped with anguish and sadness,' he wrote the morning after she left.[20] On her return through Vienna she had several audiences with the Empress. She took advantage of them to sing Stanisław's praises, and to show the portrait of himself he had given her. Both here and at Versailles, where it was also passed around, it created a favourable impression of the Polish king. Andrzej Poniatowski, who had played the part of her guide and assistant in Vienna, was sanguine that Austria was at last going to take an interest in Poland.

All this gave Stanisław heart and stiffened his resolve not to be pushed into anything, with, as it turned out, fatal consequences. Repnin was demanding that he put forward legislation enfranchising the dissenters when the Seym met in October 1766. But a strong groundswell of opinion was forming against such a measure, and against the king, who was being represented by his enemies as a godless Russian puppet. The Catholic hierarchy, led by the bishop of Kraków, Kajetan Sołtyk, agitated openly against the encroachments of the 'schismatics', and woolly heads up and down the country were filled with fanatical thoughts in defence of the faith. In July Repnin tried to persuade Sołtyk to desist, and unwisely backed this up with threats. Sołtyk's reaction was to write publicly to Stanisław, to Catherine, and to all the Catholic monarchs of Europe, complaining of the Russian ambassador's behaviour, which, he declared, was an insult to the Commonwealth and the Catholic Church.

Stanisław obliged Repnin to tender an apology. But the damage had been done. The whole country talked of nothing else throughout August and September, as the elections to the Seym drew near. Attitudes had hardened and battle-lines were drawn. Stanisław was determined not to compromise himself by embracing an unpopular and doomed cause on Russia's behalf, but he was desperate to maintain his good relations with Catherine, so he avoided taking up a position. He was on his own, since the Czartoryskis had wisely distanced themselves from Russian policy, in spite of Repnin's repeated attempts to engage their support. 'In truth, the execution of this matter is so difficult and complex, I often fall into despair,' Repnin wrote to Panin on 1 September.[21] Things were only to get worse.

Catherine was growing impatient. She had no experience of systems, like those of Poland or England, where the church hierarchy was part of the constitutional body, and therefore failed to grasp the profound implications of her demands. Brought up as a Protestant, translated into the Orthodox Church, which she viewed above all as a useful political instrument, she did not comprehend religious feeling, and could not see its importance for others. She viewed Catholicism through the eyes of Voltaire, and in the principled stand of the Polish hierarchy she saw only bigotry and lust for power. It seemed to her that Stanisław was refusing to carry out her wishes, but she noticed that he intended to pursue his own programme of reform. She sensed that she was being fobbed off, and was outraged by what she called Stanisław's 'craftiness'.[22] She reacted with characteristic vigour. On 4 September she sent Repnin new instructions; he was to press for full enfranchisement, including seats in the Senate for the dissenters, and there were to be absolutely no 'unusual novelties' – i.e. reforms – passed in the Seym.[23] 'Our Lady the Empress has seen through all the subtleties of the Polish Court,' Panin wrote to Repnin on 18 September.[24] 'The instructions given to me in the matter of the dissenters are horrific,' Repnin answered, 'truly my hair stands on end.'[25]

Stanisław saw himself as a loyal but sovereign ally of Russia, failing to grasp that Catherine and her ministry viewed him rather as a tool of their policy in Poland. 'It would be impossible to feel more keenly than I do all that I should lose if I were to forfeit the friendship and the support of the Empress, but what am I to do when I am faced with my duty?' he wrote to Rzewuski at the end of September. 'I know that it may cost me my crown and my life, I know it, but once again, I cannot betray my country.' He enjoined him to 'do the possible and the impossible' to convince Catherine of his sincerity.[26] He could not bring himself to believe that this woman whom he had loved, admired and trusted would really use force so unjustly, and he told Thomas

Wroughton as much. Wroughton was not so sure. He felt that things were getting out of hand, and so did his superiors in London.[27]

Pressed by Catherine and faced with stubborn opposition in Poland, Repnin could see no way out. He made one last attempt to bludgeon Sołtyk and several other senators into submission, and when that failed he resorted to force. 'I have decided as from today to send a courier to Major-General Saltykov with orders to march with his corps into the estates of the bishops of Kraków and Wilno, provisioning himself at their expense, for the situation in the matter of the dissenters can get no worse than it already is, and perhaps this action will make an impression and improve matters somehow,' he wrote to Panin on 24 September.[28] He threatened Stanisław with armed intervention and dethronement if he did not agree to do Russia's bidding.[29] Privately, he admitted that he was putting him in an impasse, but pleaded that matters had gone beyond his control.[30] Catherine had come to see the whole thing as a clash of wills between herself and Stanisław. Now not only her reputation but her pride as a woman was at stake. While passing on her imperious letters, Panin tried to reassure Stanisław that 'Her Imperial Majesty would be hurt if other motives were imputed to her than Your happiness, Sire, and that of Your Commonwealth.'[31]

Stanisław decided to write to her. He took great care over the letter, trying to strike a note that was friendly but not presumptuous, persuasive but not condescending, and personal but befitting his status. He explained why it was not feasible to do what she demanded, using the examples of England and the Netherlands to illustrate the point, and ended on a note of friendship aimed at reassuring her. 'You cannot have meant, in elevating my person, to raise a target for your arms,' he summed up. 'But I entreat you to take note of the fact that if all that Prince Repnin has threatened is carried out, there can be no middle course for me. I must expose myself to your blows, or I would betray my nation and my duty. You would not have wanted me to be king if I were capable of the latter. The thunderbolt is in your hand, but will you cast it on the innocent head of him who of all men has been for so long the most tenderly and the most sincerely attached to you?'[32]

Catherine was not prepared to listen to anything but a grovelling capitulation. 'Vain of past successes, giddy with present prospects, blind and incredulous to the possibility of a reverse, this court becomes every day more intoxicated with pride, more contemptuous towards other

Powers, more elated with her own,' as Sir George Macartney, the English ambassador in St Petersburg, put it.[33] Her reply to Stanisław consisted of a lecture. 'The only motive that guides me', she wrote, 'is the desire to do good for its own sake, with no other aim but your personal tranquillity and the salvation of your country.' She was 'surprised that you have found yourself embarrassed in choosing between my friendship and these duties that you imagine to be in conflict with it'. And she finished in tones of righteous indignation. 'It is useless to reason with those who do not even wish to listen. The only course that remains open to me is to leave this affair to its own fate . . . I close my eyes on the results and the consequences.'[34]

Stanisław was shattered. 'May God always keep you by my side; I shall be a better person for it,' Catherine had once said to him, and the words haunted him with bitter irony now. 'What sadness to watch one of the Creator's fine works degenerate and grow deformed,' he commented to Madame Geoffrin.[35] But he could not afford to close his eyes and await the worst, and he desperately sought a way out of the crisis. Catherine's demands on behalf of the dissenters had to be put forward in the Seym, and since he would not do it himself he devised a stratagem. He suggested that Repnin should come to the Seym and present them himself. This would have the twin advantages of divorcing the demands from the king and of making it very clear who was making them, and therefore what consequences attended their rejection. Benoit, who was promoted to the rank of minister plenipotentiary for the purpose, would do the same on behalf of his Prussian master, and his English, Swedish and Danish colleagues would follow suit. Repnin did not like the idea, but had to go along with it, since otherwise the demands would not be presented at all.[36]

On 2 October, a few days before the Seym, Stanisław held a meeting of senators in an effort to gain support for a deal he still hoped he might be able to strike with Repnin, but while most of them were prepared to back him in a compromise, nobody believed the Seym, let alone the country, would accept this.[37] The Seym opened on 6 October 1766, and at the first opportunity Sołtyk weighed in with a harangue and a proposal for a new law: that anyone suggesting to increase the rights of dissenters should be attainted. A number of deputies and senators demanded that it be entered in the statute books there and then. Stanisław managed to avert this by rising to speak. He was proud to be king of a nation which was so devoted to its faith, for which he too would gladly lay down his life, he declared. But this was not the right moment to discuss the matter or legislate on the issue, as there were a number of formal points to be got through first. He then announced the nomination of Stanisław Lubomirski as Grand Marshal of Poland, and brought on his investiture, which took two hours and cooled tempers.

Stanisław wanted to distract the Seym with political business, in the hope that this might relegate the dissenter issue. But Repnin had decided to block his reforms, and instructed a fervent republican, Michał Wielhorski, to demand the dissolution of the confederation in the Seym. The Familia had gauged Catherine's mood and decided on a change of tactic. They concluded that there was no hope of pushing through more reforms, and that further moves in that direction would probably provoke Russia into insisting on rescinding all those brought in since 1764. August Czartoryski suggested dissolving the confeder-ation immediately. This would guarantee the survival of the extant legislation, and would also make it impossible for the enfranchisement to be brought forward. It would be a neat way of defusing the whole crisis. All the members of the Familia present agreed, but Stanisław, urged on by Kazimierz, accused his uncles of betraying him and letting down the common cause. Despite their misgivings, they agreed to support him.

Since the Czartoryskis wished to keep a low profile, it was Zamoyski who presented the king's programme, the most important elements of which were the replacement of the General Tariff, abolished to placate Frederick, with a levy on spirits, and the transfer of decisions on taxation beyond the reach of the veto. The latter was brought up on 15 October, but Repnin and Benoit 'caught the alarm' in Wroughton's words.[38] They spent that evening driving round to the houses of deputies and threatening them, and in the morning Repnin had 'a lively altercation' with Stanisław. This 'had such an effect on His Majesty's health, that he was taken ill in the Senate', according to Wroughton. But the real reason for his being taken ill was that he was approached by Adam Czartoryski during a lull in the morning's debate and informed that the Familia had decided to vote against the project and to abandon the programme of reforms after all.[39]

Stanisław spent the whole of the next day in conference with them, and late in the afternoon a compromise was reached. The Familia would not resist if Repnin demanded that the confederation be dissolved, but until then they would support further reforms proposed on the king's behalf by Zamoyski, and would make a determined stand if Repnin tried to touch any of those enacted already.[40] Stanisław felt that if he showed weakness now he would never achieve anything. He was being goaded on by his friends, and particularly by his brothers. The feeling that he was battling against all the elements at once inspired a dogged determination that blinded him to the dangers of the situation. He was nearing physical and nervous exhaustion. The Seym's sessions, which began at 3 p.m., lasted late into the night, or rather into the early hours, sometimes not ending before 9 a.m. the following day. The marshal, who could not leave, actually collapsed on one occasion. Stanisław battled on, showing remarkable skill in manœuvring his own supporters and the wavering deputies of the Familia, contending with the religious fanatics led by Sołtyk. Outside the chamber, Stanisław was being ground down in the daily round of attrition with Repnin, who threatened, nagged and comforted alternately. In the last week of October Stanisław was fighting to replace the abolished Tariff with a levy on spirits, but Benoit and Repnin had worked out that this would increase the Crown's revenues dramatically, and they managed to get their clients to emasculate the measure. Stanisław was deeply upset by this reverse, and confided his sorrow to Wroughton, who urged him to abandon his programme. But Stanisław could not bring himself to give up his dream of reform.

On 4 November, Repnin came to the Seym to read out Catherine's demands on behalf of the dissenters, amid scenes of uproar which were barely contained by his own threats and Stanisław's calming speeches. Benoit followed suit a week later. On 11 November they handed the Seym a memorandum from their sovereigns protesting against the proposal to limit the veto. Stanisław was desperate but defiant. He circulated a pamphlet which he had prepared beforehand, *Considerations of a Good Citizen on the Memorandum presented by the ministers of Russia and Prussia on 11 November 1766*. It advocated resistance to foreign pressure, and although it was not signed, many, including Repnin, knew who the author was.

Stanisław was openly defying Russia. Wroughton was terrified by this 'impolitick and ill-timed heroism' and reported to London that 'I have so long loved and admired, and still love and admire this monarch for the many distinguished qualifications of his heart and head, that it gives me pain to write anything derogatory of these sentiments, but his obstinacy in this particular, as well as in the general tenor of his conduct, since the first mention of the project, has been so entirely injudicious and contrary to common policy, that I am afraid that not only his essential interests will suffer, but his reputation in foreign countries likewise.'[41]

Stanisław seems to have thought that he could rally the nation to his call, but public opinion saw him as a creature of Russia, many could not distinguish the issues, which had become fudged, and not a few took fright before the looming showdown, with the result that he found himself isolated. Those who were not abandoning him urged him to climb down. Andrzej Zamoyski explained that it was folly even to consider resistance with only 16,000 poorly equipped troops and the hetmans in opposition, while there were thousands of Russian soldiers in Poland, and many more available at a moment's notice. 'When the position of the country does not permit us to act as we should wish, then we must act as we must, and conceal the fact that we aspire to be strong,' he and Lubomirski wrote to Stanisław. 'To resist without force is to expose the nation and the Crown to obvious misfortune.'[42] But Stanisław's pride and defiance had been aroused.

So had Catherine's. She saw treachery everywhere, and railed at the 'intrigues' of the Czartoryskis. 'They really are trying to swindle us, but they won't get away with it,' she noted in the margin of one of Repnin's reports. All she could see was that those who were supposed to be making up her party in Poland were pushing through their own programme while ignoring her demands. Her patience was at an end, and she instructed Repnin to look for new allies.[43] The anti-dissenter camp, including Bishop Sołtyk, was also opposed to most of the proposed reforms, and would be happy to wreck the Seym for him. But he preferred to keep them in reserve and act through the king. He called on Stanisław and told him that he would let his soldiers loose on the population if he persisted in his stance. He had located the king's weakest point. 'I found myself in the singular, and very horrible, predicament of having to sacrifice my honour to my duty,' Stanisław wrote to Madame Geoffrin.[44] There was nothing for it but to climb down.

On 22 November, at Repnin's bidding, a cowed Seym passed an act safeguarding the veto from further encroachments. Only about a dozen deputies actually voted while 'all the others said nothing, their faces overcast with gloom'.[45] As Stanisław left the Chamber, Repnin came up to thank him for his co-operation. Stanisław could not restrain himself and burst into tears. That evening he told Wroughton that neither his life nor his crown were of any value to him any more.[46]

But if Stanisław had seen his work destroyed, Catherine and Repnin fared little better. Two days after the vote reaffirming the veto, and just before it dissolved itself at Repnin's behest, the Seym spontaneously voted in a law proposed by Sołtyk which confirmed in perpetuity all the disabilities of the dissenters. Russia had defeated her own aims.

11

Rebellion

A pall of gloom hung over Warsaw as winter turned into the spring of 1767. The carnival that year lacked gaiety, and the king did not dance. Stanisław's work lay in ruins. He was in a ridiculous position, powerless now that his Russian ally had turned against him. For all their political experience and cunning, the Familia too had got nowhere. Russia had demonstrated that she was master, but that was as far as it went. Her policy was in shreds, and her behaviour was giving other powers cause for alarm.

On 12 November 1766 Sir George Macartney had reported his misgivings over Russia's 'imperious and dictatorial' attitude, and warned that 'despair may at last, oblige the Poles to throw themselves into the hands of any other Power that can protect them'. Rumours had reached him that Austria had been proposing alliance and a marriage to Stanisław, and spies reported nocturnal comings and goings of couriers between Warsaw and Vienna.[1] Stanisław was indeed angling for Austrian support, but Maria Theresa was afraid of involvement, Joseph II was indifferent, and only Kaunitz was alarmed enough at Russia's behaviour to consider combining with Prussia in order to check it. But Frederick was nervous. On 28 December he urged Solms to persuade Panin to climb down. The interests of the dissenters were unimportant, '*une bagatelle*' as he put it, in the face of the possibility of war breaking out. And he warned that there was plenty of justification for anyone wishing to intervene in Poland. 'What would Panin say if France were to invade Holland in order to force the Estates-General to admit the Papists to the public charges?'[2]

Catherine was in no mood for compromise. 'She has been too often led to believe that the resistance she encounters in certain matters is the fault of people rather than circumstances,' Stanisław Lubomirski noted.[3] In this instance she blamed Stanisław. 'Her Imperial Majesty now perceives in all the king's protestations, actions and suggestions since his accession to the throne only a determined plan to achieve ends concealed from her,' as Panin put it, and she told Repnin to press on.[4] Repnin's youth, his lack of experience and his violent temperament ill suited his delicate job in Warsaw, and denied him the qualifications to unravel the crisis he had helped to provoke. He had painted himself into a corner. His increasingly desperate efforts to break out of this corner over the next year were to turn the crisis into a civil war and a European conflict.

In his fear of allowing the king to grow too powerful, Repnin had undermined Stanisław's authority, and his ability to promote *any* policy, let alone Russia's. Having arranged the dissolution of the Seym, he had left himself with no instrument with which to carry on his work. On 20 December 1766, Panin wrote to the Czartoryskis asking them to form a confederation which could push through the legislation on the dissenter issue and restore Russian influence. The Czartoryskis declined. The plan was unrealistic, and they would not work against the king. Repnin tried to bully them, but this produced no effect. He then changed tack and suggested to Stanisław that his uncles were betraying him, and that he should construct a confederation without them, with his brother Kazimierz as leader. Kazimierz had been discouraged by the débâcle of 1766, and now accepted with resignation, not to say cynicism, the inevitability of Russian domination in Poland. But he lacked popularity, so Repnin looked elsewhere, to the malcontents.

Stanisław's reforms had hit all the magnates very hard. They had lost their private armies, and their power to intimidate law-courts and local szlachta. They could see that the king's policies would lead not only to their own eclipse, but to the transformation of a whole way of life. This was not something they would give up without a fight.

After his discomfiture at the Convocation Seym of 1764, Karol Radziwiłł had gone into exile, while his lands were sequestered and administered in trust by the state. He had not ceased to petition

Catherine for favour, and now Repnin extended a friendly hand. He offered Radziwiłł, who was waiting in Dresden, full reinstatement. He also promised the hetmans Branicki, Rzewuski and Sapieha restoration of their former powers. He sought out members of the old Saxon party such as ex-Treasurer Teodor Wessel, Jerzy Mniszech, the Krasińskis and the Potockis, who still refused to acknowledge Stanisław as king, and even approached Bishop Sołtyk. Repnin assured them that the reforms they hated so much would be rescinded. The real bait were his heavy hints that Catherine was prepared to remove Stanisław from the throne if they co-operated. He did not go into details and managed to make it all sound very easy. As a result, at the end of February 1767, Radziwiłł wrote to Repnin agreeing to work for him.

Stanisław got wind of these negotiations, and on 3 May cornered Repnin at a ball. The ambassador was evasive, but eventually admitted that he was planning a confederation by the malcontents. Stanisław pointed out that this was a revolt against his rule, and warned him of the dangers of creating a confederation which he would never be able to control. The ambassador replied cockily that he knew how to control them. This alarmed Stanisław, who asked what the bait was. Repnin avoided answering. 'They are in my clutches, they will obey me blindly,' he declared, adding that he did not need the king and preferred to work with people who could guarantee results.[5] He promptly set about the preliminaries of his new plan. On 20 March 1767 two confederations of dissenters were proclaimed under the protection of Russian troops – one at Słuck in Lithuania and one at Toruń in Poland – numbering fewer than 500 szlachta in all. Their purpose was to demand rights for the dissenters.

Stanisław saw a chance of outmanœuvring Repnin and the malcontents before their plans were set. By calling the nation to arms against the dissenters and their Russian patrons, he might at a stroke win back the popularity and support of the vast majority of Poles and prevent the malcontents from forming their confederation. He was sorely tempted, but such a course would inevitably lead to war with Russia, with catastrophic consequences. 'I do all I can to keep my head very cool, and I tell myself fifty times a day that the pursuit of glory is foolishness,' he wrote to Madame Geoffrin. 'To do good, to aim for good results, that is what is needed, whatever people will say. Glory will come later, when the greatest good, or at least the lesser evil will have been achieved.'[6]

On 23 June the malcontents and their henchmen, assembled at Radom, proclaimed a confederation under the marshalcy of Karol Radziwiłł. They were surrounded by 15,000 Russian troops, and their manifesto was dictated to them by a Russian colonel. Its contents were vague enough to allow the leaders to dream that they would be allowed to take power and restore the good old ways of the Saxon era. They were too excited by the prospect to worry about details, and their supporters too shy to ask. It is hard to overestimate the popularity of people such as the venerable, though senile, Hetman Branicki and Karol Radziwiłł among the szlachta. Referred to by all as Karol 'My Dear' Radziwiłł on account of his habit of addressing everyone so, this affable alcoholic, warm-hearted, reckless and generous, had all the qualifications for their esteem.

The confederates of Radom were to assemble as a new Seym at Warsaw in the autumn, and in the mean time they could go home and repossess their estates. Karol Radziwiłł returned to Lithuania like a homecoming hero, although a strong Russian 'escort' did not leave his side. It really had been, as Benoit called it, '*la journée des dupes*'.[7] While Repnin still hinted at Stanisław's dethronement in private, nothing was openly stated. A delegation sent to St Petersburg by the Confederation of Radom to thank the empress for her support were surprised to discover that she had no plans to remove the king.

Catherine believed that by threatening him with the stick of the Radomians, she would bring Stanisław back to heel. While ostensibly working with the malcontents, Repnin therefore continued to press the king and the Familia throughout the spring of 1767 to collaborate. The Czartoryskis maintained an olympian aloofness. But Stanisław had realised, too late, that Catherine would stop at nothing to get her legislation on the dissenters, and he also realised that Frederick was poised to profit from any turmoil in Poland, for if Russia lost control of her Polish satellite, she would invoke Prussian assistance, and that would carry a price – to be paid by Poland. It was not in his nature to take offence at fate or seek solace in disdainful righteousness. Stanisław had his faults, but irresponsibility was not one of them. 'It is my duty not to leave the tiller while I live, however painful and bitter that job might be,' he wrote to Madame Geoffrin. He also believed in his star, and in the providential purpose of his life. 'I shall reach port, with difficulty no doubt and not without losses; but I shall get there, my heart tells me so, and my duty orders me not to relax my grip,' he added.[8]

He knew that Repnin's attempt to create a reliable party out of the malcontents would end in fiasco, and by the beginning of the summer the ambassador's cockiness crumbled as he too began to perceive it. Russia needed Stanisław, and that need was Stanisław's principal asset. Distasteful and humiliating as it might be to have to work with the likes of Karol Radziwiłł, he decided to co-operate. Catherine was so delighted at this 'return' that she declared her amenability to various concessions. 'My feelings towards Your Majesty, like my efforts to see you perfectly happy and tranquil, have never varied,' she wrote to him at the end of June.[9] To Repnin she wrote that all attacks on Stanisław must cease, and that there was to be no more talk of toppling him or reducing his prerogatives.[10] 'I do not ask of you a cooperation that would proclaim itself loudly,' Catherine assured Stanisław, sensing the delicacy of his position, 'but an interior and sincere cooperation.'[11] At the same time she reminded him that on the subject of the dissenters she was 'committed to the point of no return'. Stanisław nevertheless pressed her to reduce her demands on behalf of the dissenters to an acceptable minimum, and at the same time he put forward a new idea.

Since the very mention of tampering with the veto provoked unease in Berlin and St Petersburg, Stanisław decided to leave it alone and try another tack. It had always been his intention to create some form of cabinet government. He had originally approached this problem by the most constitutional and therefore, to the Poles at least, acceptable, means – through the gradual reform of the Seym, the Senate and the Senate Council. But he now suggested creating a council drawn from the Seym and Senate that could provide continuous government. Repnin liked the idea. The impossibility of controlling the 300 deputies and senators made him amenable to any concentration of decision-making in a smaller body. Even the malcontents liked the idea when they were consulted, since they assumed it would be a good framework for their oligarchy. Stanisław therefore went ahead and produced a draft project at the beginning of September. This envisaged a council made up of the king, the ministers and a few senators and deputies, with supplementary commissions for areas such as the army and the Treasury. Repnin referred the project to St Petersburg, where it met with approval. Stanisław began to feel hopeful once more.

At the end of the summer Karol Radziwiłł turned up in Warsaw and took up residence in his palace, surrounded by a battalion of Russian soldiers. Throughout September he and Michał Brzostowski, the marshal of the Lithuanian confederation, attended daily conferences with Stanisław, Repnin, Kazimierz Poniatowski, Michał Poniatowski and Ksawery Branicki. (Andrzej Poniatowski had left Warsaw after the end of the 1766 Seym, and settled in Vienna.) The king invited Zamoyski and Borch to attend, but they refused out of solidarity with Michał Czartoryski, Przeździecki and Stanisław Lubomirski, who had been barred at Repnin's insistence. The aim of these conferences was to prepare the ground for the enfranchisement of dissenters. A major problem was how to neutralise the Church hierarchy.

The Primate Władysław Łubieński had died in 1766, and Repnin persuaded Stanisław to nominate as his successor Gabriel Podoski, a creature as corrupt and servile as he could wish for. Most of the other bishops had acceded to the Confederation of Radom, mainly out of mistrust for the king's reformist and pro-Russian tendencies. But they had no idea that in doing so they had joined a body whose sole purpose was to enfranchise the dissenters. Bishops Sołtyk, Turski, Załuski and Krasiński continued to publish strident manifestos about the defence of the faith. Many of the deputies to the impending Seym, including those elected on the Radomian ticket, were highly susceptible to religious propaganda and increasingly unhappy about the Russian troops infesting the capital. Radziwiłł himself was in a state of confusion as to where he stood. Left to itself, the Seym would turn into a forum for protest. As Stanisław had predicted, Repnin would never be able to control it. With Stanisław's help, he devised a stratagem that would permit him to bypass it. He proposed that the Seym appoint a delegation to discuss and frame the legislation. This would then be rubber-stamped by the Seym. It was without constitutional precedent, but then virtually everything done in the past ten months had been unconstitutional.

Things got off to a poor start. At the first session of the Seym, on 2 October, one deputy protested about the presence of Russian troops.

He was arrested on leaving. The following day Radziwiłł called on Repnin to protest. 'Behave yourself, or you will meet with a similar fate,' Repnin told him.[12] On the same day Stanisław called a conference of ministers and leaders of the Familia to reveal the plan for the Seym delegation. When he had finished explaining it, there was a long silence. 'Where there is need for good counsel, there should be no silence,' he said. Lubomirski asked whether the project could be altered, but Stanisław replied that it had already been fixed. 'In that case there is no need for counsel, only for acknowledging that it is the perdition of this nation,' Lubomirski said. To which Zamoyski added: 'We should, and I propose that we do, tell our nation honestly, without mincing words, that we are submitting in everything to a neighbouring Power.' Similar sentiments were voiced by the two Czartoryskis and Przeździecki. Stanisław was dismayed. He tried to persuade them that in the circumstances it was right to embrace the lesser evil, but it was no good.[13]

On 5 October, after endless disputes about procedure, which Repnin's and Radziwiłł's actions violated at every turn, the Seym opened its session. But Repnin's plans were upset at the very outset, when the new Papal Nuncio, Angelo Durini, burst into the chamber and delivered a harangue. He roused the zeal of the deputies to such a pitch that they wanted to swear an oath in defence of the faith there and then. He showered apostolic blessings on them and left the chamber in a state of turmoil. Hearing of this, Repnin turned up to restore order. He was met with remonstrations and demands for the freeing of the arrested deputy. 'If your petitions will not move me, then neither will your barking, for I can bite as well as bark!' he yelled from the gallery.[14] The chamber quietened down and the king took his seat. Radziwiłł opened the proceedings by proposing that the Seym thank the empress for the interest she took in Polish affairs, and ask her to guarantee the Polish constitution. He then put forward the project for the Seym to hand over its powers to a delegation. Bishop Sołtyk denounced the project, seconded by Hetman Wacław Rzewuski and the bishops of Lwów and Chełm. They, and most of the chamber, protested against any delegated body being given powers to legislate on behalf of the Seym.

The next days passed in fruitless negotiation. Stanisław's influence over events was slipping, and his support in the Seym was dwindling.

His brother Kazimierz and Ksawery Branicki went about lobbying, saying that 'anyone who holds the king dear must agree to all that Moscow wants'.[15] On 8 October Stanisław sent Radziwiłł to negotiate with Michał Czartoryski. Radziwiłł called Czartoryski 'father of the nation', and invited him to join in the task of saving the country in its moment of peril. Czartoryski refused. That night Russian troops moved into his estate of Wołczyn and August Czartoryski's Wilanów. Repnin was in an evil mood, and his patience was nearing its limit. He was daily despatching orders to the Russian commander, General Krechetnikov, to occupy one estate or ravage another.[16] He told a gathering of the king's supporters that he would stop at nothing to achieve his aims, and that he did not care if he had to reduce the country to rubble with his army in the process. He ordered more troops into the capital and set up a cordon running all the way round it, which allowed people in but not out. The city itself was beginning to resemble a military encampment, with bivouacs in the streets and pickets at every corner. At night, they would stop carriages and question their occupants, either detaining them or ordering them back home.

Nothing had been resolved when the Seym reconvened on 12 October. Stanisław delivered a speech on the looming perils, stating that the choice now lay solely between the greater and the lesser of two evils, but the inflamed chamber would not listen. Getting nowhere, Stanisław adjourned the session. Repnin was at his wits' end. His threats were having no effect, and none of his clients was doing as they were told. He decided to act.

On the evening of 13 October Bishop Sołtyk was having dinner with Jerzy Mniszech. Soon after eleven o'clock, as he was preparing to go home, he was advised that there was so much soldiery in the streets it would be better to stay the night. A room was prepared. But just as the bishop was about to undress, a violent battering resounded through the palace, followed by the sound of boots pounding up stairs. The bishop went to join Mniszech in his study. The doors flew open with a crash, and Russian grenadiers burst into the room, led by Colonel Igelström, who announced that he had orders to arrest the Bishop of Kraków. Sołtyk was led out, bundled into a carriage, and driven off to Repnin's embassy under heavy escort. Igelström then went after the Bishop of Kiev. His troops forced their way in, woke up Załuski, and

159

dragged him off likewise. Another detachment of several hundred Russian troops, both foot and horse, had gone to the Rzewuski palace, which they stormed with bayonets fixed. The hetman was woken and told to dress. He and his son Seweryn were then taken off to the embassy as well. The four prisoners were immediately sent off to the Russian camp across the Vistula, whence in the morning they were despatched in haste to Kaluga in Russia. Repnin had in fact wanted to arrest Bishop Turski of Chełm, but the relatively harmless Załuski was taken instead by mistake. Another who escaped the net was Adam Krasiński, Bishop of Kamieniec, who was on his way to Warsaw, but received warning just outside the city. He immediately donned a disguise and made his way back to Kamieniec, and thence abroad.

The next morning churches filled with people, and a large crowd gathered outside Sołtyk's palace, where Igelström and his men were going through the bishop's papers. There was uproar and indignation. Every conceivable legal principle had been violated, the Seym had been affronted, as had the majesty of the king and the Commonwealth. Groups of deputies met and passed resolutions, while Repnin issued more threats and Colonel Carr let it be known that 'this is not the end of the matter, and more heads will roll'.[17] On 15 October, a body of senators and deputies came to the king, asking him to demand the release of the four senators and a guarantee of the Seym's immunity. Stanisław had already done so, but his request was dismissed by Repnin, who said that he answered for his actions only to the empress. In a letter to Stanisław, Catherine claimed that Repnin's 'act of authority' had been fully justified. 'I must show myself to Europe and above all to your nation as a just and impartial sovereign, determined to keep her promises, incapable of betraying the interests of the freedom of the Commonwealth,' she wrote.[18]

Chancellor Zamoyski declared that in the circumstances he could neither usefully serve the king with his counsel nor fulfil his ministerial function. He laid the great seal of state in its velvet bag on the table before Stanisław, who tried to talk him out of the step, but Zamoyski cut him short by stooping to kiss his hand, and left. He was replaced at Repnin's insistence by Andrzej Młodziejowski, 'a man well suited to seal the downfall of the country', according to one contemporary.[19]

At the next sitting of the Seym Stanisław Rzewuski demanded the release of his father and brother, while others clamoured for the freedom of the bishops. Michał Czartoryski and Lubomirski threatened to resign like Zamoyski. But Repnin, leaning out of the spectators' gallery, merely threatened to arrest more people and confiscate their estates. The recognition of their impotence soon cooled the ardour of the body politic. Stanisław made a speech recommending acceptance of a situation from which there was no way out, and closed the session. That evening Russian officers called on those who were expected to cause trouble, telling them they would meet with the same treatment as the four senators if they did not toe the line. On 19 October a docile Seym agreed to delegate four ministers, twelve senators and forty-eight deputies under the presidency of the Primate to discuss and agree the Russian demands. The Seym then adjourned for four months.

'I used to feel pride in saying I was a Pole, now I am ashamed of it,' people would say to James Harris, an English diplomat passing through Warsaw.[20] At the same time, an atmosphere of febrile hedonism vied with the mood of despondency that prevailed in most quarters, as Repnin's clients spent the cash with which he was retaining their support. On St Catherine's day, Radziwiłł gave a ball at which, as well as a quantity of other wines, a thousand bottles of champagne were drunk.[21] Stanisław felt the humiliation more keenly than most, but he was growing increasingly philosophical in the conviction that the more bitter the pill, the greater the merit in swallowing it. And he believed in its effects, for he was determined to exact a price for his co-operation.

The delegation nominated by the Seym, made up of a mixture of the king's men and Repnin's clients led by Primate Podoski, Radziwiłł and the new Chancellor Młodziejowski, met at Repnin's embassy, always in his presence. He was so energetic and quick to quell any protest with brutal threats that the delegation bent to his will. Stanisław used his supporters within it to influence some decisions, but in the main he elected to further his own aims outside it, by direct negotiation with Repnin. What he wanted was to ensure the survival of the reforms passed to date, and to provide Poland with an executive cabinet, both of which were acceptable to Repnin. In a letter to Catherine, Repnin argued that rescinding the king's reforms 'will not only reduce our influence here, it will destroy it; it will leave a wound in the heart of all sensible and honourable people . . . and these are the only people on whom we may rely'. The effect of these words was not lost on Catherine, who noted in the margin of the letter: 'As long as we have the means of using the liberum veto when we need to, there is no reason why we should not allow our neighbours some other system which is indifferent to us.'[22]

Having cowed Stanisław, Catherine could now afford to indulge him a little – in fact, she needed to in what had become a somewhat fluid international situation. After the arrest of the four senators, the Prussian ministry had decided that Repnin had 'spoiled things from the beginning by his misplaced violence'.[23] Cautious yet wily, Frederick wrote to Benoit instructing him to keep options open, so that Prussia might take advantage of a Russian débâcle in Poland.[24] In October Catherine wrote to Stanisław that she would like to see 'a closer intimacy' between their two countries, and Panin began to hint at a dynastic union of some sort.[25] But if these utterances were calculated to fan the dying embers of Stanisław's dreams of marrying Catherine, they did not signify a change of policy. Panin instructed Repnin to keep an eye open for any attempts at tampering with the veto, and suggested that Stanisław be left with an effective memento of his betrayal of Russia in the previous year, in the shape of some loss of power.[26] Stanisław's idea of a permanent council was a casualty of this. Frederick had smelt a rat and began warning Russia that Stanisław was up to his tricks. Panin was not prepared to stand up for Stanisław and in January 1768 he wrote to Repnin instructing him to abort the plan.[27]

The Seym met again on 1 February 1768, but since the delegation had not finished its work, it adjourned for another three weeks. Those deputies who had tried to speak up were interrupted and warned by Repnin's officers that they would be flogged, trussed and sent to Siberia. It was not until 27 February that the Seym assembled once more. 'The coup d'oeil striking,' noted Harris. 'The idea of a whole nation thus represented is aweful – but how much was my respect diminished when I saw in the same room as myself, which had a window that looked into the hall, the Russian Ambassador attended by four or five generals who watched all that passed, and seemed, by putting out their heads every now and then, to menace any that presumed to oppose!'[28]

The delegation's proposals were read out. They took the form of an 'eternal treaty' with Russia. This included legislation emancipating the dissenters. It also included a full constitution expressed in a number of 'Cardinal Laws' on the other. These defined, in a list of 'matters of state', all areas in which the veto must obtain, including currency rates and trade treaties. 'These Cardinal Laws may not be altered at any time, under any pretext, by whomsoever, not even by confederations, nor during interregna, not even by unanimous voting,' ran the text, adding that 'he who would act against any of these laws shall be regarded as an enemy of the motherland.'[29] The treaty was a mean-minded document which reads like a set of prohibitions elaborated by a nanny whose nursery rules have been bent by children more intelligent than she. When the reading was over, on 5 March, Karol Radziwiłł asked the chamber for its assent. Five or six voices mumbled agreement, the rest remained silent. Radziwiłł then closed the Seym, and later that day got roaring drunk.

The Cardinal Laws condemned Poland to constitutional stagnation. But while the veto was reaffirmed, the limitations imposed on it in 1764 were largely left intact, as were a number of the administrative changes made since. This was a minor triumph for Stanisław. And it was by no means the only one, as he had managed to put through several useful measures in the lee of the dissenter legislation. Permanent Supreme Tribunals were instituted, and a vast quantity of legal business was despatched. The szlachta's right to pass the death sentence on their peasants in local courts was abolished. Seym procedure was simplified and fixed. Acts were passed on the proper funding of the Cadet Corps, on the paving and lighting of Warsaw, the repair of roads and bridges, fortresses and arsenals, as well as the royal castles of Warsaw, Kraków and Grodno. A project by Michał Ogiński to dig an important canal was approved. Tax exemption was granted to new factories. An academy of medicine was to be established at Warsaw, and a new hospital set up in Wilno. A million złoty were earmarked for the diplomatic service. Expenditure on the army was boosted dramatically. A reorganisation of the national cavalry was approved, but shelved on account of traditionalist hostility in the ranks. Taxation was raised to cover a budget nearly three times as high as previous ones. Unfortunately Repnin also made the Seym vote vast gifts to Radziwiłł and all those who had served him.

Though bruised and battered, Stanisław was almost sanguine,

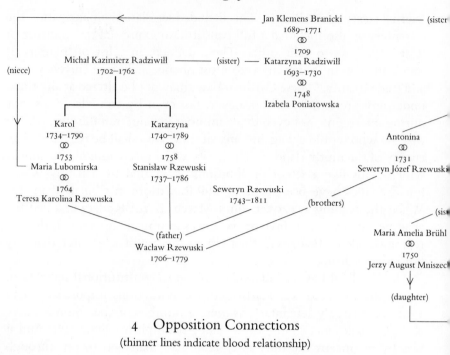

4   Opposition Connections
(thinner lines indicate blood relationship)

having saved a remarkable amount from the political shipwreck. He was far too pragmatic and long-sighted to dwell on the humiliations. 'My heart tells me that before I die I shall after all see some happier days, and that I will do some real good for my country, which may not give me credit for it until after I am gone,' he wrote to Madame Geoffrin.[30] Although the road to further reforms was blocked, he would be able to continue with the non-political parts of his programme. The crisis had been seen off, and Catherine's face had been saved. She could now go back to her preferred role. 'Her Imperial Majesty, graciously responding to the wishes and the amicable trust of the Most Illustrious Commonwealth, solemnly guarantees by this treaty for all time its constitution, form of government, freedoms and laws, and solemnly promises and binds herself and her successors on the throne of the Empire of All Russia, to support, guard and protect the Most Illustrious Polish Commonwealth in its entirety and integrity.'[31] This at least closed the door on any territorial designs Frederick might nurture.

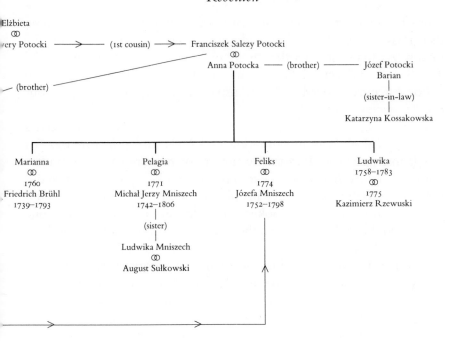

On 7 March, two days after the final session of the Seym, Repnin called on Stanisław accompanied by Primate Podoski, Radziwiłł, Franciszek Potocki and other prominent Radomians. He ceremoniously recommended them to the king's favour, declaring that 'the work of the empress is done; her friends in Poland are now and will forever remain Your Majesty's most faithful subjects'.[32] Repnin, Catherine and Panin congratulated themselves and each other on having brought the matter to a successful conclusion, and Russian troops began to withdraw at once. Their confidence could hardly have been more misplaced.

The malcontents were a motley crew united by bonds of friendship, marriage, outlook, allegiance to the house of Saxony, or just repugnance at the election of Stanisław. Most were convinced republicans who resented the encroachments of central authority under any form. These sentiments far outweighed any feelings, hostile or otherwise, towards Russia or other powers. Beneath these motives lurked a more general urge to return to the anarchy of the old days, which had suited their class so well. Those days had not necessarily been halcyon for the minor szlachta, but even they were overcome by a certain nostalgia. The Saxon era seemed like an age of innocence in contrast to the political depravity displayed by Russia and her agents in the previous couple of years.

To the masses of country szlachta unaware of the political niceties being argued in Warsaw, the king and the Familia appeared as the servile instruments of Russia, and their reforms were viewed as limitations of personal freedom. The idea of the state being strengthened did not get through to those very people, the minor szlachta, who would benefit most. 'Nobody looked at their utility, while everyone bemoaned the violence done to the freedoms, customs and ancient laws of the country, and also to the will of the nation,' noted a Scots observer.[33] From the middle of 1766, the clergy, particularly the mendicant orders, began to reinforce the swell of suspicion towards the reformers in Warsaw, denouncing the king's motives from the pulpit, representing his court as a den of vice, accusing him of every kind of debauchery, and arguing that far from being the anointed of God, he was the tool of the Devil. When news of the imprisonment of Sołtyk, Załuski and the two Rzewuskis spread through the land, responsibility was pinned on Stanisław, who now appeared to be waging war on civil liberty and the Catholic Faith. The Russian treaty of guarantee passed on 5 March 1768 was the last straw.

That the Confederation of Radom had been responsible for extending the Russian grip on the country did not, curiously enough, discredit its leaders. They had been taken in, and they laid the blame at the door of the king. There was nothing rational in it, as one contemporary pointed out:

In the midst of so many misfortunes people looked for a scapegoat. And whom did they find most guilty? The king. For what reason? For the results of the 1768 Seym, for the guarantee. Who was responsible for that Seym? Russia. Who insisted on the guarantee? Russia. Who was tricked? The Confederation of Radom. In what were they tricked? In that Russia did not help them to dethrone the king. And why did Russia promise to dethrone the king? Because he wanted to make Poland independent of Russia.[34]

Some of the malcontents, like Radziwiłł, merely wanted to get rid of the king and the Familia. Others had been more consistent, aiming to get rid of the Russian protectorate as well as the king. A number of them, including the old Hetman Branicki, Jerzy Mniszech, Teodor Wessel, Joachim Potocki, Franciszek Potocki, Franciszek Wielopolski, Adam and Michał Krasiński, and Paweł Mostowski, had been carrying on negotiations with Austria, Turkey, and, most importantly, with France, which had suddenly woken up and decided that she must reassume an active role in Poland. They had begun to hatch plans for an armed rising once the Russian troops had withdrawn. Bishop Adam Krasiński, the most clear-sighted of them, had gone to France in December 1767 in quest of French and Austrian support, without which he believed any action to be pointless.

His departure left the field open to hotter heads. While the delegation sat and negotiated with Repnin through the winter of 1767–8, people throughout the country had been meeting and plotting. Towards the end of February, a couple of hundred szlachta congregated at the little town of Bar in Podolia, where a few of the ringleaders had retired. The most senior of these was Bishop Krasiński's slow-witted and stubborn brother Michał. Another was Józef Pułaski, once a follower of the Familia, later a supporter of the Saxon dynasty, and most recently a Radomian. Disregarding the bishop's advice to do nothing until the Russian forces had left Poland, they decided the time for action had come. On 29 February, they announced at Bar the continuation of the 'true' Confederation of Radom, with a manifesto which declared that they were fighting 'In defence of the motherland, the faith and liberty' – not a sentiment any Pole could honestly quarrel with.[35]

News of this reached Warsaw on 5 March, the day the Radziwiłł Seym came to an end, but nobody was greatly alarmed. Stanisław merely ordered all units in the area to stand by.[36] Repnin instructed General Krechetnikov's corps, which was withdrawing to Russia, to swing south through Podolia. He also demanded that Stanisław take action, which the king refused to do. On 21 March Repnin summoned a group of ministers and senators to his house, and told them to request the military assistance of the empress in putting down the trouble. He wrote out a draft for them to produce at the meeting of the Senate Council of 24 March. On the morning, Repnin sent a characteristic note to Lubomirski. 'I know that the Prince Grand Marshal of the Crown will be of a different opinion at the meeting of the Senate Council, because he is always opposed to me, and he will make difficulties; but I shall take away his palace if he does.'[37]

The Senate Council listened while a copy of Pułaski's manifesto was read out, and then to a report from Tadeusz Dzieduszycki, commander of the Crown troops in the area, in which he told of how he had been surrounded by rebels who had managed to sway some of his own detachments into joining them. The Primate suggested sending out someone to parley with the confederates, and the majority were in favour of Stanisław's advice to take no action until more was known of their demands and their strength.[38] But Repnin insisted they despatch the letter to the empress requesting military support. He had his way, but Czartoryski, Lubomirski and Przeździecki refused to sign it. Repnin began to move units into strategic areas in preparation for action, and sent one to Nieśwież to keep an eye on Karol Radziwiłł.

Stanisław had no wish to be precipitated into any action. 'As far as I can see, this spark will not start a conflagration,' he wrote to Madame Geoffrin. 'It is nevertheless highly vexing to be living always with a pump in one's hand, and to tread continually on warm ashes.'[39] On 2 April, he despatched Andrzej Mokronowski to Bar to negotiate. The rebels refused to talk to Mokronowski, but Stanisław still would not commit himself to action. 'I can see quite clearly that Your Majesty is not with us in his heart, and only awaits an opportunity to turn against us,' Repnin taunted him.[40] Stanisław wanted to avoid turning the rebellion into a civil war, and therefore thought it wise to keep the Polish army disengaged. But he could not delay taking action indefinitely. Rebel units had begun to attack Polish and Russian forces, and Russian troops went into action against them. Repnin repeated his demands for Polish commitment, not because he needed the military assistance of the Polish troops, but because he wanted to implicate them, and the king, on the Russian side. A nightmare that haunted him was the possibility that Stanisław and his army might join forces with the rebels.

The idea had crossed Stanisław's mind. Pułaski had actually written asking him to join the confederation, but this was probably only a ploy.[41] Stanisław and most of his entourage felt the same aversion to join with Russia against any group of Poles, and only

Michał Poniatowski advocated complete loyalty to Russia. But Repnin knew how to manipulate the king. On 16 May in a private interview he declared that he did not need the Polish army, having enough troops of his own to put down the rebellion, but, he added with intentional brutality, his troops would take no prisoners.[42] Stanisław was now faced with the dilemma of either letting the Russians waste the country and massacre the confederates or letting his own armies take the field and assume responsibility for dealing with the rebellion. He chose the latter course.

He ordered Ksawery Branicki to assume command over all Polish contingents in the area, enjoining him to avoid battles, to separate the confederates and the Russians wherever possible, and to do little more than contain the rebellion. 'I still hope that you will have little or no blood to shed,' he wrote to Branicki on 9 June. 'The less is spilt, the greater will be your honour.'[43] The crisis brought out all that was best in Branicki, who went about the business with courage and a great deal of discretion. But he could not avoid fighting. On 9 June he forced Kazimierz Pułaski, son of Józef Pułaski, to capitulate at Berdyczów, and on 20 June he took the town of Bar. The leaders of the confederation crossed the Dniester to the safety of Turkish territory, but on the very same day a rebel force captured Kraków. A few days later, on 28 June, a peasant revolt broke out in the Polish Ukraine. Tens of thousands of szlachta were slaughtered, and in one massacre at Humań, 15,000 Poles and some 30,000 Jews were put to death.[44] This had almost certainly been provoked by Russia in order to cow the szlachta of the south-eastern provinces.

The rebellion of Bar nevertheless continued to grow. Landless szlachta flocked to the confederate ranks, driven by obscure yet passionate stirrings of patriotism and religious zeal. Anti-Russian sentiment was running high, hatred or at best mistrust of the king and the politicians in Warsaw marched behind, and a dimly perceived threat to Poland's sovereignty brought up the rear, the whole bound together with conservatism, the bitterness of the magnates, and the grievances of the poor szlachta. Fanatical monks, such as the Dominican Father Marek Jandołowicz, added a mystical dimension, turning the movement into something of a crusade. It was the epidemic nature of these feelings which guaranteed the survival of the movement, which consisted of poorly armed bands, with no supplies, no bases, no strategy and no leadership. Over the next four years some 100,000 men would take a greater or lesser part in over 500 skirmishes.[45] No sooner was an outburst stamped out in one place than it erupted in another. Kraków was recaptured by General Apraxin in August, but in September Michał Pac and Karol Radziwiłł raised the standard of revolt in Lithuania.

The epidemic also refused to respond to treatment. Radziwiłł and his 4,000 private troops were soon encircled and forced to surrender. But, having pledged his loyalty to the king and promised to go home quietly, he and his associates promptly sneaked off to Moldavia to join the other Barians. In some cases, prisoners were treated harshly. After the fall of Bar the Russians sent off 1,200 to Siberia, and several thousand more met with the same fate after Apraxin took Kraków. General Drevitch and some of the other Russian commanders were more brutal, and Russian Cossack detachments were unaccountable.[46] But on the whole, and particularly in areas where Branicki was operating, captured rebels were disarmed, forced to abjure the confederation and bound over to keep the peace. When the troops had moved on, they would slip off to join other units. So although by the autumn of 1768 the original armed outbursts had been effectively put down, the movement was in no sense smothered. Indeed, it was only just beginning to grow.

Its weakness from the beginning lay in lack of leadership. The obvious candidate was Hetman Branicki, but he was eighty years old and senile. The magnates who did join the rebellion brought valuable weight, but little else. Few of them were prepared to work together, each wanting to lead on his own, and they all had markedly different views on what they were fighting for. The original leaders, Michał Krasiński, Joachim Potocki and others, had taken refuge on Turkish territory, from where they tried somewhat ineffectually to control the movement. In the following year Bishop Adam Krasiński managed to set up a headquarters at Biała on the Austrian border. Michał Krasiński and Michał Pac were the two marshals, with Joachim Potocki and Józef Sapieha as military commanders. But a few months later they were forced to move to Prešov (Eperyesz) in Hungary. Teodor Wessel, Franciszek Wielopolski and others had meanwhile set up their own headquarters at Teschen in Austrian Silesia.

The physical difficulties of communication only exacerbated the lack of co-operation. Both of these groups spent much time arguing about manifestos and future governments. They had little control over the men actually fighting in Poland, who largely ignored them anyway. In a sense, therefore, there were two tiers to the Confederation of Bar; the szlachta in Poland who hardly knew what they were fighting for; and the malcontent magnates who had in effect recreated the Confederation of Radom abroad, with the same purpose in mind – to remove Stanisław. The young poet Franciszek Karpiński records his enthusiasm on hearing of the confederation. But when he reached the rebel camp, the first thing he heard from the lips of Joachim Potocki was that he was 'fed up with the reign of the Poniatowskis'. 'From such a prelude', Karpiński continues, 'we recognised what sort of dance this would be; it was a question neither of faith nor of liberty, as they claimed in their manifestos, but of the fact that they could not bear having a Poniatowski on the throne.'[47]

This situation still left Stanisław a hope that he would be able to wean the patriotic szlachta away from their leaders. But at this point, the whole issue became an international one. In July a Russian Cossack unit had crossed into Turkish territory in pursuit of some fleeing rebels, and promptly began a massacre of Jews at Balta. The Porte was outraged, and demanded that Russia withdraw her troops from Poland. France saw her chance of regaining influence in Eastern Europe and goaded Turkey to issue an ultimatum, demanding this time not only the withdrawal of Russian troops, but also the rescinding of the Russian treaty with Poland, complete with the dissenter legislation, the Cardinal Laws and the guarantee. Russia rejected this out of hand, and on 6 October 1768 the Porte declared war on Russia.

French diplomacy went into action, with its habitual lack of purpose. The *Secret* was now being directed by Broglie, who had changed his views since the days when he would do everything to block Stanisław. In a memorandum to Louis XV dated 17 November 1768 he argued that the Confederation of Bar was a shambles with no hope of succeeding. He put forward a plan whereby France could espouse the cause of Stanisław and bring her influence to bear on the malcontents in Poland, on the confederates, on Austria, Saxony and Turkey, to support him in defying Russia, thereby wrenching Poland decisively away from the Russian sphere of influence.[48]

French official policy, as it was conducted by Choiseul, took a diametrically opposed course. As soon as news of the confederation reached Paris, Choiseul despatched the Chevalier de Taulès to assess the viability of the movement, and, if it was worth backing at all, to give it money and offer French officers. Taulès was unimpressed by what he found, and he returned to France within a few months without having given the rebels any money. His scepticism did not deter Choiseul. At the beginning of October, Bishop Adam Krasiński was received at Versailles and given assurances of support. Austria was asked to give facilities to the rebels, and France pledged arms, money and military advisers. A new envoy, the Chevalier de Châteaufort, was sent to the Barian headquarters. His instructions, dated at Versailles 18 January 1769, reveal that France had no illusions about the Barians. 'Their uncertainties do not merit any confidence on our part,' they run. 'They are guided by personal and private motives, and there are very few of them who think of the real good of their country. They have no defined aim, no policy, no unity between themselves, no means, no resources.'[49] Choiseul did not care. He wanted to turn Poland into a battleground which would suck off Russian military resources. Châteaufort was to 'nourish in the mind of the Polish nation hatred and defiance of the Russians', and encourage them to fight. He was also to put about the view that Stanisław's election was invalid.[50]

As Choiseul explained to Mercy, now Austrian ambassador in Paris, 'It matters very little who will be king of Poland, as long as Poland remains in a state of upheaval and Russia is tied down by her as well as by the Porte for a few years.'[51] He contemplated replacing Stanisław with a Saxon prince. Austria was not happy about this policy, and Kaunitz pointed out that since neither Russia nor Prussia would ever accept the dethronement of Stanisław, France's attitude would place Austria in an impossible position.[52] France's failure to heed this warning was to cost her, and Poland, dear. It eventually faced Austria with the dilemma of having to choose between her French ally and her Russian and Prussian neighbours, and she was forced to choose the latter. It also removed the only real alternative option left to Poland.

12

Desperation

$\mathcal{S}$tanisław often represented his position in melodramatic terms, making liberal use of effective simile to picture himself as a fire-fighter or as the captain of a storm-tossed vessel. But the best simile to describe his position after the eruption of the Confederation of Bar is that he was between the hammer and the anvil.

The confederation was an amorphous phenomenon that defies definition. It was all things to all men. It was a political demonstration, a sort of phoney war of fence-sitting and calculation. Yet it was also an armed explosion of feeling ranging from impassioned patriotism to personal grievance, a tragi-comic epos marked by heroism and suffering. It had been born of muddle by illusion, and as it spread, further layers of misunderstanding and reaction accrued to render it daily more politically insoluble. Only in one sense did the issues grow clearer: the original impulse of the rebellion had been directed at the king and his reforms, but a year of fighting had turned it into an uprising against Russia. As such, it gained the attributes of a national movement and engaged the sympathy of the vast majority of Poles.

The tragedy of Stanisław's position was that he was seen as a Russian puppet by the confederates, and as a crypto-confederate by the Russians. The fact that he had been forced, back in March 1768, to sign the request for Russian military assistance against the confederation had technically cast him in the former role. Yet his evident sympathy for the rebels and his sluggish response to Russian demands convinced the Russians that he was 'a declared enemy'.[1] He continued to make approaches to the Barians and did not exclude the possibility of joining with them in a national stand against Russia.[2] Andrzej Zamoyski devised a plan whereby he himself would join the confederation, which he would have little trouble in dominating with his stature and popularity, in order then to bring it round to the king's side.[3] Ksawery Branicki worked with Stanisław on various possible means of drawing the rebels into the army, and carried on negotiations with the Porte and the Crimean Tatars, to ascertain whether they might support him rather than the Barians against Russia.[4]

The outbreak of war between Russia and Turkey in October 1768 highlighted the failure of Russia's policy. Catherine and Panin had intended Poland to be a docile ally that could be counted on in the event of such a war, and they now expected Stanisław to make available Polish troops and the fortresses of Kamieniec and Zamość, which would be useful bases for the Russian army's operations against Turkey. Stanisław later reflected that it might have saved Poland if he had complied: raising an army and marching at its head to fight the Turks might just have swept the nation behind him and out-manœuvred the Barians, and it would have restored trust between himself and St Petersburg.[5] But although he was being strongly urged by his brother Michał and others of his entourage to comply, Stanisław refused the Russian demands. Repnin was incensed. 'The king has spoken to me as a king, but it will be for the last time,' he threatened as he left what had been an acrimonious audience.[6] He could ill afford to make such threats. The Russian system in Poland was on the brink of collapse, and he knew it.

The ambassador's role was a complex one. The depth of Russian involvement in Poland and the free hand he was given made his role akin to that of a colonial governor. His personality compounded this, and he was soon behaving like a satrap. It could not have been easy for anyone, let alone a fiery young man like Repnin, to know what limits to impose on his behaviour. Any society placed in a form of colonial subjection will react with the same baffling mixture of fear, defiance and irresponsibility, and Poland was no exception. The Russian ambassador found no lack of toadies to do his work for him, and since he promoted them and pushed them into the highest offices, he created an unwelcome social phenomenon. After four years of his activities, many of the highest posts in public life were occupied by people who in normal societies spend their lives in brothels and gaming-houses. While he promoted such venal elements, the ambassador despised them. But he reserved his hatred for those who showed moral backbone: their probity was the reef on which all his calculations were wrecked. Yet he could do little to hurt people like Michał Czartoryski, Zamoyski or Lubomirski. The one person he could hurt, very deeply, and through whom he could get his own back on the whole Polish nation, was Stanisław. The fact that he genuinely liked the king could not alter this.

In their private conferences, of which Stanisław kept meticulous records, Repnin often lapsed into the most uncouth behaviour. He could do this with impunity, since he represented a formidable military power, and because he also held Stanisław by the throat financially. The Russian troops in Poland provisioned themselves in the Crown estates, for which Repnin was supposed to pay the king. It requires little imagination to see what kind of a weapon this put in the ambassador's hand. While this could not have been pleasant for Stanisław, it was as nothing to the public humiliations, which were an affront to his majesty and therefore to the whole nation. Repnin flouted etiquette, talking out of turn, sitting in the king's presence, arriving or leaving at will, and generally treating the king as if he were a person of little consequence. The Poles grew so used to it that they hardly bothered to record such outrages. Visiting foreigners were scandalised.

When he went to the theatre in Warsaw, James Harris was astonished to find the actors waiting for Repnin to arrive before beginning the play, even though the king had been sitting in his box for almost an hour. At a masquerade given by Karol Radziwiłł during the 1768 Seym, Harris records that Stanisław wanted to wait until the ballroom was ready before opening the dance, only to receive a message from Repnin, who was impatient to start the dance in another room, that 'If he does not come at once, we shall begin without him!' During a gathering at the Primate's, the conversation turned to the unfortunate topic of kings who had been forced into exile and obliged to support themselves, and Stanisław said that he should be extremely embarrassed if he were put to the trial, as he knew no way of earning his livelihood. 'Excuse me, Sir,' said Repnin, 'Your Majesty is still a very good dancer.' 'What should we think if we heard an ambassador tell

our king, "If all trades fail, your Majesty may turn dancing-master?"'
noted the shocked English diplomat.[7]

Repnin's policy had undermined Stanisław's authority and circumscribed his political influence. His offensive behaviour had encouraged all manner of malcontents to denigrate Stanisław's person and
insult his majesty. These factors had contributed greatly to building up
opposition to the king and priming his subjects for rebellion. Repnin
had made it almost impossible for Stanisław to govern. Yet
Stanisław was the major, and now the only, resource Russia possessed
in Poland.

And Stanisław had decided to put his foot down. He had been
diminished in every way, but he still had a hard core of loyal subjects.
He could also count on the Familia. The two Czartoryskis, Lubomirski,
Zamoyski, Borch, Przeździecki and others had conspicuously respected
the dignity of the Crown in Stanisław's person, which had helped to
maintain a shadow of royal authority. They also broadly concurred
with Stanisław's pragmatic policies, and, unlike the malcontents,
devoted their efforts to the survival of Poland. With their support,
Stanisław now set about regaining the political initiative.

In November 1768 he wrote to Panin suggesting the abolition of the
Russian guarantee and the repeal of the legislation on the dissenters, and
proposing that the Catholic powers be invited to mediate in the
pacification of Poland. On 1 December 1768 he instructed his envoy
Jakub Psarski to inform Catherine that 'the person of Prince Repnin is
not pleasing to the nation', and that it would be impossible to negotiate
any agreement through him.[8] On 8 December he sent the Polish army
to winter quarters, and declared Poland's neutrality in the Russo-
Turkish conflict.[9] There was no immediate reaction from St Petersburg, which was absorbed by the problems of the war with Turkey,
but in June 1769 Repnin was replaced by Prince Nikolay Volkonsky.
He was utterly unlike Repnin in character, and his views on Poland
were more conciliatory. His instructions were to rebuild the original
Russian party around the king and the Familia.[10] He let it be known
that Catherine was prepared to amend the legislation on the dissenters
and to allow a few minor reforms in return for their co-operation. But
she would not hear of the lifting of the guarantee, even less of allowing
powers such as France and Spain to have a say in Polish affairs. This did
not satisfy Stanisław.

On 6 November 1769, Stanisław held a Senate Council and then issued a formal proposal to Russia. It demanded the repeal of the Cardinal Laws passed by the last Seym, the withdrawal of all Russian units, the immediate return of the four imprisoned senators, and extensive reparations for the destruction caused by Russian troops over the past two years. In return, Poland would deal with the Confederation of Bar by herself and thereby remove the threat to the flank of the Russian armies operating against Turkey. Catherine refused to receive the Polish envoy, and ordered the sequestration of the estates of the ministers who had signed the proposal with Stanisław: Lubomirski, Michał Czartoryski, Borch and Przeździecki. This did not solve her problem. The fact remained that she now had no party in Poland. Volkonsky had gathered a dismal group of people such as Primate Podoski, Adam Poniński and other clients of Repnin's into a 'Patriotic Council', but this was no substitute. At the beginning of 1770, Catherine climbed down and let it be known to Stanisław that she would be prepared to renegotiate the Cardinal Laws, and drop the legislation on the dissenters entirely. This was a victory for the king, but it was too little and too late.

Popular belief had it that it was he who had had the four senators arrested, he who was keeping Russian troops in Poland, he who had pushed through the legislation on the dissenters and the Cardinal Laws, and matters were not improved when Russian units operating in Poland invariably proclaimed that it was on his orders they were looting private estates. Unless he could demonstrate publicly that he could cast off the Russian yoke entirely, he would be in no position to rally anyone or stabilise the situation. In a long letter dated 21 February 1770 he explained all this to Catherine in the most candid terms, and begged her to co-operate more actively in their common cause.[11]

His letter came at an unpropitious moment. Russian forces now surged ahead in the Balkans, routing the Turks everywhere on land, and winning the resounding naval battle of Chesme on the Aegean. Catherine's extraordinary luck was holding, and as she grew more confident her inclination to compromise on anything dwindled drastically. She did not bother to reply. Volkonsky ordered Stanisław to collaborate with the 'Patriotic Council'. If he refused, said Volkonsky, the four ministers, Lubomirski, Czartoryski, Przeździecki and Borch, would be imprisoned for life. Stanisław refused. 'I shall always remember with the most sincere gratitude that it was the empress who brought me to this throne,' he wrote, 'but at the same time I cannot conceal that the manner in which I am being treated at present destroys the sweetness of this gift, and fills it with the most cruel bitterness, since it is in the highest degree wounding to my royal dignity as well as my person, as it is quite impossible for me to accept that a foreign Power might have the right to punish Polish Ministers.'[12] He wrote to Catherine again, pointing out the blindness of a policy which supposed the Russian cause in Poland would benefit by imprisoning people of the calibre of Czartoryski and Lubomirski. But his letters went unanswered.

Rebuffed by Catherine, Stanisław tried negotiating with the Barians through the Catholic courts supporting them. The Papal Nuncio, Angelo Durini, had strong French connections and ensured that the Vatican remained hostile. Choiseul was struggling to keep his post in the face of the mounting influence of Madame du Barry, and, as he explained to Stanisław's envoy Joachim Chreptowicz on 1 May 1770, Poland was the least of his worries.[13] Only Vienna was sympathetic. Since the Barians had made their headquarters on Austrian territory, Austria could easily bring pressure to bear, and Andrzej Poniatowski was sanguine that something could be achieved through his good relations with Maria Theresa. The agent of the *Secret* in Vienna, Stanisław's old acquaintance Durand, was trying to persuade his masters to construct a Franco-Austrian scheme to unite the Barians and the king against Russia.[14] But Choiseul pursued his own increasingly unrealistic schemes. One of his agents was exhorting Prince Charles of Saxony to raise an army at France's expense and take the Polish Crown. Choiseul suggested that the Duke of Teschen, another son of Augustus III, should be put on the Polish throne.[15] The next moment he appears to have favoured placing Prince Charles Edward Stuart, 'Bonnie Prince Charlie', at the head of the confederation.[16] Like a chess-player who wants to upset the board to avoid defeat, he missed no opportunity of creating confusion, even provoking a war between England and Spain over the Falkland Islands. It was not until the end of 1770 that he decided to withdraw his support from the Barians, and to post Breteuil to Vienna. But he fell from power, and his successor, the Duc d'Aiguillon, despatched Breteuil to London and sent a new batch of French officers to fight in Poland.

Stanisław also kept trying to involve England, Denmark and the Netherlands, which could put pressure on Russia. He corresponded with the Yorkes, Lord Mansfield, Bentinck and others. He made use of unofficial agents such as Charles Lee, and at the end of 1769 he despatched Tadeusz Burzyński to London as envoy extraordinary, armed with a proposal for England to preside at an international congress to restore peace, not only in Poland, but between Russia and Turkey as well.[17] Burzyński was received by the Secretary of State, Lord Rochford, who was alarmed at Russian and Prussian intentions, and by George III, who professed a willingness to help. But England was loath to participate if the Catholic powers were involved, as she was suspicious of French designs.[18]

The situation in Poland itself was deteriorating, and chances of reconciliation were slipping away. With Russian troops being sucked into the Turkish war and the Polish army remaining in camp, rebel activity revived. So far, this had been largely confined to guerrilla warfare. In 1769, the rebels had taken and lost Częstochowa, then Poznań, and a second Lithuanian rising was defeated. But the situation altered in the second half of 1770. New commanders such as Józef Zaremba and Kazimierz Pułaski developed a talent for cavalry raids which harried the Russian units and left no corner of the Commonwealth outside the sweep of the rebellion. In June 1770, Colonel Dumouriez arrived to head a number of French officers who trained infantry and artillery units to supplement the mounted szlachta. Dumouriez discouraged mobile warfare and advocated the fortification of strong points such as Częstochowa, Tyniec and Lanckorona. His aim was to take over most of the Kraków area and turn it into a base for the whole movement. This strategy began to yield results in the second half of 1770 and the beginning of 1771.

The leaders of the confederation grew more confident and decided to raise the stakes. On 9 April 1770 Michał Krasiński and Joachim Potocki put their names to a document declaring Stanisław's election to have been invalid and the throne to be vacant. Flushed with the news of a couple of successful military operations, and with the fact that on 9 June the Emperor Joseph II came to Prešov to meet them, they went further. On 9 August they issued a manifesto referring to 'Stanisław Poniatowski, intruder, usurper, tyrant', and on 22 October 1770 another, declaring the throne to have been vacant since 1763, and calling on everyone to rise and persecute the usurper and his henchmen by every available means.[19] This was treason, and it precluded any further negotiation between the king and the Barians. It seriously reduced Stanisław's chances of reaching a settlement and, while it did discredit the confederation in the eyes of many courts, it did nothing to strengthen his position. 'Oh God, why has my nation misjudged me!' Stanisław wrote to Madame Geoffrin. 'It has now made it almost impossible for me to save it from the abyss.'[20]

Stanisław was living through a protracted nightmare. Both Russia, on which he had built his policy, and the Catholic powers, which he saw as a viable alternative, seemed perversely intent on undermining their own interests. He meandered between hope and despair, repeating to himself his motto 'patience and courage'. Every now and then there would be a promising glimmer in a letter from Panin, some information from Vienna, or some appearance of a change of mood at Versailles. But he was never allowed to entertain such hopes for long. His faith in himself and in his mission must have been extremely difficult to sustain.

He was a product of his times, and deeply affected by the spiritual malaises that characterised them. He understood that religious beliefs had been intellectually discredited, yet he could not live without faith in some deity. The new faith in reason and science was for him, as for so many of his contemporaries, more of a crypto-masonic creed than a conviction. The Enlightenment had taught him that man was a free agent, yet his psyche clung to superstition. Throughout his youth he had taken refuge in a reasoned fatalism. Williams had lured him out of this, not without difficulty, and taught him to value himself, to consider life as a challenge, and to forge his own destiny. Stanisław had struggled manfully to implement this teaching, but throughout the 1750s and early 1760s his life was steered and buffeted by circumstances which he could in no way control. When he ascended the throne, he made a supreme effort of assertiveness – and that had resulted in the crisis of 1766. Whatever remained of his faith in his power to order events had evaporated, and he gradually relapsed into his old fatalism.

'I feel only too painfully the thorns with which my crown is woven,' he confided in Harris. 'I would have thrown it to the devil a long time ago if I were not ashamed of abandoning my post . . . My ambition carried me away – I dared aspire to a crown, I succeeded, and I am miserable.'[21] He had been repeatedly crossed in matters of policy and frequently humiliated in his person. He was estranged from his people. An explosion in the chimney of his study in May 1769 may even have been an attempt on his life.[22] Whatever image of royalty he had laboured to project had been savagely shattered. His health was undermined by the continuous stresses. Yet somehow it held out. 'I am destined to last,' he quipped to Madame Geoffrin.[23] His letters to the old lady had grown almost confessional in tone, graphically reflecting his hopes and enthusiasms, followed inexorably by disappointment and despair. They also reveal the continuous mental exercise he put himself through of reaffirming his belief in providence and destiny, and a stoical determination to go through with whatever these had prepared for him. 'In my earliest childhood I always carried with me the presentiment of a great elevation,' he wrote to her in October 1769. This was true, as various utterances from his youth demonstrate. But he goes on to say that he had also known that 'everything that I undertook would be spoiled and almost entirely destroyed; but I would survive, I would rebuild, I would overcome in the end,' which is already a slight embellishment of his earlier convictions. Not content with this, he builds this amalgam of premonition and experience into a theory which he represents as some sort of Divine ordinance. 'My destiny has always been such: in every different passage of my life, there have always been, to begin with, some brilliant and unexpected successes, which seemed to happen of themselves, but which were short; then come long and painful reversals which bring me to the edge of the abyss, which make me reflect, and resist; and then God changes the scene, either through some expedient which He inspires in me, or by some circumstance that He ordains over my head, and then I find myself walking down a new road.'[24]

This recipe required constant repetition in the face of discouragement. 'No, no, it is not possible that God should have created me with so little venom and such a deep desire to be of use, if He did not intend my contemporaries and posterity to benefit from it,' he cried out in June 1770. The system was highly effective, and over a year later, when he was facing both complete political failure and a personal landmark in his life, he could sound almost serene. 'I have already earned many grey hairs, and the prime of my life has passed. In three months I shall be forty years old: my noon has passed, and I can now only look forward to a beautiful evening as consolation. But the lamp of hope is not extinguished in me . . . God alone knows whether this hope is well-founded; but since He keeps it alive in the depths of my heart, He must wish to keep up my courage, and He never does anything without purpose.'[25] Thus Stanisław's own hopes became the design of providence, and his convictions the fulfilment of a higher destiny. This formula gave him the courage to face any trials, the detachment to bear any humiliation, and the endurance to persevere against all odds. And these included a myriad day-to-day problems.

If it was difficult for Stanisław to keep up the semblance of royal dignity, it was even harder to maintain any normality in everyday affairs. The rebels were never in a position to take Warsaw, even though small units did occasionally foray close to the capital. Nor did they ever control any part of the country for long. But no part of the country was beyond the reach of their depredations. The preferred activity of the rebels was to loot Crown estates, to ambush convoys, posts and royal functionaries. Taxes could not be collected properly, trade and industry suffered, and, to compound the picture, the plague began to spread from the Ukraine. The revenues of the state, the Crown and of individuals loyal to it dwindled dramatically. Stanisław's own income went down from 9.5 million złoty in 1768 to 5.5 million in 1769. In 1770 it went up to 7 million, but fell to 6 million in 1771.[26] If he was giving fewer parties, he had to pay for the war and his diplomatic initiatives. Remarkably, he did not allow this to tell on his manifold activities. His accounts for 1769, when his income fell to an all-time low, reveal that he still managed to fund essential repairs to the Castle, to invest one-tenth of his income in his factories, and to service and repay debts.[27]

Amusements and distractions of every sort were an essential element in his fight for psychological survival, and they helped to ward off his nostalgia and melancholy in the face of passing time. 'I have applied my thoughts to banishing this rust of sadness that would corrode a soul of steel,' he wrote in June 1770.[28] He distracted himself with dancing, with women, but most of all with his great hobby – the arts. A letter full of gloom suddenly brightens when he comes to speak of a painting he has bought or a commissioned bust of Henri IV which has arrived. And he continued to buy throughout this period – works by Batoni,

Guido Reni, Bassano, Luca Giordano and Salvator Rosa. Amid the political obstacles and setbacks he relaxed by reviewing Fontana's drawings for a Cathedral in Warsaw or the new House of Correction, which was opened in 1771. He found solace and gratification in the work of setting up a pottery at Belweder, which started production in 1770. In the following year he instituted a practice of Thursday dinners, at which he hosted a carefully selected group of writers, artists and intellectual aristocrats, who contributed papers, readings or discussion. He also began writing memoirs which, to judge by the tone of the early chapters, were a source of amusement and pleasure. He founded a new weekly, *Entertainments Pleasant and Useful*, under the editorship of one of his secretaries, Jan Albertrandi. He continued to take a keen interest in the progress of the painter Franciszek Smuglewicz and the architect Efraim Szreger, both in Rome on bursaries granted by him, and delighted in the arrival of the painter Bernardo Bellotto and the sculptor André Le Brun, both of whom he had summoned to work at the Castle.

Stanisław only managed to complete one project during the civil war, and it is a very telling one. Using the architect Fontana, the sculptor Le Brun and the painter Bacciarelli, he rebuilt the ruined marble chamber of the Castle as an emblematic pantheon to the memory of Poland's greatest rulers. Their portraits are framed within the cladding of green and black marble, with Stanisław's own over the fireplace, facing an ornate clock, flanked by allegories of Justice and Peace. The chamber was opened on 7 September 1771, the seventh anniversary of his election, and it stated quite clearly Stanisław's constitutional pedigree, his right to rule, and the three elements on which he based his policy – time, justice and peace.

Stanisław was prepared to weather the storm for as long as it lasted, but his determination could avail him little in the face of an alarming new development. In February 1770 Austrian troops occupied the province of Spisz (Zips). This had been mortgaged to Poland by Hungary in 1412 and, never redeemed, it had remained part of the Polish Commonwealth ever since. When Stanisław protested at the incursion, Austria replied that the province belonged to the Crown of Hungary, and therefore to the Austrian monarchy. Then, in August 1770, Austrian troops marched deeper into Poland and set up a cordon against the plague which had broken out in the Polish Ukraine. Not to be outdone, Frederick also moved his troops into border areas, occupying a buffer zone in order to 'protect' his own dominions from the confederates.

With no army to speak of, there was nothing Stanisław could do. It was Russia's job to defend Polish territory. But Russia was absorbed in the Turkish war, and her Polish policy was in a state of paralysis. For month after month throughout the year 1770, Volkonsky repeatedly demanded that Stanisław dismiss the four ministers and work with the 'Patriotic Council'. In vain did Stanisław write to Catherine, explaining that this was impossible. 'It is not just your reason that I wish to touch with my request, but your heart, which is generous, compassionate, and in its very nature removed from wishing to cause suffering in others, and particularly in the best of your friends,' he wrote. 'May it therefore please Your Majesty, let similar propositions against my ministers never be repeated, and let the sequestration on their lands be lifted.'[29]

Catherine had decided that the Czartoryskis bore a heavy load of the responsibility for the failure of her policies in Poland. She resented the fact that they had never allowed themselves to be used, and she suspected their motives. 'Their whole power, importance and influence in their own country must be definitively destroyed, to its very foundations, to the point of moral annihilation,' Panin instructed Volkonsky. 'That is the irreversible policy of our court in the light of their proven treachery and lust for power.'[30] But the Czartoryskis were not so easily broken. When ordered by Catherine to resign his ministry or face execution, Michał made a public reply which was not calculated to soothe her. 'I did not receive my charge from Her Imperial Majesty, so She will forgive me if I do not see fit to resign it at Her request,' he wrote. 'I am old, very old, and She can do me very little harm by shortening the days I have left to live. But I have too much consideration for my reputation to blemish the twilight of a life which, I may say, has been lived without reproach in the service of my country, by an act that the world would rightly condemn as cowardly and self-interested.'[31]

At Stanisław's request, Lord Rochford wrote to the Russian Court interceding for the Czartoryskis and requesting that their lands be returned to them. Catherine riposted with a fierce letter to the English ambassador in St Petersburg. Her own ambassador in London called on

Burzyński and told him to pack his bags and leave or his estate would be confiscated. This did not make a good impression in London, and she was forced to climb down.[32]

But the truth remained that no other power was prepared to protect Poland, and Stanisław was thrown back on Russia. In December 1770 he sent Ksawery Branicki to St Petersburg to speak with Catherine. She was prepared to stand by Poland against Prussia and Austria if Stanisław proved his loyalty by sending his army out against the confederates and severing his diplomatic links with foreign courts. She was particularly irritated by Burzyński's presence in London, and repeatedly demanded that he be recalled.[33] Stanisław faced a grave decision. 'Never has the position of a sovereign been more critical, or his kingdom been so threatened with total dissolution,' Panin warned him in March 1771. 'I conjure Your Majesty to deem worthy of your most serious attention these few words which truth wrests from me.'[34]

In May 1771 Volkonsky was replaced with Kaspar von Saldern. He was ageing and unwell, and he took a jaundiced view of the situation in Poland. He reported that the Russian troops spent most of their time looting and carousing instead of dealing with the confederates.[35] He disbanded Volkonsky's 'Patriotic Council' and repudiated Podoski. 'The people have no respect for him, the great despise him, the weak loathe him,' he explained.[36] In a fit of pique, the Primate went off to Gdańsk with his mistress, and thence to Marseille, where they both died of indigestion. Saldern wanted to recreate a Russian party with the king and the Familia, and confided in Stanisław that on his co-operation depended Russia's will to check Prussia, which had designs on Polish territory. Stanisław took the threat seriously, and saw no option but to co-operate. He agreed to send out the Crown troops to reinforce the Russians against the confederates. But the Czartoryskis refused to believe that Russia would ever allow anything as damaging to her own interests as a cession of Polish territory to Prussia. They therefore stood firm against his blandishments and his threats, which irritated Saldern. They had enjoyed Repnin's fall, taken pleasure in Volkonsky's frustration, and could hardly conceal their glee at the irritable Saldern's rages.

These were brought on by the realisation that Russian policy in Poland had run out of options. He saw clearly that she could not extinguish the Barian movement, however many troops were devoted to the task. Dumouriez and his carefully trained army were defeated by General Suvorov in May 1771 at Lanckorona, but in June Zaremba defeated the Polish troops sent against him in obedience to Catherine's wishes. Dumouriez lost heart and went home cursing the Poles, but he was replaced by General de Vioménil and a fresh bevy of French officers. When, in September 1771, Hetman Michał Ogiński gathered a sizeable body of troops in Lithuania and declared his accession to the confederation, Saldern concluded that Russia would quite simply have to evacuate Poland.[37]

Ogiński won a battle, but was himself defeated by Suvorov at Stołowicze on 23 September, and fled to France. But more bands of confederates seemed to appear as soon as the Russian units moved on. By no stretch of the imagination could Russia be said to be in control. Not only had Austria extended her cordons into Polish territory, Frederick had chosen the moment when the Russians were occupied with Ogiński to move his own forward, taking in the Poznań area. The situation was degenerating fast, and, like a wound that is constantly irritated and not allowed to heal, began to produce unwonted suppurations, the most unpleasant of which erupted on 3 November 1771.

13

The Royal Cake

It was a Sunday evening, and Stanisław had called on Michał Czartoryski, who was indisposed. The king never took more than a platoon of lancers when driving around Warsaw, and on that particular evening he dismissed even this escort. His carriage was preceded by two mounted men carrying torches, two orderly officers, two gentlemen, and one under-equerry. An aide-de-camp rode with the king inside the carriage, which was accompanied by two mounted pages flanking the doors, two heyduks on the box, and two valets behind. It was a dark, moonless night when the royal carriage trundled out of the gates of the Czartoryski palace.

A hundred yards further on, a group of horsemen suddenly debouched from a side-street, and another clattered out of an alleyway to head off the carriage team. Shots rang out. The postillion and two heyduks fell to the ground. The aide-de-camp tried to block the carriage door and was felled by a sabre-blow to the head. A musket-ball pierced the king's coat, another grazed his head. Stanisław leapt out of the carriage and ran down the street towards the Czartoryski palace. He began to hammer on the bolted gate, then spun round to face his pursuers and drew his sword. They knocked it from his hand, seized him by the collar and dragged him off. They hoisted him on to a horse, which one of them led by the reins, while others goaded him on from behind, slashing at his pelisse with their sabres, and the whole party made off at full tilt.

Two of the king's escort had ridden back to the Castle to raise the alarm, and the guard hurried to the rescue, as did the Czartoryskis' men. But the kidnappers were already far away. At the city limits, they had to jump a wide ditch, but as the reins were being held by another rider, Stanisław's mount fell and broke its leg, throwing him into a muddy fosse. He was dragged out and put on another horse, losing his pelisse and one of his shoes in the process. The party then split up. The main body, some thirty men, rode off in one direction, while the other seven made off in another with the king. They soon got lost in the dark, and after much aimless wandering their numbers dwindled to three. At length they dismounted to rest, but two of the remaining men apparently panicked and made off with the horses, leaving Stanisław in the custody of a single man. They trudged on, the king in one drawing-room pump and one clumsy boot lent by one of the kidnappers.

The two men fell into conversation. The man, Kuzma Kosiński, was a valet who had joined the rebels after being dismissed from service. He told Stanisław that he had sworn to Pułaski himself to bring the king back dead or alive. He forced Stanisław to carry on, in the vague hope of finding the small wood in which a carriage was supposed to be waiting. After some way, the king stumbled and fell, utterly exhausted by now. Kosiński began to lament his position, and Stanisław offered him a reward if he would take him back to safety. The man was mistrustful. Trying another tack, Stanisław told him to make a run for it, promising to mislead any pursuers. Eventually, Kosiński threw himself at Stanisław's feet and, embracing them, sobbed: 'I shall never leave you. I wish to serve you from now on come what may. Dispose of me as you wish.' Stanisław promised him protection and sent him off to look for the nearest habitation. The man eventually found a mill, and carried the king over to it. When he was told that a noble traveller had been attacked by brigands, the miller gave them shelter. Stanisław scribbled a note to General Coccei, commander of the Guards, and sent the miller's boy off with it, while the miller's wife dressed his wounds. An hour or so later, Coccei turned up with a squadron of cavalry. Adam Czartoryski and his party had found the king's bloody cloak in the ditch and concluded that he had been killed, so the joy was all the greater when the miller's boy turned up with the note. Half the city spilled out, on foot, on horseback and in carriages to meet the monarch, and the hundreds of torches and shouts of joy gave his homecoming the appearance of a triumphal procession. By five o'clock in the morning Stanisław was back in his Castle.[1]

He was not badly wounded, but he was deeply shaken, not so much by the fear he had experienced as by the hatred of his person that lurked behind the attempted abduction. But his faith in Divine Providence quickly reasserted itself. 'Since the Heavens did not wish me to perish, it seems they still wish to bestow some benefit on my country through me,' he wrote to Count Bentinck in answer to his good wishes.[2] And he immediately set about exploiting the incident, with characteristic resourcefulness. An attack on the person of a monarch was an attack on the moral order, and Stanisław was confident that his unpleasant experience would elicit a reaction of solidarity from the crowned heads of Europe. It certainly discredited the Barians, both abroad and in Poland itself, where such violence would be viewed with horror even by Stanisław's enemies. When they realised this, the leading Barians began to put it about that the whole thing had been invented and stage-managed by Stanisław himself.[3]

The event was sensational enough in itself to guarantee it wide publicity all over Europe, and Stanisław did everything to help matters along. He dictated a full account which was published in several countries and languages, often with illustrations of the shocking event. His courtiers and sympathisers composed odes of thanksgiving and verse epics on the subject. Popular prints and other mementos appeared on the market. A Warsaw clockmaker marketed a commemorative lamp, pastry-cooks created puddings representing the king's happy deliverance. Stanisław dragged out his convalescence for a couple of months, giving audiences in bed with his head picturesquely bandaged. He gave the miller a spanking new mill of his own and set him up for life. He personally designed a monument for the heyduk who had died defending his royal master. Kosiński was sent off to live in Italy on a generous pension, and at the trial of the other apprehended kidnappers Stanisław made a fine speech which spared them from the rope.

'One has to be a barbarian not to love you: one would have to be blind to one's own interests not to serve you,' Voltaire exclaimed in a letter full of concern. A few days later he followed it up with another, in which he assured Stanisław that 'One feels certain that this horror will turn to your advantage.'[4] Stanisław certainly hoped so.

He realised that the attempt on his person could be the catalyst for a national reconciliation. Accordingly, he decided to call the Senate to his side and proclaim an amnesty for all rebels who were prepared to lay down their arms and take part in elections to a Seym which would set about the task of pacification. He communicated this design to Vienna, whose role would be crucial in persuading the Barian leaders, and received a signal from Stormont to the effect that Maria Theresa was in favour.[5] But Russia would have none of it. 'It is our intention that you should maintain yourself on the throne only through us,' Saldern declared. 'We view with suspicion every step you take to gather your nation about you without our involvement.'[6] Stanisław had thought that his brush with death would move Catherine and bring out something of the old feelings, but to his mortification, she replied in a matter-of-fact tone, suggesting that he improve his security arrangements.[7]

Frederick's reaction was, for all its solicitude, much more sinister. His behaviour over the past three years had been equivocal. He gave discreet encouragement to the rebels active along his border with Poland, and himself made frequent raids into Polish territory, allegedly in pursuit of confederates who had violated his own. His troops exacted contributions from towns and estates, and pressed able-bodied men into the ranks. He again started minting debased coinage for use in Poland.[8] In 1770 he occupied a considerable area of Polish territory permanently, allegedly in order to safeguard his own dominions.

The civil war in Poland suited him, since it gave substance to his view that the Poles were 'a despicable people from every point of view', and that Poland should not be left to the Poles, but rather placed under the beneficent rule of 'the Solomon of the North' as he liked Voltaire to refer to him. He displayed self-righteous indignation at their obscurantism, and even practised his poetic talents at their expense. In an epic poem begun in 1769, *Le Chant des Confédérés*, a work that occasionally rises to the level of barrack-room wit but mostly flounders in leaden caricature, Frederick brands the Polish nation as being 'just as it was at the Creation, brutish, stupid and without instruction'. The Bishop of Kiev is depicted as a crazed bigot who has a library with no books in it, only a collection of relics and a painting of the St Bartholomew's day massacre. (It is ironic that in his ignorance he should have picked on Załuski, who had collected and endowed the first public library on the European mainland.) Pułaski always flees from the battlefield and then takes his forces on an orgy of pillage and rape instead. (So much for the father of American cavalry.) And the whole is presided over by 'the pathetic Stanisław', an epithet that recurs at the end of every stanza. The inference was that it was not through him that Europe could expect Poland to be saved.

Frederick sent the work, canto by canto, to his philosopher friends. 'The poem on the Confederates is a very pleasant work, full of imagination, of action, and above all of gaiety,' wrote D'Alembert.[9] He lapped it up with much sycophantic praise, and only registered a reservation when the philosopher-king's pen scratched his chauvinism. 'My sole anxiety', he wrote, 'is that the end of the stick with which Your Majesty beats the Poles should have gone so far as to touch the French noblemen who went to assist them.'[10] Voltaire, to do him justice, was more sparing in his praise, and sat down to write something on the subject himself. His play *Les Lois de Minos* is about a king of Crete who inherits 'a grandiose slavery, a title, an empty glory, the name of majesty, the trappings of power, and no authority'. He is faced with grandees who 'only chose kings in order to insult them'. The king bravely defies custom and bigotry, and leads his people to happiness. This earns him the epithet of 'Demi-God on Earth, O great Man! O Great King!' Just in case anyone should have been in any doubt as to whom the play was about, Voltaire added notes, in which he described Stanisław as 'a wise, enlightened, humane king'.

Voltaire confessed to being 'filled with grief and pity over the horrible attempt against the king of Poland', but the receipt of Frederick's next canto cheered him up and made him laugh.[11] 'I am always surprised that you were able to make something so gay out of such a sad subject,' he complimented Frederick.[12] But Frederick was too clever not to realise that the events of 3 November 1771 had made his ribald jollity out of place. Stanisław, whose international stature was miraculously enhanced by the events, could no longer be treated as a pathetic nonentity. The next instalment of *Le Chant des Confédérés* contained an unexpected apology. 'Oh! My good king, I accuse myself of having treated you sometimes too harshly . . . I am contrite,' wrote Frederick, and from now on the 'pathetic Stanisław' became 'this good king'.

Frederick merely realigned his fire. He went into a froth of indignation at the attempt committed against his royal brother, and voiced the view that Stanisław was threatened by his own subjects and needed the assistance of his well-disposed royal neighbours. Stanisław did everything he could to counter this, by giving the impression that the majority of his people were behind him, and that the others would now be brought round peacefully. Hence all the theatricals on the theme of reconciliation. Frederick was having none of it. 'Russia must use this pretext to request my assistance in Poland; for I have guaranteed the throne to this prince, so the excuse is plausible,' he wrote to his ministers in St Petersburg, Vienna and Warsaw after Stanisław's abduction.[13] It was an excuse Frederick had been waiting for to put into effect a plan which had long been maturing in his mind and those of a number of other people.

Back in 1709 Frederick I had proposed to Peter the Great that they partition Poland between them, to which the Tsar replied in his shipyard slang: '*es sei nicht praktikabel*'.[14] Nevertheless, the acquisition of Poland's northern and western provinces remained one of Prussia's cardinal reasons of state. In February 1769 Frederick II instructed Solms to sound out Panin as to his views on the subject.[15] Interestingly enough, only a month later, Choiseul tentatively offered Frederick a slice of Poland if he would back the current, somewhat ephemeral, French design of putting a Saxon prince on the Polish throne.[16] In May 1770 Frederick personally mentioned the idea to the Austrian envoy in Berlin, and in January of the following year, his brother Prince Henry of Prussia, then visiting St Petersburg, put forward the proposal to Catherine in the form of light-hearted banter.

The plan crystallised as the international crisis deepened. Russia was at war with Turkey, which was losing. France wanted Austria to come in on the Turkish side and back the Barians, in order to defeat Russia. Frederick did not want this to happen, not because he was Russia's ally, but because an Austro-Franco-Turkish-Polish victory would block his own plans for expansion, which had to be at the expense of either Austria or Poland. But if Russia managed to detach Austria from France and Turkey by offering her prizes in Poland or Moldavia, Frederick would again be left out in the cold. His answer to the problem was to restrain Russian desire for Moldavia (which might alarm Austria and push her into Turkey's arms) by inducing Catherine to compensate herself at the expense of Poland; to wean Austria away from French influence by offering her gains in Poland; and to reward himself for his efforts by taking a slice of Poland for Prussia.

Frederick was not, on the face of it, in a very strong position to make demands or dictate terms, and his only grounds for compensation were the subsidies which, as an ally, he had been paying Russia for her war with Turkey. Nor was there any good reason why Russia, which regarded Poland as her own sphere of influence, should start ceding pieces of it to Frederick. But he did hold certain cards. One was that when France and Denmark began stirring up trouble on Russia's back doorstep in Sweden, Russia felt an acute need for a reliable ally in that area, and that ally could only be Prussia. Another was that in September 1770 the Porte formally asked Frederick, at his own suggestion, to act as mediator in bringing about peace between her and Russia. Yet another was provided by Austria's behaviour.

Austria had, with good reason, been suspicious of Prussian machinations. But Frederick arranged two meetings with Joseph II, at Neisse in August 1769, and Neustadt in September 1770, in the course of which he encouraged the young Emperor's expansionist urges. At the same time he let it be understood that Prussia would countenance the recent Austrian annexations of Spisz and other Polish lands provided he, Frederick, got something out of it. In the summer of 1770 Austria moved her troops further into Poland. This was very convenient for Frederick. Someone else had cut into the pie first, and Frederick could declare to Russia in tones of outrage that he did not intend 'to remain a peaceful spectator of such an act'.[17] Finally, and most importantly, Russia had by the middle of 1771 quite clearly lost control of affairs in Poland.

In spite of her brilliant military successes against Turkey, Russia had got herself into a difficult position. The war had been expensive and its outcome still hung in the balance while Austria hovered undecided on the sidelines. Poland was costing a great deal in money and men, without any visible results. The arrival of General de Vioménil in the summer of 1771 with more French officers, arms and funds had breathed new life into the confederation. The rebels took Kraków again, and held it. By the end of 1771 it was beginning to look as though the Barians had found a firm base. In the same year the plague swept across Russia, killing 75,000 people and causing riots in Moscow. Russia needed to make peace and repair her Polish fences. Since what Russia could gain from Turkey and her future freedom of action in

Poland both depended on Frederick's goodwill, his proposals were taken seriously. In February 1771, Panin let it be known that rather than prolong the war for another year for the sake of more gains from Turkey, Russia might indeed be satisfied with an immediate slice of Polish territory.[18]

So by the beginning of 1771 Austria had shown that she was not averse to occupying Polish territory, and Russia had given the green light in principle. But nothing was yet decided. Alternative projects, involving places as varied as Venice and Silesia, kept surfacing in the diplomatic game. In May 1771, Panin suggested a variant to Frederick's plan: Poland would be given Moldavia and Wallachia as compensation for ceding slices of her own territory, which would preclude Russia having to give these provinces back to Turkey.[19] Frederick agreed, but Austria protested. Turkey now put her own proposals to Austria: Turkey would give Wallachia to Austria, if Austria gave up her pretensions in Poland and induced Russia to give up hers. This did not suit Frederick at all, since he had no intention of giving up any of his own claims on Polish territory.

Everything hung in the balance of Austria's indecision. Kaunitz wanted to go to war against Russia rather than spoliate Poland, Joseph II wanted to remain friendly with Russia and help himself to as much territory as possible, while Maria Theresa hated the idea of both war and partition. 'No project of partition however advantageous will tempt me a moment,' she assured the English ambassador Lord Stormont in July.[20] In the summer of 1771 the Russians again scored spectacular successes against the Turks and occupied the Crimea. Alarmed at this, Austria began concentrating troops and negotiating an alliance with the Porte. Russia needed Prussia more than ever, so Frederick raised his price, demanding Gdańsk as well.

By the end of the year, Frederick was getting nervous. Russia had done so well in the war that Turkey might just give in and accept a peace dictated by Catherine. Then Catherine would no longer need Prussia. On 4 January 1772 he gave up his demand for Gdańsk and persuaded Russia to join with him in an ultimatum to Austria to the effect that if she did not go along with them, they would make war on her.[21] Austria could waver no longer, and the fear of being left out of the deal outweighed all other considerations. Joseph now upped his demands and Maria Theresa gave in to 'the cruel necessity' of partitioning Poland.[22] On 17 February 1772, a Russo-Prussian convention was signed, followed on 18 March by a preliminary agreement between the three courts. After much haggling over respective claims, the final convention was agreed and signed on 5 August.

Prussia was to get a slice of Wielkopolska, Pomerania and Royal Prussia: 36,300 square kilometres with 580,000 inhabitants. Austria would acquire 81,900 square kilometres of southern Poland, including the cities of Lwów, Przemyśl and Zamość, with 2,650,000 inhabitants. Russia awarded herself 93,000 square kilometres of the north-eastern reaches of the Commonwealth, with the cities of Vitebsk, Polotsk and Mohylów, and 1,300,000 inhabitants. 'It was the only way that remained of avoiding new troubles and of satisfying everyone,' Frederick explained.[23] The tensions that had built up between Russia, Prussia and Austria could best be defused by a carve-up of the country that lay in their midst. Such an act united all three states and all three religious denominations, Catholic, Orthodox and Calvinist, Frederick wrote to his brother Henry, 'for we shall partake of the same eucharistic host – Poland, and, even if it does not save our souls, it will certainly be of great benefit to our states'.[24]

'It is said that it is you, sire, who thought up the dismemberment of Poland, and I believe it, for there is genius in it,' Voltaire wrote to Frederick on 18 November 1772.[25] But Frederick was eager to deny all responsibility, and adopted an attitude of lofty insouciance. 'I have been given a slice of anarchy to deal with,' he wrote to D'Alembert, complaining of the nuisance.[26] To his brother, he admitted that 'in order to allay envy, I tell whoever will listen that I have seen nothing on my passage but sand, fir-trees, heather and Jews'.[27] At the same time, he took pains to spread the notion that the territory he had acquired rightfully belonged to the Prussian Crown, and that he was in effect only repossessing his own property. He put his court historians to work forging documents and had a gold medal struck to commemorate the event, with the legend *a regno redintegrato*. D'Alembert, to whom he sent one, agreed that it 'proves that Your Majesty has done no more than to enter into possession of that which belonged to him before'.[28] Voltaire laughed obligingly at Frederick's jokes about the 'royal cake' that Poland had become, and declared that since Copernicus and Hevelius had come from Toruń and Gdańsk, Frederick had an intellectual right to annexe these as well.[29] 'I should like to know for

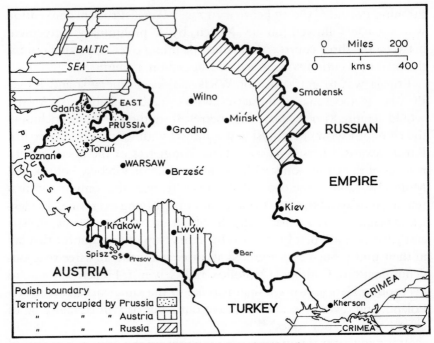

3   The First Partition of Poland, 1772

how many paltry roubles and florins he has prostituted his incense & character,' wrote Horace Walpole to a friend, '– for the florins, I will trust the King of Prussia for half of them being of base metal.'[30]

Catherine also had good returns from her patronage of intellectuals. D'Alembert expressed approval of her actions. Grimm, who had only a few years before offered his services to Stanisław, protesting 'with what zeal I should like to execute the orders of Your Majesty in everything that could depend on me', praised everything his imperial pen-friend and paymaster had done, awarding her 'the right of the strongest'.[31] 'I believe in Catherine, unique though second, I believe in her Holy Spirit,' he parodied the Creed, adding that through her he had been 'regenerated to a new life'.[32] Voltaire too caught the fashion for blasphemy. He was so excited by her victories over the Turks in 1769 that he began jumping up and down on his bed shouting 'Allah Catharina!', and then intoned the prayer: *Te Catharinam Laudamus, Te Dominam Confitemur.*[33] Both under his own name and under various pseudonyms, his pen was at her service to justify her right to send troops into Poland. 'It is the right which allows a neighbour to bring water to the burning house of his neighbour; it is the right of friend-ship; the right of respect, the right to do good when one can.'[34]

This humbug was born of ignorance and doctrinaire attitudes. People in Western Europe knew little of Poland, and what they did know was not edifying. The accepted view was that the country was an ungovernable mess, a disgrace to Enlightenment Europe. Its consti-tution was described by Voltaire as 'gothico-slavonico-romano-sarmatique'.[35] Adam Smith used it as an example of the medieval economy. Abbé Vautrin asserted that the Poles were as sophisticated as 'Persians, negroes and south-sea islanders'.[36] La Condamine thought that the country ought to be given to Prussia to civilise, while Raynal concurred that a society such as Poland 'deserves no better than to find itself oppressed'.[37] What particularly horrified Voltaire was the appar-ent Catholic intolerance reigning in Poland, which he painted in lurid terms in a number of pamphlets, describing confederates having their daggers blessed on the altar before the Black Madonna of Częstochowa as they set off to assassinate their king. Such stories made good copy, and even the London *Gentleman's Magazine* carried descriptions of non-existent religious massacres by confederates.[38]

Intolerance elicits lack of sympathy, and just as in 1945 the intoler-ance and anti-semitism imputed to the nations of Eastern Europe made Western intellectuals indifferent to their fate and amenable to the idea of giving them to Soviet Russia to 'civilise', so in 1772 most of the *philosophes* felt that the partitions not only served the Poles right, but might even bring enlightenment to the country. There were notable and worthy exceptions. Diderot was in no doubt that the partition was 'an offence to humankind'.[39] His view was shared by Rousseau, Mably and others. Eventually, even Voltaire began to have his doubts, and he never dared write another letter to Stanisław.[40]

European public opinion was not much interested in Polish affairs. 'Between a foreign cause, whatever it might be, and the cause of order, which is foreign to nobody, France and Europe will not hesitate in their choice,' observed a French diplomat.[41] The French nevertheless took the partition personally, as Edmund Burke, who was then in Paris, noted. 'I found them in a perfect frenzy of rage and indignation; not that they were hurt at the shocking and uncoloured violence and injustice of that partition, but at the debility, improvidence, and want of activity in their government, in not preventing it as a means of aggrandisement to their rivals, or in not contriving, by exchanges of some kind or other, to obtain their share of advantage from that robbery.'[42] France's alliance with Austria had supposedly been strengthened in 1770 through the marriage of the archduchess Marie-Antoinette to the Dauphin, yet in December 1771, Kaunitz declared that 'in any case, we have done as we have seen fit, and we can do very well without [France's] approbation'.[43] Louis XV told Marie-Antoinette not to mention the subject of Poland at court.[44]

France had, rather late in the day, woken up to the implications of what was being cooked up in Eastern Europe. In the spring of 1772 the Duc d'Aiguillon suggested that Stanisław place himself at the head of his nation and make a public appeal for French assistance. Since by then half the country was in the hands of foreign troops, and the rest was infested with rebels still being actively subsidised by France, such a proposal could only elicit a bitter smile in Warsaw.[45] It nevertheless gave Stanisław hope. He had tried to negotiate with the Barians in order to unite Poland in the face of the threat from outside. He had directed efforts at Vienna and Versailles in an attempt to bring the rebels round, and to block Prussian attempts at splitting the Austro-French alliance. He had tried to make Catherine see that she would in no sense strengthen her position by absorbing Polish territory, but that she would enormously increase Prussia's power by allowing Frederick to do so.[46] Now that the partition was agreed, Stanisław concentrated on breaking up the harmony between St Petersburg, Berlin and Vienna. He realised that Austria was the weakest link in the alliance.

Once Austria had agreed to the plan of partition, she was carried away by Joseph's greed. He swapped the names of rivers and towns so that agreements already reached could be used to expand the Austrian share by another 8,000 square kilometres. He viewed the acquisitions of the other powers with intense jealousy, and his correspondence with Kaunitz reveals a veritable panic not to be outstripped in cupidity. But beneath this lurked a profound unease. Kaunitz admitted to Lord Stormont that the partition was 'louche', and even Joseph agreed that it looked ignominious.[47] It was Maria Theresa who put words to the feeling. 'I shall always regard [the Polish territories] as having been bought too dearly, since they were purchased at the expense of the honour, of the reputation of the Monarchy, of our good faith and virtue,' she wrote to Joseph.[48] She was right. 'The cabinet of Vienna will one day perceive', noted the English diplomat N. W. Wraxall, 'that in consenting to the partition of Poland, they violated not less the laws of true policy, than those of morality and justice.'[49] If France had been left out in the cold, Austria's political reputation was shaken to its foundations.

Stanisław bombarded Maria Theresa with letters designed to prey on her conscience, and stirred her piety by reminding her that the partition would leave millions of Catholics under Protestant or Ortho-dox rule. But she could not change Austrian policy unless France and England took a hand in the matter, and he therefore pressed his case in that quarter. England's response to the partition was weak. The Secretary of State Lord Suffolk called it 'a curious transaction' and instructed his diplomats to show strong disapproval, but did not think it warranted any reaction.[50] But Prussia's designs on Gdańsk threatened English interests, and Stormont in Vienna, Wroughton in Warsaw and Harris in Berlin began to urge Suffolk to act. Stanisław had sent John Lind to London at the beginning of 1772 to help Burzyński's successor Franciszek Bukaty engage public opinion on Poland's side. Lind published a book and a number of pamphlets, and initiated a polemic in the editorial and correspondence columns of the press. There was much public indignation in England at the partition, loudly voiced by people such as Horace Walpole, who adduced it as proof of the existence of the Devil.[51] 'I began to lift up my prayers for Poland,' wrote Lind's friend Jeremy Bentham.[52]

By the summer of 1772 England was prepared to combine with France in order to detach Austria from the concert. Stormont, who was transferred to the Paris embassy, was to engineer the Anglo-French agreement. Stanisław then concentrated his efforts on France, with which he communicated through General Monet, now resident in Paris. 'In the name of God, let the Court of France not lose heart,' he wrote to him in August 1772.[53]

Stanisław no longer dared hope that he could avert the partition itself, and he set his sights accordingly. 'Let all the Powers, counselled by their own interest and alerted by France, demand in the strongest terms firm treaties, whose clauses will, by guaranteeing freedom to what is left of Poland, and security to her commerce, prevent the cupidity of our neighbours from being the arbiters of her destiny,' he wrote to Monet. 'In a word, let there remain a healthy germ of Poland which might, with time and circumstances, flourish. It is on this object that the wishes and attention of the interested and friendly courts must concentrate; unable to prevent the wrong today, they must prepare a remedy for the future.'[54] But the signals he began to receive from France encouraged him to raise his hopes higher.

Aiguillon was toying with the idea of armed intervention in Poland, and urged Stanisław to extend a general pardon to the Barians prior to organising a united stand. 'I persist to the end in the resolution of forgiving them sincerely,' Stanisław replied. 'The only condition I impose on them is repentance for having misjudged me.'[55] The confederates had started the year well, with Szymon Kossakowski recapturing Kraków and Zaremba defeating General Lopukhin in March. But the partition agreement pulled the carpet from under them. In April Austria ordered them off her territory. A few weeks later Kraków fell to the Russians, followed by their other strongholds at Lanckorona and Tyniec. The chances were that they might prove more tractable, particularly if France took a firm line. Although Stanisław did not really believe that she would, he was prepared to stake everything on this last chance, as he wrote to Monet in August 1772: 'I repeat once again that if I am helped, if I am given, I do not say the certitude, but merely a chance of success, I shall be ready to expose myself to anything; I am prepared for anything.'[56]

On 19 September 1772 the sensational news spread across Europe that the king of Sweden had led a coup and broken the grip of the Russian party that had controlled Sweden since 1764. The parallels with Stanisław's case were highly suggestive, and many believed he could attempt a similar venture. Ksawery Branicki fell on his knees before Stanisław and begged him to act. Versailles hinted strongly that it would back him in such a venture. Stanisław was tempted. 'You may assure the Duc d'Aiguillon that neither lack of courage nor the passive enjoyment of my crown and my life will stop me,' he wrote to Monet.[57] But the situation in Poland was entirely different from that in Sweden, which had no foreign troops in occupation. Stanisław could only act if French support materialised and the Barians could be persuaded to back him. But with the fall of Częstochowa, on 18 August 1772, the Confederation of Bar collapsed.

Thousands of rebels were taken prisoner, tortured, branded, and then sent off to Siberia or a lifetime of service in the ranks of Russian regiments. Kazimierz Puławski managed to cut through to Turkish territory and tried to create a Polish legion on the Danube, before going to America in search of a new cause. There, he would organise Washington's cavalry and lay down his life leading it at the Battle of Savannah. Many other Barians were to fight in the American cause, and Paweł Mostowski proposed to Congress to establish a 'New Poland' in Florida in which exiled Barians could live and fight for their republican values.[58] One enterprising rebel, Maurycy Beniowski, managed to escape from Russian captivity in Kamchatka, by seducing the governor's daughter and seizing a Russian ship, the *Saints Peter and Paul*, on which he hoisted the flag of Bar and set sail with a crew of fellow-rebels. The appearance of the strangely flagged vessel in the Portuguese port of Macao in September 1771 caused a mild sensation, but an even greater stir was caused by Beniowski's capture, in 1775, of Madagascar, of which he proclaimed himself emperor. Another maritime Barian, Feliks Miklaszewicz, fought for the Americans as a privateer, harrying the English in a ship named after Karol Radziwiłł.

Radziwiłł himself continued on his inglorious course, driven by the winds of circumstance. During the last moments of the rebellion, he was asked by a French officer whether he feared for his future. '*J'ai deux potences pour moi!*' proudly affirmed Radziwiłł in his best French, meaning that he could count on the benevolence of two powers. When he had stopped laughing, the Frenchman mused that the gibbets would have been more appropriate.[59]

The hard core of the confederation's leaders, including Michał Krasiński, Pac, Ignacy Bohusz, Joachim Potocki and Józef Sapieha, went into exile. Over a year later, on 25 November 1773, the ninth anniversary of Stanisław's coronation, they published their last decree, in Lindau, which protested at everything and everyone, and most of all at Stanisław. They had learnt nothing.

The French ministry had learnt nothing either. Stanisław continued to denounce the *fait accompli* of the partition. He issued a formal appeal to every court in Europe to resist the aggression, and sent Ksawery Branicki to Paris. 'You will have rendered me valuable service even if you can only ascertain that they cannot or will not do anything for us,' he wrote to Branicki, reflecting his pessimism.[60] He sensed in all of Aiguillon's professions and promises 'an appearance of intrigue and ill–will which does not lead me to expect anything good from these people'[61] He was nevertheless ready to act on the slightest signal from Aiguillon, and he prepared an audacious enterprise that would give France the excuse she needed. He made a plan to slip out of the Castle on foot, meet his acting chamberlain Franciszek Ryx at a postern, and then join his aide General Byszewski, who held a travelling-chaise in readiness. Passports for a merchant and two servants were prepared, enabling them to travel through Silesia and Bavaria to France, whose protection he would publicly invoke. If the partitioning powers should declare the throne vacant, there would have to be an election, and that would involve the whole of Europe and prevent the partition from going ahead.[62]

Aiguillon did not receive Branicki until 7 December, and told him Poland was too far away to concern France. Louis XV suggested that all Poland's problems were of her own making, and appeared oblivious of ever having taken an interest in the country at all. On the same day, Stanisław received a letter from George III. 'It is conceived in terms which are very obliging to my person, but entirely negative as to the assistance requested,' he informed Branicki.[63]

But if England's actions were no more effective than those of France, it was in England that the real import of the partition was fully realised. George III strongly believed that such behaviour by major powers was 'subversive' and bad for Europe.[64] Hume lamented 'that the two most civilized nations, the English and French, should be on the decline; and the barbarians, the Goths and Vandals of Germany and Russia, should be rising in power and renown'.[65] But it was Burke who put it in the clearest and most far-sighted terms. In an article in the *Annual Register* he pointed out that the partition was 'the first very great breach in the modern political system of Europe . . . It is not sapping by degrees the constitution of our great western republic, it is laying the axe at once to the root, in such a manner as threatens the total overthrow of the whole.' He pointed out that by destroying Poland, Germany was only laying herself open to eventual invasion by Russia, a theory echoed by Karl Marx nearly a century later, and partially realised in ours.[66] And he summed up his fears in the phrase: 'Poland was but a breakfast . . . where will they dine?'[67]

14

Readjustment

'$\mathcal{J}$f the king of Poland wishes to appear to be a great man, he will perish at the foot of his throne defending his rights,' Joseph II said to the French ambassador in Vienna, Cardinal de Rohan. 'If he is one, he will sacrifice a part in order to save the rest.'[1] The words echoed Stanisław's own convictions, but he also knew that 'whether I give way or resist, I shall be equally blamed', as he put it to Ksawery Branicki. 'In the first instance I will be reproached with weakness; in the second, all the resulting damage will be blamed on me.'[2]

There could of course be no military resistance: three neighbouring states with a combined military might of over half a million men were in occupation of his kingdom. But the blatancy of their own conduct embarrassed them, and they wanted to dress up their conquest as a voluntary cession. A new Russian ambassador, Baron Otto Magnus von Stackelberg, arrived in Warsaw to 'procure to such a cession the greatest possible appearance of authenticity'. As confederate activity had ceased, the Russian troops in Poland 'will have a free hand, and they shall remain there, in order to facilitate your negotiations', his instructions read.[3]

His arrival was welcomed by Stanisław. The new ambassador declared that he wished to make Poland happy. 'His turn of mind and his education were that of a French courtier,' Stanisław noted with approval. 'His polished tone, which contrasted with the rages of Saldern, made him all the more agreeable at first.'[4] The Prussian agent Benoit was promoted to the rank of envoy and reinforced with

General Lentulus, an arrogant busybody who treated Warsaw like a barracks. Vienna had sent Baron Reviczky, an unsympathetic, dry man who disliked his job and took solace whenever he could in his hobby, the study of Oriental languages. Even the Vatican had decided to replace the fiercely anti-Russian Durini, who was implicated in the abduction of Stanisław.[5] Giuseppe Garampi, Archbishop of Beirut, who succeeded him, would have to salvage whatever he could for the Polish Church from the non-Catholic powers taking over lands inhabited by its flock.

Stackelberg was presented to Stanisław by his predecessor on 15 September 1772. A few days later, he laid before the king a Russian declaration 'justifying' the partition on the grounds that Poland had become a risk to the peace of Europe, and demanding that Stanisław convoke the Seym and instruct it to ratify the arrangements made by his neighbours. Stackelberg pointed out that there was nothing he could do to oppose the three powers, 'whose might was sufficient to subjugate the entire globe'. He told Stanisław that if he did not co-operate he was likely to lose his throne and everything he possessed 'down to his last spoon', and that Poland would cease to exist.[6] This did not leave Stanisław much choice. They could ultimately dispense with the ratification. It was, so to speak, only the icing on the cake, and they would rather eat it without the icing than go hungry.

Stanisław nevertheless determined to make the most of the cards he did hold and play the game to the end. He refused the Russian demands outright, and convoked the Senate Council for October to frame a formal reply. This indignantly rejected Russia's justifications and demanded the immediate evacuation of the country by her troops. It also asked why the guarantor of Poland's territorial integrity was violating it within four years of pledging herself to defend it.

Stanisław's plan was to stall for as long as possible. While he did not nourish high hopes of French intervention, he wanted to leave the door open to it. And as long as the three powers felt any uncertainty as to whether they would succeed in getting all they wanted in territorial terms, they were likely to be more open to negotiation on the subject of the constitutional arrangement of what remained of Poland. Until they were in formal possession of their new acquisitions, Stanisław might bluff them into trading constitutional concessions for territory. He hoped that having diminished Poland physically, they might be inclined to allow her a more efficient form of government. Loss of land might, in effect, have its compensations.

Catherine had her own thoughts on the subject. She was disillusioned with Stanisław, with the Familia and with the malcontents. Stackelberg was to reorganise the constitutional framework in such a way that whatever clients Russia did use would be able to serve her purposes but not govern effectively. Learning from Repnin's mistakes, he picked people of no standing who would be unable to defy him. His first choice was Adam Poniński, Master of the Kitchens, a man whose self-interest was matched only by his delusions of grandeur. 'He was one of those creatures who are born and mature only in the sewers of revolutions, creatures that social philosophy should dissect and examine in depth in the interests of human instruction,' in the words of one contemporary.[7] To lead the Lithuanian collaborators, he picked Michał Hieronim Radziwiłł. Others who were to prove immensely useful to Stackelberg were the Sułkowski brothers, who had turned away from Stanisław. The elder, August, was dubbed 'the Cromwell of Wielkopolska' by Stackelberg on account of the zeal with which he now opposed the king.[8] Stackelberg also recruited Teodor Wessel and Marcin Lubomirski, and, by arranging the release of the four senators imprisoned by Repnin in 1767, won over many Barians to his side. Bishop Sołtyk returned a broken man, unhinged by his experiences. His colleague Załuski, old and tired, gave himself over to his devotions. Hetman Rzewuski buried himself on his country estate. Only his son Seweryn, whom Stanisław nominated Field-Hetman of Poland, took any interest in politics – with consequences that stretched far into the future.

Thus Stanisław found his old enemies regrouping, some of his former collaborators, such as Młodziejowski and the Sułkowskis, ranged alongside them, and a bevy of opportunists swelling their ranks. He himself was short on political support. The ageing Czartoryski uncles were relinquishing their grip, Adam was abroad, so policy was increasingly in the hands of Stanisław Lubomirski. He favoured a degree of independence from the king, and began to extend the Familia's influence and broaden its base. A significant step in this direction was the marriage on 27 December 1772 of his daughter Elżbieta to the young Ignacy Potocki, whose family had been traditional enemies of the Familia, and particularly of the Poniatowskis. The wedding was also the occasion for an insult to Stanisław. The bride was the daughter of the king's first cousin, but the groom was the nephew and ward of the redoubtable harridan Katarzyna Kossakowska, who waged a private war on Stanisław and refused to be presented to him. As she insisted on being there and persisted in her refusal to acknowledge the king, he had to stay away in order not to suffer an affront to his majesty.

It was a lonely time for Stanisław. 'He is very rarely to be seen, and dines for the most part quite alone,' reported a diplomatic agent.[9] He was also penniless. Both Benoit and Reviczky had offered him pensions as a bribe for his co-operation.[10] When he refused, they resorted to bullying, pointing out the harm they could do to the country over and above partitioning it. Frederick was again minting fake Polish coinage, and answered Stanisław's protests with the curious justification that he only did it so that his troops could pay for supplies in Poland. Complaints poured in to Stanisław from the provinces, but he could do nothing. To add insult to injury, General Lentulus told him that Frederick was only taking defensive measures, as he feared that Stanisław would become a despot.[11] Their behaviour was outrageous, particularly in the case of Benoit. A dreary man of mean birth and little consequence, treated like a low functionary by his own master, he soothed his bile by insulting a powerless king. Stanisław swallowed hard and ignored the insults, but it could not have been easy. 'The king's person and manner are strikingly engaging and manly,' noted Hugh Elliot, the future diplomat Lord Minto, who called on Stanisław at the end of September 1772. 'I never was so moved with any scene as with the first aspect of this court. Remorse and despair get the better of the forced cheerfulness with which they endeavour to veil the approach of ruin, slavery and oppression.'[12] It was against this background that the battle over the future of Poland's government began.

While most of the Barians had dreamt only of dethroning Stanisław, a few had given thought to what kind of system they should introduce if they won. Michał Wielhorski, who had represented the confederation in Paris, discussed the Polish question with the Abbé de Mably and with Jean-Jacques Rousseau. The upshot of these conversations was Mably's *Du gouvernement et des lois de Pologne* and Rousseau's *Considérations sur le gouvernement de Pologne*. Mably suggested a strong Seym, the reduction of royal power, and the abolition of the veto. Rousseau liked the idea of federative systems and believed in organs that could express the will of the people. He therefore recommended a strong role for the seymiks and retention of the veto. Wielhorski himself used the two treatises as a basis for his own project, published in 1775, which was a stew of the two French philosophers' ideas, seasoned to the taste of the Barians. Bishop Adam Krasiński's project advocated the abolition of the veto and stronger central government based on a cabinet. Józef Sanguszko suggested a permanent Seym with a reduced membership, and the limitation of the veto to matters of great moment. His former tutor Pyrrhis de Varille presented these thoughts in more coherent form in his *Réflexions politiques sur la Pologne*. Antoni Sułkowski was for a council of ministers that would rule independently of the king, a solution typical of Stanisław's enemies. Some of the projects advocated an hereditary monarchy, but most were republican in the sense the magnates understood the term. But they all betrayed the conviction that some sort of permanent executive government was needed. And this had been the basis of all Stanisław's efforts to date. The only project produced by a kindred soul was Zamoyski's, based on the English model of balance between Crown and Parliament.[13] And his arguments were backed up by the publication, in 1772, of the full text of Montesquieu's *De l'ésprit des lois* in Polish.

Stanisław had intended to develop existing institutions. He revived the Senate Council, which had become little more than a court ceremony under the two Saxon kings. He convoked it regularly and made its sittings secret. He proposed, first to Repnin, then to Saldern, the creation of a permanent council. The proposal was rejected by St Petersburg several times, but by 1772 Russia had come round to the idea in its search for an instrument through which to rule Poland without allowing any one party to gain an ascendancy.

The ground was therefore well prepared, and it seemed certain that Poland would at last acquire continuous cabinet government. The question at issue was what form this would take, and whether it would be fashioned as an instrument of the king or of an oligarchy of magnates. Stackelberg considered the various projects, and at the beginning of February 1773 sent a draft of his own to St Petersburg for approval. In his covering note, he explained that he envisaged a Poland 'happy within, insignificant with regard to the rest of Europe'.[14]

Stanisław did not like the proposals, but he was in no position to influence them. His diplomatic efforts had come to naught. Although Branicki's subsequent interviews with d'Aiguillon had been more positive, it was clear that nothing would come of the French promises. Stanisław was gravely disappointed by France. 'Her principles today are the bizarre consequence of the memory of what she has been and of the feeling of what she is, that is to say of arrogance and timidity,' he wrote in his letter recalling Branicki in February 1773.[15] It was time to abandon the first line of defence and fall back.

The Senate Council met again and for the last time on 8 February 1773. It recommended that the king call elections to the Seym, which he did. At the same time he set about defending his kingdom on paper. The three powers had published full justifications of their territorial claims. The Prussian declaration ran to some forty pages and indulged in predictably dishonest arguments hingeing on the quasi-mythical descent of a Prince Barnim of Pomerania, supported by forged documents. The Austrian declaration was an absurd concoction running to nearly a hundred pages. It lamely attempted to prove that the territory Austria was awarding herself, having some six hundred years previously belonged to the Duchy of Red Ruthenia, should in 1190 have passed to the Hungarian king Bela III, and thence on down to the house of Austria. The argument rests on tortuous interpretations of barely legible medieval chronicles and documents of dubious authenticity. The Russian declaration was the shortest. It began by stating that since the Poles resented the Russian guarantee and denounced it, Russia was no longer morally bound by it. 'In an Anarchy, where disobedience annihilates all regular government and destroys all civil law, the state itself, perpetually violated in its rights, ceases in effect to exist,' it propounded. It went on to describe how over 300,000 Russian serfs had fled into Poland, where they had been 'debauched' with liberty, cited the cost of keeping Russian armies in Poland as grounds for compensation, and mentioned in passing that Poland had in fact annexed various Russian border areas.[16]

Stanisław's replies make good reading. The Prussian claims are dismissed with hauteur, the Austrian ones with devastating historical evidence. The reply to the Russian declaration begins by stating that if Russia had merely justified her act of conquest by her superior might, Poland would have had nothing to say, but that since she had invoked rights and duties, she must be answered. In a tone of almost indulgent reproach, it points out that 'to guarantee in 1768 the territory of the Commonwealth only to appropriate it in 1772, under the pretext of injury caused over the past sixty years, are two actions that should not have issued from the same hand'.[17] Stanisław must have enjoyed composing the replies, even if they were largely irrelevant to the struggle he was about to face in the Seym.

Stackelberg wanted to ensure the election of his men, and staffed the seymiks with Russian troops. Stanisław did not encourage his supporters to stand. Only 108 deputies were returned, the lowest number in the history of the Commonwealth, and only thirty-six senators took their seats when the Seym opened. A few days before, Poniński and Michał Hieronim Radziwiłł announced a confederation with the support of only sixty deputies and nine senators, declaring that 'he who is not with us is against us'.[18] They invited Stanisław to adhere to it, but he refused. On 19 April 1773, when the Seym actually met, it turned out that his supporters were reinforced by a group of patriotic deputies bent on obstruction. On the opening day their leader, Tadeusz Reytan, attacked Poniński so vehemently that he fled from the chamber. He repeated the performance on the following day, and then changed his tactic. He and three others staged a sit-in, by barricading themselves in the Senate for thirty-eight hours. When Russian soldiers were brought in to clear them out, Reytan and his supporters made a dramatic show of passive opposition, then registered their veto and left Warsaw.

On 21 April the ambassadors of the three powers called on Stanisław and told him that if he did not join the confederation with Poniński they would give orders to their troops to start looting Warsaw. On the following day Stanisław took the floor in the Seym. He asked the chamber for guidance. There was silence. 'I do not wish to be declared the cause or become the pretext for the final destruction of the country,' he said. 'I have neither soldiers, nor means of resistance. I therefore believe that I would do well, or at least the least harm, by joining the confederation, which will do everything it wishes without me and in spite of me.'[19] While he acceded to the confederation, he attempted one last piece of obstruction by suggesting that the territorial demands of the three powers be laid before neutral powers such as France and England for their mediation. The Seym agreed and addressed a note to that effect to the three ambassadors. But they replied that unless the Seym submitted forthwith, they would partition the rest of Poland.

Stackelberg had opted for Repnin's method of bypassing the Seym. Accordingly, on 10 May 1773 Poniński read out a proposal that the Seym elect a delegation and invest it with the power to negotiate and ratify the treaties of partition on its behalf. The sting in the tail as far as Stanisław was concerned was that the proposed delegation would also be empowered to draw up a new constitution for Poland. He sprang forward to defeat the project. He told the chamber that if he were to go on resisting the cession of territory any longer, he would lay himself open to the reproach that 'in seeking vain glory in obstinate yet powerless resistance, I expose the remainder of my country to even more disastrous consequences; I am therefore making the supreme sacrifice of my self-esteem, and swallowing my pain . . . '[20] He accepted the necessity of allowing the delegation to negotiate the partition. But he could not accept giving it legislative powers. He was eloquent on the right of the Seym to decide on the future form of government, and in the process made a fine defence of the Crown's prerogatives. Poniński responded with an attack on Stanisław's despotic tendencies, and the brothers Antoni and August Sułkowski made speeches that were insulting as well as hostile. Stanisław rose to speak once again. '*Popule meus, quid feci tibi*?' he asked the Seym, wishing to know why he should be stripped of his prerogatives.[21]

For four days Stanisław pitched his eloquence against Poniński's project. But he had few supporters in the chamber, and everyone was looking to their own interests. In April he had given the vacant Vice-Chancellorship of Lithuania to Joachim Chreptowicz, but this had offended Bishop Massalski, who now sided with his opponents. He had also incurred the anger of his own brother by giving the rank of Field-Hetman, which Kazimierz coveted, to Branicki in an attempt to secure the latter's wavering loyalty. Kazimierz resigned all his charges and withdrew from politics.

The Czartoryskis and Lubomirski would not support him either. 'You have more than fulfilled all that honour and duty demanded,' Michał Czartoryski told Stanisław. 'But that is enough. We beg you to give way.' The three ambassadors delivered a note declaring that they were 'surprised and saddened' by Stanisław's resistance, and that there would be no further warnings.[22] On 14 May Poniński's project was passed by fifty-eight votes to fifty-two.[23] Stanisław announced that he would withhold his signature from the law, but, seeing the hopelessness of the situation, he gave in on 18 May.[24]

A delegation was invested with absolute power to negotiate all issues on behalf of the Seym. 'It is made up for the most part of the most corrupt subjects of the Commonwealth, most of them my enemies,' Stanisław wrote to Monet, 'so I expect only harm from all the work that is entrusted to them.'[25] He could be fairly certain that whatever form of government they did come up with, it would not be one in which he would be allowed much power. 'Cursed be the day that led me to the unfortunate position I occupy, and which I cannot abandon,' Stanisław wrote to Madame Geoffrin, complaining of constant migraines.[26] But things were not to turn out quite as expected.

The delegation began sitting on 2 June. The minutes of the fifty-four sessions make surrealistic reading.[27] At the first session, Baron Reviczky proposed to commence the reading of the new treaty with Austria, which he assumed would then be signed and sealed. Before he even started, there was a row about seating arrangements and protocol. Then came numerous complaints about the conduct of Austrian troops, allegations that they were foraging without paying, or that they had ravaged some town or estate. August Sułkowski, Marcin Lubomirski and Młodziejowski tried to bring the delegation to order, to no avail. It was not until the fourteenth session that Reviczky managed to begin reading out the proposed treaty, but he did not get far before red herrings – foraging, compensations, alleged violations – were dragged across his path, and the session was adjourned amid scenes of chaos. Reviczky left the hall cursing.

Four sessions later, they were still bickering about the wording of the preamble, and it was not until the nineteenth session, on 3 August, that the proposed treaty was actually read out. The text provoked uproar, and almost every article of it was called into question. There was a hard core of resistance, led by Michał Czartoryski, Stanisław Lubomirski, August Moszyński and Joachim Chreptowicz. Even Poniński was finding the terms of the treaty hard to swallow, and Russian clients like Antoni Czetwertyński were turning out to be masters of diversionary tactics.

'I did not come to this assembly to watch debates,' Reviczky snapped, 'and I must make it clear to you, gentlemen, that while the delegation may be allowed to alter what it sees fit in the treaties in the way of form, it will not be able to touch any of the essentials, particularly with regard to the frontiers.'[28] Two sessions later, however, they were back to their stalling tactics. Members stood up and made statements with no bearing on the issue, provoking lengthy debates while Reviczky vainly tried to bring the matter back to the case in point. It is hard not to believe that they were enjoying themselves.

Stackelberg turned up and cracked the whip, but there was little he could do. The whole point of going through the charade was to obtain the 'voluntary transfer' of the territories, so he was to a certain extent caught in a trap of his own making. At the same time, there was nothing the members of the delegation could effectively do, and they knew it. Stackelberg wore them down by vexations and confiscations. A typical incident took place after Bishop Turski had made some protest against the proposed treaty. He returned to his residence to find a platoon of Russian hussars billeted there. They lolled about on his sofas smoking and drinking with their whores, breaking or stealing his possessions.[29]

The treaty with Austria was eventually signed at the twenty-ninth session, on 21 August, after a more than usually energetic intervention by Stackelberg. At the thirty-seventh session, on 1 September, lasting seven hours, the treaty with Russia was signed. Stackelberg thanked the delegation for being 'the instruments of the happiness and tranquillity of their motherland'.[30] Five days later, the negotiations started over the treaty with Prussia, and this was not agreed on until the forty-eighth session, on 18 September 1773.

The treaties were to be ratified by the Seym, which had reassembled on 15 September. However, the deputies were in fighting mood and many came to Stanisław for guidance. He tacitly encouraged them to resist, declaring that he would refuse to break the *Pacta Conventa*, which forbade him to cede Polish territory. He was hoping that the greater the difficulty Stackelberg encountered over the cession of territory, the more tractable he would be on the question which concerned Stanisław vitally.

In the summer, the delegation had formed a sub-committee to produce a project for a new form of government. It was dominated by people such as Poniński, Młodziejowski, Bishop Massalski, the

Sułkowskis and Wessel, who outdid each other in proposing reductions to the king's prerogatives. They did not do this merely out of spite or envy. 'I hope that the Poles will be wiser than the English,' Mably exhorted them, claiming that the kings of England were accorded too much power and money.[31] In line with his view that Stanisław should have no more than 'a shadow of authority', the committee envisaged the monarch as a rubber-stamp for the decisions of a ruling council, to be rewarded with 6 million złoty from the civil list. Poniński saw himself as a sort of absolute ruler at the head of such a council, and the only point on which he was still uncertain was that of the title to be attached to this role. He suggested 'Tribune', then 'Speaker', then 'Grand Orator' (and in passing got the Seym to award him the title of Prince).

Stanisław countered by publishing, anonymously, his own project. This advocated an English-style balance between a strong Crown and a reformed Seym with extensive powers.[32] It proved popular with the Seym, which was increasingly apprehensive of government by oligarchy, and at the next session, on 21 September, many voices were raised in defence of the Crown. Poniński challenged Stanisław to give up his prerogatives willingly, and August Sułkowski followed this with a speech which was so sarcastic and impudent that Stanisław had to be bled afterwards.[33] But the chamber was with the king. On 25 September it voted to ratify the partition, but only on condition it was given back control over the constitutional issue. This elicited an ultimatum from Stackelberg and Benoit, who declared that their courts viewed any further delays as a *casus belli*. Under pressure, the Seym agreed to extend the delegation's powers until 22 January 1774, empowering it to draw up the new constitution. In the mean time it ratified the treaties of partition.

Stanisław's resistance on constitutional matters was no longer likely to provoke further encroachments on Polish territory. Indeed, now that she felt secure in the possession of her new provinces, Austria grew friendly. Both Maria Theresa and Kaunitz favoured a strong Crown and the abolition of the veto, and Reviczky began to voice this line.[34] Maria Theresa suggested that France send an ambassador to Warsaw and co-ordinate policy with Austria in an effort to 'give Poland some kind of substance'.[35] Stanisław had no agents left in Vienna to help him capitalise on this goodwill. His brother Andrzej had died in the previous year, Stormont and Canal had both been posted elsewhere. Moreover, Russia and Prussia were alarmed at Austria's apparent change of heart, and particularly at renewed rumours of a Habsburg marriage, which the Vatican was now trying to arrange for Stanisław in an attempt to draw the Catholic states of central Europe together.[36]

At the same time the uncoupling of the constitutional issues from the partition exposed Stanisław: he was no longer fighting for Polish territory, but struggling for his own survival, financial as well as political. The partitions had robbed him of the Crown lands of Mohylów, Malbork and Sambor, and of the salt-mines of Wieliczka (taken by Austria). Stanisław calculated that this reduced his revenues by just over 4 million złoty, nearly half his annual income.[37] It was understood that the Treasury would have to make up this loss from the civil list, but this would be yet another bone of contention.

He had run up debts on behalf of the state to the value of some 9 million złoty, to cover losses incurred through war, the deficit on the Mint and other shortfalls. He claimed that he had himself suffered losses of about 17 million złoty up to the beginning of 1774, and he did not include in this figure monies spent in the public interest on such things as embassies, the Guards, and so on.[38] He was also owed a great deal by Russia, since payment for forage and compensation for ravages to his estates by its troops were in arrears. 'I am dying of hunger,' he wrote to Madame Geoffrin, but he could not afford to be seen to be grasping.[39] When, in February 1774, the delegation addressed itself to the matter of his financial establishment, he showed them detailed accounts and adopted an attitude of proud aloofness. 'Examine your resources, and then see what you can, what you wish to do for me,' he told them.[40]

Among the prerogatives of which the delegation was proposing to strip him was the granting of starosties, a powerful source of influence. Poniński had suggested a Distribution Commission, to be presided over by himself, to take over that role. He announced that the starosties would be sold at nominal prices to the deserving, and set about drawing up a list of those to be 'rewarded for their services to the motherland'. People began to line up outside his door eager to prove their merit.

Poniński's resourcefulness did not stop there. The old problem of the Ostróg entail surfaced once more in the light of the general reorganisation of the country's fiscal constitution, and many hoped that the valuable estate could at last be placed in the hands of the Treasury and used to support the army. The Order of Malta sent an ambassador to register its claim. Poniński outmanœuvred him and struck a deal whereby the entail was turned into a Grand Priory of the Order, with himself as Grand Prior, providing him with a meal-ticket for life. Nor did he neglect his friends the Sułkowskis, who became Commanders of the Order.

On 10 September 1773, news had reached Warsaw of the Pope's Bull *Dominus ac Redemptor*, abolishing the Jesuits. The news caused widespread dismay, and there were suggestions that the Bull be ignored. The Pope regarded it as a purely ecclesiastical matter, and his Nuncio assumed that the estate of the Jesuits would be redistributed among the bishops. This could not be. With the University of Wilno and fifty-seven colleges throughout Poland, the Society of Jesus was the largest educational institution in the country, and the subject of education had recently become a matter for wide discussion. Stanisław had raised the idea of a national system of education at one of his Thursday dinners, and as a result Chreptowicz had produced a draft project.[41] Ironically, this suggested funding a national system of education by confiscating the wealth of all the religious orders in Poland except for the Jesuits and Piarists. In the Seym, the Kraków deputy and supporter of the king, Feliks Oraczewski, had advocated an educational system which would 'turn people into Poles, and turn Poles into citizens'.[42]

Bishops Młodziejowski of Poznań and Massalski of Wilno suggested that the Society's entire wealth be given over to education, and the Seym voted overwhelmingly in favour of this on 27 September, just before it adjourned and handed over its powers to the delegation. Stanisław was delighted. The 1,750 Jesuits in Poland represented the largest body of educated people in the country. 'Let us encourage the ex-Jesuits to serve Poland as they served their order,' he exclaimed.[43] The Jesuits themselves were in favour of such a solution, and wanted Stanisław to be in charge. Chreptowicz quickly redrafted his project to suit the new situation. But Massalski produced a counter-project, which placed the whole matter in the hands of a Commission for National Education headed by himself.

The moment the dissolution of the Jesuits was announced, people began to cast a greedy eye over the Society's vast estate. Country squires clawed back gifts or bequests made by themselves or their forbears, others invented claims on pieces of Jesuit land or simply appropriated what they could. Even the princesses of France registered a claim for bequests made by the Leszczyński family.[44] Młodziejowski suggested that a full inventory of the Society's wealth be compiled, and Poniński assumed the task himself. Since such a compilation entailed making decisions on claims put forward by individuals, he was in the happy position of taking bribes in return for excluding lands or property from the inventory. He then set about liquidating what was on the inventory, through two commissions, one under Massalski, the other under Młodziejowski. Stanisław again suggested auctioning the property to the highest bidder, but the commissions opted for selling it off at 'estimated' prices, which were extensively negotiable under pressure of friendship or bribery.

The moral climate of Polish politics was degenerating, and Poniński was in his element. He was receiving the huge sum of 2,000 ducats a month as a retainer from Stackelberg (Michał Radziwiłł was getting 1,000 and the Sułkowskis and other leaders in the delegation lesser sums).[45] He was drawing heavily on the funds of the Grand Priory of Poland and appropriating slices of Jesuit estate (church gold and silver plate were the first to go). He had awarded himself the lucrative tobacco monopoly, and he was taking countless bribes to award offices and favours. A swarm of unscrupulous scavengers assisted him in asset-stripping the state. As it became clear that vast fortunes were there for the taking, even otherwise honest people joined the scramble. Those who got the most, led by Poniński himself, gambled and spent on a gargantuan scale, creating a carnival atmosphere in the capital while the future of the country was being decided. An English diplomat noted that the Russian embassy resembled 'a club of gamesters'.[46] Poniński was an obsessive gambler, and lost on a gigantic scale. But even Bishop Massalski, who was a renowned cheat at cards, contrived to lose the huge sum of 360,000 złoty at one session in October 1773.[47]

The stakes were much higher for Stanisław. The delegation, acting on Stackelberg's orders, was empowered to revise the constitution, define his prerogatives, decide the level of his revenues, and reorganise the whole fiscal system. Since he had little influence within the delegation, he could only defend his own interests and those of the state through the Seym, but whatever support he managed to conjure up

44 Medal designed by
Stanisław in 1770, showing the
ship of state sailing in a storm
between Scylla and Charybdis

45 Stanisław in the early 1770s,
by Aleksander Kucharski

46 The marble chamber at the
Castle

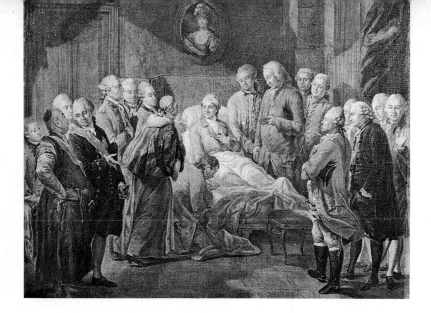

47   Stanisław recovering from the attempt on his person, by Friedrich
Lohrmann. The miller kneels at the foot of the bed, with his wife standing
behind him. The other figures, from left to right are: Tomasz
Aleksandrowicz, chamberlain and later marshal of Stanisław's court;
Marcello Bacciarelli; Kazimierz Karaś, marshal of the court; General
Coccei, commander of the Guards; 'tapissier de la cour' Susson; Dr
Boeckler; Franciszek Ryx; Johann Regemann, Adam Czartoryski's
physician; Charles Lagénie and Wilhelm Ritsch, court surgeons; Kazimierz
Poniatowski; August Moszyński; Gaetano Ghigiotti, royal secretary;
Anastazy Walewski and Józef Zabiełło, both chamberlains.

48   'Picture of Europe for July 1772', an English caricature. Stanisław
waits, bound and bowed, while Catherine, Joseph II and Frederick II
haggle over a map of Poland, with the kings of France and Spain looking
on in concern, the Sultan in chains, and George III asleep.

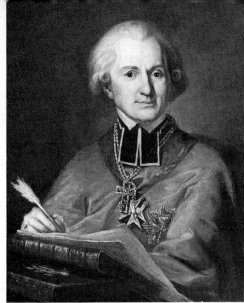

49 *Above left* Stanisław's youngest brother, Michał, soon to become Primate of Poland, by Bacciarelli

50 *Above* Adam Naruszewicz, Bishop of Smolensk, a friend and close collaborator of the king, painted by Mateusz Tokarski

51 *Left* Jacek Małachowski, a conservative and efficient Marshal of the Crown, by Józef Peszka

52 Joachim Chreptowicz, the mainstay of Stanisław's foreign policy, by an unidentified miniaturist

53   Project for parish school teachers' training college, by Marcin Knackfus, 1776

54a & b   The *Merentibus* medal

55   Two generations: a conservatively dressed szlachta couple with their son, wearing the uniform of the Cadet Corps. Detail from a painting by Bellotto.

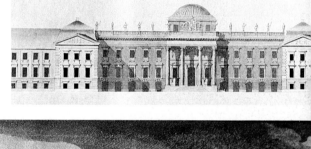

56　Merlini's project for
rebuilding the Castle, 1773

57　Second project by Merlini,
c. 1780

58　Fontana's project of 1772

59 The smaller throne room, leading to the conference room

60 The Great Hall of the Castle

61 Stanisław in the uniform of the Cadet Corps, by Bacciarelli

62   Project for the Academy of
Sciences, by Merlini, *c.* 1775

63   Marcello Bacciarelli with his
two sons, self-portrait

64   Cartoon ridiculing
Stanisław's building projects, by
Norblin. Bacciarelli, with a
donkey's head, proposes projects
to Stanisław. Various individuals
are stealing bags of coins, while
two cartloads of plans for the
Castle and Łazienki trundle past
in the distance.

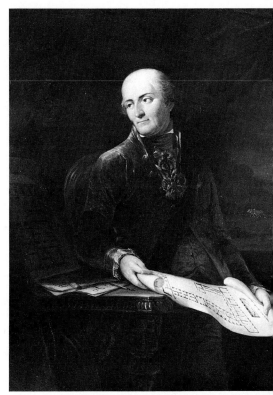

65 Project for a silk-worm breeding farm, by Szymon Bogumił Zug, 1782

66 A vase from the Belweder factory established by Stanisław, mid-1780s

67 Antoni Tyzenhauz, by an unidentified artist

68 Plans for a brewery at Dereczyn

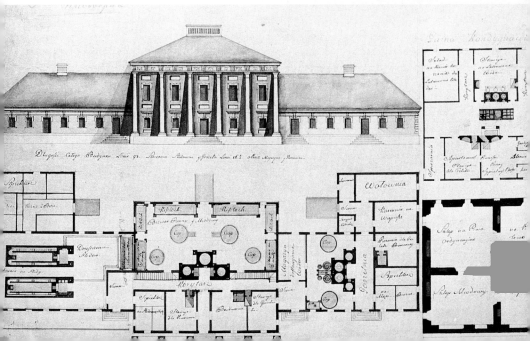

was quickly eroded by Poniński's skilful rabble-rousing, and above all by his ability to distribute largesse. Whenever he made a show of firmness, Stackelberg resorted to bullying.

On 9 December, after a meeting during which Stanisław had adamantly refused to relinquish the command of the Guards, Stackelberg announced that he would order the Russian troops in Poland to devastate the country, announcing to everyone that 'out of attachment to his own prerogatives, His Majesty the King is exposing the country to desperate dangers and is their only cause'.[48] The following day he informed Stanisław that Catherine had instructed him to depose him and to have his friends and advisers executed publicly on the market square of Warsaw unless he submitted completely. 'This last blow, I confess, has pierced my heart because it attacks my dignity and most of all because it comes straight from her whom my heart has never wronged,' Stanisław wrote to the ambassador later that day.[49]

But Stanisław did not give up. Stackelberg was increasingly irritated by the magnates, and Panin in St Petersburg had been alarmed at the idea of Poniński and his gang growing too powerful. 'There is nothing more I can get out of Russia except the sash of St Andrew,' Poniński had recently been heard to say. 'As soon as I get that, I shall leave the Russian party and become a Prussian.'[50] He intended to buy himself into Frederick's favour by arranging the secession of Wielkopolska and transferring it to Prussian suzerainty, a plan toyed with earlier by August Sułkowski.[51]

Stanisław sent Ksawery Branicki to St Petersburg to see what could be gained from direct negotiation with Catherine, but nothing came of it. On 28 March 1774 Stackelberg's project for the new constitution was read out to the delegation. Several members spoke out against it, and one pointed out that it was the death-blow to the Seym's power, echoing Stanisław's feelings. Bishop Turski and a number of others declared that they could not give their assent without the agreement of the Seym. As Prussian troops had recently moved forward once again, the delegation declared that it would not decide on anything until the three powers agreed to respect their own treaties. Stackelberg was growing impatient, and issued an ultimatum. Stanisław read this out at a public audience on 7 August, and announced that he could see no way out of accepting the main principles of Stackelberg's project.

It took another seven months of negotiations to finalise the matter, with Stanisław haggling over every point with Stackelberg and every member of the delegation fighting for his own interests. Branicki and his colleagues were looking to the powers of the hetmans, the treasurers to theirs. The sessions of the Seym grew longer, to the point where Stanisław initiated a routine of having a light supper served to him at a small table behind the throne. Stanisław found himself having to defend not only his own position, but the powers of the Seym, the Treasury and Military Commissions, and the Commission for National Education. In the Seym, he vainly tried to prevent the slashing of military expenditure by half, even offering to forgo his civil list for that year.[52] He had told Stackelberg that he would be prepared to give way on a number of his own prerogatives in exchange for the abolition of the veto. But Panin decreed that the veto must stay.[53] On 8 April 1775 the new constitution, couched in a set of Cardinal Laws, was presented to the Seym and approved. On 11 April the Seym and the delegation were wound up.

Stanisław had lost the fight. The new form of government consisted of a Permanent Council, composed of the king, the Primate, and of two bishops, eleven senators, four ministers, and eighteen deputies to the Seym, including the Marshal; thirty-six people in all. The Council was to work through five departments, of eight people each. Its members were to be elected once every two years, in a rotation of one third, by the Seym and the Senate, and would receive salaries. Majority voting obtained in the Council, and the king could not reject a measure passed by it, although he did have two votes to cast. The Council was to produce three candidates for all ministerial, episcopal and senatorial posts, out of which the king could choose one. The Council, not the king, would now name the members of the five departments: Military, Treasury, Police, Justice, and Foreign Affairs. The Council took over from the Crown the right to appoint most of the officers in the army and the distribution of the starosties. The command of the Guards passed to the Military Department. Stanisław retained the right to nominate judges and ambassadors, but little else. He was now a president, and a fairly weak one at that. He had lost many of his direct powers, and much of his influence. It is worth noting that the dissenters, over whom the crisis had started, got no more than the permission to build a few churches and to sit as local magistrates.

The first Council was chosen in equal parts by Stackelberg and Stanisław. Many of the people whom he would have liked to see in it declined, including Stanisław Lubomirski, Andrzej Zamoyski, Ignacy Potocki, Fryderyk Moszyński and Andrzej Mokronowski. Nevertheless, Stanisław began to extend his influence within the Council. With characteristic doggedness, he manœuvred his way round the obstacles erected to restrain him. Those such as Poniński and Sułkowski who had assumed that they would be in control soon found themselves powerless. Their response was to sabotage the king's activities through the departments in which they sat. In October, Stanisław fell ill under the strain. 'Violent headaches combined with a nervous fever' laid him so low that his life appeared to be in danger.[54]

The new arrangement quickly revealed itself to be unworkable. The Council was cumbersome and ineffectual, and it was resented by the Seym and the public. In no sense was it a cabinet based on the Seym, but rather a committee visited upon the country and accountable to none. Opposition to it was headed by the Familia and the disgruntled hetmans Michał Ogiński, Seweryn Rzewuski and Ksawery Branicki. The latter had returned to St Petersburg on his own initiative, to curry favour for himself, and also to intrigue against Stackelberg, whom he did not like. He had found a kindred spirit in the new favourite, Grigory Alexandrovich Potyomkin, and he returned there with Adam Czartoryski. In 1776 he went there again, this time with Ignacy Potocki. It was clear that they were hoping to become the next Russian party in Poland.

Stackelberg was worried by the state of affairs, and this pushed him into the arms of Stanisław, who was full of suggestions for reorganising the Council. This could only be done during the next session of the Seym, in the summer of 1776, but as this drew near it became obvious that the opposition were in fighting mood. There were meetings at Michał Ogiński's Słonim and Kazimierz Sapieha's Kodeń which drew members of the Familia together with sundry opponents of the king. In order to defeat them and improve the constitution, Stanisław dropped his scruples and made common cause with the Russian ambassador. Together, they drew up a list of desirable deputies, and the presence of troops at the seymiks ensured that these were elected. Stackelberg told Adam Czartoryski that if he stood for election he would have dealings with Russian grenadiers. The opposition had managed to get thirty of their men elected, led by Ignacy Potocki and Branicki's nephew Kazimierz Sapieha. But their election was declared invalid on technical grounds, and they were barred from taking their seats. A Russian detachment occupied Sapieha's estate of Kodeń to discourage him from making trouble.[55]

The Seym met on 24 August, and two days later confederated itself under the marshalcy of Andrzej Mokronowski and Michał Ogiński. Russian and Polish troops stood guard and the Seym proceeded in orderly fashion. Stanisław even managed to have gambling banned in Warsaw for the duration. 'It is time, after ten years of giddiness, for the nation to begin to trust a king whose good intentions have been proven,' Stanisław told the chamber.[56] He extolled the virtues of English cabinet government, and managed to isolate those, such as Branicki, Rzewuski and Lubomirski, who wanted to extend the role of ministers. The Council's powers were increased, the independence of the departments was curtailed, and a number of procedural improvements were made.

The main beneficiary was Stanisław, who regained personal control of the Department of Foreign Affairs, the command of the Guards, and the right to nominate all officers in the army. He recovered the right to award twenty-five of the greatest starosties, his revenues were topped up from the civil list to a total of 7 million złoty per annum, and the Treasury undertook to pay off his debts at the rate of half a million złoty a year. The principal casualty of the reforms were the hetmans, who lost most of their power and now had to swear an oath of loyalty to the king as well as the Commonwealth. When Branicki's turn came, he tried to avoid the oath, and when he had to swear it, attempted to leave out the first name of Stanisław Augustus. But he was made to repeat it.[57]

Stanisław had every reason to feel satisfaction. Through cunning, patience and tenacity, he had turned the Council which his enemies had created in order to control him into an instrument through which he could rule, or at least administer the country within the Russian hegemony. It was far from ideal, but it did have the great advantage of having defined powers, procedures and duties. Above all, it was a government, the one thing that Poland had lacked. Stanisław looked to the future with something approaching optimism.

15

Creating a
Nation

hen the smoke had cleared from the diplomatic battle-field it became clear that the position of Poland, and indeed the whole configuration of Europe, had altered far more dramatically than the mere rearrangement of frontiers would suggest. Russia had gained comparatively little in territorial terms. Austria too could hardly be said to have enlarged her empire significantly. Prussia, on the other hand, had managed to link up the two parts of her kingdom and acquire the most prosperous slice of Poland. In real terms, Prussia was the main winner. France had been humiliated, and with her, the Catholic powers. Turkey had been beaten. Austria had compromised herself, and was tied, by her complicity, into a new Northern system. This now stood unchallenged, as the only other major power that had kept her reputation intact, England, was being drawn away by the revolt of her American colonies.

For Poland, the loss of almost one-third of her territory was tragic. Over 200,000 square kilometres were signed away, and with them the country's third most important city, Lwów. Gone too were her lifeline to the sea, her natural mountain frontier in the south, and large stretches of fertile country. Her most important financial centre, Gdańsk, was physically cut off from the rest of the country. She also lost almost two-fifths of her population; nearly 4 million people became subjects of other states. Although Poland was still larger than France and three times the size of Prussia, with a population of 7.5 million, this was of scant significance in itself.

Polish statehood had received a blow quite incommensurate with the actual losses. The Commonwealth had been undergoing a crisis of sovereignty since the death of Jan III in 1696, but no land had been lost in those eighty years. And the country's technical sovereignty had been carefully respected, even with regard to her overlordship of Kurland. In 1772, Polish territorial rights were ignored and her sovereignty mocked openly. There had been a Russian guarantee hanging over Poland since 1717, but this had been in the form of a bilateral treaty. In 1772, the guarantee was shown to be something which the Poles could not reject, but which Russia could flout. And in 1775, what was left of the Polish Commonwealth was constitutionally tied to Russia by a new guarantee, making it a sort of dependency.

The English diplomat Wraxall, who arrived in Poland in 1778, felt, as did presumably his host Wroughton, that 'there is strong reason to believe that the final dissolution of Poland cannot be very remote'.[1] Mably was no less pessimistic. 'Without further trouble, and without any revolution, the rest of Poland will find itself divided, and perhaps this century must serve as the setting for this sinister event,' he mused.[2] He pointed out that the western powers could only attack Russia through Poland, Turkey or Sweden, and all three were now prostrate. To the argument that a war between Russia and Prussia, or Austria and Prussia, might produce a situation favourable to Poland, he retorted that since Poland was too weak to be of any use to either of the parties, she would not be able to exploit such a situation, while any settlement of such a dispute would inevitably entail the powers accommodating each other with the easiest gifts to make – slices of Polish territory. 'Why, I ask you, should Europe, in an effort to prevent a second partition of Poland, do what she did not do to prevent the first? It patiently suffered your decline, and it will patiently suffer your fall,' he warned the Poles.[3]

The partition was unfinished business, particularly where Prussia was concerned. Her annexations begged rounding off with Gdańsk and Toruń. And while a Polish state survived, it would never cease to dream of recapturing the lost provinces, particularly those taken by Prussia and Austria. Their only guarantee of keeping the territory taken was to close down Poland altogether. Stanisław realised this, and that is why he accepted the Russian guarantee with resignation and even a kind of relief.

The new situation did have its compensations. In 1764, Poland had been a playground for the interests of many countries, but these were now excluded by Russia. In 1776 Prussia recalled her formidable and meddling minister Benoit, replacing him with a bilious but harmless agent, a Swiss called Blanchot. And while Russia's spectacular victories against the Turks had dazzled Europe, the war had revealed internal weaknesses, highlighted by the disorders resulting from the plague and famine, and by the savage revolt of the Cossacks under Pugachov in 1773. As soon as she had managed to shackle Poland, Catherine embarked on a far-ranging programme of reorganisation and consolidation at home. She was thus content to leave Poland to itself, or rather to the discretion of her man in Warsaw.

While Repnin had been an executive of Russian policy, Stackelberg's brief was to rule Poland on behalf of Russia. He referred back to St Petersburg much less frequently than his predecessors, and the term ambassador scarcely does justice to his role. Stanisław observed that his position was more akin to that of a Roman proconsul in Asia Minor.[4] Unlike Repnin, he did not have to rage or threaten. The nation had, in Stanisław's words, sunk into 'a kind of stupor', and Russia could pull out her troops.[5]

Stackelberg thought he had the measure of Stanisław. 'He always imagines that he can be a Louis XIV, but he never will,' he said dismissively to the Nuncio.[6] He was wrong, for Stanisław had abandoned that model, and if he sought to emulate anyone in the 1770s, it was Henri IV of France. He certainly shared the French king's gifts of affability, gallantry and clemency, his concern for his subjects, and his pragmatic attitude to politics. It is true that he conspicuously lacked the firmness, the discernment and above all the frugality of his model, as Wraxall discovered for himself one evening in 1778:

After a sumptuous repast, a comedy was performed in a building constructed expressly for the occasion. The whole company, habited in fancy dress, next embarked in barges on the Vistula, attended by bands of music. An Island, fortified and defended by women in the dress of Amazons, the queen Hyppolita at their head, having presented itself to the view, a mock combat ensued, in which the king was the principal assailant. They did not however make a long, or an obstinate resistance; and Hyppolita, followed by her female train,

laid their spears at the feet of the royal Theseus; for whose diversion
they then exhibited an opera. A supper and a ball succeeded, while on
the other islands in the stream of the Vistula, were displayed fireworks and illuminations. It must be admitted that nothing more
classically elegant could have been given by the Princes of the House
of Medici, at Pisa, or at Florence.[7]

'It is apparently only in his weaknesses that he wishes to emulate the
French king,' Catherine observed drily to his ambassador Franciszek
Rzewuski.[8] Catherine and Frederick liked to mock Stanisław, yet
they were quick to panic whenever he showed the slightest sign of
breaking out of the role of royal nonentity which they prescribed for
him. Even the most apparently innocent initiatives aroused their suspicions and provoked diplomatic intervention.

Another might have been tempted to abandon his dreams and
withdraw into a life of hedonism. But it was not in Stanisław's nature
to accept defeat. He was extraordinarily hard-working, and suffered
from a compulsive urge to pursue every scheme at once. He was also
possessed of a remarkably fertile brain, and whenever one project was
shot down, another took wing. With his sense of mission and the
tenacity with which he clung to his vision of a better Poland, this added
up to a nature which would not be stifled or distracted from its chosen
aims. If his courage was sapped by the cold reality of his predicament,
his fortitude was only enhanced by adversity. But his tactics and his
outward behaviour had altered.

Stanisław had achieved a great deal in moments of defeat by
indirect means, and this taught him to give way to frontal assault, in the
conviction that the real battle would be won on the flanks. It was a
tactic that sometimes made him appear abject. This impression was
supported by his proclivity for covert, sometimes wily, methods, by
his tendency to lose his temper from impatience and his failure to react
with thunderous rage when crossed, by his sensualism, his preciosity
and his frequent recourse to tears. But any inference of his pusillani-
mity is firmly contradicted by the evidence of his daily struggle, against
insuperable odds, in a cause whose hopelessness he saw more clearly
than anyone. A few close friends understood and appreciated what he
was doing, but he was far too clever not to realise that the vast majority
of his subjects never would. In order to gain time, fool his guardians

and steal a march on history, he made a cult of patience and mastered a form of courage that consisted in swallowing humiliation in silence, slowly obviating a million petty vicissitudes, and letting the world believe he was frivolous and weak.

While the first twelve years of his reign had brought catastrophe in the form of civil war and partition, they had also yielded many positive results. There were now permanent cabinet government and administrative institutions. The Crown had lost certain prerogatives, but gained in real influence. The hetmans were left with little of either, and were invigilated by their departments. The magnates with their standing armies were a thing of the past. Stackelberg's creatures had fared little better. By 1776 Poniński had gambled away his ill-gotten gains, and was begging Stanisław for a loan. The Familia were now a faction, as they had been before Stanisław's election, and no longer a dominant party. The army, fixed since 1717 at a top figure of 18,000 men, was allowed to grow to 30,000, and its organisation was modernised. Many of the reforms brought in since 1764 had remained in place, and a number of others were passed by the Seyms of 1775 and 1776. The alarming national debt of over 28 million złoty galvanised the Seym into voting a sensible budget. The General Tariff was brought back, the poll-tax was replaced by a hearth-tax, and stamp duty was brought in.

More important to Stanisław were some of the social reforms he had managed to introduce. The law of 1505 forbidding szlachta to indulge in trade, a principle which continued to delay economic progress in many European countries, was repealed in 1775. The legislation forbidding people who did not belong to the szlachta from buying country estates was also repealed. Torture was banned from all legal proceedings, and the death penalty abolished for cases relating to sorcery. Towards the end of the 1776 Seym, Stanisław had called for a revised Code of Laws, and suggested the task be given not to a commission, but entrusted in its entirety to Andrzej Zamoyski. The Seym acclaimed the plan unanimously, and as he thanked it, Stanisław declared that he 'would note this day amongst the happiest in his life'.[9] It gave him hope that he would be able to continue modernising the state in spite of the Russian shackles.

Stanisław reconstructed his political party in 1775 under the leadership of his brother Michał, now Bishop of Płock and Coadjutor (administrator) of the Kraków diocese. It included Joachim Chrepto-wicz; Michał Mniszech, the educated and efficient nephew of the Barian Jerzy Mniszech; Stanisław's sister Izabela's consort Andrzej Mokronowski; Jacek Małachowski, and a number of others. Through his Gabinet he brought into public life people of considerable ability, such as the brothers Stanisław and Marcin Badeni, Antoni Dziekoński, Pius Kiciński, the painter's son Fryderyk Bacciarelli and many others who were to prove their loyalty to him time and again. Stanisław also developed a countrywide network of supporters. In Lithuania, he now worked through Antoni Tyzenhauz, Ludwik Tysz-kiewicz, who had married his niece, Kazimierz's daughter Konstancja, and Antoni Giełgud, whom he brought into the Permanent Council. In every palatinate he picked out intelligent young nobles and pro-moted them to positions of influence. He chose well. Through Józef Stempkowski, Palatine of Lublin, he exerted influence over Podlachia, through Tadeusz Dzieduszycki and Marcin Grocholski he gradually prised the Ukraine from the grip of the Potockis. Stanisław also kept up a vast personal correspondence with hundreds of nobles and officials throughout the country. He rewarded them with honorific posts, the title of gentleman of the bedchamber (he named no less than 743 of these), or the sash of St Stanisław.

All this enabled him to get his candidates elected to the Seym, which they dominated from the mid-1770s. In addition, Stanisław pursued an ingenious policy of using his private administrative bodies to shadow and supersede the Permanent Council's departments. Thus the Gabinet, still managed by Jacek Ogrodzki, and after 1785 by the able Pius Kiciński, gradually took over the conduct of diplomatic business from the Department of Foreign Affairs. Stanisław's Military Office, run by General Jan Komarzewski, effectively took the running of the army away from the Military Department.

Stanisław's attitude had hardened. The experiences of the first decade of his reign had shattered his illusions and dampened his enthusiasm. His faith in people had suffered, and the continual obstruc-tion and bad luck he had encountered had dug a deep well of bitterness in his heart. This did not show in his dealings with people. He was still prepared to open his heart and his mind to others; he was always ready to forgive, and – this may have been a consequence of not having a family of his own – he treated others with an increasingly avuncular indulgence. He may have been a poor judge of character, but he understood human failings, and this is why he did not nurture resentment or hatred, even towards those who had wounded him deeply.

He believed that wounds could be healed and was prepared to take the first steps in reconciliation. He went to some lengths to intercede in St Petersburg to have the lands of Barians like Michał Wielhorski and Michał Ogiński restored to them, and handed out honours to people who had fought against him. He brought August Sułkowski and others who had opposed him into the Permanent Council. In many cases, he was successful in wiping out old animosities, and gaining the friendship, or at least the grudging acceptance of people. Karol Radziwiłł, who could hardly bear to hear the king's name uttered up to 1772, came to Warsaw five years later to pay his respects and offer his co-operation. In the same year Bishop Adam Krasiński, the leading light of the Confederation of Bar, made his peace with Stanisław. Unfortunately, these gestures of forgiveness were sometimes interpreted as weakness, and some beneficiaries of his kindness treated him all the worse for it.

But while he kept the bitterness of his experiences out of his feelings towards other human beings, it had crept into his political attitudes, along with a certain cynicism. He was increasingly prepared to justify the means by the end. He had come to accept that the only option was between a greater and a lesser evil, and he embraced the latter with determination. He asked his nephew Stanisław, who had just met Lord Lyttelton in London, to 'tell him that in the days when he was kind enough to listen to the opinions and feelings of a patriot of twenty-two who spoke with all the ardour of his age; that young man did not think it possible to ever see himself reduced to half-measures, and to indulge in what the English express so well by the word "trimming".'[10] He resigned himself to a course of action that was neither glorious nor admirable, merely sensible and effective.

And it was in common sense and notions of progress that Stanisław now sought justification for his role. It is significant that he stopped courting the *philosophes* and transferred his patronage to savants. He instituted the medal *Merentibus*, which he awarded to those, in Poland and abroad, whose intellectual achievements he admired. From 1773 he paid an annual pension to the editor of the *Courrier du Bas-Rhin* in order to ensure the dissemination of favourable information about Poland.

He now corresponded with people such as Buffon, Lavater and Her-schel, and took a greater interest in new scientific discoveries than in theoretical discourse. In 1775 he suggested to Johann Formey, the Secretary of the Berlin Academy, a project to publish jointly a running Encyclopedia, to which the latest scientific discoveries could be added as they occurred. Stanisław had been elected an honorary member of the Royal Society of London in 1766. In 1785 the St Petersburg Academy elected him a member, and in 1791 the Berlin Academy followed suit.

He also founded his justifications on a reassessment of Polish reasons of state. In this he was helped by the trauma of the partition, which had shaken society out of its complacent view of Poland's past and its old faith in Divine protection. The Barians had propounded the traditional republican view of history, blaming all the disasters on 'tyrants' and suggesting that all would be well if the country returned to the 'golden freedom' of the old days. But their arguments carried less and less conviction. The chastened nation felt less sure of the old catchwords. Poems and pamphlets increasingly represented Stanisław as a wise figure, misunderstood and wronged, and the blame hitherto univer-sally heaped on him began to be apportioned elsewhere. It began to dawn on people that Polish society might itself bear some responsibility for the catastrophe.

Stanisław had used every means at his disposal to destroy the accepted notion of Poland's republican ideal state. In 1771 he wrote a pamphlet, entitled *Suum Cuique*, in which he argued that the current problems had started not in 1764 but in 1572, when the country had become a republic. He reinforced his arguments with the publication of historical documents, collated by his secretary Jan Albertrandi and his erstwhile envoy to France, Feliks Łojko. His most devoted ally in this cause was Adam Naruszewicz, an ex-Jesuit and long-term supporter of the Familia, a good poet, often referred to as the Polish Horace. In 1774 Stanisław made him Bishop of Smoleńsk, which gave him a seat in the Senate but no diocese, since this had been left in Russia. Naru-szewicz expounded the king's ideas in poetry and prose, and in the 1770s embarked on a monumental *History of the Polish Nation*. Its thesis was that Poland had flourished under hereditary monarchs who held the szlachta in check and protected the interests of the townsfolk and peasants.

As well as making the case for a strong Crown, Stanisław wanted to alter the very way in which Poles thought about themselves, their society, and their state. And the single most important instrument for bringing this about was the Commission for National Education set up on 14 October 1773. It consisted of eight people taken in equal numbers from the Senate and the Seym, all nominated by Stanisław for a term of six years. For its first complement, he chose his brother Michał, Adam Czartoryski, Andrzej Zamoyski and Joachim Chreptowicz. In order to show goodwill towards the Familia, he chose the intelligent young Ignacy Potocki; in order to placate rival ambitions he chose August Sułkowski and Antoni Poniński, a cousin of the would-be 'Grand Orator', and in order to keep him quiet, he chose as president Bishop Massalski, who had always shown a keen interest in education.

After Adam Poniński and his clients had helped themselves to large slices of the Jesuit estate, it was placed in the hands of a Liquidating Commission, and then an Administrative Commission, which frittered away more of it. In all, about two-thirds of the Jesuits' wealth was diverted into the pockets of private individuals and never reached the coffers of the Commission for National Education.[11] It was not until October 1776 that the Seym gave the Commission itself the remainder of the Jesuit estate, and Michał Mniszech was placed in charge of accounts. The situation improved markedly, and the total income of 1,852,420 złoty for the first three years was increased to 2,805,470 for the next two (1778–80).[12] In May 1778, after an inspection had shown up Massalski's malpractices, the bishop was forced to resign, and Stanisław persuaded his brother Michał, who was an excellent administrator, to assume the presidency.

Stanisław stamped his personality on the whole enterprise and fashioned it as a tool for fostering cultural and social regeneration. In this he was zealously assisted by his brother, Chreptowicz, Zamoyski and Ignacy Potocki. The day-to-day work was done by the technical committee, consisting of priests such as Antoni Popławski, Grzegorz Piramowicz, Józef Koblański and Jan Albertrandi, to which Adam Czartoryski ceded, as secretary, a tutor he had brought back from France for his son, Pierre-Samuel Dupont de Nemours. Dupont was enthusiastic about the work, declaring that he would 'create a Nation through public education', but he grew convinced that 'the first steps of the Commission were so impressive, and revealed such far-reaching plans to revive the Nation through schemes of civil and military instruction so well-appointed and so practically applied to the peasants themselves, that the foreign Powers, which commanded in the Seym, [would] seek ways of arresting the progress of such schemes.'[13] He feared that his future in Poland might not be as bright as that held out in a letter from his friend Turgot, who had just been named *Controlleur des Finances*. Dupont left at the end of December 1774, and after working for the French government, took off for America, where he founded the powder-mills that were to form the kernel of what is now the Du Pont empire. His pessimism was ill-founded.

On 20 June 1774, the Commission published its regulations for the 1,600 parish schools, which reduced catechism classes and abolished the teaching of Latin as a spoken language, replacing them with Polish and mathematics. The guidelines recommended that each parish school should employ two ex-soldiers to provide military training for peasant children, with the ultimate aim of creating citizens' militias on the Swiss model. They also advocated that peasants should be freed from labour-rents, so that they would have more time to better themselves. The curriculum of all secondary schools was revised, with Polish, logic, morality, history, law, economics and the natural sciences as the core. In 1775 regulations concerning boarding schools for girls were drawn up by Adam Czartoryski, who laid down that they should be taught Polish, history, languages and arithmetic. A general visitation of the schools in the summer of that year revealed that many teachers resented the new curriculum, for which they lacked training and textbooks. There was a shortage of teachers, since many ex-Jesuits had left the profession, while most of the monastic orders refused to take part. Many country nobles kept their children away from schools which, they believed, had been turned into dens of freethinking, and which no longer taught popular subjects such as rhetoric. But such problems were only to be expected.

The most important work of the Commission for National Education, and the most lasting, was done by the Society for Elementary Books, a sub-committee set up in March 1775. It was supervised by Ignacy Potocki, Adam Czartoryski and Zamoyski, and consisted of Popławski, Piramowicz and half a dozen former Jesuits. A list of subjects was drawn up, a competition was announced, and all the academies and learned societies of Europe were notified. The results were impressive. The competition for the mathematics primer brought in nine entries, two of them from Poland. The winner was the Genevan Simon Lhuilier, whose innovative method, published in Warsaw in 1778, was later retranslated and used in France and Germany for many decades. Rural economy yielded two texts, one by Michał Hube of Toruń, the other by Etienne de Rieule, a Frenchman settled in Poland, both of which were published, and a third, by Krzysztof Kluk, deemed too political on the peasant question and therefore printed independently. Hube also produced the physics textbook, zoology was covered by Jean Baptiste Dubois and Kluk, mineralogy by Johann Philip Carosi, diet by Doctor Curti, and Polish editions of works by Doctor Tissot and James Mackenzie dealt with health and hygiene. There was a new Latin-Polish grammar, a history of the world and a history of Greece, by the brothers Gaetan and Wincenty Skrzetuski respectively, a theory of law by Hieronim Stroynowski, and a handbook of Polish political law by Wincenty Skrzetuski. Stanisław was very keen that the young should read and ponder books dealing with the subject of statehood. He promoted translations of Mably's works on Greek history and his *Droits et Devoirs du Citoyen*, and urged the study of the reforms of Peter the Great and Joseph II.

The catechism of the new Polish educational system, the textbook on logic, was entrusted to Condillac. 'No one could better fulfil this important task,' Potocki wrote to him.[14] The manuscript was delivered, translated and published in 1778. But no manual of religious instruction was ever published. The Commission for National Education was sailing into dangerous waters here. For although most of the leading lights in it were priests or ex-Jesuits, their views were anything but orthodox. In producing his course on morality, published in 1778, Popławski based himself on the works of three Protestant and two Catholic writers.[15] He made clear his belief that religion cannot prevent evil, which can only be contained by good laws based on the 'natural order', itself prescribed by God, since He had created the world. Religion was merely the moral perfection of the natural laws, and for this reason, he held, the study of the natural sciences was more important than reading the Bible. His whole thesis was based on a rational concept of reciprocal obligations between men and their fellows and God.[16] It might have been dictated by Stanisław.

This sort of thing was bound to produce violent reactions, and there were frequent complaints from parents. The Commission had inherited a number of Protestant and Orthodox as well as Catholic schools, and planned to run them all as interdenominational establishments. But it was obliged to abandon this idea under pressure from parents. The most visceral reactions were in fact directed not so much at the religious aspects of the new methods of instruction, but at the socio-political views lurking within them. Most of the textbooks published by the Commission took for granted the rationalist beliefs of the Enlightenment. Those dealing with economics, social subjects and history questioned aspects of a social and political order that was still sacred to the average member of the szlachta. Some of them denounced servitude, and Piramowicz's manual on the duties of the parish school teacher laid down that he should awake in every peasant a feeling of self-respect, of society's obligations towards him as well as his towards society. In 1776, Bishop Massalski held an open day for local szlachta at his seminary for teachers. They were subjected to a speech by one of the teachers, who admonished them for having forgotten that the basis of their social position was the obligation of service to the Commonwealth. 'Our peasants, some noblemen say, are born to work for us,' he went on. 'Certainly. But you, you are born to work for them. Your dominion over them can be founded on nothing other than a contract of reciprocal service.'[17] The outburst of resentment on this occasion was appeased by Massalski, but the grumbling continued among parents throughout the country. Ten years later, in 1785, when Franciszek Jezierski used the occasion of a visitation of schools in the Łęczyca area to make a frankly political speech, the local szlachta protested that 'he apparently came here only in order to dishonour us and insult us in front of our children'.[18] It is surprising that such grievances never grew into anything more serious. Since instruction in most parish schools was subject to the views of the parish priest and financially dependent on the goodwill of the local landowner, a nationwide reaction could have annihilated the efforts of the Commission. One reason why no such movement developed was probably that the process of modernisation was fitful and uneven, with change creeping in gradually.

This was not how Stanisław would have liked it. His vision had been more radical and symmetrical. Long before the dissolution of the Jesuits, he had dreamt of founding a central university which would control every aspect of teaching and science. It was to have been based in Warsaw, with departments of liberal arts, medicine, law, theology, languages, fine arts, music and agriculture. It was to have superintended all schools throughout the country, as well as all hospitals and orphanages.[19] A mixture of shortage of funds and cadres forced him to abandon this plan and concentrate on the two existing universities of Kraków and Wilno (the University of Lwów and the Academy of Zamość had been lost in the partition).

The Jagiellon University of Kraków was a caricature of scholasticism and entrenched interest surrounded by a rampart of ancient rights and usage. To breach this was no easy matter, and it took all the energy and political flair of an ambitious young priest, Hugo Kołłątaj. In 1774 he became a canon of Kraków Cathedral, and offered his services to Michał Poniatowski, who was the administrator of the diocese. Poniatowski took him into the Society for Elementary Books, and in 1776 briefed him to look into the finances of the university and report on the method of teaching. Kołłątaj went to work with energy. In 1778 he reformed the philosophy faculty, and in 1780 published his programme for fundamental reform of the whole structure. The horrified academics tried to remove him by accusing him of mal-practice, but in 1782 Kołłątaj became rector of the university. He gave prominence to subjects such as social economics, political law, mathematics, physics and chemistry. With the financial backing of Michał Poniatowski, he put up new buildings, bought books and imported scientific instruments. The university became the head-school for Poland, laying down rules and curricula for all schools in its area, and sending out teachers to inspect and examine. The University of Wilno, under Marcin Poczobut, assumed the same role for Lith-uania. The universities also inspected the religious seminaries, which had their curricula amended to include a number of secular subjects. The teachers at the two universities were formed into an Academic Corps, which Stanisław wanted to develop into a countrywide organisation on military lines, but the idea met with resistance.

While Stanisław's vision had been forced to adapt to the possi-bilities, his aims were carried through in essence. The facade of the system may have lacked splendour, but the building itself was strong and enduring. And Stanisław believed in the future. 'Most of all I lay my trust in this crop which I have sown, although someone else will reap it after my death, when, because of the proper education given to children now, he will find tens of thousands of enlightened citizens freed from all superstition and so much more suitable for every purpose than when I found them,' he wrote to Feliks Oraczewski.[20]

Stanisław also strove to give artistic expression to these ideas, commissioning works of art that expressed a view on events or people. Indeed, it would be possible to reconstruct his attitudes and programme on the sole basis of his artistic legacy, from the smallest objects to the largest works. The great many medals he commissioned from his medallist, Johann Philip Holzhaeusser, testify as strongly in this respect as the great canvases of Bacciarelli or Bellotto. But his most eloquent statements were made through his work on the Royal Castle, which he now resumed with energy. Five new projects, four by Dominik Merlini and one by Efraim Szreger, were produced between 1776 and 1779. Comparison between these and the group of projects from the 1760s sheds blinding light on the change in Stanisław's thinking about the role of the monarchy and its relation to the state. All allusions to Versailles and the Louvre are absent from the new plans, which respect the existing shape of the Castle and its proximity to the old city. Szreger's project is the most interesting, since it turns the Castle into something of a capitol, with the Senate chamber as the focal point, and the courtyard resembling a forum more than a royal *cour d'honneur*. The symbolism of the decorative elements is similarly transformed, with Hercules ceding his place to God the Father, and the deities of Glory and Fame making way for statues of Polish kings.

These projects remained on paper, but in the mean time, Stanisław undertook the rebuilding of the interiors. He redecorated the Royal Apartments entirely between 1772 and 1777, spent the next six years rebuilding the Great Hall, and in 1783 moved on to the Apartments of State. In the Royal Apartments, Stanisław stressed the legitimacy of his position as king. His bedroom, completed by Dominik Merlini after Fontana's death in 1773, was panelled in yew – another reference to Saturn – and decorated with biblical scenes suggesting the sacred nature of kingship, but it has none of the baroque courtly atmosphere of earlier projects, and exudes masculine austerity. The old throne room was redecorated in 1775 by Merlini, with frescoes and paintings by Bacciarelli and Jan Bogumil Plersch, and sculptures by Giaccomo Monaldi. It featured busts of Catherine, Elizabeth I of England, Henri IV of France and Jan III Sobieski, portraits of Stanisław's parents, and allegorical paintings representing Stanisław's own virtues of courage, justice, sacrifice and wisdom. The ceiling depicted the genius of Poland reigning over the arts, agriculture and trade. The Senators' Antechamber was dominated by the theme of Stanisław's election, a painting of which by Bernardo Bellotto occupies the central position. The twenty-one other paintings by Bellotto that effectively panel the room are seemingly random views of Warsaw, but they too have a theme. One shows the Palace of the Commonwealth, another the Arsenal; four more depict churches founded by preceding elected monarchs; the rest feature the palaces of Stanisław's father's successors in the rank of Castellan of Kraków, the highest temporal post in the Senate.

Stanisław began the rebuilding of the State Apartments with the Great Hall, which was both the principal assembly room and the ballroom. He had already considered four projects for this in 1765, and in 1777 he announced a competition among his architects. Projects were put forward by Merlini, Szymon Bogumil Zug, Plersch, Szreger and Stanisław Zawadzki, but Stanisław was not satisfied with any of them. He selected Merlini's project and asked his young protégé Jan Christian Kamsetzer, fresh from his tour of Greece and Turkey, to work on it. The result was a magnificent and highly individualistic room, opened in September 1781, on the seventeenth anniversary of the election. The vast frescoed ceiling depicts Jove turning chaos into order, a favourite theme of Stanisław's, and the room is completed with two statues by Le Brun, one of Apollo, modelled on Stanisław, the other of Minerva, in which a likeness to Catherine is discernible. It was a way of stating that he still had faith, or at least wished to have faith, in her wisdom.

In the same year work began on the great Knights' Hall, which was to be a subliminal history-lesson for the magnates who would use it. He began working on the thematic content in 1773, and revised his scheme at least four times over the next eight years, after frequent consultations with Naruszewicz. The room was to be a hall of fame and achievement, dominated by six large paintings of seminal moments in Polish history, and adorned with the likenesses of thirty-two of the country's greatest kings, warriors, statesmen and men of learning. He agonised over whom to include and which medium to represent them in, and kept rearranging the order. The paintings were executed by Bacciarelli, the busts by Le Brun and Monaldi. In 1783 Kamsetzer returned from another tour, of Italy, France and England, and redesigned Merlini's project, introducing a solemn baroque tone, with a great clock supported by the figure of Chronos-Saturn and two statues, of Fame and Eternity. Naruszewicz composed a poem explaining the meaning of the chamber when it was ready, in 1786.

In the same year Stanisław redecorated the *cabinet* of the State Apartments, along his own designs, featuring portraits of all his brother monarchs. He also started, then abandoned, what was to be a formal chamber for the Permanent Council, which would stress his dominance of that body. In 1786 he rebuilt the Grand Throne Room, as a sacral interior with a clock donated by the Pope, and statues of Scipio and Hannibal, Pompey and Caesar, alluding to the crushing of pride and rebellion by legal authority.

It was an age when people were highly receptive to such allusions, and these interiors delivered a powerful message. Stanisław underlined those tendencies in history and in the life of the state which he considered to be positive, he promoted those figures of the past whom he considered to have contributed something real and, by representing Copernicus among the hetmans of the past, struck at the szlachta's monopoly of fame and merit. By reference to God and the gods of antiquity, he enhanced the sacred nature of his presence, and he used the layout of apartments and the relative importance of the rooms to suggest a hierarchy and his role within the state. By redesigning what was after all the physical centre of the Polish state, he was communicating his vision of the state to all those who entered those rooms. 'I shall not cease to work and build while there is breath in me,' he wrote to Naruszewicz, 'in order to plant and graft good seed in our motherland, although I have long since realised that it is my destiny that it will not be me who gathers the fruit.'[21]

Inherent in this abdication of personal ambition was a transference of hopes and ambitions to another. Stanisław was only in his forties, but a combination of personal factors and diplomatic obstruction had made him put aside thoughts of marriage. He nevertheless continued to build up the position of the Crown and to create court structures that would fit comfortably around a putative successor.

As to who this might be, Stanisław had begun to entertain ardent, if unavowed, designs. He had for some time been impressed by how his brother Kazimierz's son, Stanisław, was developing. The young man had the Poniatowski good looks, a natural refinement and striking intelligence. He was in many ways very close in character to his royal uncle, but he was more determined and displayed some of his father's arrogance. He had been educated by John Lind and graduated from the Cadet Corps. In 1771 he had gone to London and thence on a tour of Britain, and in the following year he spent a year studying at Cambridge. He had also travelled in France, Switzerland and Italy before returning to Warsaw in 1775. He took part in the Seym of the following year and displayed political flair. The king set him up financially, and Andrzej Zamoyski helped. Atypically for a Poniatowski, he possessed remarkable financial talents, and soon grew very rich.

In December 1776 Stanisław sent his nephew to St Petersburg, officially to obtain Catherine's support for Poland in the negotiations over a trade treaty with Prussia. But there were other, concealed, aims. On the one hand, the king wanted to undo any mischief that might have been done by the visits of Branicki and Ignacy Potocki, and, by communicating with her through this personable young man, perhaps rekindle some of her affection for him. There was also the possibility that Catherine might decide that the young man would be a convenient successor to Stanisław, and perhaps give him the Duchy of Kurland in the mean time. Stackelberg had erroneously assured him several times that such a possibility existed.[22]

Young Stanisław cut a good figure in St Petersburg, and was received graciously by Catherine, who bestowed many polite phrases and the Order of St Andrew on him. She also made the somewhat Delphic utterance that: 'The hand which may, perhaps, remove the thorns from the crown of Poland, will give a relative to the king, whose family she may bring closer to herself.'[23] But there were too many hypotheses in the statement, and in a letter telling him to return, Stanisław admitted that: 'It would appear that the success of your trip has not entirely fulfilled our hopes.'[24]

Like all Stanisław's plans, this one was never abandoned, and it was given a boost in the following year, through the agency of France. The death of Louis XV in 1774 brought about a change of attitude in that country's foreign policy, and Louis XVI's new foreign minister, the Comte de Vergennes, took a broom to the cobwebs left by Choiseul,

Aiguillon and the *Secret*. One of his first actions was to cut off all subsidies and to sever unofficial diplomatic contacts with Polish magnates. Stanisław had high hopes of the new monarch and his ministry, and in 1777 he despatched his secretary Maurice Glayre to Paris. 'The slightest move towards France was then a crime in [Catherine's] eyes,' as Stanisław put it, so Glayre's official motive was to fetch furnishings for the Castle.[25]

Madame Geoffrin was on her deathbed, so Glayre relied on the good offices of her daughter, the Marquise de le Ferté-Imbault. He made contact with Vergennes, who hinted to him that France would like Stanisław to emulate the king of Sweden and break free from Russia, with French help. 'He avoided using the word, but he made the thing sufficiently clear,' wrote Glayre.[26] The Prince de Condé approached Glayre with a view to marrying his daughter, the Princesse Louise Adelaïde de Bourbon, to Stanisław.[27] The king replied that he would prefer her to marry his nephew, which would strengthen his royal aspirations.[28] But he was sceptical about French promises and acutely aware of the dangers of defying Catherine. 'My system does not change,' he wrote to Monet in 1778, 'I am holding to Russia, and I desire very much that she should ally herself with France.'[29] This seemed likely, as France and Russia were indeed seeking a rapprochement. 'In that eventuality, there is nothing that I would not dare to hope for Poland from a ministry such as that of France today,' he wrote to Monet.[30]

Hope was what kept Stanisław going. Content in the conviction that God or Providence had put him in the post he occupied, he believed that they had not put him there in vain, and that one day history would vindicate him. This eased the pain of his wounded pride. It allowed him to bear the disappointment of having to put aside his youthful ambitions and elect a caretaker's role. It helped him endure the almost daily aggravations and petty humiliations of dealing with Stackelberg. The only thing against which it was powerless was his sense of frustration, and this could only be assuaged by work – continual, agitated, obsessive and often fruitless work.

16

Cultivating the Garden

Stanisław's was a typically eighteenth-century vision, in which politics, commerce, science and the arts complemented each other and combined to create civilisation. As he dreamed throughout his youth of regenerating his country, he was not thinking merely in terms of making it politically and militarily strong: his underlying urge was to cultivate the wilderness – a strong and pervasive theme in eighteenth-century literature. In other ages, people sought to achieve this through moral admonition; in his, it was seen in terms of spadework and manure. Civilisation had come to be equated with good husbandry. 'Happy Englishman!' Stanisław said to one visitor. 'Your house is raised, and mine is yet to build.'[1]

Not only was the house not built, the plot itself was ill-defined: the gerrymandering of the three powers in 1772 was only possible because the country had never been properly surveyed. Stanisław had engaged Hermann Perthées, a natural son of the erstwhile ambassador Keyserling, as Royal Geographer in 1764, and took a personal interest in fixing the spelling of place-names, but it was not until 1780 that Perthées was ready to start engraving his Polish Atlas. Stanisław's regulation of tariffs, weights and measures, his activation of the Mint, his road-building programme and reorganisation of the postal service, and above all his establishment of Public Order and Paving Commissions in larger towns had all been meant as tools to serve in the erection of the building. *Monitor* and other publications were intended to encourage constructive endeavour, his Poniatovian University and an Agricultural Academy, to be established by Arthur Young, to direct it.

Typical of the times was Stanisław's faith in art as a means of education and a lever for industry, his belief that an antique sculpture or a Renaissance medal had the power to mould the spirit and awaken the appreciation of form that led to good design. While he encouraged and sometimes paid for young men and women to travel abroad, he also wanted to be able to bring this kind of education to larger numbers at home. With the help of August Moszyński, a passionate collector himself, Stanisław built up a comprehensive collection of some 8,000 coins and medals, and one of the most important collections of prints and engravings in Europe, numbering over 30,000 plates. He assembled a geological collection, and built up a *cabinet de physique* consisting of 132 scientific instruments. They were housed, along with a jumble of antiquities, above his private apartments at the Castle. 'My prints and my medals are, in comparison with matters of greater import, nothing more than a pleasant distraction, but I also think of their useful side, and I would like them to become useful to others,' he wrote to Moszyński.[2] These and other objects he had acquired were to form the nucleus of a *Museum Polonicum* for which Michał Mniszech finalised the plans in 1775. The portals were to be inscribed with the motto 'From the Spirit to Utility'. This phrase, conceived by Adam Czartoryski, encapsulated the intention behind most of Stanisław's cultural activities.

As early as 1766 Stanisław's principal painter and director of works Marcello Bacciarelli had drawn up plans for a Royal Academy of Fine Arts, the running of which, he calculated, would not add very much to the costs the king would have to incur over the years in rebuilding the Castle and his other residences.[3] In the 1770s Stanisław attempted several times to further this project, and although no such academy was actually established, it did in effect exist. Stanisław had turned three great chambers on the ground floor of the Castle into a studio in which his painters and sculptors worked, and where cabinet-makers, plasterers and other craftsmen did their drawing. The studio made frequent use of the king's collections of paintings, antiquities, medals, prints and mouldings. It accepted young artists as apprentices and opened its doors to students.

Stanisław's library evinced a similar sense of purpose. Housed in an elegant functional building erected beside the Castle in 1782, it never grew to more than 15,000 volumes. But each one was chosen with care, and every so often books were removed in order to make way for more comprehensive ones. It contained only some 2,000 volumes of literature, while history was covered by 4,000, and the scientific section was among the largest.[4] The librarian, Marc Reverdil, prepared files on topics such as serfdom or constitutional law, which permitted members of the court and the Seym as well as the king to master the essentials of a subject with comparative ease. He also paraphrased longer books and wrote digests of new discoveries or theories, and read these to Stanisław as he was being dressed in the mornings. In the evenings or during sleepless nights Reverdil or one of the other readers would read literary works to him. Therein lay the secret of Stanisław's extraordinary grasp of contemporary literature, thought and scientific knowledge.

His correspondence shows an almost childlike interest in new ideas and discoveries. He badgered his diplomats to provide him with details or samples of things he had seen mentioned in the press or heard of through a visitor. When he read about Franklin's experiments, he began installing lightning conductors at Ujazdów, using kites and obelisks.[5] He was inspired not only by his own curiosity, but also by the idea of showing and making such things available to his people. Ever since his teenage trip to the Netherlands, he had been unpleasantly conscious of the backwardness of his own country, and was determined to do something about it.

The economic regeneration of Poland was no simple matter. The Commonwealth was a huge state, and economic patterns varied considerably. The concentration of population overall worked out at seventeen people to the square kilometre, but in the ethnically Polish areas of Wielkopolska, Mazovia, Kujavia and Małopolska, it was thirty. In Wielkopolska, 25 per cent of peasant rents were in cash, 10 per cent in kind, and 65 per cent in labour. The figures for Małopolska were 10 per cent, 10 per cent and 80 per cent respectively, and for Ruthenia 5 per cent, 5 per cent, and 90 per cent. In Wielkopolska, up to 15 per cent of the peasants were free landowners, a category that hardly existed east of the Bug. As a result, agricultural yields were far higher and grew much faster there than in the eastern areas. Similarly, some 30 per cent of the population in Wielkopolska was town-based,

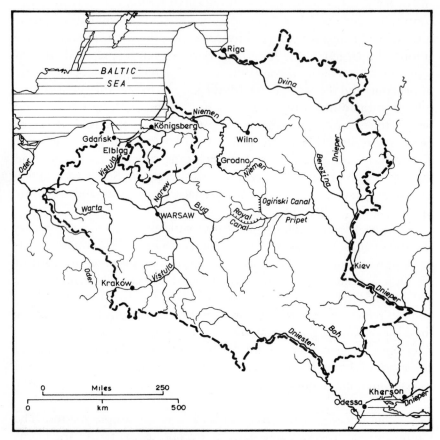

a   The navigable system of Poland-Lithuania

while in Lithuania the figure averaged out at some 5 per cent. By the last quarter of the eighteenth century, Wielkopolska was economically more developed and productive than many parts of Germany, while areas of Lithuania were still economically in the Middle Ages. The industrial sector presented a similarly uneven pattern, with iron production averaging out at 1.8 kilograms per capita. This compares with the figure of 1.2 kilograms per head for Germany, 2.8 for France, and 3.7 for England. And while the annual economic growth in countries like England and France wavered between 0.7 per cent and 0.9 per cent,

nteenth-century Poland

b   Industrial development in the second half of the eighteenth century

in Poland it stood at 0.3 per cent to 0.4 per cent over the century as a whole.[6]

Economic progress was vitiated by a whole range of political and social factors. The magnates were the only entities capable of funding development, but by the middle of the century they were increasingly short of cash, as their establishments absorbed more and more in running costs. The medium-sized landowners did better, as prices of agricultural produce continued to rise, but they were not in a position to invest their wealth in anything but land. There was still no active middle class to speak of, and no banks or other agencies which could handle investment. The cities were so impoverished and legally hamstrung that no major enterprise could issue from them.

It was the magnates who set up industries, and they were poorly equipped for it. They had no understanding of markets, no grasp of long-term investment, and no aptitude for the minutiae of business. Their ventures were usually inspired by foreign travel, and suffered from all the characteristics of dilettantism. Factories were built up too fast and sums were not done. They would import foreign masters whose expertise they were in no position to verify, with the result that they were exploited by fraudsters and fortune-hunters. As there was no developed market, each venture operated within its own. Karol Radziwiłł had a cloth-mill at Nieśwież in Lithuania which he supplied with wool from flocks on his large estate in the Ukraine, while Prot Potocki had a cloth-mill in the Ukraine, very close to Radziwiłł's sheep, which he supplied from his flocks grazing in the Lublin area.[7] This was partly because magnates still tended to think in terms of their own realms being self-sufficient, but mainly because life was not commercialised and there was too little money in circulation. Salaried labour was more expensive than it was in Paris or London, which tempted landowners to use their peasants, and this lowered efficiency and the quality of the products.[8]

Ideas on how the problem should be tackled varied enormously, but they were all heavily influenced by Physiocratism, that strange offshoot of the French Enlightenment, first formulated in the 1750s by Dr Quesnay and the Marquis de Mirabeau and their colleagues of the *Société des Économistes*. It was a curious, proto-Romantic school of applied philosophy, based on the concept of a Natural Law, a harmonious order built on the mutual duties and rights of men, the right of property for all, and an organic pattern of self-sufficiency. It favoured agriculture and held trade and industry to be unnatural and sterile, but shied away from advancing any practical substitute. It was a woolly philosophy which marked social culture and attitudes to the universe more than economic practice.

The Physiocrat Bernardin de Saint-Pierre spent two years in Poland, and when he left in 1764, he wrote a recipe for the country's economic recovery that caused a stir among his colleagues. Poland was an ideal testing-ground for their theories, since it was a predominantly agrarian economy, and they even found the form of government organic in its regionalism and grass-roots democracy. Their first Polish convert was Bishop Massalski, an enthusiast for new ideas. He returned from Paris in 1768 fired by their theories and determined to apply them at home. He also brought the Physiocrat economist Abbé Nicolas Baudeau to visit Poland. On his return to Paris, Baudeau published two works containing his recipe for the country. Massalski preached self-improvement along Physiocratic lines, telling people to plant trees, repair roads and increase yields, and imported agricultural implements from England to serve as models for local production. In 1771 he had to leave the country, having drawn too close to the Barians. He went to Paris, where he discussed the economic and political future of Poland with Mirabeau, Turgot and other leading Physiocrats.

The civil war in Poland prompted the Physiocrats to extend their philosophical system into the political field. In 1772 Baudeau presented to Aiguillon a plan for the pacification of Poland based on Physiocratic ideas, while his colleague Mercier de la Rivière sketched out for Massalski a comprehensive cure for the country. 'The basis of your government is admirable, it is of great strength,' he preached. 'To make it perfect you need do very little.'[9] He suggested the gradual enfranchisement of the peasants, the extension of land-ownership to a wider group of people, and a system of taxation based on agricultural yields. At the last session of the Senate Council, on 8 February 1773, Massalski suggested reorganising the country on these lines. Many agreed with him, and even Stackelberg liked the idea. The philosophy of the Physiocrats was turning into something of a fashion in Poland, fed by the publication in 1774 of a book on the subject by Popławski. It was popular among the szlachta, since it appeared to sanction their supremacy and reinforced their prejudice against the cities.

Stanisław was cautious. He declared himself in favour of 'the establishment of a single tax on land according to the system of the economists'.[10] But that was as far as it went. His cast of mind was much too practical and 'English' to be impressed by metaphysical notions of a natural order. His own preferred recipe for reviving Poland economically would have been the sort of state capitalism practised by his neighbours, and while the Polish state was neither centralised nor rich enough to implement this, he started factories of his own and encouraged others to do so.

The headway made in the economy during the first four years of the reign was largely cancelled out by six years of civil war, and ventures such as the Wool Manufacturing Company did not survive it. Although the partition was signed in 1772 and ratified by the Seym in 1774, the new boundaries were not finally fixed until 1778, until which date Russian and in particular Prussian troops continued to treat border areas as enemy country. The partition was economically more damaging than the loss of territory might suggest, since the surgery had been carried out without regard to local economic patterns, and areas of production were cut off from traditional markets.

Not content with the territory he had annexed, Frederick inhibited the economic recovery of Poland by all available means. In March 1775 he foisted a protectionist trade treaty on Poland whose aim was to maintain Poland as a source of cheap raw materials for Prussian industry and a market for Prussian goods. Duties of up to 50 per cent on some Polish goods and a complete ban on the import of others was to close the Prussian market to Polish industry. A transit duty of 50 per cent on timber floated down to the Baltic ports and one of 90 per cent on wool were designed to force the Poles to sell these cheaply to Prussia rather than export them overseas. Frederick also squeezed Gdańsk in order to make it desire incorporation into Prussia. He slapped a duty of 12 per cent on goods passing Marienwerder, and another 12 per cent on them as they sailed out of Gdańsk. The same goods passing Marienwerder for shipment from Elbląg, now Prussian Elbing, were only taxed at 2 per cent.

The answer for Poland was to find other outlets. Projects were drawn up in 1777 by August Sułkowski and August Moszyński for building new ports, one at Połąga, the other at Libawa in Kurland. But the idea was quashed by Catherine, who feared the unfavourable effects of competition on her own ports.[11] Russia was also nervous of allowing Polish commerce on to the Black Sea, to which the Poles turned their attention next.

In 1768 Stanisław had pushed through the Seym Ogiński's project for a canal between the Szczara and Jasiołda, to link the river system of the Black Sea to that of the Baltic. In 1775 the Treasury began work on another canal, linking the Bug with the Dnieper. In August 1777 the Porte's envoy Numan Bey arrived in Warsaw with proposals for the purchase of Polish grain, but Stackelberg forbade any negotiations.

Stanisław exerted all his influence at the Russian court to reverse this attitude, but it took time. A Polish Consulate was established at Kherson in 1783, followed by a trading house belonging to the joint-stock Black Sea Company. The Royal Canal had been opened in 1783 and the Ogiński Canal in 1784. In that year the first boat sailed from Gdańsk on the Baltic to Kherson on the Black Sea. The digging of several shorter canals and the dredging of rivers opened this outlet to goods from the whole of eastern Poland.

One reason Stanisław was keen to develop the Black Sea trade was that he wanted to use it to promote rapprochement with France. Polish trade with that country had tailed off, and by 1785 the French Consul at Gdańsk was reporting that the earlier average figure of 30,000 barrels of Bordeaux wine imported every year had sunk to 3,736.[12] Stanisław sent August Sułkowski to Paris to investigate possibilities of reviving it. France's main interest lay in ships' stores, but since the English navy could threaten the Baltic routes, a commercial relationship with Poland only became interesting if it could be conducted through the Black Sea and the Mediterranean. The Seym of 1784 passed enabling legislation, and Catherine granted favourable concessions. These included the permission to flag the Black Sea Company's ships with the Russian ensign, the only flag the Turks allowed passage through the Bosphorus. In 1785 Maître Mâteur Dantoine from Toulon carried out inspections of forests in Poland and Lithuania, and by the end of the year there were twelve Polish ships plying between Kherson and Marseille with the wood intended to build a new navy for France, the great stockpile which was burnt by Admiral Hood in 1794.[13]

The combination of devastations caused by the civil war and the Prussian trade treaty had turned what had always been a favourable balance of trade into a deficit. The 50,287 tons of corn exported through Gdańsk in 1764 had fallen to 19,000 in 1776, and the Seym of that year listened in horror as it was told that the country had exported goods to the value of 20 million złoty and imported to the value of 48.5 million. Poland's principal exports consisted of agricultural and forest produce, coarse cloth, potash, lead and vodka. It imported iron, copper, cotton, silk, spices, wine, fish, a variety of luxury goods and, after the loss of the Wieliczka mines in 1772, salt to the value of 7 million złoty per annum. In 1775 sumptuary laws were passed imposing duties on the import of luxury goods, but the only way of improving the balance of trade was to manufacture at home some of the goods that were normally imported, and this had preoccupied Stanisław for a long time.

His ventures in this direction met with mixed results. His reactivation of the abandoned Crown copper mines at Miedziana Góra, begun in 1782, was a failure. The lead-mine he opened near by produced large quantities of poor quality lead. In 1788 he fared better with a marble quarry at Dembnik near Kraków, and in 1789 he branched out into coal-mining. In 1773, after the loss of the Wieliczka mines, he established a salt company to exploit other sources, but it managed to extract no more than about 50 tons per annum during the 1780s. He also set up the joint-stock Metal Company to exploit the lead and silver deposits in the Olkusz hills. In 1768 he had founded a pottery on his own land at Belweder just outside Warsaw, but it lost him so much money that he was forced to sell it in 1780 to a couple of entrepreneurs under whom it flourished. In 1788 he set up a firearms factory on the Crown estate at Kozienice, which he wanted to turn into a model manufacturing town.

By far his most ambitious project, and one that nicely illustrates his ideal, was the development of the large Crown estate of Grodno. In 1765 he had given the farming of the Crown revenues from Lithuania to Antoni Tyzenhauz, with the brief of developing industry there. Tyzenhauz set up a cloth-mill at Grodno in 1767, followed by a linen factory run by Swiss craftsmen. In the following year he activated a silk-works under the supervision of Lyonnais and Florentine masters. In 1768 he started a factory turning out gold thread, braid, tassels, buttons and horse-tack, and another producing stockings. In the same year he established an industrial centre at Postawy producing belts, paper and copper products, a cloth-mill and an iron foundry at Brześć, another linen factory at Szawle, and a firearms factory at Mohylów. Stanisław was impressed by Tyzenhauz's work and encouraged him to expand. In 1770, Tyzenhauz added a camlet mill, a candle factory, a carriage-works, a hat factory, a tannery, an oil-works, a musket factory, and other workshops producing playing-cards, needles and lace. Stanisław wanted to import silkworms, and further plans included a mint, a pottery, a vitriol works, a sugar-factory, a mirror-works and a paper-mill. By 1780 there were fifteen factories at Grodno itself, employing about 1,500 people.[14]

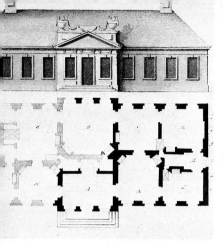

69   'Plan of a house for a married gentleman of substance,' by Marcin Knackfus

70   The ballroom of a country house at Pawłowice, by Jan Chrystian Kamsetzer

71   Country house at Walewice, by Hilary Szpilowski

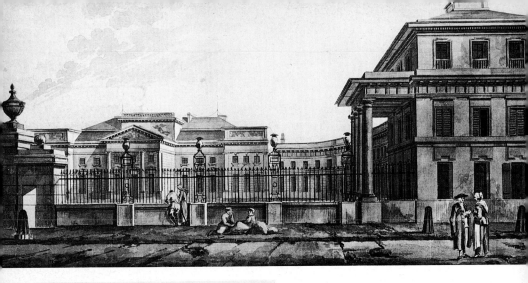

72   The Primate's palace, Warsaw, from a watercolour by Zygmunt Vogel

73   One of the customs-houses that ringed Warsaw, showing the severe neo-classicism that dominated public buildings in the 1780s

74   Miodowa Street, Warsaw, by Bellotto. On the left, the palace of the bishops of Kraków, on the right, the back of Ksawery Branicki's residence, at the very end, the Palace of the Commonwealth.

75   Stanisław Lubomirski's
suburban retreat at Natolin

76   Plans of the underground
garden of Ksawery Branicki's
villa, by Szymon Bogumił Zug,
1776

77   Michał Poniatowski's villa
at Jabłonna, drawn by Franciszek
Smuglewicz

78 Otto Fergusson Tepper, a Warsaw banker's son, with the king's dog Kiopek, by Friedrich Lohrman 1785

79 Jan Dekert, President (Mayor) of Warsaw, by Ksawery Jan Kaniewski

80 Project for the ballroom of Piotr Fergusson Tepper's town house, by Szymon Bogumił Zug, 1769

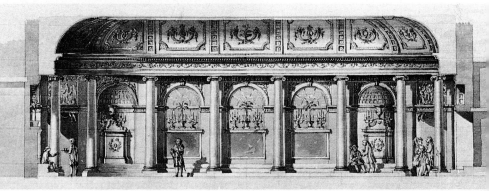

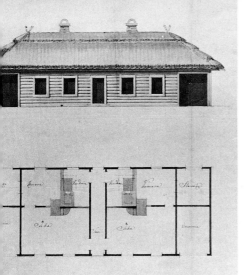

81   Plan for a house for two peasant families, *c.* 1775

82   Stanisław Poniatowski, who emancipated and endowed 400,000 peasants, by Bacciarelli, 1776

83   The regulations governing the peasant 'republic' of Pawłów

84   Paweł Brzostowski granting the deeds and statutes of the 'republic' to the peasants of Pawłow on 14 July 1767, painted by Franciszek Smuglewicz. The peasants are wearing the uniform of their militia, and in the background can be seen the hospital.

USTAWY
STOSUIACE SIĘ DO DOBREGO PORZĄDKU,
I POWINNOSCI OSIADŁYCH LUDZI
W DOBRACH PAWŁOWIE CZYLI
MERECZU
PRZEPISANE
W ROKU 1769.

85 The king's retreat at Łazienki

86 Bridge in the park of Łazienki, by Kamsetzer, 1784

87 One of the three theatres at Łazienki

88 Stanisław's sister Izabela Branicka, by Bacciarelli, *c*. 1760

89 Józef Poniatowski in the uniform of the Royal Horseguards, by Bacciarelli, 1778

90 Stanisław's mistress Elżbieta Grabowska, by Angelica Kauffman

91   Stanisław in the 1780s, by Giovanni Battista Lampi the elder

The original wool factory worked well and brought in a profit. By the 1780s it employed 400 weavers, backed up by some 600 cottage spinners, and its products were praised even by foreign observers.[15] The same was true of the linen factory, the tannery and the candle-works. The carriage-works and several others turned out high-class products, but ran at a deficit. The programme had been set in motion too fast and it was too broad; the less successful factories detracted from the viability of those with better chances by diverting resources and qualified manpower. They suffered from shortage of investment, and their products were often more expensive than better-quality imported goods. There was no developed market, and the irregularity of sales and orders pushed up costs further. Stanisław involved himself actively in these problems, writing frequent letters to Tyzenhauz and his managers on matters of detail. He wanted them to open a shop and warehouse in Warsaw, and tried to arrange exports to Turkey. He also set a fashion for the home-produced goods. He ordered the cloth for uniforms and servants' liveries at Grodno and persuaded others to do the same. He wore the lace produced there, and bought a number of hats, although he complained that they fell off when he went riding.[16]

Within a year of taking over the management of the Lithuanian Crown lands, Tyzenhauz had doubled their revenue, and by 1771 trebled it. But by the end of the 1770s he was getting late with payments. Franciszek Rzewuski, Stanisław's Court Marshal and privy purse-keeper, began to voice suspicions that all was not well. This made Tyzenhauz more secretive, and Stanisław began to have doubts. But whenever he voiced them Tyzenhauz countered by saying that he was being slandered and intrigued against by his enemies. There was something in this.

As well as being the manager of his Lithuanian lands, Tyzenhauz was the mainstay of Stanisław's political influence in Lithuania, organising canvassing at seymiks, and, from 1776, spreading royalist propaganda in a newspaper he published at Grodno. But since the partition had greatly reduced the extent of the Crown lands in Lithuania, he set out to maximise the returns of the remainder, and in doing so could not fail to tread on a few toes. The Crown lands were infested with settlers claiming freedom from rent and szlachta whose grandparents had leased estates or been granted usufruct, and who had managed to remain in possession due to the inefficiency or the venality of previous administrators. Tyzenhauz determined to clear them all out and, ignoring Stanisław's injunctions to proceed with diplomacy, managed to bring several hundred cases to court. This alienated people and started a number of running feuds, the most acrimonious being that with the Kossakowskis, a grasping family with political ambitions.

Stanisław paid a visit to Grodno in 1777 to find out for himself what was going on. He visited all the factories and other institutions, was feted and flattered, and returned to Warsaw none the wiser. He decided to stand by Tyzenhauz, but at the same time began to transfer the management of his political work in the Grand Duchy to others. Tyzenhauz's enemies were on the offensive, the Czartoryskis joined them, and even Stackelberg was dragged into the intrigue. At the beginning of 1778 Stanisław summoned Tyzenhauz to Warsaw, but this yielded little more than professions of loyalty and promises that payments would be made on time.

Stanisław defended his friend when questions about Tyzenhauz's accounting were brought up in the Seym that year, and when Bishop Kossakowski wrote a pamphlet accusing Tyzenhauz of embezzlement, Stanisław responded with another defending him. But Tyzenhauz was becoming a political liability and when, in 1780, he was unable to make the required payments on time, Stanisław reluctantly took away the management of the Crown lands. A commission was set up to investigate his activities, but came across only minor irregularities. The Seym nevertheless demanded that he stand trial. Stanisław attempted to prevent this, but he was overruled. The trial started in 1781 and dragged on to 1784 before absolving him of any malpractice. Tyzenhauz died the following year, a broken man.

Stanisław had stood by Tyzenhauz for so long because he personified a dream that was very close to his heart. 'The diamonds in your crown' is what Tyzenhauz called the Grodno establishments in a letter to Stanisław, and he was not merely referring to the factories.[17] In 1771 he had brought the Veronese architect Giuseppe Sacco to Grodno to rebuild administrative buildings all over the Crown lands. In 1773, he established a small Cadet Corps of twenty-five pupils. This was followed by schools of accountancy, architecture and surveying, a school of midwifery and a hospital. In 1774 Tyzenhauz invited the French naturalist Jean Emmanuel Gilibert to set up a school of veterinary medicine, to carry out a survey of the flora of Lithuania, and to establish a botanical garden. Gilibert arrived in 1775, and in the following year founded a Royal School of Medicine under the physician Charles Virion. This taught between fifteen and thirty pupils a year, at least a couple of whom became eminent medics. By 1778 his botanical garden contained over 1,500 species. He had created a natural history collection with some 10,000 mineral samples, and was working on a *Flora Lithuanica* according to Linnaeus. He had also gathered a library containing an edition of the *Encyclopédie* and all the most modern textbooks.

Tyzenhauz was an obsessive worker and only slept three hours a night. He ordered astronomical instruments from London for a planned observatory, and set up a printing-works, which published the three volumes of Gilibert's *Flora* in 1781, as well as a number of other scientific works. He was already thinking in terms of uniting all these institutions into one great Academy, which would be a centre of agricultural development and of experimental study in the natural sciences. Grodno had become a showpiece of progress by 1780, with elegant buildings, burgeoning industrial activity, and ambitious institutions. Tyzenhauz kept an orchestra and a *corps de ballet* which performed publicly, and he had even created a small art gallery. Visitors such as the Swiss mathematician Johann Bernouilli, John Forster (Captain Cook's Scots-Polish naturalist) and William Coxe of Cambridge heaped praise on Tyzenhauz's work.

With the demise of Tyzenhauz, the vision was taken out of Grodno. Some industries survived, uncompetitive ones collapsed. Gilibert moved to Wilno, where he taught at the university, which also inherited the books, plants, collections and instruments. It was a sad end to a fine idea, but the venture had not been fruitless. Grodno was revitalised and remained an industrial centre. Men trained there took their skills elsewhere. As Stanisław had said to William Coxe, 'The establishment at Grodno is only a beginning: I consider it only as a pledge of my future intentions.'[18]

Increasing numbers of landowners followed the king's example, with mixed results. The most successful were the Czartoryski pottery at Korzec and cloth-mill at Staszów, the Radziwiłł factories at Naliboki and Urzecz (glass), Korelicze and Biała (tapestries and furnishing fabrics), and Słuck (silk sash belts), the Sapieha silk-works at Różana, Michał Poniatowski's cloth-mills at Łowicz, Ogiński's potteries and carpet factory at Słonim, and Prot Potocki's glass-works at Cudnów. This last was the most commercially minded of all Polish magnates. He started out by building factories, then dug a canal, and moved on to create the successful joint-stock Black Sea Trading Company, with its own fleet on the warm seas. In 1785 he set up a bank in Warsaw. By this time Warsaw boasted a dozen banks, the most notable being those of Piotr Fergusson Tepper, Piotr Blank, Fryderyk Karbrit, Maciej Łyszkiewicz, and Andrzej Kapostas, and they played an important part in fuelling economic activity. In the mid-1780s a favourable balance of trade was achieved. By 1788 there was a surplus of 30 million złoty, as exports had risen to a total of 150 million, an increase of over 500 per cent in ten years.

Economic growth was reflected in the physical aspect of the country. Small towns and cities alike proclaimed their revival with fine new public buildings and merchants' houses. Wilno was transformed by a new cathedral, town hall, university buildings and town houses in the robust neo-classicism of Wawrzyniec Gucewicz, a protégé of Bishop Massalski. Lublin, Kraków, Poznań and other cities acquired important new buildings. In the countryside, not only great palaces such as Elżbieta Lubomirska's Łancut or Zofia Lubomirska's Opole Lubelskie, but hundreds of noble residences testified to good husbandry and a renewal of taste. The Prince de Ligne's quip about Polish country houses – 'a surfeit of temples, porphyry and lapis lazuli, but few doors and windows that close' – was no longer true.[19] The example set by Stanisław was followed, and the baroque and rococo styles, so redolent of the Saxon days and favoured by Barian magnates, were abandoned for a new, progressive classicism. The Stanislavian style, as it became known, was the product of the Palladian classicism of Dominik Merlini, Architect of the King and the Commonwealth after Fontana's death in 1773, of the Hellenistic influence of Jan Christian Kamsetzer and of the baroque love of contour of Stanisław himself, who harnessed them together and moulded their style. This was taken up and developed by two younger protégés of the king, Jakub Kubicki and Stanisław Zawadzki, who specialised in country houses. Stanisław Potocki, who had conducted excavations in Italy, designed a number of buildings in collaboration with his architect Piotr Aigner, and also brought Vincent Brenna to Poland.

Stanisław's passion for collecting works of art was mirrored in the activities of many of his subjects, and several outstanding collections were formed at this time. All the major living artists were commissioned, and several were brought to Poland. Some, like Jean Pierre Norblin de la Gourdaine, settled there permanently. Nurtured in this congenial atmosphere, several Polish painters flourished and achieved renown, notably Franciszek Smuglewicz, Aleksander Kucharski, Kazimierz Wojniakowski, Józef Kosiński and Aleksander Orłowski. The growing demand for decorative art acted as a spur on native artisans, and Warsaw silversmiths, clock-makers and cabinet-makers attained standards of excellence. Even the Polish musical tradition, which had suffered a long decline, revived, largely under the patronage of Michał Wielhorski and Michał Ogiński, himself a talented composer.

The chief beneficiary of all this was Warsaw. This had been a jumble of palaces and hovels with a population of no more than 30,000 at Stanisław's accession. Although it grew considerably over the next decade, the city was still not properly paved or lit. 'The metropolis seems to me, like the Republic of which it is the nominal head, to unite the extremes of civilization and of barbarism, of magnificence and wretchedness, of splendour and misery; but unlike all other great cities of Europe, these extremes are not softened, approximated, and blended by intermediate gradations,' wrote Wraxall in 1778.[20] The increasing number of fine palaces stood in a sea of mud, sheds and rubbish-tips. 'The city gives the impression of a room with beautiful furniture, all standing in the wrong place,' noted Ernst von Lehndorff during a visit in 1781.[21] Stanisław Lubomirski and Michał Mniszech, who succeeded him as Grand Marshal in 1782, worked hard at clearing waste ground and paving and lighting the streets, and by 1784 Ségur could state that 'Warsaw offered itself to my sight with all the brilliance of the capital of a great Kingdom.'[22] The city began to grow at an extraordinary rate in the 1780s, and by 1791 the population had reached about 120,000, making it the tenth-largest in Europe.

The former pattern of palaces and hovels had been broken up with merchants' residences, shops, apartment-houses and gardens. At the end of the 1780s, the city had four hospitals. There were elegant new barracks, guard-houses and toll-gates, all in the neo-classical style, to underline their civic nature. The streets in the centre were paved and lit by then, and a German traveller noted that he 'found the sort of

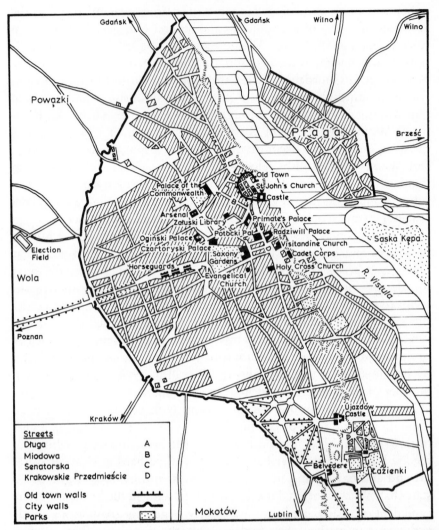

Streets
Długa   A
Miodowa   B
Senatorska   C
Krakowskie Przedmieście   D

Old town walls
City walls
Parks

5 Warsaw in the 1780s

cleanliness one only meets with in the most refined cities of civilized Europe'.[23] The city acquired a fiacre taxi service in the late 1770s. By the mid-1780s Warsaw had three hotels, the best of which, the Hotel de Pologne, was as comfortable as any in Europe. A major attraction for visiting foreigners was the lavish bath-house and brothel established on the river-bank by Jacek Jezierski in 1776, with a restaurant serving the best crayfish in Poland. Bernouilli claims that he had nowhere seen so many pineapples, and the bread, wine and coffee in Warsaw were deemed excellent by travellers, who also marvelled at the cosmopolitan nature of the city.[24] Coxe was astonished to find that even common soldiers on guard at the city gaol were fluent in Latin, while many of the citizens spoke German, French, and even English. A wave of Anglomania swept Warsaw in the late 1780s, and there was an English gentlemen's club, founded by Thomas Wroughton, who also pioneered horse-racing. On 10 May 1789 the French aeronaut and inventor of the parachute Jean Pierre Blanchard staged the first balloon flight. The spendthrift Marcin Lubomirski kept an orchestra which gave public concerts, and in 1784 opened the Foksal (Vauxhall) amusement gardens. Polish and visiting German troupes kept the capital musically up to date, and the operas of Mozart were staged in Warsaw usually within a year of their Vienna or Prague première. There were good bookshops, most notably Groell's, which stocked the most recent publications from all over Europe. Groell also ran the best of the thirty-three printing presses in Poland. 'I must confess that from the point of view of splendour and comfort, only Vienna can compare with Warsaw,' noted Johann Erich Biester, director of the Berlin Royal Library.[25] Ironically, the only institution in Warsaw which belied all this was the Załuski Library, which remained musty, overcrowded and hardly catalogued.

Some of the greatest delights of the city were to be found just outside, as every magnate complemented his Warsaw palace with a suburban villa in which to play. In the 1760s Izabela Czartoryska began staging imaginative *fêtes champêtres* at Powązki, her estate just outside Warsaw. There would be lunches served on the grass and dinners among the ruins, with hidden orchestras playing in the distance while thousands of lanterns illuminated copses and bowers, from which dancers would magically emerge to perform ballets. She gradually transformed the estate into an arcadian park, with grottos, fountains, ruined temples, triumphal arches and a colosseum. Her inspiration had come from English gardens, but she added a distinctly Rousseauesque flavour of her own. At the centre of this bucolic landscape lay a picturesque cluster of cottages, one for each of her family and friends. 'Imagine the astonishment as one is taken into a hut that from outside looks like poverty itself; the luxury inside is bewildering,' wrote Lehndorff. 'Princess Adam has, in her thatched hut, a bathroom covered in Dutch tiles. But these are not earthenware tiles costing four groats apiece, but of Sèvres porcelain, and the smallest costs a Louis d'or.'[26] Coxe claims they were of Meissen china and cost three ducats apiece. Either way, there were 600 of these tiles in her bathroom, and not the least of the splendours of the thatched cottage was that it had a lift.

A similar effect was evoked by Barbara Sanguszko's country retreat, and Elżbieta Lubomirska had her own gardens at Mokotów, scattered with gothic, Chinese and Turkish pavilions. Adam Poniński created an eccentric interior at Fawory to the north of the city, with a Turkish tent of a bedroom, a dining-room that represented a forest clearing, and, beneath it, baths set in a grotto encrusted with shells. At Jabłonna across the river, Michał Poniatowski built a small palace whose most interesting feature was a Turkish saloon 'of an oblong shape, very lofty, with a fountain in the middle, surrounded with a parterre of flowers', in Coxe's words.[27] Kazimierz Poniatowski had a residence at Solec on the banks of the Vistula underneath which stretched a labyrinth of caverns with waterfalls and steam baths. The park contained a number of ruins, a barn that turned out to be an exquisite salon, and a ruined gothic church that housed a miniature court theatre. There were also hothouses full of tropical fruit, an extensive family of pet monkeys, and a fine collection of paintings.

Stanisław had created his own retreat in the park of Ujazdów around a seventeenth-century bath-house. He laid out the gardens in the English style, making imaginative use of water to surround the bath-house, the Łazienki, to which he added apartments for himself. He used the same architect, Merlini, throughout, but experimented with styles to a surprising degree. He rebuilt the Łazienki in the classical style in 1784, but surrounded it with Chinese bridges and gazebos. The Little White House was an Italian villa, the Myślewicki Palace was neo-classical, the Trou-Madame pavilion was Chinese, the ballroom was a Turkish structure, the orangery and theatre were baroque. In spite of this astonishing diversity, there is a unity about Łazienki, as there is in all Stanisław's works, which can best be described as a unity of taste.

It is on this very idiosyncratic taste that Stanisław's great merit as a patron reposes. However many artists he employed on a project, he always managed to imbue them with his own vision of the whole. And he was not afraid of lecturing even established figures, such as Boucher, Mengs, Canova and Angelica Kauffman. It would be difficult to establish which was the dominant influence, although it is tempting to point to Italy. 'The colouring should, if possible, be that of Rubens, the contours those of Paul Veronese, particularly where the female figures are concerned, and the costumes should be in the taste of Rembrandt,' he wrote to one artist when commissioning a painting.[28] Such ideas seem out of place in the late eighteenth century. In fact, Stanisław's sculptural sense of shape, his bold use of colour and his love of classical form betray a baroque and a very Polish pedigree. However small and however restrained, all his works possess a sensual and monumental quality that echoes the tastes of the Sarmatian magnates of the previous century.

While the Polish monarchy did not, like the French, demand of the king that he live out his private life in a ritualised public display, it involved stresses of its own. The most obvious was that the king lived over the shop. The Castle was the setting for all state functions and audiences. It was also the seat of government, housing the Seym and the Permanent Council, as well as the Gabinet and Military Office. Its public nature was only exacerbated by its being the nexus of Stanisław's political party.

Stanisław's own establishment contributed to the crush. His court marshals, Kazimierz Karaś and then Tomasz Aleksandrowicz, his five acting chamberlains, his twelve pages, his negro, his Turk and most of his 275 servants were quartered there, as were his brother Michał, occasionally Kazimierz, his nephews Stanisław and Józef when they were in Warsaw, his friend Franciszek Rzewuski, and sundry mistresses. Various secretaries and political agents, such as Ogrodzki, Kiciński, Glayre and Albertrandi also inhabited reaches of the building. On the ground floor was the studio in which Bacciarelli and his artists worked, closely supervised by Stanisław, who would drop in to inspect and suggest.

Stanisław treated these people with avuncular solicitude, and the whole establishment came to resemble an extended family. 'He was always kind, reasonable and approachable to anyone, though he could be impulsive and naïve at home,' remembered one of the pages, who used to play frequent pranks on him.[29] But several hundred people living cheek by jowl in this manner could not fail to generate tensions, and there was much squabbling. Reverdil was forever complaining that he was issued with fewer candles than his rank as librarian entitled him to, but was attacked by others for being greedy with firewood, and all such grievances were laid at the feet of the king.

Stanisław would escape to Kozienice, where he spent the mornings in the woods shooting wild boar, less from love of the chase than from need of exercise, and the long winter evenings reading. When in Warsaw, he would dine informally at the houses of Sophie Leullier, General Coccei or his sister Izabela Branicka. But he was most at ease at Łazienki. There, he would spend the evenings in a small circle of family and friends, supplemented by any interesting foreign visitors, and etiquette was dropped. After dinner those who wished to played whist, while Stanisław indulged in one of his greatest pleasures – conversation. Such a dinner was, in the words of Lady Craven, 'as pleasant and cheerful as if we had been in private society'.[30] This is perhaps best illustrated by William Coxe's account of an evening at Kazimierz's villa:

We arrived at the garden about nine: it was a beautiful evening of one of the most sultry days we had experienced this summer. After walking about the grounds, we came to a grotto of artificial rock, where a spring of water dripped through the sides, and fell into a basin with a pleasing murmur. We were scarcely assembled in this delightful spot, when the king made his appearance: we rose up to meet him; the usual compliments being passed, we attended his majesty about the grounds, and then returned to the grotto, round which we ranged ourselves upon a bank covered with moss. The moon was now risen; and added greatly to the beauty of the scene. I happened to be seated next to the king (for all form and ceremony was banished), who talked with me as usual, in English, on the arts and sciences, literature and history . . . This conversation, in which I was at a loss whether to admire most the knowledge or the conde-scension of the king, was interrupted by the prince, who proposed a turn in the garden before supper: his highness led the way, and the company followed; we passed through a subterraneous passage, long and winding, with here and there a single lamp, which shed a glimmering light; we came at length to a wooden door, which seemed the entrance into some hovel; it opened, and we found ourselves, to our great astonishment, in a superb saloon, illuminated with innumerable lamps. It was a rotunda, with an elegant dome of the most beautiful symmetry; in the circumference were four open recesses between pillars of artificial marble: in the recesses were sophas, with paintings in frescoe, representing the triumphs of Bacchus, Silenus, Love, and the victory of the Empress of Russia over the Turks. As we were admiring the beauty and elegance of the rotunda, our ears were of a sudden regaled with a concert of exquisite music from an invisible band. While we were listening to this agreeable performance, and conjecturing from what quarter it came, a magnificent table was spread in the midst of the saloon with such expedition, as to resemble the effects of enchantment. We immediately sat down to supper with the king, the prince, and a chosen company: our spirits were elevated by the beauty of the saloon, by the hospitality of the prince, and by the affability of the king; who, so far from being a constraint to the society, greatly enlivened it by his vivacity, and seemed the soul of the party. I never passed a more agreeable evening.[31]

Coxe admitted to being charmed by Stanisław, and he was not alone in this. Ségur, who was no sentimentalist, noted that in 1784, Stanisław 'had conserved a measure of his good looks, a majestic figure, an eye full of refinement and gentleness, a tone of voice that went to one's soul, and the most attractive smile'.[32] Wraxall agreed. 'No prince was ever more gracious, easy and affable in his manners and address; which is the result of natural disposition, not the effect of artifice. His conversation is pleasing, and frequently displays, without the smallest affectation, extensive reading. Few individuals speak so fluently or gracefully the principal European languages.'[33] John Forster, who had just sailed round the world with Captain Cook, met Stanisław in the same year, and left a remarkable portrait of the fifty-two-year-old monarch:

He is a very handsome man, but a little pale. His nose is slightly hooked, like a hawk's, his eyes are large, black, gentle and beautiful, his forehead is finely proportioned, his mouth is sensual, and there is some streak — I know not whether of melancholy or abstraction — that pervades the whole face, a face that betrays suffering, a deep knowledge of people, and an unusual love of mankind. From the very moment one sees him one yearns to throw oneself in his arms and to say to him: 'I am your devoted friend!'[34]

Some of Stanisław's most devoted friends were foreigners, and his craving for their company was well satisfied. When Thomas Wroughton left Warsaw after more than twenty years, he was succeeded by Viscount Dalrymple, and then, in 1785, by Charles Whitworth, a handsome, clever man who became a firm friend of Stanisław's. One of the greatest socialites of contemporary Europe, the Prince de Ligne, visited Warsaw assiduously in order to get the Seym to grant him szlachta status – not because he craved it, but because his son had fallen in love with Bishop Massalski's niece and could not marry her until his credentials were verified. Another who was brought to Poland by marriage was Prince Charles of Nassau-Siegen, who had acquired fame through many adventures, including sailing round the world with the French explorer Bougainville, hunting lions in Africa and having a notorious affair with the queen of Tahiti, not to mention his audacious attack on Gibraltar in 1782. At Spa he met the witty and vivacious Karolina Gozdzka, widow of Janusz Sanguszko, and, believing her to be a formidable heiress, married her there and then. She believed she was marrying a Prince of the Empire. Although both were soon disabused, their marriage was unexpectedly happy, and they became an important fixture of Warsaw life.

In 1784 the Prince de Nassau brought Lewis Littlepage of Richmond, Virginia, to Warsaw. This colourful young man left his studies at Williamsburg to fight the English, and then went to Spain with the French army, where he met Nassau. Stanisław grew very fond of him and made him a gentleman of the bedchamber. Littlepage turned out to have acting talents, which he displayed frequently in amateur theatricals, and has the distinction of staging the Polish première of *The Barber of Seville* at the Nassaus' house.

Many of the foreigners who turned up in Warsaw were on their way to St Petersburg, but they often went no further. Warsaw was too much fun. 'The general dissolution of morals among the upper orders is not one of the least extraordinary and characteristic features of the capital and country from which I am writing,' noted Wraxall. 'Neither Petersburgh nor Naples can surpass Warsaw in these respects.'[35] The rot affected all of society, beginning with the clergy. Bishop Naruszewicz wrote erotic poetry, and, like many others, kept a mistress. Primate Ostrowski had converted a whole wing of his palace into a seraglio. These episcopal couplings bore some interesting fruit – one of Michał Poniatowski's sons, Piotr Maleszewski, was to become controller of the French army under the *Directoire*, while Primate Ostrowski produced among others the hero of the legendary cavalry charge at Somosierra in 1808, Hipolit Kozietulski.

Stanisław himself continued to philander, with perhaps less passion than before, but certainly more method. In 1778 he had a second affair with Anna Lubomirska, who had already borne him one son in the previous decade. But his other recurring relationship, with Elżbieta Lubomirska, had disintegrated for good. She had begun to meddle in politics and actively plotted against him throughout the 1770s. She had conserved her beauty, but had grown impossibly neurotic. She spent her life reclining on sofas in darkened rooms suffering from migraines, surrounded by everything that refined taste could provide, and waited on by a beautiful young Turk.[36]

The most important woman in Stanisław's life was still one of his earliest loves, Elżbieta Szydłowska. When she became pregnant in 1769, he arranged a blank marriage to General Grabowski, and she remained the *maîtresse en titre*, living in a small house hard by the Castle or in the Little White House at Łazienki. She was kind and gentle, although she could be grasping and touchy, and insisted on providing jobs and honours for her extensive family. She bore Stanisław three sons and two daughters, and he treated her for all the world like a wife.[37]

Stanisław was having fewer affairs with ladies of the court, but more than made up for this with a string of mistresses from the town and visiting actresses. Sophie Leullier, whom he had established in a small house of her own, selected and introduced them. He would either take his pleasure with them there, or move them into the Castle for a time. When he tired of them or they became pregnant, he would find them husbands. Carlo Tomatis, whose wife was one of Stanisław's mistresses, also pimped for the king and others, and his villa at

Królikarnia was little more than a high-class brothel.

A frenetic permissiveness gripped the capital, and the divorce rate shot up. A huge red-light district sprang up in the Grzybów area of Warsaw for the less exalted, and venereal disease, known in the capital as the American disease, and in the provinces as the Warsaw disease, spread alarmingly. The eminent Warsaw venereologist and ancestor of the Mountbattens, Doctor La Fontaine, claimed that six out of ten sick people in the capital were suffering from none other. But he also noted that 'pederasty, which is so very common among neighbouring nations, is unknown here'.[38]

Much of this was the fruit of the Enlightenment. The spread of the new ideas was peripatetic, and while they truly enlightened only a few, they liberated thousands from traditional constraints by destroying religious and social sanctions. Brandishing the names of Voltaire and Montesquieu, people indulged in increasingly cynical debauchery. 'If good institutions were taken up as avidly as fashions,' commented a French traveller, 'Poland would long ago have become one of the best governed and most enlightened countries in Europe.'[39]

One fashion that spread like an epidemic was Freemasonry. It had come to Poland in the first decades of the century in the baggage of noblemen returning from their travels, and the first lodge in East Central Europe was the *Red Brotherhood*, founded in 1721 by, among others, Michał and August Czartoryski. Stanisław Lubomirski and Andrzej Mokronowski became Freemasons in Paris in the 1730s, and there are unverifiable theories that Stanisław himself had been initiated in London by Charles Yorke. In 1769 Friedrich Brühl, August Moszyński and Adam Czartoryski founded a new Polish lodge, *Le Vertueux Sarmate*, into which Stanisław was initiated in 1777, under the name of *Salsinatus a Corona Vindicata*, and he mooted its change of name to *Catherine à l'Étoile du Nord*.

By the late 1780s there were over a thousand Freemasons in Poland, including most of the aristocracy, foreign diplomats, officers, merchants and members of the professions. Although many sinister allegations have been made about its possible political implications, the only practical effect of Freemasonry was to break down class barriers by facilitating contact between people of different milieux. Stanisław's only interest lay in its diplomatic potential and its charitable activities. In the early 1770s, his physician, Dr Boeckler, ran a masonic surgery giving the common people free vaccinations against smallpox. At meetings of the Grand Orient of Poland, started in 1780 by Ignacy Potocki, there were readings of scientific papers by various savants. Freemasonry also served as a cover for much charlatanry and silliness. Stanisław's former teacher Thoux de Salverte practised alchemy with August Moszyński, and it was through the masonic network that Cagliostro entered Warsaw society in 1781. He indulged in strange experiments at Adam Poniński's house at Fawory, and tried out the elixir of youth on Kazimierz Poniatowski, before being hounded out of the capital by disappointed clients.

While Warsaw life displayed all the characteristics of a society in degeneration, the country was undergoing a remarkable renaissance. Much of the wealth being generated had begun to benefit classes which had never known it before – the minor szlachta and the inhabitants of the cities. An entirely new phenomenon on the Polish scene was a number of merchant princes, people such as Piotr Fergusson Tepper, a banker grandson of a Scots immigrant – who had a fine palace in Warsaw and an exquisite villa outside but who was also welcome in every aristocratic house. A self-respecting and articulate middle class was beginning to make its mark, strongly supported by Stanisław, who ennobled merchants, doctors and artists, thereby giving them the vote. He also promoted dissenters whenever he could. This, and the greater availability of good education, were rapidly turning Poland into a modern society. And if some of the manifestations of progress were unsavoury, they did not corrupt the underlying idealism of those who thought like Stanisław, the most tangible sign of which was the changing attitude towards the less fortunate.

In 1760 Andrzej Zamoyski began freeing the peasants on his Mazovian estates of their labour obligations and renting out land to them. Within a decade, the birth-rate on these estates had doubled, and his revenues had trebled. In 1774 Bishop Massalski followed his example on some of his Lithuanian estates, and used the pulpit to urge the szlachta to show greater regard for the peasants, 'that honourable class of human society so despised in our country'.[40] A couple of years later Joachim Chreptowicz did the same. Starting in 1777 the king's nephew Stanisław Poniatowski introduced a progressive system of transferring the land to the 400,000 peasants settled on his estates, at first by giving them a share of the estates' profits, then by allowing them to pay their rent not in labour but in cash or kind, and eventually by giving them their land in return for a ground rent. He too claimed that his revenues trebled. He instituted a sinking fund in every village to compensate those who had suffered from fire or crop-failure, and one to pay for hospitals and schools. He published his system in order to encourage others to follow suit, and claims that William Pitt asked him for details with a view to introducing it into the Botany Bay settlements.[41]

Another who made his mark abroad in this respect was Tadeusz Kościuszko, who freed all the slaves a grateful Congress had given him for his services in the American War of Independence, and wrote a will bidding his friend and executor Thomas Jefferson to use his American estate 'in purchasing negroes from among his own or any others and giving them liberty in my name, in giving them an education in trades or otherwise and in having them instructed for their new condition in the duties of morality which may make them good neighbours good fathers or moders, husbands or vives and in their duties as citisens teeching them to be defenders of their liberty and their country'.[42] Jefferson found it impossible to carry out.

Many others, including Anna Jabłonowska, Jacek Jezierski (he of the brothel), Stanisław Potocki, Stanisław Małachowski, Jan Krasiński and Prot Potocki, introduced similar schemes freeing their peasants from labour duties, in many cases giving them the land they worked. Ścibór Marchocki turned his estate into a peasant co-operative. But none outdid Paweł Brzostowski. 'The principal effort of our nation should be to do justice to those who feed us,' he wrote to Stanisław, and he did not stop at pious utterances.[43] In 1769 he turned his estate of Pawłów, a few miles outside Wilno, into a self-governing peasant republic, with a senate, an army of 100 men and seven cannon, a bank, a hospital and a school. Such gestures confirmed Stanisław in his belief that given time, his vision of a modern Poland would come true.

17

The Romantic Challenge

Stanisław had accepted collaboration with Russia in the conviction that it represented the only option for the survival of Poland. But he did not follow this line of reasoning through to its logical end, and allowed emotional factors to affect his conduct. Instead of adopting an attitude of unswerving loyalty to Russia and using the power this would have given him to crush all nonconformity in Poland, he remained a reluctant collaborator, siding at heart with the opposition, which was also, in effect, opposition to his rule. This policy bore the seeds of its own destruction. Russia remained wary of him and measured out her support sparingly, while many Poles found it difficult to see in him anything other than the agent of a foreign power. Stanisław could not act otherwise. However rational and realistic his assessment of the situation, his reactions were conditioned by his wariness of Russia, by the Polish political traditions to which he was heir, by his patriotism, and by his emotional instincts.

In many respects, the system established in 1776 was highly beneficial. It provided the stability necessary for reconstruction and economic growth. The Treasury, which had struggled to raise an annual revenue of 12 million złoty before the partition, was drawing 21 million by 1787 from a country reduced by one-third. This only allowed for an army of just over 20,000 men, but Stanisław's Military Office, directed by General Jan Komarzewski, transformed it into a regular modern army, equipped to the highest standard. The buying of ranks was abolished in 1782, and it was henceforth staffed by professional officers. The political stability also allowed a couple of generations to pass through the new educational system in peace. The existence of non-political salaried jobs in the Departments of the Permanent Council and its other offshoots contributed to the emergence of an administrative cadre. Poland was beginning to function as a state. People grew used to the existence of a regular government, even if they resented the Permanent Council. From 1778 onwards there was no more need to confederate the Seym, as nobody even considered using the veto.

Most of the opponents of the Permanent Council's rule were those whose interests had suffered. The hetmans Ksawery Branicki, Michał Ogiński and Seweryn Rzewuski continually attacked the Council's Military Department, to which they had lost most of their prerogatives. Ministers resisted the encroachments of the Council and its departments on their respective domains. Other magnates merely resented the inroads the organs of state were making into their freedom of action, whittling away their pool of client szlachta, who were gradually transferring their loyalty from them to the state.

The new system defied their attempts at troublemaking. They lobbied Stackelberg and even went to Russia in search of support against the king. The ambitious young Ignacy Potocki, for instance, badgered Panin in order to obtain the vice-chancellorship of Poland, which Stanisław intended for one of his own supporters.[1] This sort of thing made life difficult, and even unpleasant, for Stanisław, but he could bear it with stoicism, except when it undermined his most cherished aims. An instance of this was the killing of Zamoyski's Code of Laws, which was printed and ready to be vetted by the Seym of 1778. It was a document with far-reaching implications: by restating extant but forgotten laws and weeding the statute books of dubious growths, it reasserted, among other things, a number of rights that were denied to the peasantry and the third estate. Since it contained no new legislation, it obviated the Cardinal Laws reaffirmed by the Russian guarantee of 1775, and opened a side door to social and economic evolution if not reform. It aroused resentment among Conservative landowners and the clergy, many of whose prerogatives it put in question. But the measure had a chance of getting through the Seym until Stanisław Lubomirski decided to join forces with Stackelberg and the Papal Nuncio. Fearing that the code would be rejected for ever, the king withdrew it.

A measure of the new stability is provided by the Sołtyk affair. Bishop Sołtyk had returned from captivity in Russia with his mind impaired, and he retired to his diocese in Kraków. He suffered from prolonged fits of depression and took little interest in anything, but he was drawn into a struggle between the chapter and Hugo Kołłątaj, backed by Michał Poniatowski, administrator of the diocese. The canons managed to enlist his support, but he began to act irrationally, and in 1781 the Permanent Council appointed a commission to look into the matter. The commission reported that he was deranged, so the Permanent Council removed him from his duties and confined him in his palace at Kielce. The opponents of the Council saw a chance of making trouble. All the elements that could have launched a national rebellion ten years before were there – a wronged bishop, a magnate oppressed by absolutism, echoes of the Russian crimes of 1767, and bonds of Barian solidarity. In the event, the affair petered out in the face of a Seym and a society which accepted the rationale of the government's action.

The Achilles' heel of Stanisław's system was Stackelberg. If Repnin had been too young for the difficult post of ambassador in Poland, Stackelberg was simply out of his depth. He was a slightly absurd figure, 'small and plump, with a physiognomy that was not at all handsome, but full of expression and cunning', in the words of the Swedish minister Lars Engeström.[2] He was extraordinarily greedy and ate so much that he suffered from protracted attacks of colic. His appetite for the ladies was similarly punished by his mistress Helena Radziwiłł, who kept him on a short rein. In his quest for popularity he professed dismay at the policy he had to implement. He would declare that he wanted posterity to say that he had made Poland happy, and boasted to Stanisław that 'if Poland was not destroyed, it is due entirely to me'.[3]

According to Stanisław, Stackelberg had the character 'of an old coquette, jealous, nagging, and taking pleasure in spreading calumny and discord'.[4] He was prodigal with invented gossip, and considered it part of his job to sow mistrust, particularly between the king and his subjects. He pestered Stanisław with advice on everything, and took umbrage when it was not followed. 'As he had infinite pretensions of every kind, as a man of standing, as a litterateur, as a connoisseur, wishing to shine everywhere and in everything, to be thought the most amiable as well as the most powerful, it became extremely difficult and painful for the king to continually satisfy this self-regard which reproduced itself under so many forms, and to bear the alternatives of quarrel and reconciliation to which Stackelberg subjected him,' Stanisław wrote, with considerable understatement.[5] The transcripts of Stackelberg's almost daily conferences with Stanisław make depressing reading. He became increasingly rude and derived the same enjoyment as had Repnin from treating a king as he would not dare treat an equal at home. He proudly told Ségur that 'his authority had no limits beyond those which the gentleness of his own character deigned to impose'.[6]

None of this would have mattered had he been more consistent and had he possessed a broader vision of his role in Poland. Stackelberg continually accused Stanisław of not being loyal enough to Russia.[7] He complained that Stanisław never gave offices or favours to those suggested by himself. He tried repeatedly to get Stanisław to dismiss Komarzewski, whose military reforms made him suspicious, and to take Russian clients into his service. He resented Stanisław's foreign contacts and kept insisting that he give up his correspondence with the provinces. 'Whatever you will lose in your relations with the provinces will be replaced a hundredfold in your relations with Russia,' he assured him somewhat inconsequentially.[8]

But Russia did not behave like an ally. She repeatedly refused to back Polish complaints against the other neighbours. Prussia did not hold to the already draconian terms of the trade treaty she had foisted on Poland, and kept imposing random sanctions. Austria simply refused to disburse the indemnities she had undertaken to pay Stanisław for the Wieliczka salt-mines. Prussian troops continually violated Polish territory. Far from supporting Poland, as she was obliged to do under the terms of the guarantee, Russia would not even mediate. And her own attitude to the new frontiers she had drawn left much to be desired. In 1783, for instance, Stanisław complained that 'a Russian detachment invaded the territory of the Commonwealth, seizing peasants in their hundreds and wreaking havoc and injustice which I recoil from describing'. The action was, as usual, justified by the steady flight of tens of thousands of Russian serfs to Poland in search of better conditions. 'Such emigration cannot be the object of complaint or entail restitution, unless it is fomented or encouraged,' Stanisław argued.[9] At the same time Russia incited subversion in Poland, by encouraging the Orthodox Bishop of Słuck, Wiktor Sadkowski, to build up a church province within Poland swearing allegiance to Catherine not Stanisław, and mentioning her, not him, in its prayers. Stackelberg would dismiss protests and counter them with complaints of his own. Being not very intelligent and by nature highly suspicious, he could not or would not comprehend Stanisław's predicament or his policy.

Stackelberg saw himself as a sort of watchdog, and his behaviour displays a fear of losing control of the situation. He awarded Russian pensions to a dozen or so people whose support he wished to retain, but there was little method in his choice. The payroll included petty spies such as the king's secretaries Karol Boskamp and Christian Friese, political nonentities such as Adam Poniński, convenient troublemakers such as Bishop Józef Kossakowski, and respectable figures like Jacek Małachowski, who took the money but followed his own conscience.

In 1775 Stackelberg pompously declared to Stanisław that 'the reign of the Czartoryskis is over and must never return', and added: 'If you give them influence in your councils, you will do yourself no good in the eyes of my sovereign.'[10] But the Czartoryskis were no longer interested in taking part in the king's councils. When, in the summer of 1777, Stanisław went to visit first his uncle August at Puławy and then Adam at Wołczyn, he felt little cordiality behind the elaborate welcome.[11] On the other hand, Stackelberg himself was drawing closer to the Familia by 1778, and it was he who in the same year demanded that Stanisław Lubomirski and several others be brought into the Permanent Council. As Stanisław noted in a letter to his new agent in St Petersburg, Augustyn Deboli, Stackelberg had found 'new friends' to play off against him.[12]

Whatever may have been the stresses and strains within the Familia in the old days, the iron hand of Michał Czartoryski had maintained consistency and unity. Despite persistent efforts, none of the Russian ambassadors had managed to prise it away from its basic community of interest with the king. This changed with Michał's death in 1775. His brother August, who had become an Austrian subject rather than sell

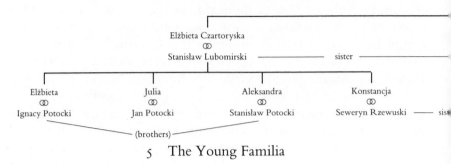

5   The Young Familia

his estate of Sieniawa, which had fallen to Austria in the partition, was thereby excluded from active political life, and remained little more than a figurehead. Stanisław Lubomirski was the effective leader of the party, and he set about refashioning it for the next generation. He began at home, with his four daughters. The first was married in 1771 to Ignacy Potocki, the third in 1776 to his brother Stanisław Potocki, the second in 1783 to their cousin Jan Potocki, and the fourth in 1782 to Seweryn Rzewuski, a sworn enemy of Stanisław, convinced that it was the king who had had him and his father arrested and deported to Russia in 1768.[13] Lubomirski wielded great influence over his cousin Adam Czartoryski, vitiated only by the constant bickering between their two wives. The only thing that seemed to bring these two ladies, both of them erstwhile mistresses of Stanisław, together was a neurotic desire to cross the king.

Lubomirski could count on the support of Michał Ogiński, and he also managed to lure Ksawery Branicki into his camp. Branicki had remained devoted to the king for many years. But he came back from his mission to Paris in 1772 'a different man' according to Stanisław: he had taken to drink again and grown very arrogant.[14] Stanisław attempted to bring him back into line, by using him as the head of his party in the delegation for the partition and granting him the baton of Grand Hetman of the Crown in 1774. He made further attempts to regain his allegiance, but Branicki was fickle. He had made friends with Catherine's favourite, Potyomkin, and therefore felt strong. He virtually led the opposition to the king at the 1782 Seym, goaded on by his sister and supported by her son, Kazimierz Nestor Sapieha, who, as Stanisław reproached her, 'distinguished himself by the spirit with which he opposed my opinions and commands'.[15] Although matters

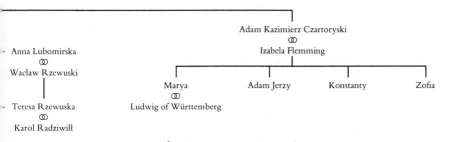

were patched up and Branicki supported the king in the following year, he began to waver again in 1784. He fell in love with Izabela Czartoryska, and although he did not apparently gain her favours, he drew closer to the Familia.

August Czartoryski died in 1782. Stackelberg is reported to have said on hearing the news that there was now nobody left in Warsaw to doff one's hat to.[16] There was certainly nobody left who could recreate the unity of the Familia, which was now little more than a collection of truculent magnates. Lubomirski died just over a year later, in August 1783. The leadership then devolved on Adam Czartoryski. He was not a strong character, and while he was clever and highly educated, his overbearing vanity had come to dominate his outlook. He enjoyed considerable prestige as the heir to his family's political tradition. He was addressed as *Cher cousin* by Catherine and Joseph II, and in 1784 the marriage of his (actually Stanisław's) daughter Marya to Prince Ludwig of Württemberg set the seal on this semi-royal status. One of Prince Ludwig's sisters was married to Catherine's son and heir Paul, while the other was engaged to Archduke Francis, the future Emperor. Czartoryski did not crave high office: his title of General of Podolia went with a large starosty he had held since his youth, and had no political significance. He seemed to want to float grandly above partisan politics. Instead, he drifted, blown this way and that by the ambitions of his wife, the machinations of Ignacy Potocki, or the blandishments of Stackelberg. He felt a nagging jealousy of the king, not so much for the office he held as for his distinction as a person and his accomplishments. For instance, the poet Karpiński found that he could never allow himself a laudatory reference to Stanisław without causing displeasure.[17]

Stanisław had, despite all unfavourable odds, managed to enhance his personal standing, and even his aura of royalty over the years. The repeated attempts to topple him had come to naught, lending him a sense of permanence. If he was a symbol of the country's powerlessness, he was also the only tangible symbol of its sovereignty. As the country prospered and the fruits of his policies became apparent, those who benefited from them – the majority of the szlachta and the third estate – came to appreciate his wisdom. Even as they longed for a more heroic figure on the throne, they could see at least that he had proved his good intentions, and they regarded him increasingly as a benign father-figure.

This was largely the doing of Stanisław himself. He had abandoned his earlier posturings, and after the partition concentrated on promoting the image of the kindly patriarch who cared for his unruly nation like an indulgent father. The life he now led was tailored to suit. There were fewer balls and courtly entertainments of the earlier sort, and his evenings were spent mainly in a small circle.

Stanisław now dressed almost exclusively in the blue and crimson uniform of the Cadet Corps, and was accompanied when he left the Castle by an adjutant, a chamberlain, and a mounted escort of gentlemen in Polish dress. He was less of a dandy and more conscious of comfort and convenience than before. His pockets bulged with boxes of sweets, a thermometer, a calendar, a box of tooth-picks, a phial of sal volatile, a penknife, scissors, a telescope, and the lorgnette he had to use constantly on account of his increasing short-sightedness. 'I always carry pencils and paper in my pockets and I note down things I do not want to forget,' he explained.[18] He also had a tiny watch sewn on to the inside of his cuff, so that he could tell the time without seeming impatient.[19] At Łazienki he wore comfortable loose clothes, and in summer a linen suit and a straw hat.

His life was that of a very grand middle-aged bachelor. He slept only six hours, sometimes taking a nap after lunch, and was usually working by eight. He read his voluminous correspondence and all the local and foreign papers in his dressing-gown, and would then listen to one of his readers as he was being dressed, an exercise during which he was attended by two chamberlains, two adjutants, two pages and three valets, who were served coffee at the same time. (Stanisław drank only Turkish coffee.)[20] He usually dined in his private rooms with no more than ten guests. The food was exquisite. Stanisław had discovered an Italian chef, Paolo Tremo, who was a virtuoso of the refined but simple dish, and grew so attached to his cooking that he usually lent him to his hosts when he dined out. Stanisław favoured light food, beginning lunch with half a dozen oysters when they were in season. He ate lamb as often as possible, in an effort to teach his subjects to acquire the taste he had himself gained in England, as the country was full of sheep reared for wool. Although he drank only water himself, his table was well served, with three bottles of Hungarian wine, three bottles of claret (Haut Brion or Margaux), two of champagne, and two of English beer.

Although he used every available minute of the day to work, Stanisław kept fit by riding regularly, and to calm his nerves he would inspect what his artists were doing, play billiards or apply himself to a small lathe at which he made bonbonnières and snuff-boxes.[21] He kept up the Thursday dinners, but eschewed entertaining on a grand scale. He still enjoyed theatrical entertainments, and as well as a theatre at the Castle, he built two at Łazienki. Here, the performers were often members of his court, or even his family.

Stanisław's family played a greater part in his life now. Although Kazimierz had retired from public life and led an increasingly debauched existence, he was still devoted to his younger brother and spent much time with him. Kazimierz's son Stanisław, in whom the king placed such hopes, was very independent in spirit and lacked the warmth and sentimentality of his royal uncle. Stanisław nevertheless continued to promote him with the aim of building up his credentials for the future, giving him the command of the Royal Footguards, a seat on the Permanent Council and, in 1787, the Treasury of Lithuania. Stanisław admired him but could not love him – certainly not as much as he loved his deceased brother Andrzej's son Józef, who turned up in Warsaw in 1778. He had been brought up mainly in Vienna and had served in the Austrian army. He took Warsaw by storm, with his good looks and his charm, and quickly became Stanisław's favourite.

The most important influence on Stanisław was now exerted by his youngest brother, Michał, who became Primate of Poland in 1784. He was lazy and cynical by nature, but he had a deep sense of duty. He had been propelled into the Church, but he took his job seriously, and as he was highly intelligent, he did a great deal for it,

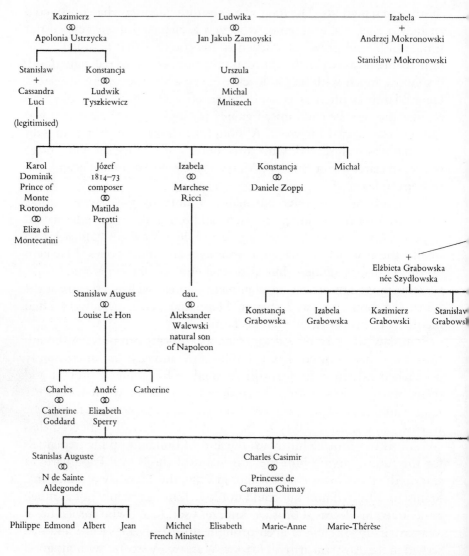

6 The Poniatowski Descent

The Romantic Challenge

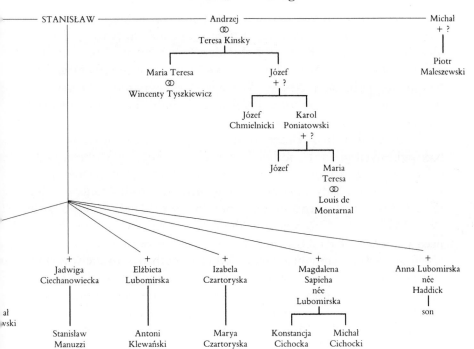

STANISŁAW —————— Andrzej —————— Michał
⊕
Teresa Kinsky

+ ?

|
Piotr
Maleszewski

Maria Teresa   Józef
⊕   + ?
Wincenty Tyszkiewicz

Józef   Karol
Chmielnicki   Poniatowski
               + ?

Józef   Maria
               Teresa
               ⊕
               Louis de
               Montarnal

+   +   +   +   +
Jadwiga   Elżbieta   Izabela   Magdalena   Anna Lubomirska
Ciechanowiecka   Lubomirska   Czartoryska   Sapieha   née
                                                   née   Haddick
                                                   Lubomirska

Stanisław   Antoni   Marya   Konstancja   Michał   son
Manuzzi   Klewański   Czartoryska   Cichocka   Cichocki

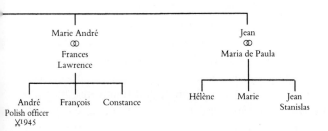

Marie André   Jean
⊕   ⊕
Frances   Maria de Paula
Lawrence

André   François   Constance   Hélène   Marie   Jean
Polish officer   Stanislas
✕1945

275

disciplining the conduct of monks and priests, making them attend retreats, and ordering them to fit lightning conductors to their spires instead of ringing bells against thunder. Stanisław was very fond of Michał, but he was also a little in awe of his cool judgment and his firmness on political questions. 'When he does something [the Primate] would not approve, he often hides it from him,' noted one of Stanisław's secretaries.[22]

Stanisław also drew closer to his sister Izabela Branicka, who had been widowed in 1771 and lived openly with Andrzej Mokronowski, by whom she had a son who passed officially as one of his nephews. She was a wise old lady, sharing strong affinities with Stanisław. She regarded herself as a royal figure, underlining the fact by adopting the style 'Madame de Cracovie', on the basis of her late husband having been Castellan of Kraków, and she took an active interest in politics. She followed the same principles as Michał, with whom she was close, and her influence over Stanisław was very marked. Stanisław's other sister, Ludwika Zamoyska, who, not to be outdone, styled herself 'Madame de Podolie', interested him less, but her daughter Urszula, who married Michał Mniszech, gained her uncle's affections and was seldom absent from his entourage.

This also included Elżbieta Grabowska, whom he saw daily. Their relationship suffered from her increasing moodiness, and in his scrawled notes to her Stanisław refers to 'frequent and heavy clouds'. But he craved her company. 'I have told Tremo to prepare supper at your house,' runs a typical note. 'If it is sunny this afternoon we shall see each other in the Saxony Gardens, if it is cold and dark, I shall pass by you before dinner *pour vous embrasser de tout mon coeur*.'[23] Her sister had married Onufry Kicki, who became Grand Equerry, a good-humoured and witty man whose company delighted Stanisław. Other regular members of the king's circle included Joachim Chreptowicz, the Moszyński brothers, and the friend of Stanisław's youth Franciszek Rzewuski, a fastidious man who was always fighting duels on arcane points of honour. He resided at the Castle throughout his life, and in 1774 became marshal of the king's court. Perhaps the most important member of this entourage was Stanisław's principal chamberlain, Franciszek Ryx, who was factotum, collaborator and confidant all in one, and whose efficiency, discretion, intelligence and total devotion to the king made him utterly indispensable to him.

Although informality reigned in his private relations, Stanisław was careful to maintain the required distance in public. At the National Theatre for instance, only an adjutant and the duty chamberlain were allowed into the king's box. Stanisław had another large box for his family and close friends, and a third for Elżbieta Grabowska – and their carriages were not to drive up to the same place as the king's. Stanisław had abandoned the brilliant ceremonial of his early years in favour of a more restrained dignity, which was none the less grandiose. 'I have seen the court of Petersburg in the full glory of its magnificence at official audiences, but although great luxury reigns there, it does not afford the same imposing spectacle as the audiences of the king of Poland surrounded by the assembled estates,' noted Karl Heinrich von Heyking, a diplomat from Kurland.[24]

But such grandeur did little to assuage the smarting national pride of the younger generation in particular. 'Petersburg had become our capital, and Warsaw the capital of a Russian province in which Russia did entirely as she pleased, observing only the niceties of title,' wrote one of them. 'Thus the Governor was called an ambassador, the Russian government was called a guarantee, the provincial council was called a Permanent Council, its chairman was called a king.'[25] Stanisław himself noted that the Polish Order of the White Eagle, which he was obliged to bestow at Catherine's whim 'had become the badge of installation or dismissal of her successive favourites'.[26] The king was cast in a thankless and unattractive role, compounded by Stackelberg's policy, which was to make him appear as odious as possible to his own people.

Few appreciated the unpleasantness of his position. 'I know full well that it is wrong to hang oneself, and that it is necessary to work at the job to which I am chained for as long as the spirit does not leave the body,' he wrote to Ignacy Krasicki in one of his moments of near-despair. 'So I must and I will work, as hard as my strength and impaired health permit.'[27] He could only take refuge in philosophical detachment and his concept of destiny to give meaning to a situation that was sometimes unbearable. He celebrated the anniversary of his miraculous escape from the kidnappers with no less solemnity than that of his coronation, for it was the clearest message Providence had uttered that he was destined to suffer yet survive. This notion became the cornerstone of his system. He transformed his humiliations into an ordeal which his duty imposed on him, and he even managed to derive a morose satisfaction from this inglorious self-immolation. To foreign friends he would represent himself as a victim of human folly and ignorance, a sort of martyr to the cause of progress. To his nation he equated himself with the state, oppressed and powerless, but destined by higher powers to survive and, one day, to see itself vindicated and free once more.

But his philosophy was undermined by its own effects. One consequence of the cultural renewal that was taking place was that concern for the country's future was no longer the exclusive prerogative of the king and a few public-spirited magnates. Polish society as a whole had begun to feel responsibility for the fate of the country, and to voice it openly. Unfortunately, this happened at a time when social and ideological changes taking place throughout Europe meant that the question was taken up with a radical intensity quite out of keeping with the political realities of Poland in the 1780s. The argument was no longer, as it had been in the 1760s, between reformers and malcontent recidivists.

A new generation bred in a climate of enlightenment created by Stanisław, educated in the schools he had reformed, imbued with the virtues he had propounded and a patriotism focused on the vision of the Polish state which he had created, rejected the mediocrity of compromise. With all the confidence of youth, it longed for action. 'From my earliest youth, in the haven of my school, I heard only of our decadence,' wrote Julian Niemcewicz.[28] Young men of his generation, encouraged by the new educational system to think and question, grew up resenting the Russian hegemony and the quietist regime of the Permanent Council. Large numbers of them congregated in Warsaw, where they came into contact with people of other classes and countries. They met in the dozens of clubs which sprang up at about this time. Some were masonic in inspiration, the Club of United Friends founded in 1784 was devoted to the cultivation of taste, the Warsaw Learned Society, founded in 1777, drew together savants and aristocrats in search of scientific knowledge, but most reflected political interests.

This generation gap was widened by ideological shifts. Stanisław and his contemporaries had been brought up on the rationalism of Montesquieu and Voltaire, which imposed a discipline of realism and even scepticism. The generation coming of age in the 1780s could not accept these: Montesquieu was Catherine's favoured political reading, Voltaire had applauded the partition. The young men had a more sentimental and idealistic vision of the world, inspired by a new literature.

Throughout the first decade of Stanisław's reign Polish literature had been singlemindedly didactic. The writings of Konarski, Krasicki, Bohomolec, Naruszewicz and others involved in *Monitor* methodically sought out and destroyed prejudice, exposed superstition and applied reason to all aspects of public and private life. The Confederation of Bar gave rise to a poetry, baroque in form and inspiration, full of chivalric ideals and pathos, which completely negated this. But the inglorious reality of the partition doused this with a wave of pamphleteering and satirical squibs. Satire dominated the literature of the 1770s, most notably that practised by Ignacy Krasicki, who revealed a formidable poetic talent. His diocese of Warmia was an autonomous principality in which the bishop was also temporal ruler, and as it had fallen to Prussia in the partition, he found himself a vassal of Frederick. This awakened his patriotism, and whenever he could avoid attending his new suzerain at Sans-Souci he would spend his summers at Łazienki. He wrote satires, fables, a couple of comic epics ridiculing religious and political bigotry, and then a novel, *The Adventures of Mikołaj Doświadczyński*, the Polish *Candide*.

Satire was also the favoured weapon of the theatre, which became a prime platform for political and ideological debate. In 1774 August Sułkowski obtained the concession for all amusements in the capital and implemented a programme of light comedy and ballets. In 1776 Franciszek Ryx bought the concession off him and built a new National Theatre, whose repertory included plays by Beaumarchais, Shakespeare, Diderot, Sedaine, Goldoni, Metastasio and Lessing, as well as Polish works. In 1783 Ryx's venture ran into financial difficulties and was taken over by Marcin Lubomirski, who concentrated on opera and ballet, but by 1785 Stanisław had provided Ryx with the backing to repossess it and move back to a more serious programme, in which pride of place was given to the Polish plays of Bohomolec, Adam Czartoryski, Józef Wybicki, and particularly the young Franciszek Zabłocki, a favourite with Stanisław.

The literature of other countries was widely accessible in translation. *Robinson Crusoe*, *Manon Lescaut* and *Gil Blas* first came out in Polish in 1769, the works of Diderot and Voltaire in the 1770s, beginning with

Zadig in 1773 and ending with *Candide* in 1780. *Gulliver's Travels* followed in 1784, and *Roderick Random* in 1785. The works of Rousseau, available only in the original or in extracts or digests in *Monitor* and elsewhere, were now published in full in Polish, as were the philosophical and political writings of Montesquieu, Beccaria, Blackstone, Helvétius, Caraccioli, Hume and Locke. While *Monitor* stopped appearing in 1785, other periodicals sprang up to transmit foreign as well as native writing. In 1782 the enterprising ex-Jesuit Piotr Świtkowski launched his monthly *Historical-Political Journal* and in 1784 he followed this up with another, the *Warsaw Magazine*. Two years later the *Trade Journal* was launched.

These extraneous influences made themselves felt in the works of the writers of the late 1770s and 1780s. A good example was the poet Stanisław Trembecki, who after a long sojourn in Paris, where he befriended a glittering array of men of letters and killed several people in a succession of duels, returned to Poland with a fine library and a set of the *Encyclopédie*. His verse progressed from a French rococo style, through a sentimental and a political phase, to a visionary pan-Slavic Romanticism. A sceptic bon-viveur who ended his life as a vegetarian hermit, he laid his considerable poetic talents at the service of Stanisław, who bestowed on him the title of gentleman of the bedchamber and gathered him into his immediate entourage. Not so Tomasz Węgierski, a younger man of great talent, also a libertine. He excelled in vicious satire, much of it aimed at the king, the court and the Permanent Council. This landed him behind bars, and his rebellious spirit then took him to America and later France, where he died young. But the mutinous note he had struck did not die away.

A new crop of talent had grown up in the 1770s with the proto-Romantic sentimentalism of Franciszek Karpiński, the lyricism of Franciszek Kniaźnin, the political vigour of Julian Niemcewicz, and the populist verve of Wojciech Bogusławski. Their attitudes were echoed in the music of the composers flourishing in Warsaw, namely Jan Wański, Feliks Janiewicz, Jan Dawid Holland, Maciej Kamieński, Jan Stefani and Józef Elsner. What distinguished them from the dozens of second-rank composers of the period is that they all introduced folk music into their concerts, symphonies and operas. This practice was not new, and folk motifs can be found in the works of Telemann, Haydn and Mozart. What was new was the authentic and even political rawness with which the peasant themes intruded into the elegance of the Polish composers' works. It was the first manifestation of nationalism in music, foreshadowing the work of Elsner's pupil Fryderyk Chopin.

The new generation of writers rejected the rationalism of the Enlightenment and the pragmatism of Stanisław's compromise. They were influenced by Rousseau, whose love of nature, respect for custom, cult of liberty, dislike of cities and trade, all struck a powerful chord in the hearts of traditionalist szlachta and young radicals alike. They were drawn towards what they saw as traditional Polish values, particularly the bucolic simplicity and the pure patriotism they imagined had underlain them in the past.

Their protest came from the heart rather than the head, and their reaction was not intellectually or politically founded. They accused a generation which was in some ways more progressive than theirs, but which couched that progressiveness in rationalist terms they found inadequate. A good example of this is the attitude towards the peasantry, which accounted for much prose and poetry in the 1780s. The young writers denounced serfdom and sang mawkishly of the hardships of peasant life, but it was their elders who actually did something about it. Those who took action on behalf of the oppressed were all, with the exception of Stanisław Poniatowski, of the older generation, and most of them were adherents of Stanisław's system of compromise within the Russian hegemony. Stanisław himself encouraged these moves and made eloquent gestures of his own. In 1774, for instance, he established out of his own pocket a fund which paid barristers to defend the poor in court for nothing.[29]

Stanisław was not a Voltairian at heart. He had originally declared war on tradition because it was being used to cloak ignorance and abuse. Now that much of this had been confounded, and his age and experience had moderated his attitudes, he too delved back into Polish history and culture in search of positive traditions. Guided by Naruszewicz's historical writings, he developed his own view of a golden Polish past. Ever desperate to find ideological support for his position, he gradually began to replace his role-model Henri IV with Kazimierz the Great (1333–70).

The young men who began to denounce the status quo at the beginning of the 1780s were therefore not revolutionaries attacking a repressive system; they were Romantics rebelling against the pragmatism of a system that wounded their sense of Poland's sovereignty – itself a product of all that Stanisław and his collaborators had achieved over the past two decades. In a book published in 1782, Karpiński refuted rationalism and advocated the primacy of sentiment. Instinct had triumphed over empiricism, and the Romantic movement was born in Poland.

Their feelings found a refuge from the capital and the court in the entourage of Izabela Czartoryska. A poorly educated girl who had no ambitions beyond enjoying herself throughout the 1760s, she achieved late maturity and found a vocation in life. She was in London in 1772 when the partition was agreed, and her husband, Adam, suggested they sell up all their property in Poland and settle either in England or France, where they would be able to live on the highest footing. 'I have told you already, and I repeat it, that by inclination and perhaps by habit I am strongly attached to Poland, and that it is there that I shall always choose to live,' she wrote back. 'One can still do some good in our country.'[30] On her return, she transformed her pleasure-grounds at Powązki into an arcadia suffused with sentimental glorification of Poland. In 1783 the Czartoryskis decided to demonstrate their disgust with the king's system by moving from Warsaw to Puławy. There they set up a court which was not merely the political centre of the new Familia, but also the forge in which its image was to be recast.

It was above all a question of style. The rococo atmosphere of Powązki was replaced with a more relaxed, English model of country life. The accent was on the natural and the picturesque, on the North (Ossian rather than Homer, Scottish mists rather than the landscape of Italy), and on innocence. Puławy rejected Stanislavian classicism and cosmopolitanism in favour of a healthy, neo-classical brand of Sarmatism, based on patriotism and a chivalric view of family. The peasantry were subsumed into this patriarchal dream, and Izabela Czartoryska began setting up hospitals and schools for them. She later wrote the first children's history of Poland for the use of these schools, and created the first museum devoted to the country's past.

History, which had been used by Stanisław to redefine the image of the Polish state, was now taken up and distorted in a strictly political and nineteenth-century manner. Puławy generated a new past for Poland, full of myth and wishful thinking, designed to give young people hope and self-assurance, but above all to shore up the crumbling prestige and the credentials of the great families, as every hero it glorified was related to them. Puławy attracted many young idealists. Kniaźnin and Karpiński settled there. Niemcewicz took service with Adam Czartoryski. Many others gravitated towards a court that had become a counterbalance to that of Warsaw. This new Athens of Polish values extended its influence all over the country throughout the 1780s as Polish society's reaction against Stanisław's inglorious policy grew. The Familia had found a new political power-base.

18

Tryst on the Dnieper

*A*bombshell burst over Warsaw on the morning of 17 January 1785, as news spread that the king's chamberlain, Franciszek Ryx, had been thrown into gaol on the previous evening, having been allegedly caught conspiring to poison Adam Czartoryski. Later that day, General Komarzewski was also detained by the Marshal's men.

Stanisław heard of Ryx's arrest while at the theatre. He was shaking with anger as he got up and left, and as soon as he was back at the Castle he instructed Glayre to investigate.[1] The capital buzzed with rumour and speculation, but nothing further was known until a few days later an anonymous pamphlet recounted in detail how the two men had approached a woman, Madame Dogrumova, and tried to bribe her to seduce Czartoryski and then poison him. The pamphlet unequivocally pointed to the king as the instigator of the plot. A few days later, Czartoryski laid before the Tribunal of the Marshalcy a formal accusation against Ryx and Komarzewski.

Soon most of the courts of Europe were abuzz with the affair. In a letter to Adam Czartoryski, the Emperor Joseph II described it as 'the most incredible, and, if one is to believe it, the most unworthy and singular business one could imagine,' and offered his protection.[2] The calibre of the people involved obscured the fundamental absurdity of the allegations, which only emerged as the court proceedings began to shed light on the affair.

Marie-Thérèse Néri alias the Baronne de Lautenbourg was a courtesan who had plied her trade all over Europe. She had been expelled from Venice, Bruges, Berlin and Hamburg, where one of her 'husbands' was hanged for his part in some sordid affair, before settling in Warsaw, where she married a Russian major called Dogrumov. The waning of her charms conjured up the prospect of diminishing resources, so she turned to intrigue for income. Some time in 1782 she had called on Fryderyk Moszyński, and told him that she had evidence of a plot by Adam Czartoryski, Ksawery Branicki and several others to poison the king. Moszyński informed Stanisław, who dismissed the story as nonsense.

Eighteen months later, she renewed her assault through Ryx. She now claimed she had proof that the assassination would take place in Grodno, during the next session of the Seym. Ryx informed Komarzewski, who took precautions to tighten security during the king's sojourn in Grodno, but nothing suspicious took place, and after the court's return to Warsaw the woman was told to get lost. She made one last attempt at convincing the two royal servants by brandishing a forged letter in their faces, but they were not impressed.

She had in the mean time ensnared an English merchant, William Taylor, in her schemes, and now changed tack. On 11 January 1785 Taylor informed Czartoryski that he, Czartoryski, was the victim of a murder plot. Czartoryski was incredulous, but the Englishman insisted so vehemently that in the end he agreed to see Dogrumova. He took Ignacy Potocki with him, and the two of them were treated by the courtesan to a hair-raising tale. She said that Ryx and Komarzewski had offered her money and an estate if she would insinuate herself into Czartoryski's favours and either poison him or stab him while they made love, and had given her a packet of poison, which she now handed over to Czartoryski. As Czartoryski and Potocki remained sceptical, she assured them that she could prove it all to them if they would come and eavesdrop on an interview she undertook to arrange with Ryx.

Accordingly, on 16 January, Stanisław Potocki went to Dogrumova's house, where he was hidden in a closet with a crack in the door. Ryx duly appeared, and Dogrumova launched into an ambivalent conversation about 'the affair', about money, poison and daggers, to which the chamberlain listened patiently, thinking she was still speaking of the alleged plot against the king. When Ryx stood up to withdraw, Taylor rushed in and put a pistol to his head. Quite what Potocki did or did not hear behind the door is uncertain, but he was swept along by Taylor's determination. The Englishman dragged his prisoner off to the house of Elżbieta Lubomirska, and Potocki followed. They burst into the crowded drawing room, and Taylor announced that he had caught Ryx red-handed plotting to murder Czartoryski. There was general astonishment. Ignacy Potocki, who was present, called for the Marshal's men and had Ryx arrested.

At the first court hearing, the whole case fell apart. Czartoryski could produce no witnesses other than Stanisław Potocki, Dogrumova and Taylor, who were all biased. The white powder had been analysed by several doctors, including Czartoryski's personal physician, and they found that it was not poison, but some kind of aphrodisiacal preparation. The case was quashed by a decree of the Tribunal dated 15 March, with the injunction that it should not be mentioned again in public. The depositions of the woman and the witnesses, as well as the pamphlets published on the affair were to be burned by the public hangman; Czartoryski had to pay damages to Komarzewski and Ryx; Taylor was fined and gaoled for six months; and Dogrumova was given a life sentence, to begin after she had been pilloried in the old market square and branded on the buttocks.[3]

Czartoryski refused to present himself to the court for the sentence, and left Warsaw in a state of dudgeon. He resigned his post as commander of the Cadet Corps to cut his last connection with the king. His sister Elżbieta Lubomirska, who had played a major part in inflating the affair, also left Warsaw, and henceforth drifted about Europe in self-imposed exile. Stanisław tried to make light of the affair and mollify his cousin's indignation. But Czartoryski was not to be conciliated and threatened to bring the matter up at the next Seym, invoking the friendship and protection of the Russian and Austrian courts. Czartoryski and the Potockis could not admit to their foolish gullibility, and therefore had to stand by the theory that the king really had been hatching a plot. Unlikely as this might seem, the idea concentrated the resentment that had been building up against Stanisław among the members of the Familia, and helped to win them a number of unexpected allies.

One was Karol Radziwiłł, not a bad man, kind and patriotic in his own way, but stupid almost beyond belief and utterly uneducated.

In the late 1770s, Radziwiłł had stopped drinking, one effect of which was that he lost his political drive. He became more amiable, and even grew quite friendly towards Stanisław. In 1784 he went out of his way to honour him by entertaining him at his seat of Nieśwież before the opening of the Grodno Seym. The king was received with gun salutes and illuminations, and put up in rooms built for the occasion. There were dinners and balls interspersed with concerts and ballets. One day, after a wolf-shoot during which Stanisław bagged over twenty beasts, there was an opera written by Karol's cousin Maciej Radziwiłł, magnificently staged with a remarkable machine representing the sun, after which there was a banquet and a drive, followed by fireworks. On the following day, after shooting three bears, Stanisław watched an elaborate recreation of the French attack on Gibraltar, staged by Radziwiłł's private forces on the Nieśwież lake with fireworks and specially constructed ships. The visit was an excuse for Radziwiłł to emphasise his vision of himself as a princely figure, but the honours paid to the king were a far cry from the insults thrown at the 'upstart Poniatowski' in the previous decade. Nevertheless, Radziwiłł felt a kinship of interests with the other magnates of the Familia.[4] Much the same was true of Bishop Massalski, who, having married his niece Helena off to Prince Charles de Ligne, fancifully plotted a royal future for the couple.

The most important new ally of the Familia was Feliks Potocki, the son of Franciszek, erstwhile arch-enemy of the Czartoryski uncles. He was rich, generous and popular. But his weak character had been traumatised by the brutality of his father. Franciszek Potocki had opposed his marriage to Gertruda Komorowska, whom he did not consider illustrious enough, and then arranged the abduction and murder of the pregnant bride after Feliks had eloped with her. Stanisław had befriended the young man in the hope of involving him constructively in the regeneration of the country 'as a good citizen and as my good friend'. Potocki professed himself ready to serve in everything, and to put the king's interest before his own. 'I lay before Your Majesty My Master all my thoughts, so that you might know my character and read my mind,' he wrote as they prepared the elections to the 1784 Seym.[5] But these sentiments were not to last. Disagreements arose between them, and by the following year Potocki too was drifting into the Czartoryski orbit.

The Seym of 1784, held in Grodno, marked a turning-point for Stanisław's system. In the previous year he had made an official visit to Siedlce in an effort to conciliate some of the ageing hetman Michał Ogiński's friends assembled there. His progress to Lithuania in 1784 was truly regal, with visits to the seats of several magnates, most notably Radziwiłł, on the way. On the way back, he graced Michał Ogiński's sumptuous artistic court at Słonim, where he was feasted with refined musical entertainments. Grodno itself was now a far cry from what Williams had seen. The royal castle was elegantly rebuilt; Tyzenhauz's buildings and a number of fine palaces, with theatres and ballrooms, had replaced the dilapidated hovels. The Seym opened in great pomp, with a sung Mass and a procession to the chamber. This was followed by an unusual ceremony in which Stanisław placed the red biretta on the head of the Papal Nuncio, Giovanni Archetti, Archbishop of Chalcedony (the king of Poland was one of four monarchs who had the right to nominate a cardinal in rotation). Stanisław had never appeared so regally established.

With the ceremonies over, the attacks on him began, directed mainly at his spending. Stanisław's finances were indeed out of control. His profligate attitude to collecting works of art and his building works were one thing. His generosity and inability to refuse help were more troublesome. 'I beg you, I advise you, I ask you, to stop throwing money out of the window,' he wrote to his nephew Józef, 'and to remember that you are not the only one, nor one in a hundred, nor even one in a thousand who ask me for it continually, and that unfortunately I do not have the science of making gold.'[6] But he kept supporting him, and the hundreds of others. Well over 10 per cent of his entire income went on pensions and assistance to various people.[7]

The real problem lay elsewhere. He had commissioned Pius Kiciński, the new director of his Gabinet, to produce a report on the finances of the royal household and suggest savings. This revealed that a vast number of people were living off the king, drawing rations of firewood, candles, and above all food, from the Castle. The kitchen, which employed twenty-eight people not counting the scullery-maids, porters, washers and turnspits, and excluding the pantry or the bakery, which had similar staffs, was a financial drain. Stanisław himself gave lunch to a dozen people every day and dinner to twice that number on Thursdays. Only rarely did he give a banquet. When the Seym was in session, several dozen of his supporters would lunch at the Castle, and although on these occasions the three oyster-openers could hardly keep up, the Seym only sat for a few weeks once a year. So, however refined and well served his table might have been, that was not the source of the problem. His brother Michał, Elżbieta Grabowska, Franciszek Rzewuski, Ogrodzki, Komarzewski, Reverdil, Glayre, Józef Poniatowski and others who inhabited the Castle also had their 'tables', and quantities of other greater or lesser royal servants would either eat at the Castle or, more often, take home whatever they fancied from the kitchens and cellars. A major reorganisation was put in hand, but the results were neither rapid nor dramatic.[8]

Stanisław's debts had grown to over 11 million złoty by 1781, principally because the original sum allocated in the state budget for repaying them was too small. But by the time this was raised, his spending had spiralled. Thus while the state devoted more than 21 million złoty to repaying the king's debts over the next six years, he ran up fresh ones to the value of more than 24 million złoty in the same period, with the result that he owed 14 million by 1787.[9] His spending was not entirely due to fecklessness, as he frequently had to patch holes in state enterprises. He also suffered from the cash shortages of the early 1780s which affected the thriftiest magnates, many of whom had had to borrow abroad.[10] The Seym was notoriously reluctant to vote higher taxes, so the king's debt assumed the nature of an irritant. 'I had to listen to some very bitter lectures,' Stanisław wrote after the 1784 Seym to August Moszyński, who was travelling in Italy. 'I must be terribly careful on the subject of finances,' he added, instructing Moszyński not to buy anything for him under any circumstances. (The instructons were ignored, and Moszyński regularly reported that he had picked up and sent back yet another 'bauble', including an Egyptian mummy.)[11]

A few months after the end of the Seym came the Dogrumova affair, and the behaviour of the Familia convinced Stanisław that his system was threatened. 'I try to calm and amuse myself by making improvements at Łazienki,' he wrote to Moszyński. 'But I must confess that an underlying sadness follows me even there, so much so that I fear that it may from now on remain a constant companion of the rest of my days.'[12] One thing that saddened him beyond measure was the death, in 1784, of Andrzej Mokronowski, whose popularity and negotiating skills had made him an invaluable supporter. 'From where you are', Stanisław wrote to Bishop Krasicki, 'you cannot know how much both I and the Commonwealth lose in him, particularly at the present moment.'[13]

Times had changed, and a collection of magnates, however rich and influential, no longer represented a political force as they had in the 1760s. 'The szlachta had come to realise that it could make its own way without the grace and favour of the magnates,' in the words of one contemporary.[14] And until the Familia could find a policy around which to deploy their influence, they could do little political damage. Nevertheless, they resumed their attacks at the Seym of 1785, and managed to field thirty-eight deputies from their camp in the Seym of 1786. They wanted to bring the Dogrumova affair before the Seym, which they hoped might reverse the ruling of the Tribunal. The Russian and Austrian ambassadors helped Stanisław put a stop to that, but the very mention of the issue rallied the fighting spirit of those opposed to the king. Bills proposed by Stanisław or the Permanent Council were strongly contested, and Stanisław had to hold back Michał Mniszech's project for a far-reaching reorganisation and democratisation of the cities lest the opposition emasculate it. 'No consideration of the public good affected them,' Glayre reported to Monet in Paris. 'Their petty interests, hidden beneath words of motherland and liberty, were the real substance of their speeches.'[15] It is true that the patriotism of the 'Patriots', as they increasingly liked to refer to themselves, was suspect. Many were dual nationals, as they had held on to estates lying in the partitioned areas. Adam Czartoryski held the rank of general in the Austrian army. He also spied for Austria, filing intelligence reports under the codename 'Abbé Sartori'.[16] But modern notions of patriotism were in their infancy, and Glayre was being less than fair. In one instance at least it was the opposition and not the king that understood the best interests of the country.

Jacek Małachowski, the new head of the Mint Commission, decided to put a stop to the outflow of silver currency and the losses to the king's purse resulting from the high silver content of the Polish złoty. He proposed adopting the very ratio that Stanisław had fought so hard to bring in exactly twenty years earlier. But Stanisław dug his heels in, apparently on the somewhat vain grounds that it was worth losing money in order to have the most valuable and finest coinage in northern Europe.[17] Happily for the country, he was defeated; the silver content of the coinage was reduced, and the Mint began to bring in a profit rather than a loss. The dramatic increase in the quantity of coinage in circulation, as the Prussians stopped melting it down, acted as an immediate tonic on trade.

After the Seym, the 'matadors of the opposition', as one observer called them, went down to Puławy to be feasted and entertained. Kniaźnin had written a play specially for the occasion, *The Spartan Mother*, in which Izabela Czartoryska in the leading role exhorted the assembled company to fight for their country.[18] The Familia still had no policy, but they had found a set of slogans and, what was possibly more important, an image which could draw support to their side. From being progressive pragmatists who had despised the old Sarmatian hangovers, the Familia now became 'Patriots', denouncing Warsaw as a rotten place and Stanisław as a Russian puppet. Like all opposition parties which lack a coherent domestic policy, they had struck the nationalist chord. And it was this that alarmed Stanisław.

He had never allowed himself to forget that Poland existed only on the sufferance of the neighbouring powers, and he kept a watchful eye on international events. Any project hatched by one or other of the three powers always raised the possibility of a new partition of Poland, as did any friction between them. The only thing that stood between Poland and perdition was the dubious Russian guarantee. Stanisław never stopped thinking up ways of turning this into a proper alliance, which would not only strengthen Poland's position internationally, but also reinforce his own position in Poland. He bombarded Panin with countless memoranda and sought new connections with the Russian court with this view in mind.

In 1781 Stanisław made one of his rare trips away from Warsaw to meet Catherine's son and heir Paul. The Grand Duke, travelling informally under the name of the Comte du Nord, was passing through Poland on the first leg of a European tour, and spent a few days as the guest of the Mniszechs at Wiśniowiec. He was accompanied by his second wife, Sophia Dorothea of Württemberg, whose brother was married to Adam Czartoryski's daughter Marya. Another connection which Stanisław pursued was with Catherine's favourite and minister for war Potyomkin. This protean and wildly contradictory figure had an enormous influence on Catherine, who treated him almost as a husband. But he was acutely aware of the precariousness of his position in the event of her death, and in this context he cast an eye on Poland. In 1775 he obtained szlachta status, and even asked Stanisław's niece, Urszula Zamoyska, recently divorced from Wincenty Potocki, for her hand in marriage.[19] But the idea did not appeal to her, and she married Michał Mniszech instead. In 1781 Potyomkin began buying land in south-eastern Poland, possibly as a refuge.

In 1782, when Russia abandoned her old Northern System and Prussia with it, Stanisław saw his chance and hastened to offer an active alliance. He pointed out that Russian suspicions had become groundless, since Poland was too weak to represent any kind of threat to Russia, and that her weakness only invited the intervention of Prussia, which would be detrimental to Russian interests. Poland needed Russia in order to survive at all, and this was the best guarantee of her loyalty. Stanisław argued that Russia should now strengthen Poland, by making the Permanent Council more efficient, extending the powers of the Crown and increasing its income, extending the Seym's sessions, and abolishing the veto.[20]

The proposal was rejected by Catherine, but in 1786, as tension mounted once more between Russia and Turkey, Stanisław decided to try again. Maurice Glayre, who thought it risky for Poland to get involved in military adventures, suggested rearranging the basis of Polish-Russian relations by offering the Polish succession to Catherine's younger grandson, the eight-year-old Constantine, who could be brought to Poland and groomed for the throne by Stanisław.[21] But Stanisław still entertained hopes for his own nephew. Also, he needed an active foreign policy in order to defuse the popular enthusiasm generated by the defiant attitudes being struck at Puławy. 'It is absolutely essential to occupy the nation, and to demonstrate to it at the same time the benefits of a close union with Russia,' he wrote as a preface to his new proposals for an alliance.[22]

Stanisław had often wished that he could explain his intentions to Catherine personally, realising that many of their misunderstandings had originated with the people through whom they had to communicate. As it happened, Catherine intended to make a grand progress through her new territories in the spring of 1787, taking in the Ukraine and the Crimea. She would be passing through former Polish territory and along the existing frontier. Stanisław instructed his minister in St

Petersburg, Augustyn Deboli, to express his ardent wish to meet her in Kiev. Stackelberg was sceptical, but in November 1786 Catherine agreed to a meeting somewhere along the Polish frontier, on the river Dnieper.[23]

Stanisław went to work on the propositions he would lay before Catherine. He would offer her an active alliance for the expected war with Turkey. Participation in the war would deflate the patriotic bombast of the opposition, and permit him to augment and equip the Polish army, which would gain valuable fighting experience. Above all, it would allow him to take a firmer grip on government at home. He did not intend to give Russia obedient support. 'One would have to be quite sure', he wrote in a set of Preliminary Reflections, 'that in the event of her concluding an offensive and defensive alliance with Russia, Poland would receive in exchange a radical improvement in her government.' On these terms he envisaged offering his ally the support of an army of 25–35,000 men under his personal command. If no concessions were forthcoming on the constitutional front, then Poland would only undertake to defend her own territory and Russia's western flank.[24]

Stanisław set off at the end of February 1787, leaving his brother the Primate in charge at Warsaw. His aunt, Michał Czartoryski's widow, had given him a holy relic along with her blessing and prayers for the favourable outcome of the undertaking.[25] The weather kept changing violently from frost to thaw. As he tried to cross the Vistula near Warka, the ice cracked and he was soaked. He had to return to Kozienice to wait for the river to freeze again. Eventually he crossed on a raft. On 4 March he reached Krasnystaw, and a few days later he was at Łabuń, staying with Józef Stempkowski, one of his most active political agents. The temperature dropped dramatically, and he continued his journey in a simple peasant sleigh, buried in a thick pile of straw and covered with furs. On 9 March he reached Wiśniowiec, in good fettle in spite of the arduous journey. But most of his suite, including Whitworth, Littlepage and Charles de Ligne, were not so lucky. 'This whole caravan got buried in the snow, and there has been no more news of them than of last year's flies,' wrote Urszula Mniszech.[26] Stanisław stayed at Wiśniowiec for four days. He was joined there by his nephew Józef Poniatowski, who diverted the company with music, and by the Prince de Ligne, who read them extracts from the memoirs he was writing. Stanisław then proceeded on his way towards Kaniów on the Dnieper.

At Chwastów on 20 March, Potyomkin came from Kiev to pay his respects. He had just been named Prince of Tauris in recognition of his role in the conquest of the Crimea, and it was he who would symbolically present to Catherine the new dominions during the forthcoming progress. He was attended by Branicki and Stackelberg, who was cringingly polite. 'The proud and pompous viceroy of Poland had become, in the Russian context, a courtier almost lost in the crowd; I seemed to behold a dethroned prince,' the French diplomat Ségur noted.[27] Potyomkin was wearing the uniform of the szlachta of the Palatinate of Bracław and his Polish decorations, and he treated Stanisław as though he were his sovereign. He told Stanisław not to worry about Ignacy Potocki, whom he referred to as '*un scélérat*', or Feliks Potocki, whom he dismissed as a fool, but interceded on behalf of Branicki, whom he described as a good fellow at heart.[28] Branicki had just married Potyomkin's niece, Alexandra Engelhardt (widely, but erroneously, believed to be Catherine's daughter), a development which Stanisław viewed with alarm. He now needed his good relations with Potyomkin in order to keep the unruly hetman under control.

Stanisław arrived at Kaniów on 24 March. His architect Kubicki had built an elegant palace in the space of two months, and was now busily designing triumphal arches and firework displays. 'Kubicki has done a good job,' noted Stanisław. 'We are all lodged quite well, and even prettily in my case.'[29] Stanisław settled down to await Catherine's arrival, and enjoyed the opportunity for a long rest in the budding countryside of the Ukraine. He celebrated Easter with the usual ceremony in the small local church, and on Maundy Thursday washed the feet of twelve local peasants and then served them dinner, as tradition dictated. He went for rides and walks, and spent his evenings playing billiards, listening to readings and making conversation with those such as the Mniszechs who were in attendance, and those passing through on their way to Kiev, such as the Venezuelan General Miranda, who told Stanisław of his plans to liberate his own country.[30] There was also a good deal of coming and going between Kiev and Kaniów. Stanisław's old friend Naryshkin came over for a day. On 28 March A.P. Shuvalov, son of the grand inquisitor who had so terrified him once, brought a letter from Catherine, and foreign minister Bezborodko turned up for a conference. He was accompanied by Stackelberg, who informed Stanisław that Catherine had read his last memorandum and liked it. Both of them returned several times over the next two weeks, and each time there was discussion of the alliance and of possible constitutional changes in Poland. Presents were exchanged, and cordiality reigned. But the talk was vague, and Stanisław was frustrated and worried lest his enemies in Kiev might steal a march on him.

The surge of interested parties towards Kiev was astonishing. Throughout the month of March the unfrequented roads of the Ukraine bore heavy traffic, and sleepy palaces, manor houses and inns opened their doors to the most illustrious and cosmopolitan travellers: 'I have never in my life met with so much gaiety, so much charm and wit,' wrote Urszula Mniszech, who had gone on to Kiev in the company of her husband, Józef Poniatowski, assorted Polish noblemen, the Prince de Ligne, Littlepage, General Edouard Dillon, the Prince de Nassau and sundry other drifting grandees. 'Our little dinners in these squalid Jewish inns are quite exquisite, and in complete contradiction to the surroundings. If one closes one's eyes one imagines oneself in Paris.'[31] Kiev itself was more like Versailles in the days of the Sun King. 'There is something here for everyone, for all types; great and little politics, great and little intrigues, great and little Poland,' wrote the Prince de Ligne. 'Certain important figures of that country, who are fooling themselves and who are being fooled, or are fooling others, all very amiable, less so it is true than their wives, wish to make sure that the empress does not know that they have insulted her during the barkings of the last Seym. They seek to catch the eye of Prince Potyomkin, which is no easy thing to do, for the prince is both blind in one eye and short-sighted.'[32] To their discomfiture, Catherine told them all that they must honour their king and obey him.[33] Feliks Potocki and Ksawery Branicki, who had the backing of Potyomkin, were well-received, but as for Ignacy Potocki and Kazimierz Sapieha, 'the empress did not even cast a glance at them', and Potyomkin reported that she thought Potocki an intriguer, and described Sapieha as '*un pisseur*'.[34]

At length, when the ice had cleared, the empress and her court embarked on a flotilla of seven galleys, each one a veritable palace, followed by eighty other vessels, and the whole circus began its progress down the Dnieper. It was a great outing, but the apparent frivolity was underlain by frantic tension, both at the court level, with everyone jockeying for position or even acknowledgment, and at the international level, as war loomed with Turkey and every power on the continent badgered its diplomats to penetrate the intentions of Catherine. But Catherine watched with a basilisk's eye, pretending to take an interest only in the amusements laid on for her along the way by Potyomkin.

The flotilla arrived off Kaniów on 6 May, greeted by an imperial artillery salute. At eleven o'clock, Alexander Bezborodko and Marshal of the Court Prince Baryatinsky came to fetch the king in a luxurious launch. 'Gentlemen, the King of Poland has asked me to commend Count Poniatowski to your care,' Stanisław said to them as he came aboard. (The king was not allowed to leave his country.)[35] He was accompanied by his nephew Stanisław, Ludwik Tyszkiewicz and the Mniszechs, that is to say by family rather than officials. When he reached Catherine's galley, those present could hardly contain their excitement, as Ségur records:

> We pressed ourselves in a circle around him, curious to see the first emotions and to hear the first words of these august persons, in circumstances so different from those in which they had last met, united by love, separated by jealousy and pursued by hatred. But our expectations were almost entirely disappointed; for, after an exchange of greetings that was grave, majestic and cool, Catherine gave her arm to Stanisław and they retired to a cabinet, where they remained closeted for half an hour. When this *tête à tête* was over, their majesties came out to join us, and as we had not been able to hear them, our inquisitive looks sought to read their thoughts on their faces; but a light cloud over their foreheads rendered this reading difficult; one could see only on the part of the empress a hint of embarrassment and unusual constraint, and, in the eyes of the king, a certain trace of sadness, which an affected smile could not entirely disguise.[36]

Catherine confessed to Urszula Mniszech that in the first moments she had found it 'impossible not to be embarrassed', but Stanisław was delighted by the meeting. 'Every time I wanted to kiss her hand,' he wrote to Pius Kiciński, 'she presented her face.'[37] The two sovereigns then stepped into a launch and pulled over to another galley, where a banquet was laid out. The feast began with Catherine rising to toast Stanisław, while the artillery of the fleet saluted. She then invested him with the Order of St Andrew. 'The lunch was very merry,' writes Ligne, who records that when it was over Stanisław looked round for his hat, but Catherine saw it first and handed it to him. 'To cover my head twice!' said the king gallantly, alluding to his crown. 'Ah! Madame, that is too much bounty and goodness.'[38]

After lunch Stanisław was conducted to a separate galley, where an apartment had been prepared for him to rest in. Later, he was rowed to Potyomkin's galley for a conference. Potyomkin said that he approved all Stanisław's plans, and begged him to admit Branicki to his favour. Stanisław replied that he would like nothing better, if only Branicki would behave himself. Branicki was summoned, and began to justify himself in such an insolent tone that Stanisław left the room. Potyomkin rushed out after him and began to make excuses for his friend. He gave Branicki a sharp reprimand, and so did Catherine when she heard about the incident. 'I will not have anyone upset the king,' she declared.

At about six in the evening, Stanisław returned to Catherine's galley, where a number of people had reassembled. Rafał Tarnowski, once a rabid Barian, now desperate to curry favour, had asked Catherine and Stanisław to be the godparents of his baby son Władysław, and they held the child over an improvised font while Bishop Naruszewicz officiated.[39] With this ceremony out of the way, Stanisław walked about the deck with Catherine, and then they retired together once again. It was now that Stanisław presented her with his detailed project for the alliance. She took the document and told him that she would give him an answer when she had read it.[40] They came back on deck, where Potyomkin and others were playing cards, and spent an hour or so in general conversation, during which the empress affirmed, in front of all those present: 'you may count on my friendship and my most amicable intentions both towards your person and your kingdom.'[41] At about nine in the evening, Stanisław was rowed back ashore, the only slight cloud on his horizon being that Catherine had pleaded weariness and declined to attend the dinner he was giving in Kaniów that night. Nor could she be enticed into staying on for two days and joining him in celebrating St Stanisław's day. She watched Kubicki's fireworks representing an eruption of Mount Vesuvius from her galley.

On the following morning, before she sailed, Catherine sent Stackelberg to Stanisław with her compliments, and with a verbal message on the subject of his project. 'The thing is good, and I like it,' it ran. 'It will be done, but one cannot deal with such matters on a galley.'[42] The fleet then weighed anchor, and Stanisław left Kaniów to go and spend a few days on the estate of his nephew Stanisław at Korsuń. His other nephew, Józef, had left to rejoin his unit on the Danube, as he was still an officer in the Austrian army. The king was eager to see the new house Stanisław was building, the first country house in Poland in the Gothick style, designed by Jan Lindsay, a native of Białystok. Stanisław also wanted to see all the improvements his nephew had made to the estates, as the young man had a remarkable talent for husbandry. But a new distraction intruded after a couple of days. As they were sitting down to dinner on 9 May, news arrived that the Emperor Joseph II, travelling incognito as Count Falkenstein through Poland on his way to meet Catherine in the Crimea, would be passing by on the following day.

Stanisław Poniatowski intercepted him at Bohusław and invited him to visit the king at Korsuń. The Emperor protested that he was not dressed for the occasion, but said that 'if the King invited Count Falkenstein to come and see him, he would consider this invitation as an order and would appear before him as he stood'.[43] This he proceeded to do, accompanied by a single attendant. 'When he came in through the door, he threw out his arms and embraced me warmly, as though we had been old friends,' Stanisław recorded. 'The conversation was consistently lively, and we talked of a hundred different things, in which I naturally tried to be as complaisant as possible, without however flattering him to his face.' As they sat side by side on the sofa, Joseph complained that he had been forced to take part in the partition by Frederick, and, taking Stanisław by the hand, he solemnly assured him that he would not touch 'a single tree' of Poland.[44] 'The king is in his society a charming man,' he wrote to Kaunitz, 'but he never leaves that air of royalty, which is a little theatrical in a Poniatowski.'[45] The monarchs parted after two hours with protestations of friendship and embraces, and as Joseph climbed back into his carriage, he embraced the king *'cordialissime'* one last time.

Stanisław was delighted. 'Laus Deo!' he wrote to Kiciński, telling him to have fifty masses said, 'for the souls of departed parents, siblings, forbears, friends and acquaintances of mine, to be said by the poorest priests'.[46] He felt that he had re-established a measure of trust between himself and Catherine, and was confident that she would respond favourably to his plans. While seeing him back to the shore, Bezborodko had reaffirmed: 'You can count on it happening, for we are agreed on everything in principle.'[47] His conversations with the unaccountable Potyomkin had been reassuring. And the interview with the Emperor could not have been more positive. 'Fear nothing,' he wrote to Stanisław Badeni, 'nobody will take even a scrap of land from us.'[48] Even France seemed well-disposed for once, and Stanisław sent Littlepage to Paris to investigate the possibilities – the American was a friend of Lafayette and knew the foreign minister Montmorin.

Stanisław was in excellent mood as he slowly wended his way home. He went first to Tulczyn, where he was received with great parade by Feliks Potocki, who freed a number of peasants from servitude in honour of the king.[49] From there he went to Wiśniowiec, then by easy stages to Krasnystaw, to stay with the Zamoyskis, and then to Kraków, where he was joined by his brother the Primate. He went to some lengths to flatter the neglected former capital, by opening institutions, visiting schools and holding court for the civic bodies. 'I'm already bored with this place,' he wrote to Kiciński after ten days, 'but there's nothing for it, I must carry on graciously.'[50]

On 20 June, his optimism was boosted by news from Kherson that Joseph and Catherine had discussed him and both expressed themselves with sympathy on his subject. It was lifted further still by a report from his nephew Stanisław, who had gone on to Kherson himself. He had had a long conversation with the Emperor, who told him that he and Catherine had agreed that Poniatowski should succeed his uncle as king of Poland, and that both countries were prepared to return some of the territory taken away in the partition.[51] 'The King of Poland must be made happy, he deserves it,' Catherine had declared.[52]

On his return to Warsaw, Stanisław continued to nurture the new cordiality. He sent Catherine the Order of the White Eagle. She sent him a portrait of herself. In the summer he staged an elaborate allegorical ballet at Łazienki with her as heroine, reports of which were graciously received in St Petersburg. A court intrigue against Stackelberg there had made the ambassador less cocky. 'He continues polite with me,' Stanisław noted, almost with surprise. Stanisław was in constant correspondence with his envoy Deboli, who tirelessly lobbied Vice-Chancellor Ostermann on the proposed treaty. But the response was sluggish and contradictory.[53]

Stanisław was eventually asked to redraft his proposals in collaboration with Stackelberg, and the outcome was a watered down version of the original. Poland would raise an army of 45,000 men, of whom 20,000 would be sent to the Turkish front and paid for by Russia. Russia would further provide 80,000 muskets, 60,000 swords, 30,000 carbines, pistols and sabres. Stanisław's earlier idea of commanding the force in person was left out. As well as helping in the war with Turkey, Poland would undertake to fight off Prussia and Sweden if either of them should attack. In return, Poland would obtain a slice of Moldavia and Bessarabia, with the Black Sea port of Ackerman, and permission to prolong the sessions of the Seym, with elections to the Permanent Council at the end of every session, to reform the finances and the judiciary, and to set up a regular police force.[54] The new project was sent off to St Petersburg on 7 October 1787, and ten days later Stanisław received an approving letter from Catherine herself which caused him 'infinite joy'. 'The more I re-read it, the more every phrase and every expression flatters and satisfies me,' he wrote to Deboli.[55] But disappointment followed the elation. The Russian chancellery began to weigh the terms and conditions of the alliance, apparently without a care for the urgency of the situation.

The death of Frederick the Great in 1786 had done nothing to alter Stanisław's conviction that Prussia was the most dangerous of Poland's neighbours. His successor Frederick William II lacked intelligence and courage, but the Prussian ministry, dominated by Hertzberg, was still in place. The outbreak of war between Russia and Turkey in September 1787 opened up a number of possible courses for Prussia to take. One was to offer to mediate in the Russo–Turkish conflict, and to gain some Polish territory in reward.[56] Another was to forge an alliance with Poland, Sweden, England and Turkey in order to lever Austria out of various areas. Undecided as to which course to take, Prussia prepared the ground by agitating in Gdańsk and clouding the waters in

Poland. Her new minister in Warsaw, Ludwig Büchholtz, began to make anti-Russian statements. 'Although it is not possible to be definite about their aim,' Stanisław wrote to Deboli on 19 September, 'one can safely say that if they do not serve to build up an actual party, they nevertheless have the effect of awakening restless spirits with the hope that something new is being planned.'[57] Russia's passivity had the effect of creating a political vacuum, and there was no lack of 'restless spirits' ready to fill it.

Snubbed in Kiev and convinced that Catherine would only work with the king, Ignacy Potocki and his friends naturally looked to Berlin. In their search for an ideological base, the Familia had moved on to constitutional ground and rediscovered Polish republican traditions. Just as the Barians had done, they sought to frame their bid for power in terms of the latest political philosophy. They could no longer rely on their prestige alone to gain support – they had to manipulate the newly politicised szlachta in more subtle ways. A crucial role in this was played by a remarkable Italian Abbé, Scipione Piattoli, who had been tutor to Elżbieta Lubomirska's children and continued as her secretary. Ignacy Potocki, Adam Czartoryski and others of the Familia congregated at Carlsbad, where she was taking the waters, and here they discussed new forms of government for Poland and schemes for bringing them about. What emerged was a plan to form a new party, a Patriotic Congress, that would win a majority in the Seym, confederate, abolish the monarchy and establish a Quattuorvirate (Czartoryski, Potocki, Karol Radziwiłł and Seweryn Rzewuski) which would rule the country. By the summer of 1787 Prussian backing for this scheme had been secured in secret talks. They began agitating throughout the country, spreading rumours that Stanisław was planning a coup to seize absolute power, and declaring that Poland ought to seek the friendship of Prussia rather than Russia.

Feliks Potocki and Branicki were hatching plans of their own with the help of Potyomkin and some unlikely bedfellows, including the arch-conservative Antoni Czetwertyński, the young radical Józef Zajączek and the former Barian Antoni Pułaski. The Prince de Ligne, who was working in the Emperor's interest, was also involved.[58] Stanisław sent Littlepage, just back from Paris, to Potyomkin's headquarters at Ochakov so as to have a spy on the spot. Potyomkin's Polish clients wanted to declare a confederation to support Russian interests, but their real aim was to take over the leadership of the country from the Permanent Council. Potyomkin, who nurtured increasingly ambitious plans for a kingdom of his own, intended the confederation as a power-base for himself. But he failed to obtain Catherine's assent. Radom had taught her to distrust confederations.

At the same time, she failed to come out firmly in support of Stanisław, because she was suspicious of his terms. 'This whole Polish project is but a trick by the king to snatch some increase in his own power,' ran a Russian memorandum on the subject.[59] She had a treaty with Austria, which was about to declare war on Turkey, so she could do without Polish troops. Catherine only wanted the Polish alliance in order to parry Prussia's influence and keep Poland quiet. 'Our main interest and the whole point of this alliance consists in distracting a large part of the gentry,' she explained to Stackelberg.[60] She was unwilling to make any move in Poland that she might have cause to regret. Ideally, she would have liked to leave everything as it was.

But Poland was in a state of frantic agitation. This was intensified by the publication that year of a book by Stanisław Staszic – an ex-priest and an illegitimate son of Andrzej Zamoyski – who revealed himself to be the most profound Polish political thinker of the century. The book, entitled *Reflections on the Life of Jan Zamoyski*, was a broad reassessment of Poland's constitution past and present, with suggestions on how it should develop. Its principal argument was that the Seym ought to sit continuously and arrogate to itself all legislative and executive power. His thinking showed a distinct break with accepted views on constitutional monarchy and put forward forcefully the idea of a sovereign Seym representing government by the people. His book came out in the same year as the Assembly of Notables met in France, and the Constitutional Convention gathered in Philadelphia. Younger men in Poland, like their contemporaries in France, America and elsewhere, needed something fresher, more exciting than the pragmatism of the *philosophes*, and his ideas met with an enthusiastic response.

This took the form of a flurry of pamphlets, in which every tenet of Polish political life was questioned, often in tones of anger and scorn. One of the most prolific authors and publishers was Jan Potocki, a brilliant, if eccentric young man who had just returned from service on the galleys of the Knights of Malta and published his travels in the Near East, and who was the first Pole to become airborne, by ascending in a balloon designed by himself, accompanied by his Turk and his poodle. 'Every day he gives birth to new pamphlets, all composed with wit, but all of them lacking in common sense and political judgment,' complained Stanisław.[61] The young man was sincerely attached to the king, but he was a cumbersome ally. He set up a discussion-club and public reading-room in his own house, and established a 'Free Press' which undertook to publish anything that other printers turned down. He was as good as his word, and the press relentlessly churned out paeans to the king, calls to arms against Russia, demands for the liberation of the peasants, denunciations of Prussia, and anything else that came his way.

A more coherent centre of agitation had formed at Hugo Kołłątaj's house at Solec. Kołłątaj had made his name by reforming the University of Kraków, and now turned his talents to politics. He was hostile to the Permanent Council, and believed the country should be ruled by a sovereign Seym in which the city classes were represented. He believed the senate should be elected, and that the king should have no more than a symbolic role. But he was a realist, and acknowledged that Poland was in no position to embark on a radical programme of transformation. In *Letters from an Anonymous Person*, he suggested that the only way forward was for the king and the opposition to reconcile their differences and carry through a 'gentle revolution' that would not upset the neighbouring powers. 'It behoves us to end this eighteenth century with humility, without a shadow of audacity,' he wrote.[62] But Jan Potocki was more in tune with the feeling of the times. 'Your nation, Sire, raises its eyes to you and fears that you bend too far beneath the weight of circumstances,' he harangued Stanisław. 'Your nation looks to you and hesitates, seeing how you bear captivity with too great a patience, how little confidence you have in it, and how you ignore its wishes.'[63]

As the year 1788 drew on, the voices of the hotheads drowned out the counsels of caution, and even Kołłątaj was pushed into more radical utterings. His house drew a number of clever young writers, most notably Franciszek Jezierski, a priest and inspector of schools, and Franciszek Dmochowski, an ex-Jesuit, the playwright Franciszek Zabłocki and Jan Śniadecki. This house, from which issued a continuous stream of political literature, was dubbed the 'Forge', and

Jezierski its Vulcan. Although they were well inclined towards the king, the issues they raised challenged the whole basis of Stanisław's system – at a moment when Russia, the cornerstone of that system, appeared to be withdrawing her support.

Stanisław could see disaster looming, as a situation began to develop that was curiously similar to that of 1768, with France's role as fomenter now taken by Prussia. He was haunted by the 'dreadful scenes' of nearly twenty years before.[64] The magnates of the opposition were full of bluster. Kazimierz Sapieha, admittedly while drunk, had declared at a dinner: 'If I could conceive of doubting my own mother as to whether I was a true Sapieha, I would dismiss that doubt, because I feel inside me a true Sapieha nature – an eagerness to oppose the king in everything.'[65] Stanisław was very agitated, and in April 1788 felt ill, suffering from spasms and fever. 'He needs rest, but cannot find it,' Dr Barnewall reported to Glayre, who had just replaced Littlepage as Stanisław's private agent in Paris. 'When I called on him this morning at six, I found he had been writing since five.'[66] Stanisław urged Deboli to press the Russian court for a definite answer to his offer of alliance, but Ostermann continued to procrastinate.[67] Stackelberg was ill and had lost his nerve. 'My situation is really critical,' Stanisław wrote to Glayre in May. 'Russia constantly tells me that she will soon do all that is necessary, but that soon has been going on for a long time.'[68]

When the final Russian proposals for the alliance did reach Warsaw, in June 1788, they were little short of an insult to Stanisław. They also pulled the rug from under his feet politically. The terms were that Poland should provide 12,000 cavalry in three brigades, which would be incorporated separately into the Russian army and fight under Russian command. There were to be no constitutional concessions and no territorial prizes of any sort in return. Catherine agreed that the 1788 Seym should be confederated, that extensive taxes could be voted, and that the army should be raised to over 40,000. Stanisław hoped that a few additional reforms might be pushed through unnoticed. But he stood little chance of selling such an alliance to his people. In July 1788, Sweden attacked Russia, and the Triple Alliance of Prussia, England and the Netherlands set to work to wean Denmark away from her Russian alliance. In such a climate, Prussian overtures in Poland looked a thousand times more alluring than the insulting Russian proposal.

In July Frederick William publicly protested against the proposed Russo-Polish alliance, stating that he could see no motive for it other than enmity towards himself. If it were only a question of Poland's security, then he was quite prepared to extend his protection to Poland as well. This produced a fever of excitement throughout the country, and hampered Stanisław in his efforts to get his men elected at the seymiks that summer. There were many more candidates than usual, as everyone wanted to take part in the forthcoming Seym, and there was a groundswell of resentment against the Permanent Council, the administration and the Russian guarantee. Matters were not helped by Russian units marching through south-eastern Poland on their way to the Turkish front. The result was that the opposition won about 40 per cent of the seats to the Seym which was to meet in October. Stanisław tried to reach an agreement at the last minute. He sent his brother Michał to Aleksandra Ogińska's Siedlce to talk to members of the Familia, and Czartoryski, who was now, under pressure from Austria, the least determined in opposing the king, came to confer with the Primate at Jabłonna. But Czartoryski and his friends were no longer in control of the movement they had started.

Stanisław worked desperately to reclaim public opinion for his Russian alliance. His friend the poet Stanisław Trembecki conjured up a vision of affinity with Russia, a sort of pan-Slavism *avant la lettre*. Stanisław himself had commissioned an equestrian statue of Jan III, to be unveiled on 14 September in commemoration of the king's victory against the Turks at Vienna in 1683. He organised an expensive and elaborate historical pageant on crusading themes, with jousts, parades and fireworks. But the event misfired, merely provoking unfavourable squibs and satires. Nobody wanted to hear of the Russian alliance any more, and the whole country was, in the words of the Papal Nuncio, in a state of '*orgasmo*'.[69]

In September Michał Ogiński and Karol Radziwiłł announced that they intended to confederate Lithuania against the king and the Russian alliance, and seek the support of Prussia. Catherine was furious. Stanisław was in despair. He had to face the approaching Seym without a policy, completely let down by his Russian ally, just as he had been in 1767. And he would have to face a chamber whose mood, reflecting that of the country, was turning violently against him and against Russia. He could see through Prussia's game clearly, but he had no weapons with which to combat it, and no influence with which to persuade his subjects of the dangers it held.

The Seym duly met on 7 October 1788 and confederated itself, under the marshalcy of Stanisław Małachowski and Kazimierz Sapieha. At the first possible opportunity, the fourth session on 13 October, the Prussian envoy Büchholtz read out a long note on behalf of his master, questioning the need for a Russian alliance, and suggesting that if Poland did need one, she could find no better ally than Prussia. If Russia persisted in her schemes, it went on, then Frederick William would invite 'the true patriots and good citizens of Poland to join him in wise and mutual action to deflect the calamities that threaten their motherland'. It assured Stanisław's enemies that: 'They can firmly count on [Frederick William] to provide them with all necessary support and the most effective assistance in order to uphold the independence, freedom and security of Poland.'[70]

19

The Great Seym

The Prussian note read out in the Seym on 13 October 1788 took the lid off the boiling pot. For the first time since anyone could remember, Poland was being addressed as a sovereign nation and offered support. Without further reflection, most of the deputies seized on this mirage of independence. Decades of patiently borne humiliation and suppressed resentment erupted into violent demonstrations of anti-Russian feeling in the general euphoria. And if Poland was to be free, she needed a proper army. At the very next session of the Seym, on 16 October, the deputy Jan Suchorzewski called for an army of 100,000 men, and his motion was deliriously acclaimed. Stanisław parried by suggesting an increase in taxation, which would determine the strength of the army Poland could realistically support, which he, and everyone else, knew to be no more than 40–50,000 men.[1] But nobody wanted to listen to such talk. 'We must decide on an army of a hundred thousand first, and ways will be found to maintain this number,' shouted one deputy, opening the debate on 20 October.[2] The heady breath of freedom was in the air. The ladies who thronged the spectators' gallery cheered the Patriots and booed those who attempted to reason against them. Anyone who wished to maintain a following was swept along. Magnates vied with each other to pledge vast offerings. Stanisław pointed out that such generosity could not begin to solve the problem, but he was ignored. The Seym decided on an army of 100,000 men, with only one vote cast against.[3] Stanisław made a gracious speech praising the patriotism of the chamber and inviting it to apply itself to the matter of taxation with all speed. The deputies gathered round to kiss his hand, and the session ended on an elevated note.

Stanisław was appalled. The vote on the army was meaningless, since the requisite funds would never be raised. It was a slap in the face to Russia, since it violated conditions set down in the treaty of partition and the Russian guarantee. It also started a damaging conflict within the Seym. The new army had hardly been voted when it dawned on people that it might constitute a formidable weapon in the king's hands. The first to spot the danger was Frederick William, who instructed Büchholtz to do everything in his power to prevent Stanisław gaining control of it.[4] On 27 October the Patriots demanded the abolition of the Military Department of the Permanent Council and the creation of a Military Commission controlled by the Seym. Stanisław's brother the Primate, who led the royal party, argued strongly against this, but could hardly make himself heard. The hetmans Branicki and Rzewuski saw an opportunity to gain control of the army for themselves. The question was fiercely contested over several sessions, and came to a head on 3 November, when Stanisław himself took the floor. The session went on for sixteen hours, and it was 4 a.m. by the time it came to the vote. Stanisław's skilful rearguard tactics appeared to pay off, and the motion was defeated in a show of hands by 149 votes to 114. But the Patriots knew that many of Stanisław's supporters were wavering, and they demanded a secret ballot. When this was taken, thirty-six of the king's supporters changed sides, and the motion was carried.[5]

The opposition was jubilant. There were demands that Russia should evacuate her military facilities in Poland, and that the Seym prolong its session indefinitely and take over the governance of the country. This was a direct challenge to the whole Russian system as it had evolved over the past seventy years, and it overflowed Stackelberg's cup. On 5 November he went to the king and demanded that he and all those still loyal to him boycott the wayward Seym. This would permit Russia to make strong representations on his behalf. Stanisław refused. Although he realised that the Seym's action was also a revolution against his own rule, he was determined not to let himself be forced into confrontation with his people.

On 6 November, Stackelberg read a note to the Seym warning that

'Her Majesty the Empress, giving up with regret the friendship which she had vowed to His Majesty the King and the Most Serene Commonwealth, cannot regard otherwise than as a violation of the treaty the least amendment of the constitution of 1775.'[6] This cracking of the Russian whip incensed the house, which wanted to declare war on Russia there and then. 'I felt this to be one of those moments when one has to go into the breach oneself,' Stanisław wrote to Glayre, and he spoke at length in favour of caution.[7] 'He who does not honour treaties gives to him with whom he made them a right to revenge without limits,' he warned. He went on to remind the deputies that the alliance which Russia had proposed allowed Poland to raise her army to 52,000 men, which was as much as the country could realistically afford. 'Therefore we should not irritate [Russia] or show her ill-will, but strive to maintain the greatest possible friendship with her.' He warned against acting in the heat of the moment and used every device at his disposal to deflect the aggressiveness of the house from the person of Catherine and her ambassador.[8] 'The next few years revealed the justice of the king's warnings,' Niemcewicz, a Patriot ringleader, later wrote, but at the time 'the king's voice seemed no more than the timorous expression of the bad habit of subservience.'[9] His speech had little effect, so he took the first opportunity to adjourn the session.

Stanisław was working behind the scenes to patch up the crumbling edifice of Russian hegemony and limit the damage. He managed to get the marshal of the Seym Stanisław Małachowski and Ignacy Potocki to join him in talks with Stackelberg aimed at reaching a compromise. But a new Prussian minister arrived in Warsaw, and raised the political temperature by several degrees. Girolamo Lucchesini was a small, thin, swarthy man with a single large black eye – the other had been lost in a chemistry experiment. 'He doesn't fight, he skirmishes,' Hertzberg wrote: 'he is a cossack of diplomacy.'[10] He was also a man of immense charm and great deviousness, and he managed to appear deeply concerned for the fate of Poland. Trembecki wrote a poem comparing Lucchesini to an organist, who only needed to push the right stops in order to get exactly the sounds he wanted from the Seym. Stanisław's two-thirds majority in the chamber evaporated, and he could only prevent his supporters from switching their allegiance by indulging their enthusiasm. On 10 November he made a speech associating himself with the Seym and its wishes. 'The king with the nation, the nation with the king, is a maxim which I have never in the course of my life been able to abandon,' he stated, coining a phrase which immediately caught on.[11] He agreed to prolong the Seym to 15 December, as they wished. He was the hero of the day. Shopkeepers began selling ribbons with his slogan embroidered on them. But Stanisław was in no mood to enjoy such manifestations. 'The health of our dear king is getting worse every day,' Anna Lubomirska wrote to Glayre. 'His depression and sadness are extreme.'[12]

Stanisław had lost control of the situation, and the Patriots, led by Ignacy Potocki, demanded the abolition of the Military Office, and, with it, of Stanisław's right to nominate officers. 'I place concord and unity with my people above all else,' he declared as he gave up this prerogative.[13] But he was wounded by the attack on his rights and also by the shabby treatment meted out to his trusted Komarzewski, who was accused of incompetence and summarily cashiered. 'The oppositionists will destroy the whole system of government beyond repair,' he complained to Deboli on 6 December.[14] Three days later the Seym abolished the Department for Foreign Affairs, replacing it with a Seym Deputation. This promptly named a series of ambassadors, an action that was at best useless and possibly harmful in Stanisław's eyes – Piotr Potocki's embassy to Turkey and that of Ignacy Potocki's brother Jerzy to Sweden, both at war with Russia, could only irritate.[15]

In its reply to the Russian note of 6 November 1788, the Seym pointed out that: 'Like any legislative authority invested with full legislative powers [it] cannot be deemed, when establishing new laws, reestablishing or amending old ones, to be violating its internal Constitution.' Catherine could hardly have enjoyed being lectured on the niceties of constitutional law, and the note's declaration that 'the Commonwealth does not wish to see the day when it loses the friendship of such a great monarch', would have done little to sweeten her temper.[16] A few days later, on 20 November, Büchholtz read out another note on behalf of Frederick William, in which the Prussian king declared that the Seym had every right to make those changes to the constitution it saw fit, and professed his willingness to protect, with arms if necessary, the independence of Poland. As a parting shot, it demanded that Russian units be evacuated forthwith from the Polish Ukraine, which they were using as a base for operations against Turkey.

Stackelberg urged Stanisław to gather his supporters and fall back on the Ukraine, where he could rally his party under the protection of Russian troops. But Stanisław was determined to stay put. He realised that the Patriots were being manipulated by Prussia, which was hoping to bring about a confrontation in Poland, from which only she would stand to benefit: she could then offer to drop her own party in Poland, in return for which a grateful Russia would permit her to annexe Polish territory. Stanisław therefore sacrificed his Russian loyalties in the interests of Polish unity. Without a party to protect in Poland, Russia could do nothing, so she meekly withdrew her troops from Polish territory and stood off. Prussia made one last effort to prise the king and the Seym apart, and to provoke Russia into action. She encouraged the Patriots to go the whole way and abolish the Permanent Council, and with it, the Russian guarantee of 1775. They needed little prompting. The Permanent Council was hated by the Patriots because it stood for the post-1772 system, and by the magnates because they saw it as the king's tool.

The matter came up in the Seym on 19 January 1789. The Primate led the royalists in a last attempt to save the Permanent Council, warning that its abolition would lead to Russian vengeance and a new partition of the country. Few were prepared to listen to reason, and the Council was abolished, by 120 votes to 11, with 62 abstentions.[17] Karol Radziwiłł ordered Stackelberg's chair to be thrown out of the spectators' gallery, and the chamber was filled with the sound of a tolling bell from the nearby Bernardine Church; one of the Patriots had rushed out to announce in this way the burial of the Russian guarantee. The bell could equally well have been tolling for Poland.

The ease with which the Russian protectorate had been seemingly shrugged off could not fail to have a galvanic effect. The atmosphere in Warsaw became that of a city at war. The Seym prolonged its session indefinitely, assumed direct rule of the country, and applied itself to its defence.

A general tax of 10 per cent on the revenue of private estates was passed, the first time the szlachta had ever been directly taxed in the history of the Commonwealth. The peasants were spared extra taxation only thanks to Stanisław's intervention. But the clergy were taxed, and lands lying within Poland but belonging to religious houses and bishoprics which had been left outside it by the partition were auctioned off by the Military Commission. On 12 March the Primate proposed a second tax on clergy lands, in order to deflect the rapacious gaze of the Seym from the funds of the Commission for National Education. The entire estate of the Bishop of Kraków was taken over to support the army, and it was decided that as bishops died, the estates of their dioceses would be similarly taken over, and the new incumbents pensioned directly by the state. In March 1789, Stanisław donated the income from the Crown estates of Grodno and Brześć to the military chest. In February 1790, he gave most of his jewellery. Others followed suit. Karol Radziwiłł offered to raise and equip a legion of 6,000 men, and Feliks Potocki one of 10,000. These ostensibly public-spirited gestures hid other designs. Radziwiłł stipulated the condition that he would command the legion, and, since he still had the uniforms and equipment of his erstwhile household army of 6,000 men, he was in effect proposing to recreate it on the state's payroll. Other offerings were more disinterested, and almost a million złoty was donated by peasants over a period of three years.[18] But none of this could suffice. The problem was, as Stanisław had pointed out, that the country could not support an army of more than about 50,000 men. His nephew Stanisław, now Treasurer of Lithuania, tried to square the circle with a project whereby a reserve of 40,000 men could in time of war supplement a standing army of 60,000, half of whom were to be on part-time duty, spending the agriculturally important months working their land. In January 1789 the Seym gave in to reason and decided that the army would only be raised to a strength of 60,000. By August 1789 it stood at more than 45,000, which shows that what could be done was done quickly.[19]

Nevertheless, a great deal of Seym time passed in exhilarating verbiage and sheer silliness. 'The love of freedom, suspicion of the king, the lack of procedural rules, and often the desire to shine with eloquence, were the cause of prolonged and harmful delays,' Niemcewicz later admitted.[20] In the early summer of 1789, for instance, someone in the chamber called for the arrest and trial of Adam Poniński. Many opposed this, and Stanisław protested that it would be a waste of time. But this only aroused the ire of the Patriots, who suggested that they were trying to shield Poniński because they had similar sins to his to hide. There was something in that, and the protesters fell silent.

Poniński was duly arrested on 8 June 1789, on charges of political

92 Ignacy Potocki, by Tokarski

93 Adam Czartoryski, by Józef Peszka, *c.* 1780

94 The Czartoryski house at Puławy, by Norblin

95 *Top left* Ksawery Branicki with his sons, after Lampi

96 *Above* Michał Ogiński, after Angelica Kauffman

97 *Left* Feliks Potocki, by Giovanni Battista Lampi the elder, *c.* 1791

98 Karol 'My Dear' Radziwiłł, by Tomasz Aleksandrowicz

99 A Polish edition of Rousseau's *Considérations sur le gouvernement de Pologne*

100 *The Revolution of North America throwing off the Yoke of Great Britain*, one of many accounts of the American struggle for independence published in Poland at the time

101 Hugo Kołłataj, one of the greatest propagandists for radical reform, by Józef Peszka

102 The National Theatre in Warsaw, depicted here in a watercolour by Zygmunt Vogel, was a prime forum for propagating political and social reform

103 Medal struck to commemorate Jan III Sobieski's victory over the Turks at Vienna in 1683, one of a number of moves by Stanisław in 1787–8 to sway public opinion towards an anti-Turkish alliance with Russia

104 Franciszek Bukaty, Polish minister in London, through whom Stanisław attempted to gain British support, by Peter Francis Bourgeois, 1792

105 Letter from Augustyn Deboli, Polish minister in St Petersburg, to Stanisław, dated 24 August 1787, in which he tells of his efforts to press home a favourable alliance with Russia. The opening passage covers innocuous information and court gossip, while the main business is communicated in code, which was standard for all diplomatic correspondence at the time.

106 & 107 Stanisław Małachowski and Kazimierz
Nestor Sapieha, the two marshals of the Great Seym,
holding their staffs of office, by Józef Peszka

108 Medal struck by Stanisław to commemorate the
vote increasing the army to 100,000 in an attempt to
align himself with the Seym's policy

109 The castle of Ujazdów, given to the army by
Stanisław as barracks for the horse artillery in the same
spirit, from a watercolour by Vogel

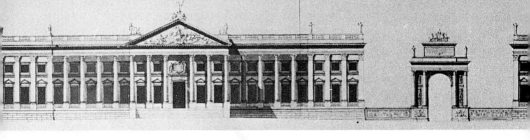

110   Merlini's last project for rebuilding the Castle, 1788, demonstrating the ever more stoical and self-effacing image of monarchy Stanisław was trying to project

111   The king's brother Michał, Primate of Poland, whose conservatism was inconvenient, was allowed to take leave of absence

112   Stanisław reviewing the troops, by Józef Peszka

113 The voting of the constitution, 3 May 1791, by Norblin. The absurd deputy Jan Suchorzewski can be seen still lying on the floor.

114 Allegory of the Constitution of 3 May, by Daniel Chodowiecki, showing Stanisław protecting tradesmen and peasants as well as the arts and justice

115 Stanisław at the time of the constitution, by Józef Pitschman

116 Project for a monument to Stanisław and the great men of Polish history, by Marcin Knackfus, 1791

irregularity, embezzlement and taking money from foreign courts. A few weeks later he managed to escape, to the quiet relief of many, but he was apprehended near the Prussian frontier and brought back. The trial, which started on 24 August, dragged on interminably, partly because of the judges' fear of letting it gather any political momentum, and Poniński was not sentenced until 1 September 1790. He was declared a criminal of state and an enemy of the Polish nation, stripped of his title, his noble status, his citizenship, and even his surname, and given four weeks to leave the Commonwealth. It was typical of the whole state of affairs that the banquet he gave on the day after being sentenced was attended by half of Warsaw, including the judges who had just sentenced him. He then left the country, travelling to Italy and thence to London, where he paraded under the name of 'Monsieur Toutcourt' (Mr Nothing).

The desire to show off patriotism produced some ridiculous effects, many of them suggested by the great ladies of Warsaw, who vied with each other for the role of Egeria. Deputies who made anti-Russian speeches were invited to dinner by the Czartoryskis and greeted with garlands by young ladies.[21] The day after the vote increasing the army, the Princesse de Nassau addressed herself to the problem of funding it by announcing that she would frame new sumptuary laws, and designed a frugal graeco-roman shift, whose only practical result was to keep the eyes of the deputies riveted to the barely clad ladies in the spectators' gallery.[22] Izabela Czartoryska riposted with a more traditional support for the old Sarmatian costume. At the end of November, she held a ceremony in her salon, during which she personally cut Kazimierz Sapieha's hair to suit the clothes, and on the following day he appeared in the Seym in Polish dress. 'It is hideous, and I think its extreme ugliness will cool some of the patriotic zeal on this point,' Anna Lubomirska reported to Glayre.[23] But she was mistaken. A few days later, Branicki also swaggered into the chamber looking like a seventeenth-century magnate in his Sarmatian fig.

Anti-Russian gestures were the height of fashion. The Masonic lodge *Catherine à l'Étoile du Nord* changed its name to *Stanisław Augustus under the Eastern Star*. But Stanisław's popularity was sinking, and while his own person was spared, his supporters were ridiculed and vilified, in pamphlets and in person. Since they were habitually given lunch at the Castle during Seym sessions, they were labelled 'roast-eaters', and openly insulted in the street. The royalists gave as good as they got. In November they amused the Warsaw public hugely by launching a multitude of hot-air balloons with 'Patriot' written on them, and the whole city watched them being blown hither and thither for a few hours until they drifted away in different directions.

This could not conceal the fact that Stanisław's own party was in disarray. Many of his younger supporters were drawn towards the Patriots, while the conservative royalists who formed the bedrock of his party took a reactionary view. He was torn himself. He was fundamentally opposed to the Seym's policy, and horrified at the impolitic way it was carried out. 'The empress is good and equitable, it is true, but she is also extremely proud,' and it would be she who decided the fate of Poland, he pointed out to his new agent in Paris, the American revolutionary Philip Mazzei.[24] But his heart went out to the young hotheads, who were in a sense his pupils, the products of his reign. Everything they did or said had its antecedent in Polish political culture, and they were influenced by that as much as by any of Rousseau's writings. Stanisław shared that political culture, and their behaviour therefore plucked a chord deep inside him. And he could not for a moment forget the anguish and the dire consequences that had attended his being alienated from his nation in 1768. 'My first duties are to my country, and therefore I cannot separate myself from my nation in anything that can lead it to real independence,' he affirmed to Mazzei. 'But the more praiseworthy this aim, the more unpleasant it is for me to see how through precocious exaltation they are alarming those very forces which are the most interested in preventing us from becoming a real Power.' He felt intense frustration at his powerlessness. 'Today I am no longer master of the ship,' he complained. 'I am carried away by the current, and God knows when I shall be able to get hold of the wheel again.'[25]

It was by no means clear which way the current would sweep the ship of state, for the Seym had developed a life of its own, as every deputy woke up and assumed an independent political line. The Russian party had vanished overnight. Stackelberg found that even his most devoted sycophants were afraid to be seen talking to him. But the Patriots also began to fall out among themselves. One of the first to go was Seweryn Rzewuski. He was disgusted that the hetmans had not been put back in charge of the army, and he had no time for the sort of democracy now reigning in the Seym. He went to Silesia to try and persuade the Prussians to invade, and later transferred to Paris, to soothe his anti-monarchist bile by watching the demolition of the Bastille.

Feliks Potocki was next. He had come to Warsaw with his head full of republican plans, expecting to be elected Marshal of the Seym. But the Patriots had already chosen Stanisław Małachowski and Kazimierz Sapieha. He was a firm believer in the Russian guarantee, and he made common cause with Stanisław in its defence. But the king's lack of determination disappointed him, while his own following among the szlachta dwindled rapidly. Potocki's pride was wounded, and he left Warsaw. He threatened to sell up his lands and seek in the United States of America the freedom which he felt was being trampled in Poland, but in the end he settled for Vienna.

His friend Ksawery Branicki also entered the fray with views rather different from those of his Patriot associates. Like Rzewuski, he was annoyed that the army was not returned to the hetmans, and fell back into the role of general malcontent. Stanisław kept a wary eye on him, knowing him to be involved in what he called 'Potyomkin's feudal projects'. Branicki had half a dozen supporters in the Seym, and also exerted a strong influence over his nephew Kazimierz Sapieha. The latter emerged as one of the leaders of the Patriotic party in the first weeks of the Seym, but he was prey to conflicting impulses, and, like his uncle, drank too much.[26] His liberal instincts were often outweighed by personal or family ambitions, and his caste atavisms were out of tune with the course events were taking. By the end of the year he was drifting closer to the king. The Patriotic party had altered accordingly. Adam Czartoryski was increasingly upstaged by the two Potocki brothers, Ignacy and Stanisław. They were joined by Stanisław Małachowski, the Marshal of the Seym, Hugo Kołłątaj, and a string of younger deputies such as Julian Niemcewicz.

These shifts were taking place against a background of momentous events abroad. In April 1789 George Washington became President of the United States of America, which set the seal on a process that had been followed with interest and much sympathy in Poland. In France, the Estates-General met in May 1789, the Bastille was stormed and fell on 14 July, and on 26 August the National Assembly voted the

Declaration of the Rights of Man. Most of Polish society naturally associated itself with any cause of liberation, and even the grandest magnates had to be seen to take their snuff from boxes inscribed with the Declaration of the Rights of Man or a portrait of Washington.

Stanisław himself followed developments in America and France closely. Back in 1765 the future American general Charles Lee wrote from Warsaw to a friend praising Stanisław's person. 'But it is still more curious to hear his opinions, which are singular for a crowned head; in short, he is as warm an advocate for the natural rights of mankind as was Algernon Sidney himself.'[27] As early as 1768 Stanisław had told Lee that England would be obliged to either harshly repress or completely relinquish her American colonies.[28] Throughout the 1770s he bombarded people like John Lind with requests for English parliamentary papers dealing with America, literature on the legal rights of the colonists, and details of events taking place there, and he welcomed Americans into his service.[29] To one of these, Mazzei, he wrote at the beginning of 1790 that 'I am more and more persuaded that Washington, and those in his country who think like him, will become the best political tutors of humankind.'[30]

Stanisław's attitude to events in France was scarcely less favourable. He was kept abreast of developments there through his cordial contacts with Lafayette, Condorcet, Sieyès and others, and above all by the frequent and detailed reports of Philip Mazzei. He welcomed the Revolution, believing that it would turn France into a stronger and beneficent influence in Europe, favourable to Poland.[31] He asserted that the behaviour of the National Assembly on 4 August 1789 was 'the best proof that this eighteenth century truly deserves to be called the century of philosophy'.[32] He sent Bertrand Barrère the *Merentibus* medal and commissioned Jacques-Louis David to paint a series of portraits of the personalities of the revolution. He was full of admiration for the conduct of Louis XVI, and opined that 'under many respects my position and that of the king of France are very similar'.[33]

But their characters were very different. Not for a moment did Stanisław reconcile himself to a passive role. In spite of having been winkled out of these areas, he began advising the Commission for Foreign Affairs and badgered the Military Commission on the subject of training and developing technical services such as the artillery. He suggested the recruitment of senior officers from abroad, but the Seym was unwilling to give commissions to anyone who did not have Polish origins or connections. In July 1789 he persuaded the Commission to approach General Friedrich Kalckreuth, who satisfied the former requirements, but Frederick William refused to let him leave the Prussian service, and suggested Prince Ludwig of Württemberg, Czartoryski's son-in-law, who was duly transferred to the Polish army with the rank of major-general.

Stanisław naturally thought of his nephew Józef Poniatowski, then serving in the Austrian army. 'God willed you to be born a Pole, and I have a claim to have replaced your father,' he wrote to him in June 1789. 'By virtue of both of these, I summon you to return to us, as quickly as possible.'[34] Józef complied, and persuaded his brother-in-arms Michał Wielhorski the younger to do likewise. On 3 October 1789 Józef was commissioned, along with Tadeusz Kościuszko, as major-general. Józef's presence was a source of great happiness to Stanisław and indeed to the whole of Warsaw society: the twenty-six-year-old was handsome, charming and well-endowed with social graces; he wore his uniforms tight and his hair curled, and wrought havoc with the young ladies. His position in the army guaranteed his uncle some influence over it. Stanisław also managed to get a proportion of the senior posts in new units reserved for Guards officers, graduates of the Cadet Corps and for those who had served him as pages, all of whose loyalty he could count on.

Reasserting influence in the Seym was more difficult. 'Twenty-five years ago, at the Convocation and Coronation Seyms, there was a great deal less enlightenment and reading among our compatriots than there is today: and for that very reason the majority had more faith in those who had some education, and allowed itself to be led,' he confided to Glayre. 'Since that time, people have read much here, but without guidance or method, and they have acquired an easy and sometimes brilliant eloquence that was very rare in the old days ... This has created in the young men who abound at this Seym the conviction that they can and must follow only their own opinions.'[35]

Apart from anything else, the sessions were exhausting by their length. As the king could not leave the chamber without closing the sessions, he had a small room built in the hall itself near his throne. He could retire to this and relieve himself, eat something or just lie down for a few minutes while votes were being counted or some windbag drivelled on. He was overworked, and beginning to feel his age. 'The length of the daily sessions deprives me of the exercise I need, and the harassment I am continually subjected to is undermining my physical strength in spite of all my philosophy,' he wrote to Mazzei.[36] To his nephew Józef, his 'dear Pepi', he confessed that he was 'overworked and very sad'.[37]

But his spirits began to rise in the summer of 1789. For one thing, Russia's passivity began to look like resignation. 'At the end of a year, I saw that the Master of Fate was giving a different course to circumstances and to the heart of a monarch whom I thought I knew better than any other,' he wrote to Glayre.[38] It is symptomatic that Stanisław commissioned Kubicki to draw up plans for a Temple of Providence. His new situation inspired a fresh view of his role, and the three musical dramas he commissioned from Paisiello that summer, unfortunately lost, would presumably have illustrated this.

As usual, it was through architecture that he expressed himself most clearly, and while the projected mausoleum for himself and his parents reaffirmed the concept of Providential origins, the two new projects for rebuilding the Castle produced by Merlini over the next two years reveal by their austere classicism a new, civic vision of monarchy. 'I still foresee some very difficult days, which will be very bitter for me,' Stanisław wrote to Mazzei in September, 'but there is a voice at the bottom of my heart which tells me that all this will after all end less badly than might now appear. *Patience and Courage* has been my motto for thirty years, and I shall hold to it.'[39]

In September 1789 Stanisław reshuffled his party and changed his tactics. His brother Michał had adopted a fatalistic view of things, and could not provide the style of leadership required by the circumstances, so Stanisław allowed him to go on the long holiday he craved, to Vienna, then Rome, Naples, and London. He also let Mniszech take a back seat. A poor speaker, with 'the voice of an old woman', he made an unfortunate impression in the parliamentary bouts with the Patriots, and he was more of a liability than an asset. The same was true of Jacek Małachowski. Stanisław replaced them with popular figures such as Joachim Chreptowicz and Pius Kiciński, and concentrated on winning over some of the Patriots. Stanisław Małachowski and Stanisław Potocki were well-disposed, and Adam Czartoryski was beginning to grow friendly. But they were dominated by Ignacy Potocki, who disliked Stanisław and referred to him in letters to friends as 'the old gossip'.[40] Stanisław courted him and gave him the ministerial post of Court Marshal of Lithuania. He also made overtures to Kołłątaj and Scipione Piattoli, who had just returned from revolutionary Paris. 'I like him,' Stanisław wrote to Mazzei. 'I think that we shall manage to make common cause.' Piattoli was growing disillusioned with the Patriots, and responded with eagerness to Stanisław's offer of the post of royal secretary. 'The more I know Piattoli, the more pleased I am with this acquisition,' Stanisław wrote only a month later.[41] Both Piattoli and Kołłątaj were to prove invaluable allies in the struggle that was about to begin.

Having abolished the Permanent Council and the king's system of patronage, the Seym had to create new administrative organs. It set up seventy-two Civil and Military Order Commissions, elected by the local szlachta and towns, through which to run the country. On 7 September 1789, the Seym nominated a deputation to revise the constitution altogether. This was presided over by the old Bishop Adam Krasiński, and included Stanisław Małachowski, Michał Kleofas Ogiński, Joachim Chreptowicz, Fryderyk Moszyński, Ksawery Działyński, Tomasz Wawrzecki, Józef Weyssenhoff and several others, but its moving spirit was Ignacy Potocki. Stanisław was vitally interested in the question, and he feared Potocki's personal ambition as well as his republican bent.

On 24 September, Małachowski and Stanisław Potocki came to the Castle and proposed collaborating on the constitution. Stanisław thanked them for their trust, but he was cautious. 'Both my age and the circumstances make me shy of ambitious designs,' he replied. 'All my desires have cooled except for one; that in these remaining days of mine I should be loved by my people and be able to work for their happiness with their approval.'[42] He slyly suggested that they make the proposals, for him to advise and comment on: he wanted Ignacy Potocki to show his hand first. At the same time, he resorted to his traditional tactic of getting others, in this case Chreptowicz, to put forward his own ideas within the deputation, and of isolating his enemies.[43]

The man who would help him more than any other in this was Hugo Kołłątaj. Kołłątaj was no monarchist, but he was no supporter of the class to which Potocki belonged either. No more than

Stanisław did he want to see a constitution that turned Poland into an oligarchy of magnates. He was in close touch with the several thousand educated and articulate citizens of Warsaw, who observed with mounting scorn the antics of the slogan-toting Seym that continued to ignore their existence. 'A minority that has no franchise from the majority cannot impose laws on it or call itself the nation,' wrote one of them, the barrister Franciszek Barss.[44] They naturally looked to the king for support, and he was ready to give it. 'Since I have been in the place I occupy, I have not ceased to say that as long as there is no contented and respected third estate from the cities, and as long as there are not peasant farmers who are less subjugated, Poland will never be what she might be, both morally and physically,' Stanisław told Mazzei.[45] This was dangerous ground, since nothing could unite the szlachta, Patriots and all, as readily as talk of emancipating other classes.

On 23 November 1789 delegates from 200 towns met and formed an association. This caused alarm. Rumours circulated that: 'The king wants to make a revolt against the szlachta by the townsfolk of Warsaw on the anniversary of his coronation and to cut off *à la Parisienne* all heads unfavourable to him.'[46] Kazimierz Sapieha wanted more troops brought into Warsaw. 'I don't want to hang!' he explained.[47] Two days later, on the anniversary of Stanisław's coronation, the civic delegates came in force to the Castle to pay their respects. On 2 December, led by the President of Warsaw Jan Dekert and dressed in black in emulation of the French *Tiers État*, they marched through Warsaw and presented a manifesto (which had been written by Kołłątaj under Stanisław's supervision) first to the king, then to the Seym Marshals Małachowski and Sapieha. It pointed out that the merchant classes had a right to be involved in legislation and to be represented in the Seym. The event made a strong impression, and not only among the szlachta and the magnates. 'While avoiding any open moves, I am trying quietly to hinder the cause of the citizens,' Lucchesini reported to Frederick William on 5 December. 'You do well,' replied the Prussian king by return. 'If the Polish cities managed to regain their ancient privileges, manufacturers from my dominions would start moving into Poland.'[48]

The original aim of Prussian policy had been to prevent the Russo-Polish alliance and provoke an internal scission in Poland which would allow Prussia to intervene and possibly gain some territory in the ensuing settlement. But Stanisław had frustrated this, while Russia had retired from the scene, leaving Poland in Prussia's sphere of influence. Prussia's policy had misfired: she wanted Polish territory, not influence. But she quickly adapted to the new situation. Russia and Austria were tied down by their war with Turkey, France was brought to her knees by the outbreak of the Revolution, Joseph II was ill, so Prussia could look towards gains from Austria instead. Frederick William began to contemplate a war against her in the spring of 1790, and sought an alliance with Poland. In the event of war, Poland could benefit by recovering the part of Poland taken by Austria in the partition, renamed Galicia by its new masters.

Stanisław had always viewed with repugnance any dealings with Prussia. He suggested to Russia and Austria that they outbid Prussia by offering Poland a more favourable alliance, but, as the Austrian ambassador in St Petersburg noted, 'everything that comes from Stanisław Augustus inspires little trust here'.[49] Stanisław then tried to persuade England to admit Poland into the Triple Alliance, of which Prussia and the Netherlands were also members. Unfortunately, the new English minister in Warsaw, Daniel Hailes, was neither as sympathetic nor as intelligent as his predecessors, and Stanisław did not like him. In January 1789 Stanisław therefore instructed Bukaty in London to suggest the idea to William Pitt. The English Prime Minister was interested, but felt that Poland should be handled by Prussia. Ignacy Potocki and the Patriots brushed aside Stanisław's misgivings and eagerly embraced the Prussian proposals. Official negotiations began in December 1789.

On 10 December 1789 a letter from Frederick William was read out in the Seym. Explaining that he 'saw more advantage in a well-ordered government in Poland which would assure the political existence of the nation', he urged the Poles to carry out constitutional reform.[50] He had radically departed from traditional Prussian policy, but Stanisław remained wary. The proposed treaty was ready in draft form at the beginning of January 1790, but Stanisław managed to delay it by insisting that clauses guaranteeing Polish economic rights be inserted, as the breakdown of relations with Russia and war with Austria would effectively cut Poland off from the whole world, leaving Prussia holding her jugular in economic terms. The Prussian response was to offer Poland all the trading concessions she wanted on condition she ceded Gdańsk and Toruń to Prussia.

When Lucchesini presented the new draft to the Seym, there was such uproar that he had to feign diplomatic illness for a few days. Frederick William agreed to reconsider the terms, but was keen to go ahead with the military alliance. Stanisław had grave misgivings, and voiced them in the Seym on 15 March. But the mood of elation and the prospect of recovering Galicia were stronger than his caution, and he was outvoted. 'If you do not sign the alliance', Lucchesini warned, 'Poland will become the theatre of the war and the price of the peace.'[51] Hailes concurred, and Stanisław gave in. The treaty, which bound Poland to support Prussia militarily and Prussia to defend Poland against any invader, was duly signed on 29 March 1790.

Stanisław's fears had been well founded. 'Now that we hold these people in our hand, and that the future of Poland depends only on our combinations, this country may serve your Majesty either as a theatre of war and as an eastern screen for Silesia, or it can become in Your Majesty's hand an object of barter at the peace negotiations,' Lucchesini wrote to his master two days after the signature of the treaty.[52] Ironically, Stanisław did everything to quell his own fears, and made light of the fact that Stackelberg was recalled a few days later. 'One has to know how to choose between the hope of improvement and the certainty of a permanent nonentity; and that is our position,' he argued to Mazzei. Russia 'continues to declare that she does not wish to avenge herself for the bad will we have been showing her over the past year, and she is allowing us some time to revive and educate ourselves.' Although he conceded that 'this Russian patience may turn into anger', he pleaded that a real alliance, even with Prussia, altered Poland's position fundamentally, since she was no longer isolated. 'And perhaps that will save us. And that perhaps is better than the state of abject submission in which we have languished till now.'[53]

The ink on the treaty was hardly dry when the situation began to shift. Joseph II had died on 20 February, succeeded by the prudent and realistic Leopold II, whose first instinct was to extricate Austria from the mess she was in. The war with Turkey was becoming an expensive burden, Austria's possessions in the Low Countries were in revolt, and there were disturbances in Hungary. She was in no condition to sustain a war against Prussia and Poland. Leopold's first action was therefore to write a conciliatory letter to Frederick William.

The Prussian king hesitated. He had taken personal command of his own army, which faced 150,000 Austrians under Marshal Laudon across the Bohemian-Silesian border, but he no longer felt very certain of success. In May General Kalckreuth came to Warsaw to assess the military value of the Polish army, and reported back that although this was high, the Poles seemed unwilling to engage it fully.[54] Through Adam Czartoryski, Leopold was agitating in Poland against the war.[55] The Swedes were making no headway against Russia, while England was prepared to exhort, and even subsidise, but not to fight. On 27 June, the tension snapped, and negotiations began. On 15 July Frederick William dropped his demand that Galicia be given back to Poland, effectively excluding Polish war aims from the settlement. Leopold immediately agreed to all his other demands, and the two monarchs signed the convention of Reichenbach on 27 July 1790.

Leopold had saved the Habsburg monarchy from disintegration. Frederick William was left with little to show for two years of diplomatic and military exertion, besides a cumbersome and now useless Polish ally. But Poland had come out of the episode worst of all: she had now antagonised Austria as well as Russia, and she had earned no points for it from Prussia. The Patriots, who had engineered the Prussian treaty, were embarrassed. The débâcle of their policy played directly into Stanisław's hands. And this at a crucial moment.

The plans for a new constitution had got bogged down in a morass of discussion. The first project to be put forward, by Ksawery Działyński, was thrown out by Potocki because it envisaged an hereditary monarchy and the emancipation of non-noble classes. In December 1789 Potocki himself had produced a set of 'Principles' for drafting the new constitution. Stanisław, to whom Potocki showed it, was not impressed. The document was Rousseauist in inspiration, translating the concept of the supremacy of the people by means of a pyramid, with the seymiks exercising control over the ministers, or 'Guardians', at the apex, supposedly giving them a stronger mandate. Stanisław did not like it, not least because it said nothing about the prerogatives of the king, merely referring to him as 'head of the nation and father of the people'. But he was polite about it and supported the one or two elements, such as a permanently sitting Seym, with which he agreed.

323

The 'Principles' were read out to the Seym on 17 December 1789. 'They did not arouse much enthusiasm,' Stanisław commented in a letter to Deboli.[56] Potocki explained this away by saying that the document was 'too metaphysical' for the deputies to grasp, but Stanisław knew it was not a question of metaphysics. The project was complicated yet vague, and many deputies suspected that the 'Guardians' would turn into another Permanent Council.

As war with Austria loomed at the beginning of April 1790, Małachowski suggested the king form an Extraordinary Administration of nine people on the grounds that firm government was 'absolutely essential in the present crisis'.[57] Stanisław was not prepared to be cast in a dictatorial role, and told Małachowski that he would accept only if Potocki put the matter through the Seym himself. But the moment it was mentioned there was talk of 'a junta' taking power, and the Seym called for a proper constitution to be prepared in time for the session of 7 May 1790. On that day Potocki turned up not with a constitution but with a speech about the will of the people and various proposals on how seymiks should be conducted. There was a stormy debate, during which he was barracked and told to get on with the work instead of talking.

Potocki seemed unable to make any headway, mainly because his ideas were theoretical and his thinking dominated by fears of allowing the Crown too much power. Stanisław was well aware of what was going on in Potocki's mind and in the deputation. Potocki's principal editorial assistant was Piattoli, who had fallen under Stanisław's spell and now believed that 'the new government must lean towards Monarchy'.[58] Potocki's ideas began to change too. 'Poland is not made for freedom,' he wrote to a friend on 12 June. 'Until it reaches a certain point, the most appropriate form of government for it will be a monarchical one.'[59] His next full project, presented to the Seym on 2 August 1790, contained, among other things, provision for an hereditary monarchy. The project, consisting of 658 articles, met with a mixed reception. Stanisław did not think much of it, and most people were confused by it. On 13 August Potocki spent ten hours trying to explain it to a group of deputies at Małachowski's house, without much success. 'One has to forget about trying to imitate ancient or modern republics, and neither Lycurgus nor Franklin suit the situation,' he wrote in a state of discouragement.[60] Stanisław watched patiently as Potocki abandoned his high-flown theories. 'The reform of our government is dragging, and will probably drag on for a long time,' he wrote to his nephew Józef at the end of August 1790, but at least he now knew that he would have a say in it.[61] He had one hand back on the rudder.

20

The Constitution

*T*he international situation confronting Poland in the summer of 1790 was deceptively tranquil, as were the style and behaviour of the new ambassador Russia sent to Warsaw in September. Yakov Ivanovich Bulgakov had instructions to 'caress the Poles' and do nothing but keep Russia's friends in readiness. 'He gives exquisite dinners in a very prettily furnished apartment, on beautiful Parisian silver, with agreeable music,' Stanisław noted, and he was polite to everyone.[1] Even Kurland judged the moment opportune to throw off the Russian hegemony and reassert her links with Poland. The apparent tranquillity was the result of Russia having got herself into a tight corner. She was heavily engaged in a war on two fronts with Turkey and Sweden. Her principal ally, Austria, had just made a separate peace with Turkey under pressure from the Triple Alliance of England, Prussia and the Netherlands. The same Triple Alliance was now putting pressure on Russia.

The rise of Russia's power had for some time been viewed unfavourably in London, and William Pitt had decided that she must be curbed in order to safeguard the existence of Poland and Turkey, and to restore stability to the Continent. Accordingly, the Triple Alliance demanded that Russia make peace with Turkey on the basis of the status quo ante, as Austria had done. Catherine refused, insisting that she must have at least Ochakov and the lands up to the Dniester which she had conquered in 1788. Lord Whitworth, now English Ambassador in St Petersburg, was convinced the time had come to force her. But England could defy Russia only if she could guarantee herself a supply of ships' stores from another source. That other source could only be Poland.

Stanisław followed international developments closely, and he was not taken in by Bulgakov's behaviour. He realised that Russia would sooner or later recover herself, and then Poland's security would depend on her dubious ally Prussia. 'In politics, despondency is a kind of treason,' he repeated to himself frequently as he contemplated his country drifting aimlessly in dangerous waters under the direction of Ignacy Potocki, and in the autumn of 1790, when he recovered his influence, he set a new course.[2] He had for some time pinned his hopes on England, for economic as much as for political reasons, and his calculations were echoed in London.

Poland would be a more convenient trading partner for England than Russia, with whom she had an annual trade deficit of about 1 million pounds a year in the 1780s. Poland imported far more English goods than Russia, while many of those imported by England from Russia originated in eastern Poland anyway, and their cost was inflated by Russian transit duties. Pitt held discussions on the subject with the Polish minister in London, Franciszek Bukaty, and Michał Kleofas Ogiński, Poland's envoy to The Hague. Any trade arrangements between Britain and Poland, however, involved Prussia, and Prussia knew how to profit from a strong position. She made it clear that she would co-operate only if she got Toruń and Gdańsk from Poland. In other words, the whole of Pitt's plan to defy Russia, which was to involve Sweden, Turkey, Denmark and the Netherlands, rested on Poland ceding Gdańsk to Prussia.

Stanisław was inclined to accept the Prussian terms if England would mediate and admit Poland to the Triple Alliance: Gdańsk had been physically cut off from Poland for the past eighteen years, and could be scooped up by Prussia at any moment. But a king of Poland could not alienate provinces of the Commonwealth, and the citizens of Gdańsk feared incorporation into Prussia. To make matters worse, one of Branicki's partisans in the Seym had tabled a motion reconfirming the inalienability of any part of the Commonwealth, and in spite of energetic action by Stanisław and the Patriots the motion was carried on 6 September 1790. Stanisław was dismayed. 'Were it not for this law', he wrote to Deboli, 'we would now have a trade treaty which would be bringing in those English millions that flow regularly into Russia.'[3] More to the point, it put additional strain on the already strained Prussian alliance. One way out of the impasse, suggested by Ignacy Potocki, was to offer the Polish succession to the junior branch of the Hohenzollerns. But Frederick William was not interested in such a solution.

Stanisław knew of Pitt's determination and believed that he would put pressure on Prussia to compromise rather than see his whole plan come unstuck. 'England is beginning to take a serious interest in us,' he wrote to Mazzei at the beginning of February 1791; and this cheered him, 'for you know that I have always been English by inclination.'[4] And the political situation at home contributed to his optimism.

Stanisław's guarded behaviour over the previous two years had paid off, and public opinion had swung back towards him. 'If I were to give even a little encouragement to the fairly general feeling among most of the szlachta against the haughty tone of the Potockis, I could do them much harm, as this ill-will towards the Potockis would immediately fuse with the szlachta's numerous marks of goodwill towards my person, whose vexation during the first year of this Seym is ascribed to the Potockis and the Prussians,' Stanisław wrote to Deboli with unmistakable satisfaction.[5] People outside the Seym were growing impatient with what they saw as its time-wasting logorrhoea. Traditional fears of royal despotism were outweighed by the realisation that there was need for a strong executive, which could only exist in the hands of the king.

The greatest contribution to this change in public opinion had come from the radicals of Kołłątaj's Forge. They were as revolutionary in their views as any member of the French Assembly. 'I believe the common people ought to be termed the first estate in the nation, or, to be precise, the nation itself,' wrote Franciszek Jezierski.[6] But they were also influenced by English political thought and the American constitution, which they publicised in articles and pamphlets, and they censured the French Assembly's attacks on the institution of monarchy. Stanisław's historically supported thesis, that the Crown provided the only true protection for the third estate and the peasantry against the szlachta, had convinced many, and even the minor szlachta had come to regard Stanisław as an ally against the magnates. Thus Kołłątaj and the radicals saw the best chance for furthering the cause of the common people in building up his position.

In his *Political Considerations for Poland* the radical agitator Józef Pawlikowski stressed that the king, 'the heart in the body of the nation', was the only agency through which the magnates' power could be broken. His sentiments were echoed by Jezierski, who in his *Catechism of the Secrets of Poland's Governance* explained that 'the king, robbed of the powers pertaining to the throne, has to bear reproaches for the misfortunes brought about by the rule of the magnates'.[7] In a pamphlet published in the autumn of 1790, Kołłątaj also defended Stanisław, writing that 'the king only had to defer to Moscow in the measure to which the impudence of the magnates forced him to'.[8] In another place, Jezierski pointed out that an ideal king should have the cunning of Frederick the Great, the conscientiousness of Joseph II and the luck of Catherine, but he stressed that a king of Poland also needed another quality. 'A monarch could have all the highest qualities, but if he does not have the heart of the one who reigns over us today, who suffers sometimes for us, sometimes with us and sometimes through us, he would be as much use as the finest clock whose parts are perfectly set but which has neither hands nor bell with which to tell the time.'[9] This sentimental note was taken up by Kołłątaj. 'The whole nation can see the purity of intention of the best of kings,' he harangued the Seym, 'from the beginning of his reign he has been famed for his goodness, yet he has never tasted the fruit of gratitude.'[10] The changing attitude to Stanisław could be measured by the way the Seym voted.

Potocki's constitutional project was debated throughout August 1790, and this debate came to a head on 13 September, when it touched on the prerogatives of the Crown. The Patriots, led by the Potocki brothers with Czartoryski in support, argued for the supremacy of the Seym. But the royalists, led by Pius Kiciński, swung the sympathy of the chamber and won a resounding victory. That same day, Czartoryski persuaded Potocki to alter his project and give the king the power, of which he had been stripped in 1775, to nominate all senators, ministers and officials. 'I am delighted to have been the instrument in a decision which has reconciled the dignity of the throne with that of the Nation,' Czartoryski wrote to Stanisław that evening. 'It would have been unseemly for the question to have been resolved in any other manner. I conjure your majesty in the name of your glory and of the public good to place yourself at our head, so that with a common effort this Seym might conclude the work of framing a good constitution.'[11] At the next session Stanisław made a long speech professing reluctance to assume too much power, and his popularity surged. Potocki was beaten. 'Let the king take hold of us, let him impose the constitution on us,' he declared in response.[12] Stanisław declined, for a number of reasons.

In their discussions on constitutional matters, a growing number of Patriots advocated adopting an hereditary monarchy in the interests of stability, and began to discuss the choice of a dynasty for Poland. The prolix Jacek Jezierski suggested inviting George III to become king of Poland, a proposal based on economic considerations. Other candidates put forward were the Duke of Gloucester and the Duke of Brunswick, and the king of Sweden also showed an interest. At the beginning of August 1790, Piattoli suggested that either the king or his nephew Stanisław marry the Prussian princess Frederica Carolina and thereby start a dynasty. Ignacy Potocki sent him to Berlin to sound out the Prussian court on the subject. He met with some interest, but Frederick William held that a strong dynasty in Poland would conflict with Prussian interests, and suggested the Wettins of Saxony, who were easy for Prussia to keep in check.[13] Having embraced the principle of an hereditary monarchy, Potocki now committed himself to it wholeheartedly. If the Elector of Saxony was the only candidate acceptable to Prussia, then so be it. He explained to Piattoli that the Elector was just a cloak under which to bring in the hereditary monarchy. 'Yes,' answered Piattoli, 'but will we be well covered by it?'[14]

Stanisław had always believed in the desirability of an hereditary monarchy, but he knew that the idea was unacceptable to Russia and provoked strong reactions at home. It stuck in the throats of people such as Seweryn Rzewuski, who had recently published a pamphlet suggesting that Poland should look to the new American constitution for a model of government. His arguments were shot down by Kołłątaj, who agreed that 'those great and virtuous souls Franklin and Washington, to whom America owes her liberty, and the entire world owes honour and admiration, have set Poland a great example,' but he pointed out that conditions in the two countries were different. 'What are we, I ask you, in relation to the Americans but an old man full of bad habits contemplating a well brought up youth whose heart has not yet been tainted by bad example?' And he pointed out that the bad habit of hereditary monarchy could be viewed in a positive light.[15]

But Stanisław took Rzewuski's lucubrations seriously, particularly as they coincided with the feelings of Feliks Potocki. He realised that Potocki was neither intelligent nor even quite balanced, but he considered him 'a very straight man of great integrity', and he was fond of him.[16] He wrote to him several times in Vienna inviting him to return to Warsaw, but Potocki was adamant. He respected the king and stressed that 'civic virtue and the love of liberty has been fostered in our hearts under Your Royal Reign', but he deplored everything the Patriots had done since 1788 – the pointless baiting of Russia, the naïve trust in Prussia, the destabilisation at home, and now the attempts at strengthening the Crown, behind which he saw sinister motives. 'Forget that You are a King, and remember that you are a Pole,' he exhorted Stanisław. 'Turn your ear away, Most Illustrious King, from those who would raise Your throne so that they might safely trample the freedoms of the nation.'[17] These were sentiments that could carry conviction with the szlachta. As Stanisław pointed out to his nephew Józef in November 1790, Potocki could easily proclaim a confederation on the lines of that of Bar, in which case not only large numbers of szlachta, but even sections of the army might join him.[18]

The Seym had sat for two years without an election, and was increasingly out of touch with feeling in the provinces. But it did not wish to dissolve itself. It therefore decided to hold elections for a new complement of deputies, who would join the existing ones, doubling the number of the lower chamber. The elections took place on 16 November 1790, and two-thirds of the 172 new deputies returned were Stanisław's candidates. The instructions from the seymiks revealed that opinion in the provinces was running against radical reform, and contemplated the idea of an hereditary monarchy and of enfranchising the non-noble classes with alarm. Many of the new intake came to Stanisław to complain of the things that had been done during the heady early days of the Seym.[19] Stanisław was the one to whom people looked more and more for guidance or reassurance, often from diametrically opposed viewpoints. He welcomed this, but it placed him in a delicate position with regard to the constitutional question.

The original deputation for the constitution had been superseded by a group who met at the house of Adam Czartoryski, including

Stanisław Małachowski, Potocki, Kołłątaj, Aleksander Linowski, Niemcewicz, Józef Weyssenhoff and Aleksander Lanckoroński, with Piattoli as their editor. And it was Piattoli who would play the crucial role. 'It is almost entirely to him that I owe the mutual confidence that became established between Marshal Potocki and myself,' Stanisław wrote to Mazzei a few months later.'And it is that which became the pivot of the revolution.'[20] Confidence is hardly the right word.

On 4 December Potocki spent several hours closeted with the king, and the upshot of the discussions was that he handed the whole job of drafting the new constitution over to Stanisław.[21] On 10 December Stanisław began dictating his own project to Piattoli, and on 20 December submitted it to Potocki. It reflected the strength of Stanisław's position as well as his views. The king was to have greater powers than in any previous project, and the cabinet was to be the chief executive of a permanently sitting Seym in which the third estate was represented.[22] The Elector of Saxony's eight-year-old daughter Maria Augusta was to be married to the king's nephew Stanisław to found the new Polish dynasty. The project was commented on by Potocki and Kołłątaj, who suggested amendments. Stanisław duly produced another, which received the same treatment, and two more, in January and February 1791. While Piattoli did his utmost to smooth the way, the differences between Stanisław and Potocki went very deep.

Stanisław's original inspiration had been English. William Coxe had been surprised by his 'extraordinary knowledge of our constitution, laws and history; which was so circumstantial and exact, that he could not have acquired it without infinite application'.[23] Over the years he had read much French political literature, but he viewed recent events in France, on which he was kept regularly and meticulously informed by Mazzei, with increasing distaste. Even his artistic pride was affronted with the arrival in January 1791 of the portraits he had commissioned from Jacques Louis David, which were clearly run up by his studio and very inferior. 'Perhaps the great Monsieur David thinks that any old daubs are good enough for wild Sarmatians as long as they come from Paris,' he wrote to Mazzei with ill-concealed pique.[24] In December 1790 he was reading Burke's *Reflections on the Revolution in France*, which had a decisive effect on his thinking at this crucial stage. England, as Stanisław wrote to Mazzei, 'is after all the happiest nation, or at least (in proportion to relative numbers) the nation in which there is the least misery and the least oppression'.[25]

Potocki, like his Barian forerunners, was addicted to Rousseau, whose notion of social contract was equated in Poland with the *Pacta Conventa* and whose concept of the primacy of the nation was understood in terms of the supremacy of the szlachta. He was also inspired by the much-vaunted logic and symmetry of French constitutional thought, a 'sublime code', an 'integral system' made up of 'laws of a superior order', unlike the 'crude, incoherent laws which do not add up to a regular system attuned with the nature of man (such as are, for instance, the laws of England)', to use Mably's words.[26] Stanisław had little time for such stuff. 'Mably is only a little less romantic than Rousseau,' he declared to Mazzei. 'That is all one can say in his favour.'[27]

The appeal of French ideas was on the wane in Poland, with more empirical views gaining ground. Staszic, who had studied under Buffon in Paris, preached evolutionary theories. 'In political matters as in the natural sciences, only *experience* is a reliable teacher of men,' he affirmed.[28] The French edition of Adam Smith's *Wealth of Nations* was selling like hot cakes in Warsaw, and its arguments also helped to draw people towards 'English' pragmatism. Stanisław was therefore in a strong position.

But he remained cautious. 'Marshal Potocki assures me that he sincerely wishes the executive power to be strengthened in my hands more than ever before,' he wrote to Deboli. 'But from such private conversations it is a long way to public action. And he has found an excuse for not doing anything, by declaring everywhere that "The king could do anything he wishes to in the Seym at present, so respected and loved is he. It is strange that the king does not know his power, or does not wish to use it." Branicki and Sapieha are saying the same thing. But I believe that if I were to step beyond the cautious behaviour I have observed until now, I should be risking much and gaining little.'[29]

Time was running out, as the international crisis had come to a head, and Poland might find herself in the midst of a war at any moment. Pitt's plan, presented in final form in Berlin in January 1791, was to deliver an ultimatum to Russia to make peace without gains. If she failed to comply, the British and Dutch fleets would sail into the Baltic, while Prussia, Poland, Sweden and Turkey advanced on land. 'Our wish to include you in this great federation is intended to succour and strengthen you, and to stop you being a staging-post for Russia, as you have been till now,' Hailes and the Dutch minister urged Stanisław. 'When this giant no longer has such a convenient passage through your country, he will stay quietly in the north and the east, and that will be of benefit to you, as you will become free masters in your own country. But if you do not desire this and will not join with us promptly, we shall be obliged to accommodate this giant and to vie with our rivals for his favour, even where this is to the greatest disadvantage of you Poles. So everything depends on your quick determination, for soon it may be too late.'[30]

Russia was diplomatically isolated, and Pitt believed she would climb down. On 27 March a courier left for Berlin bearing the ultimatum to Russia for endorsement by Frederick William. Along with the ultimatum, Pitt sent the convention between Prussia, England and Poland on the mutual alliance and the Gdańsk trade. Lord Hood hoisted his flag on HMS *Victory* at Spithead, where thirty-six ships of the line and twenty-nine others assembled. Frederick William began massing 88,000 men in East Prussia and sent his own equipages to Konigsberg in preparation for an attack on Russia. Catherine's ministers advised her to step down. Potyomkin left the army at the front and appeared in St Petersburg to persuade her to cut her losses and seek an alliance with Prussia. She resisted, going into frequent 'spasms' and 'weeping with rage' as she told him that she would not 'degrade herself' by making overtures to Frederick William, but in the end his arguments prevailed.[31] A courier was despatched with a proposal for negotiation. But it reached Berlin two days after one from London. For once it looked as though Catherine was trapped. But the one thing that did hold was her miraculous luck, and she was rescued at the eleventh hour by the intervention of the most unlikely ally – British public opinion.

Pitt had not prepared opinion for his policy, and when the first request for money to pay for the armaments came before Parliament on 28 March, the opposition, led by Charles James Fox, was spoiling for a fight. Pitt managed to win the debate that followed, but the country was with the opposition. It had no conception of the 'Eastern question', and was mystified as to why the country should go to war over 'a town and a few deserts', as Ochakov seemed to them. The

Russian ambassador Semyon Vorontsov employed an army of hacks to write articles on how British trade would suffer from such a war and conferred with members of Parliament and merchants. Alarm seized the manufacturing towns. Meetings were held in Manchester, Leeds and Nottingham, walls were daubed with 'No war with Russia' slogans in London, and letters poured in to members of Parliament and the press from the provinces. The mood of the country divided Parliament and even the Cabinet. It was pointed out that the ground had not been prepared sufficiently with Sweden and Denmark. 'How we are to get at her fleet I don't see,' Admiral Nelson wrote to William Cornwallis. 'Narrow sees & no friendly ports are bad things.'[32]

Pitt wavered, and on 31 March asked his cabinet permission to request Prussia to delay the despatch of the ultimatum to Russia. With tears in his eyes, he confessed to Ewart that this was 'the greatest mortification he had ever experienced' and that he wanted to resign.[33] He proposed softening the ultimatum to Russia, in order to allow her to keep some gains, but once it was known that England had stopped arming her fleet, Catherine knew she had weathered the storm. She ordered a marble bust of Fox, declaring that she would place it next to that of Demosthenes, since it was his eloquence that had saved Russia.[34]

The collapse of Pitt's plan raised a great question-mark over the future of Poland, and Stanisław was growing desperate to put his house in order. In the second half of February 1791, he had got down to work with Aleksander Linowski to produce the final draft of the constitution, which he submitted on 3 March. Potocki was on the offensive again, and declared that it would have to be reconsidered. He passed it to Małachowski, suggesting that Kołłątaj be asked to rewrite it, trimming away some of the prerogatives Stanisław had awarded himself. Kołłątaj's compromise, which was ready on 25 March, reduced the powers of the Crown in the legislative area and toned down the rights of the peasants and town-dwellers. Otherwise it respected all the principles of the king's project. Potocki was not happy with this compromise, but he was no longer the decisive force even among his own party, and Piattoli was urging him to forget his prejudices. The project had been shown to a wider group of senators and deputies who were sworn to secrecy, and they discussed it in the first weeks of April. The main fear expressed was that the cabinet, which had gone back to its Platonic nomenclature of 'Guardians of the

Laws', might lend itself to government by oligarchy. The upshot was that Potocki and Kołłątaj were sent back to Stanisław with a proposal to augment the powers of the Crown. The project had gone back in all essentials to that which he had sketched out in December.[35]

Nothing now remained but to arrange the passing of the constitution into law. It had always been agreed that this must be done by stealth, to avoid the risk of a rejection or referral. The proposal would come not from the king but from the Seym. The ground had been prepared for some time. On 4 January the king asked the Seym to draft new laws governing the conduct of seymiks, in order to get a necessarily unpopular part of the new constitution out of the way. The laws were passed on 24 March. These disfranchised the illiterate and all who were not landowners, their brothers and sons, or leaseholders paying a minimum of 100 złoty in tax per annum. They were based on Rousseau's concept of the active citizen, which had taken strong root in Poland over the previous two years. 'Birth can produce a nobleman', Potocki's 'Principles' had stipulated, 'but only property turns him into a citizen.'[36] This act struck off an estimated 300,000 out of a total of about 700,000 electors.

Another preparatory measure, a set of laws on the cities, was passed through the Seym just before it broke up for the Easter holiday, on 18 April. Stanisław had wanted to give them full representation in the Seym, but he had been prevailed upon by Kołłątaj and others not to force the issue. The new project, based on Zamoyski's *Code* and drafted by Chreptowicz, stipulated that the cities of the Commonwealth could elect a total of twenty-two plenipotentiaries to the Seym. Their voting rights were confined to issues affecting them directly, but they were given seats on the Seym Commissions of the Treasury, the Police and the Judiciary. The idea of giving them a vote elicited opposition in the Seym. As the debate wore on, the opposition came to embrace other points in the project. Just as it was beginning to look as though the whole proposal would have to be scrapped, on 14 April, the arch-conservative Kalisz deputy Jan Suchorzewski tabled a counter-proposal, supported by all the die-hard defenders of szlachta rights. The proposal was poorly phrased, and Stanisław realised that by altering a minor point it could in effect be turned into an endorsement of Chreptowicz's project. He rose to speak, and made a dramatic show of having changed his mind, insisting only on changing the detail in question. He thanked Suchorzewski, and waxed lyrical about the joy of finding such enlightened minds in the country. He insisted that the chamber vote on Suchorzewski's project immediately, which it did, unanimously. Stanisław gave the bemused Suchorzewski the Order of St Stanisław. The following day, outside the Castle, Stanisław was mobbed by several hundred townsfolk shedding tears of gratitude. 'I too became deeply moved, and I thanked God for this sweet grace,' he wrote to Deboli.[37]

The act extended full civic rights to the third estate. It ennobled all those who served in civic posts, all officers in the army from the rank of captain up, and all those with a certain amount of property. How radically the measure had affected the third estate can be gauged by the fact that only three weeks later the Polish minister in Vienna, Franciszek Woyna, was reporting that several Viennese merchants had approached him with a view to settling in Poland.[38] The two laws dealt with two issues unpopular with the szlachta, and at the same time dramatically altered the electorate of the country. Apart from getting these things out of the way, they also ensured the support of the cities for the forthcoming constitution.

The plan was to lay the project before the Seym soon after Easter, which fell on 24 April, when those who might be opposed to it would still be in the country. The king had chosen St Stanisław's day, 8 May, but was prevailed upon to fix on 5 May instead. The conspiracy included some sixty people by now, since a hard core of supporters had to be warned to be present, but unreliable people, such as Kazimierz Sapieha, were kept in the dark. Stanisław informed the conservative Jacek Małachowski of the plan in the hope of conciliating him, but Małachowski spilled the secret to Bulgakov. Messengers were despatched to bring various senators and deputies back to Warsaw in time, but the conspirators moved their plan forward secretly to 3 May. On the eve, there was a meeting at which the constitution was read out and explained to the supporters of the king. Others were called on during the night to ensure their acquiescence, while Kołłątaj mobilised the civic leaders of Warsaw. At the other end of town, in Bulgakov's house, Jacek Małachowski, Ksawery Branicki, Bishop Kossakowski, Bishop Massalski, Kazimierz Raczyński, Suchorzewski and several others thought up ways of disrupting the next day's session. Ironically,

Hailes and the Dutch minister Reede were now trying to persuade the Patriots to desist from bringing in the constitution.[39]

The next morning, Warsaw was in a state of subdued excitement. Extra troops had been brought in, and the Castle was surrounded by lancers under the command of Józef Poniatowski. The populace thronged the area around the Castle. Of the 182 members of the Seym present, 110 were firm supporters of the project. The session began at 11 o'clock, when Stanisław entered the chamber preceded by the dignitaries of the court and the four marshals. His entrance was greeted with prolonged cheering, which lasted while he took his seat on the throne. The grand marshal of the Crown struck the floor three times with his staff, and handed over to the marshal of the Seym, Stanisław Małachowski, who opened the proceedings with a short speech about the threatening international situation, and asked the secretary of the Deputation for Foreign Affairs to read out the most recent reports from abroad. There were shouts from the Patriots calling for immediate action, and an interruption from Suchorzewski, but Stanisław stood up and called for order.

Not to be silenced, Suchorzewski began screaming incoherently about treasonable plots to trample Polish freedoms and impose tyranny, tore the Order of St Stanisław off his breast, and threw it to the floor. At last he fell silent, whereupon Stanisław asked the secretary to proceed with the reading of the reports from the Commonwealth's diplomatic representatives in Vienna, Paris, The Hague, Dresden and St Petersburg. The picture they painted was not reassuring, and a gloomy silence fell on the chamber when he had finished. Stanisław summoned his ministers to his side and made a speech stressing the dangers surrounding the country on all sides. He said that he knew of a project that had been prepared by certain deputies that might provide a way out of the difficult situation, and called on the marshal of the Seym to read it out. Małachowski did so, and when he had finished he went on to say that 'there are two republican governments in this century: the English and the American, which has corrected the faults of the first. But the one which we intend to establish today will be finer than both, since it will combine in itself all that is most relevant in each to our own circumstances.'[40]

Stanisław then turned to the chamber and asked whether it would release him from his oath to the *Pacta Conventa*. Shouts of assent gave way to chanting of 'The King with the Nation, the Nation with the King,' but they were interrupted by Suchorzewski, who now rushed into the centre of the floor, clutching a six-year-old boy to his breast. In pathetic terms, he declared that he would rather kill his own son than let him live to see the nation enslaved. Sniggering from the benches gave way to alarm when he drew his sword, and friendly hands seized the boy from him, and then ejected Suchorzewski from the chamber. But the interruption had emboldened some of the opponents. Jacek Małachowski denounced the project as a violation of ancient laws, another deputy demanded the reconfirmation of the *Pacta Conventa*, and there followed a number of objections, not all of them unreasonable, from various deputies whose constituents were opposed to reform. A long debate commenced. The idea of an hereditary monarchy seemed to stick particularly hard in some throats.

The session had already lasted six hours, and Stanisław was growing despondent. 'I confess that by 5 o'clock, I began to think the day lost,' he later admitted.[41] Ignacy Potocki made a fine speech answering some of the objections, and the king once again took the floor. 'Whoever loves his motherland and can see through minor objections, must demand the quickest possible expedition of this act,' he said. 'To which end, most worthy Marshal, please lend the full weight of your authority. May I count this day amongst the happiest? Please call up those who are with you; show me where the will of the people lies, let me hear the true wish of the Seym.' The chamber rose and shouted: 'All of us, all of us are with the marshal. Long live the king, long live the constitution.' Małachowski turned to the chamber and asked whether there were any objections. There was silence for a while, but just as he was about to state that the act had been passed, a few deputies demanded a second reading of the project, and this inspired further queries and objections.

The measure seemed as far from being voted as ever, but then one deputy, Michał Zabiełło, got up. He was a small, quiet, but universally respected man who never spoke without making a sensible point. He now stated it had all lasted too long, and that it was time to act. 'I too am opposed to the excessive power of kings, but in this case I can see that it is circumscribed', he said, walking forward, 'and I therefore beseech Your Majesty to give your oath to it, and we shall follow your example.'[42] This had a decisive effect, and the whole chamber rose and approached the king. Stanisław asked the Bishop of Kraków to accept his oath. Silence fell as Stanisław solemnly swore to abide by the new constitution. 'The king, standing on the chair of the throne, appeared like a father surrounded by his children, who extended their hands to him, beseeching him not to delay their happiness and his own,' in Kołłątaj's words.[43]

'I now call on all those who love their motherland to go with me to church, where we may lay before God our oath and our thanks that He allowed us to accomplish such a weighty and salutory work,' Stanisław continued.[44] They duly set off for the Church of St John, cheered by the throng surrounding the Castle and filling the narrow streets of the old city. Małachowski was hoisted on to shoulders and carried in triumph. A small group of disgruntled deputies, including Branicki, remained in the chamber protesting. Noticing that Kazimierz Sapieha was keener to remain with them than go to swear to the constitution, one of the king's aides-de-camp, the powerfully built General Gorzeński, seized him and bore him triumphantly into the church. 'The day was nearing its end, and barely illuminated the church's vault, in which one could see the standards of the guilds among the people thronging the side chapels and even the altars, as well as those hung up by victorious forbears,' recorded Kołłątaj. 'The ancient tombs of valorous Poles, the very holiness of the place, the presence in it of the king, the bishops, the senators and deputies, pledging with raised arms the happiness of the nation, all this made for a spectacle that was as magnificent as it was moving.'[45]

21

The Nation with
the King

'It is a real miracle of Divine goodness,' Stanisław wrote to Mazzei on 4 May.[1] Nearly thirty years late, and long after he had given up hope of ever achieving it, what he had always longed and worked for had come about. He was genuinely astonished at himself. 'How did I, whom you know to be so prone to quandary and that kind of irresolution produced by an excess of the faculty which induces the consideration of all sides of a problem – how did I manage it?' he confided in Glayre.[2] He was guiding the destiny of his nation and fulfilling his own as he had always perceived it. He had achieved the great object of his life, and he was immensely proud of it. 'I see myself as inseparable from this Constitution,' he wrote to Ignacy Potocki, 'and whoever attacks it attacks me.'[3]

The constitution, or Government Act, was a short document consisting of eleven clauses which completely reorganised the Polish polity, turning it into a constitutional monarchy. The throne was made hereditary. Frederick Augustus Elector of Saxony, the grandson of Augustus III, was invited to start the dynasty, and since he had no son yet, his daughter was designated the Infanta of Poland. The veto was abolished, along with the right of confederation, 'being contrary to the spirit of this constitution, destructive of government, and nefarious to society'. The dualism between Poland and Lithuania was phased out. The word 'Commonwealth' was replaced by 'state', and the only mention of the Grand Duchy of Lithuania was to be found among the king's titles. Power was divided in accordance with Montesquieu's principle between the legislative Seym, the executive king, and the independently elected judiciary. The Seym was the source of political power, but since the king was the president of its upper house, the Senate, he had a share in that power. The king was also the Seym's executive, governing through a cabinet called, under Platonic inspiration, the Guardians of the Laws, *Straż Praw*, consisting of himself, the Primate and five ministers. These ministers took responsibility for the king's actions, and were directly answerable to the Seym for them. There was no prime minister, since that role was taken by the king, who also shared many of the prerogatives of the English crown and the American presidency: the executive, the power to conduct foreign policy, the power to enforce the law, the right of clemency, the right of appointment to the highest offices, and the supreme command of the army.

The system was hedged with checks and balances. The king could do nothing without the signature of at least one minister, and every minister was answerable before the Seym, which could have him dismissed by a two-thirds majority in secret ballot. The Straż therefore looked to the Seym as well as to the king. The Seym itself could have its decisions thrown out by the Senate, and it could take no action without the compliance of the executive, the king.

The section on government was prefaced with the statement that 'all authority in human society originates in the will of the Nation'. And while the nation itself was not interpreted in any radical new form, the hegemony of the szlachta was broken. The Seymik Act, which was incorporated into the new constitution, effectively limited the vote to its propertied members. The Cities Act, which was also incorporated, enfranchised a proportion of the town-dwellers. The constitution paid tribute to the peasants, referring to them as the life-blood of the nation, and although they were not emancipated, they were taken under the protection of the state. Complete freedom was extended to all immigrants of whatever estate, and to Poles who had spent time abroad – i.e. a peasant from the partitioned areas could, by escaping to Poland, become a free man.

The parallels with the English and American constitutions drawn by Małachowski were fully justified. Although there was also much in this act that originated in French thought, it was far more satisfactory than the constitution passed by the National Assembly in Paris a few months later. Stanisław could congratulate himself; the end-product hardly differed from the ideal he had sketched out more than thirty years before in his *Anécdote Historique*.

His craving for recognition came close to surfeit in the weeks that followed. Adam Czartoryski prophesied that he would go down as the best loved king in Polish history, and there seemed little reason to doubt this verdict.[4] When he entered the Seym on 5 May for the next session, he was greeted by shouts of 'Long live the saviour of the nation'. 'You should have seen at that moment the face of Stanisław Augustus, to whose countenance the hand of time has done no more than to alter the type of beauty,' Piattoli wrote to Mazzei. 'Oh! my friend, how many things you would have read in that face! The king's majesty, sustained no longer by the theoretical sense of grandeur, but by that of legitimate power and of the duties of the supreme representative of the united nation; the tenderness of the father who sees about him only his compatriots and children; the greatness of a prince who has no other object than to make his people happy and to eradicate the germs of petty passions.'[5]

The opposition melted away. Suchorzewski announced that he no longer considered himself a Pole and intended to seek liberty in America.[6] One senator and twenty-four deputies registered their protest in the Warsaw statute books. But Kazimierz Sapieha, who had been carried along against his will, came to the king on the morrow. 'I now have no credit with my mother or my uncle [Ksawery Branicki]. I am ruined,' he said. 'Only you, my king, can save me. I am now wholly yours.'[7] As the signing of the new constitution began, several deputies who had originally opposed the act now acceded to it. The Wilno deputy Korsak explained that his constituents had instructed him to resist reforms, but having done his duty, he now wished to join in the clear will of the majority. Having said this, he proposed they all go up and kiss the hand of the king who had given hope to the nation. Others emulated him. 'I was against this act, on account of my electoral instructions,' announced Szydłowski, deputy for Mielnik, when he came up to the king. 'Today, speaking from my own conviction, I declare that, seeing you, gracious Master at its head and the whole nation behind it, I declare with conviction, that I shall not desert you.'[8] Aleksander Linowski, one of the Kraków deputies, declared that 'at last a Pole can breathe freely, at last we can permit ourselves to believe that we are a nation; until now we were merely a society.'[9] Stanisław responded with one of his elegant speeches, and the Seym decreed that the feast of St Stanisław, 8 May, would be celebrated henceforth as a national holiday.

Triumphal arches were erected before the Castle and in front of the house of Stanisław Małachowski, whose name-day it was also. At eleven o'clock in the morning, Stanisław took his place on the throne to receive the greetings of people of every condition who flocked to the Castle. In the evening the citizens of Warsaw gave a public ball. 'What made this reception so pleasing', wrote a witness, 'was the sort of heartfelt union, friendship and mutual trust binding together strangers with a strong, fraternal, almost familial feeling, and the universal sympathy amongst the guests, who met and mingled as though they had been old friends.'[10] After the ball, Stanisław drove round the illuminated city in an open carriage, cheered by the jubilant population.

Over the next few days, late returning deputies were allowed to have their say about the constitution, and the majority ranged themselves behind it. People from the provinces called on the king to thank him on behalf of their cities, guilds, palatinates or simply themselves, for having laid the foundations for the nation's future happiness. The volatile but fashion-conscious Kazimierz Sapieha appeared in a bandolier with 'the Nation with the King' inscribed on it, and soon all the jewellers, bronziers, saddlers and embroiderers in Warsaw dropped all other work in order to satisfy the demand for similar accoutrements. The citizens of Warsaw announced their intention of erecting a statue of Stanisław, with the inscription 'He was the first to tear the shackles off mankind.'[11] On 17 May Kołłątaj thanked Stanisław for his nomination as Vice-Chancellor of Poland, saying that 'I am a ripe fruit of your reign, I am only an instrument of Your Majesty's great designs for the enlightenment of the nation.'[12]

Equally gratifying were the praise and congratulation from abroad. In revolutionary Paris, Stanisław was toasted in the political clubs. People such as Sieyès and Volney who had thought Poland beyond redemption registered their enthusiastic approval, and the crowds cheered the 'citizen-king' of Poland. The poet André Chénier called him '*homme-roi*' and praised him for having put into his salutary deed 'as much effort, resources and work as all other kings have hitherto employed in outraging humankind and prolonging its slavery and abjection'.[13] There were calls in the *Cercle Social* to place a bust of Stanisław next to that of Rousseau.[14]

In the United States, he already enjoyed considerable prestige: when Mazzei had expressed doubts about working for a king, Jefferson had assured him that Stanisław was well known there to be 'the finest citizen of his country'.[15] Now the American press dubbed him 'the Paragon of Kings', and Thomas Paine declared him to be unique in introducing reform voluntarily.[16] Harvard students debated on the comparative importance of the American and Polish revolutions, and soon the *New York Daily Advertiser* was noting that 'Polish morning dress has become fashionable in the city.'[17] From Lausanne, Glayre reported universal admiration, including that of Edward Gibbon, to whom he showed Stanisław's detailed account of the dramatic events in the Seym on 3 May.[18] In England, the constitution met with unanimous approval. Comparing the Polish revolution with the bloody outburst in France, Burke waxed lyrical:

Here was a state of things which seemed to invite, and might perhaps justify bold enterprise and desperate experiment. But in what manner was this chaos brought into order? The means were as striking to the imagination, as satisfactory to the reason, and sooth-ing to the moral sentiments. In contemplating that change, humanity has every thing to rejoice and to glory in; nothing to be ashamed of, nothing to suffer. So far as it has gone, it probably is the most pure and defecated publick good which ever has been conferred on mankind . . . Not one man incurred loss, or suffered degradation. All, from the king to the day-labourer, were improved in their condition. Every thing was kept in its place and order; but in that place and order everything was bettered. To add to this happy wonder (this unheard-of conjunction of wisdom and fortune) not one drop of blood was spilled; no treachery; no outrage . . . Happy people, if they know how to proceed as they have begun! Happy prince, worthy to begin with splendour, or to close with glory, a race of patriots and kings: and to leave
    'A name, which ev'ry wind to heaven would bear,
    Which men to speak, and angels joy to hear.'[19]

Even Burke's adversary James Mackintosh could not dispute this judgment. 'Let the Governors of all States compare the convulsion which the obstinacy of the Government provoked in France, with the peaceful and dignified reform which its wisdom effected in Poland,' he wrote.[20] 'Poland ought to make the French blush,' Walpole wrote to a friend. 'But that they are not apt to do on any occasion,' he added.[21] Stanisław was referred to as the gentleman-king, and he was the hero of the day. 'It is hard to describe how favourable an opinion the news has given of us with the public,' reported Bukaty.[22] This gave Stanisław great pleasure, partly on account of his enduring Anglophilia, partly because he felt that public opinion would have an effect on policy, and that England would support Poland and lean on her ally Prussia to do so too.

But Prussia's own reaction was unexpectedly enthusiastic. 'I look with favour on all the good things that have taken place in Poland, and Poland will find in me a sincere and stalwart ally,' Frederick William said to the Polish minister in Berlin, Stanisław Jabłonowski, when he read Stanisław's letter announcing the passing of the constitution.[23] To the Seym, he sent a note in which he declared: 'I strongly applaud the decisive action which the Nation has taken, and I consider it highly opportune for the consolidation of its happiness.'[24] The Berlin ministry was less enthusiastic. 'The Poles have delivered the coup de grace to the Prussian kingdom, by voting a constitution much better than the English,' Hertzberg wrote to Lucchesini. 'I think that Poland will, sooner or later, regain West Prussia, and perhaps also East Prussia. How can we defend our state, exposed from Memel to Teschen, against a numerous and well-governed nation?'[25] He went on to speculate that 'the Revolution in Poland is one of the most important events of our century, and in my opinion it will have more far-reaching consequences than that of France.'[26]

On 30 May Frederick William despatched Colonel Bischofswerder to Dresden to persuade the Elector to accept the Polish succession, and then to Milan to seek the approval of Leopold. The Emperor expressed some fears that the aristocratic order might be eroded by the reforms, but his reaction was also favourable, and Kaunitz did not share Hertzberg's fears.[27] He was relieved that Poland had been stabilised. The Convention of Vienna, signed on 25 July 1791, bound both states to accept the constitution in Poland and support the succession of the Elector. Kaunitz also wanted to bring about Russian acceptance and to cement the three powers into a fresh alliance based on the new order in Poland.

These encouraging developments misled Stanisław. 'I have good reasons for believing', he wrote to Glayre on 25 June, 'that Russia will not raise any open objections to what we have done.'[28] Glayre was inclined to agree. 'I cannot believe', he wrote, 'that [Russia] could abandon all sense of shame and employ force in order to bring back that state of affairs in which she could insult with impunity a Nation which was respected at a time when she herself was still unknown.'[29] Stanisław went further in his fancy. 'I am more and more convinced that our revolution has saved us from a second partition,' he wrote to Deboli.[30] They could not have been more wrong.

'How dare they alter the form of a government that I guaranteed!' was Catherine's first reaction. She was alarmed at the increase in the king's power, and incensed by the clause offering freedom to immigrants. 'What an Idea! That will lure most of the peasants of Byelorussia to Poland, and deprave those in the remainder of my dominions,' she exclaimed.[31] She was deeply offended with Stanisław. 'He is either led or he has fallen into imbecility to have allowed himself to be drawn into actions so nefarious and so contrary to the well-being of Poland, to probity, to gratitude,' she wrote to Grimm.[32] On 23 May, at a sitting of the Council of State she made it clear that it would be Russian policy to overthrow the Polish constitution as soon as possible. Four days later she issued a rescript to Potyomkin to make military preparations, and on 29 July she instructed him to draw up plans for an invasion, to be launched as soon as the situation on the Turkish front permitted.[33] She did not believe that the revolution that had taken place in Poland had wide support, and thought it could be reversed by a mixture of political intervention and military intimidation. Another Poniński would come in useful, she mused to Bezborodko. 'He was a scoundrel', she admitted, 'but he was convenient.'[34]

While he misjudged Catherine's response, Stanisław well knew what her objections to the constitution might be, and he also knew what formula she would use if she did decide to intervene. He acted accordingly. He did not take advantage of the extensive powers the constitution gave him in order to push through the revolution implicit in it. His watchword was 'make yourself small', as he explained to Mazzei.[35] He postponed formally notifying Russia of the new act until he could include in it the Elector of Saxony's acceptance of the Polish succession, as this would complete the *fait accompli* and at the same time add respectability to the new order in Poland. As the constitution had been prepared in secret, the Elector had not been consulted beforehand, and Adam Czartoryski was despatched to Dresden to deliver the Seym's offer and obtain his formal acceptance.

Stanisław's caution was apparent in his selection of ministers for the Straż. Jacek Małachowski had opposed the constitution on account of his pro-Russian orientation and resigned the chancellorship in protest when it became law. But Stanisław and the ex-chancellor's brother persuaded him to take back his office and a seat in the Straż. This was calculated to placate conservatives and to ensure the co-operation of Małachowski's twenty or so supporters in the Seym. Ksawery Branicki had also been opposed to the constitution, but three days after it was passed he turned up at the Castle and asked to be included as Minister for War. Stanisław knew that he had been put up to it by Bulgakov (his spies furnished him with transcripts of the ambassador's letters), and he presumably acquiesced in order to concili-ate Catherine and Potyomkin.[36] For Foreign Minister Stanisław chose not Ignacy Potocki, who was tainted in her eyes by his pro-Prussian feelings, but Chreptowicz, who shared the king's belief in the need for good relations with Russia. Potocki was given a seat, but he and the only other radical in the Straż, the Finance Minister Tomasz Ostrowski, were outnumbered by conservatives.

These gestures intended to placate Russia dovetailed with the policy Stanisław adopted at home. He strove to reconcile those opposed to the constitution, rather than to use the opportunities it offered to impose radical change. He sought out those who seemed lukewarm, and offered them posts and decorations in an effort to scotch the emergence of a group of malcontents. 'Our incomparable master is perfect, unsurpassed for this kind of business,' wrote a delighted Piattoli.[37] Stanisław again wrote to Feliks Potocki, enjoining him to return and accept the new order, but without success.

Polish historians have tended to assume that the country was united in its support for the constitution, and that the king's greatest mistake was not to have trusted his people and led them forward bravely. This is retrospective wishful thinking, based on the memoirs of leading Patriots. It was not only dyed-in-the-wool conservatives who opposed the constitution. Stanisław Poniatowski refused to be present in the Seym on the day, and on the morrow he told Piattoli over lunch that he was convinced it would merely provoke Russia into bringing about the final annihilation of Poland.[38] There was no lack of such realists, and plenty who took their pragmatism to the logical conclusion of demonstrating their disapproval as they awaited the inevitable. In the provinces, where accurate information was scarce, there was widespread mistrust of everything that had taken place in the capital on 3 May. It was a revolution that went against the grain of tradition. The deputies had not consulted with their constituents at the seymiks. Stanisław had broken the *Pacta Conventa*. The cornerstone of Polish democracy, the free elections to the throne, had been abolished in favour of an hereditary monarchy. Societies do not like violent change. Certainly the tens of thousands of landless szlachta who had lost their vote overnight and seen it given to the plebeians of the cities must have had views on the subject. The fact that esteemed figures such as Feliks Potocki and Seweryn Rzewuski, not to mention a score of other dignitaries, denounced the constitution in the most virulent terms, could not fail to have an effect.

Stanisław expected to see open opposition and even disorders. On the night of 15 July 1791 the Warsaw garrison was placed on full alert following a report that an attempt on the king's life was imminent. 'We shall guard our king day and night,' the citizens of Warsaw threatened, but he calmed them.[39] A couple of days later a man was arrested, and confessed to being involved in a plot, apparently hatched by Branicki, to abduct Stanisław. The plan was to seize him as he took his stroll in the gardens at Łazienki, bundle him into a covered three-horse kibitka which was waiting, and then make at full speed for the Russian border, where troops had been placed on alert and told to escort 'a high-ranking person' to St Petersburg.[40] This plot gave rise to rumours of others, the most picturesque of which, revealed in a French pamphlet, tells how the bishops of France sent a consignment of 10,000 daggers to Warsaw with a commando of ci-devant desperados led by an Italian priest to murder Stanisław. The plot was allegedly foiled by a Jewish courtesan who discovered their purpose and warned her beloved king of the danger threatening him.[41] Stanisław made light of the affair. 'I believe in destiny, which will cause the best guarded man to perish when she feels so inclined, and preserve the least guarded,' he wrote to his nephew Józef.[42]

But there were no other incidents, and the constitution was endorsed by the Seym with remarkable smoothness. An act enabling the Straż was passed in May; June saw regulations on the Police Commission and the internal organisation of towns; September the setting up of the Treasury Commission; October the curtailment of the Polish-Lithuanian dualism, fusing many of the separate bodies; the Seym also confirmed the 1788 Military Commission Act, the 1789 Public Order Commissions Act, and the 1791 Cities Act and Seymik Act, which, taken together, made up the bricks and mortar of the new constitution. That summer the cities held their elections and sent twenty-two deputies to the Seym.

The cities had in the main elected members of the szlachta to represent them, which softened the blow. Warsaw had compounded this by electing the wealthy landowner Ignacy Zakrzewski as its president. Stanisław was anxious nevertheless. 'The enthusiasm of the city classes needs no encouragement,' he wrote to Deboli. 'And we must now introduce a little moderation into their adulation of me, for as it is the hetmans and other malcontents are looking for any means to spread fears that I intend to wipe out the szlachta entirely through the burghers, and from there to suggest that we intend to free the peasantry from all subjection.'[43] Rumour had anticipated informed report, and on hearing that their status had been changed, some peasants refused to carry out their labour obligations. There were even cases of rioting in remote areas. This was worrying, since it might confirm country szlachta in their fears that the constitution had upset the natural order. At a meeting of the Straż on 19 July, Stanisław demanded that a strongly worded declaration be drawn up discouraging any sanguine interpretations of the constitution.[44]

But the course he was steering lacked consistency and began to alter as his emotions gained ground over his reason. Many of his closest collaborators were for moderation. His brother the Primate, whom he called back from London that summer in the hope of recasting him as the head of his party in the Seym, was a case in point. At the opening of the autumn session on 15 September 1791 he made a long speech expressing regret at not having been able to take part in the glorious act of voting in the constitution, but most of his subsequent behaviour in the Seym belied this. By the end of the year he was in frequent disagreement with Stanisław, whom he reproved for losing sight of geopolitical realities. The same was true, in varying degrees, of people such as Chreptowicz, Mniszech and Jacek Małachowski. Yet Stanisław found it difficult not to get carried away. He had slipped effortlessly into a new mode of presidential monarchy, and as he relaxed at Łazienki that summer reading Jefferson's *Notes on Virginia*, which the author had sent him, he was every inch the citizen-king enjoying a new-found fraternity with his subjects – Łazienki was unfenced and open to all, and even his new amphitheatre with its stage on the lake, completed that year, had seating for 1,000 people. Stanisław genuinely enjoyed mixing with his subjects on occasions such as the lunch for 300 lawyers given by the Warsaw bar, a form of familiarity that shocked the foreign diplomats.[45] He was also drawn by the radicalism of Kołłątaj.

'The Constitution of 3 May is to date only a collection of political laws,' Kołłątaj told the Seym on 28 June, and went on to expound a distinctly Benthamite programme for supplementing the political constitution with an economic and a moral one. The drafting of the economic constitution was entrusted to the deputation appointed by the Seym in the previous year, led by Prot Potocki and Michał Ossowski. It laid down new procedures for fixing the budget, worked out a comprehensive economic system for the country, including state investment in factories, roads and canals, and set up a national bank. It went on to study ways of turning the starosties into freeholds in order to raise money, and to move people from overcrowded areas to those with empty land. In its approach to questions dealing with the peasantry, the deputation stipulated that all work, however lowly, must be treated 'with requisite respect and just consideration'.[46]

Opinion on what to do about the peasants was sharply divided, and not just between reformers and conservatives. Staszic advocated granting them emancipation and land at once. Kołłątaj believed that the process ought to be more gradual, beginning with the removal of excessive work loads, and proceeding through education to self-improvement.[47] Accordingly, the Commission for National Education extended its control to Uniate, Orthodox, Protestant and Jewish schools, with the aim of standardising education, and adopted a more vigorous approach at the lower levels. Kołłątaj was determined to create a new Pole, with a character and set of values suited to the new state. His character-building techniques resemble nothing so much as Mussolini's *dopolavoro*, with 'national festivities, public exercises, trials of skill, games, and the multifarious activities of social life, adapted to a conscientious sense of duty'.[48] Whatever class he came from, every Pole was to earn his right to the vote through property or service. 'We have opened the door to a future freedom for many of our peasants, without granting it all to them at one stroke,' wrote Stanisław, arguing that 'we would have done a very bad thing if we had rushed the matter.'[49]

Another deputation, supervised by Stanisław himself, grasped the thorn of Jewish emancipation. Kołłątaj's project was predictably drastic, intending to propel the Jewish community into the nineteenth century at a stroke, and including compulsory shaving of beards and proscription of distinctive clothing. Stanisław's, running to eighteen closely written pages, was more humane, trusting to education and military or civic service to erode the differences.[50] Piattoli, who had ideas on everything, managed to get the Jewish delegates to agree to raise a large sum of money as a mark of gratitude for their emancipation. This would be used as a contribution to the military effort, which would silence opposition to the measure, and to settle the king's outstanding debts.[51]

Another unresolved legacy of the old structure of the Commonwealth was the huge Orthodox minority, whose hierarchy, denied political standing, tended to look to Russia. It had lain at the root of Stanisław's earliest troubles, and had surfaced again in 1789, when the Orthodox Metropolitan of Łuck, Wiktor Sadkowski, had been arrested for pro-Russian agitation. A Seym commission discussed the matter while he languished in gaol, and Stanisław was determined to solve the problem by giving the Orthodox hierarchy full political rights, including seats in the Senate for their bishops. 'Good things cannot be done as easily or as fast as I should like,' Stanisław complained to Glayre, 'but that is a problem to which I have to resign myself,' adding that 'as you can imagine, I am busier than ever.'[52]

Good things were in fact being done with surprising speed. At the local level, the Civil and Military Order Commissions were transforming the landscape. As well as governing and collecting taxes, they carried out a census, audited schools, hospitals and other public establishments, reviewed the qualifications of practising doctors, numbered houses, set up fire brigades, built bridges and developed mining and industry. None of this was enough for Stanisław. Having abandoned his original caution, he wanted to do everything at once. But his new powers, though extensive, did not permit him to bypass the Seym, and this did not share his sense of urgency. During its autumn session, which Hailes dubbed 'the dancing Seym' on account of the daily balls, the complacency of the reformers allowed the conservatives to waste much precious time.[53]

And time was not on Stanisław's side. The Elector of Saxony blew hot and cold: although Austria and Prussia had assured him of their approval, Prussia's enthusiasm was beginning to cool in the autumn of 1791, while Russia kept a Sybilline silence on the subject. His refusal to commit himself did not bode well for Poland's chances of survival. Stanisław repressed his fears, and occasionally grew quite sanguine. 'Although one should not count too much on a Nation which has been so flighty and inconsequent, which is still poorly armed, and above all not very rich, I nevertheless think that I can promise myself that if violence were attempted, it would resist courageously at my side, and possibly long enough to discourage its oppressors,' he wrote.[54] But the future of Poland would be decided by the attitude of her neighbours, and this was increasingly coloured by reactions to what was happening in France.

Inevitably, parallels were drawn between events in both countries, particularly at the courts of St Petersburg and Berlin. Stanisław himself disapproved of what was now happening in France. 'I tremble for Louis XVI,' he wrote to Mazzei in May, and his concern was not without a note of personal apprehension.[55] Most of all, however, he feared lest international opinion on the Polish revolution become tainted by association with events in Paris, which could only degrade it and encourage the self-appointed guardians of the old order to attack it. He was hailed in France as being more radical than he was, and bogus letters from him to the National Assembly were published. 'In general, both our law of 3 May and everything that has emanated from it constitute almost the exact opposite of the French revolution,' he argued, desperate to refute the damaging associations.[56]

Ignacy Potocki, Kołłątaj and other Patriots revelled in a community of spirit with France: they bandied the same language and affected a kindred style, and their posturings were meticulously, almost pruriently, reported by horrified diplomats in Warsaw. In May 1791

Kołłątaj founded the Association of Friends of the Constitution, the first organised political party in Poland. It consisted of some 200 people, most of them deputies and senators, and met regularly to co-ordinate policy and voting strategy. With its pseudo-masonic motto *Fiat Lux* and its strict set of rules (the last being that all members must subsume private convictions in the general will of the whole), it invited comparison with the Jacobin club of Paris. Ignorance confused Jacobinism with freemasonry in traditionalist minds, hence a vague but pervasive conviction that a 'sect' working through 'clubs' was out to destroy the whole moral and temporal order. Any association of people tended to induce apprehension, and there was a mild panic when a group of servants in Warsaw (including the Russian ambassador's valet) set up a union.[57]

At the beginning of July a French minister was posted to Warsaw, the first official diplomat since Paulmy. He was Marie-Louis d'Escorches, Marquis de Sainte-Croix, but, being an ardent Jacobin, he called himself Monsieur Descorches. He flouted convention, and, by refusing to address the Primate by his correct title, began a diplomatic row that strangely echoed events of thirty years before. His behaviour was calculated to annoy the already suspicious diplomatic corps, and Stanisław feared its potential consequences. Descorches floated ideas of a Franco-Polish alliance, which sent shudders down Prussian and Russian spines. In other circumstances, Stanisław would have favoured any such idea, and particularly Condorcet's scheme of a republican league of France, England, the Netherlands, Poland, Switzerland and the United States, but in the present climate, they could only jeopardise Poland's survival. The Elector of Saxony was still undecided, and the more revolutionary the situation appeared in Warsaw, the less likely he was to take up the Polish offer.

Austria, which was preparing for war with revolutionary France, continued to press Russia to join with Prussia and herself in guaranteeing the integrity of Poland and recognising the Elector's succession. Leopold and Kaunitz were afraid that Prussia might strike a bargain once their back was turned. Prussia was certainly open to suggestion: Frederick William had twice mobilised his forces and then had to return to Berlin empty-handed, and was in peril of becoming the first Prussian monarch for several generations not to add a province to the family estate. Austria offered him Hainault, Jülich and Berg if he supported her militarily against France. In February 1792, Austria and Prussia signed a fresh treaty to this end. But the wording on Poland was altered from that of the Vienna Convention of July 1791, and the two now only undertook to support *a* free constitution in Poland in the most general terms. Frederick William did not want to have his hands tied any more than was necessary. His instincts proved right, for only a few days after the signature of the treaty with Austria, he received a courier from St Petersburg bearing a very interesting piece of information. His ambassador had managed to get sight of a note from Catherine to Zubov stating that as preliminaries of peace had been signed with Turkey, all Russian forces on that front were to begin massing for an invasion of Poland: should Austria or Prussia protest, they were to be bought off with a new partition. By the end of February, the French agent in Berlin noted with surprise that there was no more talk of Prussian compensations in the west.[58] Frederick William now knew where to get his indemnities for fighting against revolutionary France.

Lucchesini was sent to Warsaw once more, this time in order to disentangle Prussia from the inconvenient alliance with Poland. In January 1792 he had a number of conversations with Stanisław, Chreptowicz, Ignacy Potocki and others, informing them privately that Prussia no longer felt bound by the alliance. Stanisław and his advisers pretended not to understand, meaning to hold Prussia to her word when the time came. Austria was alarmed at Prussia's equivocation, and persisted in her efforts to obtain Russia's acceptance of the status quo in Poland. Russia refused to give this, and urged the other two to make war on France. Catherine had viewed the progress of the French Revolution with disgust that frequently turned to anger. 'I am in a terrible rage,' she wrote to Grimm when she heard news of the French constitution of September 1791. 'I stamped my foot with rage while reading of those, those . . . horrors!'[59] And on 25 November, she told her secretary that 'I am wracking my head to push the courts of Vienna and Berlin into French affairs,' but in this she was not only inspired by her righteous anger at the French. 'There are reasons of which I cannot speak, but I want to involve them in these matters because I need to have elbow-room. I have much unfinished business, and it is necessary for them to be kept busy and out of my way.'[60] It does not require much imagination to guess where the unfinished business lay, but to Grimm she was keen to point out that, far from shirking her monarchical duty to fight Jacobinism alongside Prussia and Austria, she was going to combat it in Poland.[61] The apparent contradiction does not seem to have struck her. For if she was goading Austria and Prussia to make war on the French because they had turned a monarchy into a republic, she was going to intervene in Poland because a republic had been turned into a monarchy. Her justification was that she was obliged to succour her republican friends in Poland. 'I kept quiet as long as nobody addressed themselves to me,' she wrote, 'but now that a number of citizens request my assistance, I am in honour bound to take up their cause.'[62]

These friends consisted essentially of Feliks Potocki, Seweryn Rzewuski, the Kossakowski brothers and Ksawery Branicki. Potocki's views had hardened. He considered everything the Seym had done since 1788 as a monstrous mistake which it was his duty to put right, and held to the view that the 'fatal day of 3 May was the perdition of the nation's freedom and the end of the Commonwealth'. He fell under the influence of Seweryn Rzewuski, whose views were dominated by traditional republican canons and his personal dislike of Stanisław. He wanted to abolish the monarchy altogether, and create 'the United Provinces of Poland', a federation guaranteed by Russia.[63] Szymon Kossakowski had been one of the bravest of the Barians, and had since found congenial employment as a general in the Russian army. But he remained close to his cultivated, clever and devious brother Józef, Bishop of Livonia. Like most former Barians, they had accepted the inevitability of Russian dominion in Poland but not Stanisław's rule. Branicki could not reconcile himself to the diminution of the hetmans' powers, and saw his future in terms of a close association with Potyomkin.

Potocki and Rzewuski, who had retired to Vienna, also addressed themselves to Potyomkin after Kaunitz brushed them off. 'Deign to believe me, my dear prince,' Potocki wrote to Potyomkin in April 1791, 'that there is no human force which could deflect me from the course of doing the right thing for my country, and as I believe that one cannot do it without the constant support of the great sovereign who merits the respect and the trust of the world, and without the perfect harmony of Poland with that monarchy of which you, my dear prince, are both pillar and jewel, I shall not hesitate for a moment to come and join you.'[64] Potyomkin's plans were so inchoate and so changeable that it is difficult to be precise about them. He contemplated a kingdom of 'Dacia' carved from the Polish Ukraine and the Danubian Principalities, in which he could reign as a sort of Cossack warlord, and in 1790 drew up military plans for detaching provinces from Poland. But by the beginning of 1791 he was thinking in terms of some kind of deal with Stanisław, and in July of that year he declared to Countess Pushkin (in an attempt to gain her favours) that 'I have hopes yet of becoming king of Poland'.[65] He had a place in these plans for Branicki, Potocki and Rzewuski, and they had all kept in touch. He had established his headquarters at Jassy, where he lived like a nabob, and it was there that negotiations began after the Turks signed the preliminaries of peace with Russia in August 1791.

It was there that Potocki and Rzewuski made their way in October 1791. But on the eve of their arrival, on 16 October, Potyomkin died. Potocki wavered as to whether to persevere in their scheme, and when he met the late Potyomkin's mistress, the beautiful Greek Madame Witt, he began to lose interest in politics.[66] Rzewuski wrote to Catherine, and received encouraging replies, telling them all to stand by and wait. At this point they were joined by Branicki, who had to attend to his wife's inheritance from her uncle Potyomkin.

Stanisław let him go because he was keen to keep avenues of communication open, in order to lure this clique back to Poland. He wrote repeatedly to Feliks Potocki and Rzewuski, as did Małachowski and Ignacy Potocki. Ignacy's brother Stanisław Potocki, who had been close to his cousin Feliks, was sent to Jassy to persuade him to return. Feliks Potocki still held the rank of General of the Artillery, and Rzewuski was Field-Hetman of the Crown, so the Military Commission sent official letters recalling them both. As the letters went unanswered, there were demands that the two should be cashiered. Stanisław was opposed to such drastic steps, since 'they might serve to procure for the two insulted men such Russian protection as might later lead to other things'.[67] But when the matter was brought up in the Seym in January 1792, even such stalwart royalists as Pius Kiciński disagreed with him, and after a stormy debate, Potocki and Rzewuski were stripped of their military rank.

Stanisław's efforts to keep the Polish revolution acceptable to all had come to grief by the beginning of 1792. Not only had he failed to lure Potocki and Rzewuski back, he was finding it increasingly difficult to keep people like his own brother the Primate or Jacek Małachowski from straying into opposition. Almost everything that had been done since the previous May alienated somebody, and in January Prot Potocki's plan for selling the starosties caused a surge of anger. 'The number of malcontents is growing,' Bulgakov noted gleefully in his diary, 'everyone is blaming the king.'[68] The remarkable sense of unity that followed the passing of the constitution had given way to fear and vacillation. Many began to suspect that the revolutionary process would go too far, others were overawed by the threatening international situation. The uncertainty mounted as the elections to the Seym, due on 14 February, drew near. These would be seen as a national referendum on the constitution.

Stanisław worked hard for his favoured candidates, and the Association of Friends of the Constitution sent out 'apostles' to the provinces to canvass. Detachments of the smart new army paraded through the provinces to awaken national pride. At the instigation of the Nuncio, the Pope issued a *breve* of benediction for the constitution, which reassured the God-fearing.[69] But the malcontents had been active too, and it was widely believed that many provincial seymiks would come out in opposition. To everyone's surprise, they voted overwhelmingly in favour of the constitution, most of them swearing allegiance to it and sending separate delegations to Stanisław to thank him personally for having brought it about. Stanisław and the reformers were delighted by the unexpected landslide, which removed the need for moderation. Kołłątaj put the finishing touches to his 'moral constitution', while all the disabilities of the dissenters were lifted, and the Uniate Metropolitan was given a seat in the Senate. But the problem of getting change accepted within Poland, which had absorbed so much effort, was now urgently superseded by considerations of an international nature.

The signature of the Treaty of Jassy with Turkey on 9 January 1792 allowed Catherine to order her armies back from the Turkish front to regroup in positions from which they could invade Poland. On 28 February, she informed the Prussian and Austrian ambassadors in St Petersburg, Counts Goltz and Cobenzl, that she intended to invade Poland in order to overthrow the constitution. Cobenzl remonstrated.[70] Austria was still determined to safeguard Poland, but on 1

March the Emperor Leopold died, to be succeeded by Francis II. The new Emperor was a sickly, inexperienced and ineffectual twenty-four, while Kaunitz, now aged eighty-one, was beginning to lose his grip. Catherine could safely ignore Austria. In March she summoned Potocki and Rzewuski to St Petersburg, where she received them with great honour – Potocki was even admitted to an imperial embrace in her bedroom.[71] Szymon Kossakowski was already in St Petersburg, and a number of others joined them over the next weeks, including Antoni Czetwertyński and Jerzy Wielhorski. Branicki had been pleading in vain with Stanisław throughout February to be allowed to go to St Petersburg on family business. The king and the Straż only relented when Bulgakov let it be known that Catherine would see it as a personal affront if he were prevented from going, and accordingly on 12 March he was given three months' leave.[72]

On 9 April the Russian Council of State reached its final decision to invade Poland in May, and over the next two weeks the Polish collaborators worked, under the direction of the new favourite, Platon Zubov, on a manifesto for the confederation they would form. This was signed on 27 April 1792 in St Petersburg, but kept secret for the time being. Fortune favoured Catherine's plans. On 20 April France declared war on Austria. This was to have a decisive effect on Poland's hopes for survival.

'Notwithstanding alliances, we should look to ourselves for our principal defence,' Stanisław had argued in July 1791, but this was easier said than done.[73] Money was not the main problem, as the state's revenues had more than trebled since 1788 to a figure of 39,709,811 złoty in 1791–2.[74] Men were not lacking either, since the total number under arms worked out at only one per 150 head of population.[75] But building up an adequate store of arms was not easy, since the only two factories in Poland providing muskets (one of them Stanisław's own at Kozienice) could supply no more than 2,000 a year, while the factories in Germany were fully booked with orders from the anti-French coalition forces.[76] Disease and desertion were rife, mainly because the rapid expansion of the armed forces had not allowed for the building of adequate barracks, stables and stores, with the result that conditions were extremely bad. The infrastructure was deficient, and there was a dire lack of qualified officers. The entire officer corps represented less than 5 per cent of the total number of men.[77] Throughout 1791 Stanisław did what he could to improve matters. Large-scale manœuvres were held in the summer of 1791, by Józef Poniatowski and Kościuszko at Bracław, and by Ludwig of Württemberg at Gołąb. The latter were held in syncopation with nightly balls at nearby Puławy and accompanied by heroic pageantry, as the Czartoryskis tried to turn their son-in-law into a national hero. Although they were now at peace with Stanisław, they could not resist the temptation to further their alternative image – Izabela Czartoryska also patronised Kościuszko, building up his legend, suggesting that he was a better soldier than his commander Józef Poniatowski, and even, at one stage, toying with the idea of marrying him to her daughter Zofia.

The armed forces stood at 56,947 men in June 1791, and hardly grew at all over the next ten months in spite of Stanisław's efforts.[78] He missed the organisational skills of Komarzewski, and had to fight daily battles with the less than committed Branicki, who ignored the instruction to draw up a plan of national defence. 'Policy dictated that I should make him minister of war in the Straż,' Stanisław wrote to Deboli, 'and in the Straż we enact what amounts to a comedy.'[79] Policy also hindered another major initiative. Both the favoured republican models of America and Switzerland and the conditions existing in Poland suggested the desirability of forming local militias. Piattoli had drawn up schemes for such forces, and Stanisław was very keen to bring them into being.[80] But the idea of arming the lower orders horrified conservatives, and Ignacy Potocki prevailed upon him to drop the plan.

On 16 April 1792 the Seym passed a Defence Act, giving Stanisław wide powers to recruit officers abroad, conscript men, to take an extra 9 million złoty from the Treasury, and to raise a loan abroad of 30 million złoty. Armed with these powers, Stanisław sprang into action. On 24 April the Civil and Military Commissions of every province received instructions to provide recruits so that the army could be brought up to a full complement of 100,000 men. Within a month it had risen to about 65,000. 'I am working night and day to arm the nation,' Stanisław wrote to Deboli, adding that he only wished he had been given such powers six months earlier.[81]

*

As the Elector of Saxony continued to procrastinate, the question of the succession began to weigh heavily. It was again suggested that it should be offered to Catherine's grandson Constantine. There were also suggestions that the king's nephew Józef should succeed, after marrying either Adam Czartoryski's daughter Zofia or Ignacy Potocki's Krystyna, while Ludwig of Württemberg began to dream of the crown for himself. At the same time, the sense of uncertainty surrounding the throne bred other notions.

Stanisław had shown himself little over Christmas 1791 and most of January. He was tired and the strain of work and responsibility were beginning to tell as he finished his sixtieth year. He had the beginnings of rheumatoid arthritis, he suffered from haemorrhoids, and he often had difficulty in breathing. He spent much of the time closeted with Piattoli and others, working on various projects. On 8 February Bulgakov, who had a well-placed spy in the person of Ignacy Potocki's secretary Pierre Parandier, reported to Bezborodko that 'the king intends to deceive everyone, beginning with Potocki'.[82] Three weeks later Lucchesini was reporting to his master that Stanisław was preparing a coup to seize dictatorial powers.[83] Bulgakov despatched the same information to St Petersburg.[84] Ten days later, the Austrian ambassador Benedikt de Caché alerted his court that the coup was going to take place on 3 May, the anniversary of the constitution.[85] By the end of March Caché was certain that large numbers of peasants were going to be brought into the capital to help Stanisław impose a 'French-style equality' on his subjects, and by mid-April he was convinced that 'there can be no doubt that some very important event is being prepared, whose real significance and import will only become clear on 3 May or – as some suggest – on the eve of that great feast'.[86]

What was really going on is difficult to say, since Polish sources are cryptic on the subject. Stanisław and his closest advisers certainly gave much thought to the question of how to entrench the new system and safeguard it against possible rejection by the February seymiks. They considered extreme measures such as imposing a dictatorship by the king and the Straż. When the seymiks demonstrated the nation's wholehearted endorsement of the new order, the accent was shifted from protection to consolidation. The idea was to reinforce the powers of the Crown, and to use the occasion of the first anniversary of the constitution to hold a second coronation, at which Stanisław would be ceremonially invested in his new role and swear, not to the *Pacta Conventa*, but to the constitution. But these plans were further diluted, probably so as not to give Prussia and Austria grounds for greater alarm.

The anniversary was nevertheless to be a great day. Pope Pius VI had moved the feast of St Stanisław to 3 May, and the day became a national holiday. Stanisław devoted himself to staging the elaborate ceremonies with his usual thoroughness. He commissioned Giovanni Paisiello to write a *Te Deum* for the occasion, and attended the rehearsals. The atmosphere was marred by intelligence that had been received of a plot to assassinate him on the day. Stanisław took the threat seriously. He had been deeply affected by the stabbing of Gustavus III of Sweden at a masked ball on 16 March and his death on 9 April. He wrote out and entrusted to Stanisław Małachowski a pathetically worded political testament.[87] Extra troops were deployed on the day, and Stanisław must have been in a state of some alarm, as he spent most of it in an exposed position.

In the morning he drove in a glass carriage down the Krakowskie Przedmieście lined with guilds drawn up in military formation. In the Church of the Holy Cross, he found the whole Senate and Seym assembled, and he addressed them before Mass. 'The real and exclusive aim of this new form of government', he told them 'was none other than to ensure, as far as is humanly possible, that all the heirs of the Polish nation should in equal measure share in the common liberties and the security of their property.'[88] The only unpleasant note was struck when a hailstorm passed overhead, plunging the church into darkness and drowning out the sound of the ceremony. Stanisław then went to lay the foundation-stone of a new church of Divine Providence.

Stanisław displayed a 'joyful serenity' throughout, according to Caché, 'and everyone admired his physical endurance, for after a five-hour session he took part, on foot, in a long procession.'[89] The capital was illuminated that evening, and the king went to the performance of a new play entitled *Kazimierz the Great*, specially written for the occasion by Julian Niemcewicz. At one point, when the actor uttered Kazimierz's line that 'I shall stand at the head of my people in the moment of need,' Stanisław leant out of his box and interjected: 'I too shall stand up and not fail them.' This sally was met with wild enthusiasm, but nobody suspected how soon that moment would be upon them.

22

War

On 14 May 1792, at the little town of Targowica on the Polish frontier, Feliks Potocki, Seweryn Rzewuski, Branicki and several others proclaimed a confederation and invoked Russian aid. Two days later 97,000 Russian troops poured across the frontier. On 18 May Bulgakov delivered a note to Chreptowicz explaining that they were entering the country 'as friends, to provide assistance in the common task of resurrecting the Commonwealth in its rights and prerogatives'. The note assured that 'although Her Most Illustrious Majesty has repressed her indignation at the insults she has suffered herself, she cannot remain insensitive to the voice of complaint with which a large number of Poles has assailed her'.[1] In consequence, she demanded that the king and the Seym accede to the Confederation of Targowica forthwith.

There was predictable uproar when the note was read to the Seym on 21 May. Stanisław called for a united stand in defence of the country and the constitution, although he believed that war might yet be averted. 'It is barely credible', he said, 'that a monarch as enlightened and magnanimous as Catherine II should refuse to listen to all representations.'[2] But if it came to war, then they would have to fight. 'I intend to go myself, and to invite you to follow me in the defence of the motherland,' he exhorted the assembly.[3] Extra taxes were voted, and Stanisław was awarded another 2 million złoty for his campaign costs. A few days later he published a stirring proclamation to the army, and the Primate ordered prayers to be said in every parish.

On 29 May the Seym suspended its session, handed over all executive power to the king and the Straż, and published a declaration to the country. 'Stand by your king, your leader, your father,' it urged, 'stand by him whom you chose from your own blood and called to the sceptre, who even in venerable age will give his life and suffer great perils with you for the defence of our common motherland . . . '[4] There was an explosion of solidarity throughout the land. 'The time has come when prejudice is broken down, and man is brought closer to man,' Stanisław toasted the merchants at a banquet given by the citizens of Warsaw.[5] One astonishing manifestation of this was that the harridan Katarzyna Kossakowska finally came to the Castle to be presented to Stanisław, at last acknowledging him as king.

'I shall go with my Guards to where the shooting is,' Stanisław wrote to Deboli, but neither he nor any of his entourage believed it would come to that.[6] If Poland made a determined show of her will to fight and the Targowicans were shown to have no support within the country, if Prussia demonstrated that she would stand by the alliance, and if Austria, England and the Netherlands applied pressure, Catherine might agree to a face-saving compromise. The very fact that the diplomats of those three states were begging Stanisław to open negotiations rather than fight suggested that they felt themselves to be committed. And Stanisław was prepared to negotiate on anything – except the constitution. 'I shall not suffer any departure from the act of 3 May,' he told Deboli.[7] Although Lucchesini had done everything he could over the past three months to convince them otherwise, Stanisław and his advisers did not believe that Frederick William could refuse to honour his obligations under the treaty. This clearly stipulated that if Poland were attacked, Prussia would in the first place supply 14,000 infantry, 4,000 cavalry and a proportionate artillery park to swell the Polish army. She would then make other forces available or go into action herself.[8] On 4 May Lucchesini had handed Chreptowicz a note in which Frederick William explained that he no longer considered himself to be bound by the alliance. Stanisław believed that the Prussian king was bluffing. 'I know that Berlin is trying to frighten us into bending the knee and surrendering, in order to prevent war breaking out here, precisely because Berlin foresees that it will have to join in this war if it takes place,' he argued.[9] However unwilling he might be to defy her, Frederick William could not countenance Russia taking over the whole of Poland under his nose. 'I do not believe (whatever their present language) that the Courts of Berlin and Vienna can finally and completely refuse us their assistance,' Stanisław wrote to Józef Poniatowski.[10] This view was shared by Ignacy Potocki, who, as the architect of the Polish-Prussian alliance, went to Berlin to enforce it.

At a brief interview on 7 June, Frederick William told Potocki that he had no intention of helping Poland, 'the state of affairs having altered entirely since the Alliance which I contracted with the Republic'. He followed this up with a letter to Stanisław in which he maintained that: 'My way of thinking and the language of my ministers have never varied; and while I viewed with tranquillity the new Constitution which the Republic gave itself, independently of me and without my knowledge, I have never considered supporting or protecting it.'[11] On the following day, Frederick William having refused to see him, Potocki read out to Count Schulenberg the letter his king had sent to Stanisław and the Seym after the passing of the constitution, but Schulenberg replied that the king 'disavowed' this letter. Four days later, at a final interview, Frederick William refused to answer Potocki's questions.[12] On 14 June Lucchesini delivered Frederick William's last word on the subject to Stanisław, who found difficulty in restraining his tears as he read it.[13] 'All too often one sees people sacrifice justice to ambition in politics,' commented the French diplomat Ségur, 'but never has anyone dared to deny engagements which were so public and so recent, and to flout so openly the trust of treaties.'[14] But then Frederick William, as Catherine was fond of pointing out, was a man 'without probity, or principles, or courage, who barely knew the words for glory and honour'.[15]

Without the active participation of a major power, there could be no hope of Poland winning the war. Russia had a large war-hardened army with well-tried commanders and staffs, a functioning infrastructure, gigantic reserves of manpower, and almost endlessly renewable resources. She could afford to lose an army or even a whole season's campaigning, but she could still fight on. The theory that she could have been brought to the negotiating table by considerations of the potential cost of a protracted war can be dismissed. Catherine had always won – by pursuing her aims relentlessly and sometimes recklessly. There is no reason to believe that she might have changed the victorious habit of a lifetime. And having made up her mind that Stanisław had played her false and that the Poles had insulted her, she would have risked her throne and her empire rather than negotiate with them.

Not that there was much risk involved. The entire armed forces of the Commonwealth now stood at about 65,000 men. Accurate figures are hard to establish, since regiments were often a quarter or even a third below strength. 'I have regiments without uniforms, cannons without horses, incomplete units, quantities of sick men, chests with no money, detestable weapons, and with that a decidedly good spirit; but there is enough of that to last out one day of real action,' Józef Poniatowski wrote to his uncle.[16] Of the 65,000 theoretically under arms only about 45,000 were operational, the rest consisting of garrisons and ancillary formations. The troops were deployed in two main bodies: some 14,000 men under Poniatowski, concentrated in the Ukraine; and the army of Lithuania, of similar strength, scattered over the territory of the Grand Duchy. Poniatowski had a reserve of 5,000 men under Michał Lubomirski, and the king had his Guards corps of about 5,000 in Warsaw. New units were forming in the capital, recruits were being raised by the Civil and Military Commissions in every district, and large numbers of volunteers were expected to rally to Stanisław's banner when he set forth, as he intended to do in mid-June, to join the other forces for the main battle. 'As soon as I march, I think I can count for certain that my corps will swell like a snowball,' he wrote to his nephew.[17]

Although Stanisław had never believed in the possibility of successfully defying Russia on his own, he grew sanguine at times. 'Between a slavery that would be even more oppressive than that from which we have emerged and death, there can be no hesitation,' he wrote to Glayre.[18] This was typical of the ambivalent feelings which had been pulling him in opposite directions since the beginning of the Great Seym, and over the next months his realism often fell prey to fits of military exaltation. Similar tendencies can be detected in Ignacy Potocki, Stanisław Małachowski and Kołłątaj, all of whom were caught in the same position of conducting a war which they knew at heart to be pointless. It was only cool realists such as the Primate and Chreptowicz who never blundered into military optimism.

The person who suffered most harrowingly from this state of affairs,

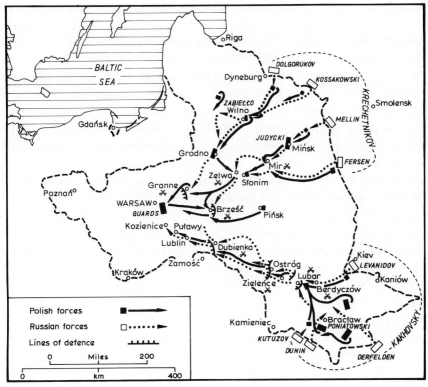

6   The War of 1792

and who was, in a sense, sacrificed to fate, was Józef Poniatowski. A born soldier, he could clearly see the hopelessness of the situation in terms of men and equipment, and of strategic and tactical options. He was a fine field-officer, but had no experience of overall command. He was only twenty-nine, and dreaded the responsibility laid on his shoulders. When in Warsaw for the anniversary celebrations at the beginning of May he had tried to relinquish his command. Stanisław would not hear of it. 'Let your valour, your wits and your love of your motherland make up for everything,' Stanisław exhorted him. 'I shall go, because I'm a Pole,' rejoined Józef, 'but I go as to my death, or worse, for I expose myself to the danger of losing my good name.'[19]

He bore up remarkably well in the circumstances. His orders were merely to cover the frontiers and if possible deny passage to the Russians, who invaded in two columns, one from the north under General Krechetnikov, the other from the south-east under General Kakhovsky. Poniatowski was loath to take risks with his untried troops. He ordered Michał Lubomirski to take his division to Dubno, and to make a strong base camp there, with a store of supplies. He intended to concentrate this force, and the army his uncle was to bring out of Warsaw, with his own before delivering a decisive blow at Kakhovsky, possibly in co-ordination with the army of Lithuania.

But the army of Lithuania's effectiveness was undermined from the start. Command of it had been given to Ludwig of Württemberg. He was thirty-six and had no wartime experience, and his appointment was based on political considerations. As the brother-in-law of the Emperor Francis II and of the Grand Duke Paul, he could lend a certain dynastic weight to the Polish cause, while his close connections with the court of Berlin might, it was hoped, draw Frederick William into some kind of action. In the event, these connections turned out to be closer than anyone thought, and had a contrary effect.

Württemberg tried to lay down his command as soon as war broke out. When his resignation was refused, he took to his bed, pleading a festering leg-injury, and issued no orders to his units to start concentrating. This insouciance was only explained when the officials of the Military Commission at Łomża intercepted a suspicious courier. It transpired that he was carrying letters to the king of Prussia in which Württemberg explained that he was deliberately keeping the Lithuanian army scattered so as to facilitate the advance of the Russians, and begging him to transmit this information and assure Catherine of his hopes of her continued favour. The incriminating letters were passed to Stanisław, who was mortified. He was anxious to hush up the affair. On 1 June he relieved Württemberg of his command, citing health reasons, and arranged for him to leave the country quickly. But the unsavoury truth seeped out, with regrettable consequences for public confidence in the conduct of the war.

General Judycki took command three days later and began to concentrate the Lithuanian forces. On 11 June he offered battle to the Russians at Mir and nearly won, but confused everyone with contradictory orders at the crucial moment. The retreat was orderly, but there was no attempt to defend Wilno, which was occupied by the Russians on 14 June. A few days later Judycki was replaced by General Michał Zabiełło, who was more energetic. He took in hand what was left of the army and made a forced march to cut off and defeat one of the Russian columns. A downpour lasting several days frustrated this plan, but at least he managed to prevent General Fersen's corps from breaking through in the centre and coming between the armies of Poland and Lithuania. He then drew back to defend the line of the Bug and liaise with the other Polish units.

But there was no real attempt being made in Warsaw to co-ordinate operations. Supreme command was vested in Stanisław, who created a 'War Council' to help him exercise it, but neither he nor the council managed to develop an overall plan or strategy. Stanisław pressed his nephew to win a battle, or 'deliver a good blow', in order to give confidence to the waverers and fatalists in Warsaw, while warning him not to take unnecessary risks. He gave a great deal of advice, much of it sensible, and attended with devoted alacrity to every request for supplies. The recruitment and armaments ordered in April were in progress, and the country's resources were not expected to be fully mobilised until the beginning of July.

The freshness and lack of experience of his army beset Poniatowski with operational and disciplinary problems, with officers unused to military service asserting their independence or showing reluctance to commit themselves for political reasons. Many of the peasant recruits had but one wish – to return to their homestead before the harvest. Poniatowski had to resort to draconian disciplinary measures and, on one occasion, even ran through a mutinous corporal with his own sabre.[20] Matters were made no easier by the equivocal attitude of the inhabitants of the territories they were operating in. 'Although the local citizens retreat and show no liking for the opposite camp, their spirit is either fearful or indifferent,' Poniatowski wrote to his uncle, 'but I believe that it would revive entirely with the arrival of Your Majesty.'[21]

Stanisław had begun sending units down to Kozienice to start forming a base camp for the four Guards regiments and two others which were completing recruitment. He was to follow himself. His chamberlain Franciszek Ryx was dusting down tents and selecting drapes, carpets, furniture and table-silver. He purchased 300 pounds of candles, quantities of linen, and supplies of every sort. Carriages were repaired and greased, and waggons built to carry all the equipment, which even included the king's sporting guns.[22] Although he was not looking forward to the discomforts involved, Stanisław was beginning to enjoy the role of military monarch, and seized the opportunity to institute a new decoration, the *Virtuti Militari*. Inevitably, he had a somewhat picturesque view of the situation and recommended the use of American tactics. 'Above all, harry and threaten constantly, that is how Burgoyne and Cornwallis were defeated,' he lectured his 'dear Pepi'.[23] But on the day Stanisław was writing those words, 14 June, Poniatowski, who had held strong positions at Lubar for two weeks, found himself suddenly outflanked by the Russians. He had to cut and run in order to save his army, and as he prepared to do so he penned a desperate letter to his uncle painting a vivid picture of the straits he was in and the unreality of trying to beat the Russians.

Stanisław seldom allowed himself to forget for long his underlying conviction that the matter could only ultimately be settled by negotiation, and by the middle of June a number of different channels of communication were open. Using Stanisław's private agent Simone Corticelli in Vienna, Feliks Potocki was inviting the king to abandon the constitution and join him in the Confederation of Targowica. Stanisław was prepared to negotiate only with Russia, but Deboli in St Petersburg could not gain access to the vice-chancellor. Stanisław wrote to Stackelberg, now in Stockholm, urging him to exert his influence at the Russian court in Poland's favour.[24] Adam Czartoryski was despatched to Vienna to seek Austrian support and to liaise with the English ambassador Sir Robert Murray Keith. Stanisław wrote to the Foreign Secretary Lord Grenville asking for England's diplomatic support, although he did not entertain high hopes of this.[25] To his surprise, however, the response was positive.[26]

English public opinion had been stirred, and a subscription was started to raise money for the Polish cause. The Lord Mayor of London launched it with 1,000 guineas, followed by William Wilberforce, Josiah Wedgwood and Richard Brinsley Sheridan.[27] Bukaty's embassy in Manchester Square was besieged by British officers volunteering to fight in Poland.[28] 'Keith in Vienna says: If only the Poles can hold out for a few weeks longer, they may find friends whom they did not know of before,' Stanisław reported to Bukaty. 'Try to find out in

London whether these words mean anything.'[29] In the mean time, he sent *Merentibus* medals to Edmund Burke and the editors of the *Sun* and the *Morning Chronicle*. Stanisław followed up every lead, and at the beginning of July even met with Descorches to examine the possibilities of French help. Piattoli had gone to Dresden, from where he opened negotiations with the Russian minister in Berlin. Meanwhile Kołłątaj tried the Russian ambassador in Warsaw, suggesting the old idea of offering the Polish succession to Constantine.

Józef Poniatowski's despairing letter from Lubar alarmed the Straż and the War Council, and at their respective meetings on 18 June both were unanimous in urging Stanisław to seek an accommodation with Russia. Orders were sent off to Poniatowski to arrange a cease-fire, and on the following day Chreptowicz presented Bulgakov with a formal proposal to negotiate. Bulgakov said that Russia would not negotiate with the king, only with the rightful leaders of the Polish nation – the Confederation of Targowica. But he suggested that the king could write directly to Catherine. This Stanisław did, after consulting with Ignacy Potocki, Chreptowicz and Kołłątaj:

Madame Ma Soeur,
I shall employ neither detours nor lengthy phrases; they suit neither my character nor my position. I will explain myself with frankness, for it is to you that I write. Be pleased to read me with kindness and attention. Be good enough to remember what I gave you in writing on your galley at Kaniów. If my efforts for the success of that plan had no effect, Your Imperial Majesty knows only too well that it is not I who is to blame. Any discussion of what followed would be superfluous here, and would remedy nothing. I therefore pass to the present moment, and I shall speak clearly.

It is your need, Madame, to have influence in Poland, and to be able to move your troops through it without hindrance every time you wish to deal with the Turks or with Europe. Our need is to safeguard ourselves from the continual revolutions which every interregnum must necessarily bring about, by making our neighbours intervene, by forcing us to arm ourselves against each other. We also need a form of government better ordered than previously.

The moment and the means to reconcile all this is here. Give us as my successor your grandson Prince Constantine; let an eternal alliance unite the two countries; let a trade treaty useful to both be joined to it . . .

I realise that you may think that the power you hold in your hand is capable of bringing about all that you demand in your declaration without any compromise. To that, I can only reply that I cannot believe that your heart, which I flatter myself to know, would prefer the means of extreme harshness to those which, while being far more gentle, would nevertheless satisfy your wishes and your glory . . .

Forgive me, Madame, if I have put neither grand phrases nor style in this letter. I dare to hope that, even if unhappily for me you were to reject my idea, you will not be wounded by my sincerity. I desire nothing more in this world than to be able to sign myself forever,

of Your Imperial Majesty
the good brother, friend and neighbour,
Stanisław Augustus rex.[30]

The letter was sent on 22 June, and there followed a long wait. Potocki and Kołłątaj got down to work on conditions and concessions on which the negotiations could hinge.

The request for an armistice had met with a haughty response. 'To demand an armistice is to presume that this is a case of war between one Power and another,' Vice-Chancellor Ostermann replied. 'This presumption bears no relation to the true state of affairs, which is that the Empress is merely acting in complete and close union with the true Commonwealth against its internal enemies.'[31] The Russian armies therefore continued to advance.

Stanisław instructed his nephew to avoid giving battle and to fall back closer to Warsaw. He decided to make his own camp outside Praga rather than at Kozienice, and ordered back those troops that had already been sent there. But on 2 July he reported that his camp would not be ready for another four or five days. 'If Zabiełło's 12,000 men were to draw closer to Warsaw, and if you were unfortunately forced to do the same, which God forbid, we would then have about 36 or 40 thousand men altogether; and with that we could perhaps do something, or at least negotiate with more honour.'[32]

Stanisław made frantic efforts to keep his nephew supplied with victuals and munitions, which was no easy task. The lack of well-oiled administrative channels and of a proper quartermastership also vitiated attempts to get the fresh recruits equipped and despatched to the front. Attempts to buy arms in Prussia and Saxony were proving fruitless. Acts of touching patriotism, such as the gift of ten cannon from the cities of Kurland, were of little use. While he struggled manfully with these pedestrian problems, Stanisław also found himself having to defend his nephew and himself from attack on the home front. The continuous retreat of the Polish forces gave rise to all sorts of suspicions. 'Several have gone so far as to voice the most insulting suspicions of me or at least of the people who are closest to me,' Stanisław complained to his nephew.[33]

He longed for him to deliver 'a good blow', but entreated him not to expose himself unnecessarily. For Stanisław the survival of the army and of his nephew were more important than any victory, and he told him not to worry about the civilians 'who would like a victory every 8 days'.[34] They soon got it. Poniatowski had escaped the Russian encirclement without any serious losses, and four days later, on 19 June, won a victory at Zieleńce. He failed to pursue his advantage after the battle, so he did not actually knock out Kakhovsky's force. But his army was beginning to function well, as officers and men gained experience and confidence. He now felt that if only he could obtain supplies and reinforcements he could engage Kakhovsky decisively. Stanisław was inordinately proud of his nephew, and greeted news of the victory with deep satisfaction. 'I embrace you a thousand times,' he wrote. 'This is the first pitched battle the Poles have won since the days of King Jan.'[35] He sent him the first gold *Virtuti Militari* decoration, and enclosed a batch for Kościuszko, Mokronowski and other officers who had distinguished themselves. 'Embrace all your brave companions-in-arms, all the new knights, for me. Oh, why can you not embrace yourself for me! But perhaps it is best so. You would smother yourself,' he wrote.[36]

Poniatowski's camp was nevertheless visited by a stream of 'commissioners' of one sort or another whose object was to check up on his loyalty. Their suspicions reflected the uncertainty that gripped the whole country. In the first weeks of the war everyone made the right patriotic noises and the sceptics were careful to hide their feelings – in May an unidentified 'Patriotic Society' plastered Warsaw with posters calling for the lynching of all 'enemies of the constitution'. The Austrian ambassador nevertheless detected much fence-sitting.[37] 'One hears many erstwhile supporters of the constitution of 3 May openly speaking against its creators and accusing them of having traded promises without coverage, deceived the nation, and brought it to its present sorry predicament,' he reported on 27 June.[38]

The structures of the nascent state stood up well, and the Civil and Military Commissions functioned loyally and efficiently throughout the war. The civic bodies and indeed the populations of the towns and cities threw themselves into the cause with enthusiasm, and merchants all over the country donated supplies of every sort. In Berdyczów, the firms of Jenni and Company and Chaim Chmielnicki gave Poniatowski horses, uniforms and even a supply of trumpets and fifes for the army. On the other hand, there were riots against recruitment in Warsaw in June, and a very high rate of desertion.[39] Poniatowski found the peasantry supine in its attitude towards his army, and in July he suggested issuing a manifesto granting freedom to the peasants in order to raise more men.[40] While there was much bluster about volunteers, few were coming forward of their own accord. On 4 July Stanisław issued a stirring call to arms, but this produced scant results. In Wilno, for instance, the call for volunteers had yielded a total of 325 men, and the picture was hardly more encouraging elsewhere.[41]

This might possibly have changed if Stanisław himself had made a decisive show of commitment to the war by taking the field. But this was something he hesitated to do. It was the first time since his election that he was in a position of real power, and the first time that his people expected him to make a decision on their behalf. This belated and unexpected trust was placed in him at the most difficult moment of his reign. His feelings had triumphed and led him to abandon his lifelong policy of loyalty to Russia, but they could not silence the voice of reason for long. He was excited by dreams of glory, and confessed to Glayre that 'the idea of meeting death together with the army was tempting,' but he felt grave doubts as to the usefulness of further operations. With his usual thoroughness he envisaged the risks inherent in every course of action, and his family, led by his brother the Primate, were exerting strong pressure on him to dissociate himself from the Patriots and the work of the Great Seym.

On 11 July the four Guards regiments marched out of Warsaw and set up camp outside Praga. Stanisław's equipment went with them, and he himself drove out to the camp. But after inspecting it and having lunch, he returned to Warsaw. The next morning a lampoon announced that 'The directors of the National Theatre have the honour to inform the despairing public that a new comedy will be performed, composed by the War Council and entitled *Expedition against the Mosquitos, or the Glorious Camp of Praga*. Immediately following this, Russian and Prussian actors will perform a tragedy entitled *The Conquest of Poland*. As the Treasury has expended some 20 million złoty on staging the tragedy, the spectacle will be free.'[42] A couple of days later he visited the camp again. 'If nothing comes from Petersburg today or tomorrow,' Stanisław wrote to Deboli, 'I shall have to take some action, so as not to lose this army of ours in vain.'[43] Two days later he despatched most of it to Brześć to help Zabiełło hold the line of the Bug.

A mood of despondency had settled on even the most active members of Stanisław's ministry. Stanisław Małachowski and the finance Minister Tomasz Ostrowski resigned from the War Council, Kołłątaj started secretly negotiating with the Targowicans, and even Ignacy Potocki was bereft of his usual defiance. 'I received your letter and read despair in it,' his brother Jerzy wrote from Stockholm on 20 July. 'You must. fight, brother, and not give way.'[44] But his exhortations arrived too late.

Poniatowski had to keep retreating in order to avoid encirclement, and whenever he took up strong positions, he would run out of ammunition and supplies after a few days. Michał Lubomirski had decided that the war was lost, and therefore earned some future Russian goodwill by secreting the large store of supplies Poniatowski had expected to find at Dubno, which would have permitted him to hold out there for a couple of weeks at least. In spite of much reinforcement, both in regular echelons and volunteers, his forces never rose above 18,000 men, due to natural attrition and desertion. On 10 July he had taken up positions along the Bug, which he held successfully for over a week. On 18 July Kakhovsky concentrated his entire force against Kościuszko's division at Dubienka, but was beaten back with heavy losses. On 14 July the army of Lithuania won a skirmish on the river Zelwa, and on 23 July it held off the Russians at Brześć. But none of these successes could influence the course of events, which would be decided by Catherine's response to Stanisław's offer.

'We are in the most painful anticipation and perplexity,' Stanisław wrote to his nephew.[45] He comforted himself with the illusion that the delay was a hopeful sign. But Catherine was not delaying because she was considering his proposals, but because she wanted to be in possession of as much of Poland as possible before she began negotiating with anyone. She was outraged by the Polish military successes and, as Deboli reported to Stanisław, 'ill-humour settled over Tsarskoe Selo' after news of Zieleńce and Dubienka.[46] The Polish proposals had been discussed by her council on 2 July, and their cornerstone, the idea of Constantine taking the Polish throne, was poorly received. Catherine saw in it no more than a ploy to gain time on the one hand, and an attempt to set Prussia and Austria against Russia on the other.[47]

Her answer arrived in Warsaw on the night of 21 July, and it flattened whatever hopes Stanisław still nourished. She rejected his proposals outright, and demanded that he accede to the Confederation of Targowica immediately. Not only was he to submit to them, he was to put his signature to a document stating that everything that had been done since 1788 had been illegal and nefarious. The document was drawn up in language calculated to wound his feelings and tarnish his reputation, since he was to denounce and disavow the greatest and most cherished achievement of his life. Stanisław sent Chreptowicz to see Bulgakov to find out whether there might be any room at all left for manœuvre, although he realised that Catherine must be in an intransigent mood.[48] Bulgakov confirmed that she would only accept complete submission.

Stanisław was in a state of terrible agitation. He oscillated between a determination to fight on to the last and a desire to abdicate, and some of his entourage feared he might try to take his own life.[49] His brothers, his sister Ludwika and other old friends managed to calm him down and dissuade him from anything drastic. It was not difficult for them to make him see reason – he was only too aware of the pointlessness of every course. But during the past two years he had suspended his natural scepticism and finally come to believe that he could achieve his Providential destiny. Although he now saw full well that it had been but a dream, he could not bear to give it up. His somewhat naïve imagination kept conjuring up plans to join the army and seek glory or death with it. 'If I were to take the army into the Sandomierz or Kraków areas, I might find a few favourable positions among the hills, but hunger and penury would find us there too,' he debated with himself.[50]

Stanisław called an extraordinary council of ministers for the following day, 23 July, and by the time it convened he had recovered his self-possession. The meeting was attended by the Primate, Ignacy Potocki, Tomasz Ostrowski, Chreptowicz, Jacek Małachowski, the two marshals of the Seym Stanisław Małachowski and Kazimierz Sapieha, Michał Mniszech, Stanisław Sołtan, Kołłątaj, Antoni Dziekoński and Ludwik Tyszkiewicz – twelve in all. Kazimierz Ponia-towski was also present, but only as an observer.

Stanisław read out Catherine's letter and summed up the situation as he saw it. He reminded them that there were now only some 30,000 troops left in the field, and that although there were reserves and more could be raised, there were no supplies for them. The arsenal and the Treasury were empty, and Prussia had blocked the import of arms purchased in Saxony. He was not being quite candid, as there were certainly more than 30,000 troops left and there was still a two-month supply of powder and shot. There was no immediate shortage of money, as taxes were being regularly collected in spite of the war, and a Dutch loan had been successfully negotiated.[51] But this was of little consequence. Even in the unlikely event that Poland could beat Russia's armies, the war would not be won, and Russia would buy Prussian assistance with a new partition. On the other hand, in her proclamation to the Confederation of Targowica, Catherine had promised to guar-antee Polish territorial integrity. So the alternatives were all-out war which would inevitably end in partition, or accession to the confeder-ation, which would plunge Poland back into the sort of subservience she had been in before 1788 but preserve the country. There was little doubt in Stanisław's mind which was the course to take, for, as he put it in a letter to Glayre, 'A kingdom is not a warship, that a captain can blow up to save his reputation.'[52]

Stanisław asked those present for their opinions. The first to speak was the Primate, who strongly advocated acceding to the confeder-ation. Ignacy Potocki said the king ought to call the nation to arms on the French model and fight to the death, or, failing that, to abdicate and flee the country. He was supported by Stanisław Sołtan and Tomasz Ostrowski, who were in favour of staking all on one last battle. Stanisław Małachowski suggested calling the Seym and letting it decide, which was not feasible.[53] Sapieha at first agreed with the Primate, but then changed his mind and sided with his colleague

Stanisław Małachowski.[54] But Mniszech, Jacek Małachowski, Tyszkiewicz, Dziekoński, Chreptowicz and Kołłątaj agreed with the Primate. Kołłątaj felt 'that Russia may sooner or later accept our project regarding Constantine, and that, having amended a few articles inconvenient to her, she will allow us to keep the constitution and all the laws passed during this Seym'.[55] On the face of it, there was not much difference between the situation now and those which obtained in 1767 and 1775. In both cases Russia had needed the king to front the confederation she had set up in order to impose her policies. Experience had shown that she did not stand by the toadies she used for this kind of work, and that, after a certain amount of compromise on both sides, the governance of Poland could be repossessed by Stanisław and those best suited to carry it on.

'And you must join the Confederation of Targowica today, not waiting for tomorrow, merciful master,' Kołłątaj urged. 'Every moment is precious, for it is bought with Polish blood.'[56] Accordingly, Stanisław sent a letter to Catherine agreeing to join the confederation and placing himself and his country at her mercy.

23

Nemesis

'The sacrifice of one's self-esteem is the most sublime of all, and the one of which only truly great men are capable,' Piattoli wrote to Stanisław from Leipzig on hearing of the capitulation. But he went on to sketch out the king's predicament with merciless clarity. 'Until now, Sire, the calamities of your reign were justified by the resistance with which you met from the nation: from 3 May that resistance ceased; and now the nation can regret only the confidence which it accorded you.' None of this would apply if Stanisław managed to surmount the crisis with the country intact. If he failed, Piattoli warned that 'I can only foresee unhappy days and the loss of your reputation for all ages to come.' If he succeeded, his act of capitulation on 23 July would go down in history as a great and noble gesture.[1] Stanisław had travelled this road before, and was relatively confident that he would be able to outmanoeuvre the Targowica clique and reach a compromise with Russia which might save some of the reforms brought in by the Great Seym. But it would be a long, lonely road.

On 24 July, as news of the capitulation leaked out, crowds gathered outside the house of Kazimierz Sapieha, who made a fiery speech denouncing the king's behaviour. They went on to look for Stanisław Małachowski and Ignacy Potocki. The first was out, the second refused to show himself. The people seemed more bewildered than angry, but the strong feelings were nevertheless alarming. Stanisław despatched a courier to his nephew, asking him to send the

379

Footguards back to Warsaw. On the morrow, even larger crowds gathered in the streets, and their mood was more aggressive, Jacek Małachowski's windows were smashed, and walls were daubed with slogans denouncing Stanisław's treachery and cowardice. Street-corner orators demanded his head, and on 28 July a drunken nobleman climbed on to the stage at the National Theatre and offered his estate to anyone who would avenge Poland's honour by assassinating the king.[2] Stanisław remained at the Castle, deserted by all save his family and Chreptowicz. 'The difficulties of his situation affect him more than ever', noted Lucchesini, 'and his health is growing visibly worse each day.'[3]

The mob had no leader, and it was baffled by the evident acquiescence of the leading Patriots in the king's policy. Kołłątaj had slipped out of the capital on the night of 24 July, making for the frontier. Over the next couple of days Potocki and a dozen or so others followed suit. The two marshals of the Seym, Małachowski and Sapieha, made formal depositions in the Warsaw statute books denouncing the Confederation of Targowica and declaring that the Seym ought to resume its sittings, but they did not exercise the right which the constitution gave them of convoking the Seym to defy the king. They too left for Saxony, leaving Stanisław to sort things out.

By the end of the week the crowds had dispersed, but the ill-will did not dissipate itself with them. 'Having considered and calculated everything, Stanisław Augustus in effect did what was best,' wrote Piotr Świtkowski, editor of the *Historical and Political Journal*.[4] This echoed the views of a silent majority, but brought little comfort. Nor did the sympathetic letters from Ignacy Potocki and Kołłątaj, who assured him that his merit in giving the country a constitution and his selflessness in standing hostage for it assured him everlasting glory. 'While a contrary fate refuses us everything, we still stand before Europe with a clear conscience; we stand before the judgment of the whole world and the furthest posterity with the greatest confidence that we will not lose our case,' Kołłątaj reassured him.[5] But Stanisław would have to swallow many a reproach before he could be vindicated, as few people could be expected to understand the motives that had led him to act as he had. The army, and his beloved nephew, were a case in point.

There was consternation when the first rumours of the king's decision reached Poniatowski's camp on 24 July. 'I expected everything, but I did not expect baseness of this kind,' he wrote to Izabela Czartoryska.[6] In spite of the difficult conditions and the shortages, morale had been high.[7] 'It is impossible to describe the dismay, the despair and the anger against the king,' wrote Kościuszko.[8] That evening they rode over to nearby Puławy in quest of more information, with generals Stanisław Mokronowski and Michał Wielhorski. It was there, under the inspiration of Izabela Czartoryska's patriotic ardour, that a plan was hatched to bring the king to the camp, by force if necessary, and to carry on a fight to the death.[9]

The following day Poniatowski received a letter from Stanisław enclosing a copy of Catherine's ultimatum and giving his reasons for acceding to the confederation. He begged his 'dear Pepi' not to upset himself, and promised that things would work out well if only he would keep the army calm and disciplined.[10] But Poniatowski had already sent Mokronowski and Wielhorski to Warsaw with a letter in which he begged his uncle to come and join him. It is possible they intended to employ force, as General Eustachy Sanguszko and his brigade, camped outside Warsaw, were standing by to escort the king.[11] But they came back with only a letter from Stanisław. 'If, which God forbid, you should persist in what you have written to me,' he wrote, 'I am lost, and, what is more, the country is lost.'[12]

Józef Poniatowski had a rigid sense of honour, and while he understood the king's argument, he found it repugnant. He was torn between opposing instincts, and sought a desperate way out. On the morning of 26 July he rode out and invited death by charging a Russian unit he encountered. He was rescued unhurt by an aide, and by that afternoon he had recovered himself. As instructed, he took steps to arrange a cease-fire with General Kakhovsky. He abandoned the plan to abduct the king. He felt bitter towards his uncle, and sent him his formal resignation from the army, as did Kościuszko and a number of other senior officers. Nor did he spare his uncle some stinging reproaches.

These were particularly wounding to Stanisław. He was quite used to being misunderstood or reviled, but found it hard to bear this from his beloved nephew. He had not taken the decision to capitulate lightly, and he had not been prompted by cowardice. He was certainly no warrior, but there is no reason to believe that he saw the prospect of a hopeless campaign, followed by exile in, say, Austria, as any more frightening than that of facing an angry Warsaw mob, of swallowing the affronts of the Targowicans, followed possibly by Russian captivity or exile. He did consider joining the army in a last desperate effort, and the idea even held strong attractions for his sometimes melodramatic imagination. 'You may be certain that I value neither my position nor my life, for I see ahead of me only the most desolate tasks. But as for joining you and seeking death in the way you suggest, I can tell you that after a week of arguing with everyone about me, I at last gave way to reason, which was bound to triumph,' he wrote to his nephew on 27 July. 'The self-esteem of a king has to give way to his first duty, which is always to do, if not the greatest good, then at least the least harm to his country.'[13]

Stanisław tried everything to make them reconsider their resignations. 'With tears in my eyes, I told him that we had earned universal esteem by fighting for our country, our government and our king, and that we would never do anything against our convictions and our honour,' Kościuszko wrote to Izabela Czartoryska.[14] Poniatowski was equally impervious. Neither would even listen to the compromise Stanisław suggested, that they take a long leave but remain in command. He had no option but to accept their resignations.

Their attitude lowered Stanisław's morale and upset his calculations, but these proved to be vain anyway. The Targowicans had assumed that they would be greeted enthusiastically by a significant proportion of the population, and Catherine had taken this for granted. Hence her official position that she was helping an allied state recover from an illegal coup. Her armies entered Poland as 'liberators': they had instructions to treat the Poles in a friendly manner and only act against the 'enemies of the Commonwealth'.[15] But not only did people not flock to the side of the Targowicans as they marched into Poland, the majority of the population denounced them as traitors. 'Your husband has disappointed me most grievously,' Catherine told Potyomkin's niece Alexandra Branicka, 'and now I see that I shall have to do everything myself with the bayonet.'[16]

The unpopularity of the Targowicans and the fact that all those least dear to Catherine had abandoned Warsaw should have played into Stanisław's hand. In sending the letter accepting the Targowica manifesto to her, not to Feliks Potocki, he had put himself forward as one who could achieve her ends in Poland more effectively than

Potocki and his associates. But Catherine no longer trusted him. 'His Polish Majesty has taken it upon himself to irritate and excite his nation against Russia,' she wrote to Grimm in August. 'There is no treachery or duplicity that he is not employing with regard to us even at this moment.'[17] This was unfortunate, as it led her to adopt a characteristically personal response, and, as Deboli reported to Stanisław, 'obstinacy and the desire to dominate outweigh any considerations of policy'.[18] Many Russians, both at court and in the army, felt sympathy for the Polish position, and Bezborodko himself favoured an indulgent approach, but he was no longer in control of Russian policy on Poland.

While offering co-operation to Catherine, Stanisław did not neglect the Targowicans. He enjoined his political supporters to adhere to the confederation, intending to take it over by sheer weight of numbers, as Potocki and his friends were having difficulty in mustering supporters. They rallied a few former Barians and some drifting malcontents such as the Chancellor of Lithuania Aleksander Sapieha and Bishop Massalski, but the only people they could count on were unscrupulous upstarts such as Józef Ankwicz and Piotr Ożarowski. Predictably, disagreements had arisen among the leaders, and Stanisław was hoping to exploit these. The day after despatching his letter of capitulation to Catherine, he wrote to Feliks Potocki in conciliatory tones, suggesting they work for Poland together. The Primate wrote to Bishop Kossakowski, pointing out the necessity for an understanding between them, and asking him to come to Warsaw for consultations. But the Targowicans did not feel confident enough to face Warsaw, and set up their seat in Grodno instead.

Feliks Potocki was in no mood for compromise. On 2 August he wrote back rejecting Stanisław's advances, in a letter that was as rude as it was incoherent. On the same day he wrote to Kakhovsky stating that 'The only way of ensuring the nation's attachment to Moscow is by deflecting all the resentment of the Poles on to the person of the king.'[19] Two days later Szymon Kossakowski, who had assumed the title of hetman, entered Warsaw with the Russian troops to accept the city's act of adherence to the confederation. He was annoyed to discover that the king's supporters had confederated the city on behalf of Targowica, thereby placing themselves in charge. The tone he took with Stanisław when he called at the Castle was so out of place that Bulgakov himself saw fit to reprimand him.[20]

Feliks Potocki ordered Stanisław to make a formal act of loyalty direct to the leadership of the confederation. Stanisław swallowed hard and did so, on 25 August, hoping that he would soon start exerting an influence over it. But the Targowicans were determined to cut him out of the political scene. While they did not dare establish themselves in Warsaw, on 9 September they set up a delegation there, under Piotr Ożarowski, an unpleasant nonentity whose career had been launched in the 1780s when he had managed to introduce his wife into Stackelberg's bed. Ożarowski set about dismantling the work of the Great Seym and imposing the new order on Warsaw in a high-handed manner, ignoring the king in most things. Stanisław tried to maintain a dignified calm, but when Ożarowski came to demand his assent to the Guards being removed from his command, he could contain himself no longer. 'You have taken so much from me already, you might as well be damned and take the Guards!' he shouted.[21] The news that the monarchy had been abolished in France on 10 August did nothing to strengthen his position.

It soon became apparent to Stanisław that Catherine had decided 'to degrade, weaken and stupefy us, to isolate us from other nations, to ruin the army, the currency and the educational system, and to reinstate the old sarmatian prejudices'.[22] And since they were good for nothing else, she would use the Targowicans as a local police force to help her armies achieve it. Every single official, judge, officer or landowner was bullied to sign a document allying himself with the confederation. If he refused, he was dismissed, penalised, robbed and often beaten up. The confederation's headquarters in Grodno issued manifestos condemning the 'crimes' of the Great Seym, and its agents went about looking for evidence of complicity in them. They began a minor reign of terror. 'It will soon be a sin to think,' the Primate warned one correspondent.[23] He himself had come under attack in his capacity as President of the Commission for National Education, an institution for which the Targowicans had little sympathy. Six months later the Commission was abolished.

Much of this execrable behaviour was the result of personal greed on the part of the Targowicans, most of whom saw their chance of personal gain as the ship of state listed and foundered. 'Having dragged us into this dirty work, sir, you cannot prevent us from taking our reward,' one of them retorted, when reproved by Feliks Potocki for looting.[24] Adam Poniński was back in Warsaw, attracted by the prospect of plunder. He was reinstated in all his titles and honours, and received a handout of cash from the Russian ambassador.

The army was persecuted in particularly malicious ways. The wearing of the *Virtuti Militari* medals was forbidden. Any officer who had distinguished himself was interrogated and hounded. Poniatowski wrote to Feliks Potocki begging him to stop these persecutions, and Kościuszko offered to stand hostage for his officers, to no avail. The confrontation between Poniatowski and Feliks Potocki threatened to upset Stanisław's attempts to conciliate the latter, so he ordered his nephew to leave the country. Poniatowski obeyed, with a heavy heart, as he complained in a letter from Austria:

I was weary of service, I was aggrieved to find myself a party or accomplice to what is presently being done in Poland, but the unhappiness I felt and the misery which I saw you suffering made my heart feel all the more keenly the attachment I feel for you. Not having to blush at my actions, and being fortunate that my position allowed me to stand aside from everything and did not even oblige me to hide my feelings, I began to see the very misfortune of my country as a solace in my position, and I told myself that if I could no longer serve my king and my country, I would at least be able to look after a dear father, I would share his sufferings and I would console him in adversity. My frank manner of thinking and of showing my feelings would help to justify his reputation in the eyes of the public, he would be pitied for the harshness of his fate and not blamed.[25]

Their relationship had developed into something far more profound and important to them both than the original tenderness felt by the uncle towards his winsome nephew and the orphaned nephew's need for a father-figure. The two had contrasting natures, made up of the same characteristics differently mixed and conditioned. As Stanisław saw himself being driven by his politically motivated compromises further and further away from his own principles, he felt a growing pride in his nephew's intransigent stand by his. It was as though this adopted son were vindicating Stanisław's own character by voicing and acting on sentiments that Stanisław would gladly have espoused himself. 'My life has been more that of a soldier than a courtier,' Poniatowski once wrote to his uncle, almost apologetically.[26] While his emotional honesty and formidable sense of honour were offended by the king's policy and produced outbursts in which he censured him for it, he admired his uncle for sacrificing his feelings to the national cause, and his greatest fear was that public opinion would not appreciate it. 'Oh Sire, why are you not, why can you not be, a private individual,' he lamented. 'How much less misery, how much more joy I should feel if I could see you enjoy one of those moments when, away from all care, from all intrigue, you can simply be yourself, loved and adored by all who surround you.'[27] It was a dream that often visited Stanisław, who liked to fantasise about retiring to the country with his favourite conversational companions.[28] 'Yes, I should certainly be happy to be able to live as a private individual with real friends, such as yourself,' he wrote back. 'But this sad scene must be played out to the end one way or another.'[29]

They were destined to remain separated by politics. Although he had left the country, Poniatowski continued a public exchange of letters, trading insults with Feliks Potocki and finally challenging him to a duel. Stanisław tried every form of persuasion to make him desist, and by December relations between them had become strained. 'You sacrifice your reputation without producing any benefits for the country,' he taunted Stanisław, who tried to calm him and persuade him to go to Italy or England.[30] But he would not hear of it and refused to withdraw his open letter to Potocki, and as a result his estate was sequestrated. 'You see where disobedience to my orders has landed you!' Stanisław wrote, pointing out that now his mother would have nothing to live on.[31] Russia demanded that Poniatowski leave Vienna and take himself further away. He would have gone to America, but he could not stand the idea of never seeing his uncle again, so he went to Brussels, where he thought of taking service in the English army.

Poniatowski was right: Stanisław was getting nowhere. In mid-October 1792, after a conference they held in Dresden, Kołłątaj, Ignacy Potocki and Piattoli sent Stanisław fulsome suggestions for the settlement he was to negotiate with Russia. From where they were it seemed that he was in a strong position to reach an understanding with Catherine over the heads of the Targowicans.[32] The trouble was that Stanisław did not know to whom to speak. In the days of

Radom, it had been Repnin who decided everything. After the partition, it had been Stackelberg. But Bulgakov was no pro-consul, and he had no brief to take a hand in the proceedings. Stanisław could not get a dialogue going with the Targowicans either. In October, the Primate and Chreptowicz had met Feliks Potocki, but he refused their invitation to negotiate with the king.

Stanisław resorted to indirect means. He suggested producing a barrage of pamphlets aimed at both Potocki and Catherine. 'The style, the titles and the angle would have to be varied,' he explained to Piattoli. 'Some would have to be addressed to the soul of Feliks, to his patriotism, his honour; others should demonstrate to Russia how much more advantageous it would be for her to win over the Poles through kindness than through oppression . . . There must be no praise for me in them, rather some slight discontent, as though I had been in too great a hurry to give in to pressure.' He was by now prepared to sacrifice his reputation, to depart from the constitution, and even to step down himself, if such means could guarantee the survival of the country, which was beginning to look doubtful.[33] Piattoli insisted that all was not yet lost, and that 'time will no doubt alter things, and you will have saved your nation and repaired your honour'. Glayre advised Stanisław to affect 'the gloomy silence of discouraged virtue'.[34] But this discouragement often gave way to moments of despair, in which Stanisław would give vent to his regret at having embarked on the course of compromise.

A mood of deep despondency settled over him. 'He is sometimes so lost in thought that it is difficult to get an answer out of him,' Ignacy Potocki's agent in Warsaw reported.[35] He was no doubt pondering the mysterious ways of Providence. He even began to study the kabbala with the assistance of a learned Jew.[36] He took refuge in morose stoicism, and diligently supervised work on the Rotunda at Łazienki, which was to be a Pantheon to those kings he admired most. He would never see it completed. He was again penniless, as revenues from Crown estates dried up and the Treasury was in the hands of the Targowicans. He cancelled all the extra tables at the Castle, and ran down his court. 'It is cruel to have to dismiss servants after 30 years,' he wrote to Glayre.[37] It could not have been much easier bearing with the worried nagging of various members of his family, and particularly Elżbieta Grabowska, who contemplated with horror the possibility of the family business folding. Such fears were not misplaced for, aside from the political imponderables, the financial situation in Poland was catastrophic. In the late autumn of 1792 one bank after another failed, starting with those of Fryderyk Karbit, Maciej Łyszkiewicz and Prot Potocki. In February 1793 it was Tepper's turn, and by the spring of that year only Piotr Blank was still solvent. Stanisław nevertheless managed to put the eloquent finishing touches to the interiors of the palace of Łazienki: the main hall over which his spirit reigned through the figure of Solomon, and, more telling still, the magnificent ballroom by Kamsetzer, in which the figures of Apollo and Hercules stonily eye their respective nemeses – in the shapes of Daphne and Dejanira.

In his fear of inactivity, Stanisław turned to writing his memoirs again, but soon abandoned these in favour of a more urgent task. As the chances of his being able to vindicate his policy by a political triumph over the Targowicans receded, he felt the need to fortify his reputation against possible attack. He dictated a short book entitled *Opinion on the King of Poland*, in which he told the story of his reign, concentrating on the events of the past four years. It contained no special pleading, merely the rational basis for his actions. It was finished in January 1793, and he sent it in secret to his agent in Gdańsk, Frederick Ernest Hennig, instructing him to publish it anonymously there. He also sent him the moulds he had secretly had made for the projected medal which Poniatowski had been given by his brother officers, with instructions for a number of pieces to be struck abroad.[38]

Stanisław could do nothing but wait for Catherine to reveal her intentions. The only reason he had acceded to Targowica was because she had promised the confederation that she would safeguard the country's territorial integrity, but her delay in making definite arrangements for the country suggested that she was considering other options. The uncertainty fostered an atmosphere which further polarised people and encouraged excesses. The Targowicans daily grew more rapacious and vengeful. They scooped up the estates not only of those like Kołłątaj whom they regarded as open enemies, but also of those like Kazimierz Sapieha, whose lands went to 'Hetman' Kossakowski, and of anyone else they could possibly implicate. They even tried to have Bishop Turski dismissed for having taken the oath in the Seym on 3 May 1791. Patriots fought back. Eustachy Sanguszko flouted the ban on wearing the *Virtuti Militari* by sporting an outsize version of the decoration and challenging anyone who so much as mentioned it. Lampoons, fliers and posters insulting the Targowicans and the Russians circulated everywhere, and Russian officers were frequently abused and sometimes set upon in the streets. The bodies of Russian soldiers were found in alleyways and out of the way spots.

The Russians responded by clamping down on anything that smelt of rebellion. Companies of troops were billeted on every house in Warsaw. People were arrested and questioned on a whim. All publications were scrutinised for subversive sentiments and newspapers were closed down. Plays were banned on the suspicion of having hidden significance. When someone thought they had seen a tricolour ribbon at a French draper's shop, this was searched and then closed down. French citizens of Warsaw had a hard time, and were interrogated at the Russian headquarters every time they received a letter from France. Both in the minds of Polish patriots and in those of their enemies, the cause of Poland was increasingly linked to that of revolutionary France. There was jubilation when Warsaw heard that the Prussian armies had been routed at Valmy on 20 September 1792. But this event did not bode well for Poland.

The Austro-Prussian alliance against revolutionary France was not a happy affair. Austria mistrusted her ally, with good reason, and kept trying to gain guarantees from her that she would not make arrangements with Russia behind her back, while at the same time fighting off Prussian greed over prizes in the west. After the coronation of Francis II as Holy Roman Emperor at Frankfurt in July, he and Frederick William had a particularly complicated bout of horse-trading about who would get what if and when the war was won. Bayreuth, Ansbach, Zweibrücken and Alsace were shunted about on paper as possibilities, while 'supplements' in Poland also came up with regularity. After Valmy, Prussia went into a sulk and declared that she could not go on fighting for putative future gains, and wanted to be indemnified at once, in Poland. She was in a strong position with respect to Austria, which needed Prussian military support, and with respect to Catherine, who wanted to see the French Revolution crushed at any cost. The only reason she was not sending her own army to France was that she needed it in Poland.

Catherine had not intended to diminish Poland further, but Prussia had to be induced to go on fighting France, and if she would only do so at a price, then the price would have to be paid. 'Jacobin' Poland would pay for the war against Jacobin France. Catherine's resistance to partition was also eroded by other factors. One was that she had realised the Targowicans were not up to ruling Poland effectively, and their inept government would have to be supported by Russian bayonets. Another was that since the death of Potyomkin in October 1791, she had fallen under the influence of the Zubov brothers and their cronies, mostly younger men with no political vision, only a limitless lust for power and wealth. One thing many of them wanted was land. Catherine also needed it. Hundreds of officers had distinguished themselves in the Turkish wars, dozens of diplomats had served faithfully over the last decades, and many officials had worked hard to consolidate the empire. The traditional reward was the grant of an estate, but there was a shortage of land available in European Russia. Eastern Poland, on the other hand, was full of rich estates with nice houses, many of them, conveniently enough, belonging to people who had supported the Great Seym and the 1792 war against Russia.[39] Catherine reached her decision on 13 December 1792, and three days later informed Goltz that Prussia would get a share of Poland. 'Our great aim is, thanks be to God, fulfilled,' Frederick William proclaimed grandly to a cabinet meeting in Berlin on 31 December. 'It required efforts to attain it, but he who risks nothing gains nothing.'[40] Quite what he had risked is hard to see.

The treaty of partition was signed on 23 January 1793, but it was to remain secret until Catherine had prepared her ground. She despatched a new ambassador, Jacob Sievers, to Warsaw, and replaced General Kakhovsky with Igelström, who had been Repnin's strong-arm man in 1768. But Prussia, ever wary of the possibility of the prize escaping her, was not inclined to wait, and sent her troops in at once, allegedly in order to defend herself against 'the overflow of *French democratism*, and of the principles of that ghastly sect' the Jacobins.

Stanisław watched the Prussian troop movements in impotent alarm. He had no influence over events, and no insight into Catherine's policy. He tried to open up a new channel of communication with her, using Littlepage, who expressed the apparently innocent desire to go to St Petersburg as a private person and had managed to convince Igelström that he was prepared to sell himself to Russia. 'He is completely of our system,' Igelström assured Sievers. 'He has all the power over the mind of the king.'[41] But the canny Sievers saw through the ploy, and denied Littlepage permission to go.[42] Stanisław was prepared to use people of mixed loyalties, such as his secretary Christian Friese, and even those of his entourage, such as Karol Boskamp, whom he knew to be Russian agents, to break out of his isolation. He was beginning to feel old and redundant. The news that arrived from Paris at the beginning of February 1793, of the execution of Louis XVI, saddened and horrified him, as it did most of Europe, but in his position he must have also found it chilling.

The only thing that cheered him was the arrival of the new Russian ambassador, for he would now at least be able to communicate with someone in a position of responsibility. He had met Sievers forty years before in London, and knew him to be cultivated and sympathetic. On 15 February 1793, Sievers called and explained that Catherine was 'displeased with him'. Stanisław replied that he had always tried to remain loyal to her, and that it was she who had repeatedly placed him in impossible situations. Sievers promised to report all this faithfully, but requested that Stanisław make preparations to go to Grodno, where a new Seym would be called in the spring. 'The empress regards Warsaw as a brazier of Jacobinism,' he explained.[43] The following day Stanisław wrote to Catherine begging to be allowed to stay in Warsaw, but the reply that arrived at the end of the month was categorical.[44] It was clear that she wanted him out of Warsaw for a reason, and that reason could only be that an announcement on Poland's fate was imminent, an announcement that was expected to produce a strong reaction.

During a conversation on 21 February, Stanisław asked Sievers outright whether there was any truth in the rumours of a new partition. The ambassador answered that he knew nothing definite. He comforted Stanisław by saying that he, Sievers, had been sent to Poland to bandage its wounds, and that he would ask for his own recall if he could not achieve anything constructive.[45]

Throughout the rest of February and the whole of March, Sievers called on Stanisław every day or so, alternately cajoling and threatening. The king produced one excuse after another for not going to Grodno, even pretending to fall ill, but Sievers threatened to cut off his revenues, so that not only he but his entire court would starve.

Stanisław had never been very good at standing up to this kind of psychological warfare, and he was tired and uncertain as to whether he could influence events either way. At the end of March, after further exchanges of letters with Catherine, he caved in, on the solemn promise that the Prussians would not be allowed to occupy Warsaw, and that all his debts, amounting now to some 34 million złoty, would be paid by Russia.[46] He had no money at all, and Sievers had to advance him some in order to pay for the journey. On 2 April Sievers wrote assuring him that as long as he went along with Catherine's wishes, Poland would be preserved and given a good constitution.[47] Stanisław only half believed him, but he set off for Grodno on 4 April 1793. Crowds of people from every estate came to pay their respects, but he was so depressed and so full of foreboding that he would never see Warsaw again that he passed quickly through the crowded rooms without raising his eyes or pausing to talk to anyone.

He broke his journey to stay with his sister at Białystok. It was while he was there that the terms of the treaty signed by Russia and Prussia were published, on 7 April. And two days later, Sievers issued a declaration on behalf of his court. It explained that 'the empress, accustomed for the past thirty years to struggle against the perpetual agitations of [Poland]', had come to the end of her extraordinary patience. It went on to affirm that the Poles 'are striving to introduce into the heart of the Commonwealth that infernal doctrine which a sect, impious, sacrilegious and at the same time absurd, has conceived for the misery and the dissolution of all societies, religious, political and civil'. The establishment of such a dangerous hotbed of these ideas in Poland had naturally alarmed her peace-loving neighbours, who had combined together 'to seek the most appropriate measure for stifling the evil at birth and for preventing its contagion from reaching their own frontiers . . . They have recognized none as more efficacious for their respective security than to restrict the Polish Commonwealth within tighter limits, providing for her a substance and proportions more appropriate to an intermediary Power.' The proclamation declared that the country would be given a suitable form of government that would prevent the recurrence of similar problems, and invited the Poles to elect a Seym that would enact this 'salutary intention'.[48]

Stanisław was handed the treaty and the proclamation by

Littlepage 3 miles out of Białystok on the Grodno road. He turned back to Białystok, where he spent a few days in a state of shock. The sheer cynicism of it stunned him. 'One monarch was demanding reward for having crushed the constitution, the other for having helped surreptitiously in its passing; each of them strained to prove their respective rights in the case, which were in effect only the right of the strongest,' as one of the Russian generals put it.[49] What staggered Stanisław most was Catherine's behaviour. Until now, all her actions had been in some way explicable to him, but her agreement to this new partition was both cynical and stupid. It shattered his basic faith in her, and with it his lifelong policy. All his calculations had been upset, and now he would have to pay the price.

The policy of the émigré Patriots in Dresden was entirely in line with Stanisław's throughout the autumn of 1792, and Kołłątaj was the most sanguine in pursuing it. He had signed an act of accession to Targowica himself before leaving Warsaw, and intended to return as soon as it was safe to do so, in order to help Stanisław infiltrate and take over the confederation. He laid all his hopes on an accommodation with Russia, and was still writing to Bulgakov on the desirability of giving the Polish succession to Grand Duke Constantine.[50] It was not until the beginning of December that he came to realise that this policy was dead. 'It has now become quite clear that we cannot expect any honest settlement from Russia, for, as I presently perceive, all the courts are now interested solely in uniting against the French, and as reward for all their costs they intend a division of Poland, Germany and France,' he wrote to Małachowski. 'So now in the whole of Europe there are only two parties: France for the freedom of peoples against all the rulers, and all the monarchs against France for despotism and old traditions.'[51]

No sooner had rumours of partition begun to circulate, than the émigrés began to dissociate themselves from the king and the policy they had been pursuing jointly with him. Those who had advised and followed him now claimed that his capitulation had led directly to partition, and that it was his cowardice that had lost Poland. A new version of the momentous council meeting of 23 July 1792 was put about. Kołłątaj and the others had wanted to fight on, there had been plenty of munitions and sufficient reserves of cash, and it had only been the king's treachery that had forced them to capitulate.[52] 'It was even said that he had listened to news of the successes of the Polish armies with annoyance rather than joy,' one contemporary recorded.[53]

In the spring, a book entitled *The Establishment and Fall of the Polish Constitution of 3rd May* began to circulate in Poland. It propounded that Stanisław had done everything he could do to sabotage the reforms and the constitution, and, when he could no longer do so, 'became an indifferent witness to what the Seym had undertaken on his as well as the Nation's behalf'.[54] The book was written by Kołłątaj, with the help of Ignacy Potocki and Franciszek Dmochowski. It was designed primarily not to insult Stanisław, but to build the platform for a new policy. In order to carry on the struggle, they had to show that victory was possible. In order to persuade people of that, they had first to persuade them that victory had been within reach in 1792, and that the Polish nation was only robbed of it by a number of circumstances, the most important being the king's betrayal.

This view of things found favour with the majority, who could not accept the implications, any more than the real causes, of Poland's weakness. 'There were still ways of beating the Russian army,' claimed Kościuszko, supporting this with the dubious assertion that if all the remaining forces and volunteers had been gathered together, an army of 60,000 men could have been fielded. Citing the entirely inappropriate example of the American war, he asserted that the struggle could have been kept going indefinitely.[55] Only Józef Poniatowski now candidly admitted that there had been no hope whatever of defeating the Russians with the army at his disposal.[56]

The frustration and bitterness felt throughout the country was translated into anger. This could only be directed at Stanisław, since the perpetrators of Targowica had vanished from the stage. When news of the partition broke, Rzewuski wrote to Catherine protesting at her betrayal, but she dismissed his letter mockingly. She answered Feliks Potocki's appeal with the bland statement that everything had changed since she had guaranteed Poland's integrity twelve months earlier. He actually fainted from the shock when he read the letter. He hurried to St Petersburg to clear up what he thought was a misunderstanding. 'How are you, dear Count Potocki?' Catherine greeted him. 'I am well, most illustrious lady,' he replied, 'but my motherland . . . ' 'Your motherland is here!' she snapped, stamping the floor with her foot.[57] After this discomfiture, Potocki lost interest and went off to attend to his new mistress, Mrs Witt. Branicki was dancing attendance on Catherine at Tsarskoe Selo, playing whist and drinking hard. Rzewuski made several patriotic speeches blaming the proposed partition on everyone but himself, and then went abroad. The only remotely honourable member of Targowica, the former Barian Michał Walewski, also made patriotic speeches and issued manifestos, but he too resigned from the confederation at the end of April and retired from the scene.

All the original Targowicans publicly blamed Stanisław for the impending partition. Many of his traditional supporters, including Chreptowicz, Mniszech and Jacek Małachowski, who had all joined Targowica with him, now resigned. It was becoming clear that he was to be the sacrificial lamb – both for the Poles and for their enemies. Even in faraway England, Burke could see what faced Stanisław:

> It was not deemed a sufficient punishment for his past offences that he was reduced to see the destruction of his dearest hopes in the downfall of his country's liberty; and to give his sanction to proceedings which his heart and reason abhorred. To fill up the measure of his anguish and shame, it was thought necessary to make him the instrument of holding up to the world his own character in the most despicable light, as a consummate hypocrite, and betrayer of his people.[58]

24

Fallen Majesty

'Poor king! He is badly lodged, badly served, he is betrayed, treated disrespectfully – and yet he is a man who truly deserves to be loved,' Sievers wrote to his daughter Lisette, adding: 'If only you knew how I persecute him!'[1] A kind man with simple tastes, Sievers did not relish his task. 'Believe me, Your Majesty,' he said to Stanisław at the beginning of May 1793, 'that nobody can feel more keenly than I do how hard is the nature of my embassy.'[2] But Sievers was also a conscientious official, and he had a job to do. 'I believe', Stanisław wrote to Antoni Dzieduszycki, 'that in his heart he realises the injustice and brutality of everything he is ordered to do, but as a Muscovite subject, he has obedience as his first duty.'[3]

His task was made no easier by a faction within Targowica, headed by 'Hetman' Kossakowski. The latter had been in league with the Zubov brothers when Potocki and Rzewuski had been banking on Potyomkin. His death left the field open to the Zubovs, and their schemes were even more bizarre than Potyomkin's had been. While Bezborodko stood by traditional Russian policy on Poland, the Zubovs subverted the Vice-Chancellor, A. I. Morkov, and began to conduct a policy of their own. In Poland, their friends the Kossakowskis and the Russian General Igelström could do much as they pleased, and there was little Sievers could do to curb them as the retirement of the original Targowicans had left him few people to work with.

'Virtue hides itself while vice swaggers abroad; and it is with this that

I have to work,' he lamented to his daughter.[4] He had to scrape the bottom of the barrel to cobble together a new party. This included people such as Antoni Sułkowski, who replaced Jacek Małachowski as Chancellor, former Barians such as Karol Radziwiłł and Antoni Pułaski, now on the Russian payroll, Michał Kleofas Ogiński, Kazimierz Plater, the king's illegitimate son Stanisław Manuzzi, Ignacy Miączyński and Stanisław Bieliński, an unscrupulous bankrupt gambler, who, in Sievers' own words, were 'ready for anything'.[5] The only people of any standing prepared to work with him were Fryderyk Moszyński and Kazimierz Raczyński.

Sievers' initial problem was to gain the co-operation of Stanisław, who refused to move from Białystok. On 10 April he wrote a long letter to the king explaining that the partition was inevitable, but that it was still possible to achieve something real for Poland. There could be no question of going back to the constitution, but Sievers assured him that the new form of government would be based on a Permanent Council more efficient than that established in 1776, with wider powers for the Crown.[6] Stanisław was sceptical. 'I foresee little actual good coming from all the charming words written to me by Sievers,' he wrote. 'An agreement for the repayment of my debts may be assured; but I do not expect either good government or the preservation of the country.'[7] But he could not remain at Białystok indefinitely, and he would certainly not be allowed to return to Warsaw now. For the first time in his life he had no policy, and the hopelessness of the situation sapped his will. His habitual political drive to influence and dominate deserted him. As the future of his country and of his kingship came into question, he began to think less as a king. His own future and that of his extended family intruded into his calculations as never before – as it did with many prominent Poles. He told Sievers that he would never sign any treaty partitioning his country, but he set off for Grodno once again.

He arrived on 22 April, to be greeted with a fifty-one-gun salute and all the honours due to a reigning monarch, but before he could recover from the journey he was assailed with requests from Sievers. He had proposed one of his secretaries, Christian Friese, as their go-between, and every day this small, thin man with his long, gloomy face would appear with a sheaf of papers to be signed. Stanisław was to be humiliated in every detail, and had to bend to countless whims. In a moment of inspired cruelty, Catherine insisted that he sign the letters calling for elections to the Seym which was to approve the partition on 3 May, the second anniversary of the constitution. 'That was horrible,' Sievers admitted.[8] On the same day Sievers announced that he would be giving a banquet in honour of the king on St Stanisław's day. Stanisław begged him not to, and refused to attend. Sievers had to carry out Catherine's order, but it was agreed that Stanisław would stay away and dine with the Mniszechs at Marcin Badeni's instead. At the end of May, he was asked by Catherine to award Orders of the White Eagle and of St Stanisław to Russian generals for their part in the Polish campaign. He complained about it in private, but complied, since every refusal of a small thing on his part was treated by her as mutiny.

On 4 May, the day after he had signed the circular convoking the Seym, Stanisław had a long conversation with Sievers, in the course of which he broke down in tears several times. He laid bare his worries and fears – about his finances, about his country, about his reputation. He said he could no longer bear his position and would gladly abdicate in favour of Grand Duke Constantine – or the Comte d'Artois, or even Feliks Potocki, if that would make Catherine look more kindly on Poland. He just wanted to go and bury himself in Rome, Naples, or somewhere far away. 'He was deeply moved, and so, to a lesser extent, was I – after all, he is a king,' Sievers wrote in his report to Catherine.[9] But he told Stanisław that abdication was out of the question, since it would provide an excuse for the interference of other powers, notably Austria.[10]

When the Austrian foreign minister Count Cobenzl had been shown a copy of the Convention of St Petersburg between Russia and Prussia setting out the partition by the Russian ambassador, his consternation was so great that he rushed to a map, dropping all pretence at diplomatic dissimulation. 'This alters the whole system of Europe!' he exclaimed. 'The revolution of France is child's play in comparison to the importance of this event.'[11] Vienna was horrified at the extent of the proposed partition, which brought Russia right into Europe, increased the size of Prussia by a third, and turned Poland into an insignificant rump. She was also far from happy at being left out of the spoils.

Prussia hinted that she would pull out of the war with France if

Austria demurred, and graciously allowed her to take the whole of north-eastern France up to the Somme in 'compensation', should she ever capture it. But Prussia had been known to change horses before, and would not fail to turn against Russia if circumstances altered. Austria invoked the support of England, which resented the relentless encroachments of the Northern Powers and remained sympathetic to Poland. As the English ambassador in Vienna pointed out, Russia's treatment of 'the Polish king's fallen majesty must at the present awful period particularly shock all men's minds'.[12]

These diplomatic flashes shed the only rays of hope on Stanisław's horizon, and this was fostered by the encouraging remarks being made by the Emperor Francis II to his minister in Vienna Franciszek Woyna. He therefore decided to force the issue. On 11 May he handed Sievers a letter for Catherine in which he announced his intention to abdicate. 'It is fitting to resign a function which one believes oneself to be unable in all honour to fulfil,' he explained.[13] Catherine's reply, addressed to Sievers, showed neither surprise nor concern. She understood that he must be getting tired, but considered the moment he had chosen to be 'highly inappropriate'. She intimated that he might be allowed to bow out when the present business had been sorted out in a satisfactory way.[14] Her off-hand response stung Stanisław, and brought home to him that he was by now too insignificant a figure even to make gestures.

Having signed the letters calling the Seym, Stanisław was allowed to go back to Białystok, where he arrived on 27 May. There, at least, he could temporarily forget the wretchedness of his position in the company of his favourite sister. To Antoni Dzieduszycki he reported that Sievers was hoping the Seym would not need to sit for more than seven days. 'I'm not sure that it might not be preferable to have a Seym of 7 hours,' Stanisław wrote, believing that it would be little more than a charade.[15] Only one bishop, Wojciech Skarszewski, and not more than a dozen senators out of a total of 136 bothered to turn up, while the 140 deputies had all been selected by Sievers. 'Our success in the election of the deputies at the seymiks has been complete,' Sievers reported. 'All those that I named or approved have been elected, and they were given those instructions which I had prescribed, I therefore have grounds to hope that there will be no more protests than a certain decency might demand.'[16] He was in for a nasty shock.

At the beginning of June 1793 Stanisław returned to Grodno for the opening of the Seym. All the foreign diplomats also turned up, as did agents of Hope & Co of Amsterdam and Barings of London – the listing Polish ship of state might drag half the banking houses of Europe down with its wreck. The Seym convened on 17 June and came to an immediate standstill when a row blew up over procedure. The performance was repeated on the following day. Every time Marshal Bieliński attempted to move the opening, a group of a couple of dozen deputies led by Adam Poniński (the unexpectedly patriotic son of Monsieur Toutcourt) barracked him on points of order. Sievers' patience gave way. He announced that he despised 'your damned laws' and ordered the arrest of Poniński and five others. On the morning of 19 June he marched into Stanisław's study accompanied by a gang of generals and issued ferocious threats, thinking that Stanisław was behind the tactics of the deputies.

Stanisław himself had been taken by surprise. 'The deputies were all elected with bayonets or with Russian money. I hardly know one-tenth of them,' he wrote to Bukaty in London, 'but by some miracle I see in them firmness, courage, and even sense and eloquence. I do not derive any great hopes from this, but any delay must in the present circumstances lend some measure of hope.'[17] He decided to make common cause with them. 'I believe it my duty to inform the estates of the Commonwealth assembled in the Seym under this confederation that I persist in the intention of not cooperating in any way in the cession of our provinces,' he declared at the first session of the Seym on 21 June.[18] His speech elicited wild enthusiasm. Sievers was livid, and gave instructions that no money should reach the king from the Treasury or the Crown lands until he bowed his head.[19]

Sievers' plan was similar to Stackelberg's after the first partition – to get the Seym to nominate a deputation to negotiate the partition with him. Just as in 1773, the Seym resisted this. On 25 June, after financial pressure had been put on him, Stanisław agreed to the principle of a deputation, but insisted that it could not cede Polish territory. This idea was thrown back and forth across the chamber for a few days, without any conclusion being reached. On 2 July Sievers had a couple more deputies arrested, and on the following day he wrote to the Primate, asking him to come to Grodno to help persuade the king of his 'error', adding that 'I should be highly mortified if I were obliged to employ methods which will appear violent and which will be only fair in order to pacify the remains of this unfortunate country.'[20] But the Primate had decided that nothing good could come of the Seym, and he remained at Jabłonna, where he was absorbed by discussions with other bishops on the future of the Polish Church. Kazimierz Poniatowski had also stayed in Warsaw, but he was occupied with giving louche parties at Foksal, and most of all with his new mistress, the actress Agnieszka Truskolaska.

The deputation was eventually appointed on 12 July, but when it reported back with the terms of the Polish-Russian partition treaty, there was a storm of protest, and the oppositionists called on Stanisław to lead them in defying Russia. 'They threaten us who wish to defend our motherland with Siberia. But Siberia will be a paradise for the righteous, for we shall see virtue shining forth even from our emaciated bodies,' the deputy Józef Kimbar exhorted Stanisław. 'They say, Sire, and I have heard it said, that it was Catherine who made you king. Show the world now that you were ordained to it by God, and that you know how to conduct yourself with honour at a time when violence engulfs everything ... Let us go together to Siberia ...'[21] Stanisław bore this nonsense with patience and understanding. 'The king would answer with particular graciousness and convincing argument, in *words of velvet* one could rightly say,' as one of the Russian generals present put it.[22] He understood the desperation of these patriots, but pointed out that going to Siberia would do nobody any good. He recommended that the Seym agree to the Russian terms, which it did, and the preliminaries were signed on 22 July.[23] That evening Sievers gave a banquet and a firework display, but his rejoicing was premature.

On the following day there were renewed protests, and the oppositionists vented their fury at Stanisław's lack of spirit. 'As I see it, Sire, you came to the throne through treachery and lewdness, you have ruled by falsehood, and you end odiously and shamelessly,' Kimbar heckled him. 'You spent your life in couplings with women, and in those skirmishes you have won for your motherland only its demise, which now faces us. Let your mistresses bury you with the same false sorrow with which you are laying our motherland in its grave. I fear nothing and speak the truth when I say that you are a traitor.'[24] The treaty was shunted back and forth in discussion between the chamber and the deputation, sent off to St Petersburg, returned, rejected, discussed, and not ratified by the Seym until 17 August, after a stormy session lasting until 3 a.m. that left Stanisław battered, bruised and thoroughly exhausted. He spent the next day sniffing salts to keep himself from fainting.

Stanisław's role in all this was not impressive. He would resist Russian demands for a few days, but then change tack and give into them. At one session, when the oppositionists stole the marshal's pen to prevent him from signing a measure, Stanisław took his own from his pocket and handed it to him. He sometimes appeared to wish only to get the whole thing over with. He had come to Grodno convinced that there was no way of avoiding the partition, and his act of defiance at the opening of the Seym had probably been intended to salvage his reputation rather than to resist the inevitable. The response from the chamber had surprised him, and the diplomatic twitchings reaching him from Vienna combined with it to raise a fleeting hope in his mind. That hope must have fuelled some audacious plans, for in his papers there are lists drawn up by him of the Polish and Russian units in and around Grodno, their respective strengths and dispositions.[25] But harsh reality and perhaps the fear of bringing perdition on himself and his family – his sister Izabela and his Mniszech and Tyszkiewicz nieces were by his side nagging about their future – shut out such ideas. He tried appealing directly to Catherine, but she bridled at what she termed 'the misguided national pride' of the Poles, and admonished him that 'the misfortunes that Poland has just experienced are merely the consequence of the fact that my efforts to spare it have been consistently misunderstood.'[26]

The alternatives were clear: Stanisław could either bow to her wishes and attempt to salvage something from the wreckage or, as the small group of patriots wanted, bring everything crashing down about him, and thereby in some nebulous way save Poland's honour and his own. It was easy for them to talk. They would get arrested for a few days, after which most would be allowed to return to the chamber. They could barrack and cause trouble with a degree of impunity, for Stanisław stood between them and Sievers, as it was on him that pressure was applied whenever things got out of hand. The pressure was constant and ubiquitous, and he was very tired. So he fought a little, and then gave way on every point, his will undermined by a thousand considerations, and most of all by the knowledge of the futility of the whole exercise.

By the end of July, when the first opposition of the Seym had been broken, life in Grodno began to grow festive. 'Alongside the signs of sadness and despair during the Seym sessions, life flows on in the houses of the very same deputies in a rushing torrent of gaiety that comes close to frenzy,' a Russian officer noted. 'The city is in a state of siege, its streets and suburbs overflowing with Russian soldiery and cossacks; there are camps, pickets and patrols everywhere. In spite of this, routs, dinners, balls, soirées, etc continue in a long and continuous sequence.'[27] Most of the deputies were on generous retainers from the Russian ambassador, and the Seym had attracted large numbers of fortune-hunters and gamblers. People took to mindless dissipation to shut out feelings of shame. Jan Ochocki was surprised as he arrived at a ball to meet a respectable married lady of his acquaintance wearing nothing but a transparent shift that concealed neither her breasts nor her legs. As he entered the ballroom he realised that her attire was not exceptional.

> The sight was really strange, and one could have thought oneself in Olympus, since one saw only Venuses, Dianas and Psyches; but then again the scene seemed to shift to Athens, with smiling Aspasias walking by, or indeed to Rome, with Vestals gliding about, or, come to that, Otaïti to judge by the number of ladies dressed, or rather undressed, *à la sauvage* but the majority were Grecian ladies, all without chemise, in the thinnest dresses with long trains, which allowed one to see and admire all the beauties with which nature had endowed them.[28]

All this contrasted starkly with the king's mood. 'He was haggard, gaunt and changed, his face was drawn and yellow, as though he had been through a heavy wasting illness, and he did not even lift his kind and expressive eyes,' writes the same Ochocki, who had not seen him for two years. 'I hardly recognized him.'[29] Stanisław avoided the balls, but tried to keep his spirits up. He went riding, he went to the theatre, he went to see a new opera by Paisiello, and like everyone else, he took great pleasure in the arrival of the young singer Madame Camelli. He read voraciously and corresponded copiously with his agents at foreign courts and with Fryderyk Bacciarelli in Warsaw. Jan Śniadecki and Marcin Poczobut came from Wilno, bringing telescopes from the observatory so he could watch the eclipse of the sun on 5 September. But in October, Valerian and Nikolay, the brothers of Catherine's favourite Platon Zubov, turned up, and the balls resumed with renewed vigour.

After the Russian treaty had been signed the Seym was presented with the proposed Prussian treaty. This caused even greater indignation, partly because of its drastic nature, partly because of Frederick William's treachery. Highly offensive to the Poles was the idea of Prussia taking over the shrine of the Black Virgin at Częstochowa, and Stanisław suggested that if this could not be avoided, the miraculous picture itself should be removed to another shrine within Poland's new frontiers. But Frederick William would have none of it – he reasoned that if he let his press-gangs loose there during the pilgrimages which drew hundreds of thousands of peasants from all over Poland, he would have acquired an unquenchable source of cannon-fodder. The Seym adopted stonewalling tactics, and to everyone's surprise, Sievers tacitly encouraged this: Catherine was annoyed at the Prussian claims, and while she did not wish to be seen openly opposing these, she wanted them challenged.[30] But Frederick William threatened once more to withdraw from the war against France, so Sievers was instructed to push through the treaty as quickly as possible. This was easier said than done.

On 2 September Sievers informed the 'Most Serene Seym' that he had ordered two battalions of grenadiers and four pieces of cannon to surround the castle, in connection with which he hoped that they would find it expedient to ratify the treaty without further delay.[31] 'What sort of an ambassador am I!' he wrote to his daughter that evening.[32] The Seym refused to comply. The furious Sievers delivered a note in which he announced the imprisonment of four deputies for making 'the most criminal excesses' in their speeches, but assuring the remaining members that he had 'never attempted to hinder the freedom of speech'.[33]

The next session, the ninety-third, began at seven o'clock on the evening of 23 September 1793, with troops surrounding the castle, their cannon trained on the chamber. General Rautenfeld sat in an armchair next to the throne, from where he could see everything and

404

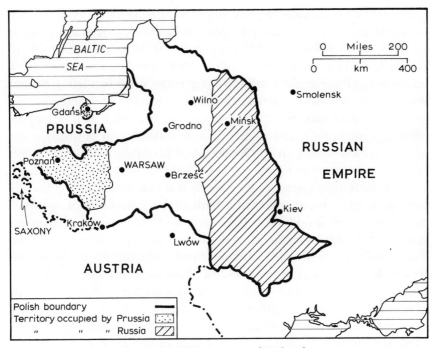

7   The Second Partition of Poland, 1793

point out to his men whom to remove.[34] Still the deputies barracked
and heckled, and it was not until midnight that Marshal Bieliński
managed to declare the session open. But his voice was drowned out as
he tried to propose the treaty to the chamber. Every trick was
employed by the obstructing deputies, and even Stanisław contributed inadvertently, by being taken ill. Sievers would not allow him to
leave the chamber, as this automatically closed the session, so wine and
broth were brought in, and he was restored *in situ*. The deputies then
resorted to a different tactic, and lapsed into silence. This allowed
Bieliński to propose the ratification of the treaty, but he could get no
response. Sievers had had enough. It was nearly four o'clock in the
morning. He instructed the marshal to ask the chamber three times
whether they approved the treaty. There was silence. With questionable logic, he then declared the treaty to have been ratified unanimously, and the second partition of Poland was deemed to have been
legalised.

405

Prussia had been awarded not only Toruń and Gdańsk, but also the whole of Wielkopolska, with the cities of Poznań and Kalisz, an area of 57,000 square kilometres, with a population of more than one million. Russia had taken a huge swathe of territory, more than 250,000 square kilometres with over three million inhabitants. What was left to Poland was a rump that lacked territorial, ethnic or economic coherence.

Sievers' next task was to get Stanisław to sign a new treaty of alliance with Russia, and he found little difficulty in persuading the king. This was signed on 16 October, and Stanisław embraced Sievers warmly, with tears in his eyes. But he had few illusions. 'The alliance made with Russia yesterday is certainly not that which I proposed six years ago, when we approached it with all the appearance of equality,' Stanisław wrote to Bukaty, 'but such as Moscow imposed on us, saying: you must sign this one, or you will have no other, and if you have no alliance with us, we will not shield you from the vexations and treacheries of every kind that it might please the Prussians to visit upon you.'[35] Grimm would have been shocked by the king's lack of enthusiasm. He congratulated Catherine on 'this treaty of alliance, of friendship, of tenderness and of intimate union', assuring her that its signature made up for all the sadness that had been caused by the execution of Marie-Antoinette on the same day. He compared Catherine's behaviour towards Poland to God's compassion for a repentant sinner, and expressed the hope that Stanisław was thanking the Almighty for granting him such a magnanimous protectress.[36]

The moment the partition was ratified, Sievers became more amenable, explaining that now Poland had been reduced in size, she would be allowed to prosper as a second-rank power, like Denmark, Sweden or Sardinia.[37] The Commission for National Education was resurrected and placed once again under the presidency of the Primate. Some of the legislation passed by the Targowicans was repealed, including the ban on wearing the *Virtuti Militari* medals.

Stanisław came to life. He requested the early withdrawal of Russian troops and began discussing the future constitution with Sievers. But his enthusiasm was short-lived. Catherine had sent Sievers detailed instructions on how to prevent Stanisław from gaining any kind of influence and ordered him to build up a new Russian party.[38] The Targowicans had played their part, and were now replaced by the Confederation of Grodno, led by Fryderyk Moszyński and Kazimierz

Raczyński. No new constitution was produced, and the Seym merely endorsed a number of Cardinal Laws put forward by Sievers. The monarchy was declared to be elective as before, the Seym was to meet for only eight weeks, and not for another four years, and the veto was reinstated in all constitutional matters. The country was to be ruled by a Permanent Council, and Stanisław was not allowed much of a say in its composition. His income was fixed at 6 million złoty, half of it earmarked for paying off his debts. 'Today I gave the last ball, on the anniversary of the king's coronation, and tomorrow we start packing,' a tired Sievers wrote to his daughter on 25 November 1793.[39]

Stanisław returned to Warsaw by way of Białystok, then stayed a couple of days with Anna Jabłonowska at Siemiatycze, with Michał Kleofas Ogiński at Sokołów and Aleksandra Ogińska at Siedlce. He drove into the capital on 9 December, warmly greeted by the inhabitants. On the following Sunday, 15 December, he held his first audience at the Castle, and this was surprisingly well attended.[40] He set about trying to influence the new Permanent Council and reclaim the governance of the country. But he soon realised that he had been excluded from it completely, and only ten days later the new English minister Colonel Gardiner was reporting that 'his spirits are worse, and his mind more agitated than whilst at Grodno'.[41] All his compromises, his calculations and his bargains had failed utterly.

'I had thought my cup of bitterness as full as it could be', he wrote to his nephew Józef on 1 January 1794, 'but I now see that I have been mistaken.'[42] Catherine had flown into a fury over the decision of the Seym in November 1793 to rescind the ban on the wearing of the *Virtuti Militari* and penned a strong note to Sievers recalling him. Threatening to order her troops to ravage the country, she insisted the Permanent Council issue a decree banning the wearing of the decoration and draw up lists of all those who had been decorated, so that they might be forced to hand in their medals, which were to be sent to St Petersburg. She even demanded that the king notify all foreign courts that the decoration had been abolished, requesting them to enforce the ban on anyone wearing it. Stanisław had to write to his nephew in Brussels asking him to send back the decoration he had taken such pleasure in awarding. He received a gloomy but defiant refusal. After much argument, however, Józef sent it back, along with his

407

orders of the White Eagle and St Stanisław.[43]

'It would appear that the intentions of the Empress are to humiliate the King of Poland by every possible means,' noted Büchholtz in a letter to Frederick William on 2 January 1794.[44] Stanisław was informed by the Permanent Council that his income would be reduced from 3 million złoty to 2 million.[45] A couple of weeks later the Permanent Council issued an edict cancelling every law that had been passed by the Seym between 1788 and 1792, and a search was instituted for all copies of the constitution and related documents. There was even talk of holding a show-trial of Stanisław Małachowski. 'His Majesty's birthday yesterday seemed more like a day of funeral than one of joy,' wrote Jan Dembowski to Ignacy Potocki on 18 January.[46] Stanisław seemed embarrassed by the good wishes being proffered, and withdrew as soon as he could, to spend the evening quietly with Bacciarelli discussing his collection of paintings: less awesome than the contemplation of his kingdom.

He had little to celebrate after thirty years on the throne. 'If I had not done as I have done, there would be no Poland at all,' he wrote to his nephew Józef in a pathetic attempt to justify his failed policy.[47] But it was not much of a Poland he had saved. 'It is hard to believe in what a difficult situation this country finds itself,' reported Johann Jakob Patz, the Saxon chargé d'affaires in Warsaw. 'All court cases are still suspended, there is no money at all; either for the army or for the civil functionaries. As for trade and business, there is complete stagnation. Most of the rich magnates are ruined, either as a result of bankruptcy, or by the ravages caused by foreign troops marching through their estates.'[48] Stanisław himself was desperately short of money, and tried to raise a loan in Holland, but nobody would risk their capital in such questionable circumstances.

The English minister, Colonel Gardiner, reported that 'a very alarming uncertainty continues.'[49] The disgraced Sievers left Warsaw on 25 January 1794. Valerian Zubov moved into his Embassy and set about kitting himself out with ambassadorial carriages and liveries, but then he too left for St Petersburg. Sievers' functions were taken over by the military commander, the violent and bad-tempered General Igelström who, being laid low with gout, never presented himself to the king, and merely summoned the Permanent Council to his bedside and issued instructions. He voided his bile by ordering arrests for 'Jacobin-

117 Plan for the Church of Divine Providence, whose foundation stone Stanisław laid on the first anniversary of the constitution, by Jakub Kubicki

118 Dial of a French pocketwatch commemorating the constitution of 3 May

119 Józef Poniatowski in 1792, wearing the cross of Virtuti Militari, by Giuseppe Grassi

120a & b The very first design of the Virtuti Militari medals, superseded within a couple of months by the cross

121 Józef Poniatowski receiving Russian standards captured at Zieleńce from General Stanisław Mokronowski, by Józef Peszka

122   Feliks Potocki, Ksawery Branicki and other traitors being hung in effigy in Warsaw in September 1794, by an unidentified painter

123   Tadeusz Kościuszko, seen here wearing the Virtuti Militari and the American Order of the Cincinnati, by an unidentified painter

124   Ignacy Wyssogota Zakrzewski, President of Warsaw, and head of the Provisional Council in 1794, by Józef Peszka

125   The standard of the Kraków battalion of Scythemen, with the legend 'They Feed and Defend'

126   A ten-złoty banknote issued by the Supreme National Council in 1794, adorned with Phrygian bonnet and other revolutionary symbols

127   'The Polish Revolution', a French print depicting people buying tricolor cockades, while others dance round a tree of liberty in the background. The shop on the right pictures 'the despair of the Tyrant of Poland, who is selling up'. Stanisław has just managed to sell one of his crowns to a man who is seen defecating into it.

128 & 129   Stanisław's sisters, Ludwika Zamoyska, 'Madame de Podolie',
and Izabela Branicka, 'Madame de Cracovie', by Bacciarelli

130   The royal castle at Grodno, built by Giuseppe Sacco 1780–3

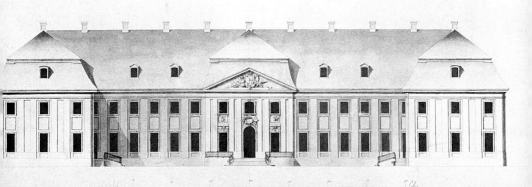

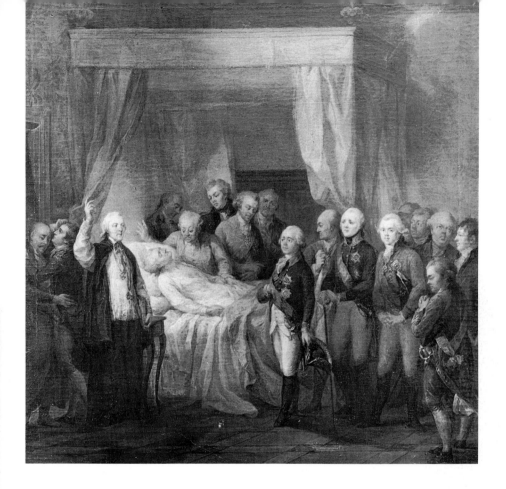

131 *Opposite page* Stanisław in St Petersburg, 1797, by Élisabeth-Louise Vigée-Lebrun

132 *Above* The death of Stanisław, by Bacciarelli. In the forefront stands Tsar Paul I, with his two sons, Alexander and Constantine.

133 The catafalque for Stanisław's lying-in-state in the Marble Palace, erected by Vincenzo Brenna

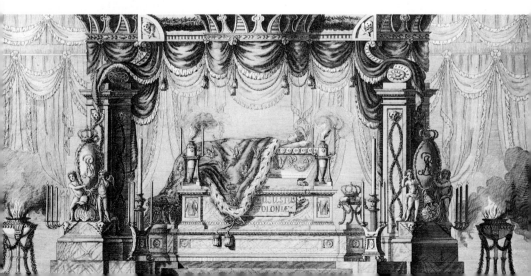

134 The parish church of Wołczyn, last resting-place of Stanisław's remains, as it was in 1939

135 'The Grave of the Motherland', an allegorical painting by Franciszek Smuglewicz, depicts Poland in chains being pushed towards the grave by various magnates, while others, including a bishop, prepare to seal it. A monument to Stanisław, clutching his constitution, is keeling over, and only Kościuszko is attempting to save the Motherland.

ism', by inspecting every tradesman's note or bill passing between Poland and France, and harassing every French doctor and valet until they swore an oath of allegiance to the imprisoned Louis XVII.

The arrangements made by Catherine for Poland were provisional in nature, and it seemed clear to most that she might close down the whole business on the slightest whim. 'There is a widespread conviction that a new partition of Poland will take place soon,' the Prussian envoy Büchholtz reported to his king the day Sievers left.[50] Stanisław certainly feared so. He began to gather material for a second volume of his *Opinion on the King of Poland* – it seemed certain that he would not be afforded another opportunity of vindicating his name – and awaited with resignation whatever Providence might decide.

Large numbers of his subjects could not affect the same resignation. Many were not given much opportunity. Anyone who had been active during the Great Seym and all those who had fought in 1792 were being financially penalised as well as persecuted, and many were left without a livelihood, with only resentment to feed on, a dangerous combination at the best of times. 'There is a most Jacobine spirit, little concealed, & often very indecently expressed,' reported Gardiner.[51] Ignacy Potocki, Kołłątaj and the other émigrés now sought the means to launch an armed rising in Poland. The necessary assistance could only come from France, and in February 1793 Kościuszko went to Paris bearing a memorandum designed to make revolutionaries salivate. 'A revolution in Poland', it argued, 'would unleash a nation which, by its topographical position, its kindred origins, customs and language, by the armed forces it could muster, would be the only one capable of rapidly spreading Republicanism through Russia, of planting and bringing to flower the tree of liberty even among the ice of Petersburg.'[52]

The authors, who included Kołłątaj, Ignacy Potocki, Franciszek Dmochowski, Józef Weyssenhoff and Józef Zajączek, were not all revolutionaries, but they all knew that a republican programme was a precondition for French support. So they declared their intention of abolishing the monarchy and the aristocratic senate, curbing the clergy and introducing full equality for all citizens. The French were not taken in, suspecting that the Poles would adopt the constitution of 3 May. But they went along with the conspirators. If the Poles thought they could use France, France would use the Poles. Pierre Parandier was sent to Dresden with instructions to assess the potential benefits to France of a 'diversion' in Poland. His instructions piously justified this on the grounds that 'the cause of the French Republic is that of all peoples'. Little had changed at the French foreign ministry since the days of the Confederation of Bar.[53]

The confusion implicit in the émigrés' plans was reflected in the situation at home. The conspirators in Warsaw were drawn principally from the Association of Friends of the Constitution, led by Ignacy Działyński and the banker Andrzej Kapostas. They were sympathetic to the king and stood by the constitution. Behind them lurked others, mostly Jacobins, who wanted to see the king punished, the Targowicans executed, and the property of the rich confiscated. They began to outnumber the conservative elements, much to the alarm of Stanisław, who was well informed. The social topography of the capital had changed dramatically over the past decade, with the richer merchants and professional classes moving into comfortable houses in newer districts or villas outside the city, while the old centre around the Castle had filled up with penniless szlachta, cashiered officers, servants and labourers – the nucleus of any upheaval. The conspirators in the provinces tended to be on the conservative side, but those of Wilno, led by the radical Colonel Jakub Jasiński, were another matter.

The conspirators therefore began the year 1794 without a clearly defined objective and without any sort of ideological unity. But they could not afford to delay. Russia had ordered the reduction of the Polish armed forces to 15,000, and Igelström wanted to carry this out at the beginning of March. The conspirators needed to take over the army as it stood, so they brought forward their plans. In February Franciszek Barss was in Paris trying to negotiate a loan, assuring the French foreign ministry that 'there is no question of bringing back constitutions based on the risible principles of monarchy or aristocracy'.[54] Meanwhile Kościuszko in Dresden held meetings with ringleaders from various parts of Poland. He had planned several risings in outlying provinces that would divert the Russian forces and allow the Polish units time to concentrate. But time was not on his side. When news came from Warsaw that Igelström had arrested a number of conspirators and was hunting down others, Kościuszko realised he could delay no longer. It was decided that the insurrection would begin on 24 March.

Igelström began reducing the Polish army at the beginning of March. On 12 March General Antoni Madaliński, whose cavalry brigade was stationed at Ostrołęka, defied the orders to start demobilising. Stanisław wrote to Madaliński begging him to submit. 'It is a king and a father who writes this letter to you,' he pleaded, but to no avail.[55] Other units joined Madaliński's, along with a number of local szlachta, and hostilities broke out between his men and Russian troops in the vicinity. When these were reinforced, he marched out and made for Kraków, where Kościuszko was due soon. Stanisław attempted to douse the fire before it spread. He wrote to Catherine, appraising her of the disturbances in Poland and trying to make them appear insignificant. 'May you not impute to the whole nation the errors of a few individuals,' he wrote, 'and may these errors not recommend to you any project which might ultimately tend towards the reduction of the extent of Poland.'[56] He wrote to his nephew in Brussels telling him not to let himself be seduced by any approaches the conspirators might make.[57] He tried to calm tempers in Warsaw, and delayed issuing any formal pronouncement condemning Madaliński. When he could put it off no longer, he insisted that it be couched in the softest possible terms. He sought out officers and prominent citizens whom he knew to be involved in the conspiracy, urging calm on them. 'All these actions, which I believe to be quite pointless, can only provoke fresh troubles and give rise to another war, whose conclusion will perhaps entail a third and final division of the country,' he told Michał Kleofas Ogiński.[58]

But things had gone too far. Kościuszko reached Kraków on 23 March and the following day proclaimed a National Insurrection against Russia. News of this brought tension in Warsaw to the highest pitch. 'A terrible storm is brewing,' Igelström wrote to Bezborodko.[59] His first reaction was to glut the city with Russian troops and order a wave of arrests. He demanded that the Permanent Council condemn the arrested men outright, which it refused to do. Igelström, who had, in Sievers' words, 'a soldier's eloquence', flew into a rage and summoned the Chancellor, Antoni Sułkowski. He gave Sułkowski such a tongue-lashing that the unfortunate Chancellor suffered a heart attack and died. Igelström only knew of the more moderate conspirators, and by arresting them he unwittingly strengthened the influence of the radicals. 'The terror of the Russians here is beyond what I can attempt to describe to Yr Ldship, and is so very apparent, that it is more likely to encourage, than to suppress any attempt to revolt,' reported Gardiner.[60]

On 12 April news spread through Warsaw of Kościuszko's victory over General Tormasov's army at Racławice on 4 April. There could be no stopping the conspirators now. In a last attempt at defusing the situation, Stanisław met Igelström and tried to persuade him to evacuate Warsaw. Igelström vacillated. He sent away his mistress and weakened his forces in Warsaw once more, but made no contingency plans against a rising. Stanisław knew that the rising was to begin on 17 April. His main reason for wanting to get Igelström to evacuate the capital was to avoid fighting in the streets. He had also floated the idea of leaving Warsaw himself with all the Polish units, in order to keep them out of it. He was frightened by the prospect of popular upheaval, which could so easily be deflected against his own person, and was intensely aware of the possibility that he might end up on the scaffold. At the same time, Stanisław could not restrain a certain admiration for those who wanted to risk everything in order to attempt the impossible, and his heart went out to them.

25

Revolution

'etween four and five o'clock on the morning of 17 April [1794], the alarm was sounded at the Castle,' records Little-page. 'I went down into the courtyard and found the king surrounded by his guards.' Stanisław seemed tense and depressed, but displayed 'the firmness and the sang-froid worthy of the son of Charles XII's companion-in-arms'.[1] Still only half-dressed, he led his only company of footguards out into the square before the Castle to take stock of the situation. But it was impossible to make out what was going on.

Led by the cobbler Jan Kiliński, the populace had stormed the arsenal and armed itself. Polish army units had joined them and brought artillery into the streets. Barricades had gone up, and there were several battles going on simultaneously. The Russians had been unprepared, and in most cases the officers were not with their units but scattered in their private quarters. Igelström was holding out with a battalion of infantry and four pieces of cannon in the Russian embassy on Miodowa Street, only a couple of hundred yards from where Stanisław stood.

A group of armed civilians marched by making for the embassy, and they called on the guards to join them. A young officer stepped forward and, assuring the king of his loyalty, declared that they must go whither their honour called. 'Your honour and your duty both oblige you to remain at your post by my side,' Stanisław retorted, but at that moment volleys of musketry coming from the embassy interrupted him, and the guards surged past him to join the fray.[2] Stanisław was now defenceless, and to make matters worse, a number of Targowicans, including the President of the Permanent Council Józef Ankwicz and Hetman Piotr Ożarowski, came to seek refuge at the Castle, followed by Bishop Massalski and other unpopular figures. Their presence only served to expose the Castle and the king to the vengeful fury of the populace.

Stanisław eventually managed to get an infantry regiment to take up positions before the Castle. He then sent his brother Kazimierz to Igelström in an attempt to arrange a Russian evacuation. But Igelström was not prepared to lay down his arms, and the insurgents would not let him go with them. Unable to stop the fighting, Stanisław turned his attention to the question of controlling the insurrection politically. That afternoon the President (mayor) of Warsaw Ignacy Zakrzewski came to the Castle and suggested Stanisław assume the leadership. Stanisław suggested that Zakrzewski himself form a provisional ruling body, and he put forward the names of moderates who might serve on it. Zakrzewski was reluctant, but in the end, to Stanisław's satisfaction, he was acclaimed by the people and carried to the Town Hall, where he convened a Provisional Council. To Stanisław's further satisfaction, his sister Izabela's son General Stanisław Mokronowski was appointed military commander of Warsaw.

That evening, amid scenes of chaos and carnage, Igelström fought his way out of his palace and took up positions in the Palace of the Commonwealth, a few hundred yards away. At the end of the next day, when that was ablaze, he decided the game was up. He ran up a white flag and then slipped out with a small group of officers and men. By the morning of 19 April all the Russians had either surrendered or evacuated the city, leaving behind well over 2,000 dead, almost as many prisoners and all their guns.[3] Polish casualties were also high, and the city was strewn with corpses. A triumphant mob roamed the streets looking for 'traitors' and looting abandoned houses. But nobody threatened the Castle. Stanisław could easily have slipped away himself, but he did not consider the option seriously, and showed no fear. On 20 April, which was Easter Sunday, the Primate celebrated Mass in the Church of St John with the king and the whole court present. The only reference to the week's events was a *Te Deum* sung in thanksgiving for the Polish victory. Later that day, however, crowds surrounded the Castle demanding the extradition of Ożarowski. Zakrzewski persuaded them to disperse by promising to fetch the traitor in an orderly manner after asking for the king's assent.

On 22 April Stanisław officially announced his adherence to the Insurrection. He had been opposed to the whole enterprise, 'But since it has happened, and the nation has demonstrated that it is resolved to run the greatest risks rather than suffer the yoke any longer, I have decided that my counsels of prudence were out of season,' he wrote to his nephew Józef, urging him to return as quickly as possible in order to take part in the fighting.[4] He admitted that there was a strong possibility that he would share the fate of Louis XVI, but this could not deter him. His old political drive flooded back and he embraced the chance of action with astonishing energy. The Swedish minister found him in high spirits when he called at the Castle that day.[5]

But not everyone was convinced by Stanisław's conversion to the cause, and the Provisional Council adopted an ambivalent attitude towards him. Its members avoided contact with him, and he noticed that they had stopped wearing the decorations he had bestowed on them. Even his former minister in St Petersburg and friend, Augustyn Deboli, now on the Council, was deferential but distant. The Council took over the Mint, then the conduct of foreign affairs, then command of the Cadet Corps. Stanisław acquiesced graciously, but it hurt him to be eased out, and he was alarmed at the Council's anti-monarchist attitudes, for he believed legitimacy to be of crucial importance. He was appalled when he learnt that they were intending to mint coins on which the words 'Liberty, Integrity, Independence' were to replace his head, and he protested vehemently.

On 24 April eight members of the Council came to the Castle and explained that the populace feared that he was planning to flee, and they asked him to show himself in public. Stanisław rode about the city all afternoon and repeated the exercise on the following day. On 29 April he went to the Church of St John for a service commemorating those who had fallen in the street-fighting. He left his box and came down to mix with the congregation. The homily imperceptibly turned into a paean of praise for the king, affirming that he had never been a traitor, and that he still had the choice to 'live with the nation and die with the nation'. 'You speak the truth,' Stanisław answered, 'and I shall do as you say.'[6] A few days later, he tried to show his goodwill by joining in the construction of earthworks, in which people of every condition were lending a hand. He appeared carrying a spade, but was harshly rebuffed by a washerwoman, who told him to keep away from the work, as everything he had ever turned his hand to had ended in catastrophe. 'His Polish Majesty's position seems to differ but little from that of the late French king,' noted the English minister Colonel Gardiner.[7]

When the messenger had arrived at Kościuszko's camp with news of the rising in Warsaw, Kołłątaj interrupted with the question 'Is the king alive?' and when the messenger answered in the affirmative, Kołłątaj said to Kościuszko: 'In that case we and our revolution are done for; the army will fight for a few months, and then Poland will fall and the king will sign her death-warrant.'[8] Kołłątaj had instituted a minor reign of terror in Kraków, and mobilised his agents in Warsaw to do the same. On 24 April they opened a Jacobin club, which held its meetings in the deserted Ogiński palace and began subverting the city proletariat, which was resentful of the gentrification that had been imposed by the Provisional Council.

The Council was finding it increasingly difficult to maintain its authority. It had to distance itself from the king and pander to the populace. On 28 April it set up an Investigating Committee to seek out and punish 'traitors'. The retreating Russians had left Warsaw a morbid present in the shape of the Russian legation's entire archive since 1767. This would undoubtedly make interesting reading for anyone trying to prove who had been an instrument of Russian policy, and Stanisław was not beyond feeling a shudder at the thought. On 1 May a representative of the Committee came to the Castle to arrest Bishop Massalski, Ożarowski and Ankwicz, and take them to the city prison in the Town Hall. Two days later news arrived from Wilno that the city had risen under the Jacobin Colonel Jasiński and expelled the Russians, and that the mob had hanged 'Hetman' Kossakowski after a summary trial.

Stanisław's only protection lay in striking the right attitude, and he took every opportunity to demonstrate that he was not afraid. 'He supports himself with great composure and great dignity,' noted Gardiner.[9] On 8 May, St Stanisław's day, he processed as usual to the Church of the Holy Cross, but few people apart from the diplomatic corps accompanied him, and the Council delegated those members who had no decorations. After the ceremony, he went for his habitual ride, which took him that afternoon to inspect the defence works in Praga. While he was there, a group of Jacobins spread the rumour that he had escaped. They whipped up a mob, which broke into the arsenal, armed itself and went out to look for him. Kiliński, who got wind of the plot, warned the Council. They sent out a troop of lancers, which encountered Stanisław riding back across the pontoon bridge over the Vistula, minutes before the mob reached him. He was escorted back to the Castle in a procession whose mood was deeply ambivalent. Cries of 'Long live the King' alternated with shouts of 'Death to the Traitor!' A shot narrowly missed him, and one of his aides was dragged from his horse and beaten nearly to death. Józef Wybicki, who was trying to shield Stanisław, had a pistol held to his head, and Kiliński himself was shot at as he covered the king with his own person. They only just managed to get Stanisław back to the Castle, where Kiliński took personal command.[10]

That night, three gibbets were erected in the old market square and a fourth outside the Church of St Anne, not far from the Castle. Throughout the night the armed mob roamed the streets shouting 'Long live the Revolution' and singing the *Carmagnole*. In the morning, it broke into the city prison from which it dragged out the hetmans Ożarowski and Józef Zabiełło, Bishop Kossakowski and Józef Ankwicz. Kossakowski screamed for mercy as he was dragged to the scaffold, urging them to hang the king instead. The Provisional Council could only restore a semblance of order by holding a rushed trial that was little more than a sanction for the lynching of the four Targowicans, and by promising to speed up the trials of the other 'traitors'. It could certainly not afford to protect the king if the mob took it into its head to harm him. This did not stop Stanisław from writing to Zakrzewski interceding for Bishop Massalski, who was in danger of hanging. 'The King of Poland is playing for very high stakes,' wrote Büchholtz to his master on 12 May, astonished at Stanisław's intrepid behaviour. 'I could not vouch that he will not meet with some misfortune.'[11]

Stanisław's principal ally was the fear, widespread among the settled population of Warsaw, that the city might be visited by horrors similar to those that had taken place in Paris in the previous year. Using pamphlets and fliers, he mounted a campaign of insinuation against the

Jacobins, suggesting that they were aiming to subvert the Insurrection from the leadership of Kościuszko and to import French ways into Poland. This obliged many of the leaders to declare for moderation, and it turned even demagogues such as Kiliński into mild conservatives. This was a minor triumph. The patriotic cobbler who had started the revolt in Warsaw was a strapping handsome fellow immensely popular with all but the most dedicated Jacobins, and he was a useful ally. Characteristically, Stanisław toyed with the idea of instituting an Order of St Kazimierz with which to decorate him and other plebeian patriots.

In an attempt to channel the energies of the mob and create a sense of solidarity between all citizens, the Provisional Council issued a poetically couched manifesto exhorting everyone to take part in building defensive earthworks. The response was edifying, with people of every condition and both sexes spilling out to toil over the fortifications. In the interests of practicality the ladies of Warsaw devised a 'working costume' that gave them freedom of movement and everyone else a stunning view of their legs.[12] But the Jacobins began to agitate against the enterprise, suggesting that only aristocrats ought to be put to work, while 'the people' should not be distracted from their revolutionary purpose. The work came to a virtual standstill, and idle mobs were once again loitering in the streets.

They were fed with a regular diet of rumour pointing to the 'treachery' of not only the king and his circle, but of all those, such as Zakrzewski, Mokronowski and even Kiliński, whom the Jacobins perceived as having sold out to him. Just as in Paris, a mood of paranoia conjured up treacherous 'conspiracies' against 'the people', and literally nobody was beyond suspicion. Restless crowds swilled around the streets manhandling respectable citizens and arresting 'spies'. Stanisław's officers were insulted and his servants beaten up when they ventured out in livery. Several times the populace invaded the courtyard of the Castle. Stanisław would appear at the window, whereupon the people would disperse. Given their contradictory feelings, he could never be sure what would happen next. He was given a citizens' guard made up of barbers, merchants, tinkers and apothecaries.[13] He fed them at his table and talked with them affably, but their presence was no guarantee of safety, and only served to make him feel like a prisoner. One of his pages claimed that he kept poison with him at all times.[14] He certainly had good reason.

Stanisław knew that the only man with sufficient authority to restore order was Kościuszko. But he could not be sure of Kościuszko's attitude – the Act of Insurrection which he had proclaimed in Kraków on 24 March had made no mention of the king. Stanisław wrote to him on 5 May professing his loyalty to the cause and suggesting that he come to Warsaw as soon as possible. He also asked Kościuszko to order the closing down of the Jacobin club, and this request was backed up by Zakrzewski and the Provisional Council. But Kościuszko was in a quandary. He was as radical as anyone in his convictions on social equality but he was no *sans-culotte*, and he nourished considerable respect and sympathy for Stanisław. He had taken the title of 'Commander' for the duration of hostilities, but he expressly deferred all constitutional matters to a future Seym. At the moment, Stanisław was an embarrassment to him. He had already written to the Council instructing them to prevent the king from escaping or communicating with anyone and to protect his person. On 8 May he issued a manifesto enjoining the Council not to allow popular ardour to cool by delaying the meting out of justice to traitors, and at the same time warned that traitors could be lurking in the clubs as well as among the aristocracy. Being fully absorbed by military matters, he delegated political direction to Kołłątaj and Ignacy Potocki, and they arrived in Warsaw on 24 May to set up a Supreme National Council.

Kołłątaj entered the capital in triumph, borne aloft by the rabble, and he ostentatiously ignored the king. But Potocki called on Stanisław two days after his arrival. 'I want your trust, and offer you mine,' Stanisław said on greeting him. Potocki made 'a very strong profession of non-Jacobinism, both from principle and from policy', but this only partly satisfied Stanisław.[15] The transcript of the conversation shows that far from being cowed, Stanisław took a managerial attitude, grilling Potocki over policy. Two days later Stanisław wrote to Kościuszko that 'I do not wish to govern or dominate any more than you and the Nation may decide to be for the benefit of the motherland', but he made it clear that he considered himself to be better qualified to decide policy than anyone else.[16] They decided against giving him power. The Supreme Council was formed on 28 May, and consisted of eight members and thirty-two deputies. It was to notify the king of its decisions at the end of each session, and he was asked to legitimate it with a formal decree. Stanisław was relieved that it was made up mainly of moderates, including Antoni Dziedu-szycki and Fryderyk Bacciarelli, who were his men. But the small group of radicals on it never slept.

A few days later the new Council issued a proclamation telling people to beware of 'false patriots'. 'Baubles offered by unclean hands are not worthy of being laid on the altar of the motherland,' it ran, a clear reference to Stanisław's donation to the cause of some jewellery on the previous day.[17] Stanisław was stung, as the donation had been a real sacrifice. 'I am only surviving at the moment by melting down my table-silver,' he protested to his nephew on 7 June.[18] All payments from the Treasury had ceased, and revenues from Crown estates could not reach Warsaw. Stanisław's beloved Kozienice had been sacked by the Russians on 17 April, and stripped of everything, including curtains, drapes, panelling and fireplaces.[19] In June, the Council gave Stanisław 120,000 złoty as payment for the precious metals he had handed over with the Mint, and decreed that he was to get a monthly pension. But he received nothing further until October, when he was given 160,000-złoty worth of valueless paper assignations.[20] Kołłątaj had taken over the Treasury, and he managed to raise the sum of 25 million złoty over the seven months of the Insurrection, at an immense cost to Poland's cultural heritage.[21] (Along with palaces and castles, churches and monasteries were stripped of their gold and silver plate, ornaments and statuary, even of their bells, whose unsuitable bronze was recast into cannon that usually exploded.) Kołłątaj was certainly not going to allow any of this to go to Stanisław, whom he regarded as a dangerous obstacle to the revolution he was attempting to carry out.

Having decided to join the Insurrection, it was in Stanisław's nature to want to lead it. He probably saw a chance to redeem the reputation he had sacrificed in 1792. But he also clearly perceived that none of those attempting to control the Insurrection were in a position to unite the nation, and that by aping French models they were throwing out a challenge to all the powers of Europe. 'One can rightly regard the war in Poland as a branch of that which the coalition Powers are sustaining against the revolutionaries of France, since those of Poland have incontestably been incited, encouraged and supported by the former and profess more or less analogous principles,' Frederick William wrote to Lucchesini. 'It is a part, and certainly a very formidable part, of this great war of the established governments against the spirit of revolution and anarchy.'[22] Stanisław was desperate to counter such assessments by expunging the Jacobin elements from the rising and giving it the appearance of a national war, with himself at its head. That was why he kept suggesting that the Supreme Council or Kościuszko declare that they stood by the universally respected constitution of 3 May. It was also why he went to great pains to make sure that all the foreign diplomats in Warsaw were accorded respect, and that Russian prisoners, their wives and dependents were treated with humanity.

Stanisław urged the English and Swedish ministers to incline their courts to support Poland, and he also looked to Austria, which was the most vulnerable to any radicalisation of the Insurrection.[23] There was some Jacobin activity in Vienna itself and stirrings of discontent in Hungary, while the Poles in Galicia might rise at any moment. Also, the supply-lines of the Austrian armies operating against France in the Low Countries ran down the Polish rivers out to the Baltic. Austria therefore took care not to antagonise the Poles, encouraging the belief that she might support them. Kościuszko had despatched an emissary to Vienna, and there was talk of offering the Polish succession to a Habsburg. But official attitudes in Vienna were not favourable. As General Joseph Harnoncourt put it, Austria would recognise the Insurrection if it succeeded and help to crush it if it failed. She was certainly not prepared to let Russia and Prussia exclude her from the booty a second time.[24]

The radicals believed that, in view of the failure of the war of 1792, the only hope for Poland lay in a people's war against all monarchy, allied in spirit to the French war of peoples against all tyrants. France did everything to encourage this trend. When Franciszek Barss addressed the Committee of Public Safety in Paris in July, he was berated for tolerating the survival of the king.[25] 'O Polish Nation, do not allow yourself to be restrained by Stanisław Augustus who has basely tricked you,' thundered '*Le Sans-Culotte*'. Do not forget that kings, noblemen and all great landowners are the mortal enemies of equality, without which there can be neither liberty nor happiness.'[26] Robespierre was against committing France to helping the Poles, while Saint Just, in an uncharacteristic outburst of concern for human life, declared that 'France would not risk the life of a single soldier to support a revolution that aims towards aristocratic or monarchical government.'[27] In effect, France was powerless to intervene in Poland's favour. But there were those in Poland, and Kołłątaj was one of them, who believed that if the king and a few dozen magnates were executed she would feel impelled to help her sister revolution, while the Polish nation itself would be fatally committed to a fight to the death. Radical priests praised Robespierre from the pulpit, and advocated the adoption of an 'early Christian' approach to private property. 'I warn you, worthy citizens, it is time to throw off the softness of heart on which our country has always prided itself so much,' Jakub Jasiński exhorted the Wilno mob. 'Pursue any traitors you can find, judge them and kill them all.'[28] He also issued a proclamation to the Russian soldiers, inciting them to kill their officers.

There were thus two diametrically opposed views of what course the Insurrection should take. 'Kościuszko is undoubtedly a good man, and a good soldier, but nature did not intend him to stand at the head of a revolution,' Ignacy Potocki admitted to the Swedish minister.[29] Staszic was more dismissive. 'He is an honest and a courageous man, but he does not know Poland well, and he understands Europe even less,' he wrote. 'He would like to be a Washington at the head of his army, but to save Poland someone more like Sulla is required.'[30] Kościuszko hovered between the two extremes. He removed Jasiński from command in Lithuania, but he feared being associated too closely with the king. Józef Poniatowski had hurried back from Brussels with his friends Generals Michał Wielhorski and Mikołaj Bronikowski. But when he came to Kościuszko's camp at Jędrzejów on 27 May to offer his services, he was received with insulting coolness.[31] Kościuszko offered him a command in Lithuania, but Poniatowski had no wish to be sent off to the periphery, and asked to be allowed to serve with Kościuszko himself. He was told to go to Warsaw and was left idle for the next six weeks.

'God is a witness that we are not making a French revolution,' Kościuszko wrote to Izabela Czartoryska in July.[32] Yet his only hope for mobilising the nation lay in turning this rising into something other than just a second round of the 1792 war. His Act of Insurrection, proclaimed on the main square of Kraków at the outset, was redolent of the American Declaration of Independence. For himself he chose a role similar to that of George Washington, and to stress that this was to be a war of liberation in more senses than one, he formed up battalions of peasant scythemen and adopted their costume himself. On 7 May from his camp at Połaniec he issued a manifesto which declared that 'the person of every peasant is free, and he can move about at will'. He halved all labour-rents and promised liberty and land to all those who fought for the country. This did not produce the hoped-for results. Peasants were slow to hear of it and they were restrained, sometimes physically, by their masters, who were unwilling to see their estates untended in any cause. In the Kraków area, where Kościuszko could enforce it, the levy yielded some 9,000 peasants, but in the Lublin region, where he could not, the figure was not more than 5,000, and other provinces yielded even less.[33] And although they were devoted to the person of Kościuszko himself, the motivation of the peasant levies left much to be desired.[34]

If the peasants were largely indifferent, the szlachta remained cagey. Many young men were prevented from taking an active part by parents fearful for their estates. Others could not get through to join the rising. The main body of the Polish army, which had been prudently stationed by the Russians down in the Ukraine, never made it. Only some 4,000 men managed to filter past the Russian units and join Kościuszko. Thousands of Poles who had been pressed into Russian service deserted and made for his camp, but most were caught and dealt with in a number of unpleasant ways.[35]

Kościuszko's victory at Racławice was an encouraging start, but it was of little consequence. He spent the next two months mostly on the move, dodging Russian and Prussian armies while he organised Polish units in other parts of the country and consolidated his own corps. On 5 June he brought this to face a smaller force under Denisov at Szczekociny. But the peasant irregulars took so long to form up that the battle could hardly begin on that day. The next morning Frederick William arrived with a large force that turned the tables radically. Kościuszko's 14,000 men, half of them irregulars, now faced over 26,000 Russians and Prussians. His twenty-four pieces of artillery were quickly silenced by the enemy's 124, and after a fierce and bloody battle, Kościuszko withdrew.

A couple of days later Zajączek with a force of 10,000, most of them scythemen, engaged General Derfelden at Chełm, and on 20 June

Michał Wielhorski, who had taken over command of the forces in Lithuania, defeated General Knorring. But Kościuszko's defeat at Szczekociny tilted the scales against the Insurrection. Ten days after the battle the Prussians occupied Kraków. This alarmed Austria, which was obliged to look to Russia to safeguard her a share in the spoils of what now looked like the inevitable demise of Poland. In the mean time, Austrian troops marched into the Sandomierz and Lublin areas. Szczekociny restored the confidence of the enemy commanders, confirmed the pessimism of many waverers in Poland, and galvanised the extremist element in Warsaw.

On 27 June Kołłątaj's associates Kazimierz Konopka and Jan Dembowski stirred up the Warsaw mob, which began erecting gibbets in front of the palaces of alleged traitors. A number were erected on the Castle square and in front of the palace of the Primate, who in fact lived with his brother at the Castle. Zakrzewski ordered the gibbets to be taken down, but the mob prevented this, broke into the city gaol and dragged out those it found there. Bishop Massalski, Stackelberg's crony Antoni Czetwertyński, the king's secretary Karol Boscamp Lasopolski, the chamberlain Stefan Grabowski, the police intendant Maciej Roguski and a police agent called Marceli Piętka were all hanged. The lawyer Michał Wulfers, who protested at the lynchings, met with the same fate, as did the public prosecutor Józef Majewski. Stanisław's friend Fryderyk Moszyński and several others were only saved by the personal intervention of Zakrzewski. But the situation was by no means under control. 'The agitation of the populace is very marked, and some dangerous explosion seems unavoidable,' noted the Swedish minister on 2 July.[36]

Stanisław despatched his equerry Onufry Kicki with a letter to Kościuszko begging him in the strongest terms to come to Warsaw. Mokronowski suggested the king should go to join Kościuszko himself, but this was hardly feasible. Only two days before, another rumour that he had escaped brought the rabble out to look for him. In fact Stanisław had abandoned the relative safety of the Castle for his beloved Łazienki, even though he was completely defenceless there. On 2 July Kościuszko replied that 'the safety of the person of Your Majesty concerns me in the highest degree', and a few days later marched into Warsaw with a body of regular infantry.[37] Late on the evening of 11 July he furtively called on Stanisław at Łazienki.

Stanisław urged him to use his dictatorial powers to restore order and impose a more sensible policy. He also begged to be allowed to go with him when he left Warsaw. Kościuszko gave him his word of honour not to leave him in the lurch, but stated that Stanisław must stay put for the time being. He then asked the king for the originals of the maps he had been making since 1776. Stanisław said he would rather give diamonds than the maps, which he had expended so much loving effort on, but allowed the Commander to take them away for copying. Kościuszko then kissed the king's hand and took his leave.[38]

The disturbances of 27–28 June had brought many liberal enthusiasts to their senses. 'This moment made me violently aware of the true nature of the common people, to whose masses that profound thinker Rousseau would have entrusted the highest powers of government,' wrote the former radical Józef Wybicki with ill-concealed disgust.[39] Kościuszko himself was horrified and acted with firmness. Over a hundred people were arrested in connection with the lynchings, and their trials began at once. Among the first to be sentenced were two priests, one of whom had worked the ropes, while the other assisted, dressed in his stole and brandishing a pair of pistols. A total of eight were hanged, with many more receiving lesser sentences.

In the second half of July 25,000 Prussians under Frederick William himself joined a force of 15,000 Russians to lay siege to Warsaw.[40] For two months Kościuszko held them off with a force of 16,000 troops and 10,000 citizen volunteers. His expertise in fortification and gunnery stood him in good stead, as he only had 230 cannon with which to defend an extended perimeter. Józef Poniatowski was at last given a command, with the task of holding the north-western sector of this perimeter against the Prussians. Stanisław was delighted, and often went up the tower of the Evangelical Church to watch the operations through his eye-glass.

The populace were kept busy defending their city, but Stanisław was still far from satisfied with the way things were going. Although the Jacobin club had been closed down at the end of June, its members had merely split into smaller groups which met in coffee-houses and billiard-rooms. 'Everyone is armed, they stalk enemies and recalcitrants, suspecting everyone, eyeing each other with mistrust,' recorded Jan Ochocki. 'Everywhere there is fear and suspicion, from which stem a kind of passion and madness, which is indescribable, fearsome.'[41]

Wherever he went he was asked to show his papers and give passwords. And these were eloquent in themselves. The Warsaw garrison's challenges and passwords for June included, along with predictably vigorous ones such as 'Unity: – strength', 'Liberty: – happiness', 'Citizenship: – loyalty', a number of others such as 'Birth: – accident', 'Personage: – shame', and 'People: – power'.[42]

The stance of the Supreme Council remained ambivalent. On 21 July Potocki assured Gardiner, who had complained about 'French methods', that they intended to bring back the constitution of 3 May as soon as the military situation permitted.[43] Ten days later he came to lunch with Stanisław, who asked him whether he saw French methods as a precondition of French support, which Potocki admitted they were actively seeking. 'No. No. No. There will be a certain similarity at the beginning, but not later,' Potocki replied. 'The French themselves know very well that it is impossible, and that it will not be.'[44] Stanisław welcomed this statement, but he did not know whether to believe it.

And whatever Potocki might say, Kołłątaj was plotting violent revolution and, according to Niemcewicz, 'he did everything in his power to destroy [the king].'[45] He worked through the populace, which went about singing ditties demanding the hanging of the king and the Primate as well as other aristocrats of doubtful allegiance. In June Kołłątaj's agents started a rumour to the effect that the papers of the Russian embassy had yielded proof of the king having tried to sell his own army to the Russians during the 1792 campaign.[46] On 11 August another rumour spread through the city that the Primate had sent Frederick William information about the defences, and the Primate's death the next day was interpreted by some as suicide. Michał had been ailing for some time. He wanted to leave the country and go to Vienna or Rome, having lost faith in the future or his ability to influence it, and while he probably was living in fear of the mob, there is no evidence that he did commit suicide.

His brother's death was a heavy blow for Stanisław. 'The king seemed more dead than alive for several days, neither eating nor sleeping,' according to one of his pages.[47] His sisters rallied round to comfort him, but nothing could make up for the loss of one who had been a close friend and valued adviser. Stanisław rarely allowed personal sorrow to intrude on his sense of duty, however, and before his brother had been laid in his grave, he had despatched a letter to the Pope. Gniezno, the archbishopric whose incumbent was the Primate, had been in Prussian hands since 1793, and he feared that Frederick William might interfere and prevent the nomination of a new head of the Church in Poland.[48]

Stanisław countered Kołłątaj's rumour-mongering with gestures. In August, he gave virtually all the money he had, 48,000 złoty, in exchange for the worthless new paper currency. He donated the remains of his table silver and his gold, bales of cloth for the army and over a thousand pounds of bronze, a thousand pounds of lead, 60,000 bricks and a piece of land for a new cannon foundry. But the Jacobins would not let up. When the Prussians surprised a weak point in Poniatowski's sector and captured a redoubt, he was accused of treachery, even though he was badly wounded, and indeed managed to recapture it. The hue and cry was such that Poniatowski resigned his command. On 25 August the *Government Gazette* began publishing lists of people whose receipts for handouts had allegedly been discovered in the papers of the Russian embassy. The king's name figured prominently. 'I have never taken any pension from any foreign court,' Stanisław protested to Kościuszko, demanding that the *Gazette* be reprimanded.[49] Although Kościuszko acquiesced and a proclamation prepared by Stanisław was published, the damage had been done. A few days later, Stanisław was once more protesting to Kościuszko, whose likeness was circulating on a print bearing an inscription hailing him as a destroyer of kings.

'In truth, even I cannot make myself obeyed in everything,' Kościuszko lamented to Stanisław during one of their evening walks in the gardens at Łazienki.[50] As he came to appreciate the real intentions of the Jacobins, he moved closer to the king's position. He was also beginning to feel the need to legitimate his role. At a solemn Mass for those who had fallen in defence of the capital Kościuszko went up to the king, bowed and took up a respectful position, standing behind his chair throughout the service. Stanisław tried to accord him precedence as they left the church, but the Commander ostentatiously declined, and followed the king out.[51]

On 2 August Frederick William had sent Stanisław an insultingly phrased call to surrender, but he was soon forced to eat his words. In the second half of August, the Poles made a number of sorties against the besieging forces. Poniatowski, who had been reinstated, delivered a raid against the Prussians, and General Jan Henryk Dąbrowski broke out with a small force and marched into Wielkopolska. He collected volunteers as he went, and wrought havoc deep in the Prussian rear. On 2 September Frederick William was obliged to raise the siege. Catherine laughed on hearing of the discomfiture of 'le gros Guillaume'.[52] She could afford to. While Dąbrowski harried Frederick William, Knorring and Derfelden took Wilno and extinguished the Insurrection in Lithuania. The combined Russo-Prussian forces operating in Poland numbered 110,000 against a grand total of 64,000 Poles under arms, most of them peasant irregulars. And she had plenty more troops available.

With Warsaw out of danger, Kościuszko marched out to try and prevent the Russian armies from concentrating, and with his departure Jacobin activity revived. The military tribunal, presided over by Kołłątaj's power-hungry and ruthless friend Józef Zajączek, was behaving more and more like the French Committee of Public Safety. It goaded the populace by arranging the hanging in effigy of Feliks Potocki, Branicki, Rzewuski and others, and exhorted it to denounce 'traitors' lurking in their midst. There followed numerous random arrests. On 12 September the tribunal sentenced to death Bishop Skarszewski of Chełm. The charge – that he had failed to resist partition at the Grodno Seym – could as easily be levelled at the king. Stanisław, who had now moved back to the Castle, wrote to Kościuszko, pointing out that aside from the extreme unfairness of the sentence, the execution of a bishop would only prejudice the world further against Poland. Kościuszko used his dictatorial powers to commute the sentence to life imprisonment, but confessed to Stanisław that his authority was being undermined and circumscribed.[53] His ability to shield Stanisław was dwindling. And even this flimsy shield was to be snatched away.

In an attempt to prevent the meeting of two Russian armies, Kościuszko took on General Fersen at Maciejowice on 10 October. His own supporting column failed to turn up at the appointed time, and he himself was wounded and taken prisoner in the rout that followed. The news was brought by a Russian officer sent to the king by General Fersen with a pass signed by the wounded Kościuszko. Fersen addressed Stanisław as the sole legitimate authority in Poland, and demanded the immediate release of all Russian prisoners. Stanisław consulted with the Council and replied that there could be no question of releasing all prisoners unconditionally, but that he would be glad to see an exchange.[54]

With the capture of Kościuszko the Insurrection entered its death-throes, and these began with a last bid for supremacy by Kołłątaj and the Jacobins. Kołłątaj founded an 'Association to Uphold the Revolution' and put forward Zajączek as a possible successor to Kościuszko, but he was turned down in favour of the moderate Tomasz Wawrzecki. The Jacobins then began to make preparations to storm the Castle, kill the king and seize power. 'The symptoms of a new revolution hovered in the air,' noted a witness.[55] The coup was planned for 28 October, but never materialised, probably because the populace had changed its mind about Stanisław.[56]

As Suvorov's main forces took up positions outside Warsaw, the city magistrates approached the king, begging him to arrange a surrender. Stanisław had no intention of being turned into the nation's scapegoat a second time, and wanted to defend the city.[57] He sent them back to the Council. But only a few hours later he was approached by the magistrates and the Council together. It was suddenly perceived, as never before, that he was the only legitimate representative of the state. At a more mundane level, his anointed status was coming to be seen as a guarantee of safety. People of every condition began slipping into the Castle with bundles of valuables, ensconcing themselves in empty servants' quarters, passages and store-rooms. Some 300 others took refuge in the English legation and another 200 in the Nunciature. The Jacobins would find few allies now. Nevertheless, regular troops which should have been manning the defences were patrolling the city in anticipation of trouble.

At dawn on 4 November, Suvorov attacked the suburb of Praga, and after three hours' fighting breached the defences. A terrible butchery then began, clearly visible and audible from the terrace of the Castle. 'Right up to the banks of the Vistula one found only dead and dying people of all estates; and the banks themselves were heaped with the bodies of soldiers, civilians, Jews, priests, monks, women and children,' wrote the Russian general Engelhardt. 'My heart froze at the sight of all this, and the loathsome picture revolted my soul.'[58] According to one Russian estimate, 20,000 people had been killed in the space of a few hours.[59] (Lieutenant Nicolas Chopin, the composer's father, was one of the few survivors.) Suvorov warned that the same fate would befall Warsaw if it did not capitulate immediately. The radicals melted away – Zajączek had been wounded and Jasiński killed at Praga, Kołłątaj had fled Warsaw – and the terrified rabble was swarming into the Castle for safety. Everyone now looked to Stanisław as their saviour.

He summoned the Council and asked what it intended to do. Wawrzecki wanted to fight on. Stanisław pointed out that it was impossible to defend a city whose population wanted to surrender. Dąbrowski suggested taking the army, the Council and the king, along with the Treasury and the national archives, and making a march for France, from where the struggle could be continued. Hardly an alluring prospect for Stanisław. Wawrzecki suggested the army evacuate the capital, leaving the king to negotiate with Russia as best he could. It was only after everyone had agreed to this plan that Stanisław assented, and he immediately sent an emissary to Suvorov. But after the meeting was over, Wawrzecki asked the king to come with him after all, and Stanisław agreed.[60] Ignacy Potocki heard of this and insisted that Stanisław must guarantee the safety of the city by staying behind.[61]

In the event, it was the people of Warsaw who decided the matter. The sight of the king's carriages being loaded spread alarm through the city and the Castle was quickly surrounded by thousands of people determined not to let him leave. By the next morning, 8 November, when Wawrzecki came to escort Stanisław out, he saw the impossibility of the plan, and only just managed to squeeze through the keening mob himself.[62]

Later that day, the Supreme Council dissolved itself and handed over all political authority to Stanisław. Wawrzecki restored the Horseguards, the Cadets and the police to the king's command before marching out in a southerly direction at the head of the remaining Polish forces. On the following morning Suvorov marched into Warsaw from the east, cringeingly greeted by the citizens, who feared a repetition of the Praga massacre. He called on Stanisław, and was perfectly deferential. It was not until the Russians had quietly taken over the whole city without slaughtering anyone that the people began to leave the Castle and go back to their homes.

Wawrzecki intended to fight on, but morale was low and the march disorderly, leaving behind it a trail of dying horses and abandoned guns. On 13 November he fought a minor engagement against the Prussians, but his army was melting away as the peasants slipped off to their homes. By 14 November it was down to 5,000 men, and Wawrzecki sent a courier to Stanisław asking him to mediate an honourable capitulation. Stanisław tried to obtain promises of leniency from Suvorov, but the Russian would not hear of any conditions. Dąbrowski wanted to make a dash for France with the remnants, but Wawrzecki took Stanisław's advice and surrendered on 16 November.

'Madam My Sister, the fate of Poland is in your hands,' Stanisław wrote to Catherine on 21 November. He told her that his country was devastated and that his people were starving, and begged her on their behalf to show mercy and forgiveness. He left himself and the political implications out.[63] Her reply was less dignified. It consisted mainly of a lecture to the effect that what had happened was the fault of corruptions emanating from France, and that all her efforts at keeping the Poles from bringing disaster on themselves had been rewarded with 'ingratitude, hatred and perfidy'. She nevertheless promised to supply food to the starving population. 'Your Majesty must know my character,' she reassured him. 'It renders me incapable of abusing the victory which the bounty of Providence and the Justice of my Cause have granted me. You may therefore anticipate with tranquillity that which reason of state and the general interest of public peace will decide as to the ultimate fate of Poland.'[64]

26

A Marble Gaol

*I*t was the end of the road, and whatever illusions Stanisław might have nourished were quickly dispelled. On 10 November, the day after Suvorov marched into the city, the king and Ignacy Potocki (who alone of the insurrectionary leaders had stayed on) wrote out a plan of pacification. It recommended a lenient approach and suggested reorganising the country into a constitutional monarchy bound to Russia by treaty.[1] But Catherine was not interested in their proposals. She ordered Suvorov to treat Poland as conquered territory. At the Castle, Polish sentries were replaced by Russian troops. All state property was confiscated. Polish banners and insignia were to be taken to Russia as booty, along with the entire Archive of the Commonwealth and even the Załuski Library.[2]

Stanisław had to beg Suvorov to stop wounded soldiers being evicted from barracks and hospitals, and to unlock the grain-stores which had been sealed up, as typhus was spreading in the wake of famine. Fortunately, Suvorov, who had been promoted to Field-Marshal and sent a gold baton by Catherine for the massacre of Praga, now showed his humane side and complied. He was less obliging, however, on other matters. He ordered the Cadet Corps to be closed down and quashed Stanisław's attempt to save it by turning it into a high school. Stanisław wanted to get the post working and to put the Mint back into production, in order to permit economic life to resume, but again he was overruled.

As he watched the last vestiges of Polish statehood being dismantled,

432

Stanisław also fretted for his subjects. He was in daily receipt of hundreds of harrowing begging-letters from friends, officers, servants and other subjects, none of whom he could help.

Catherine was determined to stamp out the Jacobin 'disease', and began by ordering the arrest and deportation to Russia of all those who had taken part in the Insurrection. Stanisław had managed to obtain from Suvorov generous terms for the treatment of officers and civilians. The field-marshal had given his word that the city's president Zakrzewski would not be touched if he returned to Warsaw, where his presence was needed. But Catherine's orders changed that, and when Zakrzewski arrived he was clapped in irons and sent off to Russia. All Stanisław could do was to give him a fur coat for the journey. Ignacy Potocki, Kiliński, Wawrzecki and over 10,000 others were sent to Russia as well in a lugubrious procession of kibitkas. (Kołłątaj had been caught and imprisoned by the Austrians.)

Stanisław's turn came on 22 December. 'The dangers to which Your Majesty has been exposed among the unbridled populace of Warsaw, make me desire that Your Majesty should at the earliest opportunity quit this guilty city,' Catherine wrote.[3] He was to go to Grodno.

Stanisław replied that he did not fear the people of Warsaw, and produced a litany of reasons for staying put.[4] He did not know that Catherine had already decided to partition the remainder of Poland, but he suspected it. He certainly knew that Prussia was eyeing Warsaw itself. His continued presence there was an obstacle, and he wanted to prolong it in the forlorn hope that friction between Russia and Prussia might yet lead to a change of plan. Catherine repeated her order, but Stanisław procrastinated, complaining of poor health, the difficulties of the journey, the fact that his carriages were in no state to undertake it, and that he had no money with which to repair them. Suvorov attended to this, so Stanisław began to draw up lists of all the people who must go with him, including his whole family and a contingent of his own Guards. He sent Antoni Dziekoński to Grodno to provide evidence that the place was unfit to receive him, but the castle was indeed well provided. Repnin, now Governor of Lithuania, categorically refused to allow Stanisław to bring his Guards, assuring him that 'the troops of Her Imperial Majesty will have the honour of attending to his well-being and paying him all the suitable honours'.[5] Repnin regarded the fallen king as still potentially dangerous, and suggested to Catherine that it would be safer to send him to Riga, where he would be cut off from all his countrymen. Sievers went further, recommending that Stanisław be sent to Orel or Voronezh.[6] 'Long experience has convinced us that Stanisław Augustus has always acted against our interests,' Repnin warned General Bezborodko, who was to be the king's gaoler in Grodno.[7]

By the new year, Stanisław had expended all his delaying tactics, and there was no longer even a flicker of hope for the survival of Poland. On 3 January 1795 Austria signed a treaty with Russia agreeing to join in Poland's final dismemberment. Foreign courts were no longer even prepared to protest. From London, Bukaty reported that Lord Grenville treated him 'as if Your Majesty and the Commonwealth no longer existed'.[8] Displaying greater probity than their courts, Colonel Gardiner, the Dutch chargé d'affaires and the Papal Nuncio called on Stanisław and announced their intention of accompanying him to Grodno, disregarding the Russian order to wind up their legations.[9]

Stanisław's departure was fixed irrevocably for 7 January 1795. The news caused genuine dismay as well as fear in Warsaw. A group of citizens collected a sum of money for him, and the Jewish community raised 50,000 złoty as a donation.[10] On the day, the people were out in force, swarming around the Castle and filling the nearby streets. That morning Stanisław heard Mass and took Holy Communion. At ten o'clock, dressed in a brown travelling coat and suede breeches, a sable pelisse lined with crimson velvet and a velvet cap, he came down into the courtyard. 'A multitude of people, including the remains of the household, stood by the great portal of the Castle in gloomy silence with tears in their eyes, waiting to take their leave of a master from whom, throughout their service they had received nothing but benefactions,' recorded one of the pages.[11] Suvorov presented the Russian guard of honour, and then Stanisław reviewed his own Guards for the last time. With tears running down his face, Stanisław gave his hand to everyone to kiss one by one. Then he climbed into a carriage, accompanied by his adjutant General Gorzeński, his valet Duhamel and Dr Boeckler. The cortège moved out under the arch of the main gate, and 'all that remained at court were tears for a good master'.

Outside the Castle, the streets were lined with Russian troops presenting arms, and behind them a crowd of citizens shouting 'Long live the King!' At one point, the crowd broke through the cordon of troops, immobilised the carriage and began to unharness the horses. Stanisław leant out of the window to speak, but at that moment a file of Russian dragoons forced its way between him and his subjects, and the carriage trundled off at a brisk trot.[12] The convoy crossed the Vistula on a raft, since the bridge had not been repaired. As his carriage climbed the opposite bank, Stanisław told the postillion to stop. He got out, and began to survey his beloved capital through an eye-glass. General Tormasov tried to get him back into his carriage, but Stanisław called for a folding stool, and remained in tearful contemplation for two hours in spite of the increasingly testy general's pleas.[13]

On 9 January Stanisław arrived at Białystok, where he hoped to rest for a few days. But he was assailed by a crowd of local szlachta and peasants, some wishing only to look on their king for the last time, most begging for financial help or redress against ravages committed by Russian soldiery. He was hustled on by his Russian escort, and continued his journey through the desolate snow-covered landscape, but not before despatching two more lengthy petitions to Suvorov on behalf of his people.

On 12 January 1795 he drove into Grodno, greeted by Repnin with full military honours and a 101-gun salute. He was taken to the castle, which was to be his prison for the next two years. Repnin's extraordinarily detailed instructions specified that while Stanisław was to be treated with all the respect due to a reigning monarch, every order he gave, however mundane, was to be vetted by his gaoler General Bezborodko or Repnin himself, who would also read every letter he sent or received. Visitors were not allowed, and anyone entering the castle, whether members of his family or his household, was to be searched. Sentries were to have loaded muskets at all times, and the hours and rounds of patrols were to be varied constantly.[14]

General Bezborodko was in daily attendance, as was Repnin, who had taken over Tyzenhauz's residence. His company was not unwelcome to Stanisław. 'Unhappiness, reflection and reading had not only made him renounce the doctrine of an *ésprit fort* which he professed in 1768, but made of him a judicious, moderate, compassionate and really good man,' he wrote.[15] Stanisław questioned him

435

incessantly about Catherine's plans. 'I keep repeating to him that the fate of Poland has been sealed,' Repnin wrote to her on 16 January. 'I gently suggest to him that since that of the Commonwealth has been decided, he ought to think of his own future . . . if he hesitates still, this is the consequence of an unjustified feeling, a tiny spark of hope, that the fate of Poland might still be altered!'[16]

That spark grew dimmer by the day, and under Repnin's skilful persuasion Stanisław began to abandon his perceived obligations. Something he would otherwise have fought against stubbornly, the liquidation of Poland's diplomatic representation, he now acquiesced in without demur. On 13 January he drafted a circular to all envoys at foreign courts. 'The saddest of realities obliges me to inform you that there is no longer any form of National authority in what we have hitherto called our motherland,' it ran.[17] But Catherine did not like the tone he took, so he obediently followed Repnin's dictation, and merely informed his diplomats that 'all form of authority having ceased to exist in Poland, your representation is terminated'.[18] To Gardiner, who was determined to follow him, and whose attendance he would in every other circumstance have done everything to promote for its symbolic value, he sent his portrait and a brief note telling him not to come.[19] Stanisław was no longer thinking of Poland, he was thinking of himself. And at the end of January he laid his thoughts before Repnin:

You can see yourself what effect sadness, the climate and age are having on my health. This requires my being removed both mentally and physically from everything that contributes ceaselessly to undermine it. An eye-witness to the most complete catastrophe of a Motherland to which I had vowed all my faculties, surrounded by every kind of misfortune which I can no longer remedy, is it not natural that I should wish to be distanced from them? If I can do no more good to my compatriots, I can no longer lead a decent existence among them . . . If I were alone, if I did not have members of my family who are the only solace left to me, I should wish to go beyond the seas and try to hide, as it were, from myself and from my memories. But in doing so I would render even more unhappy the person who loves me most, and it is something I cannot resolve to do. I can therefore see for me no other place than Italy.[20]

Catherine praised the 'wisdom and moderation' of Stanisław's wishes and promised to attend to them by May.[21] But this only partly reassured him. 'I am in no laughing mood,' Stanisław wrote to Elżbieta Grabowska, complaining of the cold and his isolation.[22] Something akin to panic took hold of him as he envisaged a long captivity in this gloomy place. 'He was rarely in his natural good humour, and a kind of sadness or melancholy suffused his face all the time,' records one of his pages. 'He only rarely smiled.'[23]

At least the regular and undemanding routine helped restore his health. He would rise every morning at eight, swallow a cup of bouillon prepared specially by Tremo, then dress, read his mail and answer letters, after which he would go for a walk on the terrace of the castle. He had lunch at two, and spent the afternoon and evening playing billiards, conversing or dictating his memoirs. He usually dined alone and retired regularly at ten, to be read to sleep. As soon as the snow melted, he began to go for drives, always tailed by a troop of dragoons and General Bezborodko in another carriage. They would watch him as he walked or stood in contemplation for hours, lost in thought, on the banks of the Niemen.

Stanisław's chief enemy was boredom, since few people were allowed to visit him, and his court was reduced by Repnin, who was intent on isolating him. General Gorzeński was ordered to leave first, then Stanisław's favourite secretary Marcin Badeni was given his marching orders. Ryx, who turned up in February, was not allowed to stay in Grodno, nor was Onufry Kicki, Equerry of the Crown and, since the death of Alexandrowicz in the previous year, Court Marshal, a dear friend and one of the few people who could bring a smile to his face. 'You will easily guess how bored I am here, and how I sigh for May,' Stanisław wrote to Elżbieta Grabowska.[24]

In February the two sons of Adam Czartoryski, Adam Jerzy and Konstanty, turned up on their way to St Petersburg. At their mother's request Repnin had persuaded Catherine not to penalise the family, on condition the two young men took service in Russia. It is symptomatic of the times that on seeing them Repnin exclaimed in horror at their 'Roman' haircuts – any departure from powder and bows was seen as evidence of Jacobin sympathies. Their sojourn in Grodno was prolonged while their hair grew, and they often called on Stanisław, who morosely went over the events of his reign with the young

Adam, reproaching himself for having failed to conserve his kingdom.[25]

He longed for Catherine to reach a decision on his future, to be allowed 'to go to the sun', as he put it to Elżbieta Grabowska, who was waiting in Vienna.[26] But Catherine would not address herself to Stanisław's future until the whole Polish question had been fully resolved. There was unholy bickering between the courts of Berlin and Vienna, as Prussia was demanding an inordinately large share, including Warsaw and Kraków. On 5 April 1795 Prussia deserted the anti-French coalition and signed the treaty of Basle with France. Prussian forces concentrated for an expected confrontation with Russia, not far from Grodno, and Stanisław's guardians considered evacuating him further away from his country. Stanisław's attention turned briefly, and without much enthusiasm, to the possibility of exploiting the situation. In September he drew up a project for a settlement of the Polish question which included a return to the constitution of 3 May, with Constantine on the throne, and a general amnesty.[27]

But at the same time he drew up more detailed projects of settlements for himself and for his family, who were penniless, as their estates had been sequestered and their Warsaw palaces ravaged. Stanisław could not help. His establishment at Grodno was paid for directly by Repnin, and he had no money of his own, since he had received no revenues over the past eighteen months. He suggested to Repnin that these should be paid him by Russia, and also that Russia should put pressure on the Emperor to pay him the money he owed him for the Wieliczka salt-mines. But the issue of his finances, like his travel plans, was bound up with the ultimate settlement of the Polish question, which was no closer to solution. But this did not stop Stanisław's family badgering him for assistance.

The one exception was his nephew Józef, who stubbornly refused to co-operate with Stanisław's efforts to get his estates back for him. Stanisław wanted him to come to Grodno, but this was impossible, because he would not swear an oath of allegiance to Catherine, or even take back the orders of the White Eagle and St Stanisław he had ostentatiously handed in along with his *Virtuti Militari* – which was interpreted as a revolutionary gesture. Stanisław pleaded with his nephew to take them back, and to grow his hair. But Józef was defiant, and Catherine ordered him to leave Poland altogether, so he moved to Vienna.

A consolation for Stanisław was the arrival, on 5 June, of his sister Izabela. He drove out to meet her, and they burst into tears as they embraced by the roadside. She was followed a few days later by his other sister Ludwika with her grandchildren, and not long after that by his nephew Stanisław, who had spent the last two years travelling in Italy. The king's natural sons Michał and Kazimierz Grabowski had also come to Grodno, and, a few weeks later, Elżbieta Grabowska herself arrived from Vienna. Repnin had relaxed his vigilance and allowed more visits, by local nobles, by Marcin Poczobut from Wilno, and by the king's faithful friend Bishop Naruszewicz. All this brought life into the castle. Kazimierz Grabowski sang duets with Joachim Chreptowicz's son Adam, plays were staged and various entertainments were devised. In August an Italian magician called Pinetti passed through and amused Stanisław greatly with his tricks. But the heavy gloom that hung over the castle could not be dispelled for long. Uncertainty and foreboding filled the days that succeeded each other interminably, punctuated by the heavy stamp of the Russian sentries whose 'flat, expressionless faces' so terrified Kazimierz's little grand-daughter Anna Tyszkiewicz.[28]

It was not until 24 October 1795 that the treaty of partition was signed by all three powers, the Prussians having at last given way and agreed to leave Kraków to Austria. They did not actually evacuate the city until January 1796 (taking with them 170 carts laden with the contents of Wawel castle, including the Polish crown jewels).[29] And it was only then that Russia allowed them to occupy Warsaw. The mistrust between the three courts was such that the final agreements were not signed for another year after that, so the question of who was to provide for Stanisław's upkeep, pay the Commonwealth's debts, and indeed what was to be done with the Polish king, remained unresolved. Having heard of his plight, the Duke of Portland communicated to Stanisław that if he had nowhere else to go he could always come to England, and that his own fortune 'would always be at the disposal of Count Poniatowski'.[30]

With the partition accomplished, Catherine decided that the time had come for Stanisław to abdicate. He was well aware that a king of Poland did not have the right to abdicate – only those who had elected him could release him from the vows sworn in the *Pacta Conventa*. He attached greater importance to symbol than most, and knew full well that his duty was to refuse to accept what had happened, and to remain, for the rest of his life, the living evidence of the violence perpetrated by the three powers. His abdication would suggest acquiescence in that act of violence and lend justification to it.

But Stanisław was tired. With his arrival in Grodno the last traces of the optimism that had sustained him through so many black moments finally deserted him, and he no longer even contemplated the possibility of a future for Poland. At the same time he transferred all his hopes from the state to the people. From the moment the Russians marched into Warsaw in November 1794, he concerned himself tirelessly with the plight of his subjects, whoever they were. He begged Repnin to stay the hand of the Russian military courts, which were dealing in particularly brutal ways with Poles from the first and second partitions who had joined the Insurrection; he tried to stop the confiscation of estates, ninety-six of which had already been taken away from their owners and given to Russian officers; and he even tried to secure the release of two of his kidnappers, who had been mouldering in the prison at Kamieniec since 1773.[31] He attended personally to thousands of petitions and requests. He wrote out generous testimonials for people who had been anything but loyal to him, he sent pathetic sums of money he could not spare to people who were in less difficult straits than himself – and he even found the time to write to George Washington to help Littlepage get a new job. His instinctive kindness shines forth from the boxes of his correspondence in this period, along with an almost reprehensible selflessness. It could not have been pleasant writing ingratiating letters to the favourite Platon Zubov on his own behalf, as he had to do, and he could reasonably have spared himself the additional humiliation of doing so repeatedly on behalf of others, such as the Czartoryskis.

Stanisław was most concerned of all for those who had served him and placed their future in his hands. An overwhelming proportion of his debts was accounted for by small sums borrowed from private individuals, tradesmen's bills and unpaid pensions. Hundreds of officers, servants, functionaries, courtiers and tradesmen had been left in the lurch, and their only hope of avoiding beggary lay in Stanisław. Repnin had made it abundantly clear that his debts would only be settled and himself and his family provided for if he obeyed Catherine in everything. Thus his public duty lay in making an empty gesture of defiance which spelt misery for thousands, and possibly for millions if it were to provoke Catherine into further repressions. It also spelt a very uncertain fate for himself and those dear to him. Unsurprisingly, Stanisław ignored his public duty in favour of his human obligations.

'There was no lack of tears, and bitter tears they were,' Repnin reported to Catherine. 'It was not the abdication itself that was their cause, but the thought of the future fate of Poland.'[32] Stanisław drafted the document himself. It glossed over the political dimension of his abdication, turning the whole exercise into something more like a transfer of obligations. It ended with the phrase: 'As We leave the throne, We acquit ourself of the last duty of Our reign in conjuring Her Imperial Majesty to accord her maternal benefactions to all those over whom We have reigned.'[33] Repnin was not satisfied, as the document did not endorse the partition, but Stanisław stood firm. In the end he agreed to add a phrase stating that his abdication was entirely voluntary. He signed it on 25 November 1795, the thirty-first anniversary of his coronation, and sent it off with a covering letter to Catherine in which he asked her to issue a public declaration to the effect that all his and the state's debtors would be paid. 'May [this act]', he concluded, 'conciliate and assure me for the rest of my days your kindness and your personal affection, which has always been the object of my first wishes, and which I preferred (as you know) to that same crown which I now place in your hands.'[34] The nervous strain of carrying out this ignominious act told on him and he took to his bed for three days.

When he had recovered he wrote to Catherine about his own future. He wanted to go to Carlsbad in the spring, and then to Vienna, from where he would like to make 'some light excursions of curiosity into Italy and Switzerland', and suggested Austria, Rome or some German principality as his permanent place of residence.[35] On 21 December she wrote back assenting to his plan. She ruled out Austria or any part of the Empire as a permanent residence, and suggested Rome, which was 'the most suitable to his political position, to his renowned taste for the arts, and for his tranquillity'. There he would be set up in suitable style and comfort, and surrounded by all the dignity which his position required, for he was to keep the title of King of Poland.[36]

Stanisław busied himself with the necessary preparations, which included disposing of his private property. Onufry Kicki came to Grodno to discuss terms for selling the Warsaw properties, including Łazienki, to the Prussian government, and in January 1796 Marcello Bacciarelli came to draw up lists and valuations of the works of art. Stanisław spent whole days shut up with Bacciarelli, deciding which of the paintings, sculptures, prints, maps and medals he would keep, and which were to be sold – a depressing task for someone who had spent so much of his life collecting. But the act of discussing the objects and assessing their artistic merit with his 'caro Marcello' was a great pleasure in itself.

Once more spring came and went, yet neither his debts nor his departure had been decided upon. In May 1796 he wrote to Catherine asking her to use her good offices with the Emperor in the matter of the sums due to him, and enquiring about how plans for his future were progressing. She wrote back promptly with cordial assurances, but nothing changed. Boredom was beginning to eat into Stanisław again. He distracted himself with his memoirs, with editing the second volume of *Opinion on the King of Poland*, prepared by Mikołaj Wolski, and with writing long letters. Fryderyk Bacciarelli wrote him lengthy despatches from Warsaw every few days retailing Warsaw and international news.

Stanisław's health was poor and he was plagued by rheumatoid arthritis. That winter he had even suffered an intermittent stroke. Above all, he was depressed. 'Happiness showed itself to us in a flash, and then vanished completely with such speed,' he said through his tears to the poet Karpiński, who visited him several times.[37] His sisters had left. His brother Kazimierz came from Warsaw in July, but was only allowed to stay for two days. After he left Sophie Leullier turned up and distracted him for a couple of weeks. Stanisław Trembecki, a constant companion, was reduced to devising a poetic tournament on the theme of Stanisław's dog Kiopek in an attempt to ward off boredom.[38] Even Repnin was suffering from melancholy. 'The contemplation of [Stanisław's] present situation unwittingly awakens a deep sense of the insignificance of things terrestrial, and of the power of the Almighty,' he wrote to a friend. 'It would be difficult to find another man who had known such happiness and such misery.'[39]

In September Repnin fell ill and left for Wilno, but not before communicating to Stanisław Catherine's decision that he must leave Grodno – not for Carlsbad, but for Moscow. Stanisław was horrified. Such a move could only signify that he was to be incarcerated in Russia for the rest of his days. With the French victorious on the Rhine and General Bonaparte sweeping through Italy driving the Austrian armies before him, Catherine would not dream of allowing the king of Poland, that potent symbol of the injustice of the three monarchies, to go wandering in Europe.

Once again Stanisław conjured up endless excuses to delay his departure for Moscow, but his gloomy forebodings were abruptly cut short on the evening of 28 November. Half-way through dinner a courier was announced, and General Bezborodko excused himself and left the table to attend to him. He returned after a while and finished dinner impassively, but once the company had risen he asked Stanisław for a word in the next room. There he announced to the king that Catherine had died on 17 November. Stanisław 'broke down with grief on hearing this sad news', an extravagant expression of eighteenth-century *sensibilité*.[40] Aside from anything else, the news plunged him into uncertainty as to his fate. God only knew what the unpredictable Paul would decree.

Stanisław did not have to wait long to find out; on 5 December Paul wrote cordially inviting him to St Petersburg. It was an order. 'To be close to you and to rejoice in your friendship with that complete confidence which only your virtuous character can inspire will be the solace of the rest of my days,' Stanisław wrote back politely.[41] By the same courier he wrote to Repnin begging him to take advantage of the new Tsar's goodwill to ask for the release from prison of Kościuszko, Ignacy Potocki, Wawrzecki and all the other leaders of the Insurrection, and also to touch on the question of his family's affairs. But a few days later he was in receipt of a letter from Repnin announcing that Paul had himself ordered the release of all the Polish prisoners, and that he had lifted the sequestrations from the estates of all the king's relatives – General Fersen was told to move out and return the estate Catherine had awarded him to Stanisław's sister Izabela. Other letters followed, informing Stanisław that Paul had assigned the Marble Palace to him as a residence after having personally gone to inspect it.[42]

Paul also announced that he had given Józef Poniatowski the rank of lieutenant-general in the Russian army and his own regiment of cuirassiers, and looked forward to greeting him in St Petersburg. Sensing that his nephew would prove awkward, Stanisław wrote to Józef's sister Teresa, who was with him in Vienna. He warned that the refusal of such magnanimity might anger the Tsar and lead him to rescind his other gestures, and that if Józef did refuse, the only way that he, Stanisław, could react would be to disavow him and never see him again. 'Is it possible that Pepi could be so hard-hearted as to inflict such mortal grief on me?' he wrote.[43] Stanisław's letter crossed with one from his nephew, who had just made the sacrifice of going to the Russian embassy in Vienna wearing his orders to swear allegiance to Paul. It was accompanied by a note from Teresa reporting that 'Pepi is in a state of anxiety and torment'.[44] His torments turned to morose defiance on receipt of his uncle's letter.

Stanisław was unmoved and wrote his nephew a stern letter ordering him to accept the Tsar's offer. To Teresa he again pointed out that her brother's obstinacy could cost them all dear. But Józef responded with a letter to the Tsar explaining that he was too ill to travel and politely declining the offer of service in the Russian army, and an emotional diatribe to his uncle in which he protested that he would never agree to wear a Russian uniform.[45] Although he complained to his nephew Stanisław (who was already in St Petersburg) of Józef's 'insane obstinacy', Stanisław relented. He wrote back thanking Józef for the sacrifice he had made over the decorations, and assuring him that he would employ 'all my eloquence so that your refusal of service might not be looked on askance'.[46]

Stanisław himself showed no eagerness to leave. 'I feel such sadness, it is so unbearable to part with my Motherland and those whom I must leave here, that I do not know how I shall bear it,' he wrote to General Byszewski.[47] His delaying excuses were swept aside by Repnin, who made it clear that the Tsar was awaiting his arrival with growing impatience. Hundreds of Poles once more descended on Grodno to beg for assistance. He could do nothing for them himself, but he accepted their petitions and made copious notes to present to the Tsar. 'I am overtaken by expenses at the moment, as everyone, alarmed at my departure, is attacking me from every side,' he wrote to Kazimierz, who was himself soliciting financial help.[48]

A few days later, on 26 January 1797, the tripartite convention settling all outstanding matters relating to the defunct Commonwealth

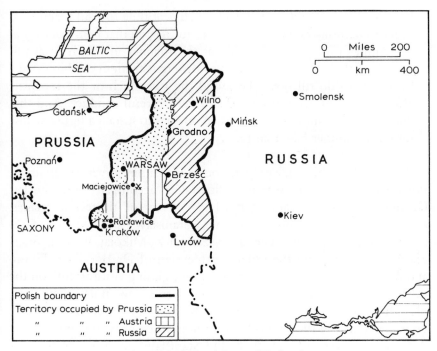

8   The Third Partition of Poland, 1795

was signed. The three powers took upon themselves Stanisław's debts, calculated now at 40 million złoty, and agreed to pay him an annual pension of 200,000 ducats. A secret protocol of this final act annihilating the Polish state bound the three powers to delete the word 'Poland' from all official documents and diplomatic correspondence, in view of 'the recognized necessity of abolishing everything that might recall the existence of a Polish kingdom'.

Stanisław faced the future with misgivings. At the age of sixty-six he was to begin a new life, and he wondered how he would manage. His health was satisfactory as long as he could pace himself, but he was afraid that it would not hold out if he were subjected to rigorous court routines, in a place whose climate had often laid him low when he was only twenty-five. More important than the change of surroundings was his change of condition, as he explained to Kazimierz's daughter Konstancja Tyszkiewicz:

I realise that I should already feel much gratitude to Paul I, and I am eager to demonstrate it. But I will admit to you that I am not easy in my mind or very confident about the manner in which to acquit myself of this role, so novel and so different from everything that I have had to do till now. To avoid the too much or the too little always requires great attention and very careful conduct. And that becomes much more difficult when one has to sustain a figure whose rank is no longer based on reality . . .[49]

After making his final preparations and handing over his affairs in Poland to Kicki, who was not allowed to accompany him, he left Grodno, on 17 February 1797. The convoy of thirteen carriages, carrying Stanisław, his two sons Stanisław and Michał Grabowski, the Mniszechs, Teresa Tyszkiewicz, Mikołaj Wolski, Stanisław Trembecki, and the usual complement of Dr Boeckler, Tremo and others, set off on a fine crisp morning, gliding comfortably on the thick snow. But a thaw set in, and after a few miles they were ploughing through muddy slush. At the first halt the carriages had to be placed back on their wheels, and the journey grew uncomfortable. Axles broke, carriages got stuck, and Stanisław's own overturned just outside Wilno, bringing on severe headaches.

At Wilno, Stanisław was greeted with military parades and fireworks, and he had to receive hundreds of nobles, each with his own tale of woe and his own petition. The journey continued, through Mitawa, Riga and Narva, in each of which the exhausted travellers were met with parades, gun salutes and delegations of dignitaries, as Paul had ordered that Stanisław be accorded the greatest possible honours. Paul also suspended court mourning for three days, so that Stanisław's entry into St Petersburg could be made with fitting pomp.

Just outside the city, on 10 March, the king's cortège was met by the Tsar's sons, Alexander and Constantine, accompanied by the two young Czartoryskis. Stanisław transferred to a Russian state coach, and entered the city with the two grand dukes riding at its doors, escorted by troops of imperial horseguards. At the door of the Marble Palace, he was greeted by the Tsar himself, who embraced him warmly and invited him into his new residence. They had an hour-long conference during which Paul told Stanisław to make all his requests directly to him, and not to any official. Stanisław promptly handed him a long list of grievances that he had been given in Grodno and Wilno. This turned out to be a mistake: Paul looked displeased and handed the document to an aide. Stanisław was nevertheless bidden to dine with the Tsar the following day, and to go with him to Pavlovsk a couple of days later.[50]

Stanisław was hardly given a moment to himself. All the Poles in St Petersburg flocked to see their king, followed sporadically by those being released from prison, including Zakrzewski, the gravely sick Kościuszko and Kiliński. Then the entire diplomatic corps in St Petersburg came to pay their respects, followed by the Russian court and nobility. Among these Stanisław noticed Ksawery Branicki, resplendent in the uniform of a Russian general.

It soon became apparent that Stanisław's role was to be more complex than anticipated. He was part honoured guest, part trophy; for while the eccentric Tsar wanted to demonstrate his magnanimity and confound his mother's meanness, he also exulted in having a king in attendance. Stanisław was therefore required to attend Paul's coronation in Moscow in April. It was an uncomfortable ten-day journey over the worst roads Stanisław had ever known – no fewer than fifteen carriages broke down on him. In Moscow he was given a palace, a bodyguard of horseguards and an adjutant in the person of Prince Gagarin. On 10 April the Tsar made his solemn entry into the city, and as he passed beneath Stanisław's window, he halted and saluted him. That evening Stanisław dined at court, seated as usual between the Tsar and the empress. The coronation took place on 16 April, and Stanisław was placed in a special pew just behind the throne. The imperial couple saluted him before taking their seats at the start of the ceremony, but the occasion was not to pass without a painful humiliation. At the height of the ceremony, Stanisław suddenly felt weak and sat down. A Russian court official promptly walked over and brusquely told him to stand up. But the Tsar continued to pay him the highest honours during the ceremonial dinners that followed the coronation, always seating him at his right hand. On 22 April Stanisław opened the great ball given by Chancellor Bezborodko by dancing the Polonaise with the empress, and a few days later the imperial family came to dine with Stanisław.

On 3 May Paul left Moscow to tour his western provinces, and Stanisław was able to relax. With characteristic curiosity, he used the remainder of his stay in Moscow to visit the Kremlin and its collections, the University, the Pokrovskaya church and the Devichy Monastir. On 9 May he left Moscow for St Petersburg. He made a slight detour to visit the Voskresensky Monastir, but his carriage got bogged down in a remote place, and he had to spend the night in it. The following day, after visiting the monastery, Stanisław bade farewell to his nephew Stanisław, who was going back to Korsuń. He bore this separation all the more easily as he hoped to see his other nephew soon. He had smoothed things out and established that Józef could come in a private capacity, and avoid causing offence at functions where a uniform was required by wearing that of the Order of Malta.[51]

Back in St Petersburg Stanisław busied himself with installing his library and the works of art that were beginning to arrive from Warsaw. He received regularly at the Marble Palace, with Urszula Mniszech playing hostess. His cook Tremo had made such an impression that all the gourmets in Russian society and the diplomatic corps fished for invitations to dinner. He often stirred from home, to visit the Hermitage, where he browsed in Voltaire's library, the various academies and art collections, the mining school, the porcelain factory and the glass-works. Although he could no longer collect, he could not resist seeking out the antique-dealers, where objects from Versailles were beginning to turn up.

But with the advent of summer his public life resumed. In July he went to Tsarskoe Selo to visit Paul, who had returned from his tour. He then accompanied the imperial family to Peterhof, where he was lodged in the pavilion of Mon-Plaisir, which must have brought back poignant memories. There were more balls, operas and dinners, pageants, parades and military exercises, at all of which Stanisław was honoured as the first person after the imperial couple. On St Alexander's day on 30 August, he took part in the ceremonies as a knight of the Order of St Alexander, but instead of the blue cloak, he wore a cloak of puce velvet doubled with ermine, whose train was carried by four Russian nobles.

An ineluctable irony pervades the official side of Stanisław's last year in St Petersburg. For it was here, where his first dreams of royal ambition were born more than forty years earlier, that he at last attained all those formal marks of regal distinction which he had sought vainly to impose while he had a throne. He was treated as an anointed monarch at a moment when everything conspired to make him face the vanity of the dreams and ambitions that had driven him through his life. Yet he faced the approaching end and his Maker with his innate quietism. 'Make me such as I must be to please you', he prayed, 'to be worthy of an easy and tranquil death, to be placed by you in a happy eternity, if not immediately, then after as little expiation as your goodness rather than your justice will wish to add to all that I have had to suffer till now.'[52]

He was prevented from retreating into a private existence, not only by Paul's punctilious observance of monarchical etiquette, but also by the Tsar's sybilline pronouncements. A strong dose of chivalry was one of the major components of Paul's unbalanced character, and he felt genuine shame at what his mother had done to Poland. He returned to the subject often with Stanisław and sometimes professed that he would do something about it. Another subject he returned to with embarrassing frequency was Stanisław's relationship with his mother. 'You will never guess what he talked to me about throughout dinner,' Stanisław said to his nephew one night. 'He tried to persuade me that he is my son. When I explained to him that this was impossible, he only insisted all the more.'[53] Given Paul's unpredictability, such conversations must have been more than just embarrassing.

The first snows fell at the end of October, and Stanisław spent more time at home. He had been joined by his sister Ludwika, and his nephew Józef assured him that he would come soon. Elżbieta Grabowska had arrived in August to settle unobtrusively into a small house near by. His sister Izabela also came for a couple of months. There were dinners every night at the Marble Palace, and even theatrical evenings, since the Tsar had placed a troupe of Italian actors at his disposal. Stanisław still attended court balls, only missing one on 5 December on account of an attack of gout. And he always danced – usually with the empress. 'I really do look after my health, which is in truth no worse than it was in Grodno,' he wrote to his sister Izabela at the end of December. 'I occasionally have the same diverse ailments, but they are no graver than they were.' His little court provided him with all the creature comforts he expected of life, and there was enough going on to keep him distracted. 'Kiopek is still very good and very sentimental, in spite of his old age, and he had the honour of being presented to [the imperial couple], and has been painted by Madame Lebrun in her portrait of Izabelka Mniszech and by her cousin Monsieur Rivière in a miniature,' he reported to Białystok.[54]

A major source of worry to Stanisław was the uncertainty attendant on the negotiations taking place in Warsaw over the sale of his property. The Prussian government was gerrymandering shamelessly over its projected purchase of Łazienki and Ujazdów, and suddenly declared that all his private property belonged to the state, since it had been acquired while he was king. This was profoundly disturbing to Stanisław, as it put in question his ability to support himself if the volatile Paul changed his mind – the prospect of being stuck in Russia without the means to move anywhere horrified him. 'The expedition of the post for Warsaw so exhausted my king, that two days after its leaving here, he was gripped several times by fits of dizziness which grew stronger every day the post arrived, bringing unpleasant news from Warsaw,' Dr Boeckler wrote.[55] By the end of January 1798 Stanisław's anxiety about his financial future was undermining his health markedly. 'I am no more than a sort of corpse,' he wrote to his friend Cardinal Antici on 22 January.[56] But on 28 January he survived the memorial service for the Duke of Württemberg, which lasted three hours in a church which, according to Stanisław's pocket thermometer, was ten degrees below freezing.[57]

On 10 February, Stanisław dined at home, in the company of the English ambassador Lord Whitworth, the Marquis de Rivière and the painter Élisabeth-Louise Vigée-Lebrun. It was, as usual, an enchanting evening, with Tremo's exquisite cuisine providing the excuse for a relaxed causerie on every topic. But the portraitist became uneasy. 'After I had been at the palace for a short time, I was struck by the singular change which I observed in the looks of our dear Prince; his left eye appeared to me so dead and lustreless that I felt terrified,' she wrote. On the stairs, as they were leaving, she told the other guests of her anxiety. 'Why? he seems in excellent health; and has been conversing in his usual spirits,' they replied. 'I have the misfortune to be a good physiognomist,' she said, 'and I noticed how curious his eyes looked: the King will not live long.'[58]

The next morning, Stanisław rose at eight o'clock, feeling perfectly well. He drank his usual cup of bouillon and almost immediately felt ill. He retired to his chaise, and thought he would vomit. Then he felt faint and came out in a sweat. Dr Boeckler put him to bed, and

Stanisław asked for a priest, who duly came. But Stanisław only had time to begin his act of contrition before the left-hand side of his face was seized by spasms. Dr Boeckler bled him and applied vesicatories to his legs. The imperial physician Dr Rogerson came, and recommended more vesicatories and an emetic, but neither produced any results. By eleven o'clock the king had lost consciousness. At one o'clock Father Juriewicz administered the last rites.

News of the attack had spread quickly, and all the Poles in St Petersburg converged on the Marble Palace. At half past two in the afternoon the Tsar himself arrived. He solicitously questioned the doctors and the chamberlain who had been on duty that morning. 'One could see on the Tsar's face a great confusion, mixed with the most sincere sorrow,' according to one of the pages.[59] He was soon joined by the grand dukes Alexander and Constantine, followed by various dignitaries of the court and members of the diplomatic corps, and the émigrés the Prince de Condé and the Duc d'Enghien, who were to have dined with Stanisław that very evening. Paul remained in attendance, lending a strangely solemn dimension to the occasion. At eight o'clock the Papal Nuncio Lorenzo Litta bestowed his absolution on the unconscious monarch. Later that night, Stanisław seemed to be breathing better, and the hopes of those surrounding his sick-bed revived. But in the early hours of 12 February the convulsions began. At five minutes to eight in the morning, Stanisław expired.

Stanisław's death was so unexpected that it aroused suspicion. Within hours there was a rumour circulating at court that he had been poisoned on the orders of the king of Prussia. As it crept into Poland, the rumour changed, turning various agencies at the Russian court into the culprits. Paul had ordered an autopsy, which was carried out on the following day, and according to Dr Boeckler, who was present, this revealed nothing untoward. 'Our good Master died quite simply of a nervous apoplexy, which was the inevitable consequence of extremely difficult and disagreeable labours to extricate himself from the tangle of disastrous machinations by which the settlement of his debts and finances were bedevilled,' he explained.[60] In plain language, he had died of a stroke.

Paul immediately put in hand preparations for the most solemn and elaborate obsequies. Stanisław's body was embalmed and dressed in the uniform of the National Cavalry, and lay for nine days in his apartments. It was then transported into a hall draped in black silk and white crêpe, and laid on a *lit de parade* under a canopy surmounted by the eagle of Poland. At the foot of the catafalque stood a throne and a stool with a crown laid on it. It was flanked by five smaller stools bearing the king's two Polish orders, the two Russian ones, and the Prussian Black Eagle.

On 22 February the official lying in state was opened by the Tsar and the two grand dukes, who placed the crown on the king's head in an elaborate ritual. Over the next four days a stream of mourners filed past to pay their respects, including Józef Poniatowski, who had thrown his principles to the wind in order to see his dear uncle one last time. On 26 February Paul presided over the ceremony of placing the body in its coffin. Yet more people filed past over the next week, and it was not until 5 March that the coffin was transferred to the Church of St Catherine. The cortège was led by a knight riding in effigy, as Polish ceremonial demanded, and Paul himself walked beside the hearse, his drawn sword pointing to the ground. The church had been draped in black, and in the nave stood another catafalque, on which the coffin was placed.

On 8 March Archbishop Litta celebrated the funeral Mass, with the Orthodox Metropolitan of all Russia and the French Bishop of Rennes. After the Mass, Stanisław's body was carried down into the vault of the church, and placed in a second coffin of gilt bronze. Paul ordered four weeks of mourning, and had the following inscription engraved on the stone covering the grave.

Stanislaus II Augustus
Rex Poloniae, Magnus Dux Lithuaniae
insigne documentum utriusque fortunae,
prosperam sapienter, diversam fortiter
tulit.
Obiit Petropoli VII kal. Feb. MDCCXCVIII
Natus Annos LXVI

Paulus I Autocrator
et Imperator totius Russiae
Amico et hospiti posuit.[61]

Epilogue

*F*ew grieved. The end of Poland and her king had been so inglorious that people did not like to dwell on it. As the century drew to its close under the twin shadows of the French Revolution and the Partitions of Poland the usual unease with which humanity faces symbolic dates was deepened by a sense of shame as well as by the uncertainties of a continent in a state of flux. In what had been Poland, people thought more of their own survival than of mourning the dead king.

Feelings of guilt pricked many, and to do him justice, Feliks Potocki owned up to his quickly. 'It is I who am responsible for everything,' he wrote to Bishop Kossakowski in May 1793.[1] But as the French Revolution turned to Terror and threatened to spill over into Poland, he and many others who believed in the established order tended to see in the regimes of Catherine, Joseph and Frederick William a guarantee of the survival of European values which, in the eighteenth century, transcended a patriotism that was still in its infancy.

The question of what had happened to Poland nevertheless had to be addressed, if not by those who had played a part in the events, then by their descendants. A nation that has allowed itself to be wiped off the map by anything other than sheer brute force must confront the shortcomings that brought this about if it wishes to continue to think of itself as a nation – and there was never any doubt that the Poles did. But the implications of such a confrontation were so complex and so unpleasant that it was easier to avoid them in favour of an altogether

453

simpler way out of the problem: to blame Stanisław for everything.

The historical basis for this had been laid by Kołłątaj, Ignacy Potocki and their friends in 1793 in their *Establishment and Fall of the Constitution of 3 May*. 'It would appear that the honour which accrued to Stanisław Augustus from the work of the constitutional Seym was too great for his character,' they wrote. 'He could not sustain a glory of which he was unworthy.'[2] They ignored the king's contribution and suggested that he had somehow undermined the work of the reformers. This notion was propagated in the memoirs of the Patriots, who needed an excuse for the failure of their own policies. Even Kościuszko began to intimate that the king had spoiled the chances of the Insurrection, in order to avoid the admission that it had been ill-conceived.

Historical truth was an early casualty. Polish valour became a byword all over Europe during the Napoleonic wars, and it was accepted as the distinguishing characteristic of the nation. Thus, the diplomat Ségur could maintain that Poland 'deserved, by her valour, a stronger king, nobler enemies, more faithful friends, and a better fate'.[3] Yet one searches in vain for displays of this virtue by the nation as a whole in 1772, 1792 or 1794. Indeed, the partitioning courts could convincingly maintain that Poland had got the king, the friends, the enemies and the fate she deserved. Unsurprisingly, the Poles could not accept such a verdict, and needed to cultivate the idea of a Poland fighting to the end. In the third decade of the nineteenth century Joachim Lelewel, the poorly informed but opinionated 'father of Polish History', could sum up Stanisław and his reign with the assertion that 'he knew all the needs and the feelings of the nation; but there was one thing he did not recognise: that the nation could not bear its shackles and needed and sought independence or death'.[4] This blatant nonsense went unchallenged for half a century.

The annihilation of Poland and the Napoleonic wars bred generations of patriots dedicated to active struggle. As they formed their legions and prepared their uprisings, each as ill-starred as that of 1794, they were in no mood for reflection on the real causes of Poland's downfall. Their own experience and the influence of the Romantic movement fuelled the anti-monarchism they had inherited from their fathers. More conservative elements, represented by the descendants of the magnates, were only too glad to see the blame for Poland's decline laid at the feet of Stanisław rather than their own parents. Adam Jerzy Czartoryski, the son of Stanisław's first cousin and reluctant rival for the throne, became president of Poland during the Insurrection of 1830 and subsequently the country's 'uncrowned king', upholding her cause from exile in Paris. It goes without saying that loyal Polish historians propounded a favourable view of the doings of the Familia and ascribed to them a role and significance that far outshone the king's.

It was not until 1868, four years after the crushing of the most hopeless and the bloodiest of all the Polish uprisings, that a sensible book on Stanisław saw the light of day. In his formidably documented study of the last years of Stanisław's reign and in subsequent books, Walerian Kalinka demonstrated the self-evident truth that however weak or even treacherous Stanisław might have been, he could not have brought a vigorous nation to perdition all on his own, and that the whole of Polish society must bear responsibility for what had happened. He was soon challenged by Tadeusz Korzoń, whose monumental survey of Stanisław's reign depicted the king as a repulsive, pleasure-seeking puppet of Catherine.

The king's reputation was inescapably caught in the conundrums of Polish politics. Kalinka's approach had found favour with a generation that rejected risings and believed, as the king had, that one could still do something useful in captivity. It also found favour in the 1890s and 1900s with the first modern Polish political party, the National Democrats, who argued, as Stanisław had, that the only hope for recovering any form of national autonomy lay in close alliance with Russia. But the rival Polish Socialist Party, led by Józef Piłsudski, believed, as Ignacy Potocki had, in using German might against Russia and, as Kościuszko had, in armed struggle. The Poland that recovered her independence as a result of the First World War was the Poland of Piłsudski, and Korzoń's unfavourable view of Stanisław became the official one. An incidental result of this was a disgraceful affair that added a new dimension to the argument.

In the spring of 1938 the Soviet authorities informed the Polish ambassador in Moscow that they were intending to demolish the Church of St Catherine in what had now become Leningrad and wished to hand over the body of the last king of Poland. This caused embarrassment in Warsaw. The remains of a king belong in the crypt of the Cathedral on Wawel hill in Kraków, where all Polish monarchs lie. But in the nineteenth century national heroes such as Kościuszko, Józef Poniatowski, and the poets Mickiewicz and Słowacki, had also been laid to rest in it. Only three years before, in 1935, the body of Marshal Józef Piłsudski had been entombed there in great pomp. The inclusion of such figures had succeeded in turning the crypt into something of a national Pantheon, and this introduced an element of merit into the question of who should be admitted to it. As far as those in government were concerned, Stanisław in no way deserved admission, particularly so soon after the grandiose burial of Piłsudski, who had struggled and fought to put back on the map the country Stanisław had signed away. They found the whole subject vaguely distasteful and highly inconvenient, so they decided to shelve it.

On 11 July 1938 the coffin containing the earthly remains of the last king of Poland arrived at the small railway border crossing of Stołpce in an ordinary goods-waggon attached to the end of a passenger train. The waggon was uncoupled and shunted into a siding. It was unsealed and the coffin opened for inspection not by customs but by a three-man commission from Warsaw, and was certified to contain the very insubstantial remains of Stanisław Augustus (two great floods had completely inundated the crypt of St Catherine's Church in the nineteenth century). Three days later another official arrived at Stołpce with a contingent of police. They waited for darkness to fall before taking the coffin from the waggon and loading it on to a small lorry which, flanked by armed policemen entirely ignorant of what was going on, took it to a new resting-place – the parish church in which Stanisław had been baptised at Wołczyn. The policemen carried his coffin into the church, in the crypt of which lay those of several Czartoryskis and Poniatowskis. As the king's coffin was too large for the entrance to the crypt, it was placed in a niche, which was promptly walled up. The parish priest was instructed to say nothing of the affair to anyone. The whole operation had resembled more the burying of stolen treasure than of a royal body.

The authorities thought they had laid the matter to rest, but they were grievously mistaken. The Soviet press agency issued a short release announcing the repatriation of the coffin, and people in Poland asked why they had heard nothing of this. The government's shabby behaviour provoked a storm, ably fomented by the opposition press. Traditionalists organised a solemn Mass for the repose of the soul of the king in the Church of St John, now Warsaw Cathedral, and demanded that the king be buried in the Wawel crypt. People who went to Wołczyn were appalled to find nothing but a whitewashed wall to look at. Seriously embarrassed by now, the government replaced the wall with an iron grille, so the coffin was at least visible, and declared they they had only placed it there temporarily while a final decision was reached. But the whole issue was soon overtaken by the advent of the Second World War.

Wołczyn changed hands several times and was the scene of heavy fighting during the spring of 1944, when it was finally 'liberated' by a punishment battalion of the Red Army. The church was damaged by military action, and the Russian soldiers looted it. They opened the coffins and even dragged some of them out of the crypt in search of gold. The area was incorporated into the Soviet Union under the Yalta agreement, and the entire Polish population was evicted in February 1945. The devastated church was eventually turned over by the Red Army, which had used it as a fuel dump, to the local collective farm, which stored chemical fertilisers there.

While the coffin and its royal contents disintegrated further under the combined assault of time and the emanations of the chemicals heaped around it, the king's memory met with a more congenial climate. The interwar period had seen the publication of documentary sources and a number of serious studies of various aspects of his reign, all of which revealed the fallacy of earlier appraisals. Postwar historians were less cavalier in their attitude to armed struggle, having just been through an object-lesson in the futility of heroism. They were more aware of the inevitability of Russian hegemony in Poland, took a less simplistic view of the king's alleged weakness, and began to appreciate both the breadth of his political activity and the wisdom of his policies. The growing interest in art history elevated Stanisław as a patron and won him a following of devoted supporters. In 1966 the distinguished historian Emanuel Rostworowski published the first measured and intelligent biography of Stanisław.

But the argument was far from being over. Another historian, Jerzy Łojek, decided to build his career on portraying Stanisław as a cynical coward. His arguments had the right mix of sensationalism and punditry to guarantee popularity with the public, and the fact that his books were poorly reviewed by fellow historians allowed him to pose as an exciting iconoclast challenging musty academe. He delighted in turning conferences and symposia into slanging-matches, knowing that he had the support of popular journalists and café philosophers up and down the country. History viewed as a morality play, in which every Pole can vicariously participate, is endlessly absorbing.

As the argument over Stanisław's merits revived, the subject of his resting-place resurfaced. In the mid-1960s several historians mooted the idea of rescuing his remains and giving them fitting burial in Poland. The Primate, Cardinal Wyszyński, agreed to admit them to the Wawel crypt, but the communist Prime Minister Józef Cyrankiewicz declared that there was no room in Poland for 'Catherine's lover' (which came well from a Soviet stooge like him), and the matter was officially buried. But while efforts to disinter it bore little fruit in Poland, a group of Byelorussian academics, in whose national territory Wołczyn now lay, took an interest in the matter. In 1987 they visited the ruined church in Wołczyn and carefully swept up what they could from the floor of the niche in which the king's coffin had lain. All they found were some remains of the coffin, buttons, shreds of the king's uniform and shoes, a surprisingly well-preserved corner of the velvet royal cloak with the Polish eagle embroidered in silver on it, and some tiny fragments of bone.

In December 1988 a delegation of Polish academics went to Wołczyn to survey the ruins, and took delivery of the box containing the remains. These relics were brought back to the Royal Castle in Warsaw, itself rebuilt from scratch after being dynamited by the Germans in 1944. A new coffin was made, identical to the one in which the king had been buried, in the hope that his scanty remains might be finally laid to rest. But the polemics started by Łojek and carried on after his death by popular journalists had once more blown up into a nationwide discussion, and a poll taken by a Warsaw daily revealed that a majority of its readership were against burying the king at the Wawel. It was then decided that Warsaw Cathedral, in which Stanisław had been crowned, would be equally appropriate and less contentious. But every time a move has been made to put the plan into action, new protests are voiced, and everything is put off once again.

The silliness of the arguments used is rivalled only by their bad taste, and the moral cowardice of both the post-communist governments and the Church hierarchy over the issue is barely credible. The final resting-place of a king is not a matter for discussion, judgment or popular vote, but a question of form and tradition, and anyone with the slightest respect for either – which the politicians, the Church and the Polish people all lay great claims to – would unhesitatingly recognise that place as the Wawel crypt. But things are not that simple.

Nations blessed with the undisputed possession and enjoyment of their own country can use history as a source of illuminating background information or merely of interesting anecdote. Those not so blessed tend to regard it as a series of processes which went wrong, and they go over it again and again, looking for the crucial mistake, like a cook who has followed instructions carefully only to find that his soufflé has failed to rise. Some historians have traced the root of Poland's downfall to the Jagiellon kings of the fifteenth and sixteenth centuries, others to the Cossack and Swedish wars of the seventeenth, but to the majority of Poles the most obviously critical moment is the reign of Stanisław Augustus, and the quest for the decisive cause of disaster inevitably centres on his person. There is a widespread conviction that if he had done one thing or left undone another, then everything would somehow have been all right.

The charges commonly levelled at Stanisław are these: that he brought Russian troops in on his side in 1764; that he served Russian interests and took money for it while he was in power; that he hindered the work of the Great Seym; that he betrayed his nation by joining the Confederation of Targowica in 1792; that he signed away parts of his country in 1773 and 1793 in return for guarantees of financial security for himself and his family; that he dithered and wept instead of charging into battle; and that he abdicated, thereby acquiescing in the final annihilation of Poland.

All but the last of these charges are groundless, and his abdication was an act of no practical significance whatsoever: his refusal would have made not one jot of difference. But generations condemned to captivity cannot see beyond the fact that it was he who signed the sentence, and in their hearts reproach him for having been able to live while his country perished. The underlying charge is that he did not die. It is not altogether clear why he is blamed while others are absolved of the same actions. It was after all the Familia, including such universally respected figures as Andrzej Zamoyski and Stanisław Lubomirski, who sought Russian backing in 1764, and this has not weighed on their reputation. In 1792 it was Kołłątaj who urged him most forcefully to join Targowica, yet Kołłątaj's radical aura is undimmed. And as for the crime of abdication, it is shared by many – beginning with Kościuszko, who by swearing an oath of allegiance to Tsar Paul formally acknowledged the demise of Poland. One might be led to conclude from all this that the Poles had embraced Saint-Just's dictum that a king cannot reign innocently. But while there may be something in this, the real explanation lies elsewhere.

Poland had lost her sovereignty by 1764 in all but name, and she had no realistic chances of regaining it. The country was politically riven, socially unprepared for common effort, economically dependent and militarily weak. Since it had nothing to offer any potential ally, it could gain nothing from any alliance. Poland's only hope of survival lay in pursuing a policy of total loyalty to the one power in whose interests it lay to protect her integrity – Russia – combined with a programme of unspectacular but profound social, economic and, where possible, political reform. This was the policy Stanisław chose, and it was endorsed by all the most intelligent public figures of the day. Despite various setbacks, it was remarkably successful, and had it been pursued methodically for another ten years, Poland would undoubtedly have entered the nineteenth century as a consolidated second-rank power in a position to take advantage of the Napoleonic wars to re-establish full sovereignty. Between 1788 and 1792 an excess of enthusiasm combined with an entirely unrealistic view of the situation impelled the Seym to pick the fruit before it was ripe, to use Stanisław's own metaphor, and to defy Russia at the very worst moment. As far as Catherine was concerned, Polish liberalism as voiced in the Great Seym and the constitution challenged the very basis of the absolute monarchy she incarnated. And she was by then the greatest power on the continent. By 1794, Polish liberalism had turned into Polish Jacobinism, apparently a pernicious offshoot of the French abomination. It mattered not how many victories Kościuszko might win – all three neighbours were prepared for a long fight to the death with this direct threat to their very existence.

Poland's position was, in a word, hopeless, and it was so because several generations had lacked the will and the energy to look after their country. But their descendants have not been prepared to accept this, and generations of historians and writers have been at pains to demonstrate that the nation had been strong and healthy, inventing an honest, patriotic Poland that had been confused and shackled by a mixture of Russian force and Stanislavian treachery. It is significant that the nineteenth-century historian Józef Szujski could label Stanisław as 'the first and the greatest of the nation's calamities', when he was demonstrably the last stage in a long process.[5]

This distortion was aggravated by the Romantic movement, which followed hard on the demise of Poland, for Stanisław was no Romantic hero – rather the disgraceful epitome of everything that the movement rejected. Polish poets of the Romantic period inherited only failure, and they did their utmost to give it meaning. Adam Mickiewicz used the symbolism of the Crucifixion to exalt Poland, which he represented as the Christ of nations, whose suffering was not only glorious but redemptive as well. As a result, the Poles began to elevate such bloody fiascos as the Confederation of Bar into expressions of triumph. Suffering or a grim death on some forgotten battlefield became ends in themselves. And Stanisław had not suffered (not gloriously, anyway) and he had not died in battle. Thus, even if he had not actually betrayed his nation, he had failed it – the Christ of nations must have its Pilate, if not its Judas. This became an article of faith for later generations, militating against any calm assessment of the king or his reign. It lurks still in the depths of the Polish psyche, and is reflected in the vexed matter of his reburial.

Stanisław was one of the most intelligent men ever to have sat on the Polish throne, and certainly the most hard-working and devoted to his country. 'No prince has ever wished as sincerely as he did to make his people happy,' as the citizens of Warsaw stated in their final proclamation before the Prussians took over their city.[6] In his day he outshone most of his countrymen and all his brother-monarchs in these aspects and in moral stature. Yet in a sense, he failed as a king. 'I should have been chancellor, not king,' he once remarked to Thomas Wroughton, and this remark touches on the root of the problem.[7] For it was his political sense, his democratic instinct to represent his people and to remain in tune with their aspirations, that caused him time and again to abandon his reasoned policy. Had he taken a monarchical view of being answerable only to himself and to God, he would have stuck like a limpet to his Russian protectress, ruthlessly repressed Barians and

Patriots alike, and almost certainly preserved his kingdom. But such an attitude was not possible in an elected king, and neither the stern Stefan Bathory nor the strong Jan III Sobieski fared any better in this respect. Stanisław did more for his country than either of these, and more than any Polish king in modern history. There can be no doubt that if his country had survived, he would be universally cited as a paragon of kingship, and there would be statues of him in every Polish town. Ultimately it was Poland's failure to survive that defeated him and condemned him to disgrace in posterity, and that failure cannot be ascribed to him.

The philosopher Immanuel Kant defined enlightenment as the liberation of man from his self-induced condition of deficiency or self-abasement. Polish society has been in such a condition since the seventeenth century, fighting a losing emotional and spiritual battle against reality. It is only when that struggle is over that the Poles will be able to look at their history with dispassionate reason. That day has yet to dawn. History is still, for most of them, a morality play and Stanisław Augustus is a key protagonist. That is why, as this book goes to print, his coffin lies under a dust-sheet on the landing of a back staircase in the Royal Castle.

Note on Polish Pronunciation

Polish words may look complicated, but pronunciation is at least consistent. All vowels are simple and of even length, as in Italian, and their sound is best rendered by the English words 'sum' (*a*), 'ten' (*e*), 'ease' (*i*), 'lot' (*o*), 'book' (*u*), 'sit' (*y*).

Most of the consonants behave in the same way as English, except for *c*, which is pronounced 'ts'; *j*, which is soft, as in 'yes'; and *w*, which is equivalent to English *v*. As in German, some consonants are softened when they fall at the end of a word, and *b, d, g, w, z* become *p, t, k, f, s* respectively.

There are also a number of accented letters and combinations peculiar to Polish, of which the following is a rough list:

ó = *u*, hence *Kraków* is pronounced 'krakooff'.
ą = nasal *a*, hence *sąd* is pronounced 'sont'.
ę = nasal *e*, hence *Łęczyca* is pronounced 'wenchytsa'.
ć = *ch* as in 'cheese'.
cz = *ch* as in 'catch'.
ch = guttural *h* as in 'loch'.
ł = *English w*, hence *Bolesław* becomes 'Boleswaf', *Łódź* 'Wootj'.
ń = soft *n* as in Spanish '*mañana*'.
rz = French *j* as in '*je*'.
ś = *sh* as in 'sheer'.
sz = *sh* as in 'bush'.
ż = as *rz*.
ź = A similar sound, but sharper as in French '*gigot*'.

The stress in Polish is consistent, and always falls on the penultimate syllable.

Glossary

CASTELLAN (*Kasztelan*) originally the king's lieutenant in a given area, later a titular office. Castellans had a seat in the Senate.

COMMONWEALTH (POLISH) comprised the Kingdom of Poland, the Grand Duchy of Lithuania, Royal Prussia, the Palatinate of Livonia and the Duchy of Kurland.

CONFEDERATION an association of szlachta who came together either in a national emergency, or as a sign of protest, or as a provincial assembly. A confederation elected a marshal and acted as a parliamentary body. If it was a nationwide movement, it would form into two branches, one Polish and one Lithuanian. A confederation could also be declared within the Seym, at which point all legislation was passed by majority voting and various practices were streamlined.

CONVOCATION SEYM extraordinary Seym elected upon the death of a king to make arrangements for the election of his successor. *See* SEYM.

CORONATION SEYM the first regular Seym after the coronation of a new monarch. *See* SEYM.

COUNT *see* TITLES.

CROWN ESTATES, CROWN LANDS (*ekonomie królewskie*) large estates belonging to the Crown, from which a part of Crown revenues were drawn.

Glossary

ELECTION SEYM   gathering to which every single member of the szlachta could come. Its sole business was the election of one of the candidates vetted by the Convocation Seym. *See* SEYM.

GABINET   Stanisław's political office. This was not part of the constitutional structure of the state.

GALICIA (AND LODOMERIA)   name given by Austria to the provinces it acquired from Poland in the partitions. A pseudo-latinisation of the duchies of Halicz and Włodzimierz.

HETMAN   the highest military rank. The Grand Hetman and Field Hetman of the Crown commanded the Polish army, the Grand Hetman and Field Hetman of Lithuania commanded the forces of the Grand Duchy. The Grand Hetman of the Crown had overall command. The Hetmans did not have ministerial rank, but could attend the sessions of the Seym at the king's side.

KAMERA   Stanisław's administrative office. This was not part of the constitutional structure of the state.

KING   the king of Poland was also Grand Duke of Lithuania, Duke of Prussia and Livonia, and vassal overlord of Kurland. He was elected for life by the whole szlachta of the Commonwealth.

KURLAND, DUCHY OF   the rump of the state of the Knights of the Sword, which acceded to the Commonwealth in 1551 as a vassal duchy.

LIBERUM VETO   *see* VETO.

LITHUANIA, GRAND DUCHY OF   comprised nine palatinates covering ethnic Lithuania and a large section of White Russia (Byelorussia, Belarus).

LIVONIA, PALATINATE OF   originally like Kurland, it was incorporated directly into the Commonwealth.

MAŁOPOLSKA (LESSER POLAND)   the southern of the two provinces making up the Kingdom of Poland.

MARSHAL OF THE COURT   *see* MINISTERS.

MARSHAL OF THE SEYM   the lower chamber of the Seym elected two marshals, one for Poland, one for Lithuania, who presided alternately and were responsible for the conduct of proceedings.

MINISTERS   the Grand Marshal of the Crown and the Marshal of Lithuania were responsible for home affairs; the Grand Chancellor of the Crown and the Chancellor of Lithuania for foreign affairs, assisted by the Vice-Chancellor of the Crown and the Vice-Chancellor of Lithuania; the Grand Treasurer of the Crown and the Treasurer of Lithuania managed the state finances, the Crown Court Marshal and the Court Marshal of Lithuania managed the royal revenues. When the Seym met in full, the ten ministers took their seats opposite the king, and gathered about him when he spoke from the throne.

PACTA CONVENTA   Conditions, drawn up by the Convocation Seym, under which the prospective monarch could rule. The king elect had to swear to honour these before his coronation. If he defaulted on them, his subjects could refuse him their loyalty.

PALATINATE *(województwo)*   administrative provincial unit.

PALATINE *(wojewoda)*   originally the royal governor of a province, later largely honorific title that went with nomination to the Senate.

PERMANENT COUNCIL   Governing body set up in 1775 at Russia's behest, and abolished by the Great Seym in 1789. The council consisted of the king, the Primate, two bishops, eleven senators, four ministers and eighteen deputies to the Seym – 36 people (plus the king) in all. Apart from the king and the Primate, all of them were elected by the Seym, and one-third of them stood down every two years. The Council worked through five Departments, of eight members each.

POLAND, KINGDOM OF   (sometimes referred to as 'the Crown') comprised the provinces of Wielkopolska (Greater Poland), which consisted of twelve palatinates; Małopolska (Lesser Poland), which consisted of eleven palatinates; and Royal Prussia, which consisted of three palatinates and the episcopal principality of Warmia.

PRIMATE   the archbishop of Gniezno, head of the Church in Poland, senior senator and, during an interregnum, supreme authority *(interrex)* in the Commonwealth.

Glossary

PRINCE   *see* TITLES.

REGIMENTARY (*regimentarz*)   senior commander of a military area, appointed by the king and not dependent on the Hetmans.

ROYAL PRUSSIA   the segment of the old state of the Teutonic Knights that had been incorporated into Poland in 1466 (the remainder became a vassal Duchy of Poland in 1520, seceded in 1656, and became part of the Kingdom of Prussia).

SENATE   upper chamber of the Seym, consisting of 136 senators, including 17 bishops, 32 palatines, 86 castellans, and one starosta, all of them appointed by the king.

SENATE COUNCIL (*senatus consilium*)   originally a governing body, it had become powerless by the eighteenth century, although it had to be convoked at regular periods for constitutional reasons. Stanisław tried to revive its role as a cabinet, but it was abolished by the legislation that brought in the Permanent Council (see above) in 1775.

SEYM (modern SEJM)   national parliament, meeting once a year for four weeks, with possible extensions. Once every three years it met not at Warsaw, but at Grodno in Lithuania. The lower chamber consisted of 178 deputies elected at seymiks. The upper (Senate) and lower chambers of the Seym would sit separately for purposes of debate, and join together to legislate, under the supreme presidency of the king.

SEYMIK   electoral assembly in one of the sixty-eight constituencies.

SPISZ (ZIPS)   Province mortgaged to Poland by Hungary in 1412. Never redeemed, it remained part of the Commonwealth until 1770, when Austria occupied it.

STAROSTA   incumbent of a starosty, originally the king's officer and judge in a given area, later an honorific title granted by the king.

STAROSTA GRODOWY   local magistrate, not necessarily the incumbent of a starosty.

STAROSTY (*starostwo*)   an estate belonging to the Crown, granted in life tenure to a deserving citizen, with the understanding that he paid one-quarter of the

467

estate's revenues into the Treasury. Originally, the granting of the estate also entailed the duty of local magistrate.

SZLACHTA   the nobility, or rather noble caste that made up almost 10 per cent of the population and enjoyed full political rights and exemption from taxation in return for its alleged preparedness to fight for the country.

TITLES   the Polish Commonwealth did not recognise titles of nobility on principle, but families of Lithuanian and Ruthene dynastic origin such as the Czartoryski, Czetwertyński, Massalski and Sanguszko were allowed to bear the title of prince. The Seym of 1764 bestowed a princely title on Stanisław Augustus's brothers, that of 1768 on the Sapieha family, and that of 1773 on the Ponińskis. The following families appearing in the text bore princely titles granted by foreign courts (usually the Holy Roman Empire): Radziwiłł, Lubomirski, Jabłonowski, Sułkowski, Ogiński. The following bore the title of count: Tarnowski, Krasicki, Flemming, Moszyński, Lanckoronski, Gorzeński, Dzieduszycki, Ankwicz, Zamoyski, Mniszech, Borch, Kossakowski, Działyński, Załuski, Wielhorski.

   The title of count used by the Poniatowskis when travelling abroad was nothing more than a polite fiction.

TRIBUNALS   the supreme courts of Poland (sitting at Piotrków) and Lithuania (sitting at Wilno) were elected annually by universal suffrage. They consisted of half-a-dozen judges presided over by a marshal, which was a fiercely disputed office.

UKRAINE   geographical area, most of which lay within the Commonwealth until 1667, when its eastern half was incorporated into Muscovy. Between 1667 and 1792, the Polish Ukraine made up the south-eastern palatinates of Podolia, Bracław and Kiev.

WARMIA (ERMELAND)   episcopal principality in Royal Prussia in which the bishop was temporal as well as spiritual ruler.

WIELKOPOLSKA (GREATER POLAND)   one of the two provinces of the kingdom of Poland.

Chronology

1696   Death of King Jan III Sobieski.

1697   Election of Prince de Conti as king of Poland.
Election of Frederick Augustus I of Saxony as King Augustus II of
Poland.

1700   Peter 'the Great' of Russia declares war on Sweden; Great Northern
War begins.

1701   War of the Spanish Succession begins.
December   Charles XII of Sweden invades Poland.

1704   Election of Stanisław Leszczyński as Stanisław I.

1706   Augustus II abdicates Polish throne.

1709   *8 July*   Battle of Poltava; Peter routs Charles XII.

1710   Augustus II reaffirmed as king of Poland.

1713   Treaty of Utrecht; end of War of Spanish Succession.

1718   Treaty of Warsaw; Russia guarantees Polish independence and
constitution.
Death of Charles XII.

1721   Treaty of Nystadt; end of Great Northern War.

1732   *17 January*   Birth of Stanisław Antoni Poniatowski.

1733   *1 February*   Death of Augustus II.
        12 September   Second election of Stanisław Leszczyński. Russia
                         intervenes; War of the Polish Succession begins.
        5 October   Election of Frederick Augustus II of Saxony as
                         Augustus III of Poland.

1734   Familia joins party of Augustus III.

1736   Pacification Seym; general acceptance of Augustus III.

1740   Accession of Frederick II 'the Great' in Prussia.
        Accession of Maria Theresa in Austria. Frederick of Prussia invades
        Silesia; War of the Austrian Succession begins.

1744   Grodno Seym; Familia attempts to bring about reform.

1748   Stanisław's journey to Netherlands.
        Treaty of Aix-la-Chapelle ends War of the Austrian Succession.
        Stanisław begins political work for Michał Czartoryski.

1750   Stanisław's journey to Berlin.
        Stanisław elected to Seym for Zakroczym constituency.

1751   Stanisław's trip to Saxony.

1752   Stanisław goes to Vienna.
        Stanisław elected to Seym for Łomża constituency.

1753   Stanisław goes to Paris.

1754   Stanisław visits England.
        Familia breaks up Seym and goes into opposition.

1755   Stanisław named Steward of Lithuania.
        June   Stanisław goes to St Petersburg.
        December   beginning of Stanisław's affair with Catherine.

1756   Frederick invades Saxony; Seven Years' War begins.
    July   Stanisław returns to Poland.
          Stanisław elected to Seym for Dyneburg.
          Stanisław posted Saxon Envoy to Russian court.

1757   *January*   Stanisław arrives in St Petersburg.

1758   Stanisław returns to Poland.
    Charles of Saxony made Duke of Kurland.
    Stanisław elected to Seym for Livonia.

1760   Stanisław elected to Seym for Przemyśl constituency.

1761   Stanisław elected to Seym for Bielsk constituency.

1762   *5 January*   Peter III succeeds to Russian throne.
    9 July   Peter III overthrown and succeeded by his wife,
               Catherine II 'the Great'.
               Charles of Saxony removed from Duchy of Kurland and
               replaced with Ernest Bühren.
    28 August   Death of Stanisław's father.
               Stanisław elected to Seym for Mielnik constituency.

1763   *15 February*   Peace of Hubertusburg ends Seven Years' War.
               Familia plans confederation to seize power.
    5 October   Death of Augustus III of Poland.

1764   *11 April*   Russo-Prussian treaty.
    7 May–23 June   Convocation Seym.
    7 September   Election of Stanisław Poniatowski as king of
               Poland.
    25 November   Coronation of Stanisław II Augustus.
    3–20 December   Coronation Seym.

1765   Foundation of Cadet Corps, Mint, etc.
    Establishment of Public Order Commissions in towns.
    Frederick establishes customs-post at Marienwerder.

1766   *October*   Dissenters' rights brought up in Seym.
    November   Russia blocks further reform.

1767   More Russian troops move into Poland.
    20 March   Dissenter confederations at Słuck and Toruń.
    23 June   Confederation of Radom.
    5 October   Seym opens.
    14 October   Repnin orders arrest of four senators.

1768   *22 February*   Treaty of Warsaw imposes Russian guarantee of Polish constitution.
    29 February   Confederation of Bar declared.
    6 October   Russo-Turkish War begins.

1769   Repnin replaced by Volkonski.

1770   *22 October*   Confederate leadership proclaims dethronement of Stanisław.

1771   Volkonski replaced by Saldern.
    3 November   Abduction of Stanisław.

1772   *17 February*   Russo-Prussian agreement on partition.
    5 August   Convention of St Petersburg arranges First Partition of Poland.
    Saldern replaced by Stackelberg.

1773   *16 April*   Poniński confederates Seym.
    30 September Ratification of Partition by Seym.
    14 October   Commission for National Education set up.

1774   Treaty of Kutchuk-Kainardji ends Russo-Turkish war.

1775   *28 March*   Permanent Council established.
    11 April   End of Partition Seym.
    13 August   Death of August Czartoryski.

1776   American declaration of Independence.
    26 August–31 October   Seym reforms Permanent Council.

1778   Outbreak of Prusso-Austrian war over the Bavarian succession.
    5 October First non-confederated Seym opens.

1780   Zamoyski's *Code of Laws* rejected.
29 November   Death of Maria Theresa. Joseph II sole ruler of
Habsburg monarchy.
All Russian troops withdraw from Poland.

1783   Death of Stanisław Lubomirski. Ignacy Potocki assumes leadership
of Familia.

1784   Russia occupies Crimea.
4 October   Grodno Seym opens; opposition to Stanisław's policies.

1785   Dogrumova affair. Opposition gathers strength.

1786   *17 August*   Death of Frederick II. Accession of Frederick William II.

1787   *6 March*   Stanisław meets Catherine at Kaniów.
16 August   Turkey declares war on Russia.
27 September   American Constitution passed.

1788   *9 February*   Austria declares war on Turkey.
June   Russian proposals for Polish alliance.
12 July   Sweden attacks Russia.
13 August   Triple Alliance of England, Prussia and the United
Provinces.
6 October   Great Seym opens.
13 October   Prussian declaration read out in Seym.
20 October   Vote to increase army to 100,000 men.

1789   *19 January*   Permanent Council abolished.
30 April   Washington becomes President of the United States.
5 May   Estates General meet in France.
14 July   Fall of the Bastille.
26 August   Declaration of the Rights of Man.
7 September   Deputation appointed to prepare new constitution.
23 November   'Black Procession' of city delegates in Warsaw.

1790   *20 November*   Death of Joseph II. Accession of Leopold II.
29 March   Polish-Prussian Alliance.
April   Stackelberg recalled from Warsaw.
27 July   Convention of Reichenbach. Austria withdraws from
war with Turkey.

1790 cont.	2 *August*	Project for reform of government presented to Seym.
	14 *August*	Sweden makes peace with Russia.
	16 *November*	Election of second complement of deputies to Seym.
	4 *December*	Ignacy Potocki hands over to Stanisław task of framing new constitution.
1791	24 *March*	New law governing seymiks.
	18 *April*	Law on Cities.
	3 *May*	New constitution voted.
	23 *May*	Russian Council of State resolves to overthrow Polish constitution.
	14 *September*	Louis XVI swears oath to new French constitution.
	16 *October*	Potyomkin dies.
1792	9 *January*	Treaty of Jassy ends Russo-Turkish war.
	14 *February*	Seymiks endorse new constitution.
	1 *March*	Death of Leopold II. Accession of Francis II.
	20 *April*	France declares war on Austria.
	14 *May*	Confederation of Targowica declared.
	18 *May*	Russia invades Poland.
	14 *June*	Russians take Wilno.
	18 *June*	Battle of Zieleńce.
	18 *July*	Battle of Dubienka.
	24 *July*	Stanisław accedes to Confederation of Targowica.
	10 *August*	Louis XVI deposed.
	24 *November*	France declared a Republic.
1793	23 *January*	Execution of Louis XVI.
	23 *January*	Russia and Prussia agree Second Partition of Poland.
	21 *June*	Grodno Seym opens.
1794	24 *March*	Kościuszko proclaims Insurrection in Kraków.
	4 *April*	Battle of Racławice.
	17 *April*	Rising in Warsaw.
	July–September	Siege of Warsaw.
	10 *October*	Kościuszko defeated and captured at Maciejowice.
	9 *November*	Warsaw capitulates.
1795	3 *January*	Russo-Austrian agreement on partition.
		Stanisław leaves Warsaw for Grodno.
		Treaty of Basel; Prussia withdraws from coalition against France.

	24 October	Russia, Prussia and Austria agree Third Partition of Poland.
	25 November	Stanisław abdicates.
1796	*17 November*	Death of Catherine.
1797	*January*	Polish legions formed in Milan.
	26 January	Tripartite convention removing name of Poland from diplomatic terminology.
	March	Stanisław leaves Grodno for St Petersburg.
1798	*12 February*	Death of Stanisław.

Notes

Abbreviations

ANP	*Archives Nationales*, Paris; *Archives Poniatowski*	BUW	*Biblioteka Uniwersytetu Warszawskiego*
AGAD	*Archiwum Główne Akt Dawnych*	*Mémoires*	Stanisław II Augustus, *Mémoires du Roi Stanislas-Auguste Poniatowski*, Vol. I, St Petersburg 1914, Vol. II, Leningrad 1924
AKP	*Archiwum Królewstwa Polskiego*		
AK	*Archiwum Kameralne*		
ML	*Metryka Litewska*		
ZP	*Zbiory Popielów*	*Mémoires Secrets*	*Mémoires Secrets et Inédits de Stanislas Auguste*, Leipsig 1862
APP	*Archiwum Publiczne Potockich*		
ASK	*Archiwum Skarbu Koronnego*	MNW	*Muzeum Narodowe*, Warsaw
AKJP	*Archiwum Księcia Józefa Poniatowskiego*	Newport	Newport Central Reference Library, Williams Papers
AXC	*Archiwum Xiążąt Czartoryskich*, Kraków	PAU	*Polska Akademia Umiejętności*, Kraków
BM	British Museum, London	PRO	Public Record Office, London
BN	*Biblioteka Narodowa*, Warsaw	SP	State Papers
BNBOZ	*Biblioteka Ordynacji Zamoyskiej*	PSI	Polish Scientific Institute, New York
BP	*Bibliothèque Polonaise*, Paris		
BPMAM	*Muzeum Adama Mickiewicza*	UV	University of Virginia, Charlottesville, Va

1 Bedchambers and Cabinets

1 *Mémoires Secrets*, pp. 7–8.
2 Voltaire to Vorontsov 28 III 68, Vorontsov, *Arkhiv Vorontsova*, Vol. V, p. 454.
3 Lésnodorski, *Polska w Epoce Oświecenia*, p. 25.

4 Korzoń, *Odrodzenie w Upadku*, p. 101.
5 Kula, *Théorie Économique*, pp. 94–5.
6 Konopczyński, *Fryderyk Wielki a Polska*, pp. 81–5.
7 Bernardin de Saint-Pierre, *Oeuvres Posthumes*, p. 14.
8 Vorontsov, op. cit., Vol. V, p. 451.
9 Coxe, *Travels*, Vol. I, p. 2.
10 Vorontsov, op. cit., Vol. V, p. 451.
11 Malmesbury, *Diaries*, Vol. I, p. 10.
12 Wraxall, *Memoirs*, Vol. II, p. 111.
13 Ségur, *Mémoires*, Vol. II, p. 155.
14 Larwood and Hotten, *History of Signboards*, p. 13.

2 Stars and Signs

1 Naruszewicz, *Liryka*, p. 81.
2 For some of the legends about Stanisław's birth see: Rulhière, *Histoire des Révolutions*, Vol. I, p. 247; also Potocka, *Wspomnienia*, pp. 42–3.
3 For the origins of the Poniatowskis, see: Mnemon, *L'Origine des Poniatowski*; also Kantecki, *Stanisław Poniatowski*; also AXC, 937; also apocryphal documents in ANP; also *Polski Słownik Biograficzny*.
4 Rulhière, op. cit., Vol. I, p. 184.
5 Voltaire, *Histoire de Charles XII*, p. 186.
6 Fabre, *Stanislas Auguste et l'Europe des Lumières*, p. 132.
7 Kitowicz, *Pamiętniki*, p. 43.
8 *Mémoires*, Vol. I, p. 8.
9 Ibid.
10 Starzeński, *Na schyłku dni*, p. 12.
11 *Mémoires*, Vol. I, p. 8.
12 Ibid., p. 11.
13 *Zabawy Szkolne*, AXC, 911.
14 *Mémoires*, Vol. I, p. 14.
15 Nieć, *Młodość Ostatniego Elekta*, p. 23.
16 Frederick to Hoffmann 28 VI 44, Zielińska, *Walka Familii*, p. 77.
17 Kazimierz Poniatowski to Ludwika Zamoyska 1 V 49, AXC, 3972 f. 463.

3 A Second Father

1 *Mémoires*, Vol. I, pp. 59–60.
2 Ilchester, *Life of Sir Charles Hanbury Williams*, p. 429.

3 Williams to Henry Fox 30 X 50, ibid., p. 215.
4 *Journal begun at Berlin in July 1750*, Newport, qM 411 012.
5 Williams to Henry Fox 22 VIII 50, Ilchester, op. cit., p. 198.
6 Williams to Capel Hanbury 12 X 52, Newport, qM 411 012.
7 Ilchester, op. cit., p. 149.
8 *Mémoires*, Vol. I, p. 43.
9 Ibid.
10 Ibid., p. 42.
11 Williams to R. Keith 29 XI 51, BM, Hardwicke, 35, 472, f. 55.
12 *Mémoires*, Vol. I, p. 44.
13 AGAD, ZP, 318, pp. 185ff.
14 Digby to Stanisław 6 III 51, ibid., 318, f. 26.
15 *Mémoires*, Vol. I, pp. 59–60.
16 Ibid., p. 61.
17 Ibid.
18 *Papers of Various Sorts bound up in 1753*, Newport, qM 411 012.
19 Williams to Capel Hanbury 12 X 52, ibid.
20 *Mémoires*, Vol. I, pp. 62–3.
21 Ibid., p. 63
22 Williams to Capel Hanbury, *Papers of Various Sorts*, Newport, qM 411 012.
23 Ibid.
24 *Mémoires*, Vol. I, p. 67.
25 Ibid., pp. 65–6.
26 Williams to Newcastle 25 XI 52, PRO, SP 88, no. 73.
27 Williams to Newcastle 16 VII 53, *Papers of Various Sorts*, Newport, qM 411 012.
28 *Mémoires*, Vol. I, p. 49.
29 Ibid., p. 69.
30 AXC, 911, ff. 353–400.

4 *Paris and London*

1 BM, Hardwicke, 35, 485, pp. 137–9.
2 Stanisław to Bentinck 25 XII 71, AGAD, ZP, 173, f. 115.
3 Stanisław to Sułkowski 5 XI 53, AXC, 798, f. 51.
4 BM, Hardwicke, 35, 485, ff. 137–9.
5 Duchesse de Brancas to Countess Brühl, AXC, 798, f. 59.
6 BM, Hardwicke, 35, 485, ff. 137–9.
7 *Mémoires*, Vol. I, pp. 95–6.

8 Aldis, *Madame Geoffrin*, p. 11.
9 Raymond Mortimer, *Channel Packet*, p. 115.
10 Stanisław to Sułkowski 4 I 54, AXC, 798, f. 43.
11 Cheverny, *Mémoires*, Vol. I, pp. 116–17; also Grimm, *Correspondance*, Vol. V, p. 220; also Maleszewski, *Essai Historique*, p. 461; also Fabre, op. cit., pp. 188–9; also Créquy, *Souvenirs*, Vol. IV, p. 49; also Komarzewski, *Coup d'Oeil*, p. 115.
12 Stanisław to Sułkowski 4 I 54, AXC, 798, f. 43.
13 Chesterfield to Stanisław 25 VII 54, AGAD, ZP, 173, f. 300.
14 Ilchester, op. cit., p. 287.
15 Walpole to John Chute, 14 V 54, Walpole, *Letters*, Vol. III, pp. 230–1.
16 *Mémoires*, Vol. I, p. 107.
17 Stanisław to Stanisław Poniatowski 25 XII 71, ANP, 340 API, 2; also Lyttelton to Stanisław 17 XII 64, AGAD, ZP, 177, f. 151; and ditto 15 X 64, ibid., f. 149.
18 *Gazetteer & Daily Advertizer*, London, 6 October 1764.
19 Askenazy, *Dwa Stulecia*, Vol. I, p. 311.
20 *Mémoires*, Vol. I, p. 112.
21 *Mémoires*, Vol. I, p. 120.
22 Joseph Yorke to Stanisław 21 IX 64, BM, Hardwicke, 35, 367, f. 160.
23 Williams to Holdernesse 12 XII 54, PRO, SP 88, no. 76.
24 See: Joseph Yorke to Chancellor 28 VIII 53, BM, Hardwicke, 35, 356, f. 175; also Williams' instructions from George II 20 VI 54, Newport, qM 411 012; also Williams to Holdernesse 16 X 54, PRO SP 88, no. 76; also Holdernesse to Williams 2 I 55, PRO, SP 88, no. 77, f. 2; and Williams to Holdernesse 6 IV 55, PRO, SP 88, no. 77, f. 136.
25 Stanisław to Charles Yorke 7 I 55, BM, Hardwicke, 35, 634.
26 Williams to Stanisław 8 I 55, AGAD, ZP, 318, f. 220.
27 *Mémoires Secrets*, p. 8.
28 *Mémoires*, Vol. I, pp. 135–6.
29 Ibid., pp. 136–7.
30 Ilchester, op. cit., p. 309.
31 *Mémoires*, Vol. I, p. 149.

5 Catherine

1 *Mémoires*, Vol. I, p. 193.
2 Stanisław Poniatowski to Ludwika Zamoyska 14 XI 55, AXC, 3972, f. 121.
3 *Mémoires*, Vol. I, p. 159.

4 Catherine II, *Mémoires*, p. 253.

5 Williams to Holdernesse 2 X 55, PRO, SP 91, no. 61, f. 131; also Bilbasov, *Istoria Ekateriny*, Vol. I, p. 322.

6 *Mémoires Secrets*, p. 8.

7 Catherine, *Mémoires*, p. 231.

8 *Mémoires Secrets*, p. 7.

9 Ibid., p. 8.

10 *Mémoires Secrets*, pp. 10–14.

11 Catherine, *Mémoires*, p. 237.

12 Williams to Catherine 9 IX 56, Catherine, *Correspondence*, ed. Goriainov, p. 137.

13 Catherine to Bestuzhev 11 IX 56, ibid., p. 159.

14 Williams to Catherine 8 IX 56, Catherine, *Correspondence*, ed. Ilchester, p. 133.

15 Catherine to Williams 18 VIII 56 and Williams to Catherine 23 VIII 56, Catherine, *Correspondence*, ed. Goriainov, pp. 45 and 76.

16 Williams to Catherine 26 XI 56, Catherine, *Correspondence*, ed. Ilchester, p. 239.

17 Catherine to Williams 14 IX 56, ibid., p. 136, also p. 143.

18 Williams to Catherine 7 X 56, Catherine, *Correspondence*, ed. Goriainov, p. 199.

19 Stanisław to Williams 17 X 56, Catherine, *Correspondence*, ed. Ilchester, p. 176.

20 Stanisław to Catherine, ibid., pp. 197–9.

21 Williams to Catherine 27 IX 56, Catherine, *Correspondence*, ed. Goriainov, p. 181.

22 Konopczyński, *Polska w Wojnie Siedmioletniej*, Vol. I, p. 393.

23 Williams to Catherine 14 XII 56, Catherine, *Correspondence*, ed. Goriainov, p. 301.

24 Williams to Catherine 22 III 57, Catherine, *Correspondence*, ed. Ilchester, p. 276.

25 Williams to Holdernesse 22 III 57, PRO, SP 91, no. 65.

26 Catherine, *Mémoires*, pp. 270–1.

27 Ibid., pp. 271–2; also Bilbasov, op. cit., Vol. I, pp. 345–7; also Nieć, op. cit., p. 175.

28 Charles of Saxony to Xavier 14 V 58, BP 74 II; also Konopczyński, op. cit., Vol. I, p. 490.

29 Bilbasov, op. cit., Vol. I, p. 390.

30 *Mémoires Secrets*, pp. 15–19.

6 King-in-Waiting

1 *Mémoires*, Vol. I, p. 350.
2 Ibid., p. 351.
3 Elżbieta Lubomirska to Stanisław 8 VI 59, AXC, 926, f. 271; also ditto 19 VI 59, ibid., f. 261; ditto 10 VII 59, ibid., f. 275; ditto 22 X 59, ibid., f. 287.
4 Paulmy's Instructions 7 IV 60, *Recueil des Instructions*, Vol. V, p. 217.
5 Przeździecki, *Diplomatie et Protocole*, Vol. I, p. 274.
6 Hennin to Tercier 30 XII 60, Broglie, *Le Secret du Roi*, Vol. I, p. 415.
7 Louis XV to Breteuil 1 IV 60, *Recueil des Instructions*, Vol. IX, p. 153; also Vorontsov to Tercier 10 II 60, Vorontsov, *Arkhiv*, Vol. IV, p. 420; also Nieć, op. cit., p. 198.
8 *Mémoires*, Vol. I, p. 373.
9 Ibid., p. 362.
10 Catherine to Stanisław 2 VII 62, Catherine, *Sochinyenia*, Vol. XII, p. 546.
11 Catherine to Stanisław 13 VII 62, ibid., pp. 547–8.
12 Catherine to Stanisław, n.d., ibid., p. 556.
13 Catherine to Stanisław 12 IX 62, ibid., pp. 558–9.
14 AXC, 798, f. 75; also Bilbasov, op. cit., Vol. II, p. 391.
15 Catherine to Stanisław 11 XI 62, Catherine, *Sochinyenia*, Vol. XII, p. 560.
16 Catherine to Stanisław 27? XII 62, ibid., p. 563.
17 Catherine to Keyserling 30 I 63, BP, 29; also ditto 1 IV 63, Solovyov, *Padenie Polshi*, p. 13.
18 Scott, *Great Britain, Poland and the Prussian Alliance*; also Halifax to Wroughton 5 IV 63, PRO, SP 88, no. 87, f. 123; also Reddaway, *Great Britain and Poland*, p. 234.
19 Wroughton to Sandwich 5 X 63, PRO, SP 88, no. 87, f. 292.
20 AXC, 798, ff. 301–2.
21 Stanisław to Voltaire 21 II 67, Voltaire, *Oeuvres Complètes*, Vol. LXVII, p. 367.
22 Buckinghamshire to Stormont 7 XI 63, Buckinghamshire, *Despatches*, Vol. II, p. 99.
23 AGAD, ZP, 177, ff. 352–92.
24 AXC, 2289.
25 Breteuil to Louis XV 16 XII 62, Broglie, op. cit., Vol. II, p. 29.
26 Stanisław to Catherine 2 XI 63, AXC 798, f. 527.
27 *Mémoires Secrets*, p. 33.
28 Catherine to Repnin 5 I 64, *Sbornik*, Vol. V, p. 131.

7 *The Election*

1 *Mémoires*, Vol. I, p. 480; also *Faits qui constatent la légitimité de l'éléction*, AGAD, ZP, 71, f. 3; also AXC, 798, ff. 579ff.
2 Stanisław to Massalski 2 IV 64, AGAD, AKP, 355, no. 9.
3 AXC, 798, f. 567.
4 Kraushar, *Repnin a Polska*, Vol. I, p. 35; also AXC, 798, ff. 601 and 605.
5 Wroughton to Buckinghamshire 20 II 64, Buckinghamshire, op. cit., Vol. II, p. 147.
6 Rostworowski, *Ostatni Król*, p. 39; also AXC 798, f. 135.
7 Rulhière, *Histoire des Révolutions*, Vol. II, p. 172.
8 Scott, *Frederick II, The Ottoman Empire, and the origins of the Russo-Prussian Alliance.*
9 Schmitt, *Materiały*, p. 34; also Korzoń, *Wewnętrzne Dzieje*, Vol. IV, p. 43.
10 Ibid., p. 35.
11 Broglie, op. cit., Vol. II, pp. 227 ff.
12 Ibid., Vol. I, p. 369.
13 Paulmy's note 16 III 64, BP 33, no. 56.
14 *Recueil des Instructions*, Vol. V, p. 243; also Paulmy to Xavier of Saxony, BP 74, no. 6.
15 Broglie, op. cit., Vol. II, pp. 265ff; Łubieński, *Pamiętnik*, Vol. II, pp. 110–11; also Łubieński, BP 33, no. 68.
16 Stanisław to Catherine 27 V 64, AXC, 798, f. 695.
17 Frederick to Solms 22 VII 64, *Sbornik*, Vol. XXII, p. 263.
18 AGAD, ZP, 50, no. 4.
19 AXC, 798, f. 709.
20 Repnin to Panin, July 64, Kraushar, *Repnin a Polska*, Vol. I, p. 59.
21 Nieć, op. cit., p. 293.
22 Kaplan, *The First Partition of Poland*, p. 42.
23 Kitowicz, *Pamiętniki*, p. 145.
24 Ibid., p. 146.
25 *Mémoires*, Vol. I, p. 505.
26 AGAD, AKP, *Pudło* 89, no. 42, f. 702.
27 Ibid., f. 703.
28 *Mémoires*, Vol. I, p. 518; also AGAD, AKP, *Pudło* 89, no. 42, f. 704; also Kitowicz, *Pamiętniki*, p. 149.
29 Kitowicz, op. cit., p. 147.
30 Catherine to Stanisław 25 IX 64, AXC, 939, ff. 635–6.

8   Stanislaus Secundus Augustus Rex

1 For the ceremonial of the coronation, see AGAD, AKP, *Pudło* 89, no. 37; also Ciampi, *Viaggi*, p. 134.
2 AGAD, AKP, *Pudło* 89, no. 35 and no. 40.
3 Schmitt, *Materiały*, Vol. I, p. 73.
4 Beales, *Joseph II*, pp. 98–9.
5 Lubomirski, *Pod władzą Repnina*, p. 97.
6 Kraushar, *Repnin a Polska*, Vol. I, p. 69.
7 Wroughton to Sandwich 22 III 65, PRO, SP 88, p. 91.
8 Stanisław to Stanisław I 27 IV 65, BP, MAM, 1088.
9 Stanisław to Mme Geoffrin 9 IX 64, Stanisław, *Correspondance inédite avec Mme Geoffrin*, p. 103.
10 Ibid., p. 113.
11 Ibid., p. 145.
12 BP, MAM, 1085.
13 Solovyov, *Padenie Polshi*, p. 38.
14 AGAD, AKP, *Pudło*, 91, f. 77.
15 Stanisław to Mme Geoffrin 15 IX 65, Stanisław, *Correspondance inédite avec Mme Geoffrin*, p. 176.
16 Ditto, 22 II 66, ibid., p. 216.
17 Korzoń, *Odrodzenie w Upadku*, p. 44.
18 Rulhière, op. cit., Vol. II, pp. 117 and 119; also *Mémoires*, p. 516; also AGAD, AKP, *Pudło*, 89, no. 42, f. 703.
19 Adam Czartoryski to Keith 5 VIII 65, BM, Hardwicke, 35,485, p. 159.
20 Stanisław to Mme Geoffrin 28 XI 64, Stanisław, *Correspondance inédite avec Mme Geoffrin*, p. 124.

9   The Constraints of Monarchy

1 Mme Geoffrin to Stanisław 24 X 64, Stanisław, *Correspondance inédite avec Mme Geoffrin*, p. 114.
2 Joseph York to Stanisław 21 IX 64, BM, Hardwicke, 35, 367, f. 160.
3 Krasicki to Stanisław 11 IX 64, AXC, 798, f. 723.
4 BUW, 122, pp. 121–6.
5 Konopczyński, *Fryderyk a Polska*, pp. 110 and 117.
6 Rostworowski, *Ostatni Król*, p. 46.
7 Lubomirski, op. cit., p. 50.
8 Ibid., pp. 50–1.
9 AGAD, AK, 612.

10 Lubomirski, op. cit., p. 96.
11 Ibid., pp. 56–7.
12 *Mémoires*, Vol. I, p. 602.
13 Malmesbury, *Diaries*, Vol. I, p. 19.
14 Rulhière, op. cit., Vol. II, p. 220.
15 Lubomirski, op. cit., p. 58.
16 AGAD, AKP, *Pudło* 89, no. 42, f. 770.
17 Rzewuski's instructions, AGAD, ZP, 50, pp. 27–8.
18 *Sbornik*, Vol. XXII, p. 314.
19 Frederick to Solms 6 X 64, ibid., p. 318.
20 Frederick to Catherine 30 X 64, Solovyov, op. cit., p. 22.
21 AGAD, ZP, 50, no. 35; also *Sbornik* XXII, no. 185.
22 Macartney to Sandwich 18 VI 65, *Sbornik* XII, no. 205.
23 Wroughton to Sandwich 4 V, 29 V & 23 X 65, PRO, SP 88, no. 91.
24 Terlecki, *Mennica*, p. 57.
25 Jobert, *La Commission d'Éducation*, pp. 146–7.
26 Stanisław to Mme Geoffrin 31 VIII 65, Stanisław, *Correspondance inédite avec Mme Geoffrin*, pp. 173–4.
27 AXC, 788, f. 327.
28 Stanisław to Mme Geoffrin 25 X 66, Stanisław, *Correspondance inédite avec Mme Geoffrin*, p. 250.
29 Zawadzki, *Polska Stanisławowska*, Vol. I, p. 62.
30 Casanova, *Mémoires*, Vol. VII, p. 220.
31 J. Heyne to Charles of Saxony, BP, 66, no. 51.

10   A Matter of Faith

1 *Sbornik*, Vol. XXII, no. 164, p. 302.
2 Stanisław to Mme Geoffrin 6 III 65, Stanisław, *Correspondance inédite avec Mme Geoffrin*, p. 144.
3 Kraushar, *Repnin a Polska*, Vol. I, p. 54.
4 Solovyov, *Padenie Polshi*, pp. 28–30.
5 Ibid., p. 30; also Catherine to Repnin 17 X 64, *Sbornik*, Vol. V, p. 134.
6 Konopczyński, op. cit., pp. 106–7.
7 Kaplan, op. cit., p. 50.
8 Panin to Repnin 14 VIII 67, Madariaga, *Russia in the age of Catherine the Great*, p. 200.
9 *Mémoires*, Vol. I, pp. 600–1; also Solovyov, *Padenie Polshi*, p. 64.
10 AGAD, ZP, 52, pp. 27 and 40.
11 Conversations between Saldern and Frederick 8 V and 13 V 66,

Solovyov, *Istoria Rossyi*, Vol. XXVII, pp. 444–9; also Saldern to Panin 17 IV 66, ibid., pp. 420–1; also Panin's exposé to Prince Henry, Beer, *Erste Theilung*, Vol. III, pp. 109–11; also Repnin to Panin 21 VIII 66, ibid., p. 426.

12 Stanisław to Mme Geoffrin 25 V 65, Stanisław, *Correspondance inédite avec Mme Geoffrin*, p. 154.

13 Catherine to Mme Geoffrin 18 VI 65, *Sbornik*, Vol. I, p. 276.

14 Stanisław, *Correspondance inédite avec Mme Geoffrin*, p. 223.

15 Grimm, *Correspondance*, Vol. V, pp. 219–20.

16 Fabre, *Stanislas Auguste et le Siècle des Lumières*, p. 308.

17 Mme Geoffrin to D'Alembert 23 VII 66, D'Alembert, *Éloges de Mme Geoffrin*.

18 Voltaire to Mme Geoffrin 3 VII 66, Stanisław, *Correspondance inédite avec Mme Geoffrin*, p. 229.

19 Ditto, 26 VIII 66, ibid., p. 239.

20 Stanisław to Mme Geoffrin 14 IX 66, ibid., p. 241.

21 Kraushar, op. cit., Vol. I, p. 128.

22 Ibid., p. 136.

23 Ibid., p. 131.

24 Solovyov, *Istoria Rossyi*, Vol. XXVII, p. 429.

25 Ibid., p. 430.

26 Stanisław to Rzewuski 24 IX 66, *Sbornik XXII*, no. 272, pp. 519–20.

27 PRO, SP 88, no. 92.

28 Solovyov, *Padenie Polshi*, p. 44.

29 AGAD, APP, 82, f. 417.

30 *Mémoires*, Vol. I, p. 536.

31 Panin to Stanisław September 66, *Sbornik*, Vol. XXII, no. 275, p. 524.

32 Stanisław to Catherine 5 X 66, *Mémoires*, Vol. I, p. 539; also AXC 798, f. 739; also AGAD, APP, 82, f. 418.

33 Macartney to Conway 5 VIII 66, *Sbornik*, Vol. XII, p. 270.

34 Catherine to Stanisław 17 X 66, *Sbornik*, Vol. XXII, p. 532; also AXC 798, f. 743.

35 Stanisław to Mme Geoffrin 6 III 65, Stanisław, *Correspondance inédite avec Mme Geoffrin*, p. 144.

36 Protocols of conferences, AXC, 653, ff. 475ff and 529.

37 Ibid., ff. 507 and 517.

38 Wroughton to Conway 18 X 66, PRO, SP 88, no. 92.

39 Stanisław to Mme Geoffrin 7 I 67, Stanisław, *Correspondance inédite avec Mme Geoffrin*, p. 262.

40 AXC, 653, f. 535; also AGAD, APP, 82, f. 245.

41 Wroughton to Conway 12 XI 66, PRO, SP 88, no. 92.

42 Lubomirski, op. cit., p. 116.

43 Catherine to Repnin 17 X 66, Kraushar, op. cit., Vol. I, pp. 161 and 168.

44 Stanisław to Mme Geoffrin 10 XII 66, Stanisław, *Correspondance inédite avec Mme Geoffrin*, p. 260.

45 Korzoń, *Wewnętrzne Dzieje*, Vol. IV, p. 46.

46 Solovyov, *Padenie Polshi*, pp. 46–7; also Wroughton to Conway 26 XI 66, PRO, SP 88, no. 92.

11   Rebellion

1 Macartney to Conway 12 XI 66, *Sbornik*, Vol. XII, p. 281, and ditto 7 XII 66, ibid., p. 288; also Heyne to Xavier of Saxony 28 I 67, BP, 66, p. 103.

2 Frederick to Solms 28 XII 66, *Sbornik*, Vol. XXII, p. 573.

3 Lubomirski's Journal, AGAD, APP, 82, f. 419.

4 Panin to Czartoryski 20 XII 66, *Sbornik*, Vol. XXXVII, p. 6.

5 AXC, 653, f. 575.

6 Stanisław to Mme Geoffrin 11 III 67, Stanisław, *Correspondance inédite avec Mme Geoffrin*, p. 276.

7 Konopczyński, *Geneza i Ustanowienie Rady Nieustającej*, p. 105.

8 Stanisław to Mme Geoffrin 1 VIII 67, Stanisław, *Correspondance inédite avec Mme Geoffrin*, p. 300.

9 Catherine to Stanisław 27 VI 67, *Sbornik*, Vol. LXVII, p. 383.

10 Catherine's rescript to Repnin 27 VI 67, ibid., p. 384; also Panin to Repnin 21 IX 67, ibid., p. 467.

11 Catherine to Stanisław 21 VIII 67, ibid., p. 429.

12 Lubomirski, op. cit., p. 121.

13 Ibid., p. 122.

14 Ibid., p. 128

15 Ibid., p. 134.

16 Krechetnikov, *Dziennik*.

17 Lubomirski, op. cit., p. 143.

18 Catherine to Stanisław 14 X 67, *Sbornik*, Vol. LXVII, p. 495.

19 Lelewel, *Panowanie Króla Polskiego*, p. 28.

20 Malmesbury, op. cit., Vol. I, p. 25.

21 Ibid., p. 15.

22 Madariaga, op. cit., p. 202.

23 Hertzberg & Finckenstein to Solms 24 X 67, *Sbornik*, Vol. XXXVII, p. 92.

24 Frederick to Benoit 129 X 67, ibid., p. 106.

25 Catherine to Stanisław 14 X 67, *Sbornik*, Vol. LXVII, p. 495; also Panin to Stanisław 6 XI 67, ibid., p. 510.
26 Panin to Repnin 29 XI 67, ibid., p. 515.
27 Solms to Frederick 12 X 67, *Sbornik*, Vol. XXXVII, p. 99; also Hertzberg and Finckenstein to Frederick 12 XII 67, ibid., p. 120; also Konopczyński, *Geneza i Ustanowienie*, p. 123.
28 Malmesbury, op. cit., Vol. I, p. 21.
29 *Volumina Legum*, Vol. VII, p. 282.
30 Stanisław to Mme Geoffrin 9 IV 68, Stanisław, *Correspondance inédite avec Mme Geoffrin*, p. 327.
31 Rostworowski, *Ostatni Król*, p. 56.
32 AXC, 653, f. 667.
33 Schmitt, *Materiały*, Vol. I, p. 65.
34 *Czasy Stanisława Augusta*, p. 42.
35 *Konfederacja Barska*, p. 4.
36 Protocols of Conferences, BN, BOZ, 877, p. 83; also Lubomirski, op. cit., p. 174.
37 Lubomirski, op. cit., p. 178.
38 Ibid., p. 179–80; also AXC 820, p. 256.
39 Stanisław to Mme Geoffrin 9 IV 68, Stanisław, *Correspondance inédite avec Mme Geoffrin*, p. 327.
40 AXC, 653, f. 695.
41 Konopczyński, *Konfederacja Barska*, Vol. I, p. 42.
42 AXC, 653, f. 693.
43 Stanisław to Branicki 9 VI 68, Stanisław, *Korespondencja z Ksawerym Branickim*, p. 12.
44 *Czasy Stanisława Augusta*, p. 55.
45 Konopczyński, *Fryderyk a Polska*, p. 127.
46 Vioménil, *Lettres Particulières*, pp. 77 and 83.
47 Karpiński, *Pamiętniki*, p. 65.
48 Broglie, *Le Secret du Roi*, Vol. II, pp. 286–8.
49 Louis XV to Chateaufort 18 I 69, *Recueil des Instructions*, Vol. V, p. 290.
50 Ibid., p. 285.
51 Choiseul to Mercy, Beer, *Erste Theilung*, Vol. III, p. 6.
52 Kaunitz to Mercy, ibid., p. 11.

12   Desperation

1 Conversations with Stackelberg, PAU, 1649, pp. 13 and 16.
2 Stanisław to Canal 5 I 71, AXC, 939, f. 531.

3 Stanisław to Zamoyski, *Skarbiec Historii Polskiej*, Vol. I, p. 182.
4 Stanisław, *Korespondencja z Ksawerym Branickim*, pp. 49–61.
5 *Mémoires*, Vol. I, p. 615.
6 Ibid., p. 616.
7 Malmesbury, op. cit., Vol. I, pp. 18–20.
8 BN, BOZ, 877, f. 106.
9 Ibid., f. 111; also Solovyov, *Padenie Polshi*, p. 90.
10 Kaplan, op. cit., p. 107.
11 *Mémoires*, Vol. I, pp. 645–9.
12 Ibid., p. 650.
13 Chreptowicz to Stanisław 1 V 70, BP, 35, p. 161.
14 Durand to Choiseul VII 70, *Konfederacja Barska*, p. 81.
15 Broglie, op. cit., Vol. II, pp. 312 and 306.
16 AGAD, ZP, 395, no. 32.
17 Lee to Stanisław 10 II 67, AGAD, ZP, 177, f. 166; also Stanisław to Burzyński 30 XII 69, AGAD, ZP, 395, f. 7.
18 Burzyński to Stanisław 16 III 70, AGAD, ZP, 216, f. 73; for British attitudes see Rochford to Wroughton, ibid., f. 113; also Cathcart to Rochford, *Sbornik*, Vol. XIX, no. 4; AGAD, ZP, 216 and 93.
19 *Konfederacja Barska*, pp. 91–2.
20 Stanisław to Mme Geoffrin 6 VII 68, Stanisław, *Correspondance inédite avec Mme Geoffrin*, p. 345.
21 Malmesbury, op. cit., Vol. I, p. 20.
22 Coccei to Sir Andrew Mitchell 20 V 69, *Skarbiec Historii Polskiej*, Vol. I, p. 397; see also note 3 of Chapter 13.
23 Stanisław to Mme Geoffrin 30 VIII 69, Stanisław, *Correspondance inédite avec Mme Geoffrin*, p. 353.
24 Ditto 7 X 69, ibid., p. 357.
25 Ditto 23 X 71, ibid., p. 409.
26 AGAD, AK, III, 587, 612, 629, 648.
27 Ibid., 612.
28 Stanisław to Mme Geoffrin 27 VI 70, Stanisław, *Correspondance inédite avec Mme Geoffrin*, p. 377.
29 Stanisław to Catherine 21 XII 70, *Mémoires*, Vol. I, pp. 652–4.
30 Rolle, *Czartoryscy i Repnin*, p. 392.
31 Malmesbury, op. cit., Vol. I, p. 31.
32 AGAD, ZP, 93, ff. 3, 7, 8 and 9.
33 AGAD, ZP, 395, ff. 26–7; also Conversation with Saldern 26 V 71, AXC, 939, f. 551; and 1 VI 71, ibid., f. 552.
34 Panin to Stanisław 22 III 71, *Sbornik*, Vol. XCVII, p. 240.
35 Saldern to Catherine 12 VI 71, Solovyov, *Padenie Polshi*, p. 122.

36 Korzoń, *Odrodzenie w Upadku*, p. 50.
37 Solovyov, *Padenie Polshi*, p. 128.

13   The Royal Cake

1 *Mémoires*, Vol. I, pp. 673ff.
2 Bentinck to Stanisław 25 XII 71, AGAD, ZP, 173, f. 115.
3 Durini's reports 16 XI 71 and 23 XI 71, *Vetera Monumenta*, Vol. IV,
  p. 410. There were two other unconfirmed reports of attempts on his
  life, one on 10 March 1768, when his carriage was supposed to have been
  attacked (see Kaleta, *Oświeceni i Sentymentalni*, p. 271), the other when a
  bomb is supposed to have gone off in his study in the first days of May
  1769 (see Charles of Kurland to Xavier 22 V 69, ANP, 340 API, 1). See
  also note 22 to Chapter 12.
4 Voltaire to Stanisław 3 XII 71, Voltaire, *Oeuvres*, Vol. LXVII, p. 374,
  and 6 XII 71, ibid., p. 375.
5 Konopczyński, *Konfederacja Barska*, Vol. II, p. 193.
6 Conferences with Saldern, AXC, 939, f. 563.
7 *Mémoires*, Vol. II, p. 3.
8 Konopczyński, *Fryderyk a Polska*, p. 168.
9 D'Alembert to Frederick 2 I 72, D'Alembert, *Lettres à Frédéric*, p. LIX.
10 Ditto 9 X 72, ibid., p. LXXVIII.
11 Voltaire to Frederick 6 XII 71, Frederick, *Correspondance*, Vol. VIII, p. 206.
12 Ditto 1 II 72, ibid., p. 210.
13 Frederick to Benoit and Solms 10 XI 71, Frederick, *Politische
   Correspondenz*, Vol. XXXI, pp. 521–3.
14 Leśnodorski, *Polska w Epoce Oświecenia*, p. 25.
15 Madariaga, op. cit., p. 221; also Kaplan, op. cit., p. 113; also *Mémoires*,
   Vol. I, p. 661 for version that Frederick employed d'Assebourg;
   Solovyov, *Padenie Polshi*, p. 149 for version that Prince Henry first
   mentioned the matter, borne out by Prince Henry's statements to Ségur,
   Mémoires, Vol. II, p. 149; also Frederick, *Mémoires depuis la Paix*, p. 26 on
   Lynar's project; also Stanisław to Deboli 3 III 92, Rok Nadziei, p. 114,
   for Stackelberg's claim that the idea was born in St Petersburg; see also
   Wraxall, op. cit., Vol. I, pp. 20ff.
16 Kaplan, op. cit., p. 115.
17 Frederick, *Mémoires depuis la Paix*, p. 35, also Kaplan, op. cit., p. 146.
18 Madariaga, op. cit., p. 19.
19 Ibid., p. 223.
20 Kaplan, op. cit., p. 150.

21 *Mémoires*, Vol. I, p. 661.
22 Beales, op. cit., p. 297.
23 Frederick, *Mémoires depuis la Paix*, p. 35.
24 Frederick to Prince Henry 9 IV 72, Frederick, *Correspondance*, Vol. XI, p. 356.
25 Voltaire to Frederick 18 X 72, Cornut, *Voltaire et la Pologne*, p. 55.
26 Frederick to D'Alembert 27 X 72, D'Alembert, *Lettres à Frédéric*, p. LXXXIV.
27 Frederick to Prince Henry 12 VI 72, Frederick, *Correspondance*, Vol. XI, p. 357.
28 D'Alembert, *Lettres à Frédéric*, p. LXXXIV.
29 Voltaire to Frederick 16 X 72, Frederick, *Correspondance*, Vol. VIII, p. 219; also 19 XI 72, ibid., p. 224.
30 Walpole to Mann 9 IX 73, Walpole, *Letters*, Vol. VIII, p. 334.
31 Grimm to Stanisław 18 IX 68, AGAD, ZP, 176, f. 179.
32 *Sbornik*, Vol. XLIV, p. 3.
33 Cornut, op. cit., p. 64.
34 Fabre, op. cit., p. 323.
35 Ibid.
36 Vautrin, *L'Observateur*, p. 256.
37 Raynal, *Commerce des Indes*, Vol. X, p. 57.
38 Fabre, op. cit., p. 356.
39 Tourneux, *Diderot et Catherine*, p. 252.
40 Voltaire to Frederick 15 II 75, Frederick, *Correspondance*, Vol. VIII, p. 313.
41 Saint-Priest, *Études Diplomatiques*, p. 13.
42 Burke, *Collected Works*, Vol. VIII, p. 247.
43 Kaunitz to Mercy 4 XII 71, Mercy Argenteau, *Correspondance Secrète*, Vol. II, p. 399.
44 Mercy to Maria Theresa 14 X 72, Maria Theresa, *Correspondance Secrète*, Vol. I, p. 378.
45 Stanisław to Monet 8 IV 72, 13 VI 72, 11 VII 72, Stanisław, *Correspondance avec Glayre*, pp. 4–16.
46 *Mémoires*, Vol. I, p. 664.
47 Beales, op. cit., p. 298.
48 Maria Theresa to Joseph 25 I 72, Maria Theresa, *Correspondance Secrète*, Vol. I, p. 307.
49 Wraxall, op. cit., Vol. II, p. 30.
50 Malmesbury, op. cit., Vol. I, pp. 82–5.
51 Walpole to Dr. G. 4 IV 76, Walpole, *Letters*, Vol. IX, p. 342.
52 Horn, *British Public Opinion*, p. 32.
53 Stanisław to Monet 15 VIII 72, Stanisław, *Correspondance avec Glayre*, p. 24.

54 Ditto.

55 Ditto.

56 Stanisław to Monet 26 VIII 72, Stanisław, *Correspondance avec Glayre*, p. 27.

57 Ditto 7 X 72, ibid., p. 46.

58 Tazbir, *Myśl Polska*, p. 121.

59 Schiedemantel to Jones 18 I 72, AXC 3877, no. 15.

60 Stanisław to Branicki 18 XI 72, Stanisław, *Correspondance avec Glayre* p. 71.

61 Ditto 9 XII 72, ibid., p. 83.

62 *Mémoires*, Vol. II, p. 136; also Stanisław to Monet 10 X 72, Stanisław, *Correspondance avec Glayre*, p. 48.

63 Stanisław to Branicki 9 XII 72, Stanisław, *Correspondance avec Glayre*, pp. 88 and p. 83.

64 George III, *Correspondence*, Vol. II, p. 428, no. 1180.

65 Horn, op. cit., pp. 18–19.

66 Ibid., p. 35.

67 Madariaga, op. cit., p. 231.

14 Readjustment

1 Glayre to Rieule 16 XII 72, Stanisław, *Correspondance avec Glayre*, p. 95.

2 Stanisław to Branicki 9 XII 72, ibid., p. 83.

3 Panin's instructions, BP, 29, IV.

4 *Mémoires*, Vol. II, p. 12.

5 Strawiński's evidence, Kaleta, *Oświeceni i Sentymentalni*, p. 110.

6 Stanisław to Monet 11 XI 72, Stanisław, *Correspondance avec Glayre*, p. 60.

7 Maleszewski, *Essai Historique*, p. 282.

8 Konopczyński, *Geneza i Ustanowienie*, p. 197.

9 Schiedemantel to NN 6 X 73, AXC, 3877, p. 37.

10 *Mémoires*, Vol. II, p. 33.

11 Correspondence with Lentulus; conversations with Saldern, PAU, 1648.

12 Hugh Elliot to Minto 30 IX 72, Elliot, *Memoir*, p. 19.

13 Konopczyński, *Geneza i Ustanowienie*, pp. 127 and 129.

14 Stackelberg to Panin 3 II 73, ibid., p. 385.

15 Stanisław to Branicki 20 II 73, Stanisław, *Correspondance avec Glayre*, p. 102.

16 *Zbiór Deklaracji*, pp. 105–22.

17 Ibid., p. 362.

18 *Mémoires*, Vol. II, p. 87.
19 Ibid., p. 94.
20 Ibid., pp. 107–8.
21 Ibid., p. 120.
22 Ibid., p. 126.
23 Konopczyński, *Geneza i Ustanowienie*, p. 208.
24 *Mémoires*, Vol. II, p. 344.
25 Stanisław to Monet 22 V 73, Stanisław, *Correspondance avec Glayre*, p. 130.
26 Stanisław to Mme Geoffrin 5 VI 73, Stanisław, *Correspondance inédite avec Mme Geoffrin*, p. 449.
27 AGAD, ZP, 312, pp. 2–170; also *Mémoires*, Vol. II, pp. 141ff.
28 AGAD, ZP, 312, p. 70.
29 Stanisław to Mme Geoffrin, 5 VI 73, Stanisław, *Correspondance inédite avec Mme Geoffrin*, p. 447.
30 AGAD, ZP, 312, p. 109.
31 Mably, *Du Gouvernement*, pp. 56 and 70.
32 Konopczyński, *Geneza i Ustanowienie*, pp. 216–17.
33 Ibid., p. 249.
34 Ibid., p. 254.
35 Maria Theresa to Mercy 31 X 76, Maria Theresa, *Correspondance Secrète*, Vol. III, p. 512.
36 Wolff, *The Vatican and Poland*, p. 15.
37 *Mémoires*, Vol. II, p. 221.
38 Ibid., p. 222.
39 Stanisław to Mme Geoffrin 5 VI 73, Stanisław, *Correspondance inér.ite avec Mme Geoffrin*, p. 449.
40 *Mémoires*, Vol. II, p. 224.
41 Ibid., p. 210.
42 Jobert, *La Commission d'Éducation*, p. 162.
43 Ibid., 164.
44 *Sbornik*, Vol. CLXV, p. 199.
45 Konopczyński, *Geneza i Ustanowienie*, p. 210.
46 Wraxall, op. cit., Vol. II, p. 110.
47 Kaleta, *Oświeceni i Sentymentalni*, p. 255.
48 Konopczyński, *Geneza i Ustanowienie*, p. 268.
49 *Mémoires*, Vol. II, p. 242.
50 Stanisław to Deboli 19 VI 75, AGAD, AKP, 70, f. 1.
51 Schiedemantel to NN 18 X 72, AXC 3877, f. 77.
52 Ibid., p. 286.
53 Konopczyński, *Geneza i Ustanowienie*, p. 325.

54 *Mémoires*, Vol. II, p. 287.
55 Ibid., pp. 309–10.
56 Ibid., p. 312.
57 Ibid., p. 334.

15   *Creating a Nation*

1 Wraxall, op. cit., Vol. II, pp. 11 and 51.
2 Mably, *De la Situation Politique*, pp. 8–9.
3 Ibid., p. 19.
4 *Mémoires*, Vol. II, p. 298.
5 Ibid., p. 274.
6 Fabre, op. cit., p. 436.
7 Wraxall, op. cit., Vol. II, pp. 53–4.
8 Ibid., p. 50.
9 *Mémoires*, Vol. II, p. 352.
10 Stanisław to Stanisław Poniatowski 25 XII 71, ANP, 340 AP I, 2.
11 Jobert, *La Commission d'Éducation*, p. 174; also AXC, 818.
12 Ibid., p. 227.
13 Ibid., pp. 27 and 187.
14 Ibid., p. 311.
15 Ibid., pp. 314–15.
16 Ibid., pp. 316ff.
17 Ibid., p. 205.
18 Ibid., p. 354.
19 Ibid., pp. 152–4.
20 Morawski, *Ignacy Potocki*, p. 17.
21 Rottermund, *Zamek Warszawski*, p. 212.
22 *Mémoires*, Vol. II, p. 463; also Ostermann to Stackelberg 21 VIII 77, *Sbornik*, CXLV, p. 467.
23 *Mémoires*, Vol. II, p. 475.
24 Stanisław to Stanisław Poniatowski 3 III 77, AGAD, AKP, 70, p. 27.
25 *Mémoires*, Vol. II, p. 277.
26 Glayre to Stanisław 23 VI 77, Stanisław, *Correspondance avec Glayre*, p. 140.
27 *Mémoires*, Vol. II, p. 478.
28 Stanisław to Glayre 27 IX 77, Stanisław, *Correspondance avec Glayre*, p. 143.
29 Stanisław to Monet 24 XI 78, ibid., p. 163.
30 Stanisław to Monet 24 IX 79, ibid., p. 167.

16   *Cultivating the Garden*

1 Coxe, *Travels*, Vol. I, p. 226.
2 Mańkowski, *Mecenat Artystyczny*, p. 23.
3 Tatarkiewicz, *O Sztuce Polskiej*, pp. 472–3.
4 Fabre, op. cit., p. 378.
5 AXC, 782, f. 572.
6 Leśnodorski, *Polska w Epoce Oświecenia*, pp. 178–91.
7 Kula, *Théorie Économique*, p. 103.
8 Kula, *Szkice*, p. 664.
9 Jobert, *Magnats Polonais*, p. 46.
10 Ibid., p. 57.
11 Ostermann to Stackelberg 18 XI 77, *Sbornik*, Vol. CLXV, p. 540.
12 Feldman, *Projekty Handlu Polsko-Francuskiego*, p. 252.
13 Ibid., p. 262.
14 Kościalkowski, *Tyzenhauz*, Vol. I, p. 264.
15 Ibid., pp. 234–5.
16 Ibid., p. 256.
17 Ibid., Vol. II, p. 390.
18 Coxe, *Travels*, Vol. I, p. 227.
19 Ligne, *Fragments de l'Histoire*, Vol. II, p. 76.
20 Wraxall, op. cit., Vol. II, p. 6.
21 Zawadzki, op. cit., Vol. II, p. 25.
22 Ségur, *Mémoires*, Vol. II, p. 157.
23 Zawadzki, op. cit., Vol. II, p. 234.
24 Ibid., Vol. I, p. 434.
25 Ibid., Vol. II, p. 208.
26 Ibid., Vol. II, p. 426.
27 Coxe, *Travels*, Vol. I, p. 224.
28 Tatarkiewicz, *Rządy Artystyczne*, p. 44.
29 Wójcicki, *Archiwum Domowe*, p. 15.
30 Craven, *Memoirs*, Vol. I, p. 91.
31 Coxe, *Travels*, Vol. I, pp. 214–18.
32 Ségur, *Mémoires*, Vol. II, pp. 164–5.
33 Wraxall, op. cit., Vol. II, p. 91.
34 Zawadzki, op. cit., Vol. II, p. 78.
35 Wraxall, op. cit., Vol. II, p. 108.
36 Ibid., Vol. II, p. 32.
37 Kraushar, *Dwa Szkice*, Vol. I, p. 71.
38 Kaleta, *Oświeceni i Sentymentalni*, p. 269, also p. 240.
39 Vautrin, *L'Observateur en Pologne*, p. 221.

40 Jobert, *Magnats Polonais*, p. 41.
41 Poniatowski, *Établissement du Cens Général*, pp. 7–8.
42 UV.
43 Stanisław, *Korespondencja Krajowa*, p. 127.

17   The Romantic Challenge

1 Panin to Stackelberg 18 IX, 75, *Sbornik* Vol. CXXXV, p. 468.
2 Zawadzki, op. cit., Vol. II, p. 132.
3 *Mémoires*, Vol. II, p. 551.
4 Ibid., p. 294.
5 Ibid., p. 293.
6 Ségur, *Mémoires*, Vol. II, p. 175.
7 *Mémoires*, Vol. II, p. 551.
8 Ibid., p. 556.
9 Stanisław to Monet 8 X 83, Stanisław, *Correspondance avec Glayre*, p. 174.
10 *Mémoires*, Vol. II, p. 305.
11 Ibid., p. 502.
12 Stanisław to Deboli 12 X 78, AGAD, AKP, 70, f. 109.
13 Conversation with Repnin 6 XII 95, AGAD, AKP, *Pudło* 91, no. 13.
14 *Mémoires*, Vol. II, p. 201.
15 Stanisław, *Korespondencja Krajowa*, p. 15.
16 Karpiński, *Pamiętniki*, p. 156.
17 Ibid., p. 168.
18 Stanisław to Mazzei 9 III 91, BP 37, p. 484.
19 Wójcicki, *Archiwum Domowe*, pp. 3–4.
20 AGAD, ZP, 66, no. 14.
21 Wójcicki, *Archiwum Domowe*, p. 15.
22 Boscamp's memorandum, Sievers, *Drugi Rozbiór*, p. 45.
23 Stanisław to Grabowska, AXC, 3157, no. 30.
24 Zawadzki, op. cit., Vol. I, p. 172.
25 *Czasy Stanisława Augusta*, p. 85.
26 *Mémoires*, Vol. II, p. 475.
27 Stanisław to Krasicki 7 I 82, Krasicki, *Korespondencja*, Vol. II, p. 86.
28 Niemcewicz, *Pamiętniki*, Vol. I, p. 82.
29 Korzoń, *Odrodzenie w Upadku*, p. 118.
30 Izabela Czartoryska to Adam Czartoryski 16 III 72, AXC, 6030.

18   Tryst on the Dnieper

1 Zawadzki, op. cit., Vol. I, p. 152.
2 Joseph II to Czartoryski 24 I 85, AXC, 6034, f. 93.
3 *Recueil des Pièces Relatives au procès entre le Prince Czartoryski et MM Komarzewski et Ryx.*
4 *Bytność Stanisława Augusta w Nieświeżu.*
5 Stanisław to Feliks Potocki 1 VII 84, Stanisław, *Korespondencja Krajowa*, p. 26; also Potocki to Stanisław n.d., ibid., p. 31.
6 Stanisław to Józef Poniatowski 23 I 88, PAU, 4582, p. 257.
7 Rymszyna, *Memoriał Kicińskiego*, p. 281.
8 AGAD, ZP, 66, nos 14, 17 & 67.
9 AGAD, AKJP, 398, p. 126.
10 Grochulska, *Warszawa na mapie Polski*, p. 195.
11 Stanisław to Moszyński 29 VI 85, Mańkowski, *Mecenat Artystyczny*, p. 61.
12 Ibid.
13 Stanisław to Ignacy Krasicki 23 VI 84, Krasicki, *Korespondencja*, Vol. II, p. 229.
14 Ochocki, *Pamiętniki*, Vol. II, p. 341.
15 Glayre to Monet 15 XI 86, Stanisław, *Correspondance avec Glayre*, p. 180.
16 AXC 6034, ff. 43ff.
17 Terlecki, *Mennica*, p. 57.
18 Niemcewicz, *Pamiętniki*, Vol. I, p. 241.
19 *Mémoires*, Vol. II, p. 464.
20 AGAD, AKP, *Pudło* 90, ks III, no. 12.
21 Stanisław, *Correspondance avec Glayre*, pp. XXXff.
22 AGAD, AKP, 352, ff. 343 and 345.
23 Stanisław to Deboli October 86 and 18 XI 86, AGAD, AKP, 378, pp. 104 and 159.
24 *Reflexions préliminaires*, AGAD, AKP, *Pudło* 90, ks III, no. 19.
25 Stanisław, *Korespondencja Krajowa* p. 208.
26 Mniszech, *Listy Pani Mniszchowej*, p. 189.
27 Ségur, *Mémoires*, Vol. II, p. 59.
28 Stanisław to Kiciński 21 III 87, BP, 38, p. 59.
29 Ditto.
30 Ditto 27 III 87, ibid., p. 77.
31 Mniszech, op. cit., p. 192.
32 Ligne, *Lettres*, Vol. I, pp. 71–2.
33 Mniszech, op. cit., p. 197.

34 Ibid., p. 199.

35 Ligne, *Lettres*, Vol. I, p. 81.

36 Ségur, *Mémoires*, Vol. III, pp. 125–6.

37 Mniszech, op. cit., p. 213; also Stanisław to Kiciński 8 V 87, Kalinka, *Ostatnie Lata*, Vol. II, p. 34.

38 Ligne, *Lettres*, Vol. I, p. 82.

39 Mniszech, op. cit., p. 214.

40 Stanisław to Kiciński 8 V 87, BP, 38, p. 165.

41 Ibid.

42 Ibid.

43 Joseph to Kaunitz 15 V 87, Joseph II, *Briefwechsel*, p. 259.

44 Stanisław to Kiciński 11 V 87, BP, 38, p. 189.

45 Joseph to Kaunitz 15 V 87, Joseph II, *Briefwechsel*, p. 259.

46 Stanisław to Kiciński 11 V 87, BP 38, p. 189.

47 Stanisław to Kiciński 8 V 87, BP, 38, p. 165.

48 Stanisław to Badeni 7 V 87, *Korespondencja Krajowa*, p. 210.

49 Stanisław to Kiciński 19 V 87, BP, 38, p. 209.

50 Ditto 27 VI 87, BP, 38, p. 281.

51 Mniszech, op. cit., p. 226; also Stanisław Poniatowski's Memoirs, ANP, 340, Ap I, 3.

52 Stanisław to Kiciński 11 VI 87, BP, 38, p. 253.

53 Deboli to Stanisław, AGAD, AKP, 269, f. 498; Stanisław to Deboli 8 VII 87, AGAD, AKP 378, f. 315; also Deboli to Stanisław, AGAD, AKP, 269, pp. 500ff; Deboli to Stanisław 12 VII 87 and 18 VII 87, AGAD, AKP, 269, ff. 515 and 528.

54 AGAD, AKP, 378, p. 444.

55 Stanisław to Deboli 17 X 87, AGAD, AKP, 378, f. 346.

56 Lord, *Second Partition of Poland*, p. 77.

57 Stanisław to Deboli 19 VII 87, AGAD, AKP, 378, f. 324.

58 Ligne, *Lettres*, Vol. I, p. 173.

59 Askenazy, *Przymierze Polsko-Pruskie*, p. 32.

60 Catherine to Stackelberg 9 VII 88, BP 29, IV, no. 104.

61 Rostworowski, *Ostatni Król*, p. 120.

62 Ibid., p. 125.

63 Ibid., p. 121.

64 AGAD, AKP, 378, f. 324.

65 Stanisław, *Korespondencja Krajowa*, p. 105.

66 Barnewall to Glayre 2 IV 88, Stanisław, *Correspondance avec Glayre*, p. 192.

67 AGAD, AKP, 269, f. 353.

68 Stanisław to Glayre 7 V 88, Stanisław, *Correspondance avec Glayre*, pp. 194–5.
69 Wolff, *The Vatican and Poland*, p. 185.
70 Hertzberg, *Recueil*, Vol. II, p. 476.

19 The Great Seym

1 Kalinka, *Sejm Czteroletni*, Vol. I, p. 183.
2 Ibid., p. 179.
3 *Dyariusz Seymu*, AGAD, AKP, *Pudło* 85, no. 4, p. 34.
4 Frederick William to Büchholtz 11 XII 88, Kalinka, *Sejm Czteroletni*, Vol. I, p. 289.
5 *Dyariusz Seymu*, AGAD, AKP, *Pudło* 85, pp. 37–8.
6 AGAD, APP, 97, f. 30.
7 Stanisław to Glayre 8 XI 88, Stanisław, *Correspondance avec Glayre*, p. 212.
8 Rostworowski, *Ostatni Król*, p. 151.
9 Niemcewicz, *Pamiętniki*, Vol. I, p. 270.
10 Solovyov, *Padenie Polshi*, p. 208.
11 Rostworowski, *Ostatni Król*, p. 152.
12 Lubomirska to Glayre 20 XII 88, Stanisław, *Correspondance avec Glayre*, p. 226.
13 Kalinka, *Sejm Czteroletni*, Vol. I, p. 292.
14 Ibid., p. 289.
15 Stanisław to Mazzei 10 XII 88, BP, 37, p. 22.
16 AGAD, APP, 97, p. 46.
17 Kalinka, *Sejm Czteroletni*, Vol. I, p. 375.
18 Korzoń, *Wewnętrzne Dzieje*, Vol. I, p. 462.
19 Ratajczyk, *Obronność*, p. 79.
20 Niemcewicz, *Pamiętniki*, Vol. I, p. 273.
21 Kalinka, *Sejm Czteroletni*, Vol. I, p. 258.
22 Lubomirska to Glayre 22 X 88, Stanisław, *Correspondance avec Glayre*, p. 210.
23 Ditto 3 XII 88, ibid., p. 223.
24 Stanisław to Mazzei 6 V 89, BP, 37, p. 90.
25 Ditto 18 II 89, ibid., p. 48.
26 Zawadzki, op. cit., Vol. I, p. 167.
27 Lee to Earl of Charlemont 1 VI 65, Haiman, *Poland and the American Revolutionary War*, p. 4.
28 Fabre, op. cit., p. 506.

29 AGAD, ZP, 212.

30 Stanisław to Mazzei 17 IV 90, BP, 37, p. 260.

31 Ditto 22 VII 89, ibid., p. 112.

32 Ditto 1 VIII 89 and 28 VIII 89, ibid., pp. 116 and 121.

33 Ditto 8 X 90, ibid., p. 387.

34 Stanisław to Józef Poniatowski, Skowronek, *Książe Józef*, p. 30.

35 Stanisław to Glayre 25 XI 89, Stanisław, *Correspondance avec Glayre*, p. 233.

36 Stanisław to Mazzei 2 V 89, BP, 37, p. 86.

37 Stanisław to Józef Poniatowski 13 V 89, PAU, 4582, f. 353.

38 Stanisław to Glayre 21 VI 91, AGAD, AKP, *Pudło* 90, Ks. III, no. 43.

39 Stanisław to Mazzei 12 IX 89 and 12 XI 89, BP, 37, pp. 128 and 163.

40 Potocki to Aloe, Rostworowski, *Legendy i Fakty*, pp. 299–301.

41 Stanisław to Mazzei 25 XI 89 and 26 XII 89, BP, 37, pp. 165 and 180.

42 Rostworowski, *Legendy i Fakty*, p. 290.

43 AGAD, AKP, *Pudło* 90, Ks. III, no. 22.

44 Korzoń, *Odrodzenie w Upadku*, p. 247.

45 Stanisław to Mazzei 21 XI 89, BP, 37, p. 161.

46 Stanisław to Deboli 28 XI 89, *Materiały do Dziejów Sejmu*, Vol. II, p. 321.

47 Ibid., p. 367.

48 Kalinka, *Sejm Czteroletni*, Vol. I, pp. 598–9.

49 Cobenzl to Kaunitz 20 II 90, ibid., Vol. II, p. 43.

50 Lord, op. cit., p. 121.

51 Stanisław to Mazzei 17 III 90, BP, 37, p. 240.

52 Kalinka, *Sejm Czteroletni*, Vol. II, p. 73.

53 Stanisław to Mazzei 27 II 90, BP, 37, p. 204.

54 Łojek, *Geneza i Obalenie*, p. 46.

55 AXC, 6034, f. 133.

56 Stanisław to Deboli 19 XII 89, Rostworowski, *Legendy i Fakty*, p. 291.

57 Potocki to Aloe 7 IV 90, AGAD, APP, 277, II, p. 217.

58 Piattoli to Stanisław 26 V 90, Ancona, *Scipione Piattoli*, p. 219.

59 Potocki to Aloe, AGAD, APP, 277, II, p. 260.

60 Ditto 14 VIII 90 and 20 VIII 90, ibid., pp. 309 and 311.

61 Stanisław to Józef Poniatowski 24 VIII 90, PAU, 4583, f. 138.

20   The Constitution

1 Kalinka, *Konstytucja*, p. 7.

2 Stanisław to Mazzei 15 XII 90, BP, 37, p. 436.

3 Stanisław to Deboli 23 XI 90, Łojek, *Geneza i Obalenie*, p. 62.

4 Stanisław to Mazzei 5 II 91, BP, 37, p. 465.

5 Stanisław to Deboli 6 XI 90, AGAD, ZP, 420, p. 960.

6 Leśnodorski, *Polska w Epoce Oświecenia*, p. 161.

7 *Kuźnica Kołłątajowska*, p. 12.

8 Rostworowski, *Ostatni Król*, p. 205.

9 *Kuźnica Kołłątajowska*, p. 97.

10 Ibid., p. 155.

11 Czartoryski to Stanisław 13 IX 90, AXC, 720, p. 709.

12 Piattoli to Stanisław 17 IX 90, Ancona, *Scipione Piattoli*, p. 231.

13 Rostworowski, *Legendy i Fakty*, p. 336.

14 Piattoli to Stanisław 23 IX 90, Bozzolato, *Un Aventuriero Onorato*, p. 350.

15 *Kuźnica Kołłątajowska*, pp. 80, 84 and 76.

16 Stanisław to Mazzei 18 III 89, BP, 37, p. 64.

17 Feliks Potocki to Stanisław 23 XI 90, AXC, 2890, p. 237; also Potocki to Stanisław Walewski 4 XII 90, ibid., p. 249.

18 Stanisław to Józef Poniatowski 5 XI 90, PAU, 4583, f. 218.

19 Stanisław to Deboli 4 II 91, Rostworowski, *Legendy i Fakty*, p. 289.

20 Stanisław to Piattoli 1 VI 91, Ancona, *Scipione Piattoli*, p. 257.

21 Rostworowski, *Legendy i Fakty*, pp. 346–354.

22 Ibid., pp. 355ff.; also Leśnodorski, *Dzieło Sejmu*, p. 185.

23 Coxe, *Travels*, Vol. I, p. 212.

24 Stanisław to Mazzei 2 III 91, BP, 37, p. 479.

25 Ditto 25 VIII 90, ibid., p. 354.

26 Mably, *Du Gouvernement*, p. 278.

27 Stanisław to Mazzei 23 III 91, BP, 37, p. 493.

28 Leśnodorski, *Dzieło Sejmu*, p. 79.

29 Stanisław to Mazzei 22 I 91, Stanisław, *Rok Nadziei*, p. 31.

30 Ditto 6 IV 91, ibid., p. 40.

31 Lord, op. cit., p. 181.

32 Ehrman, *The Younger Pitt*, Vol. II, p. 26.

33 Rose, *William Pitt*, p. 617.

34 Solovyov, *Padenie Polshi*, p. 221.

35 Kołłątaj confirms the king's authorship in his letter to Strasser 11 IX 92, Kołłątaj, *Listy*, Vol. I, p. 27; Piattoli confirms it in his letter to Stanisław 17 X 92, Ancona, *Scipione Piattoli*, p. 331.

36 Leśnodorski, *Dzieło Sejmu*, p. 130.

37 Stanisław to Deboli 20 IV 91, Stanisław, *Rok Nadziei*, p. 42.

38 Ibid., p. 179.

39 Stanisław to Deboli 4 V 91, ibid., p. 47.

40 Leśnodorski, *Dzieło Sejmu*, p. 66.
41 Stanisław to Glayre 25 VI 91, AGAD, AKP, *Pudło* 90, Ks. III, no. 43.
42 Niemcewicz, *Pamiętniki*, Vol. I, p. 398.
43 Kołłątaj et al., *O Ustanowieniu i Upadku*, Vol. I, p. 158.
44 *Czasy Stanisława Augusta*, p. 135.
45 Kołłątaj, op. cit., p. 159.

21   The Nation with the King

 1 Stanisław to Mazzei 4 V 91, BP, 37, p. 515.
 2 Stanisław to Glayre 21 VI 91, Stanisław, *Correspondance avec Glayre*, p. 250.
 3 Stanisław to Ignacy Potocki 24 VII 91, AGAD, APP, 184, f. 196.
 4 Czartoryski to Stanisław 18 VI 91, AXC, 724, no. 741.
 5 Piattoli to Mazzei 7 V 91, Ancona, *Scipione Piattoli*, p. 72.
 6 Stanisław to Deboli 7 V 91, Stanisław, *Rok Nadziei*, p. 49.
 7 Ditto 4 V 91, ibid., p. 47.
 8 Wegner, *Dzieje*, pp. 207–8.
 9 Ibid., p. 200.
10 Ochocki, *Pamiętniki*, Vol. II, p. 68.
11 Leśnodorski, *Polscy Jakobini*, p. 116.
12 Rostworowski, *Ostatni Król*, p. 240.
13 Chénier to Stanisław, 18 XI 90, Chénier, *Oeuvres Complètes*, p. 731.
14 Handelsman, *Konstytucja Trzeciego maja a Opinia Publiczna*, p. 94.
15 Mazzei, *Memorie*, Vol. I, p. 543.
16 Paine, *Works*, p. 994.
17 Haiman, *The Fall of Poland*, pp. 47 and 70.
18 Glayre to Stanisław 25 XI 91, AGAD, AKP, *Pudło* 90, Ks. III, no. 43.
19 Burke, *Works*, Vol. VI, pp. 244–6.
20 Mackintosh, *Defence of the French Revolution*, p. 344.
21 Walpole to Mary Berry 8 VI 91, Walpole, *Letters*, Vol. XIV, p. 446.
22 Bukaty to Stanisław 24 VI 91, AXC, 3998, f. 130.
23 Kiciński to Middleton 14 V 91, AGAD, AKP, 278, no. 93.
24 Frederick William to Goltz, AGAD, APP, 97, f. 212.
25 Hertzberg to Lucchesini 12 V 91, Dembiński, *Źródła*, Vol. I, p. 451.
26 Ditto 28 V 91, ibid., p. 453.
27 Stanisław Poniatowski to Stanisław 24 XI 91, AGAD, AKP, *Pudło* 90, Ks. III, no. 33.
28 Stanisław to Glayre, AGAD, AKP, *Pudło* 90, Ks. III, no. 43.
29 Glayre to Stanisław 15 IX 91, ibid.

30 Stanisław to Deboli 4 VI 90, Stanisław, *Rok Nadziei*, p. 59.

31 Deboli to Stanisław 5 III 92, ibid., p. 115.

32 Catherine to Grimm, *Sbornik*, Vol. XXIII, pp. 534–5.

33 Kalinka, *Ostatnie Lata*, Vol. II, pp. 112 and 123.

34 Catherine to Bezborodko, *Sbornik*, Vol. XLII, p. 289.

35 Stanisław to Mazzei 27 VII 91, BP, 37, p. 550.

36 Łojek, *Geneza i Obalenie*, p. 165.

37 Piattoli to Mazzei 7 V 91, Ancona, *Scipione Piattoli*, p. 71.

38 Rostworowski, *Legendy i Fakty*, p. 372.

39 Stanisław to Deboli 20 VII 91, Stanisław, *Rok Nadziei*, p. 66.

40 Stanisław, *Rok Nadziei*, p. 96; also BP, 37, p. 553; also Łojek, *Geneza i Obalenie*, pp. 188–9.

41 *Horrible Complot des Prestres*.

42 Stanisław to Józef Poniatowski 16 VIII 91, Stanisław, *Stanisław August i Książę Józef Poniatowski*, p. 34.

43 Stanisław to Deboli 24 VIII 91, Stanisław, *Rok Nadziei*, p. 76.

44 AGAD, ML, 164, p. 23.

45 Lucchesini, *Listy*, p. 125.

46 Rostworowski, *Ostatni Król*, p. 251.

47 Rostworowski, *Maj 1791–Maj 1792*, pp. 11–12.

48 Ibid., p. 12.

49 Stanisław to Deboli 24 VIII 91, Stanisław, *Rok Nadziei*, p. 76.

50 Stanisław, *Projekt do Reformy Żydostwa*.

51 Ancona, *Scipione Piattoli*, pp. 307ff.

52 Stanisław to Glayre 25 VI 91, AGAD, AKP, *Pudło* 90, Ks. III, no. 43.

53 Zawadzki, op. cit., Vol. II, p. 161.

54 Stanisław to Glayre 29 X 91, AGAD, AKP, *Pudło* 90, Ks. III, no. 43.

55 Stanisław to Mazzei 11 V 91, BP, 37, p. 517.

56 Stanisław to Bukaty 16 V 92, Kalinka, *Ostatnie Lata*, Vol. II, p. 211.

57 Lucchesini, *Listy*, p. 150.

58 Lord, op. cit., p. 240.

59 Madariaga, op. cit., p. 428.

60 Ibid.

61 Catherine to Grimm 9 V 92, *Sbornik*, Vol. XXIII, p. 567.

62 Catherine to Bezborodko, *Sbornik*, Vol. XLII, p. 157.

63 Potocki to Potyomkin 16 V 91, AXC, 2890, f. 337.

64 Ditto 20 IV 91, ibid., p. 299.

65 Deboli to Stanisław 22 VII 91, Stanisław, *Rok Nadziei*, p. 68. For Potyomkin's plans, see: Pistor, *Mémoires*, p. 2; also Stanisław to Mazzei 14 VII 90, BP, 37, p. 328.

66 Stanisław, *Rok Nadziei*, pp. 179 and 197.

67 Stanisław to Deboli 21 I 92, Stanisław, *Rok Nadziei*, p. 107.
68 Kalinka, *Ostatnie Lata*, Vol. II, p. 289.
69 Wolff, *The Vatican and Poland*, p. 212.
70 Lord, op. cit., p. 254, and Madariaga, op. cit., p. 431.
71 Deboli to Stanisław 20 III 92, Stanisław, *Rok Nadziei*, p. 121.
72 Stanisław to Deboli 14 III 92, ibid., p. 118.
73 Ditto 27 VII 91, ibid., p. 69.
74 AGAD, ASK, *Rachunki seymowe*, III.
75 Ratajczyk, *Obronność*, p. 89.
76 Kula, *Szkice*, p. 784.
77 Ratajczyk, *Obronność*, p. 218.
78 Ibid., pp. 81–3.
79 Stanisław to Deboli 8 II 92, Stanisław, *Rok Nadziei*, p. 110.
80 Ditto 27 VII 91, ibid., p. 69.
81 Ditto 9 VI 92, ibid., p. 151.
82 Bulgakov to Bezborodko 8 II 92, *Sbornik*, Vol. XLVII, p. 227.
83 Lucchesini to Frederick William 29 II 92, Lucchesini, *Listy*, p. 102.
84 Kalinka, *Ostatnie lata*, Vol. II, p. 302.
85 Caché, *Obrady Sejmu*, p. 69.
86 Ibid., pp. 74, 80, 84 and 91.
87 Łojek, *Geneza i Obalenie*, p. 281.
88 Rostworowski, *Ostatni Król*, p. 256.
89 Caché, op. cit., p. 109.

22 *War*

1 AGAD, APP, 97, no. 72.
2 Smoleński, *Ostatni Rok Sejmu*, p. 400.
3 *Czasy Stanisława Augusta*, p. 160.
4 Zahorski, *Stanisław August Polityk*, p. 274.
5 Smoleński, *Ostatni Rok Sejmu*, p. 389.
6 Stanisław to Deboli 16 V 92, Stanisław, *Rok Nadziei*, p. 143.
7 Ibid.
8 Hertzberg, *Recueil*, Vol. III, p. 4.
9 Stanisław to Deboli 16 V 92, Stanisław, *Rok Nadziei*, p. 143.
10 Stanisław to Józef Poniatowski 20 V 92, PAU, 4585, f. 7.
11 Frederick William to Stanisław 8 VI 92, AGAD, APP, 97, f. 241.
12 AGAD, APP, 97, pp. 248–62.
13 Lucchesini, *Listy*, p. 196.
14 Ségur, *Histoire du règne de Frédéric Guillaume*, Vol. II, p. 142.

15 *Sbornik*, Vol. XXIII, p. 626.
16 Józef Poniatowski to Stanisław 26 V 92, Stanisław, *Stanisław August i Książę Józef Poniatowski*, p. 296.
17 Stanisław to Józef Poniatowski 23 V 92, AGAD, AKP, 201, p. 201.
18 Stanisław to Glayre 10 IV 92, AGAD, AKP, *Pudło* 90, Ks. III, no. 43.
19 AGAD, AKP, 183, p. 22.
20 Askenazy, *Książę Józef Poniatowski*, p. 270.
21 Józef Poniatowski to Stanisław 6 VI 92, Smoleński, *Konfederacja Targowicka*, p. 127.
22 Łojek, *Geneza i Obalenie*, p. 344.
23 Stanisław to Józef Poniatowski 14 VI 92, Stanisław, *Stanisław August i Książę Józef Poniatowski*, p. 38.
24 Łojek, *Geneza i Obalenie*, pp. 353–4.
25 Stanisław to Bukaty 4 VII 92, Kalinka, *Ostatnie Lata*, Vol. II, p. 218.
26 Łojek, *Geneza i Obalenie*, pp. 383–4.
27 Libiszowska, *Życie Polskie w Londynie*, p. 156.
28 Bukaty to Stanisław 6 VII 92, AXC, 3211, ff. 11 and 13.
29 Stanisław to Bukaty 11 VII 92, Kalinka, *Ostatnie Lata*, Vol. II, p. 220.
30 Rostworowski, *Ostatni Król*, p. 292.
31 Ostermann to Bulgakov 14 VII 92, Solovyov, *Padenie Polshi*, p. 283.
32 Stanisław to Józef Poniatowski 2 VII 92, Stanisław, *Stanisław August i Książę Józef Poniatowski*, p. 93.
33 Ditto, ibid., p. 91.
34 Ditto, ibid.
35 Ditto 22 VI 92, AGAD, AKP, 201, f. 55.
36 Ditto 24 VI 92, PAU, 4585, f. 52.
37 Caché, op. cit., p. 99.
38 Ibid., p. 155.
39 Ibid., p. 141.
40 Askenazy, *Książę Józef Poniatowski*, p. 74.
41 Smoleński, p. 154; also Komarzewski, *Coup d'Oeil*, pp. 223–4.
42 Smoleński, *Konfederacja Targowicka*, p. 177.
43 Stanisław to Deboli 14 VII 92, Stanisław, *Rok Nadziei*, p. 165.
44 Jerzy Potocki to Ignacy Potocki 20 VII 92, AGAD, APP, 227, f. 463.
45 Stanisław to Józef Poniatowski 16 VII 92, AGAD, AKP, 201, f. 123.
46 Deboli to Stanisław 31 VII 92, Stanisław, *Rok Nadziei*, p. 164.
47 Madariaga, op. cit., p. 433.
48 Stanisław to Glayre 27 IX 92, AGAD, AKP, *Pudło* 90, Ks. III, no. 43.
49 Lucchesini, *Listy*, p. 232.
50 Stanisław to Bukaty 25 VII 92, AXC, 849, f. 669.

51 AGAD, ASK, *Rachunki Seymowe*, III; see also Łojek, *Geneza i Obalenie*, p. 299.
52 Stanisław to Glayre 27 IX 92, AGAD, AKP, *Pudło* 90, Ks. III, no. 43.
53 AGAD, AKP, 183, p. 402.
54 Smoleński, *Konfederacja Targowicka*, p. 212.
55 Kołłątaj to Strasser 29 IX 92, Kołłątaj, *Listy*, Vol. I, pp. 38–9.
56 AGAD, AKP, 183, p. 400.

23 Nemesis

1 Piattoli to Stanisław 4 VIII 92, Bozzolato, *Un Aventuriero Onorato*, pp. 490–3.
2 Caché, op. cit., p. 178.
3 Lucchesini, *Listy*, p. 240.
4 Dzikowska, *Pamiętnik*, p. 235.
5 Kołłątaj to Naruszewicz 1 VIII 92, Kołłątaj, *Listy*, Vol. I, p. 1; also Potocki to Stanisław 25 VIII 92, Ancona, *Scipione Piattoli*, p. 320.
6 Askenazy, *Książę Józef Poniatowski*, p. 271.
7 Józef Poniatowski to Stanisław 7 IV 93, AXC, 3972, f. 339.
8 Kościuszko, *Opis Kampanii*, p. 108.
9 Łojek, *Geneza i Obalenie*, p. 423.
10 Stanisław to Józef Poniatowski 24 VII 92, AGAD, AKP, 201, f. 127; also ditto, Stanisław, *Stanisław August i Książę Józef Poniatowski*, p. 112.
11 Sanguszko, *Pamiętnik*, pp. 22–3.
12 Stanisław to Józef Poniatowski 26 VII 92, Stanisław, *Stanisław August i Książę Józef Poniatowski*, p. 148.
13 Ditto 27 VII 92, AGAD, AKP, 201, f. 152.
14 Kościuszko to Izabela Czartoryska 5 VIII 92, *Kościuszko w Historii*, p. 92.
15 Deboli to Stanisław 13 VII 92, Stanisław, *Rok Nadziei*, p. 164.
16 Ibid.
17 Catherine to Grimm 13 VIII 92 and 26 VIII 92, *Sbornik*, Vol. XXIII, pp. 571 and 577.
18 Deboli to Stanisław 13 VII 92, Stanisław, *Rok Nadziei*, p. 169.
19 Smoleński, *Konfederacja Targowicka*, p. 239.
20 Ibid., p. 241.
21 Dembowski to Ignacy Potocki 17 XI 92, *Tajna Korespondencja*, p. 96.
22 Rostworowski, *Ostatni Król*, p. 304.
23 *Polski Słownik Biograficzny*, Vol. XXVII, p. 465.
24 *Czasy Stanisława Augusta*, p. 205.

25 Józef Poniatowski to Stanisław 6 IX 92, PAU, 4585, f. 147.

26 Ditto, n.d., MNW.

27 Ditto 6 IX 92, PAU, 4585, f. 147.

28 Stanisław to Mazzei 11 VI 91, BP, 37, p. 526.

29 Stanisław to Józef Poniatowski 12 IX 92, Stanisław, *Stanisław August i Książę Józef Poniatowski*, p. 133.

30 Józef Poniatowski to Stanisław 2 XII 92, PAU, 4585, f. 192.

31 Stanisław to Józef Poniatowski 27 III 93, ibid., f. 264.

32 Piattoli to Stanisław 17 X 92, Ancona, *Scipione Piattoli*, p. 330.

33 Stanisław to Piattoli 7 XI 92, Ancona, *Scipione Piattoli*, p. 334.

34 Glayre to Stanisław 27 IX 92, AGAD, AKP, *Pudło* 90, Ks. III, no. 43.

35 Dembowski to Potocki 10 XI 92, *Tajna Korespondencja*, p. 91.

36 Świętorzecki to Potocki 5 IX 92, ibid., p. 47.

37 Stanisław to Glayre 1 X 93, AGAD, AKP, *Pudło* 90, Ks. III, no. 43.

38 Rostworowski, *Legendy i Fakty*, p. 493.

39 Madariaga, op. cit., p. 432.

40 Lord, op. cit., p. 388.

41 Igelström to Sievers 27 III 93, Haiman, *Kościuszko*, p. 25.

42 Sievers, op. cit., pp. 66–7.

43 AGAD, AKP, 203, ff. 26–9.

44 Ibid., ff. 37–8.

45 Ibid., ff. 43–8.

46 AGAD, AKP, *Pudło* 90, Ks. IV, f. 50.

47 Sievers to Stanisław 2 IV 93, Sievers, op. cit., p. 121.

48 AGAD, AKP, 203, ff. 178–81.

49 Engelhardt, *Pamiętniki*, p. 89.

50 Piattoli to Stanisław 17 X 92, Ancona, *Scipione Piattoli*, pp. 330–1.

51 Kołłątaj to Małachowski 13 XII 92, Smoleński, *Konfederacja Targowicka*, p. 377.

52 Piattoli papers, AGAD, APP, 101, ff. 239–44.

53 *Czasy Stanisława Augusta*, p. 200.

54 Kołłątaj et al., *O Ustanowieniu*, p. 74.

55 Kościuszko, *Opis Kampanii*, p. 109.

56 Józef Poniatowski to Stanisław 7 IV 93, Stanisław, *Stanisław August i Książę Józef Poniatowski*, p. 165.

57 Rostworowski, *Ostatni Król*, p. 283.

58 Burke, *Annual Register*, p. 3.

24 Fallen Majesty

1 Sievers, op. cit., p. 69.
2 Stanisław to Dzieduszycki 10 V 93, AGAD, ZP, 7, f. 563.
3 Ditto 20 V 93, ibid., f. 448.
4 Sievers to Mrs Uxküll 18 IV 93, Sievers, op. cit., p. 160.
5 Ibid., p. 136.
6 AGAD, AKP, 203, f. 185; also AGAD, ZP, 7ff., 412ff.
7 Stanisław to Dzieduszycki 13 IV 93, AGAD, ZP, 7, f. 435.
8 Sievers to Mrs Uxküll, Sievers, op. cit., p. 193.
9 Ibid., p. 198.
10 Stanisław to Dzieduszycki 5 V 93, AGAD, ZP, 7, f. 544ff.
11 Lord, op. cit., p. 404.
12 Auckland to Grenville 26 IV 93, Auckland, *Journal*, Vol. III, p. 35; also Morton Eden to Auckland 10 VII 93, ibid., p. 78.
13 AGAD, AKP, 203, f. 263 and AKP, 359, f. 12.
14 AGAD, AKP, 359, f. 14.
15 Stanisław to Dzieduszycki, AGAD, ZP, 7, f. 578.
16 Sievers to Razumovsky 14 VI 93, BP, 29, IX, no. 6.
17 Stanisław to Bukaty 27 VII 93, Kalinka, *Ostatnie Lata*, Vol. II, p. 255.
18 AGAD, AKP, 203, f. 398.
19 Ibid., f. 401.
20 Sievers to Michał Poniatowski 3 VII 93, BP, 29, IX, no. 7.
21 Dembowski to Ignacy Potocki 24 VII 93, *Tajna Korespondencja*, p. 233.
22 Engelhardt, *Pamiętniki*, p. 90.
23 Ilovaysky, *Sejm Grodzienski*, p. 158.
24 Dembowski to Ignacy Potocki 27 VII 93, *Tajna Korespondencja*, p. 234.
25 Mann, *Stanisław August*, p. 108.
26 Ilovaysky, op. cit., p. 314; AGAD, AKP, 203, f. 479.
27 Rolle, *Stanisław August*, p. 316.
28 Ochocki, *Pamiętniki*, Vol. II, pp. 325–6.
29 Ibid., p. 337.
30 Madariaga, op. cit., pp. 437–8.
31 AGAD, AKP, 203, f. 490.
32 Sievers to Mrs Uxküll 20 IX 93, Sievers, op. cit., p. 342.
33 AGAD, AKP, 203, f. 522.
34 Engelhardt, op. cit., p. 91.
35 Stanisław to Bukaty 17 X 93, Kalinka, *Ostatnie Lata*, Vol. II, p. 263.
36 Grimm to Catherine 14 XI 93, *Sbornik*, Vol. XLIV, p. 497.
37 AGAD, AKP, 203, f. 549.
38 Ilovaysky, op. cit., p. 314.

39 Sievers, op. cit., p. 389.

40 BP, 44, p. 304.

41 Gardiner to Grenville 25 XII 93, BP, 44, p. 307.

42 Stanisław to Józef Poniatowski 1 I 94, Stanisław, *Stanisław August i Książe Józef Poniatowski*, p. 184.

43 Józef Poniatowski to Stanisław 22 III 94, PAU, 4586, f. 50.

44 Büchholtz, *Powstanie Kościuszkowskie*, p. 31.

45 Góralski, *Stanisław August*, p. 41.

46 Dembowski to Ignacy Potocki 18 I 94, *Tajna Korespondencja*, p. 310.

47 Stanisław to Józef Poniatowski 1 II 94, Stanisław, *Stanisław August i Książe Józef Poniatowski*, p. 191.

48 Patz, *Z Okien Ambasady*, p. 26.

49 Gardiner to Grenville 4 I 94, BP, 44, p. 315.

50 Büchholtz to Frederick William 25 I 94, Büchholtz, op. cit., p. 48.

51 Gardiner to Grenville 4 I 94, BP 44, p. 315.

52 Kopczewski, *Tadeusz Kościuszko w Historii*, p. 39.

53 *Recueil des Instructions*, Vol. V, pp. 329–30.

54 Kocój, *Wielka Rewolucja*, p. 128.

55 AGAD, AKP, 323, ff. 13–14.

56 Stanisław to Catherine 6 IV 94, AGAD, AKP, 203, f. 757.

57 Stanisław to Józef Poniatowski 9 IV 94, PAU, 4586, f. 58.

58 Góralski, *Stanisław August*, p. 25.

59 Igelström to Bezborodko, 5 IV 94, Bartoszewicz, *Dzieje Insurekcji*, p. 186.

60 Gardiner to Grenville 22 III 94, BP, 44, p. 363.

25   Revolution

1 AGAD, AKP, 355, III, f. 158.

2 *Dyariusz Króla Stanisława*, p. 281.

3 Zajączek, *Histoire de la Révolution*, p. 106; also Bartoszewicz, *Dzieje Insurekcji*, pp. 192 and 201.

4 Stanisław to Józef Poniatowski 19 V 94, Stanisław, *Stanisław August i Książe Józef Poniatowski*, p. 202.

5 Toll, *Powstanie Kościuszkowskie*, p. 97.

6 AGAD, AKP, 323, ff. 77 and 79.

7 Gardiner to Grenville 3 V 94, BP, 44, p. 399.

8 Schmitt, *Żywot ks Kołłątaja*, pp. 250–1.

9 Gardiner to Grenville 21 V 94, BP, 44, p. 412.

10 Góralski, *Stanisław August*, pp. 98–9; also, Sagatyński, *Pamiętnik Byłego Pazia*, pp. 12–15.
11 Büchholtz to Frederick William 12 V 94, Büchholtz, op. cit., p. 142.
12 Ochocki, *Pamiętniki*, Vol. II, pp. 384–5.
13 AGAD, AKP, 323, ff. 134–92.
14 Sagatyński, op. cit., p. 11.
15 AGAD, AKP, 323, f. 213.
16 Stanisław to Kościuszko 29 V 94, ibid., f. 222.
17 Góralski, *Stanisław August*, p. 127.
18 Stanisław to Józef Poniatowski 7 VI 94, PAU, 4584, f. 10.
19 Góralski, *Stanisław August*, p. 78.
20 Ibid., pp. 184 and 213.
21 Korzoń, *Odrodzenie w Upadku*, p. 334.
22 Frederick William to Lucchesini 25 IV 94, Leśnodorski, *Polscy Jakobini*, p. 598.
23 Toll, op. cit., p. 137.
24 Góralski, *Austria a Trzeci Rozbiór*, p. 102.
25 Kocój, op. cit., p. 144.
26 *Le Sans-Culott*, 13 V 94, p. 1815.
27 Kocój, op. cit., p. 144.
28 Mościcki, *Generał Jasiński*, p. 163.
29 Zawadzki, op. cit., Vol. II, p. 182.
30 Leśnodorski, *Polscy Jakobini*, p. 182.
31 Sanguszko, *Pamiętniki*, pp. 33–4.
32 Kopczewski, op. cit., p. 73.
33 Korzoń, *Wewnętrzne Dzieje*, Vol. I, p. 483.
34 Zajączek, op. cit., p. 114.
35 Bartoszewicz, *Dzieje Insurekcji*, p. 227.
36 Toll, op. cit., p. 170.
37 AGAD, AKP, 323, f. 353.
38 Ibid., f. 386.
39 Wybicki, *Pamiętniki*, Vol. II, p. 70.
40 Madariaga, op. cit., p. 446.
41 Ochocki, *Pamiętniki*, Vol. II, p. 373.
42 Leśnodorski, *Polscy Jakobini*, p. 272.
43 AGAD, AKP, 323, f. 437.
44 Ibid., f. 469.
45 Niemcewicz, *Notes sur ma Captivité*, p. 92; also Solovyov, *Padenie Polshi*, p. 368.
46 Patz, op. cit., p. 102.
47 Sagatyński, op. cit., p. 35.

48 Góralski, *Stanisław August*, p. 191.

49 Stanisław to Kościuszko 25 VIII 94, AGAD, AKP, 323, f. 630.

50 Ibid., ff. 449–54.

51 Góralski, *Stanisław August*, p. 203.

52 Madariaga, op. cit., p. 446.

53 Linowski, *List*, p. 61.

54 AGAD, ZP, 73, ff. 10–13.

55 Starzeński, *Na Schyłku Dni*, p. 94.

56 Góralski, *Stanisław August*, pp. 211–12.

57 AGAD, ZP,73, ff. 23ff.

58 Engelhardt, op. cit., p. 118.

59 Madariaga, op. cit., p. 447.

60 Wawrzecki to Stanisław 6 XI 94, AGAD, AKP, 202, f. 33; also Gardiner to Grenville 8 XI 94, BP, 44, p. 527.

61 Ignacy Potocki to Stanisław 6 XI 94, AGAD, AKP, 202, f. 29.

62 Patz, op. cit., p. 197.

63 AGAD, AKP, 202, f. 349.

64 Ibid., f. 735.

26 A Marble Gaol

1 AGAD, AKP, 359, ff. 53–4; also AKP, 204, no. 18.

2 *Arkhiv Tsarstva Polskavo*, p. III.

3 Catherine to Stanisław 21 XI 94, AGAD, AKP, 202, f. 735.

4 Ibid., f. 737.

5 Rolle, *Stanisław August*, pp. 304–5.

6 Siemieński, *Ostatni Rok*, p. XXIV.

7 Rolle, *Stanisław August*, p. 306.

8 Bukaty to Stanisław 3 II 95, AGAD, AKP, 355, IV, f. 5.

9 Gardiner to Grenville 10 I 95, BP, 44, p. 571.

10 Góralski, *Stanisław August*, p. 249.

11 Sagatyński, op. cit., pp. 44–5.

12 Bykowski, *Dwór Królewski*, pp. 15 and 16.

13 Ibid., p. 17.

14 Rolle, *Stanisław August*, pp. 306–12.

15 *Mémoires*, Vol. I, p. 602.

16 Rolle, *Stanisław August*, p. 340.

17 AGAD, AKP, 204, f. 11.

18 Ibid., f. 106; also AKP, *Pudło* 91, no. 2.

19 Stanisław to Gardiner 18 I 95, Dembiński, *William Gardiner*, p. 102.

20 AGAD, AKP, 204, f. 100.
21 Ibid., f. 109.
22 Stanisław to Grabowska 24 I 95, AXC, 3157, no. 85.
23 Sagatyński, op. cit., p. 57.
24 Stanisław to Grabowska 25 II 95, AXC, 3157, no. 88.
25 Czartoryski, *Pamiętniki*, p. 111.
26 Stanisław to Grabowska 28 VI 95, AXC, 3157, no. 91.
27 AGAD, AKP, *Pudło* 91, no. 17.
28 Potocka, *Wspomnienia*, p. 26.
29 Góralski, *Austria a Trzeci Rozbiór*, p. 271.
30 Gaspari to Stanisław 18 IX 95, AGAD, AKP, 355, IV, p. 28.
31 Madariaga, op. cit., p. 451; Stanisław to Repnin 27 XI 95, AGAD, AKP, *Pudło* 91, no. 10.
32 Rolle, *Stanisław August*, p. 376.
33 AGAD, AKP, *Pudło* 91, no. 9.
34 Stanisław to Catherine 25 XI 95, ibid., no. 11.
35 Ditto 27 XI 95, ibid., no. 9.
36 Ditto 21 XII 95, AGAD, AKP, 359, f. 31.
37 Karpiński, *Pamiętniki*, p. 289.
38 Kaleta, *Oświeceni i Sentymentalni*, p. 394.
39 Rolle, *Stanisław August*, p. 376.
40 Bykowski, op. cit., pp. 126–7.
41 Stanisław to Paul 13 XII 96, AGAD, AKP, 359, f. 115.
42 AGAD, AKP, 204, f. 409ff.
43 Józef Poniatowski to Paul 8 I 97, MNW.
44 Teresa Poniatowska to Stanisław 4 I 97, ibid.
45 Józef Poniatowski to Stanisław 14 I 97, ibid.
46 Stanisław to Józef Poniatowski 22 I 97, ibid.
47 Żywirska, *Ostatnie Lata*, p. 154.
48 Stanisław to Kazimierz Poniatowski 15 I 97, MNW.
49 Stanisław to Konstancja Tyszkiewicz 11 I 97, ibid.
50 *Mémoires Secrets*, Journal.
51 Stanisław to Teresa Poniatowska 2 VI 97, MNW.
52 Stanisław to Konstancja Tyszkiewicz 11 I 97, ibid.
53 Stanisław Poniatowski, *Pamiętnik Synowca*, pp. 95 and 101.
54 Stanisław to Izabela Branicka 26 XII 97, MNW.
55 Boeckler to Bacciarelli 26 V 98, *Mémoires Secrets*, p. 225.
56 Fabre, op. cit., p. 534.
57 *Mémoires Secrets*, Journal, 19/31 January.
58 Vigée-Lebrun, *Souvenirs*, Vol. I, pp. 123–4.
59 Sagatyński, op. cit., p. 89.

60 Boeckler to Bacciarelli 26 V 98, *Mémoires Secrets*, p. 225.
61 Ibid., p. 237:

Stanisław II Augustus
King of Poland, Grand Duke of Lithuania
An illustrious example of the fickleness of Fortune,
the good he accepted with wisdom, the ill he bore with courage.

Died in St Petersburg 12 February 1798
Aged 66

Paul I Autocrat and Emperor of All Russia
to his friend and guest.

Epilogue

1 Potocki to Kossakowski 26 V 93, Tokarz, *Rozprawy i Szkice*, Vol. I, p. 345.
2 Rostworowski, *Ostatni Król*, p. 8.
3 Ségur, *Histoire de Frédéric Guillaume*, Vol. I, p. 241.
4 Rostworowski, *Ostatni Król*, p. 9.
5 Bocheński, *Dzieje Głupoty*, p. 136.
6 Komarzewski, op. cit., p. 265.
7 Wraxall, op. cit., Vol. II, p. 94.

Bibliography

Primary Sources

Archival

Archives Nationales, Paris:
  Archives Françaises 340: *Archives Poniatowski.*
Archiwum Główne Akt Dawnych, Warsaw:
  Archiwum Królestwa Polskiego: Pudło 85, Pudło 89, Pudło 90, 91, 181,
    183, 193, 201, 202, 203, 204, 266, 269, 278, 323, 343, 345, 352, 355, 359,
    354, 360, 378.
  Archiwum Kameralne: III/76, 566, 587, 612, 629, 648, 669, 939.
  Metryka Litewska: VII 164.
  Zbiór Popielów: 7, 50, 51, 52, 66, 67, 71, 72, 73, 82, 93, 144, 146, 173, 176,
    177, 212, 216, 311, 312, 318, 374, 395, 397.
  Archiwum Publiczne Potockich: 82, 83, 86, 95, 96, 97, 99, 101, 184, 227, 264,
    279.
  Archiwum Skarbu Koronnego II: 90, 95, 106, 107, 111.
  Archiwum Księcia Józefa Poniatowskiego: 129, 398,
Archiwum Xiążąt Czartoryskich, Kraków:
  Rękopisy: 652, 653, 724, 782, 788, 798, 817, 818, 820, 849, 926, 939, 961,
    965, 1705, 1818, 2289, 2890, 3157, 3159, 3160, 3211, 3877, 3972, 3998,
    6030, 6034, 6036, 6067, 6103.
Biblioteka Narodowa, Warsaw:
  Rękopisy: III/3284, 3291, 3293.
  Biblioteka Ordynacji Zamoyskiej: 802, 859, 877, 3284, 6684.

Bibliography

Biblioteka Uniwersytetu Warszawskiego, Warsaw:
  Rękopisy: 122, 134, 135, 136.
Bibliothèque Polonaise, Paris:
  Muzeum Adama Mickiewicza: 1085, 1088.
  Biblioteka Polska: 29, 32, 37, 38, 44, 66, 74, 111.
British Museum, London:
  Hardwicke Papers: Add. 35356, 35367, 35472, 35479, 35485, 35634.
  Newcastle Papers: Stowe 263.
Muzeum Narodowe, Warsaw, *Archiwum: Lettres de Famille*.
Newport Central Reference Library, Newport, Gwent:
  Hanbury Williams Papers
Polish Scientific Institute, New York:
  Potocki Family Papers: Boxes 16, 17, 36, 60, 79.
Polska Akademia Umiejętności, Kraków:
  Rękopisy: 120, 1648, 1649, 1658, 2184, 2664, 4582–9, 6034.
Public Record Office, London:
  State Papers 88 (Poland), books: 68–89, 91–2, 94, 96, 98, 100, 102, 104,
    106–8, 110–11, 113–14, 117–18.
  State Papers 90 (Prussia), book 90.
  State Papers 91 (Russia), books: 60–6.
University of Virginia, Charlottesville, Va., Archive:
  Kościuszko Papers.

Printed

Akty Powstania Kościuszki, ed. S. Askenazy & W. Dzwonkowski, 2 vols, Kraków, 1918.
Alembert, Jean Le Rond D', *Lettres à Frédéric II sur le démembrement de la Pologne*, Amsterdam, 1808.
— & Morellet, M., *Éloges de Madame Geoffrin*, Paris, 1812.
Ancona, A. d', *Scipione Piattoli e la Polonia*, Florence, 1915.
Anspach, Margravine of, *Memoirs*, 2 vols, London, 1826.
Auckland, William, Lord, *Journal & Correspondence*, 3 vols, London, 1861.
Büchholtz, L., *Powstanie Kościuszkowskie w Świetle Korespondencji Posła Pruskiego w Warszawie*, Warsaw, 1983.
Buckinghamshire, John Hobart, Earl of, *Despatches and Correspondence*, ed. A. Collyer, 2 vols, London, 1900–2.
Burke, Edmund, *Collected Works*, Vols VI & VIII, London, 1826.
—, *Annual Register for the year 1795*, London, 1810.
Bytność Stanisława Augusta w Nieświeżu, Poznań, 1843.

Bibliography

Caché, Benedikt de, *Obrady Sejmu Wielkiego w Świetle Relacji Posła Austriackiego w Warszawie*, Warsaw, 1988.

Casanova, Jacques, *Mémoires*, Paris, n.d., Vol. 7.

Catherine II, Empress of Russia, *Sochinyenia*, ed. A. N. Pypin, 12 vols, St Petersburg, 1907–11.

—, *Correspondence with Sir Charles Hanbury-Williams*, ed. S. Goriainov, Moscow, 1909.

—, *Correspondence with Sir Charles Hanbury-Williams*, ed. the Earl of Ilchester & Mrs Langford-Brooke, London, 1928.

—, *Mémoires*, Paris, 1953.

Chénier, André, *Oeuvres Complètes*, Paris, 1940.

Cheverny, J. N. Dufort, Comte de, *Mémoires*, Paris, 1909.

Cieszkowski, Ludwik, *Pamiętnik Anegdotyczny*, Poznań, 1867.

Considérations Politiques et Philosophiques sur les Affaires de Pologne, London, 1774.

Cornut, R., *Voltaire et la Pologne*, Paris, 1846.

Coxe, William, *Travels into Poland, Russia, Sweden and Denmark*, 4 vols, London, 1779.

Créquy, Marquise de, *Souvenirs*, Paris, 1842.

Czacki, Michał, *Wspomnienia z roku 1788 do roku 1792*, Poznań, 1867.

Czartoryski, Adam, *Żywot J. U. Niemcewicza*, Poznań, 1860.

—, *Pamiętniki i Memoriały Polityczne*, Warsaw, 1986.

Czasy Stanisława Augusta Poniatowskiego przez jednego z posłów wielkiego sejmu napisane, Poznań, 1867.

Dembiński, B. (ed.), *Źródła do dziejów Drugiego i Trzeciego Rozbioru Polski*, 2 vols, Lwów, 1902.

Dembowski, Jan et al., *Tajna Korespondencja z Warszawy do Ignacego Potockiego 1792–1794*, ed. M. Rymszyna & A. Zahorski, Warsaw, 1961.

Dyaryusz Przyjazdu Króla Polskiego do Miasta Krakowa po widzeniu się z Józefem II i Katarzyną II na granicy Państwa swojego spisany, Kraków, 1787.

Dyariusz Króla Stanisława Augusta podczas Powstania w Warszawie 1794r, in *Rocznik Towarzystwa Historyczno-Literackiego*, Paris, 1867.

Dyariusze Seymowe z Wieku XVIII, ed. W. Konopczyński, 3 vols, Warsaw, 1937.

Engelhardt, Gen. L. M., *Pamiętniki*, Poznań, 1873.

Engeström, Lars, *Pamiętniki*, Poznań, 1875.

Frederick II, King of Prussia, *Histoire de Mon Temps*, in *Oeuvres Historiques*, Vols 2 & 3, Berlin, 1846.

—, *Mémoires depuis la Paix de Hubertsbourg*, ibid., Vol. 6.

—, *La Guerre des Confédérés*, in *Oeuvres Poétiques*, Vol. 5, Berlin, 1850.

—, *Correspondance de Frédéric II*, Vols 8–11, Berlin, 1853.

—, *Politische Correspondenz*, Vols 22–46, Berlin, 1895–1939.

—, *Briefwechsel Friedrichs des Grossen mit Voltaire*, Leipzig, 1911.

—, *Die Politischen Testament Friedrichs des Grossen*, Berlin, 1920.

Garran, J. P., *Recherches politiques sur l'état de la Pologne*, Paris, 1794.

George III, King of England, *Correspondence*, ed. J. Fortescue, 6 vols, London, 1927–9.

Grimm, F. M., von, *Corréspondance Littéraire, Philosophique et Critique*, Vols 5–7, Paris, 1829–30.

Hertzberg, E. V., *Recueil des Déductions, Manifestes, Déclarations, etc*, 3 vols, Berlin, 1788–92.

Horrible Complot des Prestres et des Aristocrates pour faire Assassiner le Roi de Pologne, n.p., n.d.

Joseph II, Holy Roman Emperor, *Joseph II, Leopold II und Kaunitz. Ihr Briefwechsel*, ed. A. Beer, Vienna, 1873.

Kalinka, W. (ed.), *Ostatnie lata panowania Stanisława Augusta*, 2 vols, Poznań, 1868.

Karpiński, Franciszek, *Pamiętniki*, Lwów, 1849.

—, *Korespondencja*, Wrocław, 1958.

Keith, Sir Robert Murray, *Memoirs and Correspondence*, 2 vols, London, 1849.

Khrapovitsky, A. V., *Dnievnik*, St Petersburg, 1874.

Kiliński, Jan, *Pamiętniki*, Warsaw, 1958.

Kitowicz, Jędrzej, *Pamiętniki, czyli Historia Polski*, Warsaw, 1971.

Kołłątaj, Hugon, *Co się to dzieje z nieszczęśliwą Ojczyzną naszą*, Warsaw, 1790.

—, *Listy*, 2 vols, Poznań, 1872.

—, *Listy Anonima i Prawo Polityczne Narodu Polskiego*, Warsaw, 1954.

Kołłątaj, Hugon & Potocki, Ignacy & Dmochowski, Franciszek, *O Ustanowieniu i Upadku Konstytucyi Polskiey 3go Maia*, 2 vols, Lwów (Metz), 1793.

Komarzewski, Jan, *Coup d'Oeil Rapide sur les causes de la Décadence de la Pologne*, Paris, 1807.

Komisja Edukacji Narodowej; Wybór Źródeł, ed. S. Tync, Wrocław, 1954.

Konfederacja Barska; Wybór Tekstów, ed. W. Konopczyński, Kraków, 1928.

Kopczewski, J., ed., *Tadeusz Kościuszko w Historii i Tradycji*, Warsaw, 1968.

Kosmowski, Stanisław, *Pamiętniki*, Poznań, 1867.

Kościuszko, Tadeusz, *Opis Kampanii przeciw Moskalom w 1792r*, Poznań, 1843.

—, *Listy do Jenerała Mokronowskiego*, Lwów, 1877.

Bibliography

—, *Odezwy i Raporta*, Kraków, 1918.

—, *Pisma*, Warsaw, 1947.

Koźmian, Kajetan, *Pamiętniki*, 3 vols, Wrocław, 1972.

Krasicki, Ignacy, *Korespondencja*, 2 vols, Wrocław, 1958.

Krasiński, Józef, *Pamiętniki*, Poznań, 1877.

Krechetnikov, Piotr, *Dziennik Wojennych Działań*, Poznań, 1874.

Kuźnica Kołłątajowska; Wybór Tekstów, ed. B. Leśnodorski, Wrocław, 1949.

Lee, Charles, *Memoirs*, Dublin, 1792.

Leopold II, Holy Roman Emperor, *Leopold II, Franz II und Catharina Ihre Correspondenz*, ed. A. Beer, Leipzig, 1874.

Lichocki, Filip, *Pamiętnik*, Poznań, 1862.

Ligne, Prince de, *Mélanges Militaires, Littéraires et Sentimentaires*, Vol. 21, Vienna, 1801.

—, *Lettres et Pensées*, 2 vols, London, 1808.

—, *Fragments de l'Histoire de ma Vie*, 2 vols, Paris, 1923.

Lind, John, *Letters Concerning the Present State of Poland*, London, 1773.

[Lind, John], *Le Partage de la Pologne en Sept Dialogues, par Gottlieb Pansmouzer*, London, 1773.

—, *Considérations Politiques et Philosophiques sur les Affaires présentes du Nord et particulièrement sur celles de Pologne*, London, 1773.

Literatura Barska, ed. J. Maciejewski, Wrocław, 1976.

Łubieński, Władysław, *Pamiętnik* in Askenazy S., *Dwa Stulecia*, Warsaw, 1910.

Lubomirski, Stanisław, *Pod władzą Księcia Repnina. Ułamki Pamiętników i Dzienników historycznych 1764–68*, ed. J. Łojek, Warsaw, 1971.

Lucchesini, Girolamo, *Listy do Fryderyka Wilhelma II*, Warsaw, 1988.

Lutostański, K. (ed.), *Les Partages de la Pologne; Recueil des Actes Diplomatiques etc*, 2 vols, Paris, 1918.

Mably, Gabriel Bonnot de, *Du Gouvernement et des lois de Pologne*, Paris, 1794.

—, *De la Situation Politique de la Pologne en 1776*, Paris, 1794.

—, *Le Banquet des Politiques*, Paris, 1795.

[Mably], *Le Destin Politique de la Pologne*, Croja, 1778.

Mackintosh, James, *Defence of the French Revolution*, London, 1791.

Mączeński, Wojciech, *Dziennik Zdarzeń w Krakowie w Czasie Konfederacji Barskiej*, Kraków, 1911.

Magier, A., *Dwór i Zarysy z Domowego Życia Króla Stanisława Augusta*, in *Archiwum Domowe*, ed. K. Wójcicki, Warsaw, 1856.

—, *Estetyka Miasta Warszawy*, Wrocław, 1963.

Małachowski, Hyacynt, *Mowy i Pisma Publiczne*, Wrocław, 1809.

Maleszewski, P., *Essai Historique et Politique sur la Pologne*, Paris, 1832.

Malmesbury, James Harris, 1st Earl of, *Diaries and Correspondence*, Vol. I, London, 1844.

Maria Theresa, Empress of Austria, *Correspondance Secrète avec le Comte de Mercy-Argenteau*, ed. A. Arneth, 3 vols, Paris, 1874.

Marshall, Joseph, *Travels*, 3 vols, London, 1772.

Masson, C. F. P., *Mémoires Secrets sur la Russie*, Paris, 1859.

Materiały do Dziejów bezkrólewia po smierci Augusta III i pierwszych lat dziesięciu panowania Stanisława Augusta Poniatowskiego, ed. H. Schmitt, 2 vols, Lwów, 1857.

Materiały do Dziejów Sejmu Czteroletniego, ed. E. Rostworowski, J. Michalski & J. Woliński, 5 vols, Wrocław, 1960–9.

Matuszewicz, Marcin, *Diariusz Życia Mego*, 2 vols, Wrocław, 1986.

Mazzei, Filippo, *Memorie della vita e peregrinazioni del Fiorentino Filippo Mazzei*, 2 vols, Lugano, 1845–6.

—, *Un Osservatore Italiano della Rivoluzione Francese: Lettere Inedite di Filippo Mazzei al re Stanislao Augusto*, Florence, 1934.

—, *Lettere a la Corte di Polonia*, 2 vols, Bologna, 1937.

Méhée de la Touche, Jean Claude, *Mémoires Particuliers*, Hamburg, 1807.

Mémoires et actes authentiques relatifs aux negociations qui ont précédé le partage de la Pologne, n.p., 1810.

Mercy Argenteau, Florimond de, *Correspondance Secrète avec L'Empereur Joseph II et le Prince de Kaunitz*, ed. A. Arneth, 2 vols, Paris, 1889.

Minto, Countess of, *A Memoir of Hugh Elliot*, Edinburgh, 1868.

Mniszech, Urszula, *Listy Pani Mniszchowej żony Marszałka W. Koronnego* in *Rocznik Towarzystwa Historyczno Literackiego*, Paris, 1866.

Moszczeński, Adam, *Pamiętnik*, Poznań, 1867.

Naruszewicz, Adam, *Liryka*, Warsaw, 1778.

—, Korespondencja, Wrocław, 1959.

Nax, J. F., *Wybór Pism*, Warsaw, 1951.

Niemcewicz, J. U., *Pamiętniki Czasów Moich*, Warsaw, 1957.

—, *Notes sur ma Captivité à Saint Petersbourg*, Paris, 1843.

Ochocki, Jan Duklan, *Pamiętniki*, 4 vols, Wilno, 1857.

Ogiński, Michał, *Mémoires sur la Pologne et les Polonais depuis 1788 jusqu'à la fin de 1815*, Paris, 1826.

Paine, Thomas, *Works*, New York, 1934.

Pan na Tulczynie; Wspomnienia o Stanisławie Szczęsnym Potockim, ed. A. Czartkowski, Lwów, n.d.

Patz, J. J., *Z Okien Ambasady Saskiej. Warszawa 1794 Roku w Świetle Relacji Dyplomatycznych Przedstawiciela Saksonii w Polsce*, Warsaw, 1969.

Pawlikowski, Józef, *Myśli Polityczne dla Polski*, Warsaw, 1789.

Bibliography

Pierwsze Lata Panowania Stanisława Augusta, in *Czas*, n.p., 1858.

Pistor, General de, *Mémoires de la Révolution de Pologne*, Paris, 1806.

Poezja Polityczna Pierwszego Rozbioru, ed. B. Wolska, Warsaw, 1967.

Polska Stanisławowska w Oczach Cudzoziemców, ed. W. Zawadzki, 2 vols, Warsaw, 1963.

Poniatowski, Józef, *Listy* in *Obraz Polaków i Polski w XVIIIw*, Poznań, 1843.

Poniatowski, Stanisław, *Établissement du Cens Général*, Rome, 1818.

—, *Souvenirs*, Paris, 1895.

—, *Pamiętnik Synowca Stanisława Augusta*, ed. J. Łojek, Warsaw, 1979.

Potocka, Anna, *Wspomnienia Naocznego Świadka*, Warsaw, 1965.

Powstanie Kościuszki z Pism autentycznych, sekretnych, dotąd drukiem nieogłoszonych wydane, Poznań, 1846.

Przyjęcie najjaśniejszego Pana Króla Stanisława Augusta w Siedlcach 1783 roku, Warsaw, 1783.

Pyrrhys de Varille, Ch. de, *Réflexions Politiques sur la Pologne*, London 1772.

Raynal, Guillaume Thomas de, *Histoire Philosophique et Politique des Établissements et du Commerce des Europééns dans les Deux Indes*, Geneva, 1780.

Recueil des Instructions données aux Ambassadeurs et Ministres de la France, Vol. V *Pologne*, Paris, 1888; Vol. IX *Russie*, Paris, 1890.

Recueil de Pièces Relatives au Procès entre S.A. le Prince Adam Czartoryski & MM Komarzewski & Ryx, Warsaw, 1785.

Roussel, P., *Politique de tous les Cabinets de l'Europe pendant les règnes de Louis XV et Louis XVI*, Paris, 1801.

Rulhière, C., *Histoire de l'Anarchie de Pologne*, Paris, 1807.

Sagatyński, Jan, *Pamiętnik Byłego Pazia króla Stanisława Poniatowskiego*, Poznań, 1845.

Sanguszko, Eustachy, *Pamiętnik*, Kraków, 1876.

Saint-Pierre, J. H. Bernardin de, *Correspondance*, Vol. III, Paris, 1826.

—, *Oeuvres Posthumes*, Paris, 1833.

Sbornik Imperatorskovo Russkovo Istoricheskovo Obschestva, Vols 1, 2, 5, 6, 7, 8, 9, 10, 11, 12, 19, 20, 22, 23, 36, 37, 42, 48, 51, 57, 67, 72, 87, 97, 135, 140, 141, 143, 145, St Petersburg, 1869–1917.

Ségur, Louis Philippe Comte de, *Mémoires*, Paris, 1826.

—, *Histoire du Règne de Frederic Guillaume II*, Vols 2 & 3, Paris, 1800.

Sievers, Jacob von, *Drugi Rozbiór Polski z pamiętników Posła Rossyjskiego*, 3 vols, Poznań, 1865.

Skarbiec Historii Polskiej, ed. Karol Sienkiewicz, 2 vols, Paris, 1839–40.

Skrzetuski, Wincenty, *Prawo Polityczne narodu Polskiego*, Warsaw, 1784.

Bibliography

Stanisław II Augustus, King of Poland, *Postanowienie y Opisanie Kondycji Orderu S. Stanisława*, Warsaw, 1765.

—, *Lettre du Roi de Pologne à l'Assemblée Nationale*, Paris, 1791.

—, *Mémoires Secrets et Inédits de Stanislas Auguste*, Leipzig, 1862.

—, *Zdanie o Królu Polskim*, in *Rocznik Towarzystwa Historyczno Literackiego*, Paris, 1868.

—, *Korespondencja między Stanisławem Augustem a Ksawerym Branickim w roku 1768*, ed. L. Gumplowicz, Kraków, 1872.

—, *Korespondencja Krajowa z lat 1784 do 1792*, Poznań, 1872.

—, *Correspondance Inédite du roi Stanislas Auguste et de Madame Geoffrin*, ed. Ch. de Mouy, Paris, 1875.

—, *Stanisława Augusta Projekt Reformy Żydostwa Polskiego*, ed. L. Gumplowicz, Kraków, 1875.

—, *Correspondance avec Maurice Glayre*, ed. E. Mottaz, Paris, 1897.

—, *Stanisław August i Książę Józef Poniatowski w Świetle własnej korespondencji*, ed. B. Dembiński, Lwów, 1904.

—, *Mémoires du roi Stanislas-Auguste Poniatowski*, ed. S. Goriainov, Vol. I, St Petersburg, 1914; Vol. II, Leningrad, 1924.

—, *Rozmowy z Ludźmi*, ed. S. Wasylewski, Lwów, 1930.

—, *Listy* in *Miscellanea z Doby Oświecenia*, ed. T. Mikulski, Wrocław, 1960.

—, *Rok Nadziei i Rok Klęski; Korespondencja Stanisława Augusta z posłem polskim w Petersburgu*, ed. J. Łojek, Warsaw, 1964.

Starzeński, M., *Na Schyłku Dni Rzeczypospolitej*, Warsaw, 1914.

Staszic, Stanisław, *Przestrogi dla Polski*, Kraków, 1926.

—, *Uwagi nad Życiem Jana Zamoyskiego*, Wrocław, 1951.

Sułkowski, Józef, *Mémoires*, Paris, 1832.

Toll, Johan Christopher, *Powstanie Kościuszkowskie w świetle korespondencji Posła Szwedzkiego*, Warsaw, 1989.

Trębicki, Antoni, *Opisanie Sejmu Ekstraordynaryjnego Podziałowego roku 1793 w Grodnie*, Warsaw, 1967.

—, *O Rewolucji Roku 1794*, Warsaw, 1967.

Trembicka, Françoise, *Mémoires d'une Polonaise*, Paris, 1841.

[Vaughan, B.], *Letters, on the Subject of the Concert of Princes, and the Dismemberment of Poland and France*, London, 1793.

Vautrin, Hubert, *L'Observateur en Pologne*, Paris, 1807.

Vetera Monumenta Poloniae et Lithuaniae, ed. A. Theiner, Vol. 4, Rome, 1864.

Vigée-Lebrun, Elisabeth-Louise, *Souvenirs*, 2 vols, London, 1879.

Vioménil, A. du Houx, baron de, *Lettres Particulières sur les affaires de Pologne*, Paris, 1808.

Voltaire, François Arouët, *Dictionnaire Philosophique*, Vol. 42, Paris, 1785.

—, *Histoire de Charles XII*, Vol. 23 in *Oeuvres Complètes*, Paris, 1785.

—, *Les Lois de Minos*, Vol. 6 in *Oeuvres Complètes*, Paris, 1785.

—, *Lettres de Souverains*, Vol. 67 in *Oeuvres Complètes*, Paris, 1785.

—, *Dissensions des Églises en Pologne*, Paris, n.d. (Joseph Bourdillon pseud.)

Volumina Legum, 12 vols, St Petersburg, 1859–89.

Vorontsov, Mikhail Larionovich, *Arkhiv Knyazya Vorontsova*, 10 vols, Moscow, 1870–6.

Walpole, Sir Horace, *Memoirs of the Reign of King George the Second*, London, 1847.

—, *Letters*, 16 vols, London, 1903–5.

Wielhorski, Michał, *Essai sur le rétablissement de l'ancienne forme du gouvernement de Pologne*, London, 1775.

Williams, Sir Charles Hanbury, *Works*, ed. H. Walpole, 3 vols, London, 1822.

Wodzicki, Stanisław, *Wspomnienia z przeszłości od roku 1768*, Kraków, 1873.

Wójcicki, K., *Archiwum Domowe*, Warsaw, 1856.

Wojda, Karol, *O Rewolucji Polskiej w roku 1794*, Poznań, 1867.

Wolski, Mikołaj, *Obrona Stanisława Augusta* in *Rocznik Towarzystwa Historyczno-Literackiego*, Paris, 1868.

Wraxall, N. W., *Memoirs of the Courts of Berlin, Dresden, Warsaw and Vienna*, 2 vols, London, 1806.

Wybicki, Józef, *Pamiętniki*, 3 vols, Poznań, 1840.

—, *Dodatek do Pamiętników odnoszący się do życia Andrzeja Zamoyskiego*, Poznań, 1842.

—, *Archiwum Wybickiego*, ed. A. Skałkowski, 2 vols, Gdańsk, 1948–50.

Zajączek, J., *Histoire de la Révolution de Pologne en 1794 par un Témoin Oculaire*, Paris, 1797.

Zawadzki, W. (ed.), *Polska Stanisławowska w oczach cudzoziemców*, 2 vols, Warsaw, 1963.

Zbiór Deklaracyi, Not i Czynności Głównieyszych które Poprzedziły i Zaszły podczas Seymu pod Węzłem Konfederacyi Odprawującego się od Dnia 18 września 1772 do 14 Maja 1773, n.p., n.d.

Secondary Sources

Aldis, J., *Madame Geoffrin, Her Salon and Her Times*, London, 1905.

Aleksandrowska, E., *Pisarze* in *Słownik Literatury Polskiego Oświecenia*, Wrocław, 1977.

Arkhiv Tsarstva Polskavo, ed. I. S. Ryabinin, Moscow, 1914.

Bibliography

Askenazy, S., *Przymierze Polsko-Pruskie*, Lwów, 1900.

—, *Dwa Stulecia*, 2 vols, Warsaw, 1910.

—, *Książe Józef Poniatowski*, Warsaw, 1974.

Backvis, C., *Stanislas Trembecki*, Paris, 1937.

—, *Les Contradictions de l'Age Stanislavien*, in *Utopie et Institutions au XVIII siècle*, Paris, 1963.

Bain, R. N., *The Last King of Poland*, London, 1909.

Bańkowski, P., *Archiwum Stanisława Augusta*, Warsaw, 1958.

Baranowski, I. T., *Komisje Porządkowe 1765–1788*, Kraków, 1907.

Bartoszewicz, J., *Zamek Bialski*, Lwów, 1881.

Bartoszewicz, K., *Dzieła*, 10 vols, Kraków, 1880.

—, *Dzieje Insurekcji Kościuszkowskiej*, Vienna, 1913.

—, *Konstytucja 3 Maja*, Warsaw, 1989.

Bartys, J. *Rzeczpospolita Pawłowska*, Warsaw, 1982.

Battaglia, O. F., *Stanisław August Poniatowski und der Ausgang des alten Polenstates*, Vienna, 1927.

Baudouin de Courtenay, R., *Nowe Materiały do Dziejów Kościuszki*, Kraków, 1889.

Bauer, K., *Blaski i Cienie Insurekcji Kościuszkowskiej*, Warsaw, 1982.

Beales, D., *Joseph II*, Vol. I, Cambridge, 1987.

Beer, A., *Die Erste Theilung Polens*, Vienna, 1873.

Bilbasov, V. A., *Istoria Ekateriny Vtoroy*, 2 vols, London, 1895.

Bocheński, A., *Dzieje Głupoty w Polsce*, Warsaw, 1988.

Bobliy, K. T., *Ocherki po Istorii Polskoi Fabrichnoi Promyshlenosti*, Vol. I, Kiev, 1909.

Bogucka, M. & Samsonowicz, H., *Dzieje miast i mieszczaństwa w Polsce przedrozbiorowej*, Wrocław, 1986.

Borkowska-Bagińska, E., *Zbiór Praw Sądowych Andrzeja Zamoyskiego*, Poznań, 1986.

Bozzolato, G., *Un Aventuriero Onorato: Scipione Piattoli*, Padua, 1964.

Bracisiewicz, J., *Stanisław August Poniatowski na Pierwszym Sejmie Rozbiorowym*, Warsaw, 1984.

Brandys, M., *Nieznany Książe Poniatowski*, Warsaw, 1960.

—, *Strażnik Królewskiego Grobu*, Warsaw, 1981.

Broglie, J. V. A., Duc de, *Le Secret du Roi*, 2 vols, Paris, 1878.

Buist, M. G., *Ac Spes non Fracta; Hope & Co 1770–1815*, The Hague, 1974.

Bykowski, P. J., *Dwór Krolewski w Grodnie*, Warsaw, 1884.

Castera, J., *History of Catharine II*, London, 1800.

Cazin, P., *Le Prince-Évèque de Warmie Ignace Krasicki*, Paris, 1940.

Chojecki, R., *Patriotyczna opozycja na sejmie 1773*, in *Kwartalnik Historyczny*, Vol. 79, Warsaw, 1972.

Bibliography

—, *Stanisław August a proces Adama Ponińskiego*, in *Przegląd Historyczny*, Vol. 63, Warsaw, 1972.

Chrapowicki, E., *Starościna Opeska*, unpublished typescript.

Ciampi, S., *Viaggi in Polonia*, Florence, 1831.

Ciechanowiecki, A., *Michał Kazimierz Ogiński und sein Muzenhof zu Słonim*, Cologne, 1961.

Cini, L., *Venezia e la Polonia nei secoli dal XVII al XIX*, Venice, 1965.

Czaja, A., *Między Tronem, Buławą, a Dworem Petersburskim*, Warsaw, 1988.

—, *Lata Wielkich Nadziei*, Warsaw, 1922.

Davis, C., *The King's Chevalier, A biography of Lewis Littlepage*, New York, 1961.

Dębicki, L., *Puławy*, 2 vols, Lwów, 1887.

Dembiński, B., *Polska na Przełomie*, Lwów, 1913.

—, *Ignatius Potocki's Mission to Berlin 1792* in *Baltic and Scandinavian Countries*, Vol. III, no. 3, Gdynia, 1937.

—, *William Gardiner: the last British Minister at the Court of Stanislas Augustus*, in *Baltic and Scandinavian Countries*, Vol. III, no. 1, Gdynia, 1937.

—, *Zmierzch Hetmana. Seweryn Rzewuski w latach 1788–93* in *Studia Historyczne ku Czci St. Kutrzeby*, Kraków, 1938.

Dernałowicz, M., *Portret Familii*, Warsaw, 1974.

Desenfans, N. J., *A descriptive catalogue of some pictures of the different schools, purchased for His Majesty the late King of Poland*, London, 1801.

Dihm, J., *Trzeci Maj*, Kraków, 1932.

—, *Sprawa Konstytucji Ekonomicznej z 1791r*, Wrocław, 1959.

—, *Kościuszko Nieznany*, Wrocław, 1969.

Drozdowski, M., *Traktaty handlowe po pierwszym rozbiorze a problem jedności gospodarczej ziem polskich*, in *Roczniki Historyczne*, Vol. 37, Warsaw, 1971.

—, *W sprawie reformy monetarnej w początkach panowania Stanisława Augusta*, in *Roczniki Dziejów Społecznych i Gospodarczych*, Warsaw, 1974.

—, *Podstawy finansowe działalności państwowej w Polsce 1764–1793. Działalność Budżetowa Sejmu Rzeczypospolitej w czasach panowania Stanisława Augusta Poniatowskiego*, Poznań, 1975.

Drozdowski, M. & Zahorski, A., *Historia Warszawy*, Warsaw, 1981.

Dzikowska, I., *Pamiętnik Historyczno-Polityczny Piotra Świtkowskiego 1782–1792*, Kraków, 1960.

Ehrman, J., *The British Government and Commercial Negotiations in Europe 1783–93*, Cambridge, 1963.

—, *The Younger Pitt*, Vol. II, London, 1983.

Eisenbach, A., *The Emancipation of the Jews in Poland 1780–1870*, Oxford, 1991.

Eversley, G. Lefèvre, Lord, *The Partitions of Poland*, London, 1915.

Fabre, J., *Stanislas Auguste et les Hommes de Lettres Français*, Kraków, 1937.

—, *Stanislas Auguste Poniatowski et l'Europe des Lumières*, Paris, 1952.

Feldman, J., *Na Przełomie Stosunków Polski-Francuskich 1774–1787*, Kraków, 1935.

—, *Projekty Handlu Polsko-Francuskiego w XVIII wieku* in *Studia Historyczne ku czci Stanisława Kutrzeby*, Vol. II, Kraków, 1938.

Fournier-Sarlovèze, K., *Les Peintres de Stanislas Auguste II*, Paris, 1907.

Francastel, P. (ed.), *Utopie et Institutions au XVIII siècle*, Paris, 1963.

Garlick, R. C., *Philip Mazzei, Friend of Jefferson*, Baltimore, 1933.

Golovkin, F., *Dvor i tsarstvovanie Pavla I*, Moscow, 1912.

Gomulski, E., *Służba dyplomatyczna w Polsce czasów Insurekcji Kościuszkowskiej*, Wrocław, 1979.

Góralski, Z., *Austria a Trzeci Rozbiór Polski*, Warsaw, 1979.

—, *Stanisław August w Insurekcji Kościuszkowskiej*, Warsaw, 1988.

Grabski, A. F., *Myśl Historyczna Polskiego Oświecenia*, Warsaw, 1976.

Grochulska, B., *Warszawa na mapie Polski Stanisławowskiej*, Warsaw, 1980.

Gruszczynski, L., *Michał Jerzy Wandalin Mniszech* in *Acta Universitatis Lodziensis, seria I, zeszyt 4*, Łódź, 1976.

Grzeskowiak, A., *Publicystyka polska lat 1772–1792 o angielskim systemie rządów*, in *Przegląd Humanistyczny*, no. 5, Warsaw, 1985.

—, *Polska myśl polityczna o systemie władzy monarchii absolutnej* in *Kwartalnik Historyczny*, Vol. 94, Warsaw, 1987.

Grzybowski, M., *Kościelna Działalnośc Michała Poniatowskiego*, in *Studia z Historii Kościoła w Polsce*, Vol. 7, 1983.

Haiman, M., *Poland and the American Revolutionary War*, Chicago, 1932.

—, *The Fall of Poland*, in *Contemporary American Opinion*, Chicago, 1935.

—, *Kościuszko, Leader & Exile*, New York, 1946.

Handelsman, M. *Konstytucja 3 Maja 1791 a współczesna opinia publiczna we Francji* in *Studia Historyczne*, Warsaw, 1911.

Hass, L., *Sekta Farmazonii Warszawskiej*, Warsaw, 1980.

—, *Wolnomularstwo w Europie Środkowo-Wschodniej*, Wrocław, 1982.

Hoffman, K. B., *Historia Reform Politycznych w Polsce*, Warsaw, 1988.

Horn, D. B., *Sir Charles Hanbury Williams and European Diplomacy*, London, 1930.

—, *British Public Opinion and the First Partition of Poland*, Edinburgh, 1945.

Hubert, S., *Poglądy na prawo narodów w Polsce czasów oświecenia*, Wrocław, 1960.

Bibliography

Ilchester, Earl of, and Mrs Langford-Brooke, *The Life of Sir Charles Hanbury-Williams*, London, 1929.

Ilovaysky, D., *Sejm Grodzieński*, Poznań, 1872.

Jędruch, J., *Constitutions, Elections and Legislatures of Poland*, Washington, 1982.

Jobert, A., *La Commission d'Éducation Nationale en Pologne*, Paris, 1941.

—, *Magnats Polonais et Physiocrates Français*, Paris, 1941.

Kaleta, R., *Oświeceni i Sentymentalni*, Wrocław, 1971.

Kalinka, W., *Sejm Czteroletni*, 2 vols, Lwów, 1884.

—, *Konstytucja Trzeciego Maja*, Lwów, 1888.

—, *Ostatnie lata panowania Stanisława Augusta*, 2 vols, Kraków, 1891.

Kantecki, K., *Stanisław Poniatowski Kasztelan Krakowski*, Poznań, 1880.

Kaplan, H. H., *The First Partition of Poland*, New York, 1962.

Kasparek-Obst, J., *The Constitutions of Poland and the United States*, Miami, 1980.

Kazimierz Pułaski, Kraków, 1931.

Klimowicz, M., *Oświecenie*, Warsaw, 1975.

Kocój, H., *Wielka Rewolucja Francuska a Polska*, Warsaw, 1987.

Konczacki, J. M., *Stanisław August Poniatowski's 'Thursday dinners' and cultural change in late eighteenth-century Poland* in *Canadian Journal of History*, Vol. 21, 1986.

Konopczyński, W., *Polska w dobie Wojny Siedmioletniej*, 2 vols, Kraków, 1909.

—, *Mrok i Świt*, Warsaw, 1911.

—, *Geneza i Ustanowienie Rady Nieustającej*, Kraków, 1917.

—, *Od Sobieskiego do Kościuszki*, Kraków, 1921.

—, *Le Liberum Veto*, Paris, 1930.

—, *Polityka i Ustrój Generalności Konfederacji Barskiej* in *Archiwum Komisji Historycznej, serya 2, Tom II*, Kraków, 1930.

—, *Konfederacja Barska*, 2 vols, Warsaw, 1936.

—, *Fryderyk Wielki a Polska*, Poznań, 1947.

Kopczewski, J. S., *Casimir Pułaski*, Warsaw, 1980.

Korzon, T., *Kościuszko*, Kraków, 1894.

—, *Wewnętrzne Dzieje Polski za Stanisława Augusta*, 6 vols, Kraków, 1897–8.

—, *Zamknięcie dziejów wewnętrznych Polski za Stanisława Augusta*, Lwów, 1899.

—, *Odrodzenie w Upadku, Wybór pism historycznych*, Warsaw, 1975.

Kościałkowski, S., *Antoni Tyzenhauz*, 2 vols, London, 1970–2.

Kostomaryov, N., *Poslyednie Goda Riechi Pospolitoi*, St Petersburg, 1886.

Kowecki, J., *Pospolite Ruszenie w Insurekcji 1794r*, Warsaw, 1963.

Kozłowski, S. A., *Józef Ks Poniatowski i ród jego*, Poznań, 1923.

—, *Przyczynek do Rodowodu Królewskiej gałęzi Poniatowskich*, in *Herold*, Warsaw, 1930.

Kraushar, A., *Książe Repnin a Polska*, 2 vols, Warsaw, 1900.

—, *Barss, palestrant Warszawski*, Warsaw, 1903.

—, *Dwa Szkice Historyczne*, 2 vols, Warsaw, 1905.

—, *Obrazy i wizerunki historyczne*, Warsaw, 1906.

Kukiel, M., *Losy polskich Insygniów Koronnych* in *Biblioteka Warszawska*, Vol. I, Warsaw, 1910.

—, *Od Wiednia do Maciejowic*, London, 1966.

Kula, W., *Szkice o Manufakturach w Polsce XVIII wieku*, 2 vols, Warsaw, 1956.

—, *Théorie Économique du Système Féodal*, Paris, 1970.

Kurdybacha, L., *Dzieje Kodeksu Andrzeja Zamoyskiego*, Warsaw, 1951.

Kwiatkowski, M., *Stanisław August Krol-Architekt*, Warsaw, 1983.

—, *Łazienki*, Warsaw, 1978.

Larwood, J. & Camden Hotten, J., *The History of Signboards*, London, 1866.

Lasocki, Z., *Wawel czy Wołczyn*, Kraków, 1938.

Łaszewski, R., *Sejm Polski w latach 1764–1793*, Warsaw, 1973.

Lebedyev, P. S., *Grafy Nikita i Piotr Paniny*, St Petersburg, 1863.

Lelewel, J., *Panowanie Króla polskiego Stanisława Augusta Poniatowskiego*, Warsaw, 1831.

Lerer, D., *La Politique Française en Pologne sous Louis XV*, Toulouse, 1929.

Leśnodorski, B., *Dzieło Sejmu Czteroletniego*, Wrocław, 1951.

—, *Nauka Polskiego Oświecenia w Walce o Postęp*, Warsaw, 1951.

—, *Polscy Jakobini*, Warsaw, 1960.

—, *Les Partages de la Pologne*, in *Acta Poloniae Historiae*, VIII, 1963.

—, *Polska w Epoce Oświecenia*, Warsaw, 1971.

Lewański, J., *Teatr, Dramat i Muzyka za Stanisława Augusta*, in *Pamiętnik Teatralny rok* IX, *zeszyt* I (33), Warsaw, 1960.

Libera, Z., *Życie Literackie w Warszawie w Czasach Stanisława Augusta*, Warsaw, 1971.

Libiszowska, Z., *Opinia Polska wobec Rewolucji amerykańskiej*, Łódź, 1962.

—, *Misja Polska w Londynie w latach 1769–1795*, Łódź, 1966.

—, *Życie Polskie w Londynie w XVIII wieku*, Warsaw, 1972.

Łojek, J., *Przed Konstytucją Trzeciego Maja*, Warsaw, 1977.

—, *Geneza i Obalenie Konstytucji 3 Maja*, Lublin, 1986.

Lord, R. H., *The Second Partition of Poland*, Cambridge, Mass., 1915.

—, *The Third Partition of Poland*, in *Slavonic Review*, London, Vol. III, no. 9.

Loret, M., *Zamach na Stanisława Augusta* in *Biblioteka Warszawska*, Vol. I, Warsaw, 1911.

Łukasiewicz, W., *Targowica i Powstanie Kościuszkowskie*, Warsaw, 1953.

Bibliography

Łukowski, J., *Liberty's Folly; the Polish-Lithuanian Commonwealth in the Eighteenth Century*, London, 1991.

Mackiewicz, S., *Stanisław August*, London, 1953.

Mączak, A., et al. (ed.), *Francja-Polska XVIII-XIXw*, Warsaw, 1983.

Madariaga, I. de, *Russia in the Age of Catherine the Great*, London, 1982.

—, *Catherine the Great*, Yale, 1990.

Majewska-Maszkowska, B., *Mecenat Artystyczny Izabelli z Czartoryskich Lubomirskiej*, Warsaw, 1976.

Mańkowski, T., *Galeria Stanisława Augusta*, Lwów, 1932.

—, *Mecenat Artystyczny Stanisława Augusta*, Warsaw, 1976.

Mann, Z., *Stanisław August na Sejmie Ostatnim*, Warsaw, 1938.

Martin, H., *Une Française à Varsovie en 1766*, Paris, 1935.

Michalski, J., *Propaganda Konserwatywna w walce z Reformą w Początkach Panowania Stanisława Augusta* in *Przegląd Historyczny*, Vol. 43, Warsaw, 1952.

—, *Schyłek Konfederacji Barskiej*, Wrocław, 1970.

—, *Rousseau i Sarmacki Republikanism*, Warsaw, 1977.

—, *Problematyka aliansu polsko-rosyjskiego w czasach Stanisława Augusta* in *Przegląd Historyczny*, Vol. 75, Warsaw, 1984.

—, *Konstytucja 3 Maja*, Warsaw, 1985.

—, *Reytan i dylematy Polaków w dobie pierwszego rozbioru*, in *Kwartalnik Historyczny*, Vol. 93, Warsaw, 1986.

Mnemon, S., *L'Origine des Poniatowski*, Kraków, 1913.

Morawski, K., *Ignacy Potocki*, Kraków, 1911.

Mortimer, R., *Channel Packet*, London, 1942.

Mościcki, H., *Generał Jasiński i Powstanie Kościuskowskie*, Warsaw, 1917.

Mrozowska, K., *Szkoła Rycerska Stanisława Augusta*, Wrocław, 1961.

Nahlik, S., *Narodziny Nowożytnej Dyplomacji*, Wrocław, 1971.

Nieć, J., *Młodość Ostatniego Elekta*, Kraków, 1935.

Nowak, J., *Satyra polityczna Seymu Czteroletniego*, Kraków, 1933.

Olszewicz, W., *Biblioteka króla Stanisława Augusta*, Kraków, 1931.

Ostrożyński, W., *Sprawa Zamachu na Stanisława Augusta*, Warsaw, 1891.

Palewski, J. P., *Stanislas Auguste Poniatowski, dernier Roi de Pologne*, Paris, 1946.

Peleński, J., *The American and European Revolutions, Sociopolitical and Ideological Aspects*, Iowa City, 1980.

Perey, L., *Histoire d'une Grande Dame au XVIII Siècle*, Paris, 1888.

Petrushevsky, A., *Generalissimus Kniazh Suvorov*, 2 vols, St Petersburg, 1884.

Popiol-Szymańska, A., *Poglądy Monetarne w Polsce od XV do XVIII wieku*, Poznań, 1978.

Bibliography

Przeździecki, R., *Diplomatie et Protocole à la Cour de Pologne*, 2 vols, Paris, 1934.

—, *Diplomatic Ventures and Adventures*, London, 1953.

Pule, M. De, *Stanislav Avgust v Grodnie*, St Petersburg, 1871.

Ratajczyk, L., *Wojsko i Obronność Rzeczypospolitej 1788–92*, Warsaw, 1975.

Reddaway, W. F., *Great Britain and Poland 1762–1772* in *Cambridge Historical Journal*, Vol. IV, no. 3, 1934.

Reychman, J., *Le commerce Polonais en Mer Noire* in *Cahiers du Monde Russe et Soviétique*, Vol. VII/2, 1966.

—, *Likwidacja Placówek dyplomatycznych polskich po II i III rozbiorze Polski*, in *Kwartalnik Historyczny*, Warsaw, 1968.

Rolle, A. J., *Stanisław August w Grodnie* in *Przewodnik Naukowy i Literacki*, Wilno, 1875.

—, *Czartoryscy i Repnin* in *Przewodnik Naukowy i Literacki*, Wilno, 1877.

Rose, J. H., *William Pitt and National Revival*, London, 1911.

Rose, W. J., *Stanisław Konarski, Reformer of Education*, London, 1919.

Rostworowski, E., *Korespondencja Szczęsnego Potockiego z Sewerynem Rzewuskim*, in *Przegląd Historyczny*, Vol. 45, 1954.

—, *Sprawa Aukcji Wojska na tle Sytuacji Politycznej przed Sejmem Czteroletnim*, Warsaw, 1957.

—, *Legendy i Fakty XVIIIw*, Warsaw, 1963.

—, *Ostatni Król Rzeczypospolitej*, Warsaw, 1966.

—, *Naprawa Rzeczypospolitej w XVIII wieku*, Warsaw, 1968.

—, *Maj 1791–Maj 1792; Rok Monarchii Konstytucyjnej*, Warsaw, 1985.

Rottermund, A., *Zamek Warszawski w Epoce Oświecenia*, Warsaw, 1989.

Rutkowski, J., *Histoire Économique de la Pologne avant les Partages*, Paris, 1927.

Rybarski, R., *Skarbowość Polski w Dobie Rozbiorów*, Kraków, 1937.

Rymszyna, M., *Memoriał Piusa Kicińskiego do Stanisława Augusta z 1786r w sprawie budżetu dworu* in *Teki Archiwalne*, Vol. 7, Warsaw, 1961.

—, *Gabinet Stanisława Augusta*, Warsaw, 1962.

Saint-Priest, A., Comte de, *Le Partage de la Pologne*, Paris, n.d.

Salmonowicz, S., *La Presse et la diffusion des Lumières en Pologne dans la seconde moitié du XVIII siècle*, in *Annales Historiques de la Révolution Française*, Paris, 1964.

Schmitt, H., *Materiały do Dziejów Bezkrólewia po Śmierci Augusta III i Pierwszych lat Dziesięciu Panowania Stanisława Augusta Poniatowskiego*, 2 vols, Lwów, 1857.

—, *Żywot i Pisma ks Hugona Kołłątaja*, Lwów, 1860.

—, *Dzieje Polski XVIII i XIX wieków osnowane na przeważnie nie wydanych dotąd źródłach*, 3 vols, Kraków, 1866–7.

Bibliography

—, *Dzieje Panowania Stanisława Augusta Poniatowskiego*, 4 vols, Lwów, 1868.

—, *Szkic Historyczny Dziejów Panowania Stanisława Augusta*, Kraków, 1872.

Schumpeter, E., *British Overseas Trade Statistics 1697–1808*, Oxford, 1960.

Scott, H. M., *Britain, Poland and the Russian Alliance* in *Historical Journal*, Vol. XIX, London, 1976.

—, *Frederick II, the Ottoman Empire and the origins of the Russo-Prussian alliance of 1764* in *European Studies Review*, no. 7, London, 1977.

Serejski, M. H., *Europa a Rozbiory Polski*, Warsaw, 1970.

Siemieński, J., *Aktualność Długów Stanisława Augusta* in *Przegląd Historyczny*, Vol. XXIV, Warsaw, 1924.

Siemieński, L., *Ostatni Rok Życia Króla Stanisława Augusta*, Kraków, 1862.

Siemieński, W., *Kuźnica Kołłątajowska*, Warsaw, 1949.

—, *Miezczaństwo Warszawskie w końcu wieku XVIII*, Warsaw, 1976.

Skałkowski, A.,*Stanisław August wobec Powstania*, Warsaw, 1926.

Skowronek, J., *Książe Józef Poniatowski*, Warsaw, 1986.

Smoleński, W., *Stan i Sprawa Żydow Polskich XVIIIw*, Warsaw, 1876.

—, *Ostatni Rok Sejmu Wielkiego*, Kraków, 1897.

—, *Pisma Historyczne*, 3 vols, Kraków, 1901.

—, *Jan Dekert, Prezydent Starej Warszawy*, Warsaw, 1912.

—, *Komisja Boni Ordinis 1765–1789*, Warsaw, 1913.

—, *Konfederacja Targowicka*, Kraków, 1913.

—, *Mieszczaństwo Warszawskie w końcu w. XVIII*, Warsaw, 1917.

—, *Studia Historyczne*, Warsaw, 1925.

—, *Przewrot Umysłowy w Polsce wieku XVIII*, Poznań, 1949.

Solovyov, S., *Istoriya Padienia Polshi*, Moscow, 1863.

—, *Istoria Rossyi s Drevnieyshikh Vremeni*, Vols 23–9, St Petersburg, 1911.

Sorel, A., *La Question d'Orient au XVIII Siècle*, Paris, 1889.

Szyjkowski, M., *Myśl J. J. Rousseau w Polsce XVIII wieku*, Kraków, 1913.

Tatarkiewicz, W., *Rządy Artystyczne Stanisław Augusta*, Warsaw, 1919.

—, *Dominik Merlini*, Warsaw, 1955.

—, *Rapports artistiques Franco-Polonais de Victor Louis à Percier et Fontaine*, Warsaw, 1958.

—, *O Sztuce polskiej XVII i XVIII Wieków*, Warsaw, 1966.

Tazbir, J., *Rzeczpospolita szlachecka wobec wielkich odkryć*, Warsaw, 1973.

—, *Myśl Polska w Nowożytnej Kulturze Europejskiej*, Warsaw, 1986.

Terlecki, W., *Mennica Warszawska 1765–1795*, Wrocław, 1970.

Tokarz, W., *Warszawa przed wybuchem powstania 17 kwietnia 1794*, Kraków, 1911.

—, *Insurekcja Warszawska*, Warsaw, 1950.

—, *Rozprawy i Szkice*, 2 vols, Warsaw, 1959.

Bibliography

Tourneux, M., *Diderot et Catherine*, Paris, 1899.

Tyszkiewicz, E., *Króla Stanisława Augusta ostatni pobyt w Grodnie* in *Rocznik Towarzystwa Historyczno Literackiego*, Paris, 1873–8.

Walicki, A., *The Age of Enlightenment and the birth of modern Nationhood; Polish Political thought from Noble Republicanism to Tadeusz Kościuszko*, Oxford, 1989.

Wasylewski, S. ed., *Stanisława Augusta Rozmowy z Ludzmi*, Lwów, 1930.

Wegner, L., *Dzieje dnia Trzeciego i Piątego Maja 1791*, Poznań, 1865.

—, *Sejm Grodzieński Ostatni*, Poznań, 1866.

Wojakowski, J., *Straż Praw*, Warsaw, 1982.

Wolff, L., *The Vatican and Poland in the age of the Partitions*, Boulder, 1988.

Woltanowski, A., *Czarna legenda śmierci prymasa Poniatowskiego* in *Kwartalnik Historyczny*, Vol. 94, Warsaw, 1987.

Żabinski, Z., *Systemy Monetarne na Ziemiach Polskich*, Wrocław, 1981.

Zahorski, A., *Stanisław August Polityk*, Warsaw, 1959.

—, *Ignacy Wyssogota Zakrzewski*, Warsaw, 1963.

—, *Warszawa w Powstaniu Kościuszkowskim*, Warsaw, 1967.

—, (ed.), *Warszawa Wieku Oświecenia*, Wrocław, 1986.

—, *Spór o Stanisława Augusta*, Warsaw, 1988.

Zaleski, B., *Karol Kniaziewicz* in *Rocznik Towarzystwa Historyczno Literackiego*, Paris, 1867.

Zgorzelska, A., *Powrót Króla*, Warsaw, 1991.

Zielińska, T., *Magnateria Polska Epoki Saskiej*, Wrocław, 1977.

Zielińska, Z., *Walka 'Familii' o Reformę Rzeczypospolitej 1743–1752*, Warsaw, 1983.

—, *O Sukcesji Tronu w Polszcze 1787–90*, Warsaw, 1991.

Zienkowska, K., *Sławetni i Urodzeni*, Warsaw, 1976.

Żuraw, J., *Myśl filozoficzna i społeczna Tadeusza Kościuszki*, Warsaw, 1979.

Żytkowicz, L., *Rządy Repnina na Litwie* in *Rozprawy Towarzystwa Przyjaciół Nauk*, Vol. X, Wilno, 1938.

Żywirska, M., *Ostatnie Lata Życia Króla Stanisława Augusta*, Warsaw, 1975.

Acknowledgments and Photograph Credits

The author and publishers are grateful to the following institutions for permission to reproduce pictures and objects from their collections: Archiwum Główne Akt Dawnych, Warsaw, pl. 105; Czartoryski Museum, Kraków, pl. 40; Historical Museum of the City of Warsaw, pl. 79; Jagiellon University Library, Kraków, pls 41, 121; Library of Kórnik, pl. 113; Museum of Art, Łódź, pls 22, 61; Museum of Fine Arts, Kaunas, pl. 132; Museum of Literature, Warsaw, pl. 34; National Library, Warsaw, pls 38, 83, 100; National Museum, Kraków, pls 6, 43, 90, 127, 128; National Museum, Poznań, pls 1, 7, 82, 112; National Museum, Warsaw, pls 5, 13, 15, 20, 29, 49, 50, 64, 67, 72, 84, 91, 93, 94, 95, 97, 102, 109, 114, 122, 129, 133; National Museum, Wrocław, pls 88, 118, 135; Ossoliński Institute, Wrocław, pl. 33; Polish Academy of Sciences Art Institute, pls 42, 59, 71, 73, 75, 134; Polish Army Museum, Warsaw, pls 123, 125; Pomeranian Museum, Toruń, pl. 49; Royal Castle, Warsaw, pls 3, 14, 19, 21, 25, 35, 39, 44, 46, 51, 54, 55, 63, 66, 68, 74, 78, 92, 96, 99, 103, 104, 106–8, 110, 115, 119, 120, 124, 126; the Trustees of the Dulwich Picture Gallery, London, pl. 45; Warsaw University Library, pls 18, 23, 26–8, 53, 56, 57, 62, 65, 69, 76, 77, 80, 81, 86, 111, 116, 117, 130.

Photograph credits: Roman Aftanazy, pl. 4; Maciej Bronarski, pls 2, 3, 18, 25–8, 35, 44, 46, 47, 51, 53–5, 57, 58, 60, 62, 63, 68, 69, 74, 81, 92, 96, 99, 104, 106, 107, 110, 113, 119, 121, 124; Maciej Ciunowicz, pl. 123; Zofia Górna, pl. 125; Ewa Kozłowska-Tomczyk, pl. 71; Edmund Kupiecki, pl. 10, 70; Zygfryd Ratajczak, pl. 7; Bożena Seredyńska, pls 5, 30, 50, 67, 84, 93, 129; Stefan Sobkowicz, pl. 87; Edmund Witecki, pl. 118.

Index

Index

Index